# Aging and Social Work

# Aging and Social Work
## The Changing Landscapes

SHARON M. KEIGHER,
ANNE E. FORTUNE, and
STANLEY L WITKIN,

Editors

NASW PRESS

National Association of Social Workers
Washington, DC

Ruth W. Mayden, MSS, LSW, *President*
Josephine Nieves, MSW, PhD, *Executive Director*

Cheryl Y. Mayberry, *Director, Member Services and Publications*
Paula L. Delo, *Executive Editor*
January Layman-Wood, *Acquisitions Editor*
Gail Martin, Editorial Associates, *Copy Editor*
Robin Bourjaily, *Proofreader*
Becky Hornyak, *Indexer*
Mia Reese-Smith, *Editorial Secretary*

Cover design by Metadog Design Group, Washington, DC
Typesetting and text design by Cynthia N. Stock, Electronic Quill Publishing Services,
Silver Spring, MD
Printed and bound by Batson Printing, Benton Harbor, MI

*Library of Congress Cataloging-in-Publication Data*

Aging and social work: the changing landscapes / edited by Sharon M. Keigher, Anne E. Fortune,
and Stanley L Witkin.
    p.  cm.
  Includes bibliographical references and index.
  ISBN 0-87101-326-6
    1. Social work with the aged.  2. Aged—Social conditions.  3. Aged—Economic conditions.  4.
Aged—Care.  I. Keigher, Sharon Marie, 1947–  II. Fortune, Anne E., 1945–  III. Witkin, Stanley L

HV1451 .A32 2000
362.6—dc21
                                    00-046-74

# Dedication
# to Celia Weisman
## A Social Worker for a Society for All Ages

Legions of friends were saddened by the unexpected death of Celia Weisman on July 5, 2000, following heart surgery, not long after she wrote the Preface for this book. Dr. Weisman, who in recent years frequently lectured around the world on the contributions that older people make to society, was an active proponent of aging in social work and a key framer of the *United Nations Principles for Older Persons.*

Dr. Weisman was a non-governmental representative at the United Nations for NASW and the International Federation of Social Workers (IFSW) during the past two decades. She had served as a chairperson of the United Nations-Non-Governmental Organizations Committee on Aging during its deliberations preparatory to the declaration and observance of the International Year of Older Persons in 1999. Her many activities at the UN included organizing its annual Social Work Day every March and constantly networking with and empowering activists and practitioners from all over the world through international organizations.

Dr. Weisman knew key social workers in many countries. She reminded audiences consistently that older people are a *resource* for societies, not a burden. When interviewed by the media last year in Finland, where she had been invited to lecture by two universities, she declared that "aging is not a disease. It's a process!" She was tickled when the newspaper headline the next day read, "Aging Not a Disease, American Expert Says."

Generously sharing her knowledge and her international contacts, Dr. Weisman often brought disparate groups together. At the Dublin meeting of the IFSW in 1997, she mobilized the Europeans present to begin sharing their many national activities in preparation for the International Year of Older Persons in 1999. Her exuberance personified what the International Year really represented.

Dr. Weisman earned her MSW from the University of Pittsburgh (1946), an MS in Education from Temple University (1941), and her DSW from Columbia University (1970). After four years with the Educational Alliance, a settlement house on New York's Lower East Side, she joined the faculty at the Wurzweiler School of Social Work at Yeshiva University where she taught for 33 years. From 1976 through 1988 Dr. Weisman directed Yeshiva University's Gerontological Institute and its Postmaster's Certificate in Advanced Gerontological Practice.

Dr. Weisman's professional writings appeared in *Social Work* and *Social Work with Groups*. She was a frequent presenter at meetings of the Gerontological Society of America and the Association for the Advancement of Social Work with Groups, and for the latter she was an ardent supporter of its Group Work Archives Project.

Dr. Weisman was an invaluable resource to a vast number of people who, like us, respected her knowledge and wisdom about aging and social work—and never knew that she was 82 years old. She had admonished us to use the term "geriatric" (with its negative connotations) sparingly. And we have tried to honor that in this book. "Retired" social workers like Celia Weisman are a precious resource social work increasingly needs to revitalize both our profession and our society "for all ages."

# Contents

❦ ❦ ❦

## V. Dignity                                                        351

# Preface

Within the framework of the International Year of Older Persons (IYOP) and its sub theme—"Towards a Society for all Ages"—this book is a most timely volume. The IYOP was launched in October of 1998, and, during 1999, it accomplished the goals of raising consciousness in the world pertaining to the demographic surge (named by Ambassador Alvarez at the United Nations as the "Age Quake") and the longevity revolution. I was privy to be at the United Nations during this period as the main representative for the International Federation of Social Workers. Along with other non-governmental representatives, I participated in the discussion and the debate as the *Principles for Older Persons* evolved, and I pondered over the meaning of this document for *Aging and the Social Work: The Changing Landscapes.*

The landscape has certainly changed and social work must be prepared to focus accordingly. Change is taking place at a rapid pace, and the predictions are for better health and better quality of life for older persons. The articles in this volume address the sub theme of the IYOP, and the five core *Principles for Older Persons* provide the guide to the formulations of new initiatives for social work.

At this point in time, we do not have reliable data on the percentage of social workers who are practicing in the field of gerontology, but we do know that this area of practice has not been a great priority for social workers. The most comprehensive data of those working with older persons have been limited to members of NASW. The analysis done by Gibelman and Schervish (1997) reveals that 4.7% of NASW members provide services for older persons as their primary practice area. Furthermore, the percentage of NASW members by area of primary practice and highest degree shows 16.7% are in the BSW category, while 4.2% are in the MSW category. This would suggest that the lesser trained social workers carry the greater numbers of older clients. Of the 13.2% that have primary practice in the health area, there is no break down to indicate how many of these services are for older persons.

Given the "age quake," the longevity factor, and some of the above statistics on what social workers do, the new agenda "Towards a Society for all Ages" poses a real challenge. The agenda has to be sufficiently broad to encompass the spectrum of aging persons ranging from the dependent and needy to the independent with other kinds of needs, as well as those who fall between these two extremes.

The concept of a society for all ages implies the notions that there is interdependency among generations and that problems of aging cut across all generations and involve different family members. The social worker has to view aging persons with a broader lens, since the impact of getting old and all that it implies will have a ripple effect in a society for all ages. The challenge, then, for the social work agenda in approaching services as well as social policies is to maintain a broad enough lens to encompass the extent of difference and range of needs among older persons. This volume should help to confront the challenge.

*Celia B. Weisman, DSW*
*Professor Emerita, Yeshiva University*
*International Federation of Social Workers*
*Main Representative to the United Nations*

### Reference

Gibelman, M. & Schervish, P. (1997). *Who We Are: A Second Look*. Washington, D.C: NASW Press.

# Introduction

## Social Work Comes of Age in the International Year of Older Persons

SHARON M. KEIGHER,
ANNE E. FORTUNE,
and STANLEY L WITKIN

The United States and the world are experiencing a profound demographic revolution that is slowly transforming societies everywhere. The world's population is moving from a state of high birth and death rates to one increasingly characterized by low birth and death rates. People are living longer and, as the numbers and proportion of older persons increase, populations are gradually growing older. Such rapid, large, and ubiquitous growth is unprecedented in the history of civilization.

Worldwide, one in ten persons is now 60 or older, and by 2050 it will be one in five. The fastest growing cohort within the older population is the oldest old. While there are 145,000 centenarians in the world today, in 2050 there will be 2.2 million. Striking differences exist among regions of the world in how rapidly this transition is occurring and in its consequent impacts. Some developed nations have already seen a squaring of the population pyramid, having maximized average life expectancy, whereas in the least developed nations, infectious diseases and other risks still limit longevity severely. One in five Europeans is 60 or over, for example, compared with only one in twenty Africans; however, in the next fifty years, in many countries that proportion will become one in four and even one in two. The pace of population aging is uneven across the world as well, happening much more rapidly now in the developing world than in already developed nations. The world's largest nations, China and India, together will account for a majority of the world's elders by 2050. A key measure of population aging is the old-age dependency ratio, the number of working age persons (15 to 64 years) per older person (65 years and older) in a given society, indicative of the "dependency burden" on potential workers. By 2050 the dependency ratio will double in the world's more developed regions, but triple in the less developed ones. The potential socioeconomic impacts of an increasing old-age dependency ratio are of major concern in policy, practice, research, and public debate.

Population aging has myriad implications; however, most of them are positive, especially for persons who can expect to experience this longevity bonus in the future. Just as older people today have been agents of positive changes in today's world, we hope that they also are its beneficiaries. To ensure this will require major rethinking of rigid distinctions that today define age and give it boundaries. "Aging is not a separate issue from social integration, gender advancement, economic stability or issues of poverty. It is connected to many other global agendas and will play an increasingly prominent role in the way society interacts with economic and social welfare institutions, family and community life and the roles of women" (UN DESA, 2000, p. 1). Our challenge is to equip ourselves and future generations with the tools to address these implications and to imagine what can be.

## Population Aging in the United States

In the United States, one of the most highly developed economies in the world, we no-tice these portentous changes largely as we feel many other phenomena, through the market. Businesses are already coping with a decline in available young people to fill jobs, universities are adapting to educating older and older students, whole communities are facing shortages of personal care workers to attend to elders with disabilities, and pharmaceutical companies are selling less infant formula and more hormone replacements. Vivid public self-consciousness keeps bringing public debates back to the urgency of preserving social security and Medicare.

Along with economic challenges, however, there are social challenges. Americans are retiring earlier and earlier and in better health than ever before, most looking forward to 20 or 30 years and more of healthy and productive life post-retirement. Disability rates among older people are actually declining. Losing a spouse and even surviving cancer are becoming normative experiences. Living with chronic illness, functional limitations, and even with unremitting pain is recognized as better than the past probabilities of mortality.

How will reasonably healthy retired persons remain productively and positively connected with their families, neighbors, and society? Perceptions of transitions that mark the boundaries of age are being altered along with family, kinship, and community structures. Four and even five-generation families are not unusual, so that the chronological rules of assuming the roles of grandparents or grandchildren are increasingly blurred. At the same time, more individuals are growing older outside of traditional family networks, some simulating family life through communities or alternative primary groups. The rhythm of the life cycle continues to develop through these different dynamics, not as tightly bound by chronological age or life stages as it once appeared to be.

Similarly, assumptions about second and third careers, volunteering, and productivity are changing. As population aging revolutionizes our social and economic infrastructure, globalization and technological advancement are revolutionizing our "tool" system—management, workplace skills, creative synthesis, political and social development. Older people are tapping into the information technology culture to varying degrees, often in multigenerational settings, and meeting educational demands to stay informed of new technologies and systems. The majority of older persons, however, mostly in developing countries—but also in isolated, still depressed regions of the U.S.—are being sidelined in this information tidal wave. The "cyber divide" is representative of other lethal socioeconomic disadvantages characterizing the life chances of still too many older Americans.

A growing proportion of American elders are people of color, most of whom live on smaller pensions (if they have them) and significantly smaller incomes, with lower prospects for well-being than whites. Many such persons cannot afford to quit working, so they are less likely to retire at all. Elderly women of color face multiple jeopardy with disproportionate probabilities of being poor and alone or singularly responsible for the care of others both younger and older than themselves.

The vast majority of Americans with disabilities still depend upon partners and family members to provide their most intimate, unscheduled personal care. What many share with their caregivers, unfortunately, is a deep abiding terror of nursing homes. Yet, all retirees face a distant future more reliant than ever on the willingness of healthy, but poorly paid younger women, many of them African Americans, Hispanic, and possibly recent immigrants, to care for them, either in nursing homes or as they "age in place" in their own homes.

While dependent older persons are far from helpless, technology and mass culture have a power to create images unhelpful to their interests. The media can do so to any group, but especially to persons viewed as "needy" by the larger culture.

> . . . the image landscape conveyed by the western media weighs heavily on the side of glorifying youth, while either omitting older persons or depicting them as stereotypes. This has a particular impact on the lives of older women, as they tend to suffer greater political, social and economic exclusion than do older men. (UN DESA, 2000, p. 3)

The media can have equally harmful effects in the portrayal of any ethnic, socioeconomic, disability, sexual orientation, or otherwise identifiable group among older people. Today's elders are the most heterogeneous older population ever, each having earned that individuality. The "new architecture of aging requires policies that remove obstacles and facilitate contributions. It requires seminal thinking and images that reflect reality and potential, not stereotypes and myths" (UN DESA, 2000, p. 3).

## The Profession's Response

Throughout the 1990s growing consensus emerged within the social work profession that the issues raised by population aging require an informed, broad-based response. In 1995, in developing a national agenda on geriatric education for all health professions, the U.S. Bureau of Health Professions commissioned a White Paper on geriatric education for social work (Berkman, Damron-Rodriguez, Dobrof, & Harry, 1995), identifying specific theoretical and strategic challenges facing the profession. The 1996 White House Conference on Aging further highlighted the essential role of social work in serving elders, and social workers were widely represented among the planners and official participants at that historic event (Saltz, 1997).

In 1998 the National Association of Social Workers established for the first time a specialty Section on Aging and began projecting new, changing priorities in its marketing for practitioners (*NASW News*, 1998). That same year Jeanette Takamura joined a long line of social workers in federal service as the Assistant Secretary for Aging at the U.S. Department of Health and Human Services and head of the nation's "aging network."

In 1999 the United Nations observed the International Year of Older Persons (IYOP), a worldwide year-long celebration of the longevity revolution of the twentieth century. In the planning since 1982, the purpose of this year was to stimulate the process of global recognition and agenda building to prepare for the demographic "age boom." As most nations began anticipating a future ripe with unprecedented prospects for long and high-quality life spans, the IYOP provided a framework for considering how those prospects will be achieved. It is no accident that the co-chairs of the U.S. observation of the UN Celebration, Rose Dobrof and Terry Hokenstad, were both social workers.

In 1999 the Hartford Foundation began a major commitment to social work, allocating $5.5 million to the development of professional geriatric specialists within the profession, infusing initiatives around faculty/researcher development, field practica experimentation, and curriculum development. Social work is definitely coming of age.

Today social workers are prominent leaders in some of the nation's largest and most important multidisciplinary organizations that advocate and promote social services for older Americans. Such organizations include the Gerontological Society of America (GSA), the American Society on Aging (ASA), the National Council on the Aging (NCOA), the Older Women's League (OWL), the National Council of Senior Citizens, the National Association of Homes and Services for the Aging, and the behemoth of them all, the American Association of Retired Persons (AARP). A significant proportion of retired women, more than any before, have worked throughout their lives and have earned their own pensions, and a significant proportion of these women have enjoyed careers as social workers. New books are speculating on the future of the profession and its possible directions relative to aging (Neysmith, S., 1999; Kaye, L., in press). Indeed, social work is scrambling to catch up with a consciousness rapidly proliferating in the popular press about the challenges wrought by aging in the work place (Goldberg, 2000; Zemke, Raines & Filipczak, 1999), retirement (Freedman, 2000), politics (Dychtwald, 1999; Rozak, 1998), and generational relations (Thau & Heflin, 1997).

## The Professional and Research Literature

A positive sign for our profession is that NASW's journals are receiving an increasing volume of high quality manuscripts relevant to the needs of, care for, and services to older persons. In large part these manuscripts reflect the research interests of academics who also publish in *The Gerontologist, Generations, Journal of Aging and Social Policy, Journal of Gerontological Social Work*, and other aging-studies journals. But most of these researchers who are social workers, or who are interested in service delivery, have a genuine desire to disseminate their findings and ideas to social work practitioners above all. It is in that interest that we devised this book. We believe this recent boomlet of articles on older persons in the social work professional literature reflects a growing consciousness within the profession.

This book includes articles on aging published in *Health & Social Work*, *Social Work*, and *Social Work Research* between late 1998 and early 2000. These articles illustrate the wide scope and impressive depth of the practice and policy issues currently before us. Even more, they suggest how the profession's agenda will be broadened in future work with old people and the society in which they live: projecting emerging human needs, research to be done, and future challenges facing the profession around aging.

Comprised largely of empirical research articles addressing the needs of various older populations and social work responses to them, this book includes articles on clinical assessment, clinical practice, case management, health care organization and delivery, innovative program developments, program evaluations, and analysis of fundamental national policies. The articles utilize a wide range of research methodologies, highlighting "best practices" throughout.

## Organization of this Book

Like all regions on the globe, North America faces profoundly new challenges as it adjusts to being an older society, a prospect few countries have ever experienced until quite recently. This book is intended to raise awareness within the social work profession of the global dimensions of population aging and the urgency of this demographic transformation locally across communities, organizations, and institutions. To do this the articles presented here all address the theme selected by the United Nations for the International Year of Older Persons, "Towards a Society for all Ages." This theme provides a rich conceptual framework for the consideration of issues around five global *Principles for Older Persons*: Independence, Participation, Care, Self-Fulfillment, and Dignity. These principles form the five major sections of this book, with each article attached to one of these principles. Since these principles were designed to promote discussion, awareness, and worldwide consensus on agenda building, they are perfect for promoting discussion and awareness within the social work profession. We hope they show how social work is part of a global movement committed to these ideals.

The Overview section provides background on the UN, its establishment of the International Year of Older Persons in 1999, and the relevance of this historical event to social development around the world. While these four articles already feel dated, they record the historical context of 1999, detailing many nascent developments that will shape an expansive future for our profession in years to come. Of particular interest to readers will be the elegant statement of the *United Nations Principles for Older Persons* and the article written by Terry Hokenstad at the end of the International Year about the U.S. observance and its activities.

Section I, **Independence,** highlights the fundamental principle upon which human well-being rests, that people have a basic right to remain independent in later life. To be independent, people need access to the basic resources vital to living decently, with continued availability of such resources in later life. Necessary resources include nutritional food, clean water, adequate housing, income, and health care. Older people need opportunities to earn, or otherwise obtain a living, to retire when they feel ready, to receive training, and to remain a vital part of the social fabric of society. They also need to live in safe environments that can adapt to their changing needs so that they may age in place without sacrificing their ability to meet other needs. Here this book features excellent analyses of the role of government in a society for all ages, income and retirement, social security, Medicare, and racial disparities in wealth acquisition for retirement. It concludes with a consumer advocacy article on knowledge social workers should share with families about the cost of funerals.

Section II, **Participation,** discusses the importance of social inclusion and societal integration in an older society. Older people must be empowered to maintain vital social roles, to make contributions to society, and to have their contributions valued and respected by society. This principle highlights the importance of retirees as volunteers in providing services and in organizing social movements. It further celebrates their interpersonal strengths as familial, neighborly, and friendly agents whose connectedness with others promotes interdependence and social cohesion and builds "social capital" beneficial to all of society. This section features articles on friendships among elders, cultural barriers to the enjoyment of benefits, and a particularly important article by the head of the U.S. Administration on Aging on the infrastructure that supports the "aging network" of services that facilitate many of these important aspects of connectedness for elders.

Section III on **Care** is the longest in this book because for social workers in the busi-

ness of doing care, this principle encompasses several important dimensions. Care includes health care and social care, as well as the legal rights of older persons to receive care and control how it is delivered. Here we highlight three specific social work responsibilities: advocating for social justice and fairness in the allocation of services, providing professional social care services, and facilitating the delivery of appropriately expert health care.

Social justice means *redressing social exclusion.* This section highlights articles on how elders currently utilize services and public benefits, barriers to access and disparities that need to be rectified. Articles cover the importance of Medicaid benefits to low-income elders, the use of services by people living at home with dementia, and the self-perceptions of Asian-Pacific Islanders about dementia, caregiving, and help-seeking. The outcome of the delivery of *professional social care* should be that elders benefit. Here articles examine the linkages between the incidence of disability and service utilization, the importance and use of standardized functional screening and assessment, emerging issues in the field of hospice care, and the effectiveness of social work with older people. Finally, in this age of managed care, the importance of *expert health care* and access to it cannot be overstated. Despite huge changes in hospital organizations, medical social workers continue to have significant roles in the design and evaluation of health care itself in order to reach and meet the needs of elders. Here several excellent evaluations address hospital services, adjustment following surgery, discharge planning, and rehospitalization. The specific patient diagnoses the section addresses include cardiac surgery, depression, hip fracture, dementia, and congestive heart failure.

Section IV, **Self-Fulfillment,** emphasizes the importance of challenges and stimulation in old age and the need for full development of potential within physical limitations. This section highlights how opportunities for growth, joy, caring, and sharing enrich life. Of particular interest to social workers is the caring work done by many elders, which, while quite unevenly distributed by gender and race, is full of meaning and power to those doing it. Articles here look closely at disparities in caregiving borne by African American and Latino grandparents and older persons caring for spouses and for other loved ones with AIDS. Highlighting caregivers' motivations and rewards, these articles emphasize the social support, information, respite, and other resources provided by social workers that sustain such care takers, reminding us as well of the limits of caregiving when it serves to deny caregivers their own self-fulfillment.

Section V is about the right to **Dignity** in old age and in death—that older people should be enabled to live free from abuse, to be respected and treated fairly, and to have control and dignity in dying. Dignity emphasizes the importance of being treated fairly regardless of one's impairments, having a right to choices in where to live or to remain at home, and how to structure daily life. Of special importance in American culture is the right to privacy and property, but of particular concern is the right to medical care, making one's own decisions about it, and controlling decisions that might prolong life and curtail suffering. Articles in this section highlight choices about living arrangements, decisions to relocate, ethical issues arising in the delivery of home care social work, decision making around death and end-of-life care, and the right to autonomy in the very last stages of life.

## References

Berkman, B., Damron-Rodriguez, J., Dobrof, R., & Harry, L. (1995). Social Work, chapter in *A National Agenda for Geriatric Education: White Papers*, U.S. Public Health Service, Health Resource & Services Administration, Bureau of Health Professions.

Dychtwald, K. (2000). *Age power: How the 21st century will be ruled by the new old*. New York: J.P. Tarcher.

Freedman, M. (1999). *Prime time: How baby boomers will revolutionize retirement and transform America*. New York: Public Affairs.

Goldberg, B. (2000). *Age works: What corporate America must do to survive the graying of the workforce*. New York: Free Press.

Kaye, L. (in press). *Perspectives on productive aging: Social work with the new aged*. Washington DC: NASW Press.

NASW News, (1998, March). NASW establishes Section on Aging. *NASW News*, p. 6.

Neysmith, S. (Ed). *Critical issues for future social work practice with aging persons*. New York: Columbia University Press.

Rozak, T. (1998). *America the wise: the longevity revolution and the true wealth of nations*. Boston: Houghton Mifflin.

Saltz, C. S. (Ed.) (1997). *Social work response to the White House Conference on Aging: From issues to actions*. New York: Haworth Press.

Thau, R. & Heflin, S. (Ed.) (1997). *Generations apart: Xers vs. boomers vs. the elderly*. Amherst, NY: Prometheus Books.

UN DESA. (2000). Implications of an aging society (adapted from *World Aging Situation 2000* by Nitin Desai). United Nations, Department of Economic and Social Affairs. http://www.un.org/esa/socdev/ageing/ageimpl.htm.

Zemke, R., Raines, C. & Filipczak, B. (1999). *Generations at work: Managing the clash of veterans, boomers, Xers and nexters at your workplace*. NY: American Management Association.

# Overview

## The Developing Agenda
## for Older Persons and
## Older Societies

❦ ❦ ❦

The articles in this section capture the historical record of 1999, the International Year of Older Persons, and the events that shaped and celebrated its observance in the United States. Encompassing both the beginning and the conclusion of that year, these articles show how both our nation and our profession were integral partners in that process.

This section opens with the elegant *United Nations Principles for Older Persons*, a statement of both ideals and practicalities. While only partially obvious to social work practitioners, these principles capture the real vitality of today's elders who are living longer and healthier lives and whose life experiences are increasingly diverse. From the interdependence enacted in dynamic and reciprocal exchanges in society through encouragement, ennoblement, and caring grows reciprocity in family, community, and society at large. This intergenerational reciprocity is the animating principle moving all nations "towards a society for all ages."

The first editorial of 1999 by the new editor-in-chief of *Health & Social Work*, Sharon Keigher, lays out that journal's agenda for 1999 in celebration of the International Year of Older Persons. It focuses on the symbolism of the event and the vivid relevance to social work of issues on the public agenda at the opening of the year: issues facing the bipartisan National Commissions on social security and Medicare, recent developments around aging at NASW and in social work education, the continuing erosion of health insurance coverage nationally, and managed care. These issues foreshadow priorities that will remain high well into the opening decade of the 21st century.

In the second article, Colleen Galambos and Anita Rosen link aging issues across the world with concerns of the social work profession. Modernization of societies and the processes of social development have very specific implications for older persons, many of them corrosive of valuation and status and negligent of basic social processes that are viewed as unproductive. "Successful aging," on the other hand, is achieved in societies that recognize and seek both the independence and contributions of elders, value multi- and intergenerational relations, and support unpaid caring work. The authors detail specific implications for social work practice deriving from the UN *Principles for Older Persons*, and wisely call on the profession to think through sound policies and programs supportive of each principle.

The third article, an editorial at the end of 1999 by Editor-in-Chief Stan Witkin, accompanied a special issue of *Social Work* on aging that featured several other articles included in this book. Witkin muses about the meaning of age, its cultural construct, its very real subjectivity, and the power of belief systems to shape and sometimes even counteract the "autonomy paradigm" and the "disease model." Witkin calls for reconsideration of current definitions and representations of old age—the taken-for-granted—and for listening for the collective, inclusive, and dignity-affirming meanings of old age in the voices of elders themselves.

Finally, Terry Hokenstad, who with Rose Dobrof co-chaired the U.S. Committee for the International Year of Older Persons, helped *Health & Social Work* close the year by reflecting on the importance and accomplishments of the UN Observance in the United States. His main message is that of Kofi Annan, Secretary General of the UN, who said, "A society for all ages is one that does not caricature older persons as patients and pensioners. Instead, it sees them as both agents and beneficiaries of development" (Annan, 1998). Reflecting on a wide range of worldwide transformations, Hokenstad notes that global interdependence has created additional dangers for vulnerable populations, including growing numbers of older persons. Global markets have produced economic dislocations, worldwide diaspora, and social exclusion. Through its International Year of Older Persons worldwide, the UN sought to raise awareness, identify specific UN policies and goals for its own agencies, and urge national governments to do the same. Implementation of the *Principles for Older Persons* will rely heavily upon national governments working closely with non-governmental organizations, including the International Federation of Social Workers, and in turn, NASW.

As 1999 ended, that work had just begun, Hokenstad notes, opening a new century "in which we hope a society for all ages will move from goal to reality."

## References

Annan, K. (1998, October). Preparations for the International Year of Older Persons. *Report of the Secretary General* (Report A/53/294). New York: United Nations.

# United Nations Principles for Older Persons

*towards a society for all ages*

International Year of Older Persons 1999

The General Assembly:

Appreciating the contribution that older persons make to their societies,

Recognizing that, in the Charter of the United Nations, the peoples of the United Nations declare, inter alia, their determination to reaffirm faith in fundamental human rights, in the dignity and worth of the human person, in the equal rights of men and women and of nations large and small and to promote social progress and better standards of life in larger freedom,

Noting the elaboration of those rights in the Universal Declaration of Human Rights, the International Covenant on Economic, Social and Cultural Rights and the International Covenant on Civil and Political Rights and other declarations to ensure the application of universal standards to particular groups,

In pursuance of the International Plan of Action on Ageing, adopted by the World Assembly on Ageing and endorsed by the General Assembly in its resolution 37/51 of 3 December 1982,

Appreciating the tremendous diversity in the situation of older persons, not only between countries but within countries and between individuals, which requires a variety of policy responses,

Aware that in all countries, individuals are reaching an advanced age in greater numbers and in better health than ever before,

Aware of the scientific research disproving many stereotypes about inevitable and irreversible declines with age,

Convinced that in a world characterized by an increasing number and proportion of older persons, opportunities must be provided for willing and capable older persons to participate in and contribute to the ongoing activities of society,

Mindful that the strains on family life in both developed and developing countries require support for those providing care to frail older persons,

Bearing in mind the standards already set by the International Plan of Action on Ageing and the conventions, recommendations and resolutions of the International Labour Organization, the World Health Organization and other United Nations entities,

Encourages Governments to incorporate the following principles into their national programmes whenever possible:

### Independence

1.  Older persons should have access to adequate food, water, shelter, clothing and health care through the provision of income, family and community support and self-help.
2.  Older persons should have the opportunity to work or to have access to other income-generating opportunities.
3.  Older persons should be able to participate in determining when and at what pace withdrawal from the labour force takes place.
4.  Older persons should have access to appropriate educational and training programmes.
5.  Older persons should be able to live in environments that are safe and adaptable to personal preferences and changing capacities.
6.  Older persons should be able to reside at home for as long as possible.

### Participation

7.  Older persons should remain integrated in society, participate actively in the formulation and implementation of policies that directly affect their well-being and share their knowledge and skills with younger generations.
8.  Older persons should be able to seek and develop opportunities for service to the community and to serve as volunteers in positions appropriate to their interests and capabilities.
9.  Older persons should be able to form movements or associations of older persons.

## Care

10. Older persons should benefit from family and community care and protection in accordance with each society's system of cultural values.
11. Older persons should have access to health care to help them to maintain or regain the optimum level of physical, mental and emotional well-being and to prevent or delay the onset of illness.
12. Older persons should have access to social and legal services to enhance their autonomy, protection and care.
13. Older persons should be able to utilize appropriate levels of institutional care providing protection, rehabilitation and social and mental stimulation in a humane and secure environment.
14. Older persons should be able to enjoy human rights and fundamental freedoms when residing in any shelter, care or treatment facility, including full respect for their dignity, beliefs, needs and privacy and for the right to make decisions about their care and the quality of their lives.

## Self-fulfillment

15. Older persons should be able to pursue opportunities for the full development of their potential.
16. Older persons should have access to the educational, cultural, spiritual and recreational resources of society.

## Dignity

17. Older persons should be able to live in dignity and security and be free of exploitation and physical or mental abuse.
18. Older persons should be treated fairly regardless of age, gender, racial or ethnic background, disability or other status, and be valued independently of their economic contribution.

# Coming of Age!

❦

## SHARON M. KEIGHER

The year 1999 marked not only the last of the 20th century, but also the 24th year of the NASW journal, *Health & Social Work*, and not insignificantly, the United Nations International Year of Older Persons. Just as 77-year-old astronaut John Glenn shot once more into outer space this past fall, consciousness about societal aging has suddenly shot into prominence around the nation and the globe, this time with special meaning for social work. This convergence of "the ages" and unprecedented attention to the field of aging make me feel especially honored to be editor-in-chief of this journal at this auspicious moment.

An "elder" baby boomer myself, I turned 52 in 1999, along with 4 million other Americans—who all surely recall the certitude with which we would never trust anyone over 30! I felt *really* old when recently told that only 42 percent of Americans today can even remember John Glenn's first orbit of the earth in 1962. Colleagues I see annually at the Gerontological Society of America whisper nervously, "We are starting to look old," recounting the signs: sagging body parts, fatigue, memory lapses, and the first symptoms of arthritis, hypertension, or diabetes. (Can cancers and cardiac failure be far behind?) Some of my "oldest" friends now count widowhood, chemotherapy, and life-saving surgeries in their list of brave life achievements. Gradually, and haltingly—as has happened to every generation before us, and will happen to Generation X as well—we begin thinking of "older" in the first person, rather than as "them."

## The International Year
## of Older Persons

The logo for the International Year uses ro-
tating concentric lines to express the vitality,
diversity, and interdependence, as well as
movement and progression implicit in this
theme. Vitality reflected in the moving lines
represents the increased ability of the mind
and spirit of older people made possible today by healthy lifestyles. The experiences
gained throughout life generate the great
diversity found among older individuals in
all societies. This combination of vitality and
diversity heralds both "a new age for old age"
and the reality of "more old age in a new age."
The concentric petals or lines draw attention to the independence and interdependence of the generations, factors that blend
to create a dynamic and reciprocal exchange
of encouragement, ennoblement, and caring.
Such reciprocity enacted in family, community, and society at large is the animating principle leading "towards a society for all ages."

This UN agenda, established clearly back
in 1982, urges the international community
to facilitate collaboration across sectors and
nations and to reach out to the development
community, the media, the private sector, and
the younger generation in our efforts to create a society for all ages.

To social workers, probably nothing could
be more fundamental to making U.S. society one for all ages than the two great political challenges. How shall we sustain our
universal social insurance system—social security and Medicare—for aging and disabled
people no longer employed?

## National Income and Health Security

In his opening remarks at the first session of
the White House Conference on Social Security in December 1998, President Clinton
noted America's responsibility for sustaining
this system of income security into the next
century. With 75 million baby boomers retiring during the next two decades, social
security, like Medicare, faces the greatest
challenge since its inception 63 years ago. By
2013 its trust fund will no longer be taking
in what it pays out. And by 2032, when the
last of the baby boomer bulge retires, the
contributions the social security system takes
in will be only enough to pay 72 percent of
benefits.

It is time to cement the intergenerational
compact implicit in this bedrock welfare
program. Today's younger Americans, who
are constantly barraged by scare rhetoric
from investment banking, insurance, and
other privatization interests, need to hear
that social security will be there for them.
Today's middle-aged and older Americans
have the responsibility to ensure that for
future generations.

President Clinton noted some of the
changing realities pushing social security to
address new unmet needs as well. When it
was founded in 1935, fully half the elderly
people were poor, but today, largely because
of it, only 10 percent are poor. Yet that poverty is felt differentially by different populations of elderly people. Women, for example,
who live longer, depend on social security for
several more years than men. Although only
4.6 percent of older married women live in
poverty, 20 percent of older women who are
single or have lost a spouse live in poverty.
And, I wish he had added that, although the
number of elderly people living in poverty
has declined, the simultaneous increase in
poverty among children to nearly 25 percent
has become a national disgrace.

President Clinton outlined the debate in
five principles he hopes will be used to judge
proposals to "reform" social security. We must:

• strengthen and protect the guarantee of social security for the next century.

• maintain universality and fairness within the system.

• finance it in a way that it can be counted on, regardless of the ups and downs of the economy or the markets.

• continue financial security for disabled and low-income beneficiaries who now are one of every three beneficiaries. And finally,

• maintain the hard won fiscal discipline now in the deficit-free federal budget.

These principles were assaulted summarily by the Republican respondents with their own version of social security reform: privatizing part of it by selling individual accounts to private investors and giving Americans the illusion that they should be able to use it individually to get rich.

A retired United Auto Workers member at the meeting pointed out that 91 percent of the shortfall projected for social security could be restored by simply removing the cap on contributions paid by high-income earners, while keeping the benefits the same. To him it's not rocket science.

The ideological positions staked out in the Social Security Conference have not been remarkably different from those of the bipartisan National Medicare Commission. Also charged with developing options for reforming the system, their recommendations are due March 3, 1999. But Medicare faces more severe financial pressures more immediately than does social security.

Initially commission members expressed strong sentiment in favor of covering at least some prescription drugs but had few ideas of how to pay for it. And since then media attention has again focused on the Republicans' only real proposal, providing "more choices," here under a fixed contribution, or "premium support" arrangement whereby government pays "most" of the health insurance premium or fees and enrollees receive a choice among private health plans. (Sound familiar?) This would inject private companies more deeply into Medicare, "allowing seniors to choose" from an array of private health plans—paying extra if they want more generous benefits (Meckler, 1998).

The question is whether "choice" among private for-profit plans can possibly guarantee that all of Medicare's 38 million beneficiaries receive certain basic benefits. Predictably, there is no consensus among the commission's 17 members, of whom at least 11 must agree to adopt any formal recommendation. So far, they cannot even agree on whether to consider reforms through 2030, the peak of the baby boomers' reliance on Medicare, or whether to just look ahead 15 or 20 years.

This commission is symptomatic of the do-nothing attitude of the 105th Congress, which obsessed for a whole year about the presidential scandal, failing to pass even a Patients' Bill of Rights for consumers of managed care. Fortunately, the Medicaid cuts that the House passed in May 1998 will die when Congress adjourns, as will the additional $12 billion in Medicaid cuts proposed by the Republicans in their large election-year tax cut package. The uncertainty about President Clinton's future and my own colleagues' ambivalence about letting him have one hang heavy over any progress possible during the next two years.

## Social Work and Services for an Aging Society

Despite the overwhelming inertia of these two high-stakes national discussions and the deadly endgame being played in Washington in December 1998, there were some groundbreaking developments during 1998 within social work in health care that are directly related to aging and intergenerational compacts. NASW, for example, has now provisionally established a Section on Aging, and action plans are coming from that group. NASW's capacity to influence policy making at the Health Care Finance Administration (HCFA) has been growing as well. Attempting to improve the professional social work requirements for mental health services in Medicare-reimbursed nursing homes, NASW lobbyists obtained a two-year delay in implementation of regulations to eliminate reimbursement for clinical social work services. They also won an indefinite delay in implementation of Medicare regulations formulated under the 1997 Balanced Budget Act (BBA) that will prevent clinical social workers from billing directly for their services. Although lobbying continues over the 1997 BBA, the public needs to hear the legitimate reasons that home health care expenses have grown so much in recent years.

Finally, last fall the John A. Hartford Foundation announced a national initiative to infuse aging content into social work curricula and raise consciousness about aging and the critically important roles for social workers in aging. For years many schools of social work, some even with major scholarships available, have bemoaned the difficulty of attracting students to careers serving older clientele. In fact, only 2.7 percent of the 35,000 students pursuing MSWs select an aging concentration, and only 2 percent of the others take any courses whatsoever in aging (John A. Hartford Foundation, 1998; Scharlach et al., 1998).

The first part of the Hartford initiative is a $574,998 two-year grant to the Council on Social Work Education (CSWE) to assess the current state of gerontological content in social work education. CSWE will develop geriatric competency standards for social work education, identify social work education models of "best practices in gerontology," and develop a national plan for moving forward.

Two other parts of the initiative as fully conceptualized would commit a total of $5.4 billion over the next five years. Social work programs around the country have bid for planning grants, from which 10 sites will be selected, for the opportunity to develop university-field site consortia of cross-site gerontological learning experiences. Finally, the foundation wants to develop gerontologically competent social work faculty committed to research and teaching about the health and support needs of elderly people. Investment in faculty expertise and leadership training is expected to enhance the profile of geriatric social work, strengthen connections between academic and practice settings, and expand available sites for student practicum training.

Members attending the fall meeting of the Association for Gerontology in Education for Social Work were elated at this news.

### Winning the Battle, Losing the War?

Just in case you think things are getting *that* much better, however, consider this. The U.S. Census Bureau reported in September 1998 that the number of Americans without health insurance climbed by another 1.5 million in 1997, from 41.7 million in 1996 to 43.2 million in 1997. That means that now 16 percent of Americans, nearly one in every six people, has no assurance of health care. The 1997 increase was equivalent to 125,000 people losing coverage every month. The uninsured rate for Hispanics, who have the highest uninsured rate of any ethnic minority population, climbed from 33.6 percent to

34.2 percent. But although uninsured people are mostly poor, nearly 11 million people in families with incomes between $30,000 and $60,000 and 5.8 million in families with incomes over $60,000 do not have health insurance either (U.S. Bureau of the Census, 1998).

This incessant rise in uninsured people year after year clearly derives from national lack of will, rather than lack of capacity, given our nation's distinction as the *only* developed country that does not guarantee health care as a right. A new catalytic factor this year in the erosion of coverage, however, has been welfare reform. Medicaid rolls around the country are falling almost as fast as state welfare rolls. Many families are losing health insurance when they are cut off welfare, but others lose it as they move from welfare to work, because many lose Medicaid even though they are still eligible for it. In addition, many states have implemented policies that discourage families from applying for welfare, and in turn, Medicaid. Reliable national data on exactly how many welfare families are losing health insurance are not yet available, but it is unlikely this "uninsurance" epidemic will end any time soon.

Even elderly people who are supposed to be protected are losing health insurance. Some 450, 000 Medicare beneficiaries have been dumped recently by their Medicare HMOs as a spate of health plans have decided not to renew their contracts with HCFA. Many of these seniors, who had enrolled in HMOs to receive prescription drug coverage and lower cost sharing, live in areas where no alternative HMOs exist. Now, faced with obtaining alternative HMO or Medigap coverage, many are caught in a Catch-22. Only four of the nation's 10 Medigap plans accept all seniors regardless of pre-existing conditions, but none of these four plans offer prescription drug coverage. "People seem to forget that Medicare was created because private insurers could not make money on the elderly population. Now managed care plans are discovering the same lesson all over again and are getting out," said Diana Archer of the Medicare Rights Center in New York (Morrow & Abelson, 1998, p. D1).

Meanwhile the top HMO executives in the largest for-profit managed care companies on average made $2 million in 1997. "The hypocrisy of the [managed care] industry on the issue of heath care costs is startling," said Ron Pollack of Families USA ("Sound Bite," 1998, p. 3). Although losing money in 1997, these companies spent millions to compensate their top executives and millions more on advertising and lobbying to kill patient protections. Then, Pollack noted, they "go around scaring the American public," threatening to raise premiums to cover the very minor costs of comprehensive patient protections ("Sound Bite," 1998, p. 3).

One can only hope that the capitalistic avarice implicit in too much of today's U.S. health care industry will implode, forcing reenergized national awareness of what's at stake in discussion of national health and income security. If it did, we could be back to basics by 2000 as, for each of us, aging becomes an ever more personal reality. By reframing our approach from the vagaries of old age to the challenges and opportunities presented to all by an aging society, we can self-consciously address ourselves to all that we all want to be at midlife.

❦ ❦ ❦

### References

John A. Hartford Foundation. (1998, June 9). *Hartford Program Initiative Proposal : Strengthening Geriatric Social Work*. New York: Author.

Meckler, L. (1998, December 3). Panel works to revamp Medicare [Online]. Available: http://www.washingtonpost.com/wp-srv/WAPO/19981230/V000901-idx.html.

Morrow, D. J., & Abelson, R. (1998, August 7). United Health Care takes $900 million charge. *New York Times* [Business Day], p. D1.

Scharlach, A., Robinson, B., Damron-Rodriguez, J., & Feldman, R. (1998). *Optimizing geronto-logical social work education* (working paper). New York: John A. Hartford Foundation.

Sound bite (Discussion with Ron Pollack). (1998, November–December). *Action for Universal Health Care*, 7(3), 3. (Available online from Families USA: http://www.familiesusa.org.)

U.S. Bureau of the Census. (1998). *Dynamics of economic well-being: Health insurance, 1993 to 1995* (P70-60, Document No. 1327). Available by fax on demand: 1-888-206-6463.

# The Aging Are Coming and They Are Us

## COLLEEN M. GALAMBOS
### and ANITA ROSEN

The United Nations (UN) General Assembly declared 1999 the International Year of Older Persons. This UN international year seeks to have each member country develop specific programs on the national and local level in relation to an intergenerational theme of "towards a society for all ages" (United Nations Division for Social Policy and Development, 1998).

The 1999 UN year comes at a time when the United States and the rest of the world are recognizing that the world's older population is growing faster than the overall total population. A statistical picture indicates that in 1991 there were approximately 332 million people ages 65 and older worldwide, but by 2000 this figure will reach 426 million (U.S. Bureau of the Census, 1993). The rate of growth of aged people is faster in developing nations compared with developed nations and can be attributed to lower mortality rates. This lower mortality rate indicates that more people survive to old age. Every month the net balance of the world's population of elderly people is increasing by a million, with 70 percent of this increase occurring in developing countries (National Institute on Aging and the U.S. Bureau of the Census, 1993). The world has never experienced such a phenomenon before—an actual demographic graying of the planet.

During the 20th century the percentage of Americans 65 and older has more than tripled, and the number has increased nearly

11 times to almost 34 million today (Administration on Aging, 1997). This enormous growth of older people will continue well into the 21st century, particularly when the Baby Boomer population begins turning 65. What are the implications of this unprecedented worldwide aging phenomenon for the social work profession and particularly social workers whose primary focus of practice is in health?

To address this question it is helpful to examine the broader conceptual framework for the International Year of Older Persons. The UN focus is on four major dimensions recognized as critical to this graying phenomenon: the situation of older people, life-long individual development, multigenerational relationships, and the relationship between development and the aging of populations (United Nations Division for Social Policy and Development, 1998). The conceptual framework is accompanied by five principles: independence, participation, care, self-fulfillment, and dignity (United Nations Division for Social Policy and Development, 1998). A brief review of some of the principles and framework issues from a global and U.S. perspective shed light on addressing the UN theme.

## The Situation of Older People

How elderly people are regarded in society varies from culture to culture and country to country and affects their care, independence, and participation. A culture's high regard for elderly people can be estimated by the extent to which societal values support positive self-esteem and status of elderly people. In industrialized societies older people are not critical to the functioning of the nuclear family, and extended care of dependent elderly people is often assumed by formal systems of long-term care (Barrow, 1996; Yadava, Yadava, & Vajpeyi, 1997). As nations become more industrialized, there appears to be a trend toward loss of role and status for elderly people, with an accompanying move toward a more nuclear family structure that minimizes the contributions of elderly people (Barrow, 1996; Yadava, Yadava, & Vajpeyi, 1997).

Evidence to support these trends can be found in the movement of industrialized countries toward health care reform (Chappell, 1997). One trend in health care reform that has universally occurred is an emphasis on reduction of health care costs (Chappell, 1997). There is an expressed concern that the aging population will be viewed as an increasing and unacceptable burden on health care systems (Chappell, 1997; McDaniel, 1997). Even industrialized countries, which have universal Medicare-type programs, are moving toward limiting the number and types of medical procedures covered by their plans (Chappell, 1997). With more emphasis on cost containment, health care may become more inaccessible to older people. For example, the current health care restructuring emphasis on health promotion disadvantages older people who cannot change the life course of the past (Bond, 1997; McDaniel, 1997) or their genetic composition. In the United States the health care system has attempted to control an acute care medical model for older Americans by shifting the burden of cost to health care providers and beneficiaries and by institutionalizing the more frail and isolated Americans at state taxpayer expense. The U.S. Medicare model does not include parity of health and mental health services, nor does it allow for reimbursement of chronic and long-term care services.

As industrialized countries move toward limiting services, increasing privatization, and using contractual services, older people may be the most disadvantaged by health care restructuring (Chappell, 1997). Some countries have instituted age rationing of health care. This type of rationing is particularly evident in life-extending measures (Bond, 1997). The United State's preoccupation with enactment of advance directives for elderly people without equal attention to advance directive enactment among younger adults also can be viewed as another such attempt to ration life-extending measures to elderly people (Galambos, 1998).

Societies must strive for policies that support productive aging. In developing countries, economically and socially productive roles for older people should be emphasized (United Nations Division for Social Policy and Development, 1998). Developed countries must strive to eliminate the negative status of retirement and formally acknowledge the unpaid productive roles of many older people. In all countries we must ensure that primary health care is available and accessible to elderly people and that there is an equal emphasis of physical, intellectual, social, emotional, mental, and spiritual well-being in the delivery of a continuum of health care services to older adults (United Nations Division for Social Policy and Development, 1998).

### Life-Long Individual Development

A recent cross-cultural comparison on the self-concept of elderly people suggests that one dimension of successful aging is a focus on new and different ways to continue leading a meaningful life (Katzko, Steverink, Dittmann-Kohli, & Herrera, 1998). In other words, an older person's ability to find a purpose in life will contribute to a positive aging experience. The literature also suggests that there is a correlation between well-being and positive health status, as well as lifestyle and health care effects from younger years on quality of aging (Bazargan & Barbre, 1994, Pruchno, 1997).

The UN's emphasis on a positive and developmentally oriented view of the older person supports the concept of productive aging and acknowledges what we know to be true about successful aging. Societies must endeavor to achieve a balance between material and spiritual well-being. The challenge is to provide income security for older people while striving to provide them with multiple and meaningful roles.

Societies can contribute to older peoples' life-long development and well-being through the support and development of mechanisms that encourage elderly people to contribute to the community and maintain independence. Among commonly described activities are work, volunteerism, continuing education, and child care activities for family members. Societies also can contribute to the well-being of older citizens through national health care programs that maintain preventive and early interventive health care and a reorientation of policy toward rehabilitation and functional status outcome criteria.

Currently, health care systems are based on an acute care medical model that focuses on short-term contacts. A functional model of health services recognizes the importance of assisting those with chronic illnesses to maintain independence and manage the normal activities of daily living. The acute care model is oriented toward "curing" disease as a basic outcome measure, whereas a functionally based model assesses outcomes related to such factors as improving a person's ability to manage daily activities and maintaining or preventing a decline in independence (Safford & Krell, 1997).

### Multigenerational Relationships

One common thread that appears in many health care reform models is a shift from reimbursed, formalized structures of care and health care delivery to increased use of less formal home and community-based services and means of support. Industrialized countries are finding that a formalized medical model of care, coupled with a rapidly increasing aging population, is becoming cost prohibitive (Bond, 1997; Chappell, 1997). At the same time developing countries are finding that informal family care providers perceive some of their tasks to be burdensome, stressful, and unmanageable financially (Baiyewu et al., 1997). In developing countries, older people without children are particularly at risk and need some type of formalized care when functioning declines (Cattell, 1990). In industrialized countries, such as the United States, smaller families and the increasing number of women who work create major financial, social, and emotional stresses on informal caregivers.

As industrialized countries look toward developing more informal care structures, public policymakers and service providers need to be attentive to supportive services for care providers and the role and status of women, who are the major providers of this care. One formidable task is to reduce gender biases in care provision across the world.

Another challenge before us is how to maintain the concept of interdependence as the populations of young and old change. As we increasingly deal with the "inverse pyramid," we must encourage each generation to actively shape the community (United Nations Division for Social Policy and Development, 1998).

## The Relationship between Development and the Aging of Populations

As developing countries throughout the world struggle with increased industrialization, advancement of the technology age, and the graying phenomenon, a concerted effort must be made to retain service models that work well and revise those that are problematic. There is increasing recognition that the provision of health and social services to elderly people should use formal and informal structures of care (Abyad, 1995; Litwin, 1994). Litwin (1994) also cautioned that formalized structures of care must be sensitive to the cultural orientation of informal caregivers, so that traditional informal support networks can be optimally supported. From an international perspective, societies must also examine what an increased reliance on informal care will mean to the role and status of women and what supportive assistance is needed in this realm.

In attempts to contain costs, health care reform models that advocate reductions in institutional care also must use home care and a variety of housing alternatives with services and adaptations (Cates, 1993; Chappell, 1997). The development of community-based models will provide more assurance that the health problems of elderly people are being managed through alternative means rather than being ignored.

Each country must explore new ways to maintain age integration within the family and the community. Each community should emphasize a culture of caring and aging in place, while maximizing opportunities for multigenerational exchanges. There should be an emphasis on housing environments that promote independence and also offer a continuum of support for changing functional levels of individuals (United Nations Division for Social Policy and Development, 1998).

Finally, policymakers in developing countries are structuring old-age security models for adoption in their countries. Lessons from the past suggest that each country must develop a model that converges with its political ideology (Williamson & Hochman, 1995). It may be an appropriate time to revisit the World Health Organization's recommendations for developing services for elderly people made in the 1980s, which suggested that the needs of elderly people in developing countries should be met in the same system of care developed for the population as a whole (World Health Organization, 1989). The challenge will be to heed these words while ensuring that the needs of all involved parties are met.

## Implications for Practice

The UN Year of Older Persons principles and conceptual structure suggest a variety of social work practice and policy implications in such areas as housing, leisure, work, and income policy. In the social work and health policy arena, the implications are many, and some alternatives to current policies have already been suggested. As for the health care practice arena, the profession would best be served by focusing on intergenerational, global perspectives regarding a year of older persons that moves "towards a society for all ages."

In general, all of the health professions, and certainly the social work profession, have not educated most of their practitioners in gerontology or geriatrics (Damron-Rodriguez, 1997). This lack of education has resulted in a dearth of trained health care practitioners with understanding of the special needs and issues of aging people. In addition, social work credentials and licenses do not require knowledge in aging, and most social workers in gerontological practice have not had formal training in gerontology content. Beyond issues of social work education and credentialling, it appears imperative for all health care social workers to avail themselves of continuing education course work

to affect practice, including differentials of practice related to diversity issues in aging. Health, mental health, and clinical practitioners will not be competent, competitive providers of services to older people and their caregivers without a current foundation of gerontological and geriatric knowledge.

The four major dimension discussed in this article also suggest a number of implications for the health care practitioner. The health care social worker can assume a number of critical roles that support the United Nations Principles for Older Persons. The most prominent are

• Advocate for the incorporation of an holistic culturally competent model of health and long-term care services. This model recognizes the important interaction of health, mental health, and social and cultural factors for people of all ages.

• Promote practices that emphasize the ethical treatment of health care patients of all ages, especially in end-of-life care. Adequate attention to psychosocial needs in ethical decision making and end-stage care is needed for patients, families, and significant others (Rosen & O'Neill, 1998; Safford & Krell, 1997).

• Advocate for basic, universal health care for people of all ages. Universal coverage will ensure access to health care for all citizens.

• Adopt new practice sites and new modes of practice that are geared toward a functionally based outcome approach to health care. This focus will address an increased demand for home and community-based services and the burgeoning development of alternative living and day care arrangements. In addition, social workers need to address the special service delivery requirements of elderly people and families with limited personal resources and of elderly people living in rural areas.

• Develop interprofessional health care practice skills. Both the increased demand for home and community-based service models and the interrelation of social, financial, medical, and mental health issues for older people require effective interdisciplinary practice skills for all social workers (Tirrito, Nathanson, & Langer, 1996).

• Advocate for responsive adult caregiving models and assume leadership roles in provision of caregiving services. Caregiving models should address the concrete provision of care and supportive services to both care receivers and care providers.

• Participate in research that focuses on innovative health care models and action-oriented studies. From the systematic collection of data, knowledge can be gained about what new service delivery models are effective in meeting the health care needs of elderly people from a holistic perspective.

• Promote education and training on "healthy aging for all" using a holistic approach to health care. This approach will ensure that the dissemination of information on healthy aging is given to the young and the old, which encourages the development of a stronger society.

The 1999 United Nations Year of Older Persons affords the opportunity to evaluate personal and professional knowledge and skills in gerontological practice. The time is now for the social work profession to strive for sound policies and programs that support each UN principle for older people. It is a time to address the rapidly growing portion of the population that uses a disproportionate share of health care services and dollars—and social work services—in medical settings. Finally, it is an occasion to take a proactive stance for the social work profession. The global aging phenomena opens new opportunities and practice arenas for health care social workers. However, the profession must seize the opportunity now, or others will fill the void.

## References

Abyad, A. (1995). Geriatrics in Lebanon: The beginning. *International Journal of Aging and Human Development, 41*(4), 299–309.

Administration on Aging. (1997). Profile of older Americans [Online]. Available: http://www.aoa.gov/aoa/stats/profile.

Baiyewu, O., Bella, A., Adeyemi, J., Ikuesan, B., Bamgboye, E., & Jegede, R. (1997). Attitude to aging among different groups in Nigeria. *International Journal of Aging and Human Development, 44,* 283–292.

Barrow, G. M. (1996). Aging, the individual, and society. Minneapolis: West/Wadsworth.

Bazargan, M., & Barbre, A. R. (1994). The effects of depression, health status, and stressful life-events on self-reported memory problems among aged blacks. *International Journal of Aging and Human Development, 38,* 351–62.

Bond, J. (1997). Health care reform in the U.K.: Unrealistic or broken promises to older citizens? *Journal of Aging Studies, 11,* 195–210.

Cates, (1993). Trends in care and services for elderly individuals in Denmark and Sweden. *International Journal of Aging and Human Development, 37,* 271–276.

Cattell, M. (1990). Models of old age among the Samia of Kenya: Family support in the elderly. *Journal of Cross-Cultural Gerontology, 6,* 375–390.

Chappell, N. (1997). Health care reform: Implications for seniors. *Journal of Aging Studies, 11,* 171–175.

Damon-Rodriguez, J. (1997). The 1995 WHCoA—An agenda for social work education and training. In C. Saltz (Ed.), *Social work response to the White House Confernce on Aging: From issues to action* (pp. 65–77). New York: Haworth Press.

Galambos, C. (1998). Preserving end of life autonomy: The Patient Self Determination Act and the Uniform Health Care Decisions Act. *Health & Social Work, 23,* 275–281.

Katzko, M., Steverink, N., Dittmann-Kohli, F., & Herrera, R. (1998). The self concept of the elderly: A cross-cultural comparison. *International Journal of Aging and Human Development, 46,* 171–187.

Litwin, H. (1994). Filial responsibility and informal support among family caregivers of the elderly in Jerusalem: A path analysis. *International Journal of Aging and Human Development, 38,* 137–151.

McDaniel, S. (1997). Health care policy in an aging Canada: The Alberta experiment. *Journal of Aging Studies, 11,* 211-227.

National Institute on Aging and the U.S. Bureau of the Census. (1993). Wall chart on global aging. Washington, DC: U.S. Department of Commerce.

Pruchno, R. (1997). Understanding the well being of care receivers. *Gerontologist, 37,* 102–109.

Rosen, A., & O'Neill, J. ( 1998). *Social work roles and opportunities in advance directives and health care decision making* [Practice Update]. Washington, DC: National Association of Social Workers.

Safford, F., & Krell, G. I. (1997). *Gerontology for health professionals: A practice guide* (2nd ed.). Washington, DC: NASW Press.

Tirrito, T., Nathanson, I., & Langer, N. (1996). *Elder practice: A multidisciplinary approach to working with older adults in the community.* Columbia: University of South Carolina Press.

United Nations Division for Social Policy and Development (1998, June 17). International Year of Older Persons 1999 [Online]. Available: http://www.un.org/esa/socdev/iyop/iyopmact.htm.

U.S. Bureau of the Census. (1993). An aging world II. *International Population Reports* (Series P95, No. 92–93). Washington, DC: U.S. Government Printing Office.

Williamson J., & Hochman, G. (1995). Innovative old age security models for developing nations: Chile & Brazil. *Journal of Aging Studies, 9,* 245–262.

World Health Organization. (1989). *Health of the elderly: Report of a WHO expert committee* (Technical Report Series No. 779). Geneva: Author.

Yadava, K.N.S., Yadava, S., & Vajpeyi, D. K. (1997). A study of aged population and associated health risks in rural India. *International Journal of Aging and Human Development, 44,* 293–315.

# How "Ripened" Are You?

## STANLEY L WITKIN

*"Are you afraid of growing old, Jacob?" asked a child, giggling while she spoke. "What grows never grows old," said Jacob.*
(benShea cited in Cole & Winkler, 1994, p. 67)

On my 13th birthday I was told, "Now you are a man," but I still felt like a kid. At 30 I felt ancient as I saw my youth slipping away. When I turned 50 I thought, "I never imagined 50 would feel this young." In each of these situations my experience of an age differed from the meaning that I or others attributed to it. Such discrepancies are common; a number cannot capture the variations among people or the depth of an individual's experience of aging. On the other hand, all of us, to varying degrees, have internalized cultural definitions associated with different chronological ages—how else could I be aware of a discrepancy?—influencing our lives in various ways. Despite the limitations of chronological age as an indicant of adulthood, maturity, wisdom, and many other attributes, it is used widely throughout society to identify, sort, admit, deny, and influence people. For some, such as those whose "number" places them into the category called "old," the implications of age-based meanings and social practices are profound. Therefore, it may be worthwhile to contemplate the implications of this form of representation, particularly for people we consider old.

Even a routine question like, "How old are you?" becomes surprisingly complex once we interrogate the taken-for-granted response: a number that indicates the sum of calendar years from the time of an individual's birth to the present. Representing age in this way is simple and consistent—the same yardstick is applied to everyone. Such a measure supports systems that value efficiency, categorization, and standardization. We can determine easily who is a child, who is an adult, and who is old. We can establish clearly eligibility for numerous programs and can determine who can vote, drink alcohol, buy cigarettes, and get a tattoo. We can produce tabulations about innumerable age-related activities and perform all manner of analyses. The costs of this reductionism are oversimplification and reification, that is, treating a symbol of age—a number—as if it were a thing rather than an arbitrary representation. Assuming that such symbols are equivalent to, or even reflect, actual material states leads people to believe, for instance, that when people reach 18 years of age they are transformed from children into adults. Chronological age-based criteria also suggest that there are different individual characteristics associated with age, such as maturity or forgetfulness, which in turn are associated with privileges (for example, the freedom to drink alcohol) or restrictions (for example, age-appropriate behavior). These characteristics and the social practices connected to them give chronological age its meaning.

Embedded in chronological age are certain assumptions about aging: that are quantitative (chronological age is expressed as a number), progressive (we get older, not younger), sequential (we cannot skip years), and singular (we can be only one age). These assumptions encourage various beliefs; for example, that aging follows a typical predictable course. They also enable social life to be organized around age groupings to which labels like "child," "adolescent," and "elderly person" are applied and normative beliefs

constructed. Thus, we nod knowingly when adolescents "rebel" against their parents (because this is what it means to be teenaged) or when older people reminisce. We express concern that someone is not "acting her age" or feel envy about a friend who "never seems to age." And we develop programs, create interventions, and conduct research to help people with these age-related problems.

Chronological age has become so important in our society that we sometimes forget that it is only one of many ways to express age. For example, rather than express our age in calendar years, we could use cellular age, subjective experience (such as how old we feel), physiological age (such as health and fitness level), spiritual age, contextual age (how old you feel in a specific situation), or all of these together. Also, we can challenge the assumptions underlying chronological age. For example, I think of age as cumulative. As I get older I incorporate all of the ages that have come before. This enables me to call on qualities associated with different periods of my life. I can be a "silly" child, contemplative adult, or exhibit the boundless idealism of youth, depending on the "age" I choose to be. From this perspective age is a choice, and the older I get the more choices I have. How different from the locked in thinking that so many have adopted—when you are age X, you must act like this, and at age Y like that. Such rigid expectations may make people more predictable and facilitate services (and sales), but at what cost?

Beliefs about aging are maintained by language. Expressions like the "decline" of old age; metaphors such as the "autumn years" or the "twilight of one's life"; and characterizations such as "old codger," "curmudgeon," "doddering," and "senile" are words reserved for older people. I am not denying that humans change over time, rather that our language not only expresses our beliefs about aging, but also constitutes what aging becomes. Even the word "aging" itself connotes meanings that may not be beneficial to certain groups. Writer and activist Meridel Le Sueur (cited in Cole & Winkler, 1994) understood this when she wrote, "I'm doing away with the word 'age.' Aging? You've heard of that? Aging or age or death? Aging? You never hear of anything in nature aging, or a sunflower saying, 'Well, I'm growing old,' and leaning over and vomiting. You know, it *ripens*, it drops its seed and the cycle goes on. So I'm ripening. For 'Age' you can say 'ripening' (p. 95).

In contemporary U.S. society, with its emphasis on youth, health, and productivity, and its unbridled faith in science, we have come to view and speak of aging in relation to these cultural values. Moody (1995) identified two scenarios, which he called the compression of morbidity and prolongevity, that express these cultural positions and give meaning to old age. The compression of morbidity scenario proposes that values of youth and middle age be extended to later life. Ideally, one is healthy up to the very end of life, and death comes quickly. Sounds pretty good to me. The problem is that this quality-of-life scenario leaves many people out. As Holstein and Cole (1996) observed, "[I]t separates the 'productive' from the 'unproductive' and by implication marginalizes those who do not measure up" (p.14). Independence rather than interdependence is the cherished value of the "autonomy paradigm" that accompanies this scenario.

In the prolongevity scenario, "instead of 'normal' or 'successful' ageing, we begin on the contrary to think of aging as a 'disease' to be conquered and cured" (Moody, 1995, p. 172). Aging no longer is a natural process, but a problem for technology to solve. One need not look very far these days to see an article in the popular press or a story in the media extolling the scientific breakthroughs that promise to redefine the limits of the human lifespan. Another exciting scenario except when once again, we consider—which as social workers we must—those who may not be the beneficiaries of these advances or whose lives are so miserable that to extend them only means the prolongation of suffering.

Just as feminist scholars once asked "whose marriage?" was the research on marital relationships describing, we might ask whose aging scenarios are these? Must aging be understood as an individual experience with options "reduced to a dichotomy of health and activity versus illness and obsolescence?" (Houtepen, 1995, p. 223). To what extent do these understandings marginalize or "problematize" the experiences of women, people with disabling conditions, people from other cultures and ethnic minority groups, or people with limited access to resources? Do not misunderstand me, I want to be healthy and live a long time. But as a white, male university professor I am a member of a privileged class for whom these aspirations are possible. As a social worker I also am obligated professionally (as well as personally committed) to consider the majority of the rest of the world for whom the probability of a long and healthy life is remote. This means not only considering the consequences of the dominant scenarios articulated earlier, particularly in relation to the allocation of resources, but imagining alternative images of aging. For example, Moody (1995) discussed another scenario which he called "recovery of the life world" in which the "meaning of old age is to be found in the finitude of human life as a condition to be voluntarily accepted through collective action, not individual choice" (p. 174). In this scenario, technology-defined life events are not assumed to be better than alternatives (Moody gives the hospice movement as an example). Decisions about resources are made with consideration to the collective good as well as our responsibility to future generations. Finding meaning in later life, according to this scenario, is not an individual act, but the collective understanding of a society whose citizens see beyond their individual desires.

We need to find ways to reverse the stereotypes and restrictive beliefs about older people. I do not think that making them more like younger people or trying to "cure" aging is the way to do this. Constructing a collective, inclusive, dignity-affirming meaning for the later part of life will come when the voices of older people, speaking for themselves, are salient. Then the achievement of old age and its many assets—even in this youth-oriented culture—may begin to be realized. Scholar, writer, and poet Ruth Harriet Jacobs (cited in Cole & Winkler, 1994) captured these sentiments in this excerpt from her poem "Don't Call Me A Young Woman":

> Don't call me a young woman;
> it's not a compliment or
> courtesy
> but rather a grating discourtesy.

> Being old is a hard won
> achievement
> not something to be brushed
> aside
> treated as infirmity or ugliness
> or apologized away by "young woman."
> I am an old woman, a long liver.
> I'm proud of it. I revel in it.
> I wear my gray hair and
> wrinkles
> as badges of triumphant survival
> and I intend to grow even older.
> (pp. 54–55)

## References

Cole, T. R., & Winkler, M. G. (Eds.). (1994). *The Oxford book of aging*. Oxford, England: Oxford University Press.

Holstein, M. B., & Cole, T. R. (1996). Reflections on age, meaning, and chronic illness. *Journal of Aging and Identity*, *1*, 7–22.

Houtepen, R. (1995). The meaning of old age and the distribution of health-care resources. *Ageing and Society*, *15*, 219–242.

Moody, H. R. (1995). Ageing, meaning and the allocation of resources. *Ageing and Society*, *15*, 163–184.

# Towards a Society for All Ages

## The International Year of Older Persons

## M. C. "TERRY" HOKENSTAD

"Towards a Society for All Ages," the theme of the 1999 International Year of Older Persons (IYOP), points to the active roles that older people should and can play in contemporary society. Populations are aging throughout the world, but the International Year focuses not so much on the demographics of aging as on the sociology of aging. Specifically, attention is being given to the societal contributions of the growing senior population.

United Nations Secretary General Kofi Annan inaugurated the International year by stating that "a society for all ages is one that does not caricature older persons as patients and pensioners. Instead, it sees them as both agents and beneficiaries of development." He pointed out the importance of a balance between supporting dependency and investing in life-long development when planning and implementing elder care policies and programs. The focus on active aging is not meant to diminish the importance of sound income-support policies and social care programs. Rather it is meant to accentuate the importance of labor market policies and volunteer programs that provide opportunities for seniors to be both active and productive members of societies.

In 1991 the United Nations General Assembly pointed toward the theme of IYOP when it adopted the United Nations Principles for Older Persons. These broad principles recognized the need for programs of care. They included the right to have access to health care and social services and to use appropriate levels of care. Yet the principles also emphasized access to appropriate education and training and the opportunity to work and make income. In addition they stated that older people should be able to seek and develop opportunities for community service and to serve as volunteers in positions appropriate to their interests and capabilities. Their focus on maintaining active social roles and remaining integrated into the society were thus principles upon which to build the theme and program for the International Year.

Governments were encouraged to incorporate the Principles for Older Persons into their national programs for aging. Then in 1992 the 42nd Plenary Meeting of the United Nations issued a proclamation that established 1999 as the International Year of Older Persons. The theme "Towards a Society for All Ages" was adopted so that attention and discussion would extend beyond the challenges of population aging to the opportunities for both the self-fulfillment of older people and the societal benefits of older populations.

## Why an International Year for Older People?

The IYOP and its theme "Towards a Society for All Ages" have particular importance as we enter a new century and a new millennium. Demographic change is and increasingly will be a major force affecting societal stability and human welfare both nationally and globally. Populations are aging and longevity is increasing around the world. Every month 1 million people turn 60 years of age. In 2000, 10 percent of the earth's inhabitants will be over 60. Two decades later one out of three humans will be 60 or older. The 80 and older age group, not the baby boomers, is the most rapidly growing part of the population in the developed world. Two-thirds of all of earth's inhabitants who have reached 80 years of age from the creation until now are alive today.

Lest one think that this is primarily a demographic trend in the developed world, developing countries will age more rapidly in the early years of the new century than developed countries have aged in the latter years of the 20th century. By 2025, 72 percent of the world's over-60 population will be in societies currently classified as developing rather than developed. Thus, the "age quake" is a global phenomenon that requires attention and action internationally as well as nationally and locally.

Societies are changing, while populations are aging. The environment in which people live is being rapidly restructured because of economic technological and societal change. Part of the change is the nature and patterns of work. As we move into a postindustrial age, physical skills become less important for most workers. Changing skills and rapidly expanding knowledge make career change likely and continuing education essential for most jobs. There is less stability in the world of work, but also greater opportunity for part-time and flexible employment.

The transformation from an industrial to an information society has implications for all, but certainly for older people. Retirement policies and pension programs have been built on an industrial model in which the rigors and tedium of the workplace plus the need to open up jobs for young people have meant that retirement in the early to middle 60s is welcome to both the worker and the society. In an information society neither the nature of the work nor the interest of the worker necessitate the same type thinking about retirement. In addition, changing population patterns may make unemployment less of an issue than underemployment in societies that reach and exceed zero population growth.

Societal change and consequent changes in patterns of education, work and leisure should provide opportunities for older people to play more active economic and social roles. The industrial age life cycle with its pattern of education in the early years, employment in the middle years, and retirement in the later years already is being modified. Life-long education is an essential part of the postindustrial age. Work patterns that are flexible in both time and place are becoming more common. Retirement remains the part of the life cycle that has been given the least attention, but it is likely that it will be transformed as there is more blending of education, work, and leisure.

Volunteerism too is changing and the demarcation between gainful employment and volunteer work as blurred as we reach the end of the century. The term "paid volunteer" may still be considered an oxymoron, but that does not change the fact that much volunteer work produces some type of remuneration. This blending of paid work and volunteer work also could encourage active aging.

Global interdependence is growing and a society for all ages is in many ways a global society as we move into the 21st century. The post–Cold War era has witnessed increased interaction across national boundaries in the economic and social spheres within an environment conducive to increased international contacts and collaboration. These contacts occur through individual exchange and cross-national cooperation, but also through a growing global network in the aging field sponsored by the United Nations and a number of international nongovernment organizations.

At the same time as creating opportunities for collaboration, globalization has resulted in additional dangers for vulnerable populations, including the growing number of older people. Transnationalization of the economy is creating forces beyond national policies and politics that have a direct effect on people's lives. Unfortunately global markets, a driving force behind both economic and social policy today, do not automatically transfer into human welfare. Economic globalization has created opportunities for enrichment for some, but has led to the impoverishment of others. Loss of jobs in some countries has been particularly hard on older workers who are most likely to be considered redundant. In addition, pension programs in many countries have been cut back because of international debt and mandated restructuring plans. Older people have been pushed into poverty because of globalization's impact on both labor market and social welfare policies.

Another global trend directly affecting seniors is the worldwide diaspora of people taking place in the 1990s and likely to continue into the new century. Immigrants, refugees, guest workers, and other uprooted people are a vivid feature of our world today. The largest human migration in the history of the world includes 20 million refugees outside of their own countries and another 20 million people uprooted in their own countries. Although the refugees are of all ages, the challenge of both relocation and social integration is particularly problematic for older people who cannot return to the workforce and whose families and social networks have been disrupted or destroyed. The refugee population, but particularly these older displaced persons, is largely marginalized from the mainstream.

The concept of "social exclusion" that is finding wide use in the international literature refers to parts of the population that are not allowed to participate fully in society, sharing its benefits and receiving full protection under the rule of law. In most countries older people are protected by pension and health care policies. In some countries, age discrimination legislation and protective services add to this security. The same cannot be said for the uprooted elderly people who have limited if any such protection. The challenge of resettling marginalized populations is especially acute for older people who are both without country and without social protection.

The International Year of Older People provides an opportunity to draw attention to such global trends that have a major impact on the lives of older people around the world. The international context is important for identifying social problems and recognizing human potential. Economic globalization and ethnic conflict create challenges that cut across national boundaries. At the same time changes in the social structure and life cycle provide opportunities for older people to be less marginalized from the societal mainstream. IYOP events and projects give attention to these trends and highlight the importance of older people as contributors to as well as beneficiaries of social development.

## What's Happening during the International Year of Older Persons

Both celebration of active aging and recognition of the challenges involved in creating societies for all ages have marked the IYOP. Events and activities have taken place around the world. The United Nations' Programme on Aging and the U.N. Nongovernmental Committee on Aging have of course figured prominently in the action of the International Year. At the same time other bodies associated with the U.N. such as the World Health Organization (WHO) and supportive of the U.N. such as the United Nations Association of the United States (UNAUSA) have been actively involved.

Many nations have developed new organizations to plan, promote, and coordinate IYOP events and activities. In the United States, the U.S. Committee for the Celebration of the United Nations International Year of Older Persons has been formed with the support of the Brookdale Center on Aging in New York City and the involvement of hundreds of volunteers who represent national, state, and local organizations in the field of aging. Working closely with the U.N.-NGO Committee on Aging and the Administration of Aging in the U.S. Department of Health and Human Services, it has become the focal point for IYOP action in the United States.

The U.S. Committee's mission is to focus attention on the challenge for our nation to ensure that the increases in life expectancy are matched by increased opportunities for older people. This includes solutions to challenges in the areas of independence, human and political rights, economic security, education, health and nutrition, employment and productive activity, housing and social services. Equally important the committee celebrates the contributions of older people to nation, community, and family. To implement this mission, the U.S. committee has sponsored both educational and celebratory events to examine the issue of societal aging and to recognize the achievements of older Americans. It also serves as a clearing house for IYOP conferences and events throughout the country.

Special mention is appropriate for two major programs of the International Year that have involved collaboration between U.N.-related organizations and the U.S. committee. On October 2, 1999, the "Global Embrace Walk" sponsored by WHO to promote active aging took place in countries around the world. A series of walk events circling the globe began at 11 A.M. in time zone after time zone. The Global Embrace highlighted the themes of the IYOP demonstrating the ability of people as they grow older to lead productive and healthy lives in their families and communities.

In addition to encouraging and coordinating walk events throughout the country, the U.S. committee sponsored its own "Age Quake" walk in New York's Central Park. This U.S. walk was billed as an intergenerational celebration and found grandparents, parents, and children walking together to celebrate. By involving both young and old, the walk event served as a reminder that today's youths and adults are tomorrow's older people. Hands were held across generations, and people were linked across nations as the cycle of life and the global embrace offered good reason to celebrate.

The "Creative Connections" project developed and sponsored by the United Nations NGO Committee on Aging has been another important area of collaboration. "Creative Connections" is an international networking project designed to increase awareness of the IYOP and to stimulate interest and action in support of International Year themes and programs. Members of the NGO committee including leadership of the U.S. committee have traveled around the globe to promote collaboration between NGOs and national governments in program implementation.

"Creative Connections" has used informal meetings convened by committee members that include representatives from government, academia, the religious community, and the civil society to begin the dialogue about aging action in different countries. Dialogue sessions have been held in a number of countries in Africa, Asia, Europe, and Latin America. In addition, the project has built a communications network including an Internet Web page and satellite downlinks to facilitate information sharing and action on behalf of older people. Networking among nations and among societal sectors within countries has resulted from these activities of the "Creative Connections" project.

On December 7th, the U.S. committee will sponsor its culminating event for IYOP. This celebration in Washington, DC, will give special recognition to both older people and elder care programs that have made extraordinary contributions to U.S. society and to America's senior population. Again, the focus will be active aging. This event will mark not only the culmination of the International Year but also the commencement of a new century—a century in which we hope a society for all ages will move from goal to reality.

# I

# Independence

❦ ❦ ❦

The five principles of the International Year of Older Persons provide a framework around which the articles in this book are presented. The first of these is the principle that people have a right to independence in their later lives, and that to live independently they must be ensured access to the resources essential to living decently. These resources include nutritionally adequate food, clean water, adequate housing, income, and health care. To achieve independence older people need opportunities to earn a living and to retire from paid employment when they feel ready, to obtain training and stay active, and to live in safe environments adaptable to their changing preferences and capabilities.

This section begins with a clarion call from Robert Hudson about the vital role of government in "a society for all ages." Specifically, Hudson explores the role of social security in providing the means for all persons unable to work or no longer working to live decently, establishing a floor under household incomes. Hudson challenges those who would privatize government by identifying their self-serving uses of population imagery, policy institutionalization, and political ideology. To counterbalance these, Hudson calls for those on the left "to reinforce and reinvigorate the place of major social insurance programs as legitimate, effective, popular and established." In a society for all ages government inevitably has a central role, along with families and the market, in equalizing the continuing life chances for all generations.

In the second article, Martha Ozawa and Yat-Sang Lum elaborate on this theme, showing why income protections are so needed in old age, especially by women. Comparing population data from 1982 and 1992, they show that marital status makes a difference in men's and women's income status at retirement and a decade later; for women, losing a spouse within 10 years of retirement makes a considerable difference in income status, a net effect specific to widowhood. "For women, widowhood before retirement had a more serious effect on income status at retirement and 10 years later, and the change between the two points than did widowhood after retirement. For men, the reverse was true." Women are increasingly likely to reach retirement age single, divorced, widowed, or without their own pension rights when they lose their husbands. This article proposes policy strategies for better securing the well-being of such retired women.

In the next article analyzing the role of social security and Medicare together, Steve Gorin shows how the lack of long-term care and prescription drug coverage further aggravate disparities in income and wealth among elders. The lack of universal health care in the United States even disadvantages elders who have Medicare, and certainly means that future generations will continue to retire disadvantaged; the most disadvantaged will not live long enough to retire.

In the fourth article, Martha Ozawa and Huan-yui Tseng address the same retirement income dilemma from the perspective of disadvantages wrought by racial discrimination over lifetimes that reduce the abilities of different groups to accumulate assets. Great disparities exist among populations in later life in terms of who has and has not accrued home equity, savings, private pensions, and other sources of wealth.

These articles might well have discussed housing alternatives and the scarcity of affordable long-term care alternatives, needs for nutrition and physical fitness, lack of accessible public transportation, and dozens of other critically important issues that currently impede the independence of older Americans. Indeed, some of these issues are addressed in other sections of this book. One distinct cost that often worries older people is that of "not being a burden on their families" in death. In the final article in this section, Mercedes Bern-Klug, David Ekerdt, and Deborah Schild Wilkinson note how little public information is available on the actual costs of making final arrangements after death. Loved ones thrust into decision making about funeral arrangements are typically still in crisis, overcome with grief, and usually ill-prepared to make what, for many, is the third most expensive decision of a lifetime (after purchasing a house and a car). Bern-Klug and her colleagues make a strong case for a social work role in gathering and providing vital information to relatives about actual cost ranges and local options, especially by discharge planners, hospital and nursing home social workers, and other advocates. They provide several sources from which to begin gathering such information.

Independence is a value singularly exalted by Americans, but an ideal still beyond the grasp of most with low incomes or physical and mental infirmities. For many older Americans, independence can still be enhanced by more sensitive and compassionate policies and better options.

# 1

# The Role of Government in a "Society for All Ages"

## ROBERT B. HUDSON

The theme of the United Nations International Year of Older Persons, 1999, was "Towards a Society for All Ages." The UN, as many social gerontology groups around the world also wish to do, wishes to promote and celebrate the ideal of older people becoming integrated into their societies, being viewed as a mainstream rather than as a marginal presence.

In the spirit of this declaration, it is instructive to juxtapose the current U.S. policy debate about the future of social security against the idea of a "society for all ages." Much irony lies in such an exercise because, as difficult as it may seem to those favoring maintenance of the universal, defined-benefit, intergenerational program that we currently have in place, those promoting the privatization of pension and health programs for elderly people see their objectives in much the same light. Because, to privatizers, the heart of mainstream society lies in families and the free market, they believe we can better integrate elderly people into society by reducing their dependence on government.

In particular, improved circumstances in the lives of many elderly people have privatizers believing that we can lessen government's central role in continuing to promote their well-being. The argument goes on to stipulate that, as a result of the key role social security itself has played in this trend, we can now reintroduce private sector mechanisms to promote economic opportunity and security among elderly people. Social security, as we have known it, was appropriate to "its time" (1935 to perhaps the early 1980s, in privatizers' view), but today it can and should move beyond its publicness and its paternalism. In short, in the views of many conservatives, substantial numbers of older people can "graduate into the private sector." In so doing, they become part of a (private) society for all ages.

The charge to liberals and progressives is not to allow the debate over the future of social security to be constructed in this manner. Specifically, the role of social insurance in U.S. life cannot be recast as dated, aberrational, and not in keeping with core American values about society and security. Whereas privatizers seek to portray social security as a prime example of public sector excess because benefits are now going to well-off elderly people, advocates must point to social security's unparalleled success in reducing poverty among elderly people. Whereas privatizers bemoan the alleged paternalism and lack of choice associated with these federal programs, advocates must remind decision makers that for decades more than 90 percent of the public has unwaveringly stated that they want either "the same" or "more" resources devoted to social security (Page, 1999). Moreover, the public would choose tax increases over benefit cuts if those were the only options available. Where privatizers would place the fate and fortunes of middle-class elderly people in the marketplace and those of low-income elderly people in "first-tier" or public assistance programs, advocates must make clear that social security prevents poverty and maintains income by incorporating all eligible beneficiaries into a single unitary and mildly redistributive system.

In short, the charge to those on the left in the emerging public debate on social security (and Medicare) is to reinforce and reinvigorate the place of major social insurance

programs as legitimate, effective, popular, and established. "Towards a society for all ages" must continue to include a central role for government as well as for families and the market.

## The Emergence of Privatization Alternatives

Given the historical realities surrounding social security, it is remarkable that privatization has today assumed such a prominent place on the menu of social security options. Three interrelated developments have made possible the ascendancy of private alternatives to social security: population imagery, policy institutionalization, and political ideology.

### *Population Imagery*

In the absence of substantial economic resources among elderly people, the privatization option could not exist. Creation of private pension, health care, and other market-based programs is predicated on there being money in the hands of older people. Until recently, the vast majority of older people did not possess such resources, and, consequently, private markets tapping elderly people and providing them with consumption and investment options were scarce.

The marginal life circumstances of elderly people historically is a well-documented tale. Extrapolating from the official measure of poverty developed by the federal government in the late 1960s, we know that something more than half of the older population were poor at the time of the New Deal (Brody, 1987). In 1967 real household income among elderly people was only $8,940 (in 1992 dollars) (Radner, 1995). As recently as 1975, half of the older people continued to have incomes less than 200 percent of the poverty level (Friedland, 1999). At the time of

Medicare's enactment in 1965, fewer than half of the older people had any form of health insurance, and Wilbur Cohen, a key architect of Medicare, stated that amassing data to show that elderly people did not have resources sufficient for paying health insurance premiums and co-payments was "like using a steamroller to overcome an ant" (Marmor, 1973, p. 17). Under these circumstances, there were very few private markets targeting older people.

In more recent years, the economic fortunes of elderly people and images of them have continued to improve. No longer can elderly people be understood as a singularly impoverished, sick, and frail population. Today, poverty among elderly people hovers around 12 percent, median income is $15,192, the percentage of elderly people with incomes less than 200 percent of the poverty level has declined to 39 percent, and over 95 percent of older Americans have acute health insurance through Medicare. In addition, roughly three-quarters of elderly people own their own homes, and roughly three-quarters of those elderly people own them mortgage free.

Highlighting these improvements in elders' collective well-being is in no way to deny the continued incidence of vulnerability among significant and easily identified subpopulations of elderly people. This "second face of aging" (Crystal, 1982) is stark and well known, certainly to social workers in health and aging. Poverty rates among old-old people are 40 percent higher than among young-old people; the median incomes of older families is 2½ times that of single older individuals; older black people are three times and older Hispanics are twice as likely to be poor than older white people; and, in the most startling composite, the poverty rate among old-old black women is 10 times the rate of poverty among young-old white men.

Stunning as these disparities may be, they are far from Exhibit A in privatizers' armamentarium. For them, the principal point remains that "the elderly" have resources they did not have decades ago. This partial reality has animated the politics of privatization surrounding social security and other programs. Privatizers would not ignore completely elderly people who are currently poor and sick, but they would "re-residualize" public efforts on their behalf. Thus, they would expand means-tested programs directed to these individuals and attempt to pull more affluent elderly people into private markets simultaneously. The principal policy consequence of simultaneously privatizing programs for the better-off while means-testing programs for the vulnerable is the systematic erosion of the nation's major social insurance program, Old Age, Survivors, and Disability Insurance (OASDI), also known as social security.

### Policy Institutionalization

The second factor furthering privatization options is found in the very growth of policies directed toward the old. In sociological jargon these programs have by now attained "institutional" status—that is, the programs are encompassing, legitimate, effective, and valued.

This was not always the case. The Old Age, Survivors, and Disability Insurance portion of the social security act, enacted during the New Deal, was smaller than the means-tested Old Age Assistance Program until the early 1950s and, in fact, came close to being eliminated during that time. Disability insurance was not enacted until 1956, and Medicare and Medicaid were created only in 1965. It was the 1965–74 decade that saw the full flowering of the aging policy we know today: passage of Medicare, Medicaid, the Older Americans Act, and the Age Discrimination in Employment Act; a 70 percent increase in social security benefits, tying future increases to the cost of living, Supplemental Security Income, the Employee Retirement Income Security Act; and creation of the National Institute on Aging. There have been few new program authorizations in the more recent period, but the expenditures and expectations surrounding each of these programs have continued to grow.

At first blush, the newfound salience of these programs should make them politically impregnable and a firewall against privatization options. That may ultimately prove to be the case, but issues surrounding their current status have partially served the privatizers' cause. The principal reason is that the programs have become by some standards "too big." In current parlance, "we can't afford them," "they are growing out of control," "they are squeezing out other needs" (especially those of children), and "they are sapping national savings and impeding economic growth." If the ultimate political opprobrium in the 1980s was "the L-word," liberalism, its replacement in the 1990s was the "E-word," entitlements. In budgetary terms, an entitlement program is one that does not require annual Congressional appropriations—expenditures mandated by law must be made, whatever the level. In political terms, entitlements have become programs that have created their own reality. They grow automatically, pulling in new claimants and beneficiaries every month— what critics see as essentially a political breeder-reactor effect.

Indeed, the argument can be and has been made that it is policies on aging, not interest groups like the American Association of Retired Persons (AARP), that are responsible for the massive political presence older people have in the United States today. The story is a complicated one, but there can be no question that most of the interest groups on aging came into being or became politically involved after most of the major aging-related programs were already in place (Quadagno, 1991; Walker, 1983). This "policy causes politics" understanding, if valid, has important implications for how privatization efforts will play out in the months and years ahead. If policy institutionalization helped galvanize the organized interests of today's elderly people, do the organized elderly people today have the size and cohesion to forestall major privatization initiatives?

## Political Ideology

The final strand of political developments fostering privatization initiatives centers on a body of conservative political philosophy that has been building since the 1970s. The creation of magazines and journals such as *The National Review* and *The Public Interest*, Washington think tanks such as the Heritage Foundation and the Cato Institute, and recent books such as *The Good Life and Its Discontents* (Samuelson, 1995) and *From Opportunity to Entitlement: The Transformation and Decline of Great Society Liberalism* (Davies, 1996) all speak to the rise of conservative thinking in U.S. political life. In Washington, Newt Gingrich, Dick Armey, and John Kasich have been the leaders of this movement.

The overall message emanating from these sources is that the federal government has become too big a part of American life, is ineffective and inefficient in what it does, is self-serving in the political alliances of like-minded liberals that it supports, and, at worst, is corrosive to the spirit of individualism and freedom that lies at the core of the American character. Government's roles and responsibilities have grown to the point where, in the view of most conservative thinkers, the government is more part of the problems we face than it is a solution to them.

Elderly people were the last social policy constituency to come under this conservative lens, largely because of their long-standing and singular vulnerability. But now because of their numbers, their well-being, and mostly because of the enormity of the programs that now exist on their behalf, older people are as legitimate targets of privatization efforts as most other population groups. And, beyond privatization, contemporary circumstances mean that older people can now be part of a residualist's society for all ages.

## New Assumptions and Old Policies

These developments in the demographic, policy, and political arenas have raised more fundamental questions about the roles and purposes of social security than have been seen at any time since the early 1950s, if not the mid-1930s. The legitimacy of these concerns is determined very much by the old political adage, "where you stand depends on where you sit."

### *Population and Policy*

Irony or not, privatization proposals build on the successes of social security in improving the lot of older people over recent decades. To conservatives, a third stage has been added to the welfare state bellwether "from relief to income maintenance," namely, "from income maintenance to investment choice." Having (and expecting in the future) a more highly educated older population and one more conversant with private investment vehicles, their view is that we can move away from simply putting collective resources into government instruments and begin putting individuals' resources into private markets. Plans that would replace the existing social

security defined benefit with mandated "personal savings accounts" (to which defined contributions would be made, but defined benefits not guaranteed) would bring about such a shift. The proposal of Sylvester Schieber, a member of the 1996 Social Security Advisory Commission, would have done this in dramatic form, albeit over a 75-year period (Schieber, 1996). More recent plans suggested by Harvard economist Martin Feldstein and by Representative Clay Shaw (R-Florida), Chairman of the House Ways and Means Committee, pull back from that proposal. They would move toward private accounts, but would maintain a full or at least partial benefit guarantee. Yet, as Roger Hickey of the Social Security Information project has noted, combining private investments with public guarantees is the perfect formula for "lemon socialism": the government absorbs the downside risks ("lemons") and the private sector is assured the upside gains ("socialism") (Kuttner, 1999).

The critical antidote liberals and progressives must administer here is that acknowledging the improved circumstances of older people does not necessarily translate into replacing security (the defined benefit) with choice (investing in one's own personal retirement account). Social security was never intended to be and is not the only source of retirement income for older people. From the New Deal to today, system proponents have always insisted on a role for individual savings and private pensions for supporting Americans in retirement. Social security is, however, the principal benefit source containing a guaranteed benefit. More critical yet, social security has become the overwhelming income source for low-income elderly people, precisely the group most dependent on the defined benefit, least interested in having private accounts, and least able to understand the various investment choices that private accounts would create.

A very different way to recognize changes in the situation of contemporary elderly people would be to reassess where the risks of old age lie today. Conservatives and privatizers have a legitimate point in citing aggregate improvements in economic well-being among today's older population. But in highlighting how things have improved, they pointedly omit where conditions have become notably more problematic. And that is in the area of health and long-term care. Older people are more readily able to meet normal consumption needs today than in the past, but they increasingly face the staggering economic and psychological costs brought about by the aging of the older population itself and through the attendant long-term care needs facing the oldest-old people.

The left's approach to "the new aging" should be moving toward establishment of public long-term care insurance while defending the core principles underlying social security. Because the catastrophic costs associated with Alzheimer's disease, stroke, and so forth dwarf the resources most older people could ever accumulate, the possibility of devoting a modest proportion of social security payments to a public long-term care insurance trust fund should be explored (Chen, 1993; Hudson, 1993). Such an approach acknowledges economic improvements among older people while addressing the devastations that can accompany very advanced age, the great late-life contingency unrecognized by social insurance in the United States.

### Politics and Policy

The politics of social security privatization will be something to behold in the months and years ahead. The outcome will hinge largely on activities along two fronts. The first centers on how the privatization issue is constructed and interpreted. Nowhere in politics will the use of language be more intriguing than in the discussions about the future of social security. Here, one person's "saving" is another's "transforming," and yet another's "dismantling." Privatizers' version of saving social security centers on their "realistic acknowledgment" of the graying of the United States, the presumed preferences of Americans to have "more choice" in their investments, and a desire "to get in on the better returns" that can be found in the stock market and other private vehicles. Beyond there being little evidence that the broad public subscribes to these views, it is something of a stretch to buy the argument that plans that would take social security from a defined-benefit to a defined-contribution plan, replace a single insurance pool with millions of private accounts, move from a pay-as-you-go intergenerational transfer to an intragenerational savings scheme, and create a two-tier program in light of the single universal one that exists today is, in fact, "saving" social security.

Those who would maintain social security largely as it is acknowledge the need for modifying the system, but their changes would be along the lines of bringing new state and local government workers under coverage, tinkering with the benefit formula, recalculating the cost-of-living adjustment, and, perhaps, investing some portion of the growing reserves in stock and bonds. Using reasonable assumptions, such moves will preserve social security for decades. Most important, this approach appears to be what the U.S. public wants. It is true that the known is often preferable to the unknown and that the public's level of knowledge about the current system or the alternatives is painfully low, but those realities hardly provide a blank check to those who would fundamentally alter the system.

The final point is related to the above. It appears increasingly that there is emerging a basic disconnect between elite ("inside the Beltway") and mass ("public") opinion—perhaps *à cause de l'affaire Lewinsky*. As is true of many arenas of public policy today, social security privatization is not a product of civics books' depiction of individuals voting, letter writing, and joining interest groups to see their bill become a law. Beyond being the source of privatization ideas and proposals, conservative think tanks and individual entrepreneurs have been the instrumental forces in disseminating and popularizing such ideas. Investment banker Peter Peterson, former Colorado Governor Richard Lamm, and business tycoon Pete DuPont all have gone from proposing to proselytizing. In a political system where campaign contributions are a protected form of free speech, this is certainly their right, but the question of representativeness—indeed, of choice—does arise.

Thus, we come to the final question, namely, whether the public will buy what the privatizers are selling. Among liberal elites (mainly academics and their think tanks), the conservatives' ideas have set off a flurry of worry and have generated proposals to largely preserve what we have come to know. It may turn out that these liberal elites are as isolated from popular thinking as are their conservative counterparts (if, for example, raising the age for full-retirement benefits surfaces in liberals' as well as in conservatives' proposals). We know that most of the public wants social security pretty much as they have known it, and we know they are very worried that it will not be.

At this point in time, it is simply too early to tell if privatizing will pass muster with the public. The early test will be if privatization catches on with those members of the public who, in economic terms, have the most to gain. Ideology varies systematically with socioeconomic status, and if any members of the public will buy social security transfor-

mation (that is, making it something quite different from what it has been), it will be those who are the better off. If this occurs, especially among those, say, age 50 and above, we will be seeing a fragmenting of the older population's political voice, a voice that polls and lore have long held to be largely one when it comes to social security. Such a development would be significant because political analysts have long wondered about the degree to which elderly people's vaunted political power ("AARP is the most powerful group in Washington") is real or imagined. As Alinsky (1946, p. 49) contended, "the perception of power is as important as the possession of power." If privatization proposals gain significant numbers of converts among the old (here, "old money"), the perception of power will begin to fade.

## Conclusion

To conservatives, privatization of social security would be a major accomplishment in a larger effort to reinstall the idea that the principal U.S. institutions related to individual well-being are the market and the family. Markets are in place to ensure economic well-being; families are the core social institution promoting social, psychological, and spiritual well-being. In such an understanding, government activity becomes a barometer of how far we have fallen from the ideal. The challenge to liberals is nothing less than making sure that the "institutional" place of social security—that is, as an accepted, expected, and legitimate program—is maintained. And by "maintained," we must mean continuation of a universal, single-tier program, assuring a defined annuity benefit, that uses the agency of government to modestly redistribute retirement benefits toward those of lower income.

## References

Alinsky, S. (1946). *Reveille for radicals.* Chicago: University of Chicago Press.

Brody, S. (1987). Strategic planning: The catastropic approach. *Gerontologist, 27,* 131–138.

Chen, Y-P. (1993). A "three-legged stool": A new way to fund long-term care. In Institute of Medicine (Ed.), *Care in the long term* (pp. 54–70). Washington, DC: National Academy Press.

Crystal, S. (1982). *America's old age crisis: The two worlds of aging.* New York: Basic Books.

Davies, G. (1996). *From opportunity to entitlement: The transformation and decline of Great Society liberalism.* Lawrence: University of Kansas Press.

Friedland, R. (1999). Demography is not destiny. *The Public Policy and Aging Report, 9,* 9.

Hudson, R. (1993). Social contingencies, the aged, and public policy. *The Milbank Quarterly, 71,* 253–277.

Kuttner, R. (1999, January 27). Clinton's dangerous dalliance. *The Washington Post,* p. A19.

Marmor, T. (1973). *The politics of Medicare.* Chicago: Aldine.

Page, B. (1999, January 27). *Is social security reform ready for the American public?* Paper presented at the Annual Meeting of the National Academy of Social Insurance, Washington, DC.

Quadagno, J. (1991). Interest group politics and the future of U.S. social security. In J. Myles & J. Quadagno (Eds.), *States, labor markets, and the future of old-age policy* (pp. 36–58). Philadelphia: Temple University Press.

Radner, D. (1995). Incomes of the elderly and non-elderly, 1967–92. *Social Security Bulletin, 58,* 82–97.

Samuelson, R. (1995). *The good life and its discontents.* New York: Random House.

Schieber, S. (1996). A new vision for social security. *The Public Policy and Aging Report, 7, 1,* 6–7, 9, 14–15.

Walker, J. (1983). The origins and maintenance of interest groups in America. *American Political Science Review, 77,* 390–406.

This chapter was originally published in the May 1999 issue of *Health & Social Work,* Vol. 24, Number 2, pp. 155–160.

# 2

# Marital Status and Change in Income Status 10 Years after Retirement

MARTHA N. OZAWA
and YAT-SANG LUM

During a time when the income levels of the American people have been stagnating, the situation of the elderly population had been an exception. As a result of increases in social security benefits in 1968, 1969, and 1970; the automatic cost-of-living adjustment that took effect in 1972; and the enactment of the Employment Retirement Income Security Act (ERISA) of 1974 (P.L. 93-406), a smaller proportion of elderly people than of nonelderly people lived below the poverty line (U.S. House of Representatives, 1996).

However, this rosy picture of elderly people's economic well-being hides the great variation among people of differing marital statuses. According to *Income of the Population 55 and Older, 1994* (Grad, 1996), the median family income of elderly couples was $27,013, but those of elderly unmarried men and women were $16,117 and $12,784, respectively. Gini coefficients of the incomes of different types of households attests to the greater income inequality among elderly people than among nonelderly people. The U.S. Bureau of the Census (1992) reported that in 1991, the Gini coefficient of the incomes of households with elderly members was .462, compared with .394 for households with children. Furthermore, the inequality in the incomes of elderly people tends to become even greater as they age, according to a longitudinal study by Ozawa (1997). In short, there are many low-income elderly people and many high-income elderly people, income inequality is greater among elderly people than among nonelderly people, and this inequality grows even greater as elderly people age. Furthermore, the findings of these studies imply that the marital-status differential is strongly related to the variation in income distribution among elderly people.

The study reported in this article explored the income status of a cohort of elderly people at the time of retirement and 10 years later and investigated the effect of marital status on the level of income at these two points, as well as on the degree of change in income status during this period. In particular, it examined:

• the income status of recently retired people of different marital statuses at the time of retirement and 10 years later.
• the degree of change in income status of these marital groups of retirees during the 10 years after retirement.
• the effect of marital status on income status at retirement and 10 years later, controlling for human capital and demographic variables.
• the effect of marital status on the change in income status during the 10 years after retirement, controlling for human capital and demographic variables.

The study investigated men and women separately, because marital status may have a differential effect on men's and women's economic status. For example, widowhood may be a devastating financial blow for women but not for men, because men's contribution to their households' incomes before they die is generally greater than women's.

## Literature Review

Recent research on the effect of marital status on the income of elderly people has focused almost exclusively on widowhood. Research in this area has been concerned with the following questions: To what extent does the death of a spouse increase the probability of the surviving spouse's becoming poor? How differently does widowhood affect the income status of widows and widowers? Does the couple's income level before the spouse's death make a difference in how far the income level drops as a result of widowhood? Do single-life versus joint-and-survivor pensions have a differential effect on the income status of widows? How does the age at which the surviving spouse is widowed affect his or her income status?

### Widowhood

A review of the literature indicated that women who eventually become widowed have a higher poverty rate before they are widowed and have an even higher poverty rate afterward than women who stay married. Widowhood raises the already high poverty rate of eventual widows by 30 percentage points (Holden, Burkhauser, & Myers, 1986), because the husbands of eventual widows tend to have lower earnings (Zick & Smith, 1991). Furthermore, widowhood abruptly increases the risk of becoming poor and increases it persistently thereafter because the tendency to fall into poverty over time is affected by widowhood, as well as by aging.

Widowhood appears to affect the income status of men and women differently. According to Burkhauser, Butler, and Holden (1991), on the death of a spouse, the chance of falling into poverty and facing a significant drop in income (measured by the income-to-needs ratio) dramatically increases for widows, but not for widowers. Also, Holden (1990) found that whereas the income of women falls sharply when their husbands die, the income of men remains stable on the death of their wives. On the other hand, Zick and Smith's (1986) study showed that the death of a spouse has negative economic consequences for both widows and widowers relative to continuously married couples. However, the small size of the sample of widowers in that study (149 widows compared to 27 widowers) casts doubt on the reliability of this finding.

Furthermore, the earlier a woman becomes widowed, the greater the woman suffers economically. Zick and Smith (1991) reported that middle-aged widows and widowers fared equally well financially, but that young widows suffered a significantly greater loss of income as a result of their husbands' deaths than young widowers did as a result of their wives' deaths. Also, Holden (1989) demonstrated that widows whose husbands chose single-life pensions not only had significantly lower incomes before they were widowed, but also faced a greater decline in their incomes afterward than their counterparts whose husbands chose joint-and-survivor pensions.

### Divorce

Although there has been little research on the effect of divorce on the income status of elderly people, studies on the effect of divorce among nonelderly people provide some insight into the situation of the elderly population. Several studies have reported that divorce results in a significantly large reduction in the family income of women, ranging from 29 percent to 55 percent (Corcoran, 1979; Duncan & Hoffman, 1985; Hoffman, 1977; Mott & Moore, 1978; Nestel, Mercier, & Shaw, 1983; Weiss, 1984). Of particular interest is that high-income women face a greater decline in family income than do low-income women as a result of divorce. For example, Weiss (1984) found that the in-comes of women who were in the top one-third of income distribution decreased 55 percent as a result of divorce, compared with 23 percent for women in the lowest one-third. Duncan and Hoffman (1985) found that after divorce the decline in the incomes of both black women and white women with relatively high incomes during marriage was greater after divorce than that of their low-income counterparts. Little or no research has been done on the income status of never-married elderly people.

### Basis of the Study

The literature indicates that widowhood results in a decline in the economic well-being of elderly people, especially elderly women; that the effect of widowhood is greater on those with greater earlier incomes; and that those who become widowed early in life are more deprived economically than those who become widowed later. The literature also seems to indicate that people who enter retirement as divorced people have considerably lower income statuses.

However, many questions remain. What is the difference in the income statuses of those who were continuously married for 10 years after retirement and the already widowed, the newly widowed, the divorced, and the never married? What changes in income status did these groups of elderly people experience during the 10 years after retirement? The present study addressed these empirical questions.

## Method

### Conceptual Framework

The concept of income status, which is the central concept of this study, needs to be explained at the outset. *Income status* is a person's income level, taking into account the number of members in the household and the economy of scale (that is, two people living together need less than twice the income of a person living alone). Thus, income status is a more appropriate indicator of economic well-being than nominal dollar figures. For the purposes of this study, then, *income status* was defined as the multiple of poverty-line income—that is, household income divided by the poverty line income of household with a particular number of members. *Poverty-line income*, as developed by the Social Security Administration, depends on the size of a household and incorporates the economy of scale. For example, if the income of an elderly couple is equal to the poverty line, then their income status is 1, and so is the income status of each person in the household. The actual dollars needed for a couple to achieve the income status of 1 is 1.261 times the dollars needed for an unmarried elderly person to achieve the income status of 1 (see Social Security Administration, 1996). Because a couple benefits from the economy of scale, a couple does not need double the income of an individual, but only a fraction more. *Income status*, as defined in this study, is the ratio of income to poverty-line income, which is often referred to as the income-to-needs ratio, or simply the "poverty ratio." In this study, we express the income statuses in poverty ratios.

When a spouse dies, the surviving spouse's income status does not necessarily decline; it may increase. If a person's income in dollars shrinks by less than 21 percent (100 − 1.00/ 1.261 × 100) as a result of the death of a spouse, his or her income status increases. This scenario often holds true when a man survives, because the portion of income attributable to his wife while both were alive is often small. The reverse is true for a woman. When her husband dies, the widow is at risk

of a decline in income status because she may lose more by the decrease in income than benefit by not having an additional mouth to feed. Thus, three forces are at work in determining the income status of elderly people: a spouse's death eliminates one mouth to feed, but also causes a drop in income, mediated by the economy of scale.

Because individuals who live alone must have incomes in dollars that are 79 percent of the incomes of couples to achieve the same income status, it is difficult for single individuals to attain the same income status as married couples. To compound the situation, individuals who have low-income status while young have more difficulty saving and investing money, ultimately resulting in low levels of income from assets in old age. As earnings decline and income from assets becomes a more important source of income, the inability to draw income from assets negatively affects the income status of elderly people. In the latter category fall those who enter retirement as divorced, widowed, and never-married people. Not only are the income statuses of these groups of individuals expected to be lower than that of married couples at the time of retirement, but the extent of the decline in their income statuses should be steeper during the 10 years after retirement.

How each marital group fares in income status at retirement and 10 years later and in the change in income status between these two is hypothesized to be mediated by individuals' human capital, which is the basis for creating individual economic capability. *Human capital*, an economics concept, means human capabilities that are conducive to generating economic output through education, work experience, and job-related training. For example, the death of a spouse would not cause as much of a decline in the income status of a surviving wife with greater human capital than of a surviving wife with less human capital, because the former already had her own economic base—in terms of earnings, retirement income, and income from assets—even before her husband's death. Similarly, not all unmarried people are doomed economically at the time of retirement or 10 years later. Those who have economic capabilities can continue to have earnings after retirement and can even increase their income from assets as they age. Thus, the investigation of the net effect of marital status on the income status of elderly people requires the incorporation of human capital variables as controls in the data analysis.

In this study, we included education, occupation in the longest-held job, and the number of quarters of covered employment as human capital variables. Education and occupation are widely recognized as indicators of human capital, and the number of quarters of covered employment is a strong indicator of labor force attachment, which, in turn, is an important part of human capital. The quarters of covered employment were as of 1977. (Before 1978, one quarter of coverage was earned for each calendar quarter in which a worker was paid $50 or more in wages for covered employment. Since 1978, quarters of coverage have been credited annually [see Myers, 1996].) We included the demographic variables age and race as controls. We also included income in 1982, because only by so doing could we estimate the net effect of marital status on the change in income status between 1982 and 1992 (Dalecki & Willits, 1991; Gillespie & Streeter, 1994).

### Data Sources and Sample

The sources of data for this study were the 1982 New Beneficiary Survey (NBS) and its follow-up survey, the 1991 New Beneficiary Followup (NBF) (Social Security Administration, 1994). The NBS had a sample of 18,136 individuals, representing about 2 million people who had become new beneficiaries of Old Age, Survivors, and Disability Insurance and Medicare between mid-1980 and mid-1981; the response rate in the NBS was 85.9 percent. The NBF interviewed 12,128 surviving NBS respondents and 1,834 surviving spouses of NBS respondents who had died since the survey; the response rate was 87.5 percent (Social Security Administration, 1994). The NBS collected information on demographic characteristics, employment history, marital status, health status, work history, current income, and assets. The NBF collected, in addition, information on employment history during the 10 years after the NBS, changes in marital status, and the economic effects of both.

For the purposes of this study, we selected individuals who started receiving social security benefits between mid-1980 and mid-1981 as retired workers, wives, divorced wives, widows, surviving divorced wives, and individuals who started receiving Medicare coverage without receiving cash retirement benefits (Medicare-only beneficiaries) during the same period. (Because of the repeal of the earnings test in 2000, this question will be moot in the future.)

We excluded all people who started receiving social security benefits as disabled workers and those who started receiving benefits before age 62 as widows or surviving divorced wives. (Under the law, some disabled widows can claim survivors insurance benefits as early as age 50, and some surviving divorced wives can claim these benefits as early as age 60.) In addition, we excluded individuals who had remarried since 1982 after they had been separated, divorced, or widowed because the number of such cases was small (*n* = 113). We included surviving spouses of the respondents who were interviewed in the NBS but were dead by the time of the NBF. Among surviving spouses, those who were under age 63 at the time of the NBS were excluded because the study focused on people who entered retirement at the time of the NBS. Following the same selection process for women and men, 8,509 respondents were selected: 4,447 women and 4,062 men.

We categorized the respondents as falling into the following five groups: (1) those who were continuously married from 1982 through 1992, (2) those who were continuously widowed from 1982 through 1992, (3) those who were continuously separated or divorced from 1982 through 1992, (4) those who were never married, and (5) those who became widowed after 1982. It is important to remember that beneficiary status was used solely as a means of selecting respondents for the study and that we used the variable marital status to categorize the respondents. For example, married women do not necessarily receive benefits as wives; many receive benefits as retired workers on the basis of their own earnings records. And not all divorced women receive divorced wives' benefits.

### Definition of Variables

*Dependent Variables.* The dependent variables were income status in 1982 and 1992 and changes in the income status from 1982 to 1992. We first transformed incomes (total money incomes) into poverty ratios by dividing the income of each aged unit by the poverty-line income of the aged unit. This way, we obtained the poverty ratios of respondents for 1982 and 1992 and calculated the difference between the two. The *aged unit* consists of the social security beneficiary and spouse, if married; it always consists of one

or two people. We used the aged unit, instead of family or household, to measure income status because the NBS and the NBF did not include incomes of people in the household other than the social security beneficiary and spouse.

Throughout the study, poverty ratios were used for analytical purposes. The concept of poverty ratio is useful because it automatically deals with price changes from 1982 to 1992, as well as the size of the aged unit and the economy of scale discussed earlier. In performing regression analyses of income status in 1982 and 1992, we further transformed poverty ratios into a natural log because the distribution of poverty ratios is skewed. Change in income status from 1982 to 1992 could take positive or negative numbers; therefore, we did not transform this variable into a natural log.

*Independent Variable: Marital Status.* Marital status was measured by dummy variables for respondents who were widowed continuously from 1982 to 1992, respondents who were separated or divorced continuously from 1982 to 1992, respondents who were never married, and respondents who became widowed after 1982. Those who were married continuously from 1982 to 1992 were assigned to the reference group.

*Control Variables.* The following demographic, human capital, and income variables were included as controls: age, race, education, occupation, quarters of covered employment, and the 1982 baseline income status. Age was the age at the time of the NBS, which was the year of initial receipt of social security benefits or Medicare, plus one. Thus, the youngest recipient at the time of the NBS was 63. For the purpose of this study, age was called "age at the time of the NBS," "age at the time of the initial receipt of social security benefits or Medicare," or simply "age at the time of the initial receipt of social security benefits." These terms are interchangeable.

Race is self-explanatory; the value of 1 was assigned to white respondents, and the value of 0 to all others. To control for gender, we analyzed the data for men and women separately. Education was measured by dummy variables for the groups of respondents who had some high school education, were high school graduates, and had at least some college education. Those who had an elementary school education were assigned to the reference group.

Occupation was the occupation in the longest-held job. It was measured by dummy variables for the groups of respondents whose longest-held jobs were managerial, technical, and operative, and for those who held no jobs. Those whose longest-held jobs were service jobs were assigned to the reference group. Quarters of covered employment was the number of quarters of covered employment accumulated throughout the respondents' work lives until 1977.

## Data Analysis

We analyzed the data in the following ways. First, we obtained descriptive statistics on the backgrounds of the respondents. Second, we generated descriptive statistics on the respondents' income status in 1982 and 1992 and the change from 1982 to 1992. Third, we performed a series of regression analyses to estimate the effect of marital status on the level of income status in 1982 and 1992 and on the change between these two years: an OLS regression analysis to investigate the determinants of income status in 1982, an OLS regression analysis to investigate the determinants of the change in income status from 1982 to 1992, and an OLS regression analy-

sis to investigate the determinants of income status in 1992. Model 1 explains which marital groups were better (or worse) off than others in 1982, when other variables were controlled. Model 2 indicates the extent to which marital status affected the change in income status from 1982 to 1992, other things being equal. Model 3 explains which marital groups were better (or worse) off than others in 1992, when other variables were controlled.

We used the weight variable that was developed by the Social Security Administration to generate descriptive statistics on all variables. This procedure was needed to adjust for the sampling, poststratification, and nonresponse biases in the NBS and NBF data sets.

The unit of analysis was the individual. The income statuses of individuals were derived from the income levels of the aged units. We assumed that both spouses in an aged unit shared economic resources equally and, therefore, had the same income status. Thus, variable income status pertains to individuals. All other variables pertained to individuals as well.

## Findings

### *Descriptive Statistics*

*Characteristics of Respondents.* There were considerable differences in some of the characteristics of the women and men (Table 2-1). For example, the percentage of women who became widowed between 1982 and 1992 was considerably higher than that of men (29.1 percent compared with 11.3 percent, respectively). Only 45.5 percent of the women, but 78.9 percent of the men, were continuously married, and 15 percent of the women, compared with 3.3 percent of the men, were continuously widowed.

**TABLE 2-1. Characteristics of the Respondents**

| Characteristic | Percentage Women | Men |
|---|---|---|
| Race | | |
| White | 91.7 | 92.3 |
| Other than white | 8.3 | 7.7 |
| Marital status | | |
| Continuously married | 45.5 | 78.9 |
| Continuously widowed | 15.0 | 3.3 |
| Continuously separated | | |
| or divorced | 5.8 | 3.5 |
| Never married | 4.6 | 3.0 |
| Widowed after 1982 | 29.1 | 11.3 |
| Education | | |
| Elementary school | 20.3 | 22.3 |
| Some high school | 19.9 | 16.5 |
| High school graduate | 34.6 | 26.6 |
| At least some college | | |
| education | 25.2 | 34.6 |
| Occupation in the longest job | | |
| Managerial | 15.2 | 29.4 |
| Technical | 33.2 | 21.2 |
| Operative | 17.5 | 43.8 |
| Service | 14.5 | 5.5 |
| No occupation | 19.5 | 0.1 |
| | Mean and Median | |
| Mean age in 1982 | 64.9 | 65.8 |
| Mean quarters of social | | |
| security coverage | 53.5 | 116.5 |
| Median quarters of social | | |
| security coverage | 54.0 | 126.0 |
| Mean poverty ratio in 1982 | 3.6 | 5.0 |
| Mean poverty ratio in 1992 | 2.8 | 4.3 |
| Median poverty ratio in 1982 | 2.8 | 3.6 |
| Median poverty ratio in 1992 | 2.2 | 3.0 |

In addition, the men had greater human capital. A higher percentage of the men than of the women (34.6 percent versus 25.2 percent) had at least some college education, and 29.4 percent of the men, but only 15.2 percent of the women, had managerial jobs in their longest-held positions. The median number of quarters of covered employment for the men was 126, compared with 54 for the women.

Measured by median poverty ratios, the men were considerably better off than were the women in both 1982 and 1992—3.6 in 1982 and 3.0 in 1992 for the men and 2.8 in 1982 and 2.2 in 1992 for the women. Furthermore, the rate of the decline of the poverty ratio from 1982 to 1992 was considerably greater for the women (20.9 percent) than for the men (16.6 percent).

*Poverty Ratios, by Marital Status.* Of all the marital groups of women, continuously married women had the highest poverty ratio in both 1982 and 1992 (Table 2-2). The poverty ratio of those who became widowed after 1982 was the second highest in 1982, but declined the most (a 30.1 percent decline) during the 10 years after that year—so much so that it dropped below that of the never-married respondents by 1992 (Figure 2-1). The median poverty ratios of those who entered retirement as already widowed individuals or as continuously separated or divorced people were considerably lower than the median poverty ratios of continuously married people, both at retirement and 10 years afterward. The economic deprivation of those who were continuously separated or divorced was particularly pronounced in both 1982 and 1992.

As in the case of the women, the men who were continuously married had the highest poverty ratio in both 1982 and 1992 (Figure 2-2). Although the poverty ratio of the men who became widowed after 1982 declined the most (18.6 percent), the reduction was not severe enough to be outranked by the other marital groups; thus, this group maintained their second rank in income status in both 1982 and 1992 (Table 2-2). Note that it was the never-married men who were the most deprived economically in both 1982 and 1992, not the continuously separated or divorced men, as was the case with women. However, because of the large decline in the poverty ratio of the continuously separated or divorced men from 1982 to

**TABLE 2-2.  Change in the Median Poverty Ratio from 1982 to 1992, by Marital Status**

| Respondent Characteristic | Poverty Ratio 1982 | Poverty Ratio 1992 | Change | % Change |
|---|---|---|---|---|
| All women | 2.82 | 2.23 | −0.59 | −20.9 |
| Continuously married | 3.26 | 2.68 | −0.58 | −17.8 |
| Continuously widowed | 2.22 | 1.84 | −0.38 | −17.1 |
| Continuously separated or divorced | 1.79 | 1.64 | −0.15 | −8.4 |
| Never married | 2.81 | 2.31 | −0.50 | −17.8 |
| Widowed after 1982 | 3.06 | 2.14 | −0.92 | −30.1 |
| All men | 3.61 | 3.01 | −0.60 | −16.6 |
| Continuously married | 3.70 | 3.11 | −0.59 | −15.9 |
| Continuously widowed | 3.11 | 2.71 | −0.40 | −12.9 |
| Continuously separated or divorced | 2.52 | 2.22 | −0.30 | −11.9 |
| Never married | 2.27 | 2.19 | −0.08 | −3.5 |
| Widowed after 1982 | 3.50 | 2.85 | −0.65 | −18.6 |

1992 (11.9 percent), the poverty ratio of this group became almost as low as that of never-married men.

Figures 2-1 and 2-2 and Table 2-2 provide useful information at the descriptive level; however they do not give information on the net effect of marital status on the re-spondents' income status. Human capital and demographic variables are also at work in determining income status. Thus, the investigation of the net effect of marital status on the income status requires a multivariate analysis in which human capital and demographic variables are controlled.

**FIGURE 2-1.  Changes in Median Poverty Ratios, 10 Years after Retirement: Women**

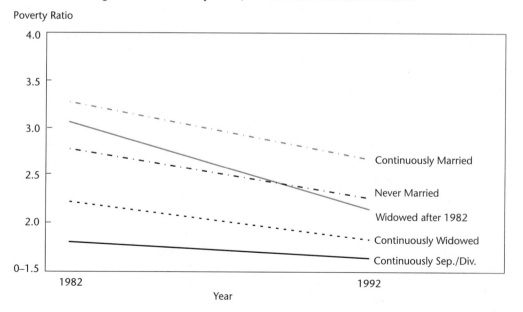

Poverty Ratio

**FIGURE 2-2. Changes in Median Poverty Ratios, 10 Years after Retirement: Men**

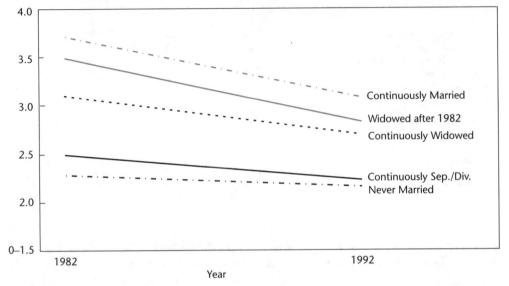

Poverty Ratio

- Continuously Married
- Widowed after 1982
- Continuously Widowed
- Continuously Sep./Div.
- Never Married

Year

### OLS Multiple Regression Analysis

It is important to clarify the meaning of regression coefficients in multiple regression analyses in which the dependent variable is transformed into a natural log and independent variables take the form of dummy variables, as in models 1 and 3. Most researchers interpret multiple regression coefficients in this situation simply as a percentage difference. A coefficient of 0.363, for example, is interpreted as "36.3 percent greater." However, Halvorsen and Palmquist (1980) warned that the traditional way of interpreting regression coefficients is wrong. They argued that

$$C = ln(1 + g) \text{ and } e^c = 1 + g$$

therefore, $g = e^c - 1$, where $C$ = regression coefficient and $g$ = relative effect.

Following this equation and applying the coefficient of 0.363, one finds the relative effect $g$ is 0.438, which can be interpreted as "43.8 percent greater." Thus, in the data analysis that follows, we used the procedure specified by Halvorsen and Palmquist. We calculated the values of the relative effect $g$ (expressed in percentage) for all coefficients for dummy variables in the OLS multiple regression analyses involving the natural log of poverty ratios as the dependent variable. (This transformation is not required for independent variables that are interval.)

*Model 1: Analysis of Poverty Ratios in 1982.* This regression model was designed to estimate the effect of marital status on income status in 1982, controlling for human capital and demographic variables. The dependent variable is the poverty ratio in 1982, and the control variables are education, occupation, quarters of covered employment, age, and race.

For both men and women, certain marital statuses made a significant difference in

TABLE 2-3. OLS Multiple Regression Analysis of the Poverty Ratio (log) in 1982

| Variable | Women[a] | | | Men[b] | | |
|---|---|---|---|---|---|---|
| | Coefficient | t | Relative Effect (%) | Coefficient | t | Relative Effect (%) |
| Intercept | −2.2965 | −8.995*** | | −3.7398 | −12.665*** | |
| Age and race | | | | | | |
| Age | 0.0411 | 10.620*** | | 0.0640 | 14.573*** | |
| White | 0.2680 | 8.620*** | 30.7 | 0.2956 | 7.545*** | 34.4 |
| Marital status | | | | | | |
| Continuously widowed | −0.3956 | −15.762*** | −32.7 | −0.1014 | −1.847 | −9.6 |
| Continuously separated or divorced | −0.6867 | −20.620*** | −49.7 | −0.2969 | −5.483*** | −25.7 |
| Never married | −0.4844 | −11.522*** | −38.4 | −0.3322 | −5.612*** | −28.3 |
| Widowed after 1982 | 0.0159 | 0.709 | 1.6 | −0.0709 | −2.228* | −6.8 |
| (Continuously married) | | | | | | |
| Education | | | | | | |
| Some high school | 0.1746 | 6.052*** | 19.1 | 0.1651 | 5.067*** | 18.0 |
| High school graduate | 0.3698 | 13.473*** | 44.7 | 0.3162 | 10.499*** | 37.2 |
| At least some college | 0.5444 | 17.750*** | 72.4 | 0.5339 | 16.508*** | 70.6 |
| (Elementary school) | | | | | | |
| Occupation | | | | | | |
| Managerial | 0.2638 | 7.655*** | 30.2 | 0.2692 | 5.550*** | 30.9 |
| Technical | 0.1510 | 5.262*** | 16.3 | 0.1096 | 2.272* | 11.6 |
| Operative | −0.0206 | −0.651 | −2.0 | −0.0338 | −0.756 | −3.3 |
| No occupation | 0.1545 | 4.672*** | 16.7 | −0.5542 | −2.132* | −42.5 |
| (Service) | | | | | | |
| Quarters of coverage | 0.0022 | 8.949*** | | 0.0015 | 5.766*** | |

Note: Reference groups are in parentheses.
a. $R^2 = 0.312$; $F = 142.416$*** $N = 4,415$.
b. $R^2 = 0.294$; $F = 119.148$*** $N = 4,022$.
*$p < .05$. **$p < .01$. ***$p < .001$.

the poverty ratios, even after the human capital and demographic variables were controlled (Table 2-3). There was no statistical difference in the 1982 poverty ratios of the continuously married and newly widowed women—those who became widowed after 1982. However, the poverty ratios of the other marital groups of women were significantly lower than that of the continuously married women. In particular, the poverty ratio of the women who were continuously separated or divorced was as much as 49.7 percent lower than that of the women who were continuously married.

In contrast, the poverty ratio of the men who became widowed after 1982 was already

significantly lower in 1982 than that of the continuously married men (6.8 percent, $p < 0.5$). However, the poverty ratios of the other marital groups of men were even lower. The never-married group was the most deprived, with a poverty ratio that was as much as 28.3 percent lower than that of the continuously married men. It is interesting that the poverty ratio of those who were continuously widowed was no different from that of those who were continuously married.

Coefficients of control variables were all as expected. Education and occupation were positively related to the poverty ratio; the greater the number of quarters of covered employment, the higher the poverty ratio; the

poverty ratio of the white respondents was
significantly higher; and the age at retirement
was positively related to the poverty ratio.
Good education seems to pay off very well
indeed. The poverty ratio of the women with
at least some college education was 72.4 percent higher and the poverty ratio of the men
with such an educational background was
70.6 percent higher than that of their respec-
tive counterparts with an elementary school
education.

The coefficients of age and no occupation (only among the women) warrant further explanation. The coefficient of age does
not necessarily mean that the older respondents had higher poverty ratios. Rather, it
means that other things being equal, those
who entered retirement later (such as people
with high wages who did not retire at age
65) tended to have high poverty ratios. The
coefficient of no occupation among the
women indicates that those with no jobs had
higher poverty ratios than those who had
service jobs, probably because some of the
women with no jobs had husbands with high
incomes.

*Model 2: Analysis of the Change in the Pov-
erty Ratio from 1982 to 1992.* This regression model was designed to estimate the
effect of marital status on the change in income status from 1982 to 1992, controlling
for human capital and demographic variables and the baseline poverty ratio for 1982.
The dependent variable is the change in the
poverty ratio from 1982 to 1992, and the
control variables are education, occupation,
quarters of covered employment, age, race,
and the 1982 poverty ratio as the baseline
poverty ratio.

The findings for women and men are considerably different (Table 2-4). Controlling
for human capital variables, demographic
variables, and the baseline 1982 poverty ratio, we found that marital status had a strong

effect on the change in the poverty ratio for
women, but not for men. Of all the nonmarried groups, the continuously separated
or divorced women had the highest negative
change in the poverty ratio from 1982 to 1992
(–1.3200), relative to the change experienced
by the continuously married respondents. In
contrast, the change for those who were widowed after 1982 was only –0.4769.

For the men, marital status affected the
change in the poverty ratio from 1982 to 1992
only a little (Table 2-4). There were no statistical differences in the change in the poverty ratios of the continuously married and
of each of the nonmarried groups, except that
for those who were continuously widowed,
there was a positive change of 1.0561 ($p < .05$),
relative to the change for the continuously
married men.

Education contributed a positive change
in the poverty ratio for both men and women.
The coefficients of other control variables
differed considerably between women and
men. For example, occupation was significantly related to the change in the poverty
ratio of women, but not of men. Age at the
time of the NBS was significantly related to
the change in the poverty ratio among the
men, but not among the women.

*Model 3: Analysis of Poverty Ratios in 1992.*
This regression model was designed to estimate the effect of marital status on the respondents' income status in 1992,
controlling for human capital and demographic variables. Thus, the dependent variable is the poverty ratio in 1992, and the
control variables are education, occupation,
quarters of covered employment, age, and
race (Table 2-5).

One major finding from this regression
analysis is that the poverty ratio of the women
who became widowed after 1982 was 17.1
percent lower ($p < .001$) in 1992 than the
poverty ratio of those who were continuously

**TABLE 2-4.** OLS Multiple Regression Analysis of the Change in the Poverty Ratio from 1982 to 1992

| Variable | Women[a] Coefficient | t | Men[b] Coefficient | t |
|---|---|---|---|---|
| Intercept | 1.2871 | 0.937 | –4.9759 | –1.919 |
| Age and race | | | | |
|   Age | 0.0383 | 1.821 | 0.1377 | 3.519*** |
|   White | 0.4917 | 2.924** | 0.8175 | 2.390* |
| Marital status | | | | |
|   Continuously widowed | –0.8778 | –6.359*** | 1.0561 | 2.212* |
|   Continuously separated or divorced | –1.3200 | –7.118*** | –0.9204 | –1.954 |
|   Never married | –0.9462 | –4.144*** | –0.3609 | –0.699 |
|   Widowed after 1982 | –0.4769 | –3.967*** | 0.2551 | 0.923 |
|   (Continuously married) | | | | |
| Education | | | | |
|   Some high school | 0.3450 | 2.222* | 0.5501 | 1.943 |
|   High school graduate | 0.7182 | 4.790*** | 1.4728 | 5.574*** |
|   At least some college | 1.3124 | 7.705*** | 2.4998 | 8.628*** |
|   (Elementary school) | | | | |
| Occupation | | | | |
|   Managerial | 0.6318 | 3.397*** | 0.5161 | 1.222 |
|   Technical | 0.3077 | 1.992* | 0.0382 | 0.091 |
|   Operative | 0.0811 | 0.478 | 0.1840 | 0.475 |
|   No occupation | 0.4330 | 2.435* | –1.3932 | –0.618 |
|   (Service) | | | | |
| Quarters of coverage | 0.0037 | 2.746** | 0.0063 | 2.723** |
| 1982 poverty ratio (log) | –4.1406 | –36.753*** | –5.0291 | –27.883*** |

*Note:* Reference groups are in parentheses.
a. $R^2 = 0.248$; $F = 96.284$*** $N = 4,408$.
b. $R^2 = 0.170$; $F = 54.689$*** $N = 4,018$.
*$p < .05$. **$p < .01$. ***$p < .001$.

married in the same year, although there was no statistical difference in the poverty ratios of these two marital groups of women in 1982 (see Table 2-3). Other than this noticeable change, there were no discernible changes in the coefficients of the independent and control variables; that is, the effects of these variables on the poverty ratio in 1992 were similar to those in 1982. The monotonously same findings regarding these coefficients mean that among women and men, the poverty ratio in 1992 is determined by the same set of variables with a similar statistical force as is the poverty ratio of 1982, with the exception of postretirement widowhood among women.

It is of interest to note that although the poverty ratio of the newly widowed women was significantly lower (17.1 percent) than that of their continuously married counterparts in 1992, the poverty ratios of the other marital groups were even lower: 42.4 percent lower for those continuously separated or divorced, 37.1 percent lower for those never married, and 31.0 percent for those continuously widowed. So, in spite of a significant negative decline in the poverty ratio from 1982 to 1992 (Table 2-4), the newly widowed women could maintain the second highest income status—lower only than the continuously married group—in the poverty ratios of all the marital groups of women in 1992.

**TABLE 2-5. OLS Multiple Regression Analysis of the Poverty Ratio (log) in 1992**

| Variable | Women[a] | | | Men[b] | | |
|---|---|---|---|---|---|---|
| | Coefficient | t | Relative Effect (%) | Coefficient | t | Relative Effect (%) |
| Intercept | −2.2552 | −8.894*** | | −3.7618 | −12.819*** | |
| Age and race | | | | | | |
| Age | 0.0347 | 10.161*** | | 0.0560 | 14.420*** | |
| White | 0.2139 | 7.621*** | 23.9 | 0.2497 | 7.196*** | 28.4 |
| Marital status | | | | | | |
| Continuously widowed | −0.3704 | −16.369*** | −31.0 | −0.0510 | −1.046 | −5.0 |
| Continuously separated or divorced | −0.5509 | −18.359*** | −42.4 | −0.2783 | −5.818*** | −24.3 |
| Never married | −0.4632 | −12.187*** | −37.1 | −0.2396 | −4.550*** | −21.3 |
| Widowed after 1982 | −0.1876 | −9.270*** | −17.1 | −0.0826 | −2.928** | −8.0 |
| (Continuously married) | | | | | | |
| Education | | | | | | |
| Some high school | 0.1566 | 6.008*** | 17.0 | 0.1400 | 4.849*** | 15.0 |
| High school graduate | 0.3326 | 13.408*** | 39.5 | 0.2981 | 11.176*** | 34.7 |
| At least some college | 0.5432 | 19.601*** | 72.2 | 0.5627 | 19.612*** | 75.5 |
| (Elementary school) | | | | | | |
| Occupation | | | | | | |
| Managerial | 0.2927 | 9.406*** | 34.0 | 0.2544 | 5.918*** | 29.0 |
| Technical | 0.1460 | 5.627*** | 15.7 | 0.1067 | 2.493* | 11.3 |
| Operative | 0.0216 | 0.756 | 2.2 | −0.0019 | −0.048 | −0.2 |
| No occupation | 0.1436 | 4.806*** | 15.4 | −0.3978 | −1.727 | −32.8 |
| (Service) | | | | | | |
| Quarters of coverage | 0.0017 | 7.401*** | | 0.0011 | 4.698*** | |

Note: Reference groups are in parentheses.
a. $R^2 = 0.309$; $F = 140.608$*** $N = 4,451$.
b. $R^2 = 0.320$; $F = 136.082$*** $N = 4,025$.
*$p < .05$. **$p < .01$. ***$p < .001$.

## Discussion

The main purpose of the study was to estimate the effects of marital status on the income status (measured by poverty ratios) of a cohort of elderly people. The results of multivariate analyses show that the net effect of marital status on income status is quite different from what the descriptive statistics project (see Table 2-1 and Figures 2-1 and 2-2). In particular, the results of the multivariate analyses indicate that the income status of newly widowed women was no different from that of continuously married women in 1982, when other variables were controlled. Widowhood after 1982 exerted a strong downward pressure on the change in

income status, relative to the change experienced by the continuously married women. Nevertheless, the degree of the negative change in income status associated with widowhood after 1982 was smaller than those for other nonmarried groups of women. As a result, the income status of newly widowed women stayed in second place, assuming that other variables were controlled, not in third place as depicted in Figure 2-1.

That the net effect of widowhood after 1982 is smaller than projected in the descriptive statistics means that descriptive statistics hide other underlying forces. For example, according to our separate analysis, newly widowed women had a considerably weaker attachment to the labor force than never-married women, with the former having only 48 quarters of covered employment, on average, and the latter having 108 quarters of covered employment. Thus, the apparently steep decline in income status among the newly widowed group, projected by descriptive statistics, was caused not only by widowhood, but by other factors.

These findings led us to focus on the economic fate of other nonmarried groups of women, particularly separated or divorced women. Separated or divorced women were the most economically deprived at retirement, experienced the sharpest declines in their income status, and stayed on the bottom of the economic ladder 10 years after retirement, assuming that other variables were controlled.

For men, marital status indeed made a difference in the income status, both at retirement and 10 years later. However, it made little or no difference in the change in income status—a distinction from the situation of women.

The net effect of widowhood is distinctly different for men and women. For women, widowhood before retirement had a more serious effect on income status at retirement and 10 years later and the change between the two points than did widowhood after retirement. For men, the reverse was true.

Another important finding was that the human capital variables—education, occupation, and labor force attachment—are all important determinants of the income status of men and women in old age. The fate of never-married women is a good example. The net effect of having never been married seems to be devastating, according to the findings, assuming all other things are equal. However, not all other things were equal. The degree of labor force attachment among never-married women was strong, as indicated by their mean quarters of covered employment (108, compared with 48 for newly widowed women and 46 for continuously married

women—data not shown in the tables). As a result, never-married women fared relatively well economically in old age because of their human capital, which mediates the effect of never having been married. As women continue to establish their own economic base by developing greater human capital through education, work, and job-related training, it is anticipated that the effect of marital status, which still is very strong, will become weaker as human capital variables gain greater force in determining women's economic fate. Achieving greater human capital, in turn, will no doubt narrow the gap in the income status of women and men that exists today.

## Implications for Social Policy

Marital status does make a difference in the level of men's and women's income status at retirement and a decade later. For women only, it also makes a considerable difference in the change in their income status during the 10 years after retirement. Thus, legislative initiatives to assist women should continue to be taken. However, future legislation in this regard may be more complicated than in the past, when widowhood was considered the major issue. This study found that the economic plight of women, both in the level of and change in their income status, who enter retirement as newly widowed or already widowed individuals is worse than that of the continuously married women. But neither group of widows fared the worst. Instead, it was the separated or divorced women who fared the worst.

In light of the complex economic situation that women face, which direction should legislative initiatives take? In the report of the Long-Term Reform Subcommittee of the Save the Social Security Coalition Women's Issues Committee (1996), *Making Social Security Work Better for Women*, the committee struck a balance between its concern for the financial needs of widows and divorced women and its concern for assisting women as individual workers. In particular, it recommended that a voluntary 125 percent survivor-benefits option (that is, 125 percent of primary insurance amount [PIA]) should be added to the benefit provisions, that a basic minimum benefit, which depends on the years of employment, should be established, that the benefit for divorced spouses be increased from the current 50 percent to 75 percent of the PIA, and that the benefit for spouses should be scaled according to the number of years of marriage.

As divorced retirees face considerable financial difficulty in retirement, the idea of an earnings sharing plan, which was hotly debated in the 1970s and 1980s, should be put to public scrutiny once again (see Burkhauser & Holden, 1982; Ozawa, 1980, 1982; U.S. Department of Health, Education, and Welfare, 1979). Under this plan, annual earnings by a husband and a wife would be combined into earnings for the couple and then divided in half each year and credited to the account of each spouse until one spouse reaches age 62 (Ozawa, 1980). This plan automatically deals not only with financial risks that women face as divorced or widowed people, but also with the internal redistribution of earnings credits to women from men, who generally earn more.

## Conclusion

Women's issues in social security, retirement, and workforce participation are complex and controversial. We anticipate that the United States will go through another round of political debate on these issues. Women's issues will become a major concern along with the dramatic increase in social security expenditures projected when the baby boomers start

to retire in less than two decades. In the meantime, the continued development of human capital among women will be in the interest of women and the nation.

## References

Burkhauser, R. V., Butler, J. S., & Holden, K. C. (1991). How the death of a spouse affects economic well-being after retirement: A hazard model approach. *Social Science Quarterly*, *72*, 505–519.

Burkhauser, R. V., & Holden, K. C. (1982). *A challenge to social security: The changing roles of women and men in American society*. New York: Academic Press.

Corcoran, M. (1979). The economic consequences of marital dissolution for women in the middle years. *Sex Roles*, *5*, 343–353.

Dalecki, M., & Willits, F. K. (1991). Examining change using regression analysis: Three approaches compared. *Sociological Spectrum*, *11*, 127–145.

Duncan, G. J., & Hoffman, S. D. (1985). Economic consequences of marital instability. In M. David & T. Smeeding (Eds.), *Horizontal equity, uncertainty, and economic well-being* (pp. 427–467). Chicago: University of Chicago Press.

Employment Retirement Income Security Act of 1974, P.L. 93-406, 88 Stat. 829.

Gillespie, D. F., & Streeter, C. L. (1994). Fitting regression models to research questions for analyzing change in nonexperimental research. *Social Work Research*, *18*, 239–244.

Grad, S. (1996). *Income of the population 55 or older, 1994*. Washington, DC: Social Security Administration.

Halvorsen, R., & Palmquiest, R. (1980). The interpretation of dummy variables in semilogarithmic equations. *American Economic Review*, *70*, 474–475.

Hoffman, S. (1977). Marital instability and the economic status of women. *Demography, 14,* 67–76.

Holden, K. C. (1989). Women's economic status in old age and widowhood. In M. N. Ozawa (Ed.), *Women's life cycle and economic insecurity: Problems and proposals* (pp. 143–169). New York: Praeger.

Holden, K. C. (1990). The joint impact of retirement and widow(er)hood: Is there double jeopardy? In *Proceedings of American Council on Consumer Interest.* New Orleans: American Council on Consumer Interest.

Holden, K. C., Burkhauser, R. V., & Myers, D. A. (1986). Income transitions at older stages of life: The dynamics of poverty. *Gerontologist, 26,* 293–297.

Mott, F. L., & Moore, S. F. (1978). The causes and consequences of marital breakdown. In F. Mott (Ed.), *Women, work and family* (pp. 113–135). Lexington, MA: Lexington Books.

Myers, R. J. (1996). *Summary of the provisions of the Old Age, Survivors, and Disability Insurance System, the Hospital Insurance System, and the Supplemental Medical Insurance System* (mimeographed). Washington, DC: Author.

Nestel, G., Mercier, J., & Shaw, L. B. (1983). Economic consequences of midlife change in marital status. In L. Shaw (Ed.), *The working lives of middle-aged women* (pp. 109–125). Lexington, MA: Lexington Books.

Ozawa, M. N. (1980). An analysis of HEW's proposals on social security. *Social Service Review, 54,* 92–107.

Ozawa, M. N. (1982). *Income maintenance and work incentives: Toward a synthesis.* New York: Praeger.

Ozawa, M. N. (1997). *Income and net worth of the elderly in the United States* (Report to the International Longevity Center, Tokyo). St. Louis: Washington University, George Warren Brown School of Social Work.

Save the Social Security Coalition Women's Issues Committee. (1996). *Making social security work better for women.* Washington, DC: Author.

Social Security Administration. (1994). *The New Beneficiary Survey data system: User's manual.* Washington, DC: Author.

Social Security Administration. (1996). *Social security bulletin: Annual statistical supplement, 1996.* Washington, DC: Author.

U.S. Bureau of the Census. (1992). *Measuring the effect of benefits and taxes on income and poverty: 1979 to 1991* (Current Population Reports, Series P-60, No. 182RD). Washington, DC: U.S. Government Printing Office.

U.S. Department of Health, Education, and Welfare. (1979). *Social security and changing roles of men and women.* Washington, DC: Author.

U.S. House of Representatives, Committee on Ways and Means. (1996). *1996 green book: Overview of entitlement programs.* Washington, DC: U.S. Government Printing Office.

Weiss, R. (1984). The impact of marital dissolution on income and consumption in single-parent households. *Journal of Marriage and the Family, 46,* 115–117.

Zick, C. D., & Smith, K. R. (1986). Immediate and delayed effects of widowhood on poverty: Patterns from the 1970s. *Gerontologist, 26,* 669–675.

Zick, C. D., & Smith, K. R. (1991). Patterns of economic change surrounding the death of a spouse. *Journal of Gerontology: Social Sciences, 46,* S310–S320.

This chapter was originally published in the June 1998 issue of *Social Work Research*, Vol. 22, Number 2, pp. 116–128.

# 3

# Saving Social Security and Medicare

## STEPHEN GORIN

A discussion of how the United States might build a "society for all ages," the theme of the United Nations' International Year of Older Persons in 1999, is not an academic exercise. The aging of the baby boomers presents difficult and unprecedented challenges. Ironically, our ability to respond to these challenges may depend on the outcome of a battle many believe we have already won.

I refer, of course, to the battle over social security and Medicare and the effort by conservatives to privatize these social insurance plans (Barker, 1999). For social workers, the importance of this battle should be clear (Hudson, 1999; Keigher, 1999; Takamura, 1999). *Social Work Speaks* (NASW, 1997) stresses the "intergenerational stake in providing adequate support for all dependent populations" and the need to obtain "public support" for "the most needy, regardless of age" (p. 19). Social security and Medicare are our most important forms of "social capital," and privatizing them would grievously damage our social fabric (Wilkinson, 1996). They also represent, in latent or embryonic form, our "society for all ages."

Unfortunately, we cannot assume that our colleagues, much less the public at large, understand the importance of these issues. As Hudson (1999) points out, the very success of social security and Medicare, and the difference they have made in the lives of older adults have fostered the illusion that most elderly people no longer need these programs. Moreover, the differences between those who support these programs and those who oppose them have become muddled. Frank Luntz, a well-known Republican pollster and the architect of the Contract with America, has advised his clients to stress their commitment to strengthening Medicare. Both political parties also have promised to protect social security.

Conservatives now frame their proposals in terms of compassion, right to choose, and bipartisanship (Starr, 1999). They no longer "ignore completely elderly people who are poor and sick" and in some cases actually advocate expanding "means-tested programs directed to these individuals" (Hudson, 1999, p. 156). In a sense, the debate has shifted from whether to preserve these programs to how to preserve them. However, we must not be fooled. The conservatives' fundamental goal—the privatization and "systematic erosion of . . . social security"—has not changed (Hudson, 1999, p. 156).

The problem for social workers and for progressives generally is developing a strategy for defending social security and Medicare. The admitted complexity of the situation should not deter us from acting. The stakes are high for both sides. Defeating privatization would not only preserve social security and Medicare but also open the door to a "society for all ages." Conversely, victory for the privatizers could throw us back a generation. This battle is one neither side can ignore.

## Myths about Privatization

It would be presumptuous to try to summarize the case against privatization in a few paragraphs. However, I will discuss briefly a few of the myths about privatization. Those interested in a full discussion of these issues should consult such important works as *Social Security in the 21st Century*, edited by Eric Kingson and Jim Schulz; *Social Security and Its Enemies* by Max Skidmore; *Social Security: The Phony Crisis* by Dean Baker and Mark Weisbrot; and *Straight Talk about Social Security* by Robert Ball and Thomas Bethell.

Other important sources include Families USA (http://www.familiesusa.org); the New Century Alliance (NCA) (http://www.ourfuture.org); the Century Foundation (http://www.socsec.org); the National Committee to Preserve Social Security and Medicare (http://www.ncpssm.org); and the Henry J. Kaiser Family Foundation (http://www.kff.org).

## Social Security

*Myth 1: Social Security Is Going Bankrupt.* This is the privatizers' central argument. The current debate revolves around the status of the social security Old Age, Survivors, and Disabilities Insurance (OASDI) and Medicare Hospital Insurance (HI) Trust Funds. These funds are financed largely through a payroll tax on employers and employees. Currently, OASDI takes in approximately $100 billion more per year than it pays out. This surplus is invested in U.S. treasury bonds and is the source of the current budget surplus. Without change, in 2015 the OASDI Trust Fund will begin paying out more than it takes in, and in 2035, it will run out of funds. However, even if the trust fund were to run out of funds, social security would still be able to meet 72 percent of its obligations through the payroll tax alone.

*Myth 2: Privatization Is the Only Way to Save Social Security.* As noted, the social security crisis has been greatly exaggerated. Privatizers argue that the only way to address this crisis, without huge tax increases, is to require individuals to invest part (or all) of their payroll deduction in private retirement accounts (Ferrara & Tanner, 1998).

Although this theory sounds persuasive, the evidence supporting it is limited. To begin with, the privatizers rely on estimates by the social security trustees that assume an unusually low rate of economic growth (Skidmore, 1999). Privatizers also assume that, during the next 75 years, real stock returns will average 7.0 percent. However, according to Diamond (1999), over the next decade, the stock market is likely to drop in value by a third before bouncing back. Under a system of private accounts, this could prove disastrous to baby boomers. If the market does not undergo such a drop, future returns will likely be lower than 7.0 percent (Diamond, 1999).

*Myth 3: Social Security Gives Workers a Poor Return on Their Investment.* This myth, of course, is related to myth 2. If social security is a poor investment, why not invest in something else? However, social security was not intended to be a form of investment, but a social insurance plan, part of a "complementary system of retirement income programs" (Ball & Bethell, 1997, p. 260). This "complementary system" refers to the famous three-legged stool, consisting of social security, pensions, and personal savings. Myth 3 also fails to place social security in its broader context. Social security provides retirement income and disability, life, and health insurance. As a result of social security, a young couple with two children "have survivors' protection worth $307,000" (Ball & Bethell, 1997, p. 277) and disability protection worth $207,000.

## Medicare

*Myth 1: Medicare Spending Is Out of Control.* This claim is as old as Medicare itself. It is true that Medicare expenditures grew rapidly during the plan's early years. However, this growth was largely the result of a reimbursement arrangement demanded by Blue Cross and the American Hospital Association as their price for supporting passage of Medicare. Without this concession, Medicare likely would have not been enacted (Hodgson, 1976).

Between 1970 and 1997, Medicare's cumulative per capita rate of growth matched that of private insurers (Moon, 1999). This does not mean that Medicare has no problems. The social security trustees (OASDI Trustees Report, 1999) predict that Medicare's HI Trust Fund will run out of money in 2015. Even if, as some argue, these figures are skewed, the aging of the baby boomers poses a serious challenge to Medicare. Moreover, despite Medicare's successes, Medicare beneficiaries must pay high out-of-pocket costs, and the program fails to cover prescription drugs and dental and nursing home care (Bodenheimer et al., 1999).

*Myth 2: Medicare Cannot Be Preserved without Fundamental Changes.* In response to the looming HI shortfall, some individuals and groups have proposed changing Medicare from a defined-benefit plan to a defined-contribution plan (Fuchs & Potetz, 1999). Currently, Medicare beneficiaries receive a specific package of benefits and services. Under a defined-contribution approach, beneficiaries would receive a premium support or voucher to buy coverage of their own. Because the voucher would cover only part of the premium cost, consumers would have an incentive "to select the plan offering the best coverage for the least cost" (Fuchs & Potetz, p. 3). This, in turn, would promote competition among providers and presumably lower costs.

Unfortunately, there is little reason to believe that such an approach would work (Neuman & Langwell, 1999). To begin with,

a competitive strategy requires informed consumers; yet perhaps as many as half of older
adults lack basic health literacy skills
(Gazmararian et al., 1999). Although health
care inflation has slowed in recent years, the
role of competition in reducing costs remains
unclear (Marquis & Long, 1999). In any
event, the growing trend toward HMO
consolidation and concentration suggests
that a competitive strategy is no longer a viable option (Crippen, 1999).

Most privatization plans are based on the
work of the National Bipartisan Commission,
chaired by Senator John Breaux (D-LA) and
Representative Bill Thomas (R-CA) (National Bipartisan Commission on the Future
of Medicare, 1999a). Although the Commission failed to agree on a final proposal, the
majority of the commission's members did
support a proposal developed by Breaux and
Thomas (National Bipartisan Commission
on the Future of Medicare, 1999b). Although
the Breaux-Thomas plan would do little to
improve the status of the HI Trust Fund, it
would likely increase costs to consumers and
reduce benefits (Bodenheimer et al., 1999).
More recently, Breaux and Bill Frist (R-TN)
have introduced the Medicare Preservation
and Improvement Act of 1999 (S. 1895)
(Senator John Breaux Press Releases, 1999).
S. 1985 is both a defined-benefit and defined-
contribution approach. Although it seems to
guarantee Medicare's current benefit package, it also exposes beneficiaries, particularly
those in traditional or fee-for-service Medicare, to potentially large cost increases.

Despite the claims of privatizers, there are
other ways to preserve Medicare, including
increasing taxes on upper-income households
and corporations, eliminating the social security cap, and closing corporate loopholes
(Bodenheimer et al., 1999). Vladeck (1999)
notes that "the baby-boomer crisis simply
goes away if one allows into the discussion

the possibility of increased taxes on the more
affluent" (pp. 25–26).

## Defeating Privatization

The debate over social security and Medicare has now moved center stage. In a bold
move, George W. Bush has proposed partially privatizing social security (Dao &
Mitchell, 2000). This would allow individuals to invest part of their payroll deduction
in individual investment accounts. Aaron et
al. (2000) conclude that Bush's plan would
likely result in benefit reductions "so substantial that they raise questions about the viability of protecting benefits for current retirees,
older workers, disabled workers, and survivors while diverting payroll taxes into individual accounts" Bush has also expressed
support for privatizing Medicare. On the
other hand, Al Gore, who NASW has endorsed, opposes privatization.

Progressives can take advantage of this
debate to build a broad coalition opposed to
privatization. People from all income groups
and backgrounds depend on and understand
the importance of social security and Medicare. The difficulty with this strategy is that,
as previously noted, conservatives stress the
need to preserve social security and Medicare. Bush promises to "honor and
strengthen Social Security" and "protect *all*
benefits for today's seniors and ensure that
Social Security is available for their grandchildren" [emphasis in original] (George W.
Bush for President Official Site, 2000).
Progressives need a way to pressure conservatives to reveal their plans before, not after,
the elections.

Campaign for America's Future (CAF), a
broad coalition of labor, civil rights, advocacy, and related organizations, has taken one
approach to this problem. CAF has called on
candidates to sign the Social Security Pro-

tection Pledge, which commits them to opposing efforts to privatize social security and Medicare and supporting measures to increase social security benefits for women (Campaign for America's Future, 2000). The co-chairs of this effort include Paul Newman, the Reverend Jesse Jackson, Robert S. Reich (former Secretary of Labor), Heidi Hartmann (National Council of Women's Organizations), Julian Bond (NAACP), and Ellie Smeal (The Feminist Majority). A coalition led by the New Hampshire NASW tested the Pledge during the New Hampshire Presidential Primary and found it extremely successful. The hope is to educate the public on a state-by-state basis and make privatization a central issue in the election.

The 2030 Center (http://www.2030.org) is also involved in the effort to defend social security and Medicare. The 2030 Center is a nonpartisan, public policy organization created by and for young adults. Their members have played a leading role in exposing the danger privatization poses to people of all ages, particularly young people. Hans Riemer, the 2030 Center's director, notes that: "Due to changes in the labor market—the growth of "temp," contract, and service-sector work—job benefits are growing scarce. Young people must frequently roll the dice and hope that they do not become sick, or pay from their own pockets for benefits that previous generations were able to win from employers. The last thing they need is to retire without the universal guarantee that social security provides today" (personal communication, June 2000).

The chief organizer for 2030 is Ann Crowley, a BSW from Plymouth State College, who also worked as an organizer for the New Hampshire Chapter of NASW. Crowley notes that 2030 has had its greatest success among social work students. According to her, "social work students quickly understand the importance of 2030's work. They know not only from their courses, but also often from personal experience the importance of preserving our nation's safety net" (personal communication, May 2000). Ann is working with NASW and other social work organizations to organize students to help lead the effort against privatization. "Young adults will pay the greatest price if privatization is enacted," says Crowley, "and we believe that they should take the lead in opposing it."

## Conclusion

The stakes in the 2000 elections were unusually high. The Social Security Act "is the basic document of the American social welfare system" (Reid, 1995, p. 2215). Whatever social security's limitations, "[a]ll generations have a common stake" in it (Kingson et al., 1986, p. 96). Privatization threatens to destroy social security. Social workers played a central role in developing social security (Louchheim, 1983). We have a special obligation to join in defending it.

## References

Aaron, H. J., Blinder, A. S., Munnell A. H., & Orszag, P. R. (2000). *Governor Bush's Individual Account Proposal: Implications for Retirement Benefits* (Issue Brief No. 11). The Century Foundation. [Online]. Available: http://www.socsec.org/facts/Issue_Briefs/bush_plan.htm.

Ball, R. M., & Bethell, T. N. (1997). Bridging the centuries: The case for traditional social security. In E. R. Kingson & J. H. Schulz (Eds.), *Social security in the 21st century* (pp. 259–294). New York: Oxford University Press.

Ball, R., & Bethell, T.N. (1998). *Straight talk about social security: An analysis of the issues in the current debate.* New York: The Century Foundation Press.

Baker, D., & Weisbrot, M. (1999). *Social security: The phony crisis.* Chicago: The University of Chicago Press.

Barker, R. L. (1999). *The social work dictionary* (4th ed.). Washington, DC: NASW Press.

Bodenheimer, T., Grumbach, K., Livingston, B. L., McCanne, D. R., Oberlander, J., Rice, D. P., & Rosenau, P. V. (1999, February). *Rebuilding Medicare for the 21st century: A challenge for the Medicare commission and Congress.* San Francisco: National Campaign to Protect, Improve, and Expand Medicare.

Campaign for America's Future. (2000). *Sign the pledge to protect social security and Medicare.* [Online]. Available: http://www.signthepledge. com/readarticle.asp?ID=632.

Crippen, D. L. (1999, February). *A preliminary review of the Premium Support Model as a foundation for Medicare reform.* Washington, DC: Congressional Budget Office.

Dao, J., & Mitchell, A. (2000, May 17). Gore denounces Bush social security plan as too risky. *New York Times,* p. A18.

Diamond, P. (1999). *What stock market returns to expect for the future?* [Online]. Available: http://www.bc.edu/bc_org/avp/csom/executive/crr/default6.html.

Ferrara, P. J., & Tanner, M. D. (1998). *Common cents, common dreams: A layman's guide to social security privatization.* Washington, DC: Cato Institute.

Fuchs, B. C., & Potetz, L. (1999). *Reforming Medicare: A framework for comparing incremental and premium support approaches.* Washington, DC: Health Policy Alternatives, Inc.

Gazmararian, J., Baker, D. W., Williams, M. V., Parker, R. M., Scott, T. L., Green, D. C, Fehrenbach, S. N., Ren, J., & Koplan, J. (1999). Health literacy among Medicare enrollees in a managed care organization. *JAMA, 281,* 545–551.

George W. Bush for President Official Site. (2000). *Issues.* [Online]. Available: http://www.georgewbush.com/issues.asp?FormMode=FullText&ID=21.

Hodgson, G. (1976). The politics of care: What is it costing you? In D. Kotelchuck (Ed.), *Prognosis negative—Crisis in the health care system* (pp. 304–316). New York: Vintage Books.

Hudson, R. B. (1999). The role of government in "A Society for All Ages" [National Health Line]. *Health & Social Work, 24,* 155–160.

Keigher, S. M. (1999). Coming of age [Editorial]. *Health & Social Work, 24,* 3–8.

Kingson, E. R., Hirshorn, B. A., & Cornman, J. M. (1986). *Ties that bind: The interdependence of generations.* Cabin John, MD: Seven Locks Press.

Kingson, E. R., & Schulz, J. H. (Eds.). (1997). *Social security in the 21st century.* New York: Oxford University Press.

Louchheim, K. (Ed.) (1983). *The making of the New Deal: The insiders speak.* Cambridge, MA: Harvard University Press.

Marquis, M. S., & Long, S. H. (1999). Trends in managed care and managed competition. *Health Affairs, 18*(6), 75–88.

Moon, M. (1999). *Beneath the averages—An analysis of Medicare and private expenditures.* Washington, DC: Kaiser Family Foundation.

National Association of Social Workers. (1997). Aging. In *Social work speaks: NASW policy statements* (4th ed., pp. 16–22). Washington, DC: NASW Press.

National Bipartisan Commission on the Future of Medicare. (1999a). *About the commission.* [Online]. Available: http//rs9.loc.gov/medicare/about.html.

National Bipartisan Commission on the Future of Medicare. (1999b). *Building a better medicare for today and tomorrow.* [Online]. Available: http//rs9.loc.gov/medicare/bbmtt31599.html.

Neuman, P., & Langwell, K. M. (1999). Medicare's choice explosion? Implications for beneficiaries. *Health Affairs, 18*(1), 150–160.

OASDI Trustees Report. (1999). [Online]. Available: http://www.ssa.gov/OACT/TR/TR99/trtoc.html.

Reid, F.N. (1995). Social welfare history. In R.L. Edwards (Ed.-in-Chief), *Encyclopedia of social work* (19th ed., Vol. 3, pp. 2206–2225). Washington, DC: NASW Press.

Senator John Breaux Press Releases (1999, November 9). *Sens. Breaux and Frist submit bipartisan Medicare reform bill.* [Online]. Available: http://www.senate.gov/~breaux/releases/991109.html.

Skidmore, M. J. (1999). *Social security and its enemies.* Boulder, CO: Westview Press.

Starr, P. (1999, November 23). America's parliamentary election. *American Prospect,* pp. 1, 11.

Takamura, J. C. (1999). Getting ready for the 21st century: The aging of America and the Older Americans Act [National Health Line]. *Health & Social Work, 24,* 232–238.

Vladeck, B. C. (1999). Medicare & political reform. *Health Affairs, 18*(1), 22–36.

Wilkinson, R. G. (1996). *Unhealthy societies: The afflictions of inequality.* Routledge: London and New York.

This article was originally published in the February 2000 issue of *Health & Social Work,* Vol. 25, Number 1, pp. 69–73.

# 4

# Differences in Net Worth between Elderly Black People and Elderly White People

MARTHA N. OZAWA
and HUAN-YUI TSENG

With the arrival of the 21st century, the public stance on the economic well-being of elderly people is changing. The philosophy behind the Social Security Act of 1935 was to help the nation share the risk of losing earnings because of old age and to pool the resources to ensure income security in old age for everyone. But the financial viability of social security began to be questioned in the 1970s, and since then, the idea of the privatization of social security has gained currency. Indeed, the centerpiece of one of the three reform proposals—the Personal Security Account (PSA) plan—made by the Advisory Council on Social Security, 1994–1996 (1997) is the privatization of a large part of social security. The spread of individual retirement accounts (IRAs), 401(k) plans, and Keogh accounts compounded the development of individual responsibility to ensure individuals' income security in old age.

The combination of the growing financial difficulty in funding social security benefits on a pay-as-you-go basis for an increasing number of elderly people and the spread of IRAs is forcing many countries to adopt the full or partial privatization of social security. Australia and some Latin American countries already have some forms of IRAs instead of traditional social security systems. Sweden allows individuals to shift part of their payroll taxes into private accounts (Feldstein, 1997).

As the traditional form of social security is minimized, the economic well-being of elderly people will depend increasingly on what they have in the form of private pensions and private wealth. Indeed, even now, income stratification among the elderly population is determined not by the amount of social security benefits, but by the amount of income from assets and from private pensions or annuities. Government data indicate that the highest fifth of aged individuals (individuals or couples) draw 24.4 percent of their total income from asset income, compared with only 2.7 percent for the lowest fifth. Likewise, the top fifth received 10.5 percent of their total income from private pensions or annuities, compared with 1.7 percent received by the bottom fifth (Glad, 1996).

The present study focused on the net worth of white and black elderly people. Financial assets, such as stocks and bonds, can generate income (Ozawa, 1997). The ownership of a home provides in-kind income, in the form of rent-free housing. Furthermore, the holding of a large net worth, whether liquid or not, generates an intangible sense of economic well-being. Thus, the investigation of net worth of white elderly people versus black elderly people provides vital information to assess these two groups' economic security in old age.

The specific questions the study addressed were these:

- What is the level of net worth held by white and black people 10 years after retirement?
- Controlling for other variables, what are the racial differences in net worth held 10 years after retirement?

- What are the differential effects of lifetime earnings and human capital variables (education, occupation, and labor force attachment) on the net worth of white men and black men?
- What are the differential effects of lifetime earnings and human capital variables (education, occupation, and labor force attachment) on the net worth of white women and black women?

## Conceptual Framework and Review of the Literature

The purpose of this study was to estimate the net effect of race on net worth in old age and to investigate whether lifetime earnings and human capital variables have a differential effect on the level of net worth of elderly white people and black people. Thus, the independent variables used in the study were race, lifetime earnings, and human capital—education, occupation, and labor force attachment—that is, attributes that contribute to people's performance in the economy. Whether an individual fares well in the economy depends on the level of education, type of job, and degree of attachment to the labor force (Cain, 1966, 1986).

In this study, both lifetime earnings and human capital variables were included as independent variables. Because lifetime earnings are determined partly by human capital variables, which creates the problem of endogenuity, these two sets of variables should not be included in the same regression model. Therefore, we developed two models of regression—one including lifetime earnings and the other including human capital variables.

In addition to these independent variables, other demographic variables that are known to affect the dependent variable were included as controls: gender, marital status, age, and the number of children raised. Number of children was included because raising children incurs extra living expenses, which results in fewer opportunities to accumulate assets (Smith, 1989).

To summarize, the framework was as follows:

- dependent variable: net worth in old age
- independent variables: race, lifetime earnings, and human capital variables—education, occupation and labor force attachment
- control variables: age, gender, marital status, and number of children raised

The literature supports the inclusion of the variables just listed. Smith (1997), using the Asset and Health Dynamics among the Oldest Old (AHEAD), found that the median net worth of black elderly households was $17,000, compared with $90,000 for their white counterparts. The distribution of financial assets was just as skewed: The median of financial assets of white elderly households was $10,500, but that of black elderly households was zero. Smith (1995) also found a similar pattern of inequality in net worth among households of nonelderly people approaching retirement. Eargle (1992) noted a great variation in wealth holding by race, with black people having only a small fraction of the wealth of white people.

In their study on net worth of families headed by people ages 24 to 34, Blau and Graham (1990) indicated that the following variables explain why the net worth of black people is so small: lower current income and permanent income (the expected level of income, given the economic and social backgrounds of the respondent). The study also found that these income variables, although significant, have a relatively weaker influence on black people's net worth than on white people's. Moreover, it demonstrated that even assuming that black people had the same level of incomes and the same degree of adverse locational and demographic characteristics,

a large portion of the gap in wealth—78 percent—would remain. In the same vein, Oliver and Shapiro (1989) showed that given the same income level, the net worth of black families is only a fraction of that of white families. For example, the median net worth of black families with annual incomes of $45,000 to $59,999 was only 42 percent of that of their white counterparts.

On the basis of their research findings, Blau and Graham (1990) speculated that there were two major reasons for the great disparity in net worth of black and white families. First, the amount of inherited wealth and the amount of intergenerational transfers when parents are still alive are significantly smaller among black families than among white families. Second, black families tend to have more liquid assets (such as bank checking accounts and savings accounts) than other types of assets (such as business assets and home equity) that have higher rates of return. Therefore, black families find it more difficult to accumulate assets.

Lifetime earnings are expected to affect net worth in old age. People with low earnings are unable to set aside money to accumulate net worth. Lifetime earnings is the most appropriate indicator of what economists call "permanent income" (see Blau & Graham, 1990), which measures the enduring level of income of one's life. Ozawa, Lum, and Tseng (1999) indicated that lifetime earnings were significantly related to the level of net worth among people ages 73 and older, particularly among men. Smith (1997) found a strong correlation between family income and net worth among those ages 70 and over. Several studies demonstrated that the distribution of net worth is considerably skewed in favor of people with high incomes. Smith (1997) found that the net worth of the top 10 percent of household income distribution was $384,000; of the median, $7,800; and of the lowest 10 percent, $150. Eargle's (1992) study showed that the median net worth of the bottom quintile of elderly people was only $25,200, of which $21,700 represented home equity, but the median net worth of the top quintile was $343,000, of which home equity was $175,000. Del Bene and Vaughn (1992) reported that contingency assets (that is, assets minus home equity) were small among low-income people; only 16 percent of poor people had contingency assets in excess of $5,000.

The literature indicates that education has a positive influence on net worth. Better education is expected to provide people with skills in and knowledge of saving and investing. Ozawa et al. (1999) found that when other variables were controlled, the net worth of people with at least some college education was 435 percent greater than the net worth of those with an elementary school education. Smith (1997) noted a similar relationship between education and net worth.

Occupation also is expected to make a difference in net worth in old age. Ozawa and Law (1993) found, for example, that although physicians have higher lifetime earnings, their annual income in old age was lower than that of lawyers, implying that physicians did not do well in saving and investing while they practiced medicine. For another example, professors in many private universities receive free tuition benefits for their children's education, effectively freeing up their financial resources for accumulating assets. Furthermore, the degree of labor force attachment is expected to make a difference in net worth in old age. Strong attachment to the labor force means that earnings are steady throughout a person's working life, providing a stable lifestyle, which is conducive to setting aside part of earnings for savings and investment.

The literature also indicates that there is a great disparity in the net worth of men and women. In her study of net worth among people ages 73 and older, Ozawa (1997) found that in 1992, the median net worth of men was $130,823, compared with $79,318 for women ($146,301 versus $88,702 in 1996 dollars). Because there is a great difference in the amount of net worth that men and women hold, it is important to disaggregate the data by gender when studying racial differences in net worth.

Marital status is expected to make a difference in net worth in old age. For example, divorce results in the division of net worth previously held jointly by spouses. Widowhood also may cause a decline in net worth because of the extraordinary expenditures incurred by the death of a spouse. People who never marry may be at a disadvantage in accumulating net worth as well, because they do not benefit from the economy of scale in consumption expenditures that married couples generally enjoy. A multiple regression analysis by Ozawa et al. (1999) of the net worth of elderly people ages 73 and older indicated that the net worth of nonmarried individuals was significantly smaller than that of married people and that divorced people had the least net worth.

Ozawa et al. (1999) also found that age was positively related to net worth among men and women when other variables were taken into account. At the descriptive level, however, Radner (1993) stated that the median net worth of the old-old (ages 80 and over) was less than that of the young-old (ages 65 to 69). The difference stems from the fact that Radner used a univariate variable whereas Ozawa et al. used a multivariate variable.

## Method

### Data Source

The source of data for the study was the New Beneficiary Data System (NBDS), which allowed us to merge the data from the 1982 New Beneficiary Survey (NBS) and the 1991 New Beneficiary Followup (NBF). The NBS had a sample of 18,136 individuals, representing about 2 million people who had become new beneficiaries of Old Age, Survivors, and Disability Insurance (OASDI) or Medicare or both between mid-1980 and mid-1981; the response rate was 85.9 percent. The NBF interviewed 12,128 surviving NBS respondents and 1,834 surviving spouses of NBS respondents who had died; the response rate was 87.5 percent (Maxfield, 1985; Social Security Administration, 1994).

The NBS collected information on demographic characteristics, employment history, marital status, health status, work history, current income, and assets. The NBF collected, in addition, information on employment history during the 10 years after the NBS, changes in marital status, and their economic effects. Furthermore, the NBF data file included administrative data on annual earnings from 1951 through 1991, as well as other data, such as the Primary Insurance Amount, Medicare expenditures, and Supplemental Security Income applications and denials.

For the purposes of our study, we selected individuals who started receiving OASDI benefits between mid-1980 and mid-1981 as retired workers, wives, divorced wives, widows, and surviving divorced wives and individuals who started receiving Medicare coverage without receiving cash retirement benefits (Medicare-only beneficiaries) during the same period and survived long enough to be interviewed in the NBF, which collected data between November 1990 and July 1992. We excluded all people who started receiving social security benefits as widows or surviving divorced wives before age 62. We further selected those who were either white or black. Thus, the sample was 8,352, of whom 686 were black and 7,666 were white.

### Dependent Variable: Net Worth

The dependent variable was the level of net worth held in 1992 by the respondent and his or her spouse, if married. Net worth—the total assets minus debts—consists of money market accounts, certificates of deposit, savings or credit union accounts, checking accounts, bonds, stocks and mutual funds, IRA/Keogh accounts, home equity (market value of home minus mortgage), business equity, professional practice equity, farm equity, and rental property/vacation home/commercial property/land.

### Independent variables

*Race.* The value of 1 was assigned to black respondents, and the value of zero, to white respondents.

*Lifetime Earnings.* To develop this variable, earnings in covered employment in each year from 1951 to 1991 were indexed to the 1992 consumer price index and then summed.

*Education.* Education was measured by dummy variables for the groups of respondents who had some high school education, completed high school, and had at least some college education. Those who had an elementary school education were assigned to the reference group.

*Occupation.* Occupation meant the occupation in the job held the longest. It was measured by dummy variables for the groups of respondents whose longest jobs were managerial, technical, precision production, operative, and farming and for those who held no jobs. Those whose longest jobs were service jobs were assigned to the reference group.

*Labor Force Attachment.* This variable was measured by two variables—quarters of covered employment from 1937 through 1977 and the number of years with earnings from 1982 through 1991. The former measured the degree of labor force attachment before the initial receipt of social security or Medicare benefits, and the latter measured the degree of labor force attachment thereafter. That the data for the quarters of covered employment ended in 1977 and did not include the quarters for 1978 through 1981 constituted a limitation of this study.

### Control Variables

*Marital Status.* Marital status was measured by dummy variables for respondents who were (1) widowed, (2) separated or divorced, and (3) never married. Those who were married were assigned to the reference group.

*Age, Gender, and Number of Children.* Age was the age at the time of the NBF, which was the year of the initial receipt of social security benefits or Medicare, plus 11. The value of 1 was assigned to men, and the value of zero, to women. The variable for the number of children was self-explanatory.

The following variables were measured at the time of the NBS: gender, race, education, and occupation. The rest of the variables were measured at the time of the NBF.

### Data Analysis

We used the weight variable that was developed by the Social Security Administration to generate descriptive statistics on all variables. This procedure was needed to adjust for the sampling, poststratification, and nonresponse biases in the NBS and NBF data sets. The unit of analysis was the individual. In performing OLS regression analysis, net worth and lifetime earnings were logged because the distribution of these variables was skewed. To deal with the endogenuity problem mentioned earlier, we developed Model 1 and Model 2 for regression analysis—one including lifetime earnings and the other including variables related to human capital.

### Findings

#### Descriptive Statistics

*Characteristics of Respondents.* The sample comprised 92.6 percent white respondents and 7.4 percent black respondents (Table 4-1). The proportion of females was larger among black people (55.4 percent) than among white people (51.0 percent). A smaller percentage (46.1 percent) of black people than of white people (65.1 percent) were married.

Educational achievement differed as well, with 13 percent of black people having at least some college education, compared with 31.2 percent of white people. Similarly, the types of occupations that black people and white people had in their longest jobs differed greatly. For example, whereas 24.9 percent of white respondents had managerial jobs, only 10 percent of black respondents did. The mean number of children raised by black respondents was 3.2, compared with 2.5 raised by white respondents.

The median amount of lifetime earnings of black people was $223,573, compared with $490,169 for white people. The median number of quarters of covered employment from 1937 to 1977 was 76 for black people, compared with 95 for white people. The median number of years with earnings from 1982 to 1991 was zero for both black and white people; the mean number of years with earnings was 2.2 and 2.3, respectively.

*Level of Net Worth.* The median net worth of black people was considerably smaller than

TABLE 4-1. Characteristics of Elderly Respondents (from the NBS and NBF)

| Characteristic | Percentage | | |
| | All (N = 8,352) | White (N = 7,666) | Black (N = 686) |
|---|---|---|---|
| Race | | | |
| White | 92.6 | — | — |
| Black | 7.4 | — | — |
| Gender | | | |
| Male | 48.7 | 49.0 | 44.6 |
| Female | 51.3 | 51.0 | 55.4 |
| Marital status | | | |
| Married | 63.8 | 65.1 | 46.1 |
| Widowed | 25.8 | 25.0 | 35.5 |
| Separated/divorced | 6.4 | 5.9 | 13.2 |
| Never married | 4.0 | 4.0 | 4.6 |
| Education | | | |
| Elementary school | 21.0 | 18.7 | 49.1 |
| Some high school | 18.9 | 18.5 | 23.7 |
| High school graduate | 30.3 | 31.6 | 14.2 |
| At least some college | 29.8 | 31.2 | 13.0 |
| Occupation | | | |
| Managerial | 23.8 | 24.9 | 10.0 |
| Technical | 28.6 | 30.2 | 9.7 |
| Service | 12.6 | 10.3 | 40.1 |
| Operative | 15.4 | 14.7 | 23.8 |
| Farmer | 3.6 | 3.5 | 4.7 |
| Precision production | 11.9 | 12.2 | 8.4 |
| Never worked | 4.1 | 4.2 | 3.3 |
| | Mean | | |
| Age | 73.8 | 73.8 | 73.7 |
| Number of children raised | 2.6 | 2.5 | 3.2 |
| Covered earnings, 1951–91 | $440,402 | $451,263 | $300,634 |
| Education | 11.5 | 11.7 | 8.8 |
| Quarters of covered employment, 1937–77 | 85.0 | 85.7 | 74.9 |
| Years with earnings, 1982–91 | 2.3 | 2.3 | 2.2 |
| | Median | | |
| Age | 75 | 75 | 74 |
| Number of children raised, 1982 | 2 | 2 | 2 |
| Lifetime earnings, 1951–91 | $457,138 | $490,169 | $223,573 |
| Education | 12 | 12 | 9 |
| Quarters of covered employment, 1937–77 | 93 | 95 | 76 |
| Years with earnings, 1982–91 | 0 | 0 | 0 |

Notes: NBS = New Beneficiary Survey and NBF = New Beneficiary Followup (Social Security Administration). Percentages do not necessarily add up to 100 due to rounding.

that of white people: $16,091 versus $110,839 (Table 4-2). The gender differential in net worth was greater among white people than among black people on the basis of either mean or median figures.

### Multivariate Analysis

It is important to clarify the meaning of regression coefficients in multiple regression analyses in which the dependent variable is

**TABLE 4-2. Net Worth of Elderly White People and Black People, 1992 (in 1992 dollars)**

| Respondent Categories | Net Worth | |
|---|---|---|
| | Mean | Median |
| All | 218,325 | 100,899 |
| White | 232,175 | 110,839 |
| Men | 300,024 | 144,214 |
| Women | 166,306 | 85,911 |
| Black | 40,091 | 16,091 |
| Men | 48,748 | 18,785 |
| Women | 32,665 | 15,452 |

transformed into a natural log and independent variables take the form of dummy variables. Most researchers interpret multiple regression coefficients in this situation simply as a percentage difference. A coefficient of 0.363, for example, is interpreted as "36.3 percent greater." However, Halvorsen and Palmquist (1980) warned that the traditional way of interpreting regression coefficients is wrong. They argued that

$$C = ln(1 + g)e^c = 1 + g$$

therefore,

$$g = e^c - 1$$

where $C$ = regression coefficient and $g$ = relative effect.

Following this equation and applying the coefficient of 0.363, the relative effect $g$ is 0.438, which can be interpreted as "43.8 percent greater." Thus, in the data analysis that follows, we used the procedure specified by Halvorsen and Palmquist (1980). We calculated the values of the relative effect $g$ (expressed in percentage) for all coefficients for dummy variables in the OLS regression analyses involving the natural log of net worth as the dependent variable. (This transformation is not required for independent variables that are interval.) We listed relative effects in percentage terms after coefficients.

*OLS Regression Analysis of Net Worth for All Respondents.* A regression analysis for all the respondents was performed to estimate the racial difference in net worth, controlling for other variables. In model 1 (Table 4-3), which includes lifetime earnings as an independent variable, the net worth of black people was found to be 95.4 percent smaller ($p < .001$) than that of white people, when other variables were controlled. In model 2, which includes variables related to human capital instead of lifetime earnings, the racial difference in net worth was –89.8 percent ($p < .001$). Under either model, it seems clear that the black–white difference in net worth is significant.

Lifetime earnings were strongly and positively related to net worth in old age ($p < .01$). This finding indicates that those who had earned more during their working lives did have larger net worth in their old age.

Model 2 (Table 4-3) shows the coefficients of human capital variables. Education exerted a strong, positive effect on net worth in old age. For example, the net worth of those who had at least some college education was 305.2 percent greater ($p < .001$) than that of those with an elementary school education. Also, the type of job was strongly related to net worth. The net worth of those who had managerial jobs in their longest-held jobs was 189.7 percent greater ($p < .001$) than the net worth of those who had service jobs. Caution is in order with regard to the coefficient of "never worked," which was larger than that for "services." This anomalous relationship was due to the fact that many women in the sample had never worked (8.6 percent; data not shown), some of whom might have been married to men with a sizable net worth. In separate data analyses, we found that the net worth of women who had never worked was significantly higher than that of those who had service jobs, but the net worth of men

TABLE 4-3. OLS Multiple Regression Analysis of Net Worth (Log): All Respondents

| | Model 1 | | | Model 2 | | |
|---|---|---|---|---|---|---|
| Variable | Coefficient | Relative Effect (%) | t value | Coefficient | Relative Effect (%) | t value |
| Intercept | 3.576*** | | 3.986 | 5.626*** | | 6.124 |
| Black | −3.079*** | −95.4 | −29.711 | −2.286*** | −89.8 | −21.581 |
| Male | 0.189** | 20.8 | 2.762 | 0.007 | 0.7 | 0.094 |
| Age | 0.107*** | 11.3 | 8.829 | 0.054*** | | 4.344 |
| Marital status | | | | | | |
|   Widow/widower | −1.120*** | −67.4 | −15.812 | −0.962*** | −61.8 | −13.668 |
|   Separated/divorced | −2.712*** | −93.4 | −25.272 | −2.506*** | −91.8 | −23.750 |
|   Never married | −1.927*** | −85.4 | −13.438 | −1.715*** | −82.0 | −12.318 |
|   (Married) | | | | | | |
| Number of children raised | −0.150*** | | −10.131 | −0.093*** | | −6.304 |
| Lifetime earnings, 1951–91 (Log) | 0.031** | | 3.205 | | | |
| Education | | | | | | |
|   Some high school | | | | 0.574*** | 77.5 | 6.332 |
|   High school graduate | | | | 1.067*** | 190.7 | 12.299 |
|   At least some college | | | | 1.399*** | 305.2 | 14.784 |
|   (Elementary school) | | | | | | |
| Occupation | | | | | | |
|   Managerial | | | | 1.064*** | 189.7 | 9.640 |
|   Technical | | | | 0.900*** | 146.0 | 8.938 |
|   Precision production | | | | 0.782*** | 118.5 | 6.477 |
|   Operative | | | | 0.326** | 38.6 | 2.960 |
|   Farmers | | | | 1.279*** | 259.3 | 7.569 |
|   Never worked | | | | 0.721*** | 105.7 | 4.106 |
|   (Services) | | | | | | |
| Quarters of covered employment, 1937–77 | | | | 0.005*** | | 6.051 |
| Years with earnings, 1982–91 | | | | 0.032*** | | 3.786 |
| N | 8,352 | | | 7,890 | | |
| $R^2$ | 0.221*** | | | 0.289*** | | |
| F | 296.142 | | | 177.492 | | |

Note: Reference groups are in parentheses.
*$p < .05$. **$p < .01$. ***$p < .001$.

who had never worked was as low as the net worth of those who had service jobs (data not shown). The variable quarters of covered employment from 1937 to 1977 was significantly and positively related to net worth ($p < .001$); so was the number of years with earnings from 1982 to 1991 ($p < .001$).

*OLS Regression Analyses of Net Worth of White Men Compared with Black Men.* There were amazingly different regression results for black men and white men (Tables 4-4 and 4-5).

Model 1 (Tables 4-4 and 4-5) shows that when other variables were controlled, both

lifetime earnings and human capital variables (education, occupation, quarters of covered employment from 1937 to 1977, and years with earnings from 1982 to 1991) exerted a positive and significant effect on the net worth of white men, but for black men, only quarters of covered employment from 1937 to 1977 ($p < .05$) had bearing on net worth in old age.

Although the number of children raised was just a control variable, its differential coefficients for white men and black men are interesting. For white men, the more children raised, the smaller the net worth

TABLE 4-4. OLS Multiple Regression Analysis of Net Worth (Log): White Men

| | Model 1 | | | Model 2 | | |
|---|---|---|---|---|---|---|
| Variable | Coefficient | Relative Effect (%) | t value | Coefficient | Relative Effect (%) | t value |
| Intercept | −3.115** | | −2.778 | 2.359* | | 2.211 |
| Age | 0.157*** | | 11.022 | 0.097*** | | 6.822 |
| Marital status | | | | | | |
|   Widow/widower | −0.680*** | −49.3 | −6.827 | −0.607*** | −45.5 | −6.389 |
|   Separated/divorced | −2.377*** | −90.7 | −15.440 | −2.238*** | −89.3 | −15.294 |
|   Never married | −1.514*** | −78.0 | −7.623 | −1.111*** | −67.1 | −5.766 |
|   (Married) | | | | | | |
| Number of children raised | −0.109*** | | −6.135 | −0.079*** | | −4.658 |
| Lifetime earnings, 1951–91 (Log) | 0.258*** | | 8.319 | | | |
| Education | | | | | | |
|   Some high school | | | | 0.401*** | 49.3 | 3.853 |
|   High school graduate | | | | 0.763*** | 114.5 | 7.999 |
|   At least some college | | | | 1.056*** | 187.6 | 10.409 |
|   (Elementary school) | | | | | | |
| Occupation | | | | | | |
|   Managerial | | | | 1.376*** | 296.1 | 9.408 |
|   Technical | | | | 1.109*** | 203.2 | 7.572 |
|   Precision production | | | | 0.991*** | 169.3 | 6.831 |
|   Operative | | | | 0.662*** | 93.8 | 4.378 |
|   Farmers | | | | 1.596*** | 393.1 | 8.950 |
|   Never worked | | | | 0.707 | 102.8 | 0.371 |
|   (Services) | | | | | | |
| Quarters of covered employment, 1937–77 | | | | 0.004*** | | 4.871 |
| Years with earnings, 1982–91 | | | | 0.037*** | | 4.120 |
| N | 3,875 | | | 3,859 | | |
| $R^2$ | 0.126** | | | 0.206*** | | |
| F | 92.758 | | | 62.240 | | |

Note: Reference groups are in parentheses.
*$p < .05$. **$p < .01$. ***$p < .001$.

($p < .001$), but for black men, there was no such relationship.

These regression results indicate that for black men, the level of education, the type of jobs they had during their working lives, and how much they earned in their lifetime had no effect on how much net worth they eventually had in old age. Only quarters of covered employment from 1937 to 1977—one of the indicators of labor force attachment—was related to net worth ($p < .05$). In contrast, the level of net worth for white men clearly was determined by education, occupation, labor force attachment, and lifetime earnings. The levels and the significance of

these variables were all high ($p < .001$), and the directions of these variables were in the predicted directions.

*OLS Regression Analyses of Net Worth of White Women Compared with That of Black Women.* We found a strong contrast in the regression results for white women and black women as well. With the exception of years with earnings from 1982 to 1991, all human capital variables had a significant effect on the net worth of white women; but the effect of these variables on the net worth of black women was much weaker (Tables 4-6 and 4-7). In particular, for black women, only the following variables were significant: high

**TABLE 4-5. OLS Multiple Regression Analysis of Net Worth (Log): Black Men**

| | Model 1 | | | Model 2 | | |
|---|---|---|---|---|---|---|
| Variable | Coefficient | Relative Effect (%) | t value | Coefficient | Relative Effect (%) | t value |
| Intercept | −3.544 | | −0.429 | 9.150 | | 1.127 |
| Age | 0.096 | | 0.922 | −0.019 | | −0.177 |
| Marital status, 1991 | | | | | | |
| Widow/widower | −1.655* | −80.9 | −2.526 | −1.319* | −73.3 | −1.997 |
| Separated/divorced | −3.507*** | −97.0 | −5.049 | −3.378*** | −96.6 | −4.735 |
| Never married | −1.658 | −81.0 | −1.328 | −1.573 | −79.3 | −1.263 |
| (Married) | | | | | | |
| Number of children raised | −0.123 | | −1.563 | −0.073 | | −0.932 |
| Lifetime earnings, 1951–91 (Log) | 0.438 | | 1.799 | | | |
| Education | | | | | | |
| Some high school | | | | 0.311 | 36.5 | 0.468 |
| High school graduate | | | | −0.051 | −5.0 | −0.065 |
| At least some college | | | | 0.864 | 137.3 | 0.946 |
| (Elementary school) | | | | | | |
| Occupation | | | | | | |
| Managerial | | | | 1.918 | 580.9 | 1.826 |
| Technical | | | | 0.882 | 141.5 | 0.923 |
| Precision production | | | | −0.256 | −22.6 | −0.331 |
| Operative | | | | −1.099 | −66.7 | −1.686 |
| Farmers | | | | −1.104 | −66.8 | −1.108 |
| Never worked | | | | 0.000 | — | — |
| (Services) | | | | | | |
| Quarters of covered employment, 1937–77 | | | | 0.014* | | 2.180 |
| Years with earnings, 1982–91 | | | | −0.048 | | −0.618 |
| N | | 275 | | | 271 | |
| $R^2$ | | 0.115*** | | | 0.167*** | |
| F | | 5.819 | | | 3.395 | |

Note: Reference groups are in parentheses.
*$p < .05$. **$p < .01$. ***$p < .001$.

school education ($p < .05$), college education ($p < .001$), technical job ($p < .05$), and precision-production job ($p < .05$). It is noteworthy, however, that college education made an enormous difference in net worth of black women: These women's net worth was 1,023.9 percent greater ($p < .001$) than the net worth of black women with an elementary school education. On the other hand, lifetime earnings exerted a strong and significant effect on the net worth of black women ($p < .01$), but not on the net worth of white women. This difference was an interesting contrast.

Again, it is interesting to note that in both models 1 and 2, the number of children had

a negative effect on the net worth of white women ($p < .001$ in both models), but for black women, this variable was significant only in model 1 ($p < .01$).

The findings illustrate the great differences in the situations of white people and black people. The difference in the net worth of white men and black men is particularly vivid. Lifetime earnings and human capital variables made little or no difference in the amount of net worth that black men had in old age (Table 4-5). In contrast, the coefficients for white men were all significant and in the expected directions (Table 4-4). What white men did in their economic lives while

TABLE 4-6. OLS Multiple Regression Analysis of Net Worth (Log): White Women

| Variable | Model 1 | | | Model 2 | | |
|---|---|---|---|---|---|---|
| | Coefficient | Relative Effect (%) | t value | Coefficient | Relative Effect (%) | t value |
| Intercept | 4.798*** | | 3.625 | 5.648*** | | 4.055 |
| Age | 0.096*** | | 5.336 | 0.052** | | 2.761 |
| Marital status | | | | | | |
| Widow/widower | −1.154*** | −68.5 | −12.628 | −1.006*** | −63.4 | −10.727 |
| Separated/divorced | −2.819*** | −94.0 | −19.797 | −2.633*** | −92.8 | −18.303 |
| Never married | −1.873*** | −84.6 | −10.000 | −1.878*** | −84.7 | −10.087 |
| (Married) | | | | | | |
| Number of children raised | −0.180*** | | −7.642 | −0.083*** | | −3.307 |
| Lifetime earnings, 1951–91 (Log) | 0.003 | | 0.324 | | | |
| Education | | | | | | |
| Some high school | | | | 0.783*** | 118.8 | 5.537 |
| High school graduate | | | | 1.374*** | 295.3 | 10.063 |
| At least some college | | | | 1.695*** | 444.6 | 11.213 |
| (Elementary school) | | | | | | |
| Occupation | | | | | | |
| Managerial | | | | 0.903*** | 146.6 | 5.634 |
| Technical | | | | 0.812*** | 125.2 | 6.046 |
| Precision production | | | | 0.879*** | 140.7 | 3.348 |
| Operative | | | | 0.329* | 39.0 | 2.030 |
| Farmers | | | | 1.186** | 227.4 | 2.685 |
| Never worked | | | | 0.798*** | 122.2 | 4.053 |
| (Services) | | | | | | |
| Quarters of covered employment 1937–77 | | | | 0.005*** | | 3.853 |
| Years with earnings, 1982–91 | | | | 0.016 | | 1.111 |
| N | | 3,791 | | | 3,370 | |
| $R^2$ | | 0.122*** | | | 0.203*** | |
| F | | 87.704 | | | 53.253 | |

Note: Reference groups are in parentheses.
*$p < .05$. **$p < .01$. ***$p < .001$.

they were young was all related to the amount of net worth they had in old age.

## Discussion and Implications

This study revealed an enormous difference in the amount of net worth of white people and black people in old age. Even when other variables were held constant, the net worth of black people was about 90 percent smaller (−95.4 percent in model 1 and −89.8 percent in model 2) than the net worth of white people (Table 4-3). Furthermore, the explanatory power of the independent variables under investigation is quite different for white people and black people. What is the most striking is that for white men, lifetime earnings and human capital variables were related to net worth as expected, but for black men, there was little or no relationship between the dependent variable and these independent variables, except the degree of labor force attachment from 1937 to 1977.

Another interesting finding was that although the lifetime earnings of white men did make a difference in their eventual net worth in old age, this variable did not make a difference in the net worth of white women. But for black people, the opposite was true: This variable had a positive effect

**TABLE 4-7. OLS Multiple Regression Analysis of Net Worth (Log): Black Women**

| | Model 1 | | | Model 2 | | |
|---|---|---|---|---|---|---|
| Variable | Coefficient | Relative Effect (%) | t value | Coefficient | Relative Effect (%) | t value |
| Intercept | 19.599*** | | 3.838 | 21.036*** | | 3.939 |
| Age | −0.160* | | −2.359 | −0.171* | | −2.419 |
| Marital status | | | | | | |
| Widow/widower | −2.277*** | −89.7 | −4.729 | −2.247*** | −89.4 | −4.594 |
| Separated/divorced | −2.130*** | −88.1 | −3.434 | −2.376*** | −90.7 | −3.760 |
| Never married | −3.216*** | −96.0 | −3.476 | −3.191*** | −95.9 | −3.444 |
| (Married) | | | | | | |
| Number of children raised | −0.183** | | −2.635 | −0.137 | | −1.872 |
| Lifetime earnings, 1951–91 (Log) | 0.195** | | 3.075 | | | |
| Education | | | | | | |
| Some high school | | | | 0.284 | 32.9 | 0.571 |
| High school graduate | | | | 1.432* | 318.8 | 2.429 |
| At least some college | | | | 2.419*** | 1,023.9 | 3.398 |
| (Elementary school) | | | | | | |
| Occupation | | | | | | |
| Managerial | | | | 0.134 | 14.4 | 0.186 |
| Technical | | | | 1.319* | 274.0 | 2.013 |
| Precision production | | | | 3.951* | 5,098.3 | 2.463 |
| Operative | | | | 0.125 | 13.3 | 0.206 |
| Farmers | | | | 0.916 | 149.8 | 0.566 |
| Never worked | | | | −0.451 | −36.3 | −0.454 |
| (Services) | | | | | | |
| Quarters of covered employment, 1937–77 | | | | 0.006 | | 1.161 |
| Years with earnings, 1982–91 | | | | 0.073 | | 1.108 |
| N | | 411 | | | 390 | |
| $R^2$ | | 0.098*** | | | 0.169*** | |
| F | | 7.321 | | | 4.749 | |

*Note:* Reference groups are in parentheses.
*$p < .05$. **$p < .01$. ***$p < .001$.

on black women's net worth, but not on black men's.

From these findings, we can say that the net worth of white men is an end result of the amount of their human capital and how much they earned in their lifetimes. Albeit to a much lesser degree, such an observation applies to black women as well. For white women, what really counts is human capital. For black men, neither human capital variables nor lifetime earnings make much difference.

Caution should be exercised in interpreting the findings for two reasons. First, the relatively weak coefficients of the independent variables for black people, in part, may be due to the relatively small sample of black people. Even taking this phenomenon into account, however, it seems clear that the black–white differences in the level of net worth and in the determinants of net worth remain.

Second, the proportion of variance explained by the regression models in the study was relatively small. For example, the $R^2$s for models 1 and 2 were only 0.115 and 0.167, respectively (Table 4-5). This means that these regression models explained only a fraction of the variance in the dependent variables. It is possible that the inclusion of other types of variables may increase the predictive power of the regression models.

Third, the racial difference in net worth that was found in this study may not be present among black elderly people and white elderly people in general, because this study focused on elderly people ages 73 and older. However, a study by Ozawa (1997), which used both cross-sectional and longitudinal data from the NBDS, found that the same degree of racial difference was present among these elderly people 10 years earlier—that is, when they were ages 63 and older. A subsequent study by Ozawa et al. (1999), which used the two-stage regression technique, supported Ozawa's (1997) findings.

With these cautionary notes in mind, you should ask: Why do black people have so little net worth in old age, and why are the economic activities in their working lives not related to the amount of net worth they have in old age? The answer may be a culmination of many events that black people undergo throughout their lives and from generation to generation. As Blau and Graham (1990) argued, the black people in this study might have had little inheritance from their parents or financial help from their parents to buy homes. Also, even if they had financial resources, they might have had them in liquid forms, such as savings accounts at banks. (People need to invest in stocks and bonds instead to have high rates of return, although stocks and bonds are riskier forms of investment.) On top of all this, the doors to investment institutions might have been closed to black people because of racial discrimination in the business practices of these institutions (Jackman & Jackman, 1980; Kain & Quigley, 1972). Thus, the composition of their assets—if they had assets—might have been different from that of white people's assets, resulting in lower rates of returns.

Profound policy implications can be drawn from the findings of this study. Because black people's assets are so small, they will have little or no income from assets. As a result, social security benefits will constitute a major part of their retirement income. Thus, the PSA plan, if adopted, may have an adverse effect on black people.

The PSA plan attempts to transform the current OASDI into a two-tier system, with the first tier providing a flat-amount benefit (equivalent to 65 percent of the poverty line) and the second tier consisting of large-scale individualized retirement accounts, financed by 5 percentage points of the OASDI employee payroll tax.

Because black workers, on average, receive considerably lower wages than do white workers (U.S. Department of Commerce, 1998), 5 percent of the taxable payroll that they would put in their individual retirement accounts would be small in absolute terms. With this in mind, suppose black people have the same likelihood of investing in the equity market, allocate the same proportion of their financial resources to the equity market, and obtain the same rate of return in their equity investment as do white people. Even under the best circumstances, as assumed here, a vital policy question remains: Would the proportionately same return be good enough for black people from the social policy point of view?

The OASDI, as designed, purports to provide low-wage earners with disproportionately higher rates of return than with high-wage earners. This policy reflects the social adequacy principle embedded in the benefit formula. But under the privatized system of social security, the benefits would be determined by individuals' investment behavior. Under such a scheme, black people would be expected to have a lower rate of return on their investment—let alone the proportionately same rate of return, because they tend not to invest their money in the equity market, which is known to yield a higher rate of return than do other types of investments (Ozawa & Lum, 1999).

The crucial vehicle that may mitigate the anticipated disadvantage of black people would be the first-tier flat-amount of social security benefits that the PSA plan incorporates. As mentioned earlier, the first-tier flat-amount benefits would be equal to 65 percent of the poverty line, which is further adjusted by the years of work in covered employment—with 35 years being considered full, lifetime work. Thus, the issue is whether the flat-amount benefits would offset the anticipated poor investment outcomes among black workers so that the combination of first-tier and second-tier benefits would provide proportionately *higher* rates of return for black people. Unfortunately, this flat-amount benefit, which is about $410 in today's dollars, may be inadequate to achieve this goal. Although this is an empirical question that needs to be investigated further, the prognosis seems poor.

❧ ❧ ❧

## References

Advisory Council on Social Security, 1994–1996. (1997). *Report of the 1994–1996 Advisory Council on Social Security: Vol. 1. Findings and recommendations*. Washington, DC: Author.

Blau, R. D., & Graham, J. W. (1990). Black–white differences in wealth and asset composition. *Quarterly Journal of Economics, 105*, 321–339.

Cain, G. G. (1966). *Married women in the labor force: An economic analysis*. Chicago: University of Chicago Press.

Cain, G. G. (1986). The economic analysis of labor market discrimination: A survey. In O.

Ashenfelter & R. Layard (Eds.), *Handbook of labor economics* (Vol. 1, pp. 694–785). New York: Elsevier Science.

Del Bene, L., & Vaughn, D. R. (1992). Income, assets and health insurance: Economic resources for meeting acute health care needs of the aged. *Social Security Bulletin, 55*(1), 3–25.

Eargle, J. (1992). *Household wealth and asset ownership: 1988* (Current Population Reports, Series P-70, No. 22). Washington, DC: U.S. Department of Commerce, Bureau of the Census.

Feldstein, M. S. (1997). The case for privatization. *Foreign Affairs, 46*, 24–38.

Glad, S. (1996). *Income of the population 55 or older, 1994*. Washington, DC: Social Security Administration.

Halvorsen, R., & Palmquiest, R. (1980). The interpretation of dummy variables in semilogarithmic equations. *American Economic Review, 70*, 474–475.

Jackman, M. R., & Jackman, R. W. (1980). Racial inequalities in home ownership. *Social Forces, 63*, 1221–1234.

Kain, J. F., & Quigley, J. M. (1972). Housing market discrimination, home ownership, and savings behavior. *American Economic Review, 72*, 263–277.

Maxfield, L. D. (1985). Income of new retired workers by age at first benefit receipt: Findings from the New Beneficiary Survey. *Social Security Bulletin, 48*(7), 7–26.

Oliver, M. L., & Shapiro, T. M. (1989). Race and wealth. *Review of Black Political Economy, 17*(4), 5–25.

Ozawa, M. N. (1997). Income and net worth of the elderly in the United States. In International Longevity Center (Ed.), *Economic conditions of the elderly and the safety net* (pp. 170–260). Tokyo: Shinkodo Press.

Ozawa, M. N., & Law, S. W. (1993). Earnings history of social workers: A comparison to other professional groups. *Social Work, 38*, 542–551.

Ozawa, M. N., & Lum, Y. S. (1999, November 20). *Taking risks in investing in the equity market: Racial and ethnic differences.* Paper presented at the 52nd Annual Scientific Meeting of the Gerontological Society of America, San Francisco.

Ozawa, M. N., Lum, Y. S., & Tseng, H. Y. (1999). Net worth at retirement and 10 years later. In S. S. Nagel (Ed.), *The substance of public policy* (pp. 245–275). New York: Nova Science.

Radner, D. B. (1993). Economic well-being of the old old: Family unit income and household wealth. *Social Security Bulletin, 56*(1), 3–19.

Smith, J. P. (1989). Women, mothers, and work. In M. N. Ozawa (Ed.), *Women's life cycle and economic insecurity: Problems and proposals* (pp. 42–70). New York: Greenwood Press.

Smith, J. P. (1995). Racial and ethnic differences in wealth using the HRS. *Journal of Human Services, 30,* S158–S183.

Smith, J. P. (1997). Wealth inequality among older Americans. *Journal of Gerontology 52B* (Special issue), 74–81.

Social Security Administration. (1994). *The New Beneficiary Survey data system: User's manual.* Washington, DC: Author.

U.S. Department of Commerce. (1998). *Statistical abstract of the United States, 1998.* Washington, DC: U.S. Government Printing Office.

This chapter was originally published in the June 2000 issue of *Social Work Research*, Vol. 24, Number 2, pp. 96–108.

# 5

# What Families Know about Funeral-Related Costs

## Implications for Social Work Practice

MERCEDES BERN-KLUG,
DAVID J. EKERDT, and
DEBORAH SCHILD WILKINSON

Most deaths in the United States occur in an institutional setting; 60 percent occur in hospitals, and another 17 percent occur in nursing homes (National Center for Health Statistics, 1996). Social workers in these settings may find themselves in the position of working with families immediately before or after a death. Social workers also are involved in the care of the nation's 61,000 hospice patients (Haupt, 1997). In addition to the important roles of counselor and therapist, social workers also are called on to be discharge planners and advocates. This article addresses ways in which the social work role of the latter two might be enhanced. From the perspective of Kelley R. Macmillan, hospital social worker and doctoral student, University of Kansas School of Social Welfare (personal communication, March 17, 1998), helping families understand their final arrangement options might be thought of as "final discharge planning."

Leming and Dickinson (1990) reported that survivors commonly experience shock, denial, and disorganization following the death of a loved one. These normal reactions to death can contribute to the stressfulness of making final arrangements. Despite these facts, the social science literature describing how to help families face funeral- and burial-related decisions (final arrangements) is practically nonexistent.

In this study of the characteristics and experience of survivors responsible for making final arrangements, we determined the extent to which survivors were familiar with costs of commonly purchased final arrangement merchandise and services and the factors influencing familiarity with those costs. The findings of this study underscore the need for consumer-oriented information about final arrangements and have implications for social work practice.

## Background

There are at least seven factors that contribute to the uniqueness of making final arrangements. These factors distinguish final arrangements from other purchasing experiences and from other family rituals such as weddings, first communions, or bar mitzvah ceremonies.

1. The person or people responsible for making final arrangements or for overseeing the arrangements in the event that arrangements were made before the death are typically in crisis and overwhelmed by grief (Clark, 1987; Scheible Wolf, 1995). It is difficult to think clearly on what may be the saddest day of one's life.

2. Final arrangements can be expensive. Norrgard and DeMars (1992) reported that the national average costs for an open casket service followed by an earth burial are between $5,000 and $6,000. Lino (1990) reported that final arrangements are typically the third most expensive consumer purchase of a lifetime, behind the cost of a house and the cost of a car.

3. The finality of the decisions contributes to the uniqueness of making final arrangements. Whereas returns or exchanges are common when purchasing other merchandise, the same is not true of caskets, vaults, and grave markers.

4. Survivors often are pressed for time when it comes to making final arrangements. After a death there is a short window of time for making final arrangements. In general survivors are faced with making the decisions during a one- or two-hour meeting with a funeral director within 24 hours of the death (Bern-Klug, 1996). One local cemeterian estimated that there are more than 70 tasks to be completed after a family death and about half are time-pressured issues that must be dealt with before the final disposition of the body can take place (personal communication with William Riley, Kansas City Catholic Cemeteries, May 11, 1997).

5. Confusion about the primary purpose of the funeral may exist. Dawson, Santos, and Burdick (1990) reported that the functions served by a funeral include providing public recognition that a death has occurred, providing a framework in which to support those most affected by the death, and providing a means of disposing of the body. In addition, funerals also can serve as a way to pay respect for a deceased loved one. The purchase of merchandise and services may vary depending on what the arranger perceives as the primary purpose of the funeral.

6. The person buying the merchandise and services usually has much less experience and knowledge about options and costs than does the person selling: "In many cases a bereaved and less-than-clearheaded consumer is faced with purchasing services and merchandise from a funeral director who is thoroughly familiar with the situation and well prepared to meet its demands. This creates a serious imbalance in what might have been, with preplanning, a more normal purchasing situation" (Nelson, 1983, p. 1).

Supporting the notion that final arrangement information generally is confined to members of the funeral industry, we found a Wirthlin Group (1990) study on behalf of the Allied Industries Joint Committee (a collection of funeral directors, casket makers, cemetery owners, and grave marker makers) that asked a nationally representative sample of adults where they would turn for information about funeral and burial options. Of those who had never made final arrangements, 58 percent reported they would go to a funeral director for the information, and 13 percent indicated they did not know where to get funeral arranging information. Of those who had made final arrangements, 72 percent said they received the information from a funeral director, 18 percent said from friends and family members.

7. There seems to be a lack of clarity in our society about the "etiquette" of final arrangements. Is it in poor taste to compare funeral home costs? Can one bargain with a funeral director over the price of a casket? Is it acceptable to decline permission to have a loved one embalmed? With whom, besides the funeral director, can one discuss the need for a sealed vault?

The same seven factors that contribute to the uniqueness of making final arrangements also can contribute to the stressfulness of the task. Even in situations in which the decedent had preplanned final arrangements, someone—usually a grief-stricken family member—must oversee the arrangements. That survivors are under stress, that the funeral home environment is unfamiliar, and that people are not sure what is expected of them creates a classic person-in-environment challenge with ample opportunity for social work intervention.

## Role for Social Workers

This article introduces information about final arrangements to augment the impor-

tant work already conducted by social workers with dying individuals and their families in health care settings, such as help with advance directives and grief counseling. It is our impression that few social workers, and typically no other professionals in the health care setting, have at hand the knowledge of costs and local options needed to assist families with final arrangements. Social workers, with their experience in public benefits, consumer advocacy, and discharge planning, possess the skills necessary to fulfill the important and overlooked tasks of sharing information about local options and costs and information about consumer rights related to final arrangement purchases. If families who experience a death in an institution are to have access to this important information before calling a funeral home, someone in the institution must assume the responsibility. Social workers have the skills to help families sort through their personal goals for final arrangements and to serve as advocates to families in the process of making final arrangements. Although some social workers have been helping families with final arrangements, very little has been published in the literature about this important function.

Final arrangements can be regarded as a consumer issue (Federal Trade Commission, 1988), an income security issue (Norrgard & DeMars, 1992), and a client self-determination and autonomy issue. Chichin, Ferster, and Gordon (1994) described a program in which social workers helped frail isolated home care clients communicate their funeral and burial plans and reported that clients appreciated the "opportunity to exercise autonomy even beyond the moment of death" (p. 148). Helping families understand their consumer rights and the variation in local options and costs of final arrangements represents an important and untapped role for social workers.

The overall study—the Funeral Information Project—was primarily a descriptive study supported by research funds from the AARP Andrus Foundation. The goal of the Funeral Information Project was to increase general knowledge of how families face funeral-related decisions and costs associated with the death of an older adult loved one. This article focuses on a more narrow set of questions about family familiarity with costs. (For other results from the Funeral Information Project, please consult Bern-Klug, 1996; Bern-Klug, Ekerdt, & Nakashima, 1999; and Bern-Klug, DeViney, & Ekerdt, in press). This article addresses the following research questions: What are the characteristics of survivors responsible for final arrangements of decedents ages 50 and older? How much experience have these survivors had with making final arrangements? How familiar are these survivors with the cost of merchandise and services commonly purchased from a funeral director or cemeterian? What factors influence whether a survivor will have some idea of total final costs?

We hypothesized that the following attributes of the respondent would be positively associated with having some idea of total final costs: increasing age, being a man, having experience making final arrangements with a funeral director, and a decedent who preplanned final arrangements. We assumed that the older a person is the more likely he or she will have had an opportunity to learn about final arrangements, that middle-age and older men may have more experience purchasing costly items than women in the same group, that experience with making final arrangements can be generalized, and that if the decedent had preplanned his or her final arrangements, the person responsible for them might have previously discussed not only the plans for but possibly the costs of the arrangements. This study is part of a larger research project designed to find out about experiences in making and paying for final arrangements. (For a detailed description of the methodology, refer to Bern-Klug et al., 1999.)

## Method

### Sample

The sample recruitment consisted of identifying eligible obituaries published in the *Kansas City Star* between June 1 and July 15, 1995, and then working with local funeral directors to identify the survivor most responsible for making the final arrangements. In the cases in which the final arrangements were made before death, we were interested in the survivor most responsible for overseeing the final arrangements. The person who signed the final funeral home bill was considered the person most responsible for the final arrangements. There were three criteria for inclusion in the study: decedent's age reported as 50 or older; decedent was listed as a Kansas City metropolitan area resident; the obituary did not indicate that a funeral home located outside the Kansas City area was used.

The 62 local funeral homes were asked to forward a letter to the persons who signed the final bill (the key arrangers) informing them of the study and inviting their participation. Letters were mailed to families about three to five months after the death. Forty-six of the 49 locally owned funeral homes participated. None of the 13 funeral homes owned by a large Texas-based chain would forward the letter. Seventy-two obituaries did not list a funeral home.

*Response Rates.* There were 991 obituaries that fulfilled the study criteria. Of these, we were able to contact 832 families and received 163 returned completed questionnaires. The obituaries were sorted into three groups based on how contact was established. The response rate of the three groups varied considerably:

1. obituaries listing a participating funeral home—Of the 645 letters that funeral directors agreed to forward to families, eight were returned by the post office as undeliverable. We received 101 completed questionnaires (16 percent).

2. obituaries associated with nonparticipating funeral homes—The project staff was able to locate an address for a next-of-kin mentioned in 123 of the 274 obituaries. We received 36 completed questionnaires (29 percent) (13 percent of eligible cases).

3. obituaries that did not mention a funeral home at all—Of the 72 obituaries, survivor addresses were found for 44. Completed questionnaires were received from 22 families (50 percent) (30 percent of eligible cases).

*Follow-up.* A reminder letter was mailed to nonrespondents for whom we had an address. Funeral directors did not agree to forward a reminder letter from the project.

### Instrument

The research tool was a self-administered 20-minute questionnaire developed with input from local funeral directors, county extension aging specialists, hospice personnel, Widowed Persons Services volunteers, and social scientists. It was pilot tested with widowed hospice volunteers.

### Important Terms

*Final arrangements* refer to activities associated with the care and disposition of a human body following death, as well as the arrangements associated with a ceremony following the death.

*Key arranger* is the person who signed the final funeral home bill. In the cases in which the funeral home would not forward a letter from us and when no funeral home was listed in the obituary, we explained in the cover letter that we were looking for the person "most responsible for making or overseeing the final arrangements." Almost all (99 percent) respondents reported that they were one of the people most responsible for making or overseeing arrangements.

*Preplanner* is a decedent who the key arranger reported had made final arrangements with a third party (a funeral director, cemeterian, or other person) or had discussed final arrangement wishes with the family. A *nonpreplanner* is a decedent who did not make or discuss final arrangement preferences.

*Final arrangements total cost* is the combined cost of funeral home and cemetery-related costs or any costs associated with the care and disposition of the body.

### Data Analysis

Descriptive statistics, chi-square, and *t* tests were used to address the first three research questions. The fourth research question, "What factors influence whether a survivor will have some idea of total final costs?" was analyzed using multiple logistic regression. Goodness of fit for the models was measured by examining the chi-square of -2 log likelihood. Interaction terms were tested. SPSS for Windows Release 6.1 was used for all analyses. Norušis (1993a, 1993b) was consulted for interpretation of SPSS results.

## Findings

### Final Costs

Although the cost of final arrangements was not a key variable in this study, we present some cost information for background. Respondents reported combined funeral and burial-related costs ranging from $195 to $14,000. Whereas the mean total cost for the sample was $5,600, average costs varied considerably by type of disposition. For the three-fourths of decedents whose bodies were placed in a casket and buried in a grave plot, the mean cost was $6,500. The mean cost for decedents who were cremated was $2,300. (A more detailed discussion of final costs can be found in Bern-Klug et al., in press.)

### Characteristics of Key Arrangers

Most key arrangers were either an adult child (47 percent) or a surviving spouse (42 percent) of the decedent. If the decedent was married at the time of death, the surviving spouse was the key arranger in practically all cases (91 percent), and an adult child served as key arranger 8 percent of the time. For the 54 percent of decedents who were divorced, widowed, or never married at the time of death, the key arranger was usually an adult child (79 percent). In those cases in which an adult child was not the key arranger of a nonmarrried decedent, another 6 percent of arrangers were siblings of the decedent, and the remaining 14 percent listed themselves as "other," most of whom were nieces.

The vast majority (84 percent) of respondents (that is, the key arrangers) identified themselves as "non-Hispanic white," reflecting the racial and ethnic distribution of the Kansas City metropolitan area. The reported age of key arrangers ranged from 22 to 83, with a median age of 61. Most (63 percent) of the key arrangers under age 60 were adult children of the decedent, and 20 percent were surviving spouses. About half (54 percent) of the key arrangers age 60 and older were surviving spouses, and 35 percent were adult

children. Most of the key arrangers were women (68 percent). Sixty-five percent of adult children were women compared with 72 percent of spouses (not a statistically significant difference). The gender of the decedent was not related to having a spouse or an adult child as the key arranger.

Key arrangers did not meet alone with the funeral director to make plans in most cases. Family members and friends accompanied 80 percent of the key arrangers. Adult children were included among those who met with the funeral director (either as the key arranger or to accompany the key arranger) in 70 percent of the cases in this study.

### Experience Making Final Arrangements

Most key arrangers in this study were not novices when it came to making final arrangements. Two-thirds reported having met with a funeral director on behalf of at least one other person before the current death. A statistically significant higher percentage of surviving spouses reported experience compared with adult children (71 percent compared with 61 percent) (Table 5-1). Not only did a higher percentage of spouses report experience, but spouses as a group also reported a higher frequency of meetings with funeral directors. Indeed, half the surviving spouses had made plans with a funeral director on behalf of two or more people; only 18 percent of adult children reported the same. There was no statistically significant relationship between age of key arranger and experience. Women had less experience than men ($p < .05$), 38 percent of women were final arrangement novices, only 18 percent of men were.

Key arrangers were less likely to report experience with cemetery arrangements than funeral home arrangements. About half the key arrangers (42 percent of spouses and 51

**TABLE 5-1. Percentage of Key Arrangers Reporting Experience with Funeral Directors and Cemeterians**

|  | Funeral Director* | | Cemeterian* | |
|---|---|---|---|---|
|  | Spouses n = 69 | Children n = 75 | Spouses n = 67 | Children n = 73 |
| None | 29 | 39 | 42 | 51 |
| One person | 20 | 43 | 19 | 39 |
| Two people or more | 51 | 18 | 39 | 10 |

*p < .001.

percent of children) reported never having met with a cemeterian to make arrangements. Surviving spouses were about as likely to report no experience as they were to report experience on behalf of two or more people; 19 percent of spouses had only one prior experience. (A different distribution for children, with only 10 percent reporting two or more experiences is presented in Table 5-1.)

Respondents were asked the extent to which the decedent had communicated his or her final arrangement preferences. Most decedents (73 percent) were classified as preplanners because they either finalized their arrangements with a third party (for example, funeral director, cemeterian, or memorial society) before death (42 percent) or because they discussed their preferences with their family, although they had not pre-arranged with a third party (31 percent). The remaining 27 percent of respondents reported that their loved one did not discuss final arrangement preferences. Chi-square tests failed to show a statistically significant relationship between whether the decedent had preplanned and the age of the decedent, the age of the key arranger, or spouse/adult child status. Almost all (93 percent) decedents who were cremated were preplanners, compared with 69 percent of those who were buried (p < .01).

The survey also asked, "In your opinion, is making final arrangements before death

helpful to survivors?" The answers to this question varied by gender, but not by age or spouse/adult child status. Sixty-eight percent answered "extremely helpful," including 73 percent of women, 56 percent of men, 77 percent of adult children, and 65 percent of spouses. About a quarter of the sample (23 percent) reported, "somewhat helpful," and 9 percent indicated "not helpful."

### *Familiarity with Costs*

Respondents were asked if, before they met with the funeral director, they had "some idea" or "no idea at all" of the costs of commonly purchased items listed in Table 5-2. Nearly half the key arrangers reported no idea of costs of individual items or of the total cost. Women were more likely to report a lack of familiarity than were men when it came to the cost of caskets and grave markers. The difference between men and women approached statistical significance for other costs as well: opening and closing a grave, body transportation, and total costs. Knowledge of total costs was not related to age of respondent or to spouse/adult child status.

On further examination of the bivariate relationships between knowledge of total costs and other variables, we found that hav-

**TABLE 5-2. Percentage of Key Arrangers with No Idea of Funeral Items Costs**

| Item | Total n = 148 | Men n = 47 | Women n = 101 | p value |
|---|---|---|---|---|
| Caskets | 46 | 33 | 53 | .02 |
| Vaults | 59 | 52 | 61 | .31 |
| Flowers | 45 | 40 | 48 | .37 |
| Cemetery space | 44 | 35 | 46 | .22 |
| Grave open/closing | 63 | 52 | 68 | .08 |
| Grave marker | 56 | 42 | 61 | .03 |
| Body transportation | 69 | 58 | 73 | .06 |
| Total arrangements | 52 | 40 | 57 | .05 |

*Note: p determined by chi-square analysis.*

ing had the experience of meeting with a funeral director to make plans was related to
reporting some idea of total costs. Sixty-one
percent of experienced key arrangers reported some knowledge of total costs compared with 17 percent of arrangers who did
not have experience. If the decedent was a
preplanner, the key arranger was more likely
to report some knowledge of total costs (55
percent compared with 28 percent).

Knowledge of total costs was not related
to actual final costs, that is, the mean cost of
final arrangements was statistically the same
for arrangers with no idea and those with
some idea of total costs ($5,727 compared
with $5,362). Also, type of disposition (burial
or cremation) was not related to key
arranger's knowledge of final costs.

### Predicting Knowledge of Total Costs with Logistic Regression

Four independent variables were tested for
their association with having some idea of
final costs: respondent's age, respondent's
gender, respondent's experience with making
arrangements with a funeral director, and
decedent's status as preplanner. Other than
age, which was a continuous variable, the remaining variables were all dichotomous. The
interaction of gender and age was not statistically significant and therefore was not included in the model.

Neither gender nor age of the key arranger
contributed significantly to distinguishing
key arrangers with some idea from those with
no idea of total final costs (Table 5-3). When
age and gender are dropped from the model
(model 2), the remaining two independent
variables remain highly significant. The odds
of having some idea of total final costs were
nine times greater (CI = 3.82, 22.98) for
people reporting prior experience with a funeral director and were four times higher (CI

**TABLE 5-3. Reporting "Some Idea" of Total Final Costs: Logistic Regression Results**

| Variable | Odds Ratio | 95% CI | p value |
|---|---|---|---|
| Respondent's gender | .68 | .29, 1.56 | .39 |
| Respondent's age | .74 | .52, 1.05 | .09 |
| Prior experience making funeral arrangements | 11.08 | 4.29, 28.59 | .001 |
| Decedent had preplanned | 3.36 | 1.33, 8.49 | .01 |

Goodness of fit measures: −2 log likelihood 158.99; goodness of fit 148.86. Model $\chi^2(4) = 41.954$, $p < .0000$.

= 1.64, 9.86) for key arrangers associated with
a decedent who had preplanned.

## Discussion

### Characteristics of Key Arrangers

One of the major findings of this study is the
large extent to which adult children are involved, either as the key arranger or by accompanying the key arranger, in making
parents' final arrangements. With the age
range of key arrangers spanning five decades
(from age 22 to age 83), it is clear that adults
of all ages are being called on. In terms of
distributing consumer-oriented information
about final arrangements, we need to avoid
the tendency to target only older people and
to broaden the population served to adults
of all ages. A special effort is called for to alert
adult children of the possibility of being included in—or responsible for—the final arrangements of parents (especially when the
parent is divorced or widowed).

Women were key arrangers in more than
half the cases. We do not know if women are
more likely to be key arrangers or if they are
more likely to respond to this type of survey.
Anecdotal information from funeral directors
supports the notion that women are more
likely than men to be involved with making
or overseeing funeral arrangements on be-

half of a loved one. Consumer-oriented information should be inclusive of women.

### Experience Making Final Arrangements

Although most key arrangers reported experience meeting with a funeral director, there were many people in the position of being responsible for final arrangements who had no prior experience, especially adult children, 39 percent of whom reported no prior experience. The level of experience with cemeteries is lower than it is for funeral homes. This may not be as pressing a concern for families, at the time of death, because in many cases the plot has been purchased years before the death, and the grave marker can be purchased well after.

Compared with men, women were more likely to report a lack of experience with funeral homes. This finding coupled with the finding that women are overrepresented as key arrangers suggests that efforts should be made to provide women with exposure to funeral homes and information about final arrangement options and costs.

More research on key arrangers also is needed. Social workers need to know the process by which the key arranger is selected, by whom, and the time frame. Social workers need to learn from key arrangers how they feel about fulfilling this role. What aspects of the role are most stressful, rewarding, or important? How best can these people prepare for the role?

Most of the decedents associated with this study were classified as preplanners because they either made final arrangements with a funeral director, cemeterian, or memorial society or because they had discussed their preferences with the family. Despite the fact that we classified nearly three-quarters of the decedents as preplanners, it is important to underscore that most people (58 percent) had

not finalized their arrangements. Even in those situations in which arrangements had been finalized, a survivor remained responsible for ensuring that the plans were carried out as specified. It is not clear why women survivors were more likely to find preplanning "extremely" helpful; perhaps by finding out in what ways preplanning is helpful, we can illuminate this finding. It is important to note that with the increased marketing efforts that funeral homes across the country are putting into selling "pre-need" funeral insurance, we can expect the number of people paying for prearrangements to increase. Our results indicate that preplanning was found to be helpful to survivors; this finding does not speak to prepaying.

Nine percent of key arrangers reported that preplanning was not helpful. One daughter wrote in the margin of the survey that it was not helpful for her to know that her father wanted to be cremated because she was not comfortable cremating him (and did not cremate him after all). A surviving husband explained that his wife had always said she wanted to be entombed in a mausoleum. After her death the family learned the cost of her wish. They could not afford to entomb her; she was buried in a grave plot. In both cases the potential for strong and lingering feelings of guilt clearly exists. Evidently, it is not enough that people state their final arrangement preferences. People should be encouraged to explore the options and costs and then discuss their preferences with those who may be responsible for carrying them out.

We cannot always know when death will strike. We encourage families to discuss the issue of final arrangements on a regular basis so members will be somewhat prepared to make these decisions, even in the event of a sudden death. Because circumstances, options, and preferences change, families should revisit these discussions every couple of years.

## Familiarity with Costs

Despite the fact that most final arrangements costs range from $3,000 to $7,000, about half the people responsible for making or for overseeing final arrangements reported that before meeting with the funeral director they had "no idea" of those costs. This finding supports results from the Wirthlin Group (1990) study, which indicated that most people turn to a funeral director to learn about final arrangements and that many people who have not yet planned a funeral do not know where to get information about final arrangements. Although we expect funeral directors to provide information, we believe that sources of information—without a financial interest in the purchase—should be available to educate families about their options and the associated costs. Video tapes, books, seminars, magazine articles, and other methods of communicating information should be developed by consumer advocates (including social workers) to educate families about final arrangements. Although the American Association of Retired Persons (AARP) has taken a leadership role in providing consumer-oriented information on final arrangements, more information is needed.

## Factors Influencing
## Knowledge of Total Costs

A major, although not surprising, finding is that people who have had the experience of making final arrangements were far more likely to report some idea of total final costs. It is notable, however, that despite the fact that they had already been in the position to make final arrangements, more than one-third of the people with experience reported no idea of total costs. It is not so much that experience puts people in the position of

knowing costs as it is that lack of experience puts people at a serious disadvantage. Whereas 39 percent of experienced arrangers reported no idea of total costs, 83 percent of those with no experience reported no idea.

The same logic follows for understanding the relationship with preplanning decedents. Key arrangers with preplanning decedents had about an equal chance of reporting no idea of final costs, whereas 72 percent of key arrangers associated with nonpreplanners reported no idea.

The logistic regression results showed that key arrangers with funeral home experience were nine times more likely to report having some idea of total final costs compared with those with no experience. Respondents associated with a decedent who had made final arrangements or discussed preferences were four times more likely to report some idea of final costs. Although we cannot directly affect a person's experience level, these findings indicate social workers can and should encourage families to discuss their final arrangement preferences.

In this study, emphasis has been placed on the key arranger having some idea of total costs, and yet the data failed to show an association with this variable and the actual cost of arrangements. Does having an idea of final costs before meeting with a funeral director make a difference for the survivor? We are not sure, because this preliminary descriptive study did not ask all the questions necessary to understand the importance of cost knowledge. We assume that having some idea of total costs before meeting with the funeral director puts the family member in a better position to understand the options, to serve as his or her own advocate, and to make an informed purchase of a package costing several thousand dollars. Also, bear in mind that 73 percent of decedents were preplanners (93 percent of decedents who were cremated were preplanners). A better question for a future study might be, "What is the relationship between knowledge of final costs of the preplanner (as opposed to the key arranger) and his or her final costs?"

A future study might ask respondents to describe the extent to which they understood final arrangement options and the costs. Even people with experience making final arrangements may be shocked to learn about the possible variation in final costs based on burial versus cremation (reported earlier) or among funeral homes. A 1995 study of funeral home costs in the Kansas City area found large cost variations for comparable items (Funeral and Memorial Society Report, 1995). For example, although the median cost of staff and equipment for a graveside service among 62 funeral homes was $200, the prices ranged from $65 to $3,440. Even long-time memorial society advocates were taken aback by the price differences.

## *Limitations of the Study*

The low response rate may affect the generalizability and trustworthiness of the findings. This shortcoming is exacerbated by the lack of published studies that deal with the research questions explored here. More studies are needed to validate the findings. The results from this study undertaken in a large metropolitan city in the Midwest should not be assumed to hold true in rural areas or other regions of the country. The results are not intended to be generalizable to final arrangements on behalf of decedents under age 50. The small number of African American respondents and representatives from other racial and ethnic groups did not allow for statistical tests of differences. Future studies are needed to build an understanding of final arrangements among subpopulations, including religious denominations.

## *Implications for Social Workers*

Our findings clearly show that some of the people responsible for final arrangements have no experience with such matters and that about half have no idea what to expect in terms of costs. Many times a family must decide what to do with the body while the decedent lies in a hospital bed or in the morgue. Many people do not have the time or the clearheadedness to be their own advocate at that point. In the midst of all the other decisions that families face at the time of death, a social worker with information about local final arrangement options and costs can make an important difference.

The Federal Trade Commission requires that all funeral homes provide a "General Price List" to anyone who requests it in person. Social workers can educate themselves about local options and costs by collecting these price lists and sharing the information with colleagues (such as chaplains, nurses, representatives from places of worship, and clients). A local chapter of the Funeral and Memorial Society (if available) may have already collected local price information and may have information about crematories, body donation programs, and cemeteries.

The finding that people with experience meeting with a funeral director were more likely to have some idea of final costs points to another potential social work role. Social workers can encourage families to talk about their final arrangement making experiences, in the hope that this might be an effective method of sharing the experience, and thereby help prepare more people for the position of key arranger. Such encouragement may help to change the perceived etiquette regarding final arrangement discussions. From our experience providing community presentations about final arrangements, we found that many people are

eager for information and willing to share experiences, given "permission" to do so.

Another important role for clinical social workers, particularly relevant in the
hospice setting, is to help individual clients
and their families enhance the meaningful-
ness of final arrangements by helping the
family sort through their own personal goals
for the service, including which merchandise and services to purchase. Doka (1984/
85) and Huan (1980) mentioned the importance of personalizing and individualizing
funeral rituals.

Social workers serving as community advocates, especially on behalf of impoverished
individuals and families, also have a stake in
understanding local options and costs. They
can serve an important role by being involved
in sharing the information with the community and informing people of their final arrangement rights, including indigent burial
options and Title XIX (Medicaid) rules affecting funeral and burial trusts. Laws regulating
the sale of pre-need funeral home insurance
or trusts and laws governing the transfer of
human remains are made at the state level and
should be reviewed to ensure that consumer
interests are well served. The ratio of public
members to funeral directors on state governing boards also should be reviewed.

Regardless of the area of practice, with
over 2 million deaths per year in the United
States (Rosenberg, Ventura, Maurer, Heuser,
& Freedman, 1996), the need and opportunity clearly exists for social workers to play
an active role in helping families with final
arrangements, which would augment the
many important activities that health setting–
based social workers are already undertak-
ing in the area of end-of-life care for the dying
individual and his or her kin.

🌿 🌿 🌿

# References

Bern-Klug, M. (1996). *Funeral-related options and costs: A guide for families*. Kansas City: University of Kansas.

Bern-Klug, M., DeViney, S., & Ekerdt, D. (in press). Variations in funeral-related costs of older people and the role of preneed funeral contracts. *Omega: Journal of Death and Dying*.

Bern-Klug, M., Ekerdt, D., & Nakashima, M. (1999). Helping families understand final arrangement options and costs. In B. deVries (Ed.), *End of life issues: Interdisciplinary and multidisciplinary*. New York: Springer.

Chichin, E. R., Ferster, L., & Gordon, N. (1994). Planning for the end of life with the home care client. *Journal of Gerontological Social Work, 22*, 147–159.

Clark, E. (1987). The rights of the bereaved. In A. H. Kutscher, A. C. Carr, & L. G. Kutscher (Eds.), *Principles of thanatology* (pp. 187–210). New York: Columbia University Press.

Dawson, G. D., Santos, J. F., & Burdick, D. C. (1990). Differences in final arrangements between burial and cremation as the method of body disposition. *Omega, 21*(2), 129–146.

Doka, K. J. (1984/85). Expectation of death, participation in funeral arrangements, and grief adjustment. *Omega, 15*(2), 119–129.

Federal Trade Commission. (1988). *Report of the Survey of Recent Funeral Arrangers*. Washington, DC: Market Facts, Inc.

Funeral and Memorial Society Report of the Greater Kansas City Chapter of the Funeral and Memorial Societies of America (1995, November), page 3 of price list insert.

Haupt, B. J. (1997, March 6). Characteristics of patients receiving hospice care services: United States, 1994. *Advanced Data*, No. 282. Atlanta: Centers for Disease Control and Prevention/ National Center for Health Statistics.

Huan, D. L. (1980). Perceptions of the bereaved, clergy and funeral directors concerning bereavement. *National Reporter, 3*, pp. 7–8.

Leming, M. R., & Dickinson, G. E. (1990). *Understanding dying, death, & bereavement*. Fort Worth: Holt, Rinehart & Winston.

Lino, M. (1990, July). The $3,000 farewell. *American Demographics*, p. 8.

National Center for Health Statistics. (1996). *Vital statistics of the United States, 1992* (Vol. 2: Mortality, Part A). Washington, DC: Public Health Service.

Nelson, T. C. (1983). *It's your choice: The practical guide to planning a funeral*. Glenville, IL: American Association of Retired Persons/Scott Foresman and Company.

Norrgard, L., & DeMars, J. (1992). *Final choices: Making end-of-life decisions*. Santa Barbara, CA: ABC-CLIO.

Norušis, M. J. (1993a). *SPSS for Windows: Base systems user's guide* (Release 6.0). Chicago: SPSS, Inc.

Norušis, M. J. (1993b). *SPSS for Windows: Advanced statistics* (Release 6.0). Chicago: SPSS, Inc.

Rosenberg, H. M., Ventura, S. J., Maurer, J. D., Heuser, R. L., & Freedman, M. A. (1996). *Births and deaths in the United States, 1995* (Monthly Vital Statistics Report, Vol. 45, No. 3, Suppl. 2). Hyattsville, MD: National Center for Health Statistics.

Scheible Wolf, S. (1995). Legal perspectives on planning for death. In H. Wass & R. A. Neimeyer (Eds.), *Dying: Facing the facts* (pp. 163–182). Washington, DC: Taylor & Francis.

Wirthlin Group. (1990). *American attitudes and values affected by death and death care services* (Report to the Allied Industries Joint Committee). McLean, VA: Author.

This article was originally published in the May 1999 issue of *Health & Social Work*, Vol. 2, Number 2, pp. 128–137.

# II

# Participation

❦ ❦ ❦

The United Nations agenda for older persons calls for special attention to issues of social integration, or the inclusion of persons of all ages within the vital fabric of society. In this endeavor, elders should be recognized as priceless treasures with knowledge and skills to share with younger generations. Opportunities need to be created for older persons to volunteer in organizations, to associate freely with others in organizing, to improve their own situations, and to create social movements. Social policies, institutions, and social workers have special roles in and obligations to facilitating and promoting such engagement with elders. While social workers recognize the importance of social support and friendships, the maintenance of such important interpersonal connectedness usually requires at least benign societal infrastructures. Increasingly, however, the maintenance of social contracts requires positive and proactive social efforts, communication and transportation, public and neighborhood space where interpersonal contacts can be made, and social activities that generate beneficial interdependence. The creation of such social cohesion, or "social capital," has spillover benefits in civic engagement by and for people of all ages (Putnam, 2000).

Next to family support, adult friendships are most vital to life satisfaction for older people. In the first article in this section, Darcy Clay Siebert, Elizabeth Mutran, and Donald Reitzes review essential aspects of post-retirement friendships, including their differential gender dimensions. Persons with abundant social support are in better mental and physical health, literally enjoying a survival advantage. By following a random sample of pre-retirement persons from 1992 to 1994, the authors were able

to question whether the friend role is significantly predictive of well-being and related to
differences in social support and gender.
They tracked their respondents' transitions
to retirement and examined "identity meanings" (the shared meanings one attributes to
oneself in a particular role) and commitment
(respondents' sense of belonging to the role
of being a friend). Their findings highlight
the importance of reciprocity in friendships,
the ability to provide and receive support, and
the unique strengths of long-term friendships
in sustaining self-identify over a life span by
providing self-esteem that familial dependency relationships sometimes erode. "Aging adults seek friends who can reduce the
discrepancy between their perception of who
they are and the negative identity meanings
they might receive from family and others."
Recognizing the ability of friends to counteract other losses and deficiencies, the authors suggest ways that social workers might
create opportunities to enhance friendship
identities. Enhancement of existing positive
support is more effective than creating new
kinds of support. And helping roles have particular salience for isolated and older women
with disabilities with fewer natural opportunities to help others because of failing health
and lack of financial resources.

In the second article, Dona Reese, Robin
Ahern, Shankar Nair, Joleen D. O'Faire
Shrock, and Claudia Warren-Wheat point to
the other side of the participation paradigm
by highlighting the insidiously destructive
effects of "social exclusion." Distinct institutional barriers exist within hospice, a particularly important health care program;
ethnic and racial minorities represent only
5-7 percent of hospice patients. Reese and
colleagues present historical and cultural reasons that might explain this disparity, but still
find it troubling. Using participatory action
research, they set out to understand these
reasons through discussion with African
American pastors. Their qualitative analysis

identifies cultural, spiritual, and institutional
barriers that deter African Americans from
using hospice services. Cultural barriers include a variety of values held about medical
care that conflict with hospice philosophy,
such as not believing in palliative care, pre-
ferring life-sustaining treatment, and holding cultural beliefs opposed to accepting
terminality. Spiritual beliefs include a preference for prayer. Institutional barriers included lack of knowledge about available
services, lack of health insurance and other
resources, lack of trust generally in the health
care system, and lack of diversity among hospice health care staffs. These authors make
solid recommendations to social workers
about reframing these barriers in practice in
order to adapt hospice to the needs and beliefs of African Americans who truly would
benefit from it. This means embracing spiritually sensitive practice and acknowledging
a raft of areas of potential convergence with
African American beliefs in the values underlying hospice provision.

Finally, in this section Jeanette Takamura,
Director of the U.S. Administration on Aging, reminds us of the importance of institutionalizing mechanisms for generating social
support, in this case through the Older
Americans Act and its "aging network" of
service agencies, membership organizations,
and community-based programs. While Dr.
Takamura acknowledges that services in the
United States are not equitably distributed,
these inequities constantly challenge us to
seek out increasingly subtle forms of discrimination in access to services and to rem-
edy them.

### References

Putnam, R. (2000). *Bowling Alone: The Collapse and
Revival of American Community*. New York:
Simon & Schuster.

# 6

# Friendship and Social Support

## The Importance of Role Identity to Aging Adults

DARCY CLAY SIEBERT,
ELIZABETH J. MUTRAN,
and DONALD C. REITZES

Popular and scholarly interest in social support has grown in the past decade, building on earlier research and theory (Antonucci & Akiyama, 1987b, 1991, 1995; Armstrong & Goldsteen, 1990; Blieszner & Bedford, 1995; Bosse, Aldwin, Levenson, Spiro, & Mroczek, 1993; Field & Minkler, 1988; Forster & Stoller, 1992; Johnson & Troll, 1994; Matt & Dean, 1993; O'Connor, 1995; Shye, Mullooly, Freeborn, & Pope, 1995; Turner, 1994; Wykle, Kahana, & Kowal, 1992). Contributing to this trend is the growing attention to social support for older adults, particularly among social workers and health care practitioners who work with increasing numbers of aging clients. It is critical to continue this focus of inquiry as baby boomers age and formal support systems become increasingly overextended. This body of research has generated a number of unifying themes, but it has produced ambiguous findings as well. Our current research sheds light on the issues by explaining how role identity theory is an integrating concept and offers applications for practitioners by revealing how clients' identities and commitment to the friendship role have a strong influence on their life satisfaction.

Despite the explosion of social support research, there is a lack of consensus in defining, operationalizing, and measuring it (Antonucci & Akiyama, 1995; Forster & Stoller, 1992; Jackson & Antonucci, 1992). Measures of social support can include structural features such as size and composition of the support network, frequency of interactions, content and quality of support, and perceptions of its adequacy. Because these measures are not standardized, researchers regularly call for further specification of both measures and concepts (Dean, Matt, & Wood, 1992). Past research also varies by method, with a reliance on cross-sectional data (Adams, 1987; Antonucci, 1989) and few studies with longitudinal designs to address issues of causal ordering (Dean et al., 1992; Matt & Dean, 1993). Diverse research questions with few replications (Israel & Antonucci, 1987), combined with the variety of measures and methods, create a body of work that lacks clarity and is difficult to interpret.

It is most impressive that despite these variations, a number of consistent findings emerge. Scholars agree that social support, however operationalized, is definitely important to health and well-being (Berkman & Syme, 1979; Jackson & Antonucci, 1992), particularly for aging adults (Minkler & Langhauser, 1988). Older adults with few social ties have increased risk of dying earlier (Berkman & Syme, 1979), whereas those with social support have a survival advantage (Forster & Stoller, 1992). Older adults who see themselves as socially engaged and supported are in better mental and physical health than those socially isolated (Carstensen, 1991).

Differences between the contributions of family and friends to older adults' well-being are a popular focus of study that also results in consistent findings. Family members make up half or more of individuals' social support networks, and the proportion of family are even higher for closest supporters (Antonucci, 1994). Despite this, researchers regularly offer evidence that friends' support is more important than family support to older adults' well-being (Larson, Mannell, & Zuzanek, 1986; Lee & Shehan, 1989; O'Connor, 1995; Wood & Robertson, 1978). This apparent contradiction often is explained by hypothesizing that because family relationships are obligatory and friendships are voluntary, older adults cannot terminate a stressful family relationship, although they can end a friendship (Antonucci & Akiyama, 1995; Lee & Shehan, 1989). However, evidence that older adults' friendships tend to be stable and very long term (Field & Minkler, 1988) would seem to mitigate this explanation.

It is generally agreed that social relations also differ by gender (Antonucci & Akiyama, 1987a; Matt & Dean, 1993; Wright, 1989). Women tend to have more extensive support networks, provide and receive more support, and are more satisfied with their friendships (Antonucci, 1994; Field & Minkler, 1988). Men tend to report receiving more support from their spouses and less from other family members and friends (Antonucci & Akiyama, 1991). A recurring theme in the literature is that men and women value reciprocity in relationships (Antonucci & Akiyama, 1991; Tilburg, 1992) but that women are more affected by their perception of reciprocity than men are (Antonucci, 1994).

Researchers have explored the theoretical explanations for both the diversity and consistency of research results and introduced several important unifying conceptualizations. The "convoy" model, prominent in the literature and termed to create the image of protective layers, characterizes social support as three concentric circles surrounding the individual. The innermost ring consists of the closest and most important providers of support, the middle ring contains the important but not most intimate supporters, and the external ring includes supporters who are close because they occupy a particular role such as coworker (Antonucci & Akiyama, 1987b). Researchers argue that convoys may function to the detriment or benefit of the individual depending on whether they are a support or a burden (Antonucci, 1994), thus having a substantial influence on well-being (Antonucci & Akiyama, 1995).

The life span perspective is embedded in the convoy model, recognizing that as people age, they continue to develop and experience many changes individually and in their relationships, thus taking their personal history and relationship experiences along with them (Antonucci & Akiyama, 1995). Individuals form attachments to others that wax and wane over time. Thus, consistent with the life span perspective, both change and continuity can characterize membership in one's convoy (Carstensen, 1991; Levitt, Coffman, Guacci-Franco, & Loveless, 1994).

Selectivity is a notion that emerged from the findings that although some older adults' support networks constrict with losses over time (Kahn, 1979) and they interact with others less frequently (Bosse et al., 1993), the perception of support remains stable (Bosse, Aldwin, Levenson, Workman-Daniels, & Ekerdt, 1990). Selectivity theory uses a continuity model (Dean et al., 1992), viewing decreases in older adults' social interactions not as a result of losses and ill health, as healthy older adults also report reduced social activity, but rather as the culmination of an adaptive process of selection (Carstensen, 1991). Older adults' friends tend to be long-term friends (Field & Minkler, 1988), and

they clearly prefer familiar friends to acquaintances they do not know well (Carstensen, 1991). Unlike decremental theories that view empirical results as confirmation that aging is a process of decline and withdrawal (Dean et al., 1992), selectivity theory assumes that reduced social interactions are functional and a continuation of a long process of selecting to interact with others to meet life-cycle goals (Carstensen, 1991).

Despite the many ways these frameworks and theories help to explain the diverse findings in social support research, a number of process issues remain unresolved. People identify family members as their closest supporters yet also report that friends contribute more to their well-being. Older adults cull their networks by choosing to interact with certain members yet continue to feel well supported. This study furthers this discussion and integrates these concepts by introducing the perspective of role identity theory, particularly as applied to adults approaching retirement years.

Stryker and colleagues offered a comprehensive description of role identity theory (Stryker, 1980; Stryker & Serpe, 1994; Stryker & Statham, 1985). In brief, role identity theory is grounded in symbolic interactionism and the notion that we all identify and categorize people into social positions to organize our universe. Each of us occupies multiple roles arranged hierarchically in order of salience, and role identity is the character and role we devise for ourselves as an occupant of a particular social position. Role identity is our perception—how we see ourselves being and acting in a particular position—so in this manner we actively create our own role identities. Others' expectations and appraisals of us support our role identity when they confirm our imagined view of ourselves. The reactions of those close to us carry the most weight; consequently, our role identities are affected as people enter or leave our convoy of relations. Because role support can be unstable and discrepancies regularly occur between our idealized identity and the support we receive, we constantly search for legitimization of the roles to which we are especially committed. Social exchanges can result in positive, negative, or neutral support for our role identities, so we strive to find ways to maximize positive support, particularly when a role identity is threatened (Thoits, 1991). In this fashion, it is our own internalized role identities that motivate our behaviors. The degree to which others' feedback matches our view has great influence on how we feel about ourselves; the greater the discrepancy, the more we seek positive support for our expectations of ourselves.

Clearly, this theory provides insight into the mechanism by which affective exchanges with others can influence individual choices of support network members and whether they are a benefit. Role identity also helps integrate existing social support concepts by clarifying some of the ambiguous findings while explaining how the social support process contributes to well-being. Using these established theories to guide our thinking, given the previous empirical findings highlighting differences by gender and in support from relatives and friends, we asked the following specific research questions:

- Is the friend role significant in predicting well-being?
- Is the friend role related to differences in social support and gender?

The answers have implications for practitioners working with adults in preparation for retirement and older age.

## Sample

### Methods

Data for this analysis were collected during a five-year longitudinal study, Roles and Self: Factors in Development and Retirement, designed to investigate working people's transition into retirement. We obtained the sample from the driver registrations maintained by the North Carolina Department of Motor Vehicles, whose records were estimated to include more than 80 percent of the targeted age group in the population and an even higher percentage of full-time workers in that age group. Names were randomly drawn from the records in proportion to the population of the three counties represented in the study. After mailing introductory letters, postcards requesting telephone numbers and work status, and using other intensive means of locating phone numbers, we telephoned 1,331 men and women who met the eligibility criteria of age, full-time employment, and residence. Of these, 60 percent of men and 64 percent of women consented to participate in the study, for a response rate of 62 percent. Thus, the baseline sample consisted of 826 respondents ages 58 to 64, working at least 35 hours per week and residing in the Raleigh–Durham–Chapel Hill area of North Carolina. A comparison of participants with the U.S. census figures for this metropolitan area found them to be similar, but our sample slightly underrepresented African Americans, people with no college education, precision workers and laborers, and consequently, people with incomes under $25,000. However, as our sample was restricted by design to full-time workers, the population would be expected to have higher educational levels, occupational status, and incomes than the census population that includes unemployed and part-time workers.

The study gathered two waves of data from in-depth telephone interviews in 1992 and 1994. Because participants were working 35 hours or more at the start of the study and the goal of the study was to track the transition to retirement, we contacted each respondent in the baseline sample at six-month intervals following the initial interview to ascertain changes in employment status and to support their ongoing participation in the study. The July 1994 wave of data included 309 respondents who identified themselves as retired and 438 who reported continuing to work full time. Fifty-four respondents decided to drop out of the study, and 14 died, for a loss of 68 cases and an attrition rate of 8.2 percent. Data from the first wave of interviews of these remaining respondents are included in this analysis.

### Variables

Our variable for general well-being was life satisfaction, measured as a scale of seven items scored on a four-point continuum from 1 = very dissatisfied to 4 = very satisfied. Respondents were asked about their satisfaction with where they lived, leisure activities, marital or dating relationships, friendships, health, relationships with their children, and work. Reports of satisfaction level were averaged across the domains relevant for a given respondent, thereby avoiding the loss of cases because the respondent was unmarried, childless, and so forth. This global measure was reliable ($\alpha$ = .73).

The next variable central to our analysis—identity—reflects the respondent's identity meanings as a friend. *Identity meanings* are the shared meanings one attributes to oneself in

a particular role. We adapted a multidimensional identity measure suggested by Mortimer, Finch, and Kumka (1982) for friend identities. Ten adjective pairs were organized in a semantic differential five-point format (Osgood, Succi, & Tannenbaum, 1957) after the leading phrase, "As a friend I am. . . ." The pairs included social–solitary, confident–anxious, happy–sad, open–closed, warm–cold, competent–not competent, relaxed–tense, successful–unsuccessful, active-inactive, and interested in others–interested in self. This scale also was reliable ($\alpha$ = .89).

*Commitment* refers to the respondent's commitment or sense of belonging to the role of being a friend. It was composed of nine items measured on a four-point scale ranging from 1 = strongly disagree to 4 = strongly agree. Items included statements such as "I'm very committed to my friends," "It is important to me that I succeed in being a friend," and "If I could, I would give up being a friend" (recoded). Again the reliability was good ($\alpha$ = .86). A moderate correlation between commitment and identity existed ($r$ = .47), so the variables represent related but distinct measures.

We assessed the composition of the respondents' social network through two variables, friend support and relative support. We asked respondents to name three close support people not living with them and to identify whether each was a relative (child, sibling, parent, or other relative) or a friend (current coworker, friend not a coworker, or other).

Two other typical measures of social support were (1) density of the network and (2) frequency of contact with network members. Our study measured density by the response to one question asking whether the support people named by the respondent were close to one another. Frequency of contact was separated into two measures, frequency of visits and frequency of calls and letters. Both variables offered responses on a six-point scale: 1 = "less than once a year," 2 = "one to five times a year," 3 = "every month or two," 4 = "every two to three weeks," 5 = "once a week," and 6 = "more than once a week." For the few respondents that named two rather than three social support people, the missing information for the unnamed support person was replaced with the mean of that respondent's other scores on this measure.

Control variables included income, which was based on one question that asked total household income and offered 10 response categories ranging from "$7,500 or less" to "$200,001 and over." Education was determined by highest grade completed in school, reported in years. Occupation represented a score on a 100-point occupational prestige scale constructed with the 1980 census occupational classifications and the 1989 National Opinion Research Center prestige scores. Scores can range from 75 for attorneys and 86 for physicians to 19 for news vendors and 9 for shoe shiners (National Opinion Research Center, 1991; U.S. Bureau of the Census, 1982). Gender and marital status were dummy variables with female = 1 and married = 1.

## Findings

Our analysis began with an investigation of the variables of interest, including *t* tests for differences by gender (Table 6-1). Commitment to the friendship role was reasonably normally distributed, whereas the high mean for friend identity reflected a distribution skewed toward higher scores. The other continuous variables were relatively normally distributed as well, although the frequency variables were somewhat skewed toward higher scores. This information needs to be taken into account when considering the re-

sults of the statistical analysis. Both means for frequency fall in the category "every two to three weeks"; for life satisfaction it falls in "satisfied"; and the density mean is nearest to "two are close."

The *t* tests established that the women in the sample had less education, lower income, and less occupational prestige and tended to be unmarried. This finding reinforces previous research that concluded that aging women have fewer resources (Arber & Ginn, 1991; Field & Minkler, 1988). Also reflective of earlier studies (Israel & Antonucci, 1987) are the ambiguous results of the variables related to the structural aspects of support networks. As we were making multiple comparisons, we used a Bonferroni-Holm correction (Toothaker, 1991) to determine the appropriate level of significance. With this correction, the "friend support" differences by gender were not significant ($p = .034$), but those for "relative support" were significant ($p = .009$). It is interesting that women were more committed to the role of friend and had stronger identity meanings as a friend, despite not having named friends as their support people more often. Density of the support network also was not significantly different for men and women, although the frequency of contact was significantly different for contact by calls and letters but not for face-to-face visits.

Our next step was to explore other possible relationships among the variables. An examination of a correlation matrix of all variables suggested a number of very strong relationships (Table 6-2). It is telling that even when using the Bonferroni-Holm correction for our large number of comparisons, many correlations were statistically significant. Some of the more predictable results were that education, income, and occupational prestige are positively related to each other. Of interest is that respondents who scored

**TABLE 6-1. Summary of Descriptive Statistics of Analysis Variables**

| | Men | | | | Women | | | | Total | | | |
|---|---|---|---|---|---|---|---|---|---|---|---|---|
| Variable | % | M | SD | N | % | M | SD | N | % | M | SD | N |
| Life satisfaction**** | | 3.43 | .37 | 356 | | 3.32 | .39 | 397 | | 3.37 | .38 | 753 |
| Identity** | | 42.54 | 6.37 | 354 | | 43.90 | 5.65 | 394 | | 43.25 | 6.03 | 748 |
| Commitment** | | 28.49 | 3.31 | 353 | | 29.21 | 3.32 | 394 | | 28.87 | 3.33 | 747 |
| Friend support^NS | | 1.36 | 1.12 | 356 | | 1.20 | .99 | 397 | | 1.28 | 1.05 | 753 |
| Relative support* | | 1.54 | 1.12 | 356 | | 1.75 | 1.00 | 397 | | 1.65 | 1.06 | 753 |
| Density^NS | | 1.94 | .82 | 343 | | 1.97 | .80 | 392 | | 1.96 | .81 | 735 |
| Frequency see^NS | | 4.45 | 1.16 | 353 | | 4.55 | 1.05 | 395 | | 4.50 | 1.10 | 748 |
| Frequency call**** | | 4.61 | 1.07 | 353 | | 5.11 | .84 | 395 | | 4.87 | .99 | 748 |
| Occupation**** | | 52.06 | 13.80 | 355 | | 46.54 | 11.65 | 396 | | 49.15 | 13.00 | 751 |
| Income**** | | 5.76 | 1.77 | 349 | | 4.50 | 1.64 | 387 | | 5.10 | 1.82 | 736 |
| Education**** | | 15.14 | 3.46 | 356 | | 13.81 | 2.51 | 397 | | 14.44 | 3.07 | 753 |
| Married**** | 91 | | .27 | 356 | 55 | | .50 | 397 | 73 | | .45 | 753 |

Note: NS indicates a nonsignificant t test with Bonferroni-Holm correction for multiple comparisons.
*p < .05. **p < .005. ****p < .0001.

high on those variables appeared to be in touch with their support people less frequently. It also seems that respondents who relied on friends for support had less dense networks and called their supporters less often than those who relied on relatives for support. A number of other interesting trends were visible, but the evidence that the structural measures of frequency of contact and network composition (friend or family) were unrelated to life satisfaction, whereas gender and role were associated with life satisfaction, were most relevant to our study.

Theory guided our decision to look at roles, and previous findings focused our attention on friendship. Our correlations and mean comparisons statistically supported the theoretical reasoning that the friendship role is important. However, several relationships remain unexplained. The t tests showed women had greater role commitment as a friend and had more positive identity meanings as a friend, both strongly correlated with life satisfaction, yet women scored lower than men on the life satisfaction scale. To explore these relationships further, we conducted a

regression analysis. Variables strongly correlated with life satisfaction—gender, marital status, income, and density of the support network—along with education and occupational prestige, which historically have been related to life satisfaction, were entered in step 1 of a hierarchical regression analysis. Next, the commitment and identity variables were entered to determine what effect they would have on life satisfaction above and beyond that of the controls (Table 6-3).

The analysis indicates that being married ($\beta = .181$) and having a higher income ($\beta = .131$) both positively influence life satisfaction. Although the other background variables were not significant, density of the social support network ($\beta = .131$) exerted a positive effect. The addition of commitment to the friendship role ($\beta = .119$) and friendship identity ($\beta = .237$) in step 2 of the analysis increased the $R^2$ from .097 to .190 (Table 6-3). It is important to note that the identity variable exerted the strongest positive influence of all variables. Thus, the results of the regression analysis clearly indicate that commitment to friendship and identity as a friend

TABLE 6-2. Correlations among Analysis Variables

| Variable | 2 | 3 | 4 | 5 | 6 | 7 | 8 | 9 | 10 | 11 | 12 | 13 |
|---|---|---|---|---|---|---|---|---|---|---|---|---|
| Commitment | .475**** | .212***** | .149***** | -.105** | .025 | .135*** | .121*** | .046 | .007 | -.062 | -.079* | .107** |
| Identity | — | .275***** | .034 | .002 | .114** | .191**** | .146**** | -.101* | -.114** | -.145**** | -.044 | .112** |
| Life satisfaction | | — | .015 | .003 | .124*** | .063 | .068 | .108** | .224**** | .062 | .244**** | -.146**** |
| Friend support | | | — | -.945***** | -.578**** | -.267***** | .147**** | .101* | .082* | .138*** | .037 | -.077** |
| Relative support | | | | — | .578**** | .295***** | -.144**** | -.127*** | -.079* | -.163**** | -.058 | .095* |
| Density | | | | | — | .270**** | .013 | -.082* | -.060 | -.129*** | -.002 | .022 |
| Frequency call | | | | | | — | .405**** | -.087* | -.135**** | -.154**** | -.172**** | .252**** |
| Frequency see | | | | | | | — | -.148**** | -.145**** | -.215**** | -.011 | .042 |
| Occupation | | | | | | | | — | .502**** | .577**** | .098* | -.212**** |
| Income | | | | | | | | | — | .449**** | .407**** | -.347**** |
| Education | | | | | | | | | | — | .116** | -.217**** |
| Married | | | | | | | | | | | — | -.408**** |
| Gender | | | | | | | | | | | | — |

Note: Boldface indicates significant correlations when using Bonferroni-Holm correction.

$*p < .05$. $**p < .005$. $***p < .001$. $****p < .0001$.

**TABLE 6-3. Summary of Hierarchical Regression Analysis for Variables Predicting Life Satisfaction**

| Variable | B | SE B | β |
|---|---|---|---|
| Step 1 | | | |
| Married | .153 | .035 | .181**** |
| Income | .028 | .010 | .131* |
| Education | −.005 | .006 | −.044 |
| Gender | −.029 | .031 | −.038 |
| Occupation | .001 | .001 | .044 |
| Density | .062 | .017 | .131*** |
| Step 2 | | | |
| Married | .153 | .034 | .180**** |
| Income | .031 | .010 | .146** |
| Education | −.001 | .005 | −.008 |
| Gender | −.047 | .029 | −.061 |
| Occupation | .001 | .001 | .031 |
| Density | .051 | .016 | .108** |
| Commitment | .014 | .004 | .119** |
| Identity | .015 | .003 | .237**** |

Note: $R^2$ step 1 = .097 and $R^2$ step 2 = .190.
*$p < .05$. **$p < .005$. ***$p < .001$. ****$p < .0001$.

significantly contribute to life satisfaction, even when controlling for gender and the background variables traditionally associated with well-being. Gender itself had only an indirect effect through its association with other variables. Gender was negatively associated with all structural variables such as marital status, education, income, and occupational prestige but positively related to the friendship variables. The friendship role identity appeared to bolster and compensate for structural differences, leaving gender with no direct effect.

## Discussion

The results of our study of preretirement-age adults clarify previous equivocal or puzzling findings about older adults and social support. The data highlight the ambiguity of how structural properties of social support, such as frequency of contact and composition of the network, fail to influence life satisfaction and suggest that some other

mechanism may be at work. The role measures emerged as both significant and stronger than either structural or background variables and thus may provide some insight.

The convoy framework illustrates how attachments are made throughout the life span and that friends and family are a part of a dynamic support system through time. The individual's ability to provide as well as receive support is key, given the value set on reciprocity. However, as people age, family may contribute more instrumental help than can be repaid, leading to feelings of obligation (Antonucci, 1989). Role identity theory suggests that increased reliance on family members threatens older adults' self-perception as competent, giving people while bolstering their role identities as needy dependents. This may account for the consistent, if puzzling, finding that family members do not contribute to older adults' feelings of well-being despite being named more often as key supporters and providing substantial support (Larson et al., 1986).

Friends, especially long-term friends, could contribute in quite a different manner. They have accepted each other as friends for quite some time, sharing historical context and exchanging positive support during their most productive years. Emotional support is important in friendships (Armstrong & Goldsteen, 1990; Quam, 1983), and reciprocal affective support is one of the few variables uniquely contributing to well-being (Israel & Antonucci, 1987). Aging adults seek friends who can reduce the discrepancy between their perception of who they are and the negative identity meanings they might receive from family and others. Friends can offer the positive identity support only such peers could provide, and aging adults are committed to this role. With friends, they can shift from a less positive identity to the reassuring identity of friend, exchanging meaningful feedback and having their positive self-perceptions legitimized.

However, contact with friends can decrease and continue to dwindle with age (Levitt, Weber, & Guacci, 1993), yet Carstensen (1991) argued that the positive effect of friendship support remains stable even in very old age. Our results also show that respondents naming more friends as supporters had less phone contact with them and less dense networks, so how can these friends be more supportive than family when they are not in touch even to exchange affective support? Again, role identity theory may provide an explanation. Friends who knew each other "back when" continue to contribute to identities as competent peers, despite current circumstances. They need not frequently be present or in contact because it is the identity—just knowing that one has been chosen as a friend—that implies positive appraisals (Lee & Shehan, 1989) and contributes to a positive sense of self. Need for this kind of role support increases in importance as aging adults experience the eroding capabilities and negative feedback that contradict their identity perceptions. It follows that older adults will continue to become more selective, choosing to retain those friends who contribute positively to identity. Consistent findings that perceived quality of social support is more important than quantity confirms this tendency toward selectivity (Antonucci & Akiyama, 1991; Field & Minkler, 1988; O'Connor, 1995).

## Implications for Social Workers

Given the empirical evidence and the guidance of theory, a number of implications for practitioners are clear. The population is graying rapidly, and the very old are the fastest growing group in the United States (Field & Minkler, 1988). During this time of life, aging adults face the loss of support for their role identities through retirement, loss of family relationships, and erosions of functioning. The role as friend is enduring even when others are lost. Friends provide a sense of continuity between the past and present, and help older adults adapt (Francis, 1990). Because our results show that the friend role is more important in predicting life satisfaction than background variables such as income and marital status, practitioners designing preretirement and other interventions for older adults might focus on creating opportunities to enhance friendship identities in addition to strengthening family and instrumental support.

A limitation of our study may be that the sample was restricted to full-time workers transitioning into retirement, and as such may underrepresent social work clients seen in the public sector. Although this may be true, our sample did include participants with lower levels of education, occupational prestige, and income and thus included the diversity of the baby boomer cohort that is our imminent aging population. Because of the sheer numbers of people entering older age, social workers in all practice settings will be working with older adults more frequently. Role identity theory and its life span perspective can be a useful addition to social work practice, particularly for those clients who have experienced financial losses along with the typical losses of role and support. Practitioners can counterbalance the rising costs and diminishing formal resources available to older clients by recognizing the importance of positive role identities, particularly friendship identities, to clients' well-being. Interventions that reinforce friendship support and role identity at earlier life stages will prepare social work clients for older age by providing the long-term relationships and thus the identity that is shown to have more influence on life satisfaction than income or education.

Social workers also should keep in mind that the support services they typically offer might conflict with clients' self-perception as competent adults (Forster & Stoller, 1992). New and unfamiliar social contacts can behave in ways that could erode rather than strengthen an older person's self-perceptions (Carstensen, 1991), so interventions focusing on enhancing existing positive support would be more effective and efficient than creating or linking a client with novel support.

Also important to consider is that aging women are more likely to be the primary caregiver to a spouse, to experience the death of a male partner, to be poor, and to live alone (Carstensen, 1991). Heller, Thompson, Vlachos-Weber, Steffen, and Trueba (1991) reported that the older women in their sample had few opportunities to participate in socially useful roles that could accommodate their failing health and lack of financial resources. They confirmed that support appraisals from friends enhanced health by conveying the perception of being valued and affirmed despite current circumstances. Clearly, interventions must carefully target each individual's multiple internalized role identities and be focused and detailed in ways to facilitate positive outcomes, particularly for vulnerable, aging women.

## Conclusion

Social support and role identity theory should be the focus of continued study. Future research about interventions with aging adults should center on identifying meaningful activities that strengthen existing positive role identities before creating new ones (Heller et al., 1991). Also of value would be continued examination of commitment to various roles, to further explore our findings that although women rely on relatives for support, it is identity as friend that contributes to well-being. Finally, because the experiences of aging women differ greatly from those of men, future research also is needed to further examine those differences in the context of role identity theory.

## References

Adams, R. (1987). Patterns of network change: A longitudinal study of friendships among elderly women. *Gerontologist, 27,* 222–227.

Antonucci, T. C. (1989). Understanding adult social relationships. In K. Kreppner & R. M. Lerner (Eds.), *Family systems and life span development* (pp. 303–317). Hillsdale, NJ: Lawrence Erlbaum.

Antonucci, T. C. (1994). A life-span view of women's social relations. In B. F. Turner & L. E. Troll (Eds.), *Women growing older* (pp. 239–269). Thousand Oaks, CA: Sage Publications.

Antonucci, T. C., & Akiyama, H. (1987a). An examination of sex differences in social support among older men and women. *Sex Roles, 17*(11 & 12), 737–749.

Antonucci, T. C., & Akiyama, H. (1987b). Social networks in adult life and a preliminary examination of the convoy model. *Journal of Gerontology, 42,* 519–527.

Antonucci, T. C., & Akiyama, H. (1991). Social relationships and aging well. *Generations, 15*(1), 39–45.

Antonucci, T. C., & Akiyama, H. (1995). Convoys of social relations: Family and friendship within a life span context. In R. Blieszner & V. H. Bedford (Eds.), *Handbook of aging and the family* (pp. 355–371). Westport, CT: Greenwood Press.

Arber, S., & Ginn, J. (1991). *Gender and later life: A sociological analysis of resources and constraints.* Newbury Park, CA: Sage Publications.

Armstrong, M. J., & Goldsteen, K. S. (1990). Friendship support patterns of older American women. *Journal of Aging Studies, 4,* 391–404.

Berkman, L. F., & Syme, S. L. (1979). Social networks, host resistance, and mortality: A nine-year follow-up study of Alameda County residents. *American Journal of Epidemiology, 109*, 186–204.

Blieszner, R., & Bedford, V. H. (1995). *Handbook of aging and the family.* Westport, CT: Greenwood Press.

Bosse, R., Aldwin, C. M., Levenson, M. R., Spiro, A., & Mroczek, D. K. (1993). Change in social support after retirement. *Journals of Gerontology, 48*, 210–218.

Bosse, R., Aldwin, C. M., Levenson, M. R., Workman-Daniels, K., & Ekerdt, D. J. (1990). Differences in social support among retirees and workers: Findings from the normative aging study. *Psychology and Aging, 5*(1), 41–47.

Carstensen, L. (1991). Selectivity theory: Social activity in life-span context. *Annual Review of Gerontology and Geriatrics, 11*, 195–217.

Dean, A., Matt, G. E., & Wood, P. (1992). The effects of widowhood on social support from significant others. *Journal of Community Psychology, 20*, 309–325.

Field, D., & Minkler, M. (1988). Continuity and change in social support between young-old and old-old or very-old age. *Journal of Gerontology, 43*, 100–106.

Forster, L. E., & Stoller, E. P. (1992). The impact of social support on mortality: A seven-year follow-up of older men and women. *Journal of Applied Gerontology, 11*(2), 173–186.

Francis, D. (1990). The significance of work friends in late life. *Journal of Aging Studies, 4*, 405–424.

Heller, K., Thompson, M. G., Vlachos-Weber, I., Steffen, A. M., & Trueba, P. E. (1991). Support interventions for older adults: Confidante relationships, perceived social support, and meaningful role activity. *American Journal of Community Psychology, 19*, 139–147.

Israel, B. A., & Antonucci, T. C. (1987). Social network characteristics and psychological well-being: A replication and extension. *Health Education Quarterly, 14*, 461–481.

Jackson, J. S., & Antonucci, T. C. (1992). Social support processes in health and effective functioning of the elderly. In M. L. Wykle, E. Kahana, & J. Kowal (Eds.), *Stress and health among the elderly* (pp. 72–95). New York: Springer.

Johnson, C. L., & Troll, L. E. (1994). Constraints and facilitators to friendships in late, late life. *Gerontologist, 34*, 79–87.

Kahn, R. (1979). Aging and social support. In M. W. Riley (Ed.), *Aging from birth to death: Interdisciplinary perspectives* (pp. 77–91). Boulder, CO: Westview Press.

Larson, R., Mannell, R., & Zuzanek, J. (1986). Daily well-being of older adults with friends and family. *Psychology and Aging, 1*, 117–126.

Lee, G. R., & Shehan, C. L. (1989). Social relations and the self-esteem of older persons. *Research on Aging, 11*, 427–442.

Levitt, M. J., Coffman, S., Guacci-Franco, N., & Loveless, S. C. (1994). Attachment relationships and life transitions: An expectancy model. In M. B. Sperling & W. H. Behrman (Eds.), *Attachment in adults: Clinical and developmental perspectives* (pp. 232–255). New York: Guilford Press.

Levitt, M. J., Weber, R. A., & Guacci, N. (1993). Convoys of social support: An intergenerational analysis. *Psychology and Aging, 8*, 323–326.

Matt, G. E., & Dean, A. (1993). Social support from friends and psychological distress among elderly persons: Moderator effects of age. *Journal of Health and Social Behavior, 34*, 187–200.

Minkler, M., & Langhauser, C. (1988). Assessing health differences in an elderly population: A five-year follow-up. *Journal of the American Geriatrics Society, 36*, 113–118.

Mortimer, J. T., Finch, M. D., & Kumka, D. (1982). Persistence and change in development: The multidimensional self-concept. *Life Span Development and Behavior, 4*, 263–313.

National Opinion Research Center. (1991). *General social surveys, 1972-1991: Cumulative codebook.* Chicago: N.O.R.C.

O'Connor, B. P. (1995). Family and friend relationships among older and younger adults: Interaction motivation, mood, and quality. *International Journal of Aging and Human Development, 40*(1), 9–29.

Osgood, C. E., Succi, G. J., & Tannenbaum, P. H. (1957). *Measurement of meaning*. Urbana: University of Illinois Press.

Quam, J. K. (1983). Older women and informal supports: Impact on prevention. *Prevention in Human Services, 3,* 119–133.

Shye, D., Mullooly, J. P., Freeborn, D. K., & Pope, C. R. (1995). Gender differences in the relationship between social network support and mortality: A longitudinal study of an elderly cohort. *Social Science and Medicine, 41,* 935–948.

Stryker, S. (1980). *Symbolic interaction: A social structural version*. Menlo Park, CA: Benjamin/Cummings.

Stryker, S., & Serpe, R. T. (1994). Identity salience and psychological centrality: Equivalent, overlapping, or complementary concepts? *Social Psychological Quarterly, 57,* 16–35.

Stryker, S., & Statham, A. (1985). Symbolic interaction and role theory. In G. Lindzey & E. Aronson (Eds.), *The handbook of social psychology* (pp. 311–378). New York: Random House.

Thoits, P. A. (1991). On merging identity theory and stress research. *Social Psychological Quarterly, 54*(2), 101–112.

Tilburg, T. V. (1992). Support networks before and after retirement. *Journal of Social and Personal Relationships, 9,* 433–445.

Toothaker, L. E. (1991). *Multiple comparisons for researchers*. Newbury Park, CA: Sage Publications.

Turner, H. A. (1994). Gender and social support: Taking the bad with the good? *Sex Roles: A Journal of Research, 30*(7 & 8), 521–542.

U. S. Bureau of the Census. (1982). *1980 census of population: Alphabetical index of industries and occupations*. Washington, DC: U.S. Government Printing Office.

Wood, V., & Robertson, J. F. (1978). Friendship and kinship interaction: Differential effect on morale of the elderly. *Journal of Marriage and the Family, 40,* 367–375.

Wright, P. H. (1989). Gender differences in adults' same and cross-gender friendships. In R. G. Adams & R. Blieszner (Eds.), *Older adult friendships* (pp. 197–221). Newbury Park, CA: Sage Publications.

Wykle, M. L., Kahana, E., & Kowal, J. (1992). *Stress and health among the elderly*. New York: Springer.

This chapter was originally published in the November 1999 issue of *Social Work*, Vol. 44, Number 6, pp. 522–533.

# 7

# Hospice Access and Use by African Americans

## Addressing Cultural and Institutional Barriers through Participatory Action Research

DONA J. REESE, ROBIN E. AHERN,
SHANKAR NAIR, JOLEEN D. O'FAIRE SCHROCK,
and CLAUDIA WARREN-WHEAT

Hospice developed in the United States in the 1970s as a grassroots movement to promote more humane care for dying people. Hospice philosophy stresses patient self-determination, acceptance of death, and palliative rather than curative care. In addition, it advocates for dying in the home surrounded by loved ones, rather than in an institution surrounded by technology. Social workers provide hospice care in collaboration with an interdisciplinary team of professionals, who attend to biopsychosocial and spiritual needs of patients and families. Nationwide, ethnic and racial minorities represent only 5 percent to 7 percent of the hospice patient population.

A need for hospice care in the African American community is justified by the higher cancer mortality rate (Lowe, Barg, & Bernstein, 1995) and the prevalence of the AIDS virus among African Americans (Infeld, Crum, & Koshuta, 1990). This article describes a project that was conducted within the context of a participatory action research project, aimed at increasing

African American access to and use of hospice. This article provides research results that address gaps in the literature and discuss implications for social work practice and policy.

## Literature Review

The hospice literature reflects a number of barriers to hospice access and use for African Americans. The literature in this area contains mainly nonempirically based discussion papers, as well as surveys of hospice staff and records, rather than studies carried out directly with African Americans. Before discussing these barriers, however, two issues must be considered. First, we may not assume that the African American population is homogeneous, because there is wide variability among African Americans in terms of income, education, employment, geographic region, and country of origin (Dowd, Poole, Davidhizar, & Giger, 1998; Lowe et al., 1995). Within this diversity, however, a cultural unity may be detected that traditionally has characterized many African American families (Nobles, 1974), and during the great stress of terminal illness, patients who normally do not adhere to ethnic culture may resort to traditional modes of behavior (Harwood, 1981). It may be argued, thus, that it is useful for social workers to be informed about traditional African American cultural characteristics while avoiding stereotypes and unquestioning assumptions about clients.

Second, within the European American population, hospice is not well recognized or understood (Burrs, 1995). The general population is unfamiliar with hospice (Mor, Hendershot, & Cryan, 1989), and physician barriers to hospice referral abound, including inadequate physician training (Miller, Miller, & Single, 1997), availability of a program, and Medicare requirements, including a six-month prognosis and a requirement for a 24-hour family caregiver in the home (Miller et al., 1997). Because referral to hospice is primarily by the physician (Gordon, 1995; Infeld et al., 1990), most terminally ill patients do not have their care provided through hospice programs. In 1995 only 37 percent of all people who died of cancer-related causes in United States and 31 percent of all who died of AIDS-related causes were cared for by hospices (National Hospice Organization, 1995).

Despite these barriers to hospice care for the population as a whole, hospice access and use are skewed toward European Americans. Medicare regulations describe patients and families from mainstream America and create barriers for disadvantaged groups. For example, European Americans are more likely to have the required full-time caregiver in the home (Gordon, 1995). Medicare regulations also require certification of terminality by a physician, and African Americans use emergency room care over a regular physician, regardless of other demographic factors such as income or insurance coverage (Heckler, 1985; Neighbors & Jackson, 1987). Additional information is needed about whether current managed-care approaches will change this pattern.

Another barrier to access is that many African Americans lack knowledge about hospice services (Burrs, 1995; Harper, 1995). In addition, lack of trust by many African Americans in the health care system as a whole (Lundgren & Chen, 1986; Neubauer & Hamilton, 1990) is a barrier to hospice use. African Americans often fear that they will receive experimental or inferior care (Burrs, 1995), do not want to be treated like "guinea pigs" (Harris, Gorelick, Samuels, & Bempong, 1996), and relate past experiences with being treated disrespectfully by health care professionals (Griffin & Bratton, 1995). African Americans often show a general reluctance to go outside of their family and circle of friends for help with medical crises (Harper, 1990; Lundgren & Chen, 1986) and often hesitate to welcome strangers from hospice into their homes (Gordon & Rooney, 1984). Lack of diversity among health care staff is cited as part of this problem (Burrs, 1995; Gordon & Rooney, 1984).

Another barrier to use has to do with values about medical care and extent of agreement with hospice philosophy. African American attitudes often are inconsistent with the hospice philosophy of palliative rather than curative care (Klessig, 1992; Neubauer & Hamilton, 1990; Ita [Reese], 1995–96). African Americans often see longevity as an intrinsic good (Klessig, 1992) and have expectations of living a long life (Kalish & Reynolds, 1976). Most prefer curative care (Ita, 1995–96) and all life-sustaining measures until death (Klessig, 1992), and many have not established a "do not resuscitate" order (Ita, 1995–96). In addition, most African Americans prefer not to die in the home, in opposition to hospice philosophy (Burrs, 1995; Gordon, 1995; Ita, 1995–96).

We found no literature on the influence of state regulations on access and use of hospice care. Medicaid covers only 7 percent of hospice patients, whereas Medicare covers 65 percent (National Hospice Organization, 1995). State policy on hospice coverage under Medicaid may be an important underlying factor in the small proportion of Medicaid patients in hospice and an important barrier to African American access and use.

Value differences between African Americans and European Americans may be based to an extent on mistrust of health care professionals' motives for suggesting palliative rather than curative care, but may be based to a large extent on differences in religious beliefs. Despite the well-documented importance of the church in African American society (Frazier & Lincoln, 1974; Griffin & Bratton, 1995; Pipes, 1981; Raboteau, 1978), African American religious beliefs have largely been neglected in empirical studies of barriers to hospice care.

## Traditional African American Religious Beliefs

Explanations of the importance of religion to African Americans may be found in their history. African slaves were stripped of their social heritage by being captured, shipped, and sold without any regard for family or tribal affiliations. Any attempt to preserve or use their native languages or religious traditions was discouraged or prohibited (Frazier & Lincoln, 1974). Christianity was forced on the slaves and used to justify slavery. But the new Christian religious beliefs, practices, and traditions formed a new basis of social cohesion, creating solidarity and a sense of union among these strangers from a variety of African nationalities. Despite prohibition of any assembly of slaves without the presence of European Americans, the "invisible institution" of the African American church took root through secret meetings in secluded places (Raboteau, 1978). The church became the most important social institution in African American culture and has remained a source of social stability through the disruptive effects of emancipation and migration to northern urban areas. The pastor, as the leader of this institution, has played a significant leadership role in African American culture (Frazier & Lincoln, 1974).

It may be helpful here to summarize some common beliefs pertaining to death and dying. Traditionally, African Americans believe in the omnipotence of God (Burrs, 1995; Cooper-Lewter & Mitchell, 1992). Illness and death are God's will and are not necessarily affected by treatment (Creel, 1991;

Dowd et al., 1998; Pipes, 1981). At the same time, God is benevolent and has miraculous powers—God is able to cause recovery or turn into good ends whatever may occur (Burrs; Cooper-Lewter & Mitchell, 1992; Creel, 1991). Another traditional belief is the belief in a better life after death, without sickness, disease, poverty, or hunger, a life in which victims of injustices will be compensated (Cooper-Lewter & Mitchell, 1992; Creel, 1991; Frazier & Lincoln, 1974). Thus, traditionally there is little apprehension at the prospect of dying; rather a sense of joy may be detected (Cooper-Lewter & Mitchell, 1992; Creel, 1991). When a death is expected, the dying person is surrounded by the community, which offers comfort and support (Creel, 1991; Dowd et al., 1998). According to Burrs, the tradition of honoring and respecting the great spirit of African ancestors leads to discomfort with death in the home.

It should be noted that traditional African American beliefs have changed over time (Frazier & Lincoln, 1974). Beliefs of the upper and middle classes have broken away from the traditional African American belief system, as have beliefs of many northern urban African Americans. Despite these changes, the church continues to function as an important element in African American society, providing a refuge for the masses of African American people (Frazier & Lincoln, 1974). Most African Americans consider themselves religious, seek health care advice from their pastors (Griffin & Bratton, 1995), and use religion as a coping strategy (Mailick, Holden, & Walther, 1994). When researchers asked African Americans what their immediate response would be to a diagnosis of cancer, they replied, "I would prepare to meet my maker" (Dignan, Michielutte, Sharp, Young, & Daniels, 1991, p. 75). Pipes (1981) stated that the African American pastor is traditionally the leader of the African Ameri-

can community, and it is to him or her that the great majority of African Americans still look for guidance. A 1997 Gallup Social Audit (Gallup Organization, 1997) reported that 71 percent of African Americans attended mostly or all-African American congregations, that 73 percent of African Americans were Protestants (48 percent Baptist), and that 9 percent were Catholic; only 8 percent had no religious affiliation.

European Americans often have failed to honor and respect traditional African American beliefs. Frazier and Lincoln (1974) characterized mainstream America's attitude as one of condescending amusement. During the Civil War, some observers were appalled at what they interpreted as resignation among the slaves. The patience in sickness was so general and remarkable, it seemed like apathy (Creel, 1991). European American researchers have regarded the African American belief system as "fatalistic" and "pessimistic" (Rana, Knasel, & Haddy, 1992) and potentially interfering with preventive health practices (Dignan et al., 1991). As noted earlier, hospice researchers have found some conflicts between traditional African American beliefs and hospice philosophy. A purpose of this project was to gain understanding of such conflicts and to develop some solutions for culturally sensitive practice.

## Action Research Model

This project is an example of the use of research as a tool for social action. Participatory action research is increasingly in use in the social work field (Hick, 1997; Wagner, 1991) and is consistent with a strengths perspective and social work values regarding integrating social action efforts into practice. Models of participatory action research vary, but hallmarks are transferring of power to the research participants (Sarri & Sarri,

1992), engaging the participation of the community in research activities (Hick, 1997), producing knowledge that is useful to service providers and clients (Penuel & Freeman, 1997), and using the knowledge for social change (Malekoff, 1994) or change in service approaches (Martinez-Brawley & Delevan, 1993; Rapp, Shera, & Kisthardt, 1993).

Our model consisted of seven strategies: (1) literature review, (2) integration with social work education, (3) collaboration with respondents, (4) collaboration with practitioners, (5) ongoing social action efforts, (6) qualitative study, and (7) quantitative study. We integrated our project with social work education through the use of independent studies, graduate research assistantships, class projects, lectures, and discussions. We engaged in ongoing collaboration with respondents and practitioners, setting several meetings between the ministerial association and local health care providers to discuss the problem and to present results of the study. Definition of the problem, as well as the quantitative measure, was based on the input of the target population, which was gathered during these meetings as well as through the qualitative interviews. The project ultimately benefited the target population by forging a new connection between the African American community and local health care providers, by developing an understanding of existing barriers, and by collaboratively developing a plan for solutions to the barriers.

## Qualitative Study

The purpose of the qualitative portion of the study was to explore unexpected reasons for the lack of participation of African Americans in hospice. Qualitative study uses an inductive method of inquiry in which theory and working hypotheses are developed after the data are collected. Qualitative methods allow for in-depth input from respondents that is not restricted by the closed-ended questions used in quantitative methods. Thus, we see qualitative methodology as an important component of participatory action research.

Because of the importance of the church in African American communities and the importance of the pastor as a community leader, we selected African American pastors for the qualitative sample. Six Christian pastors were recruited from four Baptist, one Christian Methodist Episcopal, and one Catholic congregation in a midwestern city of 100,000 population. Their beliefs largely represented the traditional African American belief system, with the Catholic pastor being somewhat more nontraditional. The pastors were recruited through the local African American ministerial association and were asked an open-ended question, "Why do you think there are very few African American patients in hospice?" Interviews lasted for approximately one hour and were tape recorded. Transcripts of the interviews were then typed from the tape recordings.

Glaser and Strauss (1967) outlined criteria for rigor of qualitative analysis, which include "comparing and contrasting" responses to develop major themes and presenting results to the respondents to verify credibility. To further establish trustworthiness and credibility of findings, Lincoln and Guba (1985) suggested using "triangulation," in which the researcher consults additional sources of data to assess consistency with the conclusions from the original source of data. Trustworthiness and credibility are the focus in qualitative research, rather than validity and reliability, which apply to quantitative research. Transferability of results to similar contexts is the goal, rather than generalizability. Because an attempt was not made to generalize to the population through inferential statistics, the large sample typical of survey research was not necessary.

In this study the qualitative analysis was conducted manually by the senior researcher, based on the method described earlier. The transcripts from the tape-recorded interviews were analyzed for major themes. The resulting categories were collapsed further into two overriding classifications: (1) cultural barriers to hospice care and (2) institutional barriers to hospice care. A second researcher conducted an independent analysis to check on the reliability of the coding, with similar results. After the data were analyzed, a second interview was conducted with each respondent to focus on themes that emerged during the analysis. Open-ended questions were still used, but they were focused on asking the respondents for feedback on the credibility and trustworthiness of the researchers' findings. In all cases, the participants agreed with the researchers' conclusions. The themes were used to develop a quantitative measure, which was used in the subsequent quantitative phase of the study. The quantitative findings were used as triangulation to examine the credibility of the qualitative findings.

Results of the qualitative study indicated the existence of cultural barriers and institutional barriers to hospice access and use for African Americans. Cultural barriers included differences in values regarding medical care and differences in spiritual beliefs between African Americans and European Americans. Institutional barriers included lack of knowledge of services, economic factors, lack of trust by many African Americans in the health care system, and lack of ethnic diversity among health care staff. Results also included many recommendations for dismantling these barriers, which are summarized in the Discussion.

## *Cultural Barriers*

*Differences in Values Regarding Medical Care.* Participants reported African American values regarding medical care that differ from hospice philosophy, stating that many African Americans do not agree with the hospice philosophy of palliative care in the home. Participants described a preference for life-sustaining treatment (chemotherapy, resuscitation, life support, artificial nutrition, and hydration) as opposed to palliative care. African Americans often prefer not to plan for death (that is, legal wills, living wills, funeral plans, DNR orders, powers of attorney, plans for dependents, and so forth). Participants stated that there is a cultural belief system opposed to accepting terminality, planning for it, or discussing it with others. They described a long cultural tradition of using home remedies rather than going to a doctor. Finally, participants reported a cultural value that one's own people—church and family—should provide care in terminal illness, rather than strangers.

*Differences in Spiritual Beliefs.* Participants stated that many African Americans would rather pray for a miracle than accept terminality. They also explained that acceptance of terminality in this culture, while everyone around the patient is praying for a miracle, would be seen as a lack of faith. Finally, they reported a belief that God determines whether you live or die, not medical treatment or the lack of it.

## *Institutional Barriers*

*Lack of Knowledge of Services.* Most of the African American pastor participants themselves were not familiar with hospice. One of the participants emphasized that if the pastors, on whom people rely for advice if a family member is dying, are unaware of hospice, it is highly unlikely that the African American community in general would be aware of hospice care.

*Economic Factors.* The respondents indicated that many African Americans do not have health insurance and do not believe they can afford hospice care.

*Lack of Trust by African Americans in the Health Care System.* Respondents thought that African Americans, especially elderly African Americans, have a lack of trust in the health care system. They reported that the African American community is aware of the infamous Tuskegee study in which African American men with syphilis were observed through the course of their illness without being offered treatment. One respondent indicated a reluctance to seek medical treatment, lest he or she "end up being a guinea pig in one of their experiments." Other respondents indicated awareness of neglectful and inhumane treatment in public health care facilities that provide care for poor people. As mentioned earlier, there was a sense that many African Americans would rather care for themselves at home with home remedies or pray for a miracle than seek health care from the health care system.

*Lack of Diversity among Health Care Staff.* Participants reported that fears of the health care system are compounded by the lack of diversity among health care staff. There was strong concern expressed by the pastors about the lack or complete absence of African American staff working for local health care providers. There was a concern that African American patients have a "friendly face" to comfort them and share an understanding of cultural differences and fears.

Consistent with the inductive method of inquiry, we developed a hypothesis on the basis of the qualitative conclusions: Barriers to hospice access and use exist to a greater degree in the African American population than in the European American population. This hypothesis was tested in the quantitative study described below.

## Quantitative Study

The purpose of the quantitative portion of the study was to test the above research hypothesis statistically. A sample of 127 respondents was recruited to accomplish this, including hospice patients, churchgoers, and non-churchgoers. Hospice patients were recruited from four volunteer home hospices in the East, Southeast, and Midwest, and from one inpatient hospice in the Midwest. Churchgoers and non-churchgoers were recruited from a midwestern city of 100,000 population. An attempt was made to recruit equal numbers of hospice patients, churchgoers, and non-churchgoers, and equal numbers of African Americans and European Americans in each subgroup. Difficulty in recruiting African Americans and hospice patients, however, resulted in fewer respondents as well as a lack of probability sampling for these subgroups. African American churchgoers were recruited from the Protestant and Catholic congregations of the pastors who participated in the qualitative phase of the study. African American non-churchgoers were recruited from the telephone book and from a housing development in the same community. European American churchgoers and non-churchgoers were randomly selected from the rolls of one Protestant church and from the phone book in the same midwestern community.

The rationale for choosing respondents from church rolls was based on the importance of the church in African American society. First, we considered it important to have the help of the pastors in recruiting the African American sample. Second, we hoped that the sample of churchgoers would represent the traditional African American perspective, which according to the literature is held by the vast majority of African Americans. We also were interested in learning the views of African Americans who do not attend church; thus, an attempt was made to control for the influence of church attendance by including subsamples of both churchgoers and non-churchgoers. The selection criteria for the subsample of non-churchgoers consisted of having attended church three or fewer times during the previous year. The rationale for this criterion was that many African Americans, who are not otherwise involved in churches, nevertheless attend church three times during the year to celebrate major holidays—Christmas, Easter, and Mother's Day.

The questionnaires were either read to respondents or self-administered, depending on their physical or reading ability. Two measures developed for this study were used— The Hospice Barriers Scale and The Hospice Values Scale. The Hospice Barriers Scale lists statements representing barriers to hospice care, with respondents circling "agree" or "disagree." Items included in this scale were derived from major themes resulting from the qualitative phase of this study. The scale itself was not tested for validity, but the barriers that made up the qualitative conclusions were taken to the African American pastors for their input. All participants agreed that these were the barriers to hospice access. The scale was tested for reliability (Cronbach's alpha = .64).

The Hospice Values Scale is a Likert-type scale that measures the extent to which respondents agree or disagree with statements representing the hospice philosophy regarding medical treatment in terminal illness.

This scale was developed by the senior author for previous research (Ita, 1995–96), and has not been tested for validity, other than seeking feedback from colleagues regarding face validity. Reliability was tested (Cronbach's alpha = .75).

As mentioned above, ethnicity, hospice status (whether a hospice patient), and church attendance (whether a churchgoer) were controlled for through sampling. In addition, the demographic variables of gender, education, age, and income also were included to test for any possible effects.

Quantitative testing supported the research hypothesis—that barriers to hospice existed to a greater degree in African American than in European American respondents. Multiple regression indicated that ethnicity predicted the Hospice Barriers Scale score—African Americans had a higher mean score than European Americans. This result was true regardless of their gender, education, age, income, or hospice status ($R^2$ = .18, $F$ = 4.28, $p$ = .000). Higher income also predicted the level of hospice barriers, regardless of ethnicity— higher income predicted a lower score on the Hospice Barriers Scale (Table 7-1).

In addition to multiple regression on the Hospice Barriers Scale score, a second multiple regression test was conducted regarding effects of the same variables on the Hospice Values Scale score. In this test, ethnicity predicted the Hospice Values Scale score—African Americans disagreed with hospice philosophy. This again held true regardless of gender, education, age, income, or hospice status. Hospice status and level of education also predicted the Hospice Values Score, regardless of ethnicity ($R^2$ = .346, $F$ = 10.591, and $p$ = .000). Hospice patients and those with a higher level of education held values more similar to hospice philosophy.

Three $t$ tests also were conducted to test for any possible effects of patient status, in-

**TABLE 7-1. Predictors of Hospice Barriers Scale and Hospice Values Scale Scores**

| Variable | Hospice Barriers Scale | | | Hospice Values Scale | | |
|---|---|---|---|---|---|---|
| | Beta | t | p | Beta | t | p |
| Whether a hospice patient | .017 | .156 | .438 | .260 | 2.753 | .004 |
| Ethnicity | .216 | 2.378 | .010 | −.401 | −4.967 | .000 |
| Age | −.053 | −.529 | .299 | −.007 | −.074 | .470 |
| Education | −.124 | 1.338 | .092 | −.259 | −3.144 | .001 |
| Income | .244 | −2.617 | .005 | −.048 | −.580 | .282 |
| Gender | −.080 | −.948 | .172 | .008 | −.112 | .456 |

Notes: Hospice Barriers Scale model statistics: $R^2$ = .176, $F$ = 4.280, $p$ = .000 one-tailed; Hospice Values Scale model statistics: $R^2$ = .346, $F$ = 10.591, $p$ = .000 one-tailed.

Variables were coded as follows: hospice patient = 1, African American = 1, female = 1.

patient status, and church attendance. Results revealed the following:

- Patient Status—There was no difference on hospice barriers based on whether the respondent was a hospice patient [$t(125)$ = 1.397, $p$ = .082]. As expected, however, there were significant differences in hospice values, with hospice patients having values more similar to hospice philosophy [$t(125)$ = 4.992, $p$ = .000].

- Inpatient Status—Whether the patient was an inpatient or home hospice patient did not influence the score on hospice barriers [$t(40)$ = 1.449, $p$ = .155] or hospice values [$t(40)$ = −1.252, $p$ = .218].

- Church Attendance—$t$ tests were conducted to test for differences among the nonhospice patients only ($n$ = 85), based on church attendance. Results indicated that church attendance did not predict differences regarding hospice barriers [$t(83)$ = −.519, $p$ = .302]. Church attendance did predict differences regarding hospice values [$t(83)$ = −5.036, $p$ = .000], with non-churchgoers holding values more similar to hospice philosophy.

## Discussion

When considering the results of this study, it must be kept in mind that much of the African American churchgoing sample was selected from churches with a traditional religious perspective and will not reflect the views of more nontraditional African Americans. The small, nonprobability sample prevents generalizing even to the traditional African American population. Results of this study are consistent with literature about barriers to African Americans' access to hospice, however, documenting explanations presented in nonempirical discussion papers, providing a study directly with African Americans, and addressing a gap in our knowledge about the influence of African American religious beliefs on hospice access and use. Differences were found on hospice barriers and hospice values by ethnicity, even when controlling for a number of other variables. The demographic variables of income and education did influence barriers and values, supporting assertions in the literature about the influence of socioeconomic status on African American belief systems. Perhaps a larger sample would have produced a larger influence of demographic variables, but the literature also provides evidence of persistent negative African American views of the health care system regardless of socioeconomic status.

Perhaps because the measures in this study were driven by perspectives of respondents, the study did not examine policy issues at the state and private managed-care organization levels. In addition, reliability statistics for the Hospice Barriers Scale were not impressive ($\alpha = .64$). Further research is needed to clarify the influence of policy on hospice access and use barriers and to further develop measures of hospice barriers.

## Implications for Social Work Practice

The model of participatory action research used in this project has several implications for practice. Such a practitioner–researcher–client partnership can benefit all involved. Practitioners often face great time and resource constraints that make it difficult for them to implement macro-level interventions. These constraints may be a source of frustration when the effects of larger social forces limit the impact of micro-level interventions. Practitioners may welcome a partnership with researchers who have resources to help them address a social problem on the community level. At the same time, researchers may welcome practitioners' input about practice problems and help in facilitating access to data. Finally, the major purpose of participatory action research is to promote better services for clients by seeking their input about social problems and then using this input to influence social policy.

In this project, most African American respondents, especially those with lower socioeconomic status, expressed disagreement with hospice philosophy. Their spiritual beliefs precluded an acceptance of death. They preferred not to talk about death or to plan for it. They preferred not to be involved in the health care system, but rather to be cared for by their own people. They expressed agreement with the Hospice Barriers Scale item, "If I were dying, I would rather turn to my church and family than a hospice." Some might argue, based on this, that if African

American people do not want hospice, it should not be forced on them.

We agree, nevertheless, with African American leaders who have emphasized a need for hospice care in their communities. Rather than concluding that African American culture and hospice philosophy have irreconcilable differences, we would urge the hospice community to find ways to adapt hospice to the needs of African Americans. As hospice moves into the 21st century, it will need to learn how to reach this population more effectively.

This project indicates a need for social work practice with African Americans that honors diversity of belief, consistent with a growing body of social work literature calling for spiritually sensitive practice (Canda, 1988; Cowley, 1993; Smith, 1995). We must move beyond the ethnocentricity that characterizes African American beliefs as pessimistic and fatalistic, and views their traditional religious orientation with condescending amusement rather than respect.

We believe areas of convergence may be found between hospice philosophy and traditional African American perspectives. Rather than viewing their stoicism in the face of death and reliance on God's will as "resignation," one might interpret these as an ability to transcend individual situations (Creel, 1991) and to accept one's own death without fear. Some African Americans may feel that since God is in charge, life-sustaining treatment may not determine whether one lives or dies. These views are consistent with the hospice philosophy of acceptance of death without great fear and of preference for palliative rather than curative care. The large supportive family network (Dowd et al., 1998) lends itself to the family support needed at home during hospice care, but Medicare regulations need to be changed to reflect the lack of full-time caregivers in the home. Considering that the African American church is the major social institution for the majority of African Americans and that pastors represent the leadership of this institution, it is reasonable to think that efforts toward social action and public education will be more successful if conducted collaboratively with pastors (Pipes, 1981) and organized through the church (Griffin & Bratton, 1995; Harris et al., 1996).

Recommendations for dismantling the barriers to hospice care for African Americans should incorporate the following:

• Respect cultural differences regarding medical treatment preferences.

• Provide facts about reality of life-sustaining treatment, equal quality, and lower cost of hospice care.

• Look for areas of convergence between hospice philosophy and African American beliefs.

• Present hospice as compatible with caring for one's own, death as homecoming, God's will.

• Conduct public education campaigns— television, community festivals, newsletters, church presentations.

• Use churches as referral sources.

• Develop programs to follow patients from active treatment to palliative care.

• Provide hospice care to African Americans in nursing homes.

• Train African American pastors to serve as community representatives.

• Keep patient and family informed, seek their input about every aspect of the treatment plan.

• Use realistic, practical language rather than communicating in a sterile and mechanical way.

• Acknowledge that there may be mistrust; address the issue directly rather than ignoring it.

• Involve African American pastors on boards of directors of hospices.

• Eliminate or make accessible the Clinical Pastoral Education requirement for hospital chaplains.

• Actively recruit African Americans for full-time positions as hospice chaplains and other staff.

❦ ❦ ❦

## References

Burrs, F. A. (1995). The African American experience: Breaking the barriers to hospices. *Hospice Journal, 10*(2), 15–18.

Canda, E. (1988). Spirituality, religious diversity, and social work practice. *Social Casework, 69,* 238–247.

Cooper-Lewter, N., & Mitchell, H. (1992). *Soul theology: The heart of American black culture.* Nashville: Abingdon Press.

Cowley, A. (1993). Transpersonal social work: A theory for the 1990s. *Social Work, 38,* 527–534.

Creel, M. (1991). Gullah attitudes toward life and death. In J. Holloway (Ed.), *Africanisms in American culture.* Bloomington: Indiana University Press.

Dignan, M., Michielutte, R., Sharp, P., Young, L., & Daniels, L. A. (1991). Use of process evaluation to guide health education in Forsyth County's project to prevent cervical cancer. *Public Health Reports, 106*(1), 73–77.

Dowd, S., Poole, V., Davidhizar, R., & Giger, J. (1998). Death, dying and grief in a transcultural context: Application of the Giger and Davidhizar assessment model. *Hospice Journal, 13*(4), 33–56.

Frazier, E. F., & Lincoln, C. E. (1974). *The Negro church in America/The Black Church since Frazier.* New York: Schocken Books.

Gallup Organization. (1997). *Special reports: Black/white relations in the United States.* Princeton, NJ: Author.

Glaser, B., & Strauss, A. (1967). *Discovery of grounded theory: Strategies for qualitative research.* Chicago: Aldine.

Gordon, A. K. (1995). Deterrents to access and service for blacks and Hispanics: The Medicare hospice benefit, healthcare utilization, and cultural barriers. *Hospice Journal, 10*(2), 65–83.

Gordon, A. K., & Rooney, A. (1984). Hospice and the family: A systems approach to assessment. *American Journal of Hospice Care, 1*(1), 31–33.

Griffin, L., & Bratton, L. (1995). Fewer black kidney donors: What's the problem? *Social Work in Health Care, 22*(2), 19–42.

Harper, B. C. (1990, Spring). Doing the right thing: Three strategies for increasing minority involvement. *Hospice*, pp. 14–15.

Harper, B. C. (1995). Report from the National Task Force on Access to Hospice Care by Minority Groups. *Hospice Journal, 10*(2), 1–9.

Harris, Y., Gorelick, P. B., Samuels, P., & Bempong, I. (1996). Why African Americans may not be participating in clinical trials. *Journal of the National Medical Association, 88*, 630–634.

Harwood, A. (Ed.). (1981). *Ethnicity and medical care.* Cambridge, MA: Harvard University Press.

Heckler, M. (1985). *Report of the Secretary's Task Force on Black and Minority Health* (Vol. 1, Executive Summary, U.S. Department of Health and Human Services). Washington, DC: U.S. Government Printing Office.

Hick, S. (1997). Participatory research: An approach for structural social workers. *Journal of Progressive Human Services, 8*(2), 63–78.

Infeld, D. L., Crum, G. E., & Koshuta, M. A. (1990). Characteristics of patients in a long-term care hospice setting. *Hospice Journal, 6*(4), 81–104.

Ita, D. (1995–96). Testing of a causal model: Acceptance of death in hospice patients. *Omega, 32*(2), 81–92.

Kalish, R., & Reynolds, D. (1976). *Death and ethnicity: A psychocultural study.* Farmingdale, NY: Baywood.

Klessig, J. (1992). The effect of values and culture on life-support decisions. *Western Journal of Medicine, 157*, 315–322.

Lincoln, Y., & Guba, E. (1985). *Naturalistic inquiry.* Beverly Hills, CA: Sage Publications.

Lowe, J., Barg, F., & Bernstein, M. (1995). Educating African-Americans about cancer prevention and detection: A review of the literature. *Social Work in Health Care, 21*(4), 17–36.

Lundgren, L. M., & Chen, S-P. C. (1986). Hospice: Concept and implementation in the black community. *Journal of Community Health Nursing, 3*, 137–144.

Mailick, M. D., Holden, G., & Walther, V. (1994). Coping with childhood asthma: Caretakers' views. *Health & Social Work, 19*, 103–111.

Malekoff, A. (1994). Action research: An approach to preventing substance abuse and promoting social competency. *Health & Social Work, 19*, 46–53.

Martinez-Brawley, E., & Delevan, S. (1993). Centralizing management and decentralizing services: An alternative approach. *Administration in Social Work, 17*(1), 81–102.

Miller, K., Miller, M., & Single, N. (1997). Barriers to hospice care: Family physicians' perceptions. *Hospice Journal, 12*(4), 29–41.

Mor, V., Hendershot, G., & Cryan, C. (1989). Awareness of hospice services: Results of a national survey. *Public Health Reports, 104*, 178–182.

National Hospice Organization. (1995). *Hospice fact sheet.* Arlington, VA: Author.

Neighbors, H. W., & Jackson, J. S. (1987). Barriers to medical care among adult blacks: What happens to the uninsured? *Journal of the National Medical Association, 79*, 489–493.

Neubauer, B. J., & Hamilton, C. L. (1990). Racial differences in attitudes toward hospice care. *Hospice Journal, 6*(1), 37–48.

Nobles, W. (1974). Africanity: Its role in black families. *Black Scholar, 5*(9), 10–17.

Penuel, W., & Freeman, T. (1997). Participatory action research in youth programming: A theory in use. *Child and Youth Care Forum, 26*(3), 175–185.

Pipes, W. (1981). Old-time religion: Benches can't say "Amen." In H. McAdoo (Ed.), *Black families* (pp. 54–76). Beverly Hills, CA: Sage Publications.

Raboteau, A. (1978). *Slave religion: The "Invisible Institution" in the antebellum South.* New York: Oxford University Press.

Rana, S., Knasel, A., & Haddy, T. (1992). Cancer knowledge and attitudes of African American and white adolescents: A comparison of two secondary schools. *Journal of the Association for Minority Physicians, 3*(1), 13–16.

Rapp, C., Shera, W., & Kisthardt, W. (1993). Research strategies for consumer empowerment of people with severe mental illness. *Social Work, 38,* 727–735.

Sarri, R., & Sarri, C. (1992). Organizational and community change through participatory action research. *Administration in Social Work, 16*(3/4), 99–122.

Smith, E. (1995). Addressing the psychospiritual distress of death as reality: A transpersonal approach. *Social Work, 40,* 402–412.

Wagner, D. (1991). Reviving the action research model: Combining case and cause with dislocated workers. *Social Work, 36,* 477–482.

This chapter was originally published in the November 1999 issue of *Social Work,* Vol. 44, Number 6, pp. 549–559.

# 8

# The Aging of America and the Older Americans Act

## JEANETTE C. TAKAMURA

Thirty-four years after the establishment of three of the four major federal programs for older Americans, national policymakers in the executive and legislative branches are engaged in crafting and advancing proposals to modernize, redirect, and secure social security (enacted in 1935), the Medicare program (enacted in 1965), and the Older Americans Act (OAA, P.L. 89-73, enacted in 1965). These proposals were introduced for public discussion and congressional action in 1999, an auspicious year for older Americans—the United Nations International Year of Older Persons.

Motivating factors underlying the flurry of activity around these programs for older Americans can be readily identified. They include a growing measure of apprehension about some of the more obvious economic, social, and other consequences that would result from inattention to an unprecedented longer living population. Specifically, the potential policy and program effect of the aging of 76 million baby boomers is beginning to develop a critical mass of interest as more sectors realize that the boomers will make up the largest generation of older people the world and our nation have ever seen. The interest of both the public and the private sectors in managing and containing the costs of health and long-term care, providing quality care for

The perspectives presented in this article are solely those of the author and do not, as such, represent the views of the federal government, the U.S. Department of Health and Human Services, or the Administration on Aging.

consumers, and ensuring the availability and
viability of a mix of provider organizations and
programs also are motivating factors. Finally,
aging issues, in particular a desire for long-
term care reform, already are being promoted
as a core concern for the 2000 election.

Possibly the most complex discussions in
the nation's capital have to do with the Medicare program. Although the Medical Trust
Fund has declared the solvency of the trust
fund until 2015 instead of 2008, there is abiding interest in adjusting the benefits package
and other features to be more responsive to
emerging health care needs and issues. Unfortunately, the Bipartisan Medicare Commission, charged with the daunting task of
reviewing the Medicare program and developing policy and program recommendations,
was unable to arrive at a consensus before it
adjourned.

The plan articulated by the commission
co-chairs, Senator John Breaux (D-LA) and
Representative Bill Thomas (R-CA), called
for raising the eligibility age for beneficiaries from 65 to 67 and included a modest prescription drug benefit administered as a
means-tested Medicare benefit. The Breaux-
Thomas plan also proposed "premium support" or higher premiums, that is, the shifting
of costs to program beneficiaries through
higher premiums for Medicare, and envi-
sioned a new administering bureaucracy but
did not address the long-term solvency of the
fund. Dissenting members did not embrace
premium support and called for more generous prescription drug coverage.

As an alternative, a set of guiding principles and a proposal have been offered by
the Clinton administration. The administration has called for a more "competitive"
Medicare program, has emphasized the need
to "smooth-out provisions in the Balanced
Budget Act that may be affecting Medicare
beneficiaries' access to quality services"
(*President Clinton's Plan*, 1999), and has called

for the use of 15 percent of the budget sur-
plus over the next 15 years to underwrite
modernization of the program. Proposed
new benefits include a $1,000 prescription
drug benefit for both older and disabled
Americans and free preventive health services, such as mammograms, prostate cancer
screenings, and diabetes self-management.
Close scrutiny of all options may be expected
to precede legislative action in the remaining days of the first session of the 106th
Congress.

Policy decisions that result in the modernization of social security, Medicare, and
OAA will determine very much the quality
of life of the nation's longer lived, increasingly diverse, predominantly female older
Americans and their families in the 21st century. Despite ongoing comparisons of public or private sector strategies, there is strong
consensus that social security must be "saved"
for future generations of older Americans.
For women, economic security in old age
may hinge on whether gender equity and
other issues are addressed satisfactorily
through social security reform.

One set of policy proposals on which this
article is focused calls for the reauthorization
of the OAA, the singular federal policy vehicle dedicated solely to the quality of life of
older Americans and their family members.
OAA is best known for its nutrition, transportation, and long-term care ombudsman
programs. The act established the nationwide
Aging Network composed of 57 state and 655
local agencies on aging, 225 Native American Indian tribal organizations representing
more than 300 tribes, more than 2,000 senior centers, and 27,000 providers of services
through which older people and their families in communities all across the United
States are served.

The reauthorization proposal submitted
by the Clinton administration through the
Administration on Aging in the Department

of Health and Human Services (HHS) would sanction three new initiatives to meet better the diverse needs of current and future older people and their families: a National Family Caregiver Support Program, opportunities to modernize OAA services and programs, and a Life Course Planning Program. Together, the initiatives offer an indication of some potential foci for social work practice with older Americans and their families in the new century.

## Demographic Imperative

Although the percentage of older adults in the United States has tripled since 1900, the elderly population is expected to double between now and 2030. But older Americans are not just greater in number, they are also living much longer. In fact, the age 85 and over population has grown 31 times larger since the turn of the century. Moreover, the most rapidly growing group of older people in the United States is that of adults 100 years of age and older. The U.S. Census Bureau (1996, 1998) points to a doubling of the number of people 100 years and older since 1990. The Census Bureau has suggested that the expected continuation of this trend may result in a centenarian population of 834,000 by 2050, from an estimated 70,000 currently. However, because human longevity is not yet part of the mind-set of the general population, most older people are "surprised survivors" (Hagestad, 1998).

Women make up the majority of older people and have a life expectancy at birth that is approximately seven years longer than men's. Although there are within-group differences in life span and in health status by race and ethnicity, as a group women account for four out of five people 100 years of age and older. As might be expected, women are more likely to experience chronic illnesses and disabilities because of their longer lives.

They are also more likely to be single, live alone, and be poor in their older years than men are. Yet, access to the resources and tools that are necessary to be able to prepare adequately for the advanced years has not been readily available to most women.

Demographers have predicted dramatic increases in the number of ethnic minority older people in the next century. From 1997 to 2030, it is expected that American Indians, Eskimos, and Aleuts will register a 159 percent increase in the number of older people. African American older people will increase by 134 percent over the same period, whereas increases of 368 percent and 354 percent are anticipated for Hispanic and Asian and Pacific Islander Americans, respectively. Thus, the older American population of the 21st century will look vastly different from the profile of older Americans at the turn of this century.

## Older Americans Act

OAA has provided the policy foundation for the development of a nationwide infrastructure of state and local agencies dedicated to advocacy, planning, and policy and program design and implementation on behalf of older Americans. OAA services are meant to be gap filling and are targeted to people in greatest economic and social need, with special attention to low-income members of ethnic minority groups. Much of the development of the home- and community-based services system for long-term care and supportive assistance, congregate and home-delivered nutrition services, and local to national information and assistance system may be traced to the OAA and authorizations provided under its various sections (Title III, Grants for State and Community Programs on Aging, authorizes the assistant secretary for the Administration on Aging to provide funds to states for a variety of services, including supportive services and senior centers under Part B, congregate nutrition services under Part C-1, and home nutrition services under Part C-2.)

The special needs of Native American, Alaskan Natives, and Native Hawaiian older people are acknowledged in Title VI of the OAA, which calls for grants to tribal organizations and to an organization that represents Native Hawaiians. Consumer protection services—the Long-Term Care Ombudsman, older persons rights and legal assistance development, adult protective services, and outreach, counseling, and assistance programs for insurance and public benefits—are addressed through Title VII, Allotments for Vulnerable Elder Rights Protection Activities. As might be expected, the need for OAA services exceeds the supply.

The reauthorization and FY2000 budget proposals transmitted this year to Congress by the administration through HHS Administration on Aging offers three new initiatives intended to support essential work that must occur at the macro, mezzo, and micro levels to ensure that the nation, its communities, its families, and its individual citizens understand, are given the best possible opportunity to prepare for, and have available resources that can be of assistance in dealing with population as well as individual longevity. These initiatives call for the establishment of a National Family Caregiver Support Program, the establishment of life-course planning as a nationwide focus of the Aging Network, and the modernization of OAA programs and services. A 19 percent increase in funding also has been requested to meet needs, which exceed current service capacity.

## Growing Need for Caregiver Support

A number of surveys have documented the extent to which family caregivers are involved in the provision of long-term care to older relatives with functional limitations. For example, a survey by the National Alliance for Caregiving and the American Association of Retired Persons (AARP) estimates that there are 22.4 million households involved in caregiving to older people (National Alliance for Caregiving and AARP Family careging in the U.S.—findings from a national survey, 1997). For nearly two-thirds to three-fourths of elderly Americans with impairments, their caregivers are their sole source of assistance (Alexcih, 1997; Doty, 1986).

Although disability levels have dropped over the past decade (Manton, Corder, & Stallard, 1997), the sheer size and the anticipated longevity of the future elderly population will make long-term care an even more compelling issue for the American family in the 21st century. If the growth in the 85 and older population continues to rise at dramatic rates, for example, the need for long-term care will not decline. Moreover, geographic mobility of family members, work force participation by women, delayed childrearing, and the older parent and grandparent-to-child ratio are among the realities that will continue to shape the ongoing availability of informal caregivers.

Caregivers of older relatives are themselves coping with a variety of demands and concerns. As an example, among caregivers to older persons in the National Alliance for Caregiving/AARP study, about 52 percent were employed full-time. More than 50 percent of these caregivers reported conflicting work and caregiving demands that resulted in their rearranging work schedules, reducing work hours, or taking unpaid leaves of absence. Many primary caregivers also have described their own health as fair to poor (Mui, 1995; Pruchno, Peters, & Burant, 1995; Schulz et al., 1997). In relation to this and to indications of caregiver burden, stress, and depression, Tennstedt (1999) cautions, however, that we must differentiate between the experience of caregivers of people with dementia and of people with other chronic illnesses and disabilities. Tennstedt notes, in this regard, that caregivers of people with dementia are more likely to experience higher levels of burden, stress, and depression.

Although most family caregivers tend not to use formal services to augment their assistance, recent studies have found that the use of adult day care by the care recipient reduces caregiver stress and that with counseling and support provided to caregivers, care recipients with Alzheimer's disease are able to live at home for an additional year before requiring institutionalization (Mittleman, Ferris, Shulman, Steinberg, & Levin, 1996; Zarit, Stephens, Townsend, & Greene, 1998).

In recognition of the demands associated with caregiving, the HHS, through the Administration on Aging, has proposed to establish a National Caregiver Support Program through an amendment to Title III-D of the OAA. The nationwide program would be implemented through the existing Aging Network and would ensure that caregivers of older people in every state and territory would have access to information; assistance; counseling, support groups, and caregiver education; daytime and overnight respite services through adult day care, residential care, and other options; and supplemental services as required. The proposal has been introduced by Senator Tom Daschle (D-SD) through Senate Bill 10 and by Senators Charles Grassley (R-IA) and John Breaux (D-LA) through Senate Bill 707 and in the House by Representatives Matthew Martinez (D-CA) and Henry Waxman (D-CA).

## The Need for Life Course Planning

A 1999 AARP poll of Americans ages 18 and older reveals that the majority of the people surveyed expect to live to 80 years of age, would like to live to about 91 years, but do not wish to be centenarians. Ninety percent of survey respondents believe that how they age is somewhat within their control and, reflecting an interest in maintaining their health and in remaining active, 84 percent report that they are exercising and engaged in some form of activity that promotes good health. Although those polled anticipate that life will be better for the much older person in the 21st century, they are fearful of the possibility of poor health and financial insecurity in old age (AARP, 1999).

The trepidations expressed by the AARP study respondents are not misplaced. If retirement income security is a measure of preparedness for successful aging, then the findings of the 1997 Retirement Confidence Survey suggest that we have a well-intentioned but "naively unprepared population" (Employee Benefit Research Institute, 1997). Although almost 70 percent of U.S. workers are saving for retirement, only 27 percent have any notion of the financial resources they will need—beyond the benefit level provided by social security—to retire when and how they desire. Furthermore, the survey found that only 36 percent of all workers have sought to determine how much retirement income they will need when they retire. Moreover, a review of the study data indicates that the confidence expressed by some respondents in their preparedness may not be well founded.

In a context of increasing longevity, individuals and families without access to knowledge and tools to plan adequately for their later years of life are likely to experience disastrous consequences in the years ahead. Already there is reason to believe that baby boomers will live longer than their financial resources will last (AARP, 1999). Similarly, women, who have longer life expectancies, lower lifetime earnings, smaller pensions, and are more reliant on social security than are men, have not been able to plan or prepare for their old age. Unfortunately, the premises that undergird current retirement and pension policies and practices, as well as community planning and individual and family lifestyles, plans, and behaviors, do not yet reflect life expectancy that will be even more commonplace in the next century.

The second new policy and program initiative developed by the Administration on Aging and presented in its OAA reauthorization proposal calls for the establishment of a nationwide Life Course Planning Program, which would be implemented by states. Specifically, the Life Course Planning Program would establish comprehensive public information and counseling programs to advise middle-aged and older people and their families about the critical aging issues for which they must prepare. Because states and area agencies are required to develop state and area plans that document the needs of older people and their families, identify program and service responses, and seek community input throughout the plan development process, the Life Course Planning Program would require the Aging Network to use a multiyear planning process to initiate discussions of general community preparedness for and responsiveness to its own aging population. States also would be expected to systematize, strengthen, and promote the coordinated use of services that address various facets of concerns that can determine whether an individual is able to age successfully, that is, concerns that are best addressed by legal services, pension benefits counseling, health insurance counseling, elder protective services, senior centers, long-term care ombudsmen, consumer awareness and protection, and other network services and programs.

The coordination and systematizing of these services through the proposed Life Course Planning Program would enable the Aging Network to better inform, counsel,

and assist older people and their families in identifying, navigating through, understanding, negotiating, and selecting from among the array of options for financial security, housing arrangements, assistive devices, health and long-term care, social activities, personal safety, and general consumer goods and services with which many older people are confronted and with which as many are not familiar. Through the Life Course Planning Program, the Administration on Aging and the Aging Network would serve as access points at the national, state, and local levels to provide information, consumer protection, counseling, and education to communities, families, and individuals. The Aging Network would strive, from a longevity perspective, with public and private sector partners, to increase awareness of health risk factors, promotion of good health, and disease prevention; reduce health disparities among older ethnic minority Americans; increase opportunities for active aging; protect the legal and other rights of older people; and increase the financial literacy and preparedness of middle-aged and older Americans.

## Modernizing Older Americans Act Services and Programs

Through the early 1990s, major discretionary funding support was available under Title IV of the OAA for the testing of new service delivery models and innovative programs. Since then, Title IV funding levels have been significantly lower and appropriations have been earmarked by Congress for specific purposes, organizations, or geographic localities. Among the innovations tested under Title IV during the 1970s and 1980s, area agencies on aging, the congregate and home-delivered meals program, the PACE program, and the long-term care ombudsman program occupy important places in the existing constellation of aging services and programs. Area agencies on aging and the meals and long-term care ombudsman programs were piloted and later written into the OAA to be permanent structures and service programs. For example, authorization for area agencies on aging is in Title III-B, Section 321, Supportive Services and Senior Centers. Authorization for congregate nutrition services is in Title III-C1, Congregate Nutrition Services, and III-C2, Home-Delivered Nutrition Services. Authorization for the Long-Term Care Ombudsman Program is provided under Title VII, Allotments for Vulnerable Elder Rights Protection Activities, Chapter 2—Ombudsman Programs.

Scientific discoveries and effective new technologies, models, and strategies that have implications for service and program interventions are available and will continue to emerge in the new century. For the Aging Network to have the opportunity and the resources required to incorporate research findings and technological and other innovations in a timely, outcome-oriented manner, the Administration on Aging has proposed that states be permitted to request the use of the greater of 4 percent or $300,000 of Title III OAA funds to underwrite service and program innovation initiatives.

## Implications for Social Work Practice

Interest in policies and programs that address the needs of older people worldwide is reflected in the declaration of 1999 as the International Year of Older Persons by the United Nations and by the discussions that center around proposals to reform Social Security and Medicare and to reauthorize the OAA. In each case, there is consensus that programs serving older Americans must be modernized. Without a doubt, a motivating force for modernization has been the sheer number of people who will come of age in

2011, when the baby boomers begin to reach age 65.

For the social work profession, there will be numerous opportunities to provide leadership in and work on behalf of what will be a very diverse population of older adults and their family members. Although older women and ethnic minorities will require special attention because they will continue to be most at risk in their later years, three general clusters of need were identified in this discussion: long-term care and caregiver support; life course planning; and the modernization of services and programs for older Americans.

Although rates of physical disability are decreasing among older Americans, the size of the elderly population and extended longevity mean that long-term care will remain a significant concern. In this domain, research clearly shows that both caregivers and older people with functional limitations will have multiple needs, ranging from the need of the caregiver for clinical services to deal with stress and depression to the need to develop policies and programs for evidence-based, outcome-oriented services.

An even larger area requiring development is life course planning. As noted, society's preparedness for the effect of an aging population and increased longevity is yet to be realized. Communities will need to examine the implications of the ongoing aging demographic revolution from a systems perspective, identify policy and program options, and commit to creating "a society for all ages" to which the United Nations International Year of Older Persons is aimed—a society in which citizens are able to function as independently as possible and remain productive and contributory through to the latest years of life. In addition, Americans of all ages must anticipate the possibility of long life and have access to critical information and resources to be able to plan for their own life course.

Third, there is much work to be done to ensure that all aging services and programs integrate and use recommendations and technologies emerging from multi-disciplinary research. As an example, the growing body of research on diverse segments of the elderly population and their caregivers must be translated and integrated into programs and services as outcome-oriented interventions. Even simple assistive devices to enhance the quality of life of older people with functional limitations are neither widely known nor widely used. Their availability and utility must be routinely incorporated in care plan discussions and consumer awareness initiatives.

The real challenge facing the social work profession will be whether it can prepare an adequate number of professionals with requisite levels of substantive knowledge and skills to meet the diverse needs of current and emerging populations of older Americans. Will social work education programs be able to revise curricula to permit this to occur? Will there be a sufficient number of continuing education courses to educate practitioners in meeting the needs of an aging America? All of us will experience the consequences of the answers to these questions in the 21st century. The new century is one in which we can create a world in which longevity and aging present real opportunities for millions of Americans.

❦ ❦ ❦

## References

Alexcih, L. M. (1997). What it is, who needs it, and who provides it? In B. L. Boyd (Ed.), *Long-term care: Knowing the risk, paying the price* (pp. 1–17). Washington, DC: Health Insurance Association of America.

American Association of Retired Persons. (1999). *"Stealing Time" study: A summary of findings* [Online]. Available: http://research.aarp.org/health/pbs_1.html.

Doty, P. (1986). Family care of the elderly: The role of public policy. *The Milbank Quarterly, 64,* 34–75.

Employee Benefit Research Institute. (1997). *Big dreams, small savings, little planning: Results of the 1997 Retirement Confidence Survey.* Washington, D.C.: Author.

Hagestad, G. (1998). *Towards a society for all ages: New thinking, new language, new conversations.* Keynote address at United Nations, New York.

Manton, K., Corder, L., & Stallard, E. (1997). Chronic disability trends in elderly United States populations, 1982–1994. *Proceedings of the National Academy of Science, 94,* 2593–2598.

Mittleman, M. S., Ferris, S. H., Shulman, E., Steinberg, G., & Levin, B. (1996). A family intervention to delay nursing home placement of patients with Alzheimer's disease: A randomized controlled trial. *JAMA, 276,* 1725–1731.

Mui, A. (1995). Perceived health and functional status among spouse caregivers of frail older persons. *Journal of Aging and Health, 7,* 283–300.

National Alliance for Caregiving and AARP (1997). *Family caregiving in the U.S.—Findings from a national survey.*

Older Americans Act of 1965, P.L. 89-73, 87 Stat. 60.

*President Clinton's plan to modernize and strengthen Medicare for the 21st century* [Fact Sheet] (1999). Washington, DC: White House.

Pruchno, R. A., Peters, N. D., & Burant, C. J. (1995). Mental health of coresident family caregivers: Examination of a two-factor model. *Journal of Gerontology—Psychological Sciences, 50B,* P247–P256.

Schulz, R. S., Newsom, J., Mittleman, M., Burton, L., Hirsch, C., & Jackson, S. (1997). Health effects of caregiving: The caregiver health effects study, an ancillary study of the cardiovascular health study. *Annals of Behavioral Medicine, 19,* 110–116.

Tennstedt, S. (1999). *Family caregiving in an aging society.* Paper presented at the U.S. Administration on Aging Symposium, "Longevity in the New American Century," Baltimore, MD [Online]. Available: http://www.aoa.dhhs.gov/caregivers/FamCare.html.

U.S. Bureau of the Census. (1996). Population projections of the United States by age, sex, race, and Hispanic origin: 1995 to 2050. (Current Population Reports, P25–1130). Washington, DC: U.S. Government Printing Office.

U.S. Bureau of the Census. (1998). *U.S. population estimates by age, sex, race, and Hispanic origin: January 1, 1997.* Washington, DC: U.S. Government Printing Office.

Zarit, S. H., Stephens, M. P., Townsend, A., & Greene, R. (1998). Stress reduction for family caregivers: Effects of adult day care use. *Journal of Gerontology, 53B,* S267–S277.

This chapter was originally published in the August 1999 issue of *Health & Social Work,* Vol. 24, Number 3, pp. 232–238.

# III
# Care

❦  ❦  ❦

In western industrialized societies, family care, state care, and, most recently, market care, have all become vital to the maintenance of healthy life and well-being for older people. Both health care and social care are necessary, along with legal protections and choices regarding how care is provided. In the provision of both health and social care, social workers have special roles with regard to three distinct aspects of care for older adults: advocating for social justice and fairness in the allocation of services, providing actual professional social care services, and facilitating the receipt of appropriately expert health care. The articles in this section are presented to highlight current knowledge about competent social work practice today regarding all three of these aspects of care.

### Redressing Social Exclusion

Social justice, an over-riding social work value, suggests that even in capitalistic societies care should be allocated and utilized in accordance with peoples' needs. But, gross disparities do exist in America in the patterns by which elders utilize health care and social services. Some encounter barriers to access that deter their use of services or discourage it. Older people can be disadvantaged by material poverty as well as by the stigma and incapacity associated with debilitating conditions.

Articles 9, 10, and 11 all address the differential use of services by subpopulations of elders who are disadvantaged in various ways. The first article highlights the crippling implications of poverty and the consequent importance of Medicaid coverage for low-income older people. Yat-Sang Lum and Hong-jer

Chang use a nationally representative sample from the AHEAD study (Asset and Health Dynamics among the Oldest Old) of the National Institute of Aging to identify low-income elders and examine how the effects of Medicaid coverage vary by race, ethnicity, and gender. Medicaid-covered elders are from 1.0 to 2.1 times more likely to use health services because the coverage makes services affordable. Yet troubling disparities in use by race, ethnicity, and gender occur for the three services examined here: home health care, physician visits, and hospitalization.

The second article addresses the same questions from the point of view of health and human service use by community-dwelling elders with dementia. In this article, Ronald Toseland, Philip McCallion, Todd Gerber, Caroline Dawson, Susan Gieryic, and Vincent Guilamo-Ramos examine health and social service use by a random sample of caregivers of persons with dementia. Identifying a sample through the New York State dementia registry, they found that, contrary to prevailing assumptions, caregivers reported fairly high levels of service use across the 33 services identified. Yet nearly three-fourths indicated that additional services would still reduce the likelihood of institutionalization of the recipient; their own needs for assistance were very great. Despite their use of formal services, many caregivers lacked knowledge about services available and needed help accessing them. Social workers have a vital role in providing such service information, making referrals, and linking caregivers with local support centers and networks specific to their situations.

Finally, Kathryn Braun and Colette Browne shed light on the growing diversity of cultural and health beliefs in American society and how much these matter. They examine how traditional values and practices among Asian and Pacific Islanders (API) reflect perceptions of diseases and use of health services. They focus on how the perceptions of dementia, caregiving, and help-seeking among the five major ethnic groups in Hawaii—Chinese, Japanese, Filipino, Vietnamese, and Native Hawaiian (actually at least 30 distinct cultural groups)—differ in important ways. These five ethnic groups are extremely uneven in terms of income, and Native Hawaiians have especially high mortality rates compared with non-Native Hawaiian residents. This study adds to previous research on Asian Americans (conducted mainly in California). It concludes by emphasizing the importance of fine-grained cultural knowledge for social work practice, policy, and research.

## Benefiting from Professional Social Care

Social workers' most significant arena of work is in actually arranging and providing social care. Activities such as screening and assessment, particularly of function and of disability among the old, are becoming increasingly sophisticated. At the same time, they risk becoming increasingly mechanized and having their purposes displaced or compromised. Social care is the arena in which the social work profession needs to critically examine the adequacy of its preparation for emerging professional opportunities in care management, hospice, psychiatry, and in-home care services. The profession needs to embrace the responsibility for evaluating services and practices and measuring their effectiveness. Articles 12, 13, 14, and 15 in this section illustrate the complexity of that challenge as they highlight potential improvements in the effectiveness of social care.

The first article, by Lee Slivinske, V. L. Fitch, and N. W. Wingerson, sets the stage for considering the profound needs of older disabled persons and the conundrum of devising appropriate measures of need and eligibility criteria for long term care (LTC) and services. To test the optimum criteria for eligibility for access to the LTC service network, these authors assess the ability of elderly individuals to care for themselves and their actual patterns of long-term care services use. Using data from a purposive sample of eight home care and institutional care providers, the authors surveyed 547 elderly consumers, obtaining subjective and evaluative measures of level of functioning, including assessments of activities of daily living (ADLs), instrumental activities of daily living (IADLs), and demographic characteristics. In the article, they examine the efficacy of using ADL-IADL dependencies and cognitive and behavioral impairments as eligibility criteria for entry into the service network, examining four different approaches: measuring individual ADL-IADL limits, counting the number of ADL-IADL disabilities, using Likert-type ADL-IADL scales, and using a comprehensive eligibility model. It is worth speculating on the implications of the fact that the most variation was explained when the comprehensive assessment model was used, including literally all of the study variables.

The second article in this section addresses the use of another assessment instrument, the SF-36, a standardized health-related quality-of-life questionnaire with thirty-six questions about social functioning. The SF-36 has been validated and found to be particularly reliable as a screening instrument identifying need for social work assessment in primary care. Barbara Berkman, Susan Chauncey Horky, William Holmes, Ann Daniels, Evelyn Bonander, Suzanne Sampson, and Mark Robinson emphasize that early identification of elderly hospital clinic patients needing nonmedical services can really facilitate the delivery of timely and appropriate services. Their team used the SF-

36 on a sample of patients at Massachusetts General Hospital to determine if the instrument could be shortened even further. They conclude that there is a great need for screening instruments that can expedite delivery of psychosocial services to elderly patients seen in general medical settings. "Social workers using reliable and valid standardized screening mechanisms to identify patients in need of psychosocial assessment can offer timely appropriate services ... saving the patient and the doctor time and money." The SF-36 is one such standardized instrument that can identify patients with significant IADL problems related to poor quality of life, and the authors urge its wider use in social work practice with older people.

The next article in this section addresses the preparation of social workers for hospice care, an important and growing arena of practice largely funded by Medicare and consequently shaped by that program's prescriptive regulations. Pamela Kovacs and Laura Bronstein's national survey of hospice social workers assesses the academic preparation, on-the-job training, and personal experiences that have prepared workers for their present positions. Hospice social workers spend more time with terminal cancer patients than do social workers in any other settings, becoming involved when persons have been given six months or less to live and are no longer pursuing curative treatment. With Medicare regulations mandating that hospice provide treatment with interdisciplinary teams and that social work be included in those teams, the demand for hospice social workers can only grow in the future. As members of these interdisciplinary teams, social workers have the privilege and the challenge of addressing the psychosocial needs of terminally ill cancer patients and their families and friends

Hospice social workers viewed a wide range of courses as important in preparing them for oncology work. On-the-job training focusing on medical terminology, interdisciplinary collaboration, death and dying, and the integration of personal experiences are important for continuing growth and success in this work. The combined generalist-specialist approach seems to work well in preparing such practitioners, but there is need for increased attention to interdisciplinary collaboration, and exploratory research to help social workers integrate their work with the personal experiences that often bring them to this field, enhancing their use of self in practice. Finally, continuing education for social work with people living with and dying from cancer is especially important for this challenging field of practice.

Finally in this section, Amanda Grenier and Kevin Gorey remind us of the many research strategies available for examining the effectiveness of social work interventions with older people. Their meta-analysis of 42 social work research presentations at the annual scientific meetings of the Gerontological Society of America (GSA) found that 69 percent of older clients or their caregivers participating in studied interventions did better than the average clients in comparison groups. This finding replicates a recent meta-analysis of published research on the effectiveness of social work interventions. Such findings add to a growing body of interventions research with specific populations, even though conference presentations at the Gerontological Society of America were less likely to have evaluated the health impacts of organizational or community practice. Meta-analyses and other research approaches can synthesize a range of findings about interventions, demonstrations, and innovations that are all-important in extending knowledge about the social care needs of an aging society.

## Obtaining Expert Health Care

Social workers need to be tireless in their critical evaluation of the American health care system and its outcomes for older patients. Whether considered core members of interdisciplinary teams, as in hospice care (see Kovacs and Bronstein above), or simply facilitators of medical care, as they are under Medicare provision of psychiatric home care (Byrne, 1999), social workers certainly bring "added value" to health care interventions (see Grenier and Gorey above). However, changes in technology and knowledge require of practitioners continual professional development. Medical social workers face constantly changing challenges to their traditional roles in discharge planning, interdisciplinary practice, team leadership, monitoring hospital readmissions, and preventing medical crises.

Articles 16, 17, 18, and 19 highlight these challenges by examining health care organizations and their outcomes. Such research is urgently needed to facilitate organizational adaptations and improvements. The first two articles here examine standard hospital inpatient practices to improve them. The second two focus on measuring the adequacy of health care systems of hospital discharge planning and of home care itself.

The three empirical articles here examine the classic roles of medical social workers in primary prevention, adjustment to illness, primary care, and risk reduction, but go beyond traditional practice methods by embracing systemic results. Case by case, hospital social workers assess patients' capacities to obtain adequate care after hospitalization: who will provide care at home, what is their capability to do specific tasks, and how often and how well must tasks be done? But, for over two decades social work researchers have been calling for empirical studies of post-hospital home care and readmissions by disease categories to improve the accuracy of findings and the design of more systematic interventions (Kane, 1994; Berkman & Abrams, 1986). These studies highlight the importance of choosing one diagnosis for study and the improved quality and more refined knowledge possible as social work research methods improve in sophistication.

In the first article, Catherine Kohm, Diane Neil-Pollinger, and Fatima Sheriff describe redesigning social work activities in a cardiac care unit in Toronto, Canada. Given Canada's universal health insurance and public funding for community care, it is noteworthy that formal and informal home care are barely mentioned in this article. Instead, this article focuses on "re-engineering" social work activities to improve efficiency within the hospital, a site needing continuous improvement regardless of systems context.

In the second article, Sheryl Itkin Zimmerman, David Smith, Ann Gruber-Baldini, Kathleen Fox, Richard Hebel, John Kenzora, Gerald Felsenthal, and Jay Magaziner examine the risks of depression following hip fracture, one of the most common and debilitating accidents to befall older people, especially women. Following 272 people aged 65 and over, the authors carefully identify risk factors for depression while in the hospital and again two months post-discharge. They identify a plethora of social factors possibly contributing to resilience or remediable by social work interventions. The implications for social work practice, and especially for research, are great, suggesting significant potential for risk reduction.

The third article, by Sherry Cummings, reports findings of a study to identify reasons for failure of hospital discharge plans for dementia patients. Medicare and other health insurance cover medical and functional needs, but not cognitive and social deficits, and dementia patients typically have a complex constellation of post-discharge needs. Finding about one-third of the discharge plans to be inadequate, this study identified factors related to inadequate discharge plans and patient readmission. The following variables typically contributed to inadequacy: discharge to a non-specialty nursing home, longer length of stay, inability to obtain needed resources, inability to accept the diagnosis of dementia, and high level of functional impairment. Social workers most accurately predicted plan failure for male patients whose caregiver had little social support. Unlike most other diseases of old age, dementia is progressively degenerative, essentially an uninsurable condition, and profoundly costly for family caregivers.

Discharge plans and subsequent care requirements again are the focus of the last article by Enola Proctor, Nancy Morrow-Howell, Hong Li, and Peter Doré. They investigate the post-hospital experiences of elders with congestive heart failure (CHF), the most prevalent diagnosis among Medicare patients and most common diagnosis requiring care at home that contributes to hospital readmissions. They followed 253 elderly Medicare patients discharged to home after a hospitalization for congestive heart failure through four telephone contacts over a 14-week period to check on medication compliance and other aspects of care. The study points to the importance of home care, both formal services and family care, in reducing risk of readmission and general health. This article assesses patient perceptions of the adequacy of formal care through skilled nursing and functional assistance from family, testing research-driven hypotheses about the relationship between health care adequacy and readmission.

These articles each exemplify research that best demonstrates the contribution social work can make to national organizational health care priorities. By optimizing quality, enhancing patient outcomes, and reducing unnecessary health expenditures, not only can health care for elders be improved, but a better health care system becomes possible for all.

## References

Berkman, B. & Abrams, R. D. (1986) Factors related to hospital readmissions of elderly cardiac patients, *Social Work, 31* (2), 99–103.

Byrne, J. (1999, February). Social work in psychiatric home care: Regulations, roles and realities, *Health & Social Work 24* (1), 65–71.

Kane, R. A. (1994). A study of post acute care, Final Report, May 1994. Minneapolis, MN: Institute for Health Services Research.

# 9

# The Effect of Medicaid Coverage on Use of Health Services by Low-Income Elderly People

YAT-SANG LUM and
HONG-JER CHANG

Since they were enacted by Congress in 1965 as Titles XVIII and XIX of the Social Security Act, the Medicare and Medicaid programs have improved access to health care for millions of disadvantaged people. Medicare provides almost universal health insurance coverage for elderly people aged 65 or older and disabled workers who meet the eligibility requirements. Medicaid, on the other hand, provides health insurance coverage for millions of low-income people. Some people may be eligible for both Medicare and Medicaid. In 1994, among the 35 million Medicaid recipients, 4 million were low-income elderly people and a majority of them were dual eligibles—they were covered by both Medicare and Medicaid (Health Care Financing Administration, 1996). Low-income elderly people may be eligible for Medicaid if they belong to one of the following four categories: those who receive cash benefits from the federal Supplemental Security Income program (SSI), those who have excessive medical or long-term care expenses relative to income, those who have income below the federal poverty threshold and limited financial assets (qualified Medicare beneficiaries), and those who have income between 100 and 120 percent of the federal poverty threshold and limited financial assets (specified low-income Medicare beneficiaries). In 1994 Medicaid covered about 20 percent of elderly people with incomes below 150 percent of the federal poverty threshold

(Health Care Financing Administration, 1996). Compared with recipients in other age groups, low-income elderly people had the highest per-user Medicaid payments. Although only 11.5 percent of the Medicaid recipients were low-income elderly people, they accounted for 31 percent (33.6 billion) of the total payments (Health Care Financing Administration, 1996). The interdependence of Medicaid and Medicare, the disproportionate share of Medicaid expenditures by low-income elderly people, and the rapidly increasing elderly population have made health care for low-income elderly people a pressing concern for policymakers. However, despite the fact that the United States spends billions of dollars every year on health care for low-income elderly people, we know very little about them and about how Medicaid coverage affects their use of health services.

The objective of this study was to investigate the effect of Medicaid coverage on use of health services by low-income elderly people. In particular it investigated

• the effect of Medicaid coverage on the probability of using three types of health services: home health services, visits to a physician, and hospital inpatient stays
• the effect of Medicaid coverage on the number of physician visits and the number of nights in hospital among those who made at least one physician visit or had at least one hospital night, respectively
• the differential effect of Medicaid coverage on the probability of using these health services and the volume of health services used by elderly people of different races, ethnic groups, and gender.

## Review of the Literature

Since the early 1980s, there have been a large number of studies on the factors affecting the use of health services by elderly people (see

Wan, 1989; Wolinsky & Arnold, 1988, for review). In general, these studies found that health and medical needs were the most important predictors of the use of health services by elderly people. Elderly people who had poor self-reported health, more difficulties with activities of daily living (ADLs) or instrumental activities of daily living (IADLs), and more medical conditions were more likely to use health services, and among those who used services, elderly people who had more health and medical needs used more services (Coulton & Frost, 1982; Levkoff, Cleary, & Wetle, 1987; Lum, Chang, & Ozawa, 1997; Nelson, 1993; Strain, 1991; Stump, Johnson, & Wolinsky, 1995; Wan, 1989; Wan & Odell, 1981; Wolinsky & Coe, 1984; Wolinsky & Johnson, 1991; Wolinsky, Miller, Prendergast, Creel, & Chávez, 1983). Other significant predictors include age (Ellencweig & Pagliccia, 1994; Hansell, Sherman, & Mechanic, 1991; Wolinsky & Coe, 1984; Wolinsky, Mosely, & Coe, 1986), education (Lum, Chang, & Ozawa, 1997; Wolinsky & Coe, 1984), and private health insurance coverage (Lum, Chang, & Ozawa, 1997; Wolinsky & Coe, 1984; Wolinsky & Johnson, 1991).

### *Medicaid Coverage*

Medicaid coverage was one of the most commonly used covariates in these studies. Studies consistently found that having Medicaid coverage was positively associated with both the probability of using health services and the volume of health services used (Lum, et al., 1997; Miller et al., 1996; Stump et al., 1995; Wolinsky & Coe, 1984; Wolinsky & Johnson, 1991; Wolinsky, Stump, & Johnson, 1995). Using data from the 1978 Health Interview Survey, Wolinsky and Coe (1984) found that elderly people who had Medicaid coverage made more physician visits and had more hospital nights. Using data from the Longitudinal Study of Aging, Wolinsky and Johnson (1991) found that elderly people who had Medicaid coverage were more likely to use home health services, make physician contacts, and use hospital services. They also found that among those who used services, elderly people who had Medicaid coverage made more visits to a physician and had more nights in a hospital. Using data from three large national surveys, Miller et al. (1996) found that Medicaid coverage was associated with higher probability of using home health services across all three studies.

In a more recent study, Lum et al. (1997) found that elderly people who had Medicaid coverage were more likely to use home health services and hospital services; among those who made physician visits, elderly people who had Medicaid coverage made more visits. However, Medicaid coverage had no significant effect on the probability of making physician visits and had a negative effect on the number of hospital nights among those who used hospital services. Lum et al. also found that the effect of Medicaid coverage varied by race and ethnicity: African American elderly people who had Medicaid coverage were more likely to use home health services and hospital services; Hispanic elderly people who had Medicaid coverage were more likely to use hospital services. However, Medicaid coverage had no significant effect on the use of any health services by white elderly people. All these studies shared a common limitation—they used elderly people in general as their samples and did not focus on low-income elderly people.

Among these studies, many researchers routinely used gender and race as control variables in their multivariate analyses (Coulton & Frost, 1982; Ellencweig & Pagliccia, 1994; Nelson, 1993; Strain, 1991; Stump et al., 1995; Wolinsky & Coe, 1984; Wolinsky & Johnson, 1991). By doing so,

they assumed that the effects of gender and race could be modeled by a few dummy variables in their models. In other words, these researchers assumed homogeneity within race and gender (Wolinsky, 1994)—there was no interaction between race, gender, and other explanatory variables in predicting the use of health services by elderly people.

### *Effect of Race*

The findings on the effect of race in these studies were not conclusive. An early study by Wolinsky and Coe (1984) found that elderly people of color made more physician visits but used fewer hospital services than white elderly people. A few recent studies found that race had no significant effect on the use of any health services by elderly people (Stump et al., 1995; Wolinsky & Johnson, 1991). Other studies, however, found that white elderly people were more likely to receive health services than African American elderly people. Using 1986 physician claims data for a 5 percent national sample of Medicare enrollees aged 65 years or older, Escarce, Epstein, Colby, and Schwartz (1993) found that white elderly people were more likely to receive 23 types of health services and to have access to higher technology or newer services than African American elderly people. Similarly, using data from 1986 Medicare patients, Goldberg, Hartz, Jacobsen, Krakauer, and Rimm (1992) found that the sex- and age-adjusted coronary artery bypass grafting rate for white elderly people was much higher than the rate for African American elderly people.

A few researchers did address the heterogeneity within race, either by using the interaction terms between race and other explanatory variables in their multivariate analyses (Nelson, 1993; Wolinsky & Johnson, 1991) or by analyzing their multivariate models separately for each racial group (Lum et al., 1997; Miner, 1995). Wolinsky and Johnson (1991) found that the effects of health measures on the use of health services varied by race. Having difficulty with basic ADLs had a stronger effect on the number of physician visits for African American elderly people than for white elderly people. Among African American elderly people, having difficulty with advanced ADLs was associated with using more home health services but with a lower probability of using hospital services. Furthermore, having lower body disability had more significant effects on both physician visits and hospital contacts among white elderly people than among African Americans. Miner (1995) found that living in the South, owning a home, and residential stability were negatively associated with the use of health services by white elderly people but not among African Americans. Living in a suburban area had a significant positive effect on the use of health services among African American elderly people but not among white elderly people. Lum et al. (1997) found that being widowed, separated, or divorced was associated with higher probability of using home health services only among white elderly people but not among African American or Hispanic elderly people; Medicaid coverage was associated with a higher probability of using home health services and hospital services only by elderly people of color but not by white elderly people.

## Effect of Gender

Many studies also found that elderly women were less likely to use hospital services than elderly men (Lum et al., 1997; Nelson, 1993; Strain 1991; Wolinsky & Johnson, 1991), and, when hospitalized, women had shorter stays in hospitals than men (Nelson, 1993; Wolinsky & Johnson, 1991). Gender had no significant effect on the probability of mak-

ing physician visits (Lum et al., 1997; Nelson, 1993; Wolinsky & Johnson, 1991) and using home health services (Lum et al., 1997). However, among those who made at least one physician visit, elderly women made fewer visits than elderly men (Wolinsky & Coe, 1984; Wolinsky & Johnson, 1991). Lum et al. (1997) found that gender differences in the use of health services existed only among elderly people of color. Using a national representative sample of elderly people aged 70 or older, they found that being male was associated with a higher probability of using home health services but with a lower probability of making physician visits among African American elderly people but not white or Hispanic elderly people. They also found that being male was associated with a higher probability of using hospital services among African American and Hispanic elderly people but not among white elderly people.

## Limitations of Earlier Studies

Several shortcomings in the existing body of literature should be addressed. First, many of these studies focused on the entire elderly population and ignored the difference between low-income elderly people and elderly people in general. As a result, we do not know whether the findings in earlier studies can be applied to low-income elderly people. Second, many researchers assumed homogeneity within race and gender (Wolinsky, 1994). In other words, they assumed that Medicaid (or other explanatory variables) had similar effects on the use of health services across different racial and gender groups. We know very little about how the effect of Medicaid coverage varied by race, ethnicity, and gender of elderly people. Third, previous studies included very limited variables on economic resources. Some studies did include family income as an enabling factor.

However, family income is not a precise measure of economic resources, because a larger family may need more income than a smaller family to attain the same economic well-being. Poorly measured economic variables may lead to serious biases in statistical analysis.

### Purpose of the Present Study

To address the problems enumerated, we used a national representative sample of low-income elderly people to examine the racial, ethnic, and gender differences in the relationships between Medicaid coverage and use of health services by this population. We first repeated the traditional dummy variable approach to model the effect of Medicaid on the probability of using health services and the volume of health services used among the users. We then grouped the Medicaid recipients into six categories according to their race, ethnicity, and gender and developed six dummy variables to capture racial, ethnic, and gender differences in the effect of Medicaid coverage. This strategy serves three important purposes. First, it adds to the existing body of literature by providing a national assessment of factors affecting the use of health services by low-income elderly people. Second, it allows us to focus on the effect of Medicaid coverage on the use of health services among low-income elderly people. Third, it allows us to examine how the effect of Medicaid coverage varies by race, ethnicity, and gender.

### Conceptual Model

We used the behavioral model of health services utilization developed by Andersen and his colleagues to guide our analysis (Andersen, 1968, 1995; Andersen & Newman, 1973). The behavioral model is the most widely adopted conceptual model for studying the use of health services by elderly people (Wolinsky, 1994). In general, it considers the use of health services as a function of the predisposing, enabling, and need characteristics of an individual. *Predisposing characteristics* are exogenous demographic and social structural characteristics that reflect an individual's propensity to use health services. Demographic characteristics usually are measured by age, gender, and marital status. Social structural characteristics usually are measured by race, ethnicity, education, and employment. *Enabling characteristics* are the means necessary to use services and include family resources and community resources. Family resources usually are measured by income, health insurance coverage, and existence of a regular source of care. Community resources usually are measured by the physician to population ratio, population density, and the hospital bed to population ratio. *Need characteristics* refer to the medical and health needs that activate the actual use of health services: both perceived and objective health status measures. Perceived health status usually is measured by self-reported health status, whereas objective health status usually is measured by number of medical conditions, ADLs, and IADLs. Both ADLs and IADLs are widely used in health services research as measures for the ability to perform personal care and self-maintenance activities.

The major focus of this study was on the effect of Medicaid coverage on use of health services by low-income elderly people. Medicaid supplements Medicare coverage by paying for the premium, copayments, and deductibles. It also covers some health services not covered by Medicare. We hypothesized that Medicaid coverage improved the access and use of health services by low-income elderly people. However, because

Medicaid is a means-tested program and is widely perceived as "welfare," we believed that individuals with different sociocultural backgrounds might have different attitudes toward use of this program. The stigma of welfare recipients may discourage some elderly Medicaid recipients from seeking health care. Therefore, we hypothesized that the effect of Medicaid on use of health services varied across different racial, ethnic, and gender groups.

## Data Source and Sample

The data were taken from the first wave of the Asset and Health Dynamics among the Oldest Old Study (AHEAD). AHEAD is funded by the National Institute on Aging and is the most recent large-scale collaborative effort between the federal government and the academic community to study the effects and interrelationships of changes and transitions for older Americans in the health, financial, and family domains. It has a national representative sample of 8,222 community-based elderly people aged 70 and older and their spouses. The sample is fully representative of all noninstitutionalized individuals over 70 years old in the United States. The data collection began in October 1993 and continued through July 1994. Among those who were between 70 and 79, about 72 percent of the interviews were completed by telephone. Personal interviews were used as alternative when the household lacked a telephone, the respondent was unable to be interviewed over the phone, or when the respondent preferred a personal interview. Among those who were aged 80 or over, 70 percent of the interviews were conducted by personal interview. The response rate was over 80 percent (University of Michigan Survey Research Center, 1994). Detailed information about AHEAD and the quality of data

has been reported in a special issue of the *Journal of Gerontology, Series B: Psychological and Social Sciences* (volume 52B) in May 1997 (Gerontological Society of America, 1997) and, therefore, will not be repeated here.

The sample for this study included only non–Hispanic white respondents, non–Hispanic African American respondents, and Hispanic respondents. We defined *low-income elderly people* as respondents who were aged 70 or older at the time of the AHEAD interview and who had household income at or below 120 percent of the federal poverty threshold, resulting in a final sample size of 1,542 respondents.

## Measurements

### *Dependent Variables*

The dependent variables were health services utilization in a 12-month period before the AHEAD interview. We included three health services in this study: (1) home health services, (2) visits to a physician, and (3) hospital inpatient stays. The use of these services was measured by three dummy variables—the dummy variable for home health services, the dummy variable for physician visits, and the dummy variable for hospital services. The volume of services used was measured by two continuous variables—the number of nights in the hospital and the number of physician visits. In performing regression analysis, we transformed these two variables into natural logs because their distributions were positively skewed.

*Medicaid Coverage.* To answer the first two research questions, we used a dummy variable to measure the effect of Medicaid coverage on the probability and the volume of health services use. The reference group was respondents who were covered by Medicare but not by Medicaid. To answer the third research question, we measured the effect of Medicaid by six mutually exclusive dummy variables for (1) African American men who were covered by Medicaid, (2) African American women who were covered by Medicaid, (3) white men who were covered by Medicaid, (4) white women who were covered by Medicaid, (5) Hispanic men who were covered by Medicaid, and (6) Hispanic women who were covered by Medicaid.

*Covariates—Predisposing Factors.* Marital status was measured by a dummy variable for respondents who were widowed, so non-widowed respondents were assigned to the reference group. Race and ethnicity were measured by two dummy variables for respondents who were African American and Hispanic; thus, white respondents were assigned to the reference group. Education was measured by two dummy variables for respondents who were high school graduates and respondents who had at least some college education; those who did not graduate from high school were assigned to the reference group. "Male" and "age" were self-explanatory.

*Enabling Factors.* Private health insurance coverage was measured by a dummy variable for respondents who had private health insurance coverage, including major health insurance, Medigap, and others. Respondents who had Medicare coverage but no private health insurance coverage were assigned to the reference group. The *poverty ratio* is the ratio between the respondent's household income and the corresponding poverty threshold. Economic resources were measured by a poverty ratio. The concept of the poverty ratio is useful for analytical purposes because it automatically deals with the size of the family on the basis of economy of scale. In performing regression analysis, we transformed the poverty ratio into a natural log because its distribution was positively skewed.

*Need Factors.* Following the suggestions of Johnson and Wolinsky (1993, 1994), we included self-reported health status, number of medical conditions, difficulty with basic ADLs, difficulty with household ADLs, difficulty with advanced ADLs, lower-body disability, and upper-body disability as our need variables. The self-reported health status was the self-perceived health status given by the respondents. It ranged from 1 = poor health to 5 = excellent health. The number of medical conditions included the following diseases or health problems: diabetes, cancer, chronic lung disease, heart problem, stroke, psychiatric problem, and arthritis. The difficulty with basic ADLs was a dummy variable with 1 assigned to respondents who had difficulty in any of the following tasks: walking across a room, dressing, bathing, eating, getting in and out of bed, and using the toilet. The difficulty with household ADLs was a dummy variable with 1 assigned to respondents who had difficulty preparing hot meals and shopping for groceries. The difficulty with advanced ADLs was a dummy variable with 1 assigned to respondents who had difficulty making telephone calls, taking medications, and managing money. The lower-body disability was a dummy variable with 1 assigned to respondents who had difficulty performing any of the following tasks: walking several blocks, climbing one flight of stairs, and pushing and pulling large objects. Upper-body disability was a dummy variable with 1 assigned to respondents who had difficulty picking up a dime from a table.

### Data Analysis

First, we obtained descriptive statistics on all variables for the sample. We used the weight variable to generate descriptive statistics to adjust for the oversampling in the AHEAD data. Second, we estimated a two-part model for health services use (Manning et al., 1981). In the first part we performed logistic regressions to estimate the effect of Medicaid coverage on the probability of using health services by low-income elderly people. In the second part we performed OLS regressions to estimate the effect of Medicaid coverage on the number of physician visits and number of hospital nights by those who had at least one physician visit or one hospital night, respectively. Finally, we repeated the two-part model by using the six race–ethnicity–gender dummy variables for Medicaid coverage to examine how the effect of Medicaid coverage on use of health services varied by race, ethnicity, and gender of the respondents. This dummy-variables approach is a modification of the interaction-terms approach frequently used by researchers to address similar research questions. The regression coefficients of these dummy variables are mathematically related to the regression coefficients from the interaction-terms model—one can obtain regression coefficients of these dummy variables by summing up regression coefficients of the Medicaid variable and the corresponding product terms from the interaction-terms model. However, the interpretations of regression coefficients of these dummy variables are more straightforward than coefficients from a three-way interactions model (race–gender–Medicaid coverage).

## Results

Table 9-1 provides the definitions of variables as well as the descriptive statistics of the respondents. About 16 percent of low-income elderly people had used home health services and more than 86 percent had made physician visits in the year before the AHEAD interview. About 25 percent had used hospital services in the year before the interview. Among those who used hospital services, low-income elderly people stayed an average of

10.8 nights in the hospital. Among those who made physician visits, low-income elderly people made an average of six visits. Twenty percent of the respondents were covered by Medicaid. Their average age was 79 years. About 21 percent of Medicaid participants were African American and about 9 percent were Hispanic.

### Use of Health Services

Medicaid coverage had a significant effect on the likelihood of using all three health services. Compared to those who did not have Medicaid coverage, respondents who had Medicaid coverage were 2.0 times more likely to use home health services, 1.9 times more likely to make physician visits, and 2.1 times more likely to use hospital services (Table 9-2). The results also showed that low-income elderly people who had Medicaid coverage were as likely as those who had private health insurance coverage to make physician visits; however, they were more likely to use home health services and hospital services.

Race and gender had significant effects on the probability of making physician visits and using hospital services. Compared to white respondents, African American and Hispanic respondents were 1.9 times more likely to make physician visits. Also, compared to white respondents, Hispanic respondents were 37 percent less likely to use hospital services. Compared to female respondents, male respondents were 1.5 times more likely to use hospital services.

### Volume of Services Used

Medicaid coverage had a significant negative effect on the number of hospital nights and a significant positive effect on the number of physician visits (Table 9-3). Many researchers interpret the regression coefficients of dummy variables in semilogarithmic regres-

**TABLE 9-1. Descriptive Statistics and Definitions of the Variables Used in the Study (N = 1,542)**

| Variable | M | % | Definition |
|---|---|---|---|
| **Dependent variable** | | | |
| Home health services | | 15.9 | = 1 if respondent had used home health services |
| Physician visits | | 86.8 | = 1 if respondent had made physician visits |
| Hospital services | | 25.1 | = 1 if respondent had used hospital services |
| Hospital nights | 10.83 | | No. of nights in hospital among those who used hospital services |
| Number of physician visits | 6.03 | | No. of physician visits among those who made at least one visit |
| **Predisposing factor** | | | |
| Age | 79.21 | | Average age at the time of interview |
| African American | | | = 1 if respondent was African American |
| Hispanic | | 21.1 | = 1 if respondent was Hispanic |
| Male | | 8.8 | = 1 if respondent was a man |
| Widowed | | 22.3 | = 1 if respondent was a widow/widower |
| High school graduate | | 64.7 | = 1 if respondent was a high school graduate |
| At least some college | | 21.4 | = 1 if respondent had at least some college |
| Need factor | | 11.2 | |
| Self-rated health status | 2.66 | | Average self-rated health status from 1 to 5. |
| Number of medical conditions | 1.30 | | Average number of medical conditions |
| Basic ADLs difficulty | | 41.4 | = 1 if respondent had difficulty with basic ADLs |
| Household ADLs difficulty | | 31.1 | = 1 if respondent had difficulty with household ADLs |
| Advanced ADLs difficulty | | 26.9 | = 1 if respondent had difficulty with advanced ADLs |
| Lower-body disability | | 61.8 | = 1 if respondent had lower-body disability |
| Upper-body disability | | 10.8 | = 1 if respondent had upper-body disability |
| Enabling factor | | | |
| Private health insurance | | 53.7 | = 1 if respondent had Medigap |
| Medicaid coverage | | 20.0 | = 1 if respondent had Medicaid coverage |
| African American men | | 1.6 | = 1 if respondent was an African American man and covered by Medicaid |
| African American women | | 7.2 | = 1 if respondent was an African American woman and covered by Medicaid |
| White men | | 2.3 | = 1 if respondent was a white man and covered by Medicaid |
| White women | | 11.0 | = 1 if respondent was a white woman and covered by Medicaid |
| Hispanic men | | 1.3 | = 1 if respondent was a Hispanic man and covered by Medicaid |
| Hispanic women | | 3.5 | = 1 if respondent was a Hispanic woman and covered by Medicaid |
| Poverty ratio | 0.81 | | Income to poverty threshold ratio |

sion equations as relative effects or, when multiplied by 100, percentage effects. For example, respondents who had Medicaid coverage made 22.1 percent (0.221 × 100) more physician visits than those who were covered by Medicare but not by Medicaid. However, Halvorsen and Palmquist (1980) showed that such interpretations were incorrect and that the correct estimates of the relative effects and the percentage effects should be equal to $g = (\exp.(c) - 1)$ and $100 \times g = 100 \times (\exp.(c) - 1)$, respectively, where $g$ is the relative effect and $c$ is the regression coefficient. Using these two equations, we calculated that respondents who were covered by Medicaid had 20.9 percent fewer hospital nights but

**TABLE 9-2. Results of Logistic Regression on the Probability of Using Three Health Services by Low-Income Elderly People**

| Variable | Home Health Services | | Physician Visits | | Hospital Services | |
|---|---|---|---|---|---|---|
| | Coefficient | Odds Ratio | Coefficient | Odds Ratio | Coefficient | Odds Ratio |
| Intercept | −4.103*** | | −0.671 | | −0.467 | |
| Predisposing factor | | | | | | |
|   Age | 0.013 | 1.013 | 0.015 | 1.015 | −0.020 | 0.980 |
|   African American | −0.007 | 0.993 | 0.641** | 1.897 | −0.300 | 0.741 |
|   Hispanic | −0.016 | 0.984 | 0.637* | 1.890 | −0.457* | 0.633 |
|   White) Male | 0.262 | 1.299 | −0.380 | 0.684 | 0.394* | 1.483 |
|   Widow | 0.139 | 1.149 | 0.122 | 1.130 | 0.252 | 1.286 |
|   High school graduate | 0.106 | 1.112 | 0.440 | 1.552 | −0.178 | 0.837 |
|   At least some college | 0.011 | 1.011 | 0.738* | 2.092 | 0.345 | 1.411 |
|   (Less than high school graduate) | | | | | | |
| Need factor | | | | | | |
|   Self-rated health status | −0.113 | 0.893 | −0.109 | 0.897 | −0.225** | 0.799 |
|   Number of medical conditions | 0.249*** | 1.283 | 0.681*** | 1.975 | 0.325*** | 1.384 |
|   Basic ADLs difficulty | 0.502* | 1.651 | 0.439 | 1.551 | 0.425** | 1.530 |
|   Household ADLs difficulty | 1.001*** | 2.722 | 0.048 | 1.049 | 0.415* | 1.515 |
|   Advanced ADLs difficulty | 0.451* | 1.569 | −0.161 | 0.851 | −0.091 | 0.913 |
|   Lower-body disability | 0.225 | 1.252 | 0.019 | 1.020 | −0.036 | 0.965 |
|   Upper-body disability | 0.093 | 1.097 | 0.707 | 2.028 | 0.083 | 1.087 |
| Enabling factor | | | | | | |
|   Private health insurance | −0.075 | 0.927 | 0.651*** | 1.916 | 0.209 | 1.233 |
|   Medicaid | 0.710*** | 2.034 | 0.647* | 1.910 | 0.727*** | 2.068 |
|   Poverty ratio | −0.064 | 0.938 | 0.156 | 1.169 | 0.397 | 1.488 |
| N | 1,514 | | 1,513 | | 1,515 | |
| Model $\chi^2$ (df = 17) | 240.596*** | | 144.559*** | | 192.744*** | |

*Note:* Reference groups are in parentheses.

*$p < .05$. **$p < .01$. ***$p < .001$.

made 24.7 percent more physician visits than those who were covered by Medicare but not by Medicaid. Similarly, Hispanic respondents made 13.8 percent more physician visits than white respondents.

### Race, Ethnicity, and Gender

Already shown is that Medicaid had significant effects on the probability of using all three health services. The results in Table 9-4 show that the effect of Medicaid coverage varied by race, ethnicity, and gender of the respondents. Compared to those who did not have Medicaid coverage, African American women who had Medicaid cover-

age were 2.4 times more likely to use home health services; white women who had Medicaid coverage were 2.1 times more likely to use hospital services; Hispanic men who had Medicaid coverage were 4.2 times more likely to use home health services and 4.4 times more likely to use hospital services. Because we had already controlled for the effect of race, ethnicity, and gender in our regression models, these results could be interpreted as differential effects of Medicaid coverage among different racial, ethnic, and gender groups.

The effect of Medicaid coverage on the volume of health services used varied by the race, ethnicity, and gender of the respondents

TABLE 9-3. Results of OLS Regressions on the Volume of Health Services Used by Low-Income Elderly People

| Variable | Hospital Services | | Physician Services | |
|---|---|---|---|---|
| | Coefficient | t | Coefficient | t |
| Intercept | 3.284*** | 4.915 | 2.044*** | 7.771 |
| Predisposing factor | | | | |
| Age | −0.014 | −1.650 | −0.003 | −0.890 |
| African American | 0.021 | 0.181 | 0.045 | 0.990 |
| Hispanic | −0.025 | −0.154 | 0.129* | 2.084 |
| (White) Male | 0.194 | 1.677 | −0.043 | −0.920 |
| Widow | 0.127 | 1.188 | 0.046 | 1.151 |
| High school graduate | −0.261* | −2.010 | 0.017 | 0.366 |
| At least some college | −0.268 | −1.763 | −0.004 | −0.074 |
| (Less than high school graduate) | | | | |
| Need factor | | | | |
| Self-rated health status | −0.069 | −1.408 | −0.129*** | −7.013 |
| Number of medical conditions | 0.017 | 0.402 | 0.086*** | 4.895 |
| Basic ADLs difficulty | 0.056 | 0.465 | −0.053 | −1.156 |
| Household ADLs difficulty | 0.364** | 3.038 | 0.053 | 1.081 |
| Advanced ADLs difficulty | −0.120 | −1.053 | 0.015 | 0.328 |
| Lower-body disability | 0.060 | 0.438 | 0.052 | 1.128 |
| Upper-body disability | −0.059 | −0.442 | 0.114* | 2.003 |
| Enabling factor | | | | |
| Private health insurance | −0.023 | −0.199 | −0.013 | −0.304 |
| Medicaid | −0.235* | −1.988 | 0.221*** | 4.488 |
| Poverty ratio | −0.214 | −1.310 | −0.037 | −0.605 |
| N | 378 | | 1,280 | |
| $R^2$ | 0.096 | | 0.176 | |
| F | 2.255** | | 15.875*** | |

Note: Reference groups are in parentheses.
*$p < .05$. **$p < .01$. ***$p < .001$.

(Table 9-5). Using the equations suggested by Halvorsen and Palmquist (1980), we calculated that African American men who had Medicaid coverage had 51 percent fewer hospital nights than those who were not covered by Medicaid; African American women who had Medicaid coverage made 19.5 percent more physician visits, and white women who had Medicaid coverage made 40.0 percent more physician visits, other things being equal.

## Discussion

Although Medicare provides almost universal health insurance coverage for elderly people in the United States, its beneficiaries are required to pay copayments and deductibles out-of-pocket for the health services they receive. Over the years, elderly people have spent an increasingly higher percentage of their family incomes on these out-of-pocket medical expenses (Moon & Mulvey, 1996). Some of them may now find it difficult to afford the health services they need. As a result, many elderly people supplement their Medicare coverage by private health insurance, so that their lives may not be ruined by unexpected high medical expenditures. For low-income elderly people, Medicaid provides a safety net because it pays for the premium, copayments, and deductibles

**TABLE 9-4. Results of Logistic Regression on the Probability of Using Three Health Services by Low-Income Elderly People, by Race and Gender**

| Variable | Home Health Services Coefficient | Home Health Services Odds Ratio | Physician Visits Coefficient | Physician Visits Odds Ratio | Hospital Services Coefficient | Hospital Services Odds Ratio |
|---|---|---|---|---|---|---|
| Intercept | −3.929*** | | −0.707 | | −0.384 | |
| Predisposing factor | | | | | | |
| Age | 0.012 | 1.012 | 0.016 | 1.016 | −0.021+ | 0.980 |
| African American | −0.177 | 0.838 | 0.603* | 1.828 | −0.242 | 0.785 |
| Hispanic | −0.256 | 0.774 | 0.565 | 1.760 | −0.580+ | 0.560 |
| (White) Male | 0.191 | 1.211 | −0.342 | 0.711 | 0.302+ | 1.353 |
| Widow | 0.141 | 1.152 | 0.123 | 1.131 | 0.260+ | 1.297 |
| High school graduate | 0.113 | 1.119 | 0.447* | 1.563 | −0.175 | 0.839 |
| At least some college | 0.025 | 1.026 | 0.730* | 2.076 | 0.343 | 1.409 |
| (Less than high school graduate) | | | | | | |
| Need factor | | | | | | |
| Self-rated health status | −0.117 | 0.889 | −0.109 | 0.896 | −0.226** | 0.798 |
| Number of medical conditions | 0.253*** | 1.287 | 0.679*** | 1.971 | 0.330*** | 1.391 |
| Basic ADLs difficulty | 0.491* | 1.634 | 0.424* | 1.528 | 0.434** | 1.544 |
| Household ADLs difficulty | 1.029*** | 2.797 | 0.055 | 1.056 | 0.412* | 1.510 |
| Advanced ADLs difficulty | 0.445* | 1.561 | −0.151 | 0.860 | −0.089 | 0.915 |
| Lower-body disability | 0.233 | 1.263 | 0.037 | 1.038 | −0.037 | 0.964 |
| Upper-body disability | 0.092 | 1.097 | 0.687 | 1.988 | 0.076 | 1.079 |
| Enabling factor | | | | | | |
| Private health insurance | −0.127 | 0.881 | 0.633** | 1.883 | 0.209 | 1.233 |
| Medicaid coverage | | | | | | |
| African American men | 1.157 | 3.181 | 0.312 | 1.366 | 1.059 | 2.884 |
| African American women | 0.895** | 2.447 | 0.952 | 2.591 | 0.448 | 1.566 |
| White men | 0.494 | 1.639 | −0.036 | 0.965 | 0.745 | 2.106 |
| White women | 0.416 | 1.516 | 0.756 | 2.130 | 0.736** | 2.088 |
| Hispanic men | 1.424* | 4.152 | 1.760 | 5.814 | 1.483** | 4.406 |
| Hispanic women | 0.818 | 2.266 | 0.310 | 1.363 | 0.728 | 2.070 |
| (Without Medicaid coverage) | | | | | | |
| Poverty ratio | −0.072 | 0.931 | 0.129 | 1.138 | 0.367 | 1.443 |
| | | | | | | |
| N | 1,514 | | 1,513 | | 1,515 | |
| Model $\chi^2$ (df = 22) | 243.740*** | | 148.473*** | | 196.001*** | |

*Note:* Reference groups are in parentheses.
*$p < .05$. **$p < .01$. ***$p < .001$.

of Medicare. In other words, it improves the affordability of health services for low-income elderly people.

This study examined the effect of Medicaid coverage on use of health services by low-income elderly people and how it varied by their race, ethnicity, and gender. We found that Medicaid coverage did associate positively with the use of health services by low-income elderly people. Those who had

Medicaid coverage were 1.9 to 2.1 times more likely to use health services, other things being equal. Medicaid coverage was also associated with fewer hospital nights and more physician visits among those who used hospital services and those who made at least one physician visit, respectively. These results from low-income elderly people were consistent with findings from elderly people in general in earlier studies. It is clear that Med-

**TABLE 9-5. Results of OLS Regression on the Volume of Health Services Used by Low-Income Elderly People, by Race, Gender, and Education**

| Variable | Hospital Services | | Physician Services | |
|---|---|---|---|---|
| | Coefficient | t | Coefficient | t |
| Intercept | 3.039*** | 4.473 | 1.995*** | 7.545 |
| Predisposing factor | | | | |
| Age | −0.012 | −1.370 | −0.003 | −0.806 |
| African American | 0.133 | 0.922 | 0.082 | 1.589 |
| Hispanic | 0.218 | 0.821 | 0.168* | 2.069 |
| (White) Male | 0.243 | 1.809 | −0.020 | −0.399 |
| Widow | 0.142 | 1.310 | 0.048 | 1.182 |
| High school graduate | −0.261* | −2.008 | 0.016 | 0.331 |
| At least some college | −0.274 | −1.801 | −0.008 | −0.136 |
| (Less than high school graduate) | | | | |
| Need factor | | | | |
| Self-rated health status | −0.071 | −1.441 | −0.127*** | −6.908 |
| Number of medical conditions | 0.025 | 0.600 | −0.086*** | 4.843 |
| Basic ADLs difficulty | 0.036 | 0.299 | 0.056 | −1.209 |
| Household ADLs difficulty | 0.365** | 3.010 | 0.049 | 1.004 |
| Advanced ADLs difficulty | −0.133 | −1.159 | 0.016 | 0.347 |
| Lower-body disability | 0.065 | 0.478 | 0.055 | 1.184 |
| Upper-body disability | −.059 | −0.440 | 0.112* | 1.967 |
| Enabling factor | | | | |
| Medigap | 0.015 | 0.127 | 0.000 | −0.001 |
| Medicaid coverage | | | | |
| African American men | −0.714* | −2.148 | −0.015 | −0.085 |
| African American women | −0.284 | −1.243 | 0.178* | 2.126 |
| White men | −0.333 | −0.967 | 0.181 | 1.020 |
| White women | −0.033 | −0.206 | 0.322*** | 4.341 |
| Hispanic men | −0.339 | −0.879 | 0.139 | 0.861 |
| Hispanic women | −0.603 | −1.799 | 0.192 | 1.644 |
| (Without Medicaid coverage) | | | | |
| Poverty ratio (log) | −0.234 | −1.412 | −0.038 | −0.619 |
| N | 378 | | 1,281 | |
| $R^2$ | 0.110 | | 0.179 | |
| F | 1.998** | | 12.451*** | |

Note: Reference groups are in parentheses.
*p < .05. **p < .01. ***p < .001.

icaid coverage did make health services more affordable to low-income elderly people. However, improving affordability and use of health services are only intermediate goals toward the final goal of improving health outcomes. Future studies should address the effect of Medicaid coverage on the health outcomes of low-income elderly people.

Although Medicaid coverage improves affordability and use of health services for low-income elderly people, this study found that its effect varied by their race, ethnicity, and gender. Medicaid coverage was positively associated with the probability of using home health services for African American women and Hispanic men, but not for African American men, white men, white women, and Hispanic women. It was also positively associated with the probability of using hospital services for white women and Hispanic men, but not for the other four groups. Among those who used hospital services, Medicaid coverage was associated with fewer hospital nights for African American men, but not for the other five groups. Among those who made visits to a physician, Medicaid coverage was associated with more physician visits for African American women and white women.

Although we showed that the effect of Medicaid on use of health services varied by race, ethnicity, and gender of respondents, this study did not provide answers to why such differences exist. One possible explanation is that some low-income elderly people may have seen Medicaid as an inferior health insurance and were reluctant to use it. Another possible explanation is that some elderly Medicaid recipients may be reluctant to use health services because of the stigma attached to welfare recipients. Future studies need to focus on the mechanism behind the differential effects of Medicaid coverage. It is also unknown why African American men who were covered by Medicaid had fewer hospital nights than those who were not covered by Medicaid. Was the hospital system pushing them out quicker than other patients who were not Medicaid recipients? We do not know why a pushing-through effect like this may affect only male African American Medicaid recipients, but not Medicaid recipients in other racial and gender groups. More studies are needed before we can explain the cause of such differences more precisely.

Like many earlier studies using the behavioral model, the $R^2$s of OLS regressions in this study were low. It seems that the behavioral model does not explain much of the variance in volume of health services used, possibly because only individual characteristics were included in the model. The latest revision of the behavior model (Andersen, 1995) did include factors related to the health services delivery system. However, the AHEAD data we used did not contain information on the health services delivery system. This is one of the major limitations of using secondary data, because researchers usually have little control over research design and data collection procedures. Future research should address this problem more adequately by collecting more detailed information on the characteristics of health care providers and the delivery system.

## Conclusion

Since its inception more than 30 years ago, the Medicare program has focused exclusively on acute care. There is no coverage for prescription drugs or long-term care. Although during the past three decades, the health care needs of elderly people have shifted from acute care to maintenance health care for chronic conditions, the Medicare benefit package remains almost unchanged. As a result, Medicare now pays for a lesser share of the total health care expenditures of its beneficiaries. In other words, elderly people now pay more out-of-pocket expenses for their health care than they did 30 years ago (Moon & Mulvey, 1996; National Academy of Social Insurance, 1997). The mismatch of the Medicare benefit package and the health care needs of elderly people have led to a booming market of private supplemental health insurance. Although low-income elderly people who cannot afford the private supplemental health insurance have Medicaid as their last resort, the findings of this study show that Medicaid does not work equally well in improving affordability and use of health services among different racial, ethnic, and gender groups. As the number of older Americans increases rapidly, this population will also become more racially and ethnically diverse (U.S. Bureau of the Census, 1996), so providing affordable health insurance coverage and health services for low-income elderly people has become a pressing challenge for policymakers. Higher priority should be given to restructuring and integrating the benefit packages of both Medicare and Medicaid so that they can provide better health care to low-income elderly people. Knowledge about the differential effect of Medicaid coverage by race, ethnicity, and gender is essential for policymakers to restructure and integrate the Medicare and Medicaid benefit packages for this growing population.

## References

Andersen, R. M. (1968). *A behavioral model of families' use of health services*. Chicago: Center for Health Administration Studies.

Andersen, R. M. (1995). Revisiting the behavioral model and access to medical care: Does it matter? *Journal of Health and Social Behavior, 36*, 1–10.

Andersen, R. M., & Newman, J. F. (1973). Societal and individual determinants of medical care utilization in the United States. *The Milbank Quarterly, 51*, 95–124.

Coulton, C., & Frost, A. K. (1982). Use of social and health services by the elderly. *Journal of Health and Social Behavior, 23*, 330–339.

Ellencweig, A. Y., & Pagliccia, N. (1994). Utilization patterns of cohorts of elderly clients: A structural equations model. *Health Services Research, 29*, 225–245.

Escarce, J. J., Epstein, K. R., Colby, D. C., & Schwartz, J. S. (1993). Racial differences in the elderly's use of medical procedures and diagnostic tests. *American Journal of Public Health, 83*, 948–954.

Gerontological Society of America. (1997). Asset and Health Dynamics among the Oldest Old (AHEAD): Initial results from the longitudinal study. *Journal of Gerontology, Series B: Psychological and Social Sciences, 52B*(Special issue).

Goldberg, K. C., Hartz, A. J., Jacobsen, S. J., Krakauer, H., & Rimm, A. A. (1992). Racial and community factors influencing coronary artery bypass graft surgery rates for all 1986 Medicare patients. *JAMA, 267*, 1463–1477.

Halvorsen, R., & Palmquist, R. (1980). The interpretation of dummy variables in semilogarithmic equations. *American Economic Review, 70*, 474–475.

Hansell, S., Sherman, G., & Mechanic, D. (1991). Body awareness and medical care utilization among older adults in HMO. *Journal of Gerontology: Social Sciences, 46*, S151–S159.

Health Care Financing Administration. (1996). *Health Care Financing Review: Medicare and Medicaid statistical supplement, 1996*. Washington, DC: U.S. Government Printing Office.

Johnson, R. J., & Wolinsky, F. D. (1993). The structure of health status among older adults: Disease, disability, functional limitation, and perceived health. *Journal of Health and Social Behavior, 34*, 105–121.

Johnson, R. J., & Wolinsky, F. D. (1994). Gender, race, and health: The structure of health status among older adults. *Gerontologist, 34*, 24–35.

Levkoff, S. E., Cleary, P. D., & Wetle, T. (1987). Differences in determinants of physician use between aged and middle aged persons. *Medical Care, 25*, 1148–1160.

Lum, Y. S., Chang, H. J., & Ozawa, M. N. (1997). *The effect of race and ethnicity on the use of health services by older Americans*. Unpublished manuscript, Washington University, St. Louis.

Manning, W. G., Morris, C., N., Newhouse, J. P., Orr, L. L., Duan, N., Keerler, E. B., Leibowitz, A., Marquis, K. H., Marquis, M. S., & Phelps, C. E. (1981). A two-part model of the demand for medical care: Preliminary results from the Health Insurance Study. In J. van der Gaag & M. Perlman (Eds.), *Health, economics, and health economics* (pp. 103–123). New York: North-Holland.

Miller, B., Campbell, R. T., Davis, L., Furner, S., Giachello, A., Prohaska, T., Kaufman, J. E., Li, M., & Perez, C. (1996). Minority use of community long-term care services: A comparative analysis. *Journal of Gerontology: Social Sciences, 51B*, S70–S81.

Miner, S. (1995). Racial differences in family support and formal service utilization among older persons: A nonrecursive model. *Journal of Gerontology: Social Sciences, 50B*, S143–S153.

Moon, M., & Mulvey, J. (1996). *Entitlements and the elderly: Protecting promises, recognizing reality.* Washington, DC: Urban Institute Press.

National Academy of Social Insurance. (1997). *Securing Medicare's future: What are the issues?* Washington, DC: Author.

Nelson, M. A. (1993). Race, gender, and the effect of social supports on the use of health services by elderly individuals. *International Journal of Aging and Human Development, 37*, 227–246.

Strain, L. A. (1991). Use of health services in later life: The influence of health beliefs. *Journal of Gerontology: Social Sciences, 46B*, S143–S150.

Stump, T. E., Johnson, R. J., & Wolinsky, F. D. (1995). Changes in physician utilization over time among older adults. *Journal of Gerontology: Social Sciences, 50B*, S45–S58.

U.S. Bureau of the Census. (1996). *65+ in the United States* (Current Population Reports, Special Studies, P23-109). Washington, DC: U.S. Government Printing Office.

University of Michigan Survey Research Center. (1994). *Codebook: Assets and Health Dynamic among the Oldest Old (AHEAD).* Ann Arbor: University of Michigan.

Wan, T. T. H. (1989). The behavioral model of health care utilization by older people. In M. Ory & K. Bond (Eds.), *Aging and the use of formal health services* (pp. 52–77). New York: Routledge.

Wan, T., & Odell, B. (1981). Factors affecting the use of social and health services for the elderly. *Aging and Society, 1*, 95–115.

Wolinsky, F. D. (1994). Health services utilization among older adults: Conceptual, measurement, and modeling issues in secondary analysis. *Gerontologist, 34*, 470–475.

Wolinsky, F. D., & Arnold, C. L. (1988). A different perspective on health and health services utilization. *Annual Review of Gerontology and Geriatrics, 8*, 71–101.

Wolinsky, F. D., & Coe, R. M. (1984). Physician and hospital utilization among noninstitutionalized elderly adults: An analysis of the Health Interview Survey. *Journal of Gerontology, 39*, 334–341.

Wolinsky, F. D., & Johnson, R. J. (1991). The use of health services by older adults. *Journal of Gerontology: Social Sciences, 46B*, S345–S357.

Wolinsky, F. D., Miller, D. K., Prendergast, J. M., Creel, M. J., & Chávez, M. N. (1983). Health services utilization among the noninstitutionalized elderly. *Journal of Health and Social Behavior, 24*, 325–337.

Wolinsky, F. D., Mosely, R. R., II, & Coe, R. M. (1986). A cohort analysis of the use of health services by elderly Americans. *Journal of Health and Social Behavior, 27*, 209–219.

Wolinsky, F. D., Stump, T. E., & Johnson, R. J. (1995). Hospital utilization profiles among older adults over time: Consistency and volume among survivors and decedents. *Journal of Gerontology: Social Sciences, 50B*, S88–S100.

This chapter was originally published in the March 1998 issue of *Social Work Research*, Vol. 22, Number 1, pp. 31–43.

# 10

# Use of Health and Human Services by Community-Residing People with Dementia

RONALD W. TOSELAND, PHILIP MCCALLION,
TODD GERBER, CAROLINE DAWSON,
SUSAN GIERYIC, and VINCENT GUILAMO-RAMOS

It was projected that there would be 2.3 to 5.8 million older people with Alzheimer's disease and other dementias residing in community settings in the United States by 2000 (Brookmeyer, Gray, & Kawas, 1998; Evans et al., 1990; Khachaturian & Radebaugh, 1996). The number of people with Alzheimer's disease alone is expected to quadruple by 2050, at which time it will affect one in 45 Americans (Brookmeyer et al.). When family members are available, they provide most of the support and supervision needed by cognitively impaired older adults (Gwyther, 1996). But many community-dwelling cognitively impaired older adults need support and assistance from health and social services agencies because they do not have family caregivers. Also, as dementia progresses, professional health and human services often are needed to supplement and support the care provided by family members.

Many social workers already play a vital role in meeting the biopsychosocial needs of community-residing people with dementia. Because social workers work in an array of public, private, and voluntary health and human services agencies, they serve in intake, assessment, and intervention capacities. For example, hospital and nursing home social workers frequently work with caregivers when a crisis occurs and when increasing care needs exceed caregivers' capacity. Similarly, social workers in family services agencies and employee assistance programs often are called on to work with caregivers of people with dementia. Although some social workers have played an important part in the development of services and service options for people with dementia and their families, there is increasing concern that not enough social workers are involved in these efforts. Indeed, many social workers report a need for more knowledge and skills in aging services (Klein, 1996; Peterson & Wendt, 1990). With support from the John A. Hartford Foundation, several organizations recently undertook initiatives for faculty, field education, and curriculum development to respond to these needs and to encourage social work leadership (O'Neill, 1999). Consistent with these initiatives, the present study was undertaken to develop a more complete picture of services use by people with dementia and their family caregivers and to explore areas for additional social work intervention.

Although there is a growing body of literature on the use of formal health and human services by community-residing, cognitively impaired older adults and their family caregivers, a review of the literature for this study failed to yield a comprehensive picture of services use. Most of the studies that have been conducted have asked caregivers about their use of particular services, such as home care or respite care (Adler, Kuskowski, & Mortimer, 1995; Cotrell, 1996; Cox, 1997; Gill, Hinrichsen, & DiGiuseppe, 1998; Ginther, Webber, Fox, & Miller, 1993; Gonyea & Silverstein, 1991; Kosloski & Montgomery, 1992; Penning, 1995). The majority of these studies conclude that there is a need for services but that they are used little. Other studies have examined a range of health and human services, but these were designed to identify factors that predict services use rather than to provide a comprehensive picture of services use (Bass, Looman, & Ehrlich, 1992; Biegel, Bass, Schulz, & Morycz, 1993; Buckwalter, Russell, & Hall, 1994; Caserta, Lund, Wright, & Redburn, 1987; Cox, 1993; Ferran, Wilson, & Doran, 1996; Gill et al., 1998; Gonyea & Silverstein, 1991; Hinrichsen & Ramirez, 1992; Mullan, 1993; Wenger, 1994).

To serve as effective care coordinators and information and referral agents and to take a greater role in designing and delivering services, social workers need to know more about the services use patterns and needs of older adults with dementia. This article is the first in a planned series of reports analyzing data on services use among a random sample of dementia patients and their caregivers drawn from a dementia registry with reporting requirements mandated by New York state law.

## Method

### Participants

A random sample of primary caregivers of community-residing people with dementia was obtained from 1995, 1996, and 1997 reports to the New York State Alzheimer Disease and Other Dementias Registry (NYSADODR). NYSADODR is the oldest state registry and has a number of strengths that make it ideal for this study. The full range of dementias and all stages of dementia are represented in the database. The NYSADODR is ethnically, racially, and demographically diverse. Because reporting to the registry is mandatory, the likelihood of underreporting by physicians and other reporters is reduced (Macera, Still, Brandes, Abramson, & Davis, 1991).

We used a multistage process for compiling the sample. First, a series of filters were applied to the reports to remove individuals known to be deceased or residing in nursing homes, hospitals, or out of state. Second, a random sample of reports was selected, and reporters were contacted by mail to determine whether they had any objection to the New York State Department of Health (NYSDOH) contacting the next-of-kin listed in the registry report and to answer any questions about the study. Third, NYSDOH staff contacted next-of-kin and asked whether they were primary caregivers; if they were, staff obtained informed consent. Fourth, consenting caregivers' names were forwarded to staff of the Ringel Institute, who were trained to conduct the interviews. To protect privacy, however, care recipient-identifying data were kept confidential and not released.

A random sample of 785 primary caregivers of community-residing individuals with dementia were identified and screened by NYSDOH staff, and their names and telephone numbers were given to the research interviewers. Telephone interviews were conducted with a total of 608 of these individuals, a response rate of 77.5 percent. Of the nonrespondents, 106 declined to be interviewed, 44 missed three or more scheduled interviews, 20 could not be located, and seven were too ill to be interviewed.

### Interviews and Instrument

Primary caregivers who agreed to participate were sent a letter introducing the study, as well as a copy of the telephone interview protocol. Interviews were conducted by telephone by trained interviewers. Interviews took from 45 to 90 minutes to complete. Because of the length of the interview and the health status of some of the primary caregivers, they were given the option of completing the interview in one or more telephone contacts.

*Services Use Variables.* The survey instrument included a comprehensive list of 33 health and human services that had been identified in earlier studies as potentially useful to individuals caring for older people in community settings (Toseland, 1990; Toseland et al., 1996). Written definitions for each type of service were developed for use by telephone interviewers. Services use was measured by current services use—that is, whether services were used during the past year; future services use—that is, whether the caregiver thought they would use services in the next year; the frequency of services use; and the duration of services use. Data also were collected about caregivers' attitudes toward the need for services, satisfaction with services use, and barriers to services use.

*Demographic Variables.* Demographic characteristics of the caregivers were collected during the telephone interviews, and data on the demographic characteristics of care recipients were obtained from registry reports.

*Caregiving Variables.* Data were collected on the nature of the caregiver-to-care recipient relationship, on whether the caregiver and care recipient shared the same household, on the duration of caregiving, and on the amount and type of care provided by the primary caregiver and by other household members. Caregiver burden also was assessed by using the Screen for Caregiver Burden (SCB) (Vitaliano, Maiuro, Ochs, & Russo, 1989; Vitaliano, Russo, Young, Becker, & Maiuro, 1991), a 25-item scale that assesses objective and subjective burden on five-point Likert scales that range from 0 = did not occur to 4 = severe distress. The SCB has good reliability and validity.

*Health and Functional Status Variables.*
Caregivers were asked how long care recipients had had symptoms of dementia. They also were asked to assess care recipients' stage of dementia by using the Global Deterioration Scale (Reisberg, 1985), an assessment tool that enables trained interviewers to assess dementia in terms of seven functional assessment stages that range from very mild cognitive decline to very severe cognitive decline. The scale has good reliability and validity (Gottlieb, Gur, & Gur, 1988; Reisberg, Ferris, deLeon, & Crook, 1982). The functional status of the care recipients also was assessed using seven items from the Physical Activities of Daily Living section of the multidimensional Older Americans Research and Services Center Instrument (Fillenbaum, 1978), which has well established reliability and validity. Caregivers also were asked to rate their own health status, the effect of their health status on caregiving, and the effect of caregiving on their health status.

*Other Variables.* Care recipients' problem behaviors were assessed by using three broad behavior categories underlying the Cohen-Mansfield Agitation Inventory (CMAI) (Cohen-Mansfield, Marx, & Rosenthal, 1989): physically aggressive behaviors, physically nonaggressive behaviors, and verbally aggressive behaviors. Caregivers were asked how often the care recipient exhibited each group of behaviors on six-point Likert-type scales that ranged from 1 = never to 6 = several times an hour. Caregivers were asked to indicate whether the care recipient lived in an urban, suburban, or rural area and whether they used public or private transportation services to help the care recipient get to medical and social services appointments. Caregivers also were asked about the care recipients' health care insurance coverage.

## Results

Demographic data are presented about the primary caregivers who responded to the telephone survey and the care recipients suffering from dementia (Table 10-1). Our data show that caregiving was very demanding for study respondents. The average caregiver in the study had been providing care for more than five years and offered an average of 46 hours of personal care and a variety of other types of assistance each week. More than 68 percent of the respondents lived with the care recipient, and more than 14 percent were caring for another disabled family member. More than 28 percent of respondents reported that their health was fair or poor, 51 percent reported that health limitations affected their ability to provide care, and 25 percent of respondents reported that caregiving had a negative effect on their own health. Results from the CMAI indicated that almost 25 percent of care recipients had exhibited physically aggressive behaviors such as hitting, 50 percent had exhibited physically nonaggressive behaviors such as wandering, and 57 percent had exhibited verbally aggressive behaviors such as yelling. It is not surprising, therefore, that respondents also reported very high levels of objective ($M = 10.4$; $SD = 4.8$) and subjective burden ($M = 39.1$; $SD = 11.6$) on the SCB (Vitaliano et al., 1991; personal communication with P. Vitaliano, 1998). In fact, Vitaliano et al. indicated that a total SCB score—that is, adding subjective and objective burden of "42 is quite high for caregivers of both age groups (that is, those under and over age 65)" (p. 80). Thus, the mean SCB score of $M = 49.5$ for this study sample indicates a very high burden level.

Although not shown in Table 10-1, data indicate that female care recipients were

**TABLE 10-1. Selected Characteristics of Study Participants (N = 785)**

| Variable | Caregiver | | Care Recipient | | Registry Data | |
|---|---|---|---|---|---|---|
| | n | % | n | % | n | % |
| Gender | | | | | | |
| Female | 443 | 73.0 | 362 | 59.5 | 14,327 | 64.0 |
| Male | 165 | 27.0 | 246 | 40.5 | 8044 | 36.0 |
| Race or ethnicity | | | | | | |
| White | 525 | 86.3 | 531 | 87.3 | 18,847 | 84.2 |
| Black | 52 | 8.6 | 53 | 8.7 | 2080 | 9.3 |
| Hispanic | 20 | 3.3 | 5 | .8 | 1051 | 4.7 |
| Other | 11 | 1.8 | 19 | 3.1 | 377 | 1.7 |
| Marital status | | | | | | |
| Married | 459 | 75.5 | 276 | 45.4 | 6234 | 27.9 |
| Single | 58 | 9.5 | 36 | 5.9 | 3163 | 14.1 |
| Divorced or separated | 50 | 8.3 | 32 | 5.3 | 2447 | 10.9 |
| Widowed | 41 | 6.7 | 264 | 43.4 | 10,527 | 47.1 |
| Education | | | | | | |
| Some high school | 64 | 10.5 | 246 | 40.7 | | |
| High school degree | 169 | 27.8 | 197 | 32.6 | | |
| Some college | 158 | 26.0 | 60 | 9.9 | | |
| College graduate | 217 | 35.7 | 102 | 16.9 | | |
| Relationship | | | | | | |
| Spouse | 225 | 37.0 | | | | |
| Adult child | 300 | 49.3 | | | | |
| Other | 83 | 13.7 | | | | |
| Global Deterioration Scale | | | | | | |
| Mild (1–3) | | | 124 | 20.4 | | |
| Moderate (4–5) | | | 292 | 48.0 | | |
| Severe (6–7) | | | 192 | 31.6 | | |

| | M | SD | M | SD | M | SD |
|---|---|---|---|---|---|---|
| Age | 60.6 | 13.3 | 78.1 | 10.0 | 80.7 | 11.3 |
| Duration of symptoms (months) | 62.8 | 56.8 | | | | |

*Note:* For education of care recipients (n = 605), three caregivers could not assess the amount of education of the care recipient.

much more likely than male care recipients to be cared for by adult children (64.1 percent compared with 24.8 percent), whereas male care recipients were much more likely than female care recipients to be cared for by a spouse (62.6 percent compared with 19.1 percent). Because men do not live as long as women, they are likely to be cared for by their wives, but widows are more likely to be cared for by an adult child, who is usually a woman (78 percent). Data based on all reports to the registry during 1996 suggest that, with the exception of more married people and fewer Hispanic individuals, the random sample obtained for this study was representative of the entire registry population. Data from two national studies (Marks, 1996; National Alliance for Caregiving and the American Association of Retired Persons [AARP], 1997) also suggest that the sample in this study is representative of people providing care to those with chronic illnesses.

## Use of Services and Projections for Future Use

The most frequently used health services were outpatient and inpatient health care, home health aides, and visiting nurse services. As can be seen in Table 10-2, these services were used by a high percentage of respondents. Overall, respondents indicated that care recipients currently were using an average of 3.2 health services. Frequency and

**TABLE 10-2. Use of Health and Human Services**

| Type of Service | Current Use (%) | Future Use (%) |
|---|---|---|
| Health | | |
| Outpatient health | 81.1 | 83.1 |
| Inpatient health | 47.9 | 37.0 |
| Home health aide | 46.7 | 57.2 |
| Visiting nurse | 45.7 | 44.2 |
| Emergency response systems | 36.7 | 35.0 |
| Outpatient mental health care | 18.1 | 21.1 |
| Alzheimer's Disease Asst. Center | 7.9 | 27.3 |
| Personal medical alert system | 7.7 | 18.6 |
| Inpatient mental health care | 4.1 | 7.9 |
| Nursing home | 3.9 | 22.9 |
| Human | | |
| Homemaker | 35.4 | 46.1 |
| Legal | 31.3 | 35.7 |
| Information and referral | 30.8 | 48.4 |
| Church, mosque, or synagogue | 28.3 | 34.0 |
| Home modification assistance | 23.8 | 33.1 |
| Library | 23.8 | 36.5 |
| Transportation | 22.7 | 33.7 |
| Alzheimer's Association | 20.2 | 45.6 |
| In-home respite | 19.2 | 43.5 |
| Agency on aging | 16.9 | 33.2 |
| Adult day care | 15.5 | 26.2 |
| Senior center | 15.5 | 22.0 |
| Financial assistance | 15.3 | 28.0 |
| Meals on wheels | 13.8 | 19.1 |
| Individual counseling | 13.7 | 25.3 |
| Educational programs | 12.2 | 34.2 |
| Support group | 12.2 | 33.2 |
| Recreation | 8.2 | 20.9 |
| Home energy assistance | 6.1 | 17.1 |
| Out-of-home respite | 5.8 | 23.0 |
| Telephone reassurance | 4.8 | 16.4 |
| Family counseling | 3.5 | 13.0 |
| Caregiver resource center | 3.3 | 28.0 |
| Other health and human services | 5.9 | 17.8 |

duration of use of health services also was quite high. For example, the 47 percent of the sample respondents who reported using home health aides indicated that they had been using this service for an average of 27.2 months and an average of 5.2 days per week. As might be expected for a community sample, however, some health care services, such as nursing homes and inpatient mental health, were used infrequently.

With regard to human services, homemaker, legal, information and referral, and caregiver support offered by churches, mosques, and synagogues were used by more than 25 percent of the respondents. Overall, respondents indicated that care recipients currently were using an average of 3.7 human services. Frequency and duration of use of human services programs also was quite high. For example, the 35 percent of the sample that reported using homemaker services indicated that it had been using the service for an average of 44.4 months and an average of 4.3 times per week. In contrast, Caregiver Resource Center, family counseling, and telephone reassurance programs were used by less than 5 percent of the sample.

With the exception of inpatient health care, caregivers consistently projected that they would use more services in the next year (Table 10-2). In fact, for 16 of the 33 services categories, more than twice as many respondents indicated that they would use a service during the next year. Some of the services projected to have the largest increases in use included nursing home, out-of-home respite, family counseling, telephone reassurance, educational programs, support group programs, and two programs unique to New York State, Caregiver Resource Centers and Alzheimer's Disease Assistance Centers.

Caregivers also were asked whether they currently were using other health or human services and what other services they might use in the future. Caregivers mentioned many different types of services, including tax relief programs, podiatry services, hospice care, laboratory services, adult homes, and volunteers.

### Satisfaction with Services

Caregivers expressed a high level of satisfaction with the services they used during the past year (Table 10-3). It is noteworthy, however, that services that were used infrequently tended to receive lower satisfaction ratings. For example, out-of-home respite was used infrequently, and almost 20 percent of those who used the service expressed at least some dissatisfaction. Similarly, inpatient mental health care, nursing home care, Caregiver Resource Centers, and family counseling were used infrequently, and when they were used, these services received lower satisfac-

**TABLE 10-3. Satisfaction with Health and Human Services**

| | | % | | | |
|---|---|---|---|---|---|
| Type of Service | n | Very Satisfied | Somewhat Satisfied | Somewhat Dissatisfied | Very Dissatisfied |
| Health | | | | | |
| Emergency response system | 217 | 84.8 | 12.9 | .5 | 1.8 |
| Personal medical alert system | 47 | 76.6 | 12.8 | 8.5 | 2.1 |
| Visiting nurse | 277 | 74.4 | 19.5 | 4.7 | 1.4 |
| Outpatient health care | 490 | 72.7 | 21.6 | 4.7 | 1.0 |
| Home health aide | 283 | 69.3 | 25.4 | 4.2 | 1.1 |
| Nursing home | 24 | 62.5 | 16.7 | 8.3 | 12.5 |
| Alzheimer's Disease Asst. Center | 47 | 61.7 | 27.7 | 4.3 | 6.4 |
| Inpatient health care | 289 | 56.1 | 29.8 | 8.3 | 5.9 |
| Outpatient mental health care | 110 | 51.8 | 33.6 | 8.2 | 6.4 |
| Inpatient mental health care | 25 | 40.0 | 32.0 | 20.0 | 8.0 |
| Human | | | | | |
| Telephone reassurance | 29 | 89.7 | 10.3 | 0.0 | 0.0 |
| Home modification assistance | 145 | 86.2 | 12.4 | .7 | .7 |
| Church, mosque, or synagogue | 172 | 84.9 | 10.5 | 2.3 | 2.3 |
| Recreation program | 49 | 81.6 | 14.3 | 4.1 | 0.0 |
| Homemaker | 214 | 76.6 | 18.7 | 4.2 | .5 |
| Library | 145 | 75.2 | 22.1 | 1.4 | 1.4 |
| Adult day care | 90 | 74.4 | 18.9 | 4.4 | 2.2 |
| Education program | 74 | 74.3 | 17.6 | 4.1 | 4.1 |
| Legal | 190 | 72.6 | 21.6 | 3.7 | 2.1 |
| Meals on wheels | 84 | 72.6 | 17.9 | 6.0 | 3.6 |
| Home energy assistance | 37 | 70.3 | 21.6 | 8.1 | 0.0 |
| Transportation | 138 | 69.6 | 25.4 | 4.3 | .7 |
| Senior centers | 93 | 72.0 | 23.7 | 3.2 | 1.1 |
| Support group | 74 | 68.9 | 17.6 | 6.8 | 6.8 |
| In-home respite | 117 | 68.4 | 25.6 | 3.4 | 2.6 |
| Individual counseling | 83 | 65.1 | 22.9 | 8.4 | 3.6 |
| Alzheimer's Association | 123 | 65.0 | 26.0 | 4.1 | 4.9 |
| Agency on aging | 103 | 60.2 | 24.3 | 5.8 | 9.7 |
| Out-of-home respite | 35 | 60.0 | 20.0 | 11.4 | 8.6 |
| Family counseling | 21 | 57.1 | 28.6 | 4.8 | 9.5 |
| Financial assistance | 93 | 57.0 | 32.3 | 9.7 | 1.1 |
| Information and referral | 187 | 56.1 | 34.2 | 6.4 | 3.2 |
| Caregiver resource center | 20 | 50.0 | 30.0 | 5.0 | 15.0 |
| Other health and human services | 35 | 85.7 | 11.4 | 2.9 | 0.0 |

tion ratings than most of the services that were used more frequently.

## Need for Services

At first, it appears that there is relatively little need for particular services that currently were not being used (Table 10-4). Out-of-home respite, in-home respite, adult day care, and Alzheimer's Association services received the highest need scores, but only about 10 percent of those who did not use these services expressed a high need for them. These data, however, may be somewhat misleading. For example, 73 percent of the sample respondents said that they had a need for at least one additional service. Of those that expressed a high need, 49 percent expressed a need for one service, 26 percent expressed a need for two or three services, and 30 percent expressed a need for four services or more. Also, in response to the question,

**TABLE 10-4. Need for Health and Human Services**

| Type of Service | n | % | | | |
|---|---|---|---|---|---|
| | | *High* | *Moderate* | *Low* | *None* |
| Health | | | | | |
| Home health aide | 324 | 9.0 | 13.3 | 14.5 | 63.3 |
| Nursing home | 584 | 7.9 | 8.9 | 15.9 | 67.3 |
| Alzheimer's Disease Asst. Center | 561 | 7.5 | 13.5 | 20.1 | 58.8 |
| Emergency response system | 385 | 6.8 | 13.0 | 18.2 | 62.1 |
| Visiting nurse | 330 | 5.8 | 7.9 | 16.1 | 70.3 |
| Personal medical alert system | 560 | 4.3 | 8.4 | 14.3 | 73.0 |
| Outpatient mental health care | 498 | 3.4 | 7.2 | 14.9 | 74.5 |
| Outpatient health care | 115 | 2.6 | 6.1 | 25.2 | 66.1 |
| Inpatient mental health care | 583 | 2.1 | 2.6 | 9.9 | 85.4 |
| Inpatient health care | 316 | 1.0 | 8.5 | 18.0 | 71.5 |
| Human | | | | | |
| Out-of-home respite | 571 | 11.2 | 10.7 | 15.9 | 62.2 |
| In-home respite | 490 | 10.6 | 15.5 | 17.6 | 56.3 |
| Adult day care | 512 | 10.2 | 11.3 | 17.6 | 60.9 |
| Alzheimer's Association | 485 | 10.1 | 15.3 | 23.9 | 50.7 |
| Support group | 534 | 9.0 | 16.9 | 19.5 | 54.7 |
| Homemaker | 392 | 8.7 | 10.5 | 16.1 | 64.8 |
| Caregiver resource center | 588 | 7.8 | 13.9 | 18.0 | 60.2 |
| Information and referral | 419 | 7.4 | 16.0 | 22.2 | 54.4 |
| Financial assistance | 515 | 6.6 | 10.3 | 11.5 | 71.7 |
| Recreation program | 557 | 6.6 | 9.3 | 19.2 | 64.8 |
| Education program | 535 | 6.5 | 17.2 | 19.8 | 56.4 |
| Home modification assistance | 462 | 6.1 | 9.3 | 15.8 | 68.8 |
| Senior centers | 514 | 6.0 | 13.4 | 14.6 | 66.0 |
| Home energy assistance | 570 | 5.6 | 9.8 | 11.8 | 72.8 |
| Agency on aging | 504 | 5.4 | 14.3 | 18.7 | 61.7 |
| Transportation | 469 | 5.1 | 7.5 | 10.9 | 76.5 |
| Individual counseling | 524 | 4.8 | 10.3 | 17.7 | 67.2 |
| Legal | 418 | 4.5 | 6.9 | 15.6 | 73.0 |
| Family counseling | 587 | 3.7 | 8.5 | 13.5 | 74.3 |
| Telephone reassurance | 577 | 2.9 | 7.1 | 15.3 | 74.7 |
| Church, mosque, or synagogue | 436 | 2.8 | 7.3 | 16.1 | 73.9 |
| Meals on wheels | 524 | 2.5 | 6.5 | 9.2 | 81.5 |
| Library | 463 | 1.5 | 12.7 | 19.4 | 66.3 |
| Other health and human services | 552 | 6.0 | 5.8 | 13.2 | 75.0 |

"Would additional services help reduce the likelihood of the institutionalization of the care recipient," 39 percent responded that it would help "a great deal," and an additional 33 percent responded that it would "help somewhat." Similarly, in response to a question about the ease of community care, 29 percent responded that additional services would make it "much easier" to provide care in the community, and an additional 36 per-cent indicated that it would make it "somewhat easier."

### Impediments to Services Use

Not knowing where to obtain services was, by far, the most important impediment to service use cited by study participants (Table 10-5). A substantial proportion of the respondents did not know where to obtain services

TABLE 10-5. Impediments to Health and Human Services Use

| Type of Service | n | Do not know where to ob-tain services | Cost | Access | Willing-ness | Other |
|---|---|---|---|---|---|---|
| Health | | | | | | |
| Alzheimer's Disease Asst. Center | 561 | 55.4 | .5 | 7.7 | 4.3 | 7.7 |
| Personal medical alert system | 561 | 41.5 | 1.6 | 3.0 | 5.9 | 9.6 |
| Home health aide | 323 | 31.3 | 12.0 | 1.5 | 9.3 | 6.2 |
| Outpatient mental health care | 498 | 29.1 | 1.4 | 2.2 | 7.8 | 2.4 |
| Inpatient mental health care | 583 | 25.7 | 1.0 | .7 | 3.6 | 2.2 |
| Outpatient health care | 115 | 20.0 | .9 | 2.6 | 5.2 | 5.2 |
| Visiting nurse | 330 | 14.5 | 3.9 | 3.6 | 5.5 | 4.8 |
| Emergency response system | 385 | 14.3 | .3 | .8 | 3.1 | 3.9 |
| Inpatient health care | 317 | 11.7 | .6 | .3 | 1.9 | 2.5 |
| Nursing home | 583 | 10.3 | 5.2 | 2.1 | 13.9 | 7.0 |
| Human | | | | | | |
| Telephone reassurance | 576 | 62.2 | .7 | 4.7 | 5.2 | 7.6 |
| Caregiver resource center | 588 | 56.1 | 1.0 | 8.3 | 3.4 | 4.8 |
| Home modification assistance | 462 | 50.9 | 3.0 | 3.5 | 2.2 | 8.4 |
| Out-of-home respite | 571 | 50.3 | 7.5 | 5.4 | 12.4 | 12.2 |
| In-home respite | 490 | 47.3 | 9.0 | 5.9 | 8.1 | 12.6 |
| Alzheimer's Association | 485 | 46.8 | .4 | 9.9 | 5.0 | 6.4 |
| Homemaker | 393 | 45.5 | 11.5 | 1.0 | 6.1 | 7.4 |
| Information and referral | 419 | 44.4 | 4.5 | 6.2 | 4.8 | 6.2 |
| Agency on aging | 505 | 42.0 | .6 | 6.3 | 4.6 | 3.4 |
| Education program | 534 | 41.6 | .6 | 10.9 | 4.3 | 9.9 |
| Support group | 534 | 41.0 | 0.0 | 13.3 | 9.4 | 12.0 |
| Family counseling | 587 | 37.8 | 2.9 | 4.9 | 9.4 | 3.6 |
| Individual counseling | 524 | 36.8 | 4.2 | 5.2 | 9.4 | 3.6 |
| Adult day care | 513 | 35.7 | 4.9 | 8.8 | 22.8 | 13.8 |
| Home energy assistance | 569 | 33.0 | 1.2 | 10.7 | 1.8 | 6.5 |
| Transportation | 468 | 31.6 | 2.8 | 4.7 | 5.1 | 8.1 |
| Recreation program | 557 | 31.2 | 1.1 | 9.2 | 16.5 | 12.4 |
| Financial assistance | 514 | 24.6 | 1.4 | 7.8 | 2.1 | 7.0 |
| Meals on wheels | 524 | 23.1 | 1.0 | 2.3 | 7.1 | 9.9 |
| Legal | 418 | 16.7 | 5.0 | 1.0 | 2.9 | 4.3 |
| Senior centers | 514 | 16.0 | 1.0 | 7.6 | 24.3 | 13.2 |
| Church, mosque, or synagogue | 436 | 10.3 | 0.2 | 3.0 | 8.7 | 3.4 |
| Library | 463 | 8.0 | 0.0 | 4.5 | 4.5 | 12.5 |
| Other health and human services | 552 | 71.4 | 2.2 | 4.9 | 1.6 | 1.8 |

in their communities. For example, despite the fact that there is an Area Agency on Aging in each county of New York State and information and referral is a central part of the mission of these agencies, 42 percent of those that had not used Area Agency on Aging services did not know where to obtain this service. Similarly, more than 50 percent of the sample indicated that they did not know where to obtain out-of-home respite services, 47 percent did not know where to obtain in-home respite services, and 44 percent did not know how to obtain information and referral services.

With the exception of homemaker and home health aide services, respondents indicated that cost was not a major barrier to services use. Access was defined broadly to include lack of transportation and other physical impediments to services use, inconvenient location or hours of operation, strict eligibility rules, and other factors that prevented caregivers from accessing services. Lack of access to services was not found to be a major impediment to the use of most services. It was cited, however, as more of a problem for the use of support groups and educational programs than for other services. Some caregivers who cited access to support groups and educational programs as a problem spontaneously mentioned that they did not feel comfortable leaving the care recipient alone to use these services. Almost 11 percent of the caregivers also mentioned that access problems prevented them from using home energy assistance programs. For this service, caregivers mentioned that strict eligibility rules prevented them from using the service, although they were having trouble paying heating bills.

Willingness to use a particular service by the caregiver, the care recipient, or a combination of the two was cited as a substantial barrier for a few services. For example, of the 24 percent that were unwilling to use senior centers, some spontaneously indicated that the care recipient was too impaired, and others indicated that they did not believe that the care recipient would be welcome. Almost 23 percent of the respondents who were not using adult day care indicated that they were unwilling to use the service. This figure included those who indicated that they had tried to get the care recipient to use the service but met with resistance, those who indicated that the care recipient was too impaired, and those who did not feel comfortable having others provide care. Caregivers also were asked about other impediments to services use. Impediments that were most often cited included the care recipient being too impaired to use a service and the caregiver being too busy with caregiving activities to use services.

## Discussion

The results of this study do not support the findings of previously reviewed studies, which indicated that caregivers of community-dwelling people with dementia use few health and human services. Data from this study indicate a high level of services use and services use of long duration and high frequency. The results, for example, revealed that the average survey respondent used 6.9 community services—that is, 3.7 human services and 3.2 health services. In contrast to earlier studies, the more comprehensive list of services used in this study may have enabled us to gain a more complete picture of the range of services caregivers draw on and that social workers may help them obtain. Discrepancies between this study and earlier studies also may be because of the nature of the samples used to estimate services use. In earlier studies that relied on nonprobability, homogenous samples may have been composed of a greater number of people in earlier stages of dementia. In any case, the results of this study underscore the vital importance of health and human services in helping caregivers for older people with dementia in community settings.

Findings about the high level of services use by or on behalf of people with dementia lend support to the few economic studies that have revealed the high cost of caring for people with dementia in community settings (Fox, 1997). For example, Weinberger et al. (1993) concluded that "the expense of caring for patients with progressive dementia living at home may be higher than previously estimated and frequently involves out-of-pocket expenses paid directly by patients and family caregivers" (p. 338). Similarly, in a study of people with dementia, depression and anxiety disorders, and physical disabilities, it was concluded that "dementia was the most expensive disorder per sufferer in terms of formal services" (Livingston, Manela, & Katona, 1997, p. 56). Although providing additional community health and social services for people with dementia would not be without cost, from a societal perspective, the hours informal caregivers spend assisting people with dementia in activities of daily living, supervision, and so forth have a considerable social cost (Fox, 1997). For example, it has been found that a significant number of informal caregivers make accommodations in their work schedules, reduce their time at work, or stop working at least temporarily because of caregiving responsibilities (National Alliance for Caregiving and AARP, 1997).

Findings about the frequency of use of particular health and human services should be interpreted cautiously. Although we provided respondents with definitions of each service, some respondents may not have remembered all the services they used. Also, there is some overlap among services. For example, a support group might be sponsored by the Alzheimer's Association. A respondent may have remembered attending the support group but may not have realized that it was developed under the auspices of the Alzheimer's Association. Thus, the respondent's use of the support group would be captured, but the respondent's use of the Alzheimer's Association would not be captured.

Despite the high level of services use, caregivers reported elevated subjective and objective burden levels. Indeed, caregivers reported spending a very substantial amount of time in caregiving activities over a long period, many reported health limitations and difficulties dealing with care recipient problem behaviors, and some also reported having other caregiving responsibilities. All of these factors are likely to increase a family caregiver's need for additional assistance, despite existing services use. If out-of-home placements are to be delayed, the quality of life for people with dementia maintained, and caregiver distress reduced, these data challenge social workers to increase their already considerable efforts to reach out proactively to caregiving families and to help them remove barriers to needed services. The challenge to social work is all the more pressing given that 73 percent of respondents identified a high need for at least one additional service and that 72 percent reported that additional services would help a great deal or somewhat to avoid having to institutionalize the care recipient. However, the reported levels of existing services use suggest that properly designed outreach efforts have a high probability of connecting families with needed services. Indeed, the experiences of the interviewers reinforce this belief. As will be reported in a subsequent article, many caregivers agreed to requests by the interviewers to refer them to local Alzheimer's Association chapters so that their services needs could be addressed.

Removal of barriers to services use is a key objective for social workers. The results of this research suggest that the lack of use of certain health and human services resulted from a lack of knowledge on the part of caregivers. A high percentage of respondents indicated that they did not know how to obtain services. When interviewers described the types of services that were available, caregivers frequently mentioned that they would use one or more of them. For example, few respondents knew about the existence of the 17 regional Caregiver Resource Centers supported by the New York State Office on Aging, but once information was provided about them, many respondents indicated that they would use a center's services. These findings suggest that social workers have an important role to play in helping caregivers become better informed about services. They also suggest that human services agencies that have information and referral services as a core mission, such as Area Agencies on Aging and local Alzheimer's Association chapters, need more support to do an effective job of reaching out to caregivers of people with dementia.

Another reason for the relative lack of use of certain human services, such as out-of-home respite, may be caregiver-perceived or actual satisfaction levels. Although caregivers were generally reluctant to express dissatisfaction with services, they expressed a higher level of dissatisfaction with respite services than with many other services. Spontaneous comments from the respondents suggested that they believed that staff were not always well equipped to handle the cognitive and physical disabilities and the behavior of care recipients. Although not reflected in the satisfaction data (Table 10-3), similar comments were made by many respondents as they described their attempts to use homemaker and home health aides. Therefore, as clinicians, administrators, and advocates, social work-

ers can play an important role in helping ensure that respite care and other health and human services are better able to accommodate the needs of people with dementia. For example, in-service training programs are now available for social workers to use in training nurses aides and other paraprofessionals, so that they, in turn, can communicate and interact more effectively with people with dementia (see, for example, Toseland & McCallion, 1998).

The interviewers were impressed with the devotion of caregivers to care recipients and their eagerness to do whatever they could to provide high quality care, despite the stress they endured. Social workers could support and enhance caregivers' efforts by offering educational programs and by teaching effective communication and interaction strategies while they serve in care coordination, consultation, and other helping roles. A number of programs are now available to help family members communicate and interact more effectively with people with moderate-to-severe dementia and also to address agitation and other behavioral symptoms (Feil, 1993; McCallion, Toseland, & Freeman, 1999; Teri, 1990).

Caregivers also need to be empowered to negotiate with health and human services systems. Despite the relatively low percentage of respondents citing high cost, lack of access, and other impediments to services use, caregivers often expressed spontaneously to interviewers that they felt powerless when attempting to confront the bureaucratic system about services needs or problems. Social workers play a key role in helping caregivers identify and effectively negotiate barriers to services use (McCallion & Toseland, 1993). However, many respondents to the survey spontaneously expressed their bewilderment about the patchwork of health and human services offered in their community and their confusion about where to turn for assistance. The high percentage of caregivers who lacked knowledge about services suggests that social workers should expand their information and referral efforts and encourage allied professionals and paraprofessionals to do the same.

Research is needed on innovative ways to configure and deliver community services to dementia sufferers and their caregivers. For example, respondents to the survey seemed to really appreciate the opportunity to have someone to talk with about their responsibilities and burdens. Yet, relatively few used counseling or support group services. Many indicated that they did not have the time or the help with caregiving activities that would enable them to use these services. Alternative services delivery methods, such as offering telephone or computer support groups and counseling services, may enable caregivers to obtain services that they are not currently able to use.

Social workers are suited uniquely to work with people with dementia and their caregivers because of their ability to integrate biological, social, psychological, environmental, and economic concerns and because of their emphasis on comprehensive assessment and intervention (O'Neill, 1999). The results of this study show both the multiple roles that social workers can play in helping people with dementia and their families and the opportunities for knowledge building and the future development of social work services that the John A. Hartford initiative is designed to support.

## References

Adler, G., Kuskowski, M., & Mortimer, J. (1995). Respite use in dementia patients. *Clinical Gerontologist, 15,* 17–30.

Bass, D., Looman, W., & Ehrlich, P. (1992). Predicting the volume of health and social services: Integrating cognitive impairment into the modified Andersen framework. *Gerontologist, 32,* 33–43.

Biegel, D., Bass, D., Schulz, R., & Morycz, R. (1993). Predictors of in-home and out-of-home services use by family caregivers of Alzheimer's disease patients. *Journal of Aging and Health, 5,* 419–438.

Brookmeyer, R., Gray, S., & Kawas, C. (1998). Projections of Alzheimer's disease in the United States and the public health impact of delaying disease onset. *American Journal of Public Health, 88,* 1337–1342.

Buckwalter, K., Russell, D., & Hall, G. (1994). Needs, resources, and responses of rural caregivers of persons with Alzheimer's disease. In E. Light, G. Niederehe, & B. Lebowitz (Eds.), *Stress effects on family caregivers of Alzheimer's patients: Research and interventions* (pp. 301–315). New York: Springer.

Caserta, M., Lund, D., Wright, S., & Redburn, D. (1987). Caregivers to dementia patients: The utilization of community services. *Gerontologist, 27,* 209–214.

Cohen-Mansfield, J., Marx, M., & Rosenthal, A. (1989). A description of agitation in a nursing home. *Journal of Gerontology: Medical Sciences, 44,* M77–M84.

Cotrell, V. (1996). Respite use by dementia caregivers: Preferences and reasons for initial use. *Journal of Gerontological Social Work, 26,* 35–55.

Cox, C. (1993). Service needs and interests: A comparison of African American and white caregivers seeking Alzheimer assistance. *American Journal of Alzheimer's Care and Related Disorders & Research, 8,* 33–40.

Cox, C. (1997). Findings from a statewide program of respite care: A comparison of service users, stoppers, and nonusers. *Gerontologist, 37,* 511–517.

Evans, D., Scherer, P., Cook, N., Albert, M., Funkenstein, H., Smith, L., Hebert, L., Branch, L.,

Chown, M., Hennekens, H., & Taylor, J. (1990). Estimated prevalence of Alzheimer's disease in the United States. *The Milbank Quarterly, 68*, 267–289.

Feil, N. (1993). *The validation breakthrough*. Baltimore: Health Professions Press.

Ferran, J., Wilson, K., & Doran, M. (1996). The early onset dementias: A study of clinical characteristics and service use. *International Journal of Geriatric Psychiatry, 11*, 863–869.

Fillenbaum, G. (1978). *Multidimensional functional assessment: The OARS methodology* (Prepared by Duke University for the Study of Aging and Human Development). Durham, NC: Duke University.

Fox, P. (1997). Service use and cost outcomes for persons with Alzheimer's disease. *Alzheimer's Disease and Associated Disorders, 11*, 125–134.

Gill, C., Hinrichsen, G., & DiGiuseppe, R. (1998). Factors associated with formal service use by family members of patients with dementia. *Journal of Applied Gerontology, 17*, 38–52.

Ginther, S., Webber, P., Fox, P., & Miller, L. (1993). Predictors of case management for persons with Alzheimer's disease. *Journal of Applied Gerontology, 12*, 139–154.

Gonyea, J., & Silverstein, N. (1991). The role of Alzheimer's disease support groups in families' utilization of community services. *Journal of Gerontological Social Work, 16*, 43–55.

Gottlieb, G., Gur, R. E., & Gur, R. C. (1988). Reliability of psychiatric scales in patients with dementia of the Alzheimer type. *American Journal of Psychiatry, 145*, 857–860.

Gwyther, L. (1996). Care for families facing Alzheimer's disease: Primary care practice implications from research. In Z. S. Khachaturian & T. S. Radebaugh (Eds.), *Alzheimer's disease: Cause(s), diagnosis, treatment, and care* (pp. 324–330). Boca Raton, FL: CRC Press.

Hinrichsen, G., & Ramirez, M. (1992). Black and white dementia caregivers: A comparison of their adaptation, adjustment, and service utilization. *Gerontologist, 32*, 375–381.

Khachaturian, Z., & Radebaugh, T. (Eds.). (1996). *Alzheimer's disease: Cause(s), diagnosis, treatment, and care*. Boca Raton, FL: CRC Press.

Klein, S. (Ed.). (1996). *A national agenda for geriatric education: White papers*. Rockville, MD: Health Resources and Services Administration.

Kosloski, K., & Montgomery, R. (1992). Perceptions of respite services as predictors of utilization. *Research on Aging, 15*, 399–413.

Livingston, G., Manela, M., & Katona, C. (1997). Cost of community care for older people. *British Journal of Psychiatry, 171*, 56–69.

Macera, C., Still, C., Brandes, D., Abramson, R., & Davis, D. (1991). The South Carolina Alzheimer's Disease Patient Registry: A progress report. *American Journal of Alzheimer's Care and Related Disorders & Research, 6*, 35–38.

Marks, N. F. (1996). Caregiving across the lifespan: National prevalence and predictors. *Family Relations, 45*, 27–36.

McCallion, P., & Toseland, R. (1993). Empowering families of adolescents and adults with developmental disabilities. *Families in Society, 74*, 579–589.

McCallion, P., Toseland, R., & Freeman, K. (1999). An evaluation of the family visit education program. *Journal of the American Geriatric Society, 47*, 1–12.

Mullan, J. (1993). Barriers to the use of formal services among Alzheimer's caregivers. In S. Zarit, L. Pearlin, & K. Schaie (Eds.), *Caregiving systems: Informal and formal helpers* (pp. 241–259). Hillsdale, NJ: Lawrence Erlbaum.

National Alliance for Caregiving and the American Association of Retired Persons. (1997, June). *Family caregiving in the U.S.: Findings from a national survey* (Final Report). Bethesda, MD: Author.

O'Neill, J. (1999, January). Aging express: Can social work keep up? *NASW News, 44*, p. 3.

Penning, M. (1995). Cognitive impairment, caregiver burden, and the utilization of home health services. *Journal of Aging and Health, 7*, 233–253.

Peterson, D., & Wendt, P. (1990). Employment in the field of aging: A survey of professionals in four fields. *Gerontologist, 30,* 679-685.

Reisberg, B. (1985). Alzheimer's disease update. *Psychiatric Annals, 15,* 319–322.

Reisberg, B., Ferris, S., deLeon, M., & Crook, T. (1982). The global deterioration scale for assessment of primary degenerative dementia. *American Journal of Psychiatry, 139,* 1136–1139.

Teri, L. (1990). *Managing and understanding behavior problems in Alzheimer's disease and related disorders.* Baltimore: Health Professions Press.

Toseland, R. (1990). Long-term effectiveness of peer-led and professionally led support groups for family caregivers. *Social Service Review, 64,* 308–327.

Toseland, R., & McCallion, P. (1998). *Maintaining communication with persons with dementia.* New York: Springer.

Toseland, R., O'Donnell, J., Engelhardt, J., Hendler, S., Thomley, J., & Jue, D. (1996). Outpatient geriatric evaluation and management: Results of a randomized trial. *Medical Care, 34,* 624–640.

Vitaliano, P., Maiuro, R., Ochs, H., & Russo, J. (1989). A model of burden in caregivers of DAT patients. In E. Light & B. Lebowitz (Eds.), *Alzheimer's disease treatment and family stress: Future directions for research* (pp. 267–291). Washington, DC: U.S. Government Printing Office.

Vitaliano, P., Russo, J., Young, H., Becker, J., & Maiuro, R. (1991). The Screen for Caregiver Burden. *Gerontologist, 31,* 76–83.

Weinberger, M., Gold, D., Divine, G., Cowper, P., Hodgson, L., Schreiner, P., & George, L. (1993). Expenditures in caring for patients with dementia who live at home. *American Journal of Public Health, 83,* 338–341.

Wenger, G. (1994). Dementia sufferers living at home. *International Journal of Geriatric Psychiatry, 9,* 721–733.

This article was originally published in the November 1999 issue of *Social Work,* Vol. 44, Number 6.

## Asian and Pacific Islander American Population

Asian and Pacific Islander (API) Americans are the third largest ethnic minority group in the United States, numbering about 7.3 million in 1990 (U.S. Bureau of the Census 1991a, 1991b). Among residents age 65 and older the API elderly group is the fastest

# 11

# Perceptions of Dementia, Caregiving, and Help Seeking among Asian and Pacific Islander Americans

### KATHRYN L. BRAUN and COLETTE V. BROWNE

Alzheimer's disease, which causes progressive memory loss and dependence, is estimated to affect 4 million Americans (Yeo & Gallagher-Thompson, 1996). Social workers, regardless of the setting in which they work, will find themselves working with more families affected by this disease. At the same time, the United States is becoming more ethnically diverse, and social workers are seeking to broaden their understanding of culturally diverse views of specific health problems, the family's role in providing care, and how help is sought. In an attempt to help expand knowledge in this area, this article pulls together findings from the literature and from research in Honolulu on the perceptions of five Asian and Pacific Islander (API) American groups—Chinese, Japanese, Filipino, Vietnamese, and Native Hawaiian—on dementia, caregiving, and help seeking. Implications for practice, policy, and research are discussed.

## Asian and Pacific Islander American Population

Asian and Pacific Islander (API) Americans are the third largest ethnic minority group in the United States, numbering about 7.3 million in 1990 (U.S. Bureau of the Census, 1991a, 1991b). Among residents age 65 and older, the API elderly group is the fastest growing, projected to have more than tripled between 1980 and 1995 (Young & Gu, 1995). Far from being a homogeneous group, the API label encompasses more than 30 distinct ethnocultural entities, each with its own language and customs (Wykle & Kaskel, 1991).

Among the largest Asian American groups are Chinese, Filipino, Japanese, Koreans, and Vietnamese. Their immigration patterns were influenced by U.S. labor needs and foreign policy. Chinese, Japanese, Korean, and Filipino immigrants initially came to fill low-paying jobs, especially in California and Hawaii, but their immigration was curtailed by the Oriental Exclusion Act of 1924. Immigration rules were relaxed during and following times of war when foreign brides of U.S. servicemen and citizens of countries who helped the U.S. cause were allowed to enter the country. The Immigration Act of 1965 liberalized U.S. immigration policy, allowing 20,000 immigrants per year per country, regardless of race or ethnicity, for purposes of occupational immigration (if their skills are needed in the U.S. labor market), family reunification, and vulnerability to political and religious persecution. Because unmarried children under age 21, spouses, fiancées, and parents of U.S. citizens are exempt from the quota limitation, each country can actually send more than 20,000 immigrants per year (Min, 1995).

Among Pacific Islander Americans, the largest groups are Native Hawaiians and Samoans (Young & Gu, 1995). Both of these groups became Americans by virtue of colonization. The Kingdom of Hawaii was overthrown by the U.S. military in 1893 and was administered by the U.S. Department of the Interior until it became a state in 1959 (Blaisdell & Mokuau, 1991). American Samoa became a U.S. Territory in 1900. It was first administered by the Department of the Navy as a coaling station; later it came under the Department of the Interior. American Samoa elected its first governor in 1977 (McDermott, Tseng, & Maretzki, 1980).

The API American group has been called a "model minority" because, as a whole, data on social status suggest that API Americans are better educated and better off financially than other ethnic minority groups (Gelfand, 1994; Markides, 1987; U.S. Department of Health and Human Services, 1985). Researchers who have taken a closer look at the data, however, have found extreme unevenness within the API designation. For example, the 1980 census indicated that a good proportion of API American households had annual incomes of $50,000 or higher; but at the same time, a greater percentage had incomes at or below poverty level compared to European Americans (Lin-Fu, 1988; Liu & Yu; 1985). U.S. residents of Samoan and Southeast Asian descent have been found to be at particularly high risk of poverty (Morioka-Douglas & Yeo, 1990). In educational attainment, the API American group boasted the highest percentage of women age 25 and older who had completed college in 1980; but at the same time, 7.5 percent of them had fewer than five years of elementary school, compared to 2.5 percent among European Americans (Lin-Fu, 1988). This disparity has been referred to as the "bipolar nature" of API status in which the successes of some API groups mask the severe problems of other API groups (Lin-Fu, 1988; Tanjasiri, Wallace, & Shibata, 1995). Even stereotyping within an API group is difficult, because immigration from a single country has likely occurred in several waves; great differences are seen between recent immigrants and those whose families have lived here for several generations (Fabrega, 1969).

Health and service utilization data on API Americans are also likely to be aggregated and suggest that API Americans are healthy and use fewer services than other ethnic groups, especially European Americans. For example, combined data from the 1976–1978 and the 1989–1991 National Health Interview Surveys (NHISs) suggested that more API respondents perceived their health as excellent or good and that fewer reported limitations in activities compared with all other groups (Liu & Yu, 1985; Tanjasiri et al., 1995). Again, a closer look at the data gives a different picture. Although in the 1976–1978 NHISs there was little difference between APIs and white people in number of physician visits per year, the API respondents reported much greater emergency room use and longer hospitalizations than the other group, suggesting that APIs are less likely to have a regular source of care or that they wait too long to use it (Liu & Yu, 1985).

The majority of studies on API utilization of mental health services have found that APIs are underrepresented in both inpatient and outpatient settings (Matsuoka, 1990; Sue, 1994). Frequently mentioned in the mental health literature is a tendency for Asian American groups to somaticize mental distress, in part because of the shame and stigma attached to mental illness (for example, Browne, Fong, & Mokuau, 1994; Sue, 1994; Takamura, 1991).

Looking specifically at dementia, investigators believe that the age-specific prevalence of dementia is similar throughout the world (White, 1992). Thus, the age-specific prevalence among API Americans should match that of the U.S. population as a whole: about 3 percent of people ages 65 to 74, 19 percent of people ages 75 to 84, and 47 percent of all adults age 85 and older (Evans et al., 1989). In terms of seeking help for dementing conditions, however, it appears that caregivers in ethnic minority communities use fewer services than white caregivers (U.S. Congress, Office of Technology Assessment,

1990) and that API groups are underrepresented in California's system of dementia diagnosis and treatment centers (Yeo, Gallagher-Thompson, & Lieberman, 1996).

Specific to API perceptions of Alzheimer's and use of dementia-related services, a search of the literature found very little outside of a book on ethnicity and dementia edited by Yeo and Gallagher-Thompson (1996), which includes chapters on California-based clinical experiences with Chinese, Filipino, and Japanese families.

This article adds to the California-based work by presenting findings from work in Hawaii that has been exploring these issues through key informant interviews and focus group research. Specific methods and timing for each study have been presented elsewhere (Braun, Takamura, Forman, Sasaki, & Meininger, 1995; Braun, Takamura, & Mougeot, 1996). The article presents a compilation of findings about five API groups—Chinese, Japanese, Filipino, Vietnamese, and Native Hawaiian. Information on the immigration and colonization experience of each group is included to aid in understanding culturally specific health perceptions and help-seeking behaviors.

## Chinese

### *History of Immigration*

Chinese immigration to the U.S. began in the mid-1800s. The first large influx (of almost 300,000) was primarily males from southern China who heard of the discovery of gold and the availability of jobs in California. Another 5,000 came to Hawaii during the same period to work on the sugar plantations. Not long thereafter, a series of laws were promulgated in the United States to discourage further Chinese immigration, including the Chinese Exclusion Act of 1882 and the Oriental Exclusion Act of 1924, keeping the total number of U.S.-resident Chinese at below 100,000 for five decades (Wong, 1995).

Immigration restrictions began to relax in the 1940s, in part to recognize China's position as a U.S. ally in World War II. The Immigration Act of 1965 allowed 20,000 immigrants per year per country (mostly from Taiwan); it was amended in 1981 to allow an additional 20,000 from mainland China and to increase the quota for Hong Kong to 5,000. From 1980 to 1990, the Chinese population in the United States doubled, to 1,645,472. The majority (43 percent) live in California, and another 17 percent live in New York (Wong, 1995).

### Chinese Cultural Traditions and Values That Affect Caregiving and Help-Seeking Patterns

Traditional Chinese beliefs, based on Confucian thought, center around the harmony, unity, and survival of the family. Hierarchy is important, and family members have prescribed roles according to gender, age, and birth order. For example, men have more authority than women, children must obey and care for their parents without question or resentment, and the first-born son has the greatest authority and responsibility among siblings. Although elder care was traditionally provided by the wife of the first-born son, today all children are expected to display filial piety and to repay their parents for sacrifices they have made for them (Braun & Browne, 1998; Char, Tseng, Lum, & Hsu, 1980; Elliott, Di Minno, Lam, & Tu, 1996; Huang, 1991).

In this tradition, the family is viewed as more important than the individual. Thus, personal mistakes reflect badly on the entire family and cause shame or loss of face (*min chi* in Cantonese). Problems of mental instability, acting-out behaviors, and even AIDS

and poverty are considered shameful (Sue, 1994). Traditional forms of coping within this structure include activity, endurance, looking the other way, and not thinking too much (Huang, 1991). Children are taught to avoid disclosing private concerns to outsiders, and the Chinese believe that problems are rarely resolved by talking (Lin, 1985; Ryan, 1985).

Discussion of physical ailments, however, is more acceptable. Thus, it is not uncommon to see mental health problems somaticized among Chinese Americans, especially recent immigrants (Chang, 1985; Cheung, 1982). In traditional Chinese medicine, illness is seen as an imbalance between *yin* (the female element) and *yang* (the male element). Therapeutic interventions involve bringing these forces into balance, and foods or herbs with strong *yin* and *yang* qualities may be prescribed (Char et al., 1980). More recently, investigators and practitioners have found Chinese Americans to use Western and Chinese medical services together (Braun & Browne, 1998; Char et al., 1980; Hessler, Nolan, Ogbu, & New, 1975).

### Chinese Views of Dementia and Associated Help-Seeking Patterns

Work in China by Ikels (1993) presents a perspective on why dementia may not be considered a problem in families of recent Chinese immigrants. Given the traditional practice of living in extended families and the hierarchical power structure based on age, having an elder develop dementia is not always seen as negative, especially if it results in the elder's loss of power over the household. In addition, loss of function in old age is expected, and sometimes dementia symptoms are attributed to sensory losses about which, in many parts of China, little can be done. Findings from work with Chinese Americans in California suggested that recent immigrants may interpret dementia symptoms as mental illness (which is shameful), as retribution for individual or family sins, as an imbalance of *yin* and *yang*, as improper alignment of the house (according to *feng shui*), and as possession by an evil spirit (Elliot et al., 1996). These perspectives suggest that help seeking for dementia symptoms among Chinese immigrants might be delayed.

In Honolulu-based work, recent immigrants who participated in our focus groups recognized dementia symptoms and told about their experiences with older adults who were forgetful, talked about the past, talked a lot, repeatedly asked the same question but knew the words to all the old songs, wandered and got lost, and needed 24-hour supervision so they would not leave the stove on and burn down the house. Informants believed that these behaviors were a natural part of old age, but that symptoms were exacerbated by the elder's move to a new environment. Respondents noted that "those who move here experience a decline in status, loss of peers, and depression. They are homesick for the food, good cultural events, and people who speak the same language" (Braun, Takamura, et al., 1995, p. 124). Cantonese phrases shared with us by informants included *chi zin* (mixed-up behavior), *lo yan chi oi zeng* (confusion in old age), *fàn lo wang tong* (old return to youth), and *sun fa* (confused and of a different spirit). The phrase *tse ling sung son* was also mentioned; this translates roughly as "godnessless spirit" and reflects a belief that if a person's behavior is unexplained, then his or her body is possessed by an evil spirit (or godnessless).

Related to help seeking, key informants and focus group participants reminded us about respecting the hierarchy within families and about the importance of eating the correct foods and balancing *yin* and *yang* to resolve illness. New immigrants said, "We usually handle problems ourselves, but if the problem is serious, we can ask a professional, preferably one that is bilingual and bicultural" (Braun, Takamura, et al., 1995, p. 123).

## Japanese

### *History of Immigration*

Significant immigration from Japan started after the Chinese Exclusion Act of 1882, when Hawaii sugar plantations looked to Japan for a new source of cheap labor. Between 1882 and 1908, almost 150,000 Japanese came to Hawaii, and about 30,000 came to California, primarily as agriculturalists. Two policy initiatives—the Gentlemen's Agreement of 1908 and the Oriental Exclusion Act of 1924—effectively halted immigration from Japan until the 1950s, when U.S. servicemen began bringing home Japanese wives. The Immigration Act of 1965 allowed 20,000 Asians per country to immigrate to the United States, but new immigration from Japan is low, only about 5,000 Japanese nationals a year. Today, fully two-thirds of all Japanese Americans are U.S. born, compared with about 37 percent of all API Americans. In 1990 about 847,562 Americans were of Japanese descent, with 52 percent living in California and 41 percent living in Hawaii (Nishi, 1995).

### *Japanese Cultural Traditions and Values That Affect Caregiving and Help-Seeking Patterns*

As in the traditional Chinese culture, traditional Japanese culture emphasizes the importance of interpersonal relationships and interdependence (*amae*). The preservation of harmony and suppression of conflict are critical factors in positive social relationships (Fujita, Ito, Abe, & Takeuchi, 1991). Also emphasized are filial piety (*oyakoko*) and the obligation (*giri*) family members have for each other, especially to parents. Caring for parents is to be done with gratitude, recognizing the balance in reciprocating for the care parents provided in childhood. Not acting accordingly brings great shame (*haji*) to the family name (Takamura, 1991). Help seeking, however, may be inhibited by the strictures of *giri;* that is, the expectation that all help would be provided from within the family may result in resistance to obligating oneself to an "outside" provider of help (Braun & Browne, 1998; Fujita et al., 1991).

There are critical differences among the various generations of Japanese Americans (Tempo & Saito, 1996). Those *issei* (members of the first generation to come to the United States) who are still alive may not speak English and most likely hold to traditional Japanese ways. Many of the *nisei* (second generation) grew up during the Depression and were incarcerated during World War II. After the war Japanese Americans in Hawaii and California were able to find work, enter government, and run for office. But many *nisei* became distrustful of the U.S. government following the disruption that accompanied internment; few out-married and many still subscribe to traditional Japanese values. In contrast, members of the *sansei* (third) and *yonsei* (fourth) generations are more Americanized; few speak Japanese and out-marriage rates are about 50 percent (Nishi, 1995).

### Japanese Views of Dementia and Associated Help-Seeking Patterns

Japanese words used to label people with dementia symptoms are *kichigai* (from *ki* = behavior and *chigai* = different), which means crazy or insane and is mostly used to describe someone with psychiatric problems, and *bokeru*, which is a verb meaning to go senile or to become forgetful in old age. Although

little has been written on Japanese American perceptions of dementia, the mental health literature provides clues as to how Japanese Americans may cope with dementia symptoms. In traditional culture, Japanese attach much stigma to emotional and mental problems, which are attributed to genetics, punishment for past behavior (karma), or poor guidance from the family unit (Shon & Ja, 1982). Such problems are often denied and the affected family member hidden. Talking to an outsider would make the person stand out even more and would cause *haji* (shame and loss of face) for the family.

Mental health practitioners have noticed a general tendency to somaticize illness and to deny the possibility of an emotional component, even when it is quite obvious to the practitioner (Rogers & Izutsu, 1980).

Another Japanese concept that comes to bear is *shikata ga nai*, meaning that the situation cannot be helped and nothing more can be done (Fujita et al., 1991; Tempo & Saito, 1996). Given these traditions, it would be unexpected for Japanese Americans of the issei and nisei generations to seek help for family members exhibiting dementia symptoms until they were quite unmanageable. California-based work confirms the notion that shame and in-group problem-solving strategies keep Japanese Americans from seeking help for family members with dementia symptoms (Tempo & Saito, 1996). Work in both California and Hawaii has found that members of the sansei and yonsei generations are more open to discussing dementia and seeking help for parents and grandparents.

### Filipinos

#### History of Immigration

At the turn of the century, two events occurred that sparked immigration by Filipinos to the United States. With Spain's loss in the Spanish-American war, the Philippines was ceded to the United States in 1892. At the same time, immigration of cheap labor from China and Japan was being curtailed. Immigration of Filipino laborers was attractive to U.S. agricultural interests, as well as to Filipinos whose country had suffered during years of war. Between 1906 and 1934, almost 120,000 Filipinos came to work on Hawaii sugar plantations, and another 45,000 arrived on the West Coast. Relatively fewer Filipinos immigrated between 1934, when the Philippines was granted commonwealth status, and the passage of the Immigration Act of 1965. Since then, immigration from the Philippines has escalated, and, since the late 1980s, more than 50,000 Filipinos a year have been admitted. In 1990 Filipino Americans numbered over 1.4 million, with 52 percent residing in California and 12 percent in Hawaii (Agbayani-Siewert & Revilla, 1995).

### *Filipino Cultural Traditions and Values That Affect Caregiving and Help-Seeking Patterns*

Several traditional Filipino values are relevant to understanding caregiving and help-seeking behaviors. *Bahala na* refers to the belief that most things are outside individual control and in the hands of God. *Pakikisama* refers to smooth interpersonal relationships and reflects a high value on harmony and avoiding conflict. It can result in giving into peer pressure and "going with the flow" so as not to cause displeasure. *Hiya* connotes loss of face or shame. *Utang na loob* refers to a debt of gratitude within relationships—for example, children are indebted to parents forever because they raised them, and if someone does another a favor he or she can expect a favor in return (Billones & Wilson, 1990; Braun & Browne, 1998; Ponce &

Forman, 1980). Also, the vast majority of Filipinos are Catholic, and these religious values reinforce traditional respect for hierarchy and reliance on God.

In traditional Filipino culture, health problems and accidents are attributed to outside factors such as overwork, exposure, anxiety, punishment from God, curses, souls of the dead, or evil persons. Thus, Filipinos may try home remedies, prayer, and faith healing in conjunction with Western medicine. The literature suggests that Filipinos tend to somaticize emotional and mental distress and that Filipinos underutilize mental health services. Once in the health care system, however, Filipinos tend to ascribe great status to health professionals, often resulting in reserved, quiet behaviors during health examinations. It is also likely, however, to result in high compliance with prescribed treatment (Billones & Wilson, 1990; Braun & Browne, 1998; Ponce & Forman, 1980; Ying & Hu, 1994).

Children are expected to care for their parents until death. In our Hawaii-based work, informants reflected the value of *utang na loob* in saying "they gave birth to us, raised us, all those good things, now we must care for them . . . everyone is going to have this responsibility with older people" (Braun, Takamura, et al., 1995, p. 123). Although the California-based work suggested that children may be called on for assistance by birth order (McBride & Parreno, 1996), focus groups in Hawaii found no expectation for a particular child to care for parents; rather it appeared acceptable that a parent live for a time with one child and then with another.

Billones and Wilson (1990) found that Filipino elders may return to the Philippines to receive care, rather than enter an institution. This sentiment was echoed by Hawaii-based informants who said, "We do not like to seek help from the government or announce our problems in church. We care for our own within our extended family network to the extent possible. . . . I would rather return to the Philippines and scout out a nephew to care for me than ask for help from the government" (Braun, Takamura, et al., 1995, p. 123).

### Filipino Views of Dementia and Associated Help-Seeking Patterns

In Filipino focus groups in Hawaii, participants expressed familiarity with dementia symptoms, recounting experiences with older adults who had lost control of themselves, wandered, given away their money, needed to be watched 24 hours a day, and remembered clearly the past but not the present. Several descriptive words and phrases were provided by informants. In Tagalog, the country's national language, phrases included *nagbabalik sa pagkabata*, meaning going back to childhood, and *tumatandang paurong*, meaning growing old backwards. *Ulianin*, referring to occasional forgetfulness, was also used. In severe cases, one might refer to the person's mind as *wala na* (gone, there is none) or *tapos na* (done or finished). In Ilokano, the language spoken in the northwestern provinces, the suggested word was *kabaw*, which is apparently quite broad and can be used in reference to someone who is forgetful, retarded, or otherwise impaired mentally. Informants believed that these behaviors were a natural consequence of the aging process and that nothing could be done about them, saying that role reversals were expected. Even if a parent has severe dementia symptoms, continued parent care is the norm. The values of *bahala na* and *utang na loob* are evident in this statement: "God does not give jobs to you that you cannot do. If your parents need care, you can do it" (Braun, Takamura, et al., 1995, p. 123).

## Vietnamese

### History of Immigration

Unlike the previously described groups, Vietnamese immigration to the United States did not start until 1975 with the fall of Saigon to the Vietnamese Communists. That year, about 131,000 Vietnamese who were friendly to U.S. forces were dispersed to sponsoring individuals and community groups who helped them get oriented and find jobs (Matsuoka, 1991). Starting in 1978, members of the general Vietnamese population started fleeing the country and, after substantial periods of time in refugee camps, some of these "boat people" entered the United States. The Orderly Departure Program, established in the 1980s, allowed controlled immigration directly from Vietnam for political prisoners, Amerasians, and those whose family members are U.S. citizens (Rumbaut, 1995).

The 1990 Census estimated the Vietnamese population in the United States at 614,547, a 134 percent increase over 1980. About 46 percent of Vietnamese Americans live in California, and 11 percent live in Texas (Min, 1995; Rumbaut, 1995).

### Vietnamese Cultural Traditions and Values That Affect Caregiving and Help-Seeking Patterns

Traditional Vietnamese culture is influenced by two religious philosophies, Buddhism and Confucianism, which emphasize a respect for authority, social order, loyalty, and filial piety. There is a strong expectation for individuals to defer to the goals of the group, especially those of the family. In Vietnam, extended families live together in compounds. Because few live to old age, it is seen as a blessing, and older persons are expected to sit back, enjoy their accomplishments, and give advice. If disabled, old people are cared for within the extended family (Matsuoka, 1991).

For adults, fathers support the household and represent the family in the community, whereas mothers are generally responsible for everything inside the house. Women are somewhat subservient to men and join their husband's household after marriage. Adolescents gain self-worth through close relationships with family adults, rather than through associations with peers. They are expected to contribute to family goals and care for their parents when needed (Braun & Browne, 1998; Matsuoka, 1990; Rutledge, 1992).

There is a growing body of literature about mental health needs of immigrants from Vietnam, as well as those from Cambodia and Laos. Ying and Hu (1994) found that Southeast Asians were overrepresented in the mental health system in Los Angeles. Common mental health problems for this group include posttraumatic stress disorder, depression, and anxiety (Flaskerud & Hu, 1994; Kinzie et al., 1990; Ying & Hu, 1994). As in other Asian cultures that tend to somaticize mental distress, Southeast Asians often present to the mental health system with complaints of pain and sleep disorders (Flaskerud & Hu, 1994; Kinzie et al., 1990). Gold (1992) interpreted these symptoms in terms of the great disruptions that these refugees have experienced, including war and loss of family and livelihood in their home countries and, in the United States, poor English skills, underemployment, and poverty. Acculturation to the United States has also resulted in the undermining of traditional values within the family and role reversal and loss of status for older immigrants (Lin, Tazuma, & Masuda, 1979; Tran, 1991).

### Vietnamese Views of Dementia and Associated Help-Seeking Patterns

Work in Hawaii suggests that Vietnamese in America have experience with older people who have dementia-related symptoms. For the most part, respondents saw these symptoms as a natural part of aging. Male informants were more likely to explain symptoms in mechanical terms ("The mind is like a motor engine and so of course when we get old we will lose memories and get confused; if you don't run it every day, it becomes damaged."), whereas female informants felt symptoms were exacerbated by culture shock ("This problem is really connected to our stressful and new way of life we have to deal with here and our mind's ability to adjust.") (Braun et al., 1996, pp. 222–223).

A number of Vietnamese words relating to mental capacity were identified that could help practitioners find out what might be causing symptoms. *Lú lân* refers to confusion related to retardation. *Lãng trí* and *dãng trí* refer to the slipping away of memory and loss of memory caused by the absence of the mind. *Mât trí nhó* means the mind is lost already; to distinguish if it is lost quickly, as in multi-infarct dementia, the phrase *mât trí giác* would be more appropriate. In contrast, *binh tâm thân* connotes mental illness or high anxiety, and *diên* translates as crazy. Overall, however, there was a sense that Alzheimer's disease was not a critical issue for the Vietnamese community. In the course of focus group interviews in Honolulu, a number of more important issues surfaced, including social isolation, inability to speak English, underemployment, crowded living conditions, unfamiliarity with and disapproval of American culture coupled with a widening language and culture gap between parents and their children, and involvement of children in gang activities (Braun & Browne, 1998; Braun et al., 1996).

Whether or not an older family member had dementia symptoms, there was no question that the person would be cared for at home. Informants would not seek medical advice for dementia symptoms, because they believed nothing could cure them.

But informants also recognized that they were in a new culture, with no desire or expectation to return to Vietnam, and that they must be open to new ways, including learning about and taking advantage of services available to residents and citizens. An informant said, "In Vietnam, we have no government services for old people but we have services here; the government provides. In Vietnamese culture, we would not let the parents live alone; we would care for them. But if they have the privilege to live in senior housing [here] and we can get it, OK. They will be more comfortable" (Braun et al., 1996, p. 224).

Respondents also discussed the importance of cultural festivals and recommended that educational efforts be presented at festival-related events (Braun & Browne, 1998).

## Native Hawaiians

### History

The Hawaiian people (or *kanaka maoli*) are of Polynesian extraction, sharing a common ancestry with indigenous people across the South Pacific, from New Zealand to Easter Island (Blaisdell & Mokuau, 1991). After contact with the West in 1778, the native population was reduced drastically as Hawaiians contracted and died from measles, tuberculosis, venereal diseases, leprosy, influenza, and other infectious diseases (Stannard, 1989). The importation of labor to Hawaii from China, Japan, and the Philippines (and other countries) was partly in response to the decimation of the Hawaiian population and, starting in the 19th century, non-Hawaiians have outnumbered Hawaiians in Hawaii (Blaisdell & Mokuau, 1991). Despite increased attention to Hawaiian health, mortality rates for Native Hawaiians continue to be significantly higher than for non-Hawaiian residents of the state (Braun, Look, & Tsark, 1995).

In 1990 the number of Hawaiians in the United States approached 300,000; 70 percent reside in Hawaii (where they make up about 18 percent of the state's population), and about 14 percent reside in California (Asian American Health Forum, 1990).

### Native Hawaiian Cultural Traditions and Values That Affect Caregiving and Help-Seeking Patterns

Family relations and help-seeking behaviors are clearly influenced by a number of traditional Hawaiian values. These include *mana* (energy that permeates and links all things), *lokahi* (harmony and unity), *pono* (rightness or proper order), *'ohana* (extended family and social supports), *kokua* (mutual help and cooperation), and *kuleana* (role). In traditional Hawaiian families, each member had his or her *kuleana*; these roles are very explicit and based on age, gender, class, and ability. As in most oral cultures, *kupuna* (elders) are respected by younger people as teachers and keepers of knowledge (Blaisdell & Mokuau, 1991).

In traditional Hawaiian culture, illness and other misfortune are thought to be caused by an imbalance of *mana* or loss of *pono*. A well-known Hawaiian problem-solving method is *ho'oponopono* (to correct or to restore *pono*), which involves prayer, a definition of the problem, self-scrutiny on the part of those out of balance, a determination of restitution, and forgiveness (Blaisdell & Mokuau, 1991). Dreams were also considered as important sources of information, used to solve problems and to forecast events and behaviors. Severe mental distress was sometimes interpreted as a type of possession, and the family would seek help from a *kahuna*, or Hawaiian healer (Braun & Browne, 1998; Young, 1980).

Spiritual health is considered to be more important than physical health, and Hawaiians are usually very accepting of people who have any kind of illness or disability. Help-seeking is compromised by feelings of fatalism about illness and perceived conflicts between Hawaiian values and those of the Western health care system (for example, specialization, economic gain, and emphasis on the individual) (Braun, Look, et al., 1995). In addition, Native Hawaiians tend to live in communities that are far from major medical centers, and they are less likely to have comprehensive health insurance. Federal legislation in the 1980s established Native Hawaiian Health Care Systems on each of the major Hawaiian islands, as well as scholarships to support the training of Native Hawaiian health care providers. These efforts have resulted in a significant increase in community-based primary care that is culturally responsive; it is hoped that these services will have a big effect on health status (Braun, Look, et al., 1995).

### Native Hawaiian Views of Dementia and Associated Help-Seeking Patterns

In interviews with Hawaiians, we found that most participants had seen older adults with dementia symptoms. Several of our participants were service providers themselves and knew about Alzheimer's disease. They thought that many of their clients, however, would just attribute dementia symptoms to old age. They recited a saying in pidgin, "more *makule*, more *pupule*," which translates roughly as "the older you get, the more mixed up you get." Regardless of cause, there was an expectation that the elder would be cared for at home by the *'ohana* and that someone would be acknowledged as accepting this honorable *kuleana*. This person does not necessarily have to be a daughter or daughter-in-law, because the role would go to the

person that the family thought could carry it out best. The designated caregiver would have control of the care and would be expected to call together the *'ohana* to discuss major decisions or problems.

Respondents said that medical care for dementia symptoms would more likely be sought if the family considered the physician to be a friend or a friend-of-a-friend. These findings concur with other studies related to help seeking among Hawaiian families (Braun, Mokuau, & Tsark, 1997).

### Implications for Practice, Policy, and Research

Implications of these findings include the recognition of diversity among and within API American groups, information about which can help increase cultural sensitivity of providers who serve API groups; the need for policy initiatives that provide for more outreach and education to specific API groups about dementia; and the need for more research about API Americans in general, as well as research specific to dementia and use of dementia-care services.

#### Practice

The diversity within the API population, which encompasses at least 30 distinctive cultural groups, cannot be overstressed. This article has provided the briefest review of only five API groups. It also emphasized traditional perceptions of dementia, caregiving, and help seeking, rather than describing the variation of perceptions within ethnic groups. This is an important consideration, because differences within API groups may be as significant as across-group differences. For example, the values and behaviors of a sixth-generation Chinese American more likely would resemble those of a fourth-generation

Japanese American than those of a Chinese person who has just immigrated from rural China.

Some of the other factors, besides timing of immigration, that influence culturally linked health behaviors include socioeconomic status, language spoken at home, extent to which the community (and family) is ethnically homogenous, educational attainment, and expectations about returning to one's ancestral home (Braun & Browne, 1998).

Social workers in health settings who work with individuals of different cultures are encouraged to seek out ways to increase their awareness of cultural values and other factors that affect each group's perception of health and illness and service-use patterns. At the same time, they must use caution to avoid stereotyping of Asian and Pacific Island populations. Koenig and Gates-William (1995), in their work with dying patients, presented guidelines that have implications for working with dementia families:

- Assess the language used to discuss the patient's disease.
- Determine whether decisions are made by the patient or by the larger family unit.
- Consider the relevance of religious beliefs.
- Assess the patient's and family's degree of fatalism versus an active desire for control of events.

In light of a call to recognize cultural differences, it is interesting that several of our API informants in Hawaii stressed a need to "socialize" our different ethnic groups to American ways. A Filipino informant was adamant that providers reach out to the local Filipino community to say that, *bahala na* aside, there are things that can be done about health problems, that preventive care is important, and that seeing a doctor about a family member's dementia symptoms is necessary.

Our Vietnamese informants appeared open to learning how to take advantage of the U.S. health and social service systems. A bilingual Chinese provider made a similar statement in relation to living wills—that is, that service providers must make efforts to explain the concept to new Chinese immigrants despite a hesitance among this group to discuss death and dying (Braun & Nichols, 1997). These same informants asked that outreach efforts and educational materials be offered in the language of the target group and be presented within contexts meaningful to the group. Yet there was an acknowledgment that new immigrants need to learn American ways if they are going to be successful. This perspective supports a two-dimensional view of acculturation (that is, new Americans can adhere to traditional cultural values and understand and follow American norms simultaneously) (Nagata, 1994). They do not have to give up one set of values for the other, and both will influence service acceptability and utilization (Braun & Browne, 1998).

*Policy*

In the area of policy, social workers are committed to ensuring that patients and their families receive the services that would benefit them. Ube and Sue (1991) recommended three possible approaches to increasing service attractiveness and fit. The most expensive, and perhaps for some groups the most effective, approach is to develop parallel services specifically for the target group. Sue (1994) described successful programs in San Francisco and Los Angeles where the language, signs, food and drinks, and providers were of the culture being served.

Specific to dementia services, Elliott et al. (1996) described programs within Chinese agencies and hospitals that provide outreach, education, diagnostic services, and treatment, and Tempo and Saito (1996) described a Japanese American community senior center, all in the San Francisco area.

In Hawaii, parallel services have been established for Native Hawaiians through the Native Hawaiian Health Systems, which fund programs and clinics in Hawaiian communities using Hawaiian health care providers (Braun, Look, et al., 1995).

The second approach is for mainstream providers to add bilingual workers to their facilities and programs. This approach is facilitated by university admission policies and financial aid programs that support individuals from ethnic minority groups in their pursuit of advanced degrees in health and social welfare. In testing the effectiveness of this approach, Sue (1994) found that API clients stayed in treatment longer and had better outcomes when matched with providers of the same ethnicity who spoke the same language. The Honolulu chapter of the Alzheimer's Association has taken this route through a contract with Ameri-Corps, which allows the association to employ bilingual VISTA workers in outreach to specific ethnic communities (Braun, Takamura, et al., 1995).

The third approach is for mainstream providers to obtain training for their workers in cultural awareness and sensitivity, emphasizing listening skills and nonjudgmental helping strategies (Mokuau & Shimizu, 1991). For educational institutions cross-cultural awareness and sensitivity training need to be part of the curriculum. This type of training should continue within health and social service agencies, keeping practitioners abreast of findings related to value-linked behaviors, to resources that can facilitate work with individuals of different cultures (for example, translation services), and to increasing appreciation of diversity and the capacity to listen.

In addition, patient education and outreach materials should be produced in the appropriate language and recognizable context for specific groups.

## Research

Clearly, more research on API perceptions of dementia and service use must be conducted and published. If culturally sensitive outreach materials and services are to be developed, the profession needs to base them on information gathered directly from these groups, not on assumptions or stereotypes about elderly people of color. This article has sketched out what we have learned about select API groups, but much more needs to be learned. At least in Hawaii-based work, use of qualitative methods, especially focus group interviews (we call them "talk-story" interviews) have been well received by participants and have revealed a great deal of information about the groups' worldviews, attitudes, and practices. However, large-scale studies of socioeconomic and health status are also needed (Liu & Yu, 1985; Tanjasiri et al., 1995; Yu & Liu, 1992).

Currently, few national studies offer API respondents the opportunity to specify to which API group they belong. Even when these data are collected, API respondents are usually undersampled. Researchers who are concerned with improving our knowledge of the API American groups have recommended that federal agencies fund studies that expand and standardize API racial or ethnic classification, develop more culturally appropriate survey measures, oversample API populations, and support a thorough collection and analyses of API data in states where 68 percent of all API Americans live—California, Hawaii, New York, Illinois, and Texas (Liu & Yu, 1985; Tanjasiri et al., 1995; Yu & Liu, 1992).

## Conclusion

Dementia is a serious concern faced by elderly people, their families, and the social workers who serve them. As the nation's cultural diversity increases, researchers and practitioners need to learn more about the histories and traditional cultures of residents of color and gain an understanding about how culturally linked values affect health and help-seeking behaviors related to dementia. Gaining insights into clients from ethnic minority groups can help social workers increase the cultural competence of their own practices and of the facilities within which they work.

## References

Agbayani-Siewert, P., & Revilla, L. (1995). Filipino Americans. In P. G. Min (Ed.), *Asian Americans: Contemporary trends and issues* (pp. 134–168). Thousand Oaks, CA: Sage Publications.

Asian American Health Forum. (1990). *Asian and Pacific Islander American California proportionate mortality ratios.* (Monograph Series 2). San Francisco: Author.

Billones, H., & Wilson, S. (1990). *Understanding the Filipino elderly.* Toronto: Ryerson Polytechnical Institute.

Blaisdell, R. K., & Mokuau, N. (1991). *K naka Maoli*: Indigenous Hawaiian. In N. Mokuau (Ed.), *Handbook of social services for Asian and Pacific Islanders* (pp. 131–154). New York: Greenwood Press.

Braun, K. L., & Browne, C. (1998). Cultural values and caregiving patterns among Asian and Pacific Islander Americans. In D. Redburn & R. McNamara (Eds.), *Social gerontology* (pp. 155–182). New York: Greenwood Press.

Braun, K. L., Look, M., & Tsark, J. U. (1995). Native Hawaii mortality rates. *Hawaii Medical Journal, 54,* 723–729.

Braun, K. L., Mokuau, N., & Tsark, J. U. (1997). Cultural themes in health, illness, and rehabilitation among Native Hawaiians. *Topics in Geriatric Rehabilitation, 12*(3), 19–37.

Braun, K. L., & Nichols, R. (1997). Death and dying in four Asian American cultures: A descriptive study. *Death Studies, 21,* 327–360.

Braun, K. L., Takamura, J. C., Forman, S., Sasaki, P., & Meininger, L. (1995). Developing and testing outreach materials on Alzheimer's disease for Asian and Pacific Islander Americans. *Gerontologist, 35*(1), 122–126.

Braun, K. L., Takamura, J. C., & Mougeot, T. (1996). Perceptions of dementia, caregiving, and help seeking among recent Vietnamese immigrants. *Journal of Cross-Cultural Gerontology, 11,* 213–228.

Browne, C., Fong, R., & Mokuau, N. (1994). The mental health of Asian and Pacific Islander elders: Implications for mental health administrators. *Journal of Mental Health Administration, 21*(1), 52–59.

Chang, W. (1985). A cross-cultural study of depressive symptomatology. *Culture, Medicine, and Psychiatry, 9,* 295–317.

Char, W. F., Tseng, W. S., Lum, K. Y., & Hsu, J. (1980). The Chinese. In J. F. McDermott, W. S. Tseng, & T. W. Maretzki (Eds.), *People and cultures of Hawaii: A psychocultural profile* (pp. 53–72). Honolulu: University Press of Hawaii.

Cheung, F. K. (1982). Psychological symptoms among Chinese in urban Hong Kong. *Social Science and Medicine, 16,* 1339–1344.

Elliott, K. S., Di Minno, M., Lam, D., & Tu, A. M. (1996). Working with Chinese families in the context of dementia. In G. Yeo & D. Gallagher-Thompson (Eds.), *Ethnicity and the dementias* (pp. 89–108). Bristol, PA: Taylor & Francis.

Evans, D. A., Funkenstein, H. H., Albert, M. S., Scherr, P. A., Crook, N. R., Chown, M. J.,

Herbert, L. E., Hennakens, C. H., & Taylor, J. D. (1989). Prevalence of Alzheimer's disease in a community population of older persons. *JAMA, 262,* 2551–2556.

Fabrega, H. (1969). Social psychiatric aspects of acculturation and migration: A general statement. *Comprehensive Psychiatry, 10,* 314–392.

Flaskerud, J. H., & Hu, L. T. (1994). Participation in and outcome of treatment for major depression among low income Asian-Americans. *Psychiatry Research, 53,* 289–300.

Fujita, S., Ito, K. L., Abe, J., & Takeuchi, D. T. (1991). Japanese Americans. In N. Mokuau (Ed.), *Handbook of social services for Asian and Pacific Islanders* (pp. 61–78). New York: Greenwood Press.

Gelfand, D. E. (1994). *Aging and ethnicity.* New York: Springer.

Gold, S. J. (1992). Mental health and illness in Vietnamese refugees. *Western Journal of Medicine, 157,* 290–294.

Hessler, R. M., Nolan, M. F., Ogbu, B., & New, P. K. (1975). Intraethnic diversity: Health care of the Chinese-Americans. *Human Organization, 34,* 253–262.

Huang, K. (1991). Chinese Americans. In N. Mokuau (Ed.), *Handbook of social services for Asian and Pacific Islanders* (pp. 79–96). New York: Greenwood Press.

Ikels, C. (1993). *The experience of dementia in China* (Working Paper Series on International Mental Health). Cambridge, MA: Harvard University, Center for the Study of Culture and Medicine.

Kinzie, J. D., Boehnlein, J. K., Leung, P. K., Morre, L. J., Riley, C., & Smith, D. (1990). The prevalence of posttraumatic stress disorder and its clinical significance among Southeast Asian refugees. *American Journal of Psychiatry, 147,* 913–917.

Koenig, B. A., & Gates-William, J. (1995). Understanding cultural difference in caring for dying patients. *Western Journal of Medicine, 163,* 244–249.

Lin, K. M., Tazuma, L., & Masuda, M. (1979). Adaptational problems of the Vietnamese refugees, Part 1: Health and mental health status. *Archives of General Psychiatry, 36,* 955–961.

Lin, T. Y. (1985). Mental disorders and psychiatry in Chinese culture. In W. S. Tseng & D.Y.H. Wu (Eds.), *Chinese culture and mental health* (pp. 369–393). San Diego: Academic Press.

Lin-Fu, J. S. (1988). Population characteristics and health care needs of Asian Pacific Americans. *Public Health Reports, 103,* 18–27.

Liu, W. T., & Yu, E.S.H. (1985). Asian/Pacific American elderly: Mortality differentials, health status, and use of health services. *Journal of Applied Gerontology, 4,* 35–64.

Markides, K. (1987). *Aging and ethnicity.* Newbury Park, CA: Sage Publications.

Matsuoka, J. K. (1990). Differential acculturation among Vietnamese refugees: Implications for social work practice. *Social Work, 35,* 341–345.

Matsuoka, J. K. (1991). Vietnamese Americans. In N. Mokuau (Ed.), *Handbook of social services for Asian and Pacific Islanders* (pp. 117–130). New York: Greenwood Press.

McBride, M. R., & Parreno, H. (1996). Filipino American families and caregiving. In G. Yeo & D. Gallagher-Thompson (Eds.), *Ethnicity and the dementias* (pp. 123–136). Bristol, PA: Taylor & Francis.

McDermott, J. F., Tseng, W. S., & Maretzki, T. W. (1980). *People and cultures of Hawaii: A psychocultural profile.* Honolulu: University Press of Hawaii.

Min, P. G. (1995). *Asian Americans: Contemporary trends and issues.* Thousand Oaks, CA: Sage Publications.

Mokuau, N., & Shimizu, D. (1991). Conceptual framework for social services for Asian and Pacific Islander Americans. In N. Mokuau (Ed.), *Handbook of social services for Asian and Pacific Islanders* (pp. 21–36). New York: Greenwood Press.

Morioka-Douglas, N., & Yeo, G. (1990). *Aging and health: Asian/Pacific Island American elders*

(Working Paper Series No. 3). Stanford, CA: Stanford Geriatric Education Center.

Nagata, D. K. (1994). Assessing Asian American acculturation and ethnic identity: The need for a multidimensional framework. *Asian American and Pacific Islander Journal of Health, 2*(2), 108–124.

Nishi, S. M. (1995). Japanese Americans. In P. G. Min (Ed.), *Asian Americans: Contemporary trends and issues* (pp. 95–133). Thousand Oaks, CA: Sage Publications.

Ponce, D., & Forman, S. (1980). The Filipinos. In J. F. McDermott, W. S. Tseng, & T. W. Maretzki (Eds.), *People and cultures of Hawaii: A psychocultural profile* (pp. 155–183). Honolulu: University Press of Hawaii.

Rogers, T., & Izutsu, S. (1980). The Japanese. In J. F. McDermott, W. S. Tseng, & T. W. Maretzki (Eds.), *People and cultures of Hawaii: A psychocultural profile* (pp. 73–99). Honolulu: University Press of Hawaii.

Rumbaut, R. G. (1995). Vietnamese, Laotian, and Cambodian Americans. In P. G. Min (Ed.), *Asian Americans: Contemporary trends and issues* (pp. 232–270). Thousand Oaks, CA: Sage Publications.

Rutledge, P. J. (1992). *The Vietnamese experience in America*. Bloomington: Indiana University Press.

Ryan, A. S. (1985). Cultural factors in casework with Chinese-Americans. *Social Casework, 66,* 333–340.

Shon, S. P., & Ja, D. A. (1982). Asian families. In M. McGoldrick, J. K. Pearce, & J. Giordano (Eds.), *Ethnicity and family therapy* (pp. 208–228). New York: Guilford.

Stannard, D. E. (1989). *Before the horror: The population of Hawaii on the eve of Western contact.* Honolulu: University of Hawaii Press.

Sue, S. (1994). Mental health. In N.W.S. Zane, D. T. Takeuchi, & K.N.J. Young (Eds.), *Confronting critical health issues of Asian and Pacific Islander Americans* (pp. 266–288). Thousand Oaks, CA: Sage Publications.

Takamura, J. C. (1991). Asian and Pacific Islander elderly. In N. Mokuau (Ed.), *Handbook of social services for Asian and Pacific Islanders* (pp. 185–202). New York: Greenwood Press.

Tanjasiri, S. P., Wallace, S. P., & Shibata, K. (1995). Picture imperfect: Hidden problems among Asian Pacific Islander elderly. *Gerontologist, 35,* 753–760.

Tempo, P. M., & Saito, A. (1996). Techniques of working with Japanese American families. In G. Yeo & D. Gallagher-Thompson (Eds.), *Ethnicity and the dementias* (pp. 89–108). Bristol, PA: Taylor & Francis.

Tran, T. V. (1991). Sponsorship and employment status among Indochinese refugees in the United States. *International Migration Review, 25,* 536–550.

Ube, L., & Sue, S. (1991). Nature and scope of services for Asian and Pacific Islander Americans. In N. Mokuau (Ed.), *Handbook of social services for Asian and Pacific Islanders* (pp. 3–19). New York: Greenwood Press.

U.S. Bureau of the Census. (1991a). *Population of metropolitan areas by race and Hispanic origin: 1990* (CB-91-229). Washington, DC: U.S. Department of Commerce.

U.S. Bureau of the Census. (1991b). *Race and Hispanic origin: 1990 census profile number 2.* Washington, DC: U.S. Department of Commerce.

U.S. Congress, Office of Technology Assessment. (1990). *Confused minds, burdened families: Finding help for people with Alzheimer's disease and other dementias* (Publication No. OTA-BA-403). Washington, DC: U.S. Government Printing Office.

U.S. Department of Health and Human Services. (1985). *Report of the Secretary's Task Force on Black and Minority Health, Volume 1.* Washington, DC: U.S. Government Printing Office.

White, L. (1992). Toward a program of cross-cultural research on the epidemiology of Alzheimer's disease. *Current Science, 63,* 456–469.

Wong, M. G. (1995). Chinese Americans. In P. G. Min (Ed.), *Asian Americans: Contemporary trends and issues* (pp. 58–94). Thousand Oaks, CA: Sage Publications.

Wykle, M., & Kaskel, B. (1991). Increasing the longevity of minority older adults through improved health status. In Gerontological Society of America (Ed.), *Minority elders: Longevity, economics, and health* (pp. 24–31). Washington, DC: Gerontological Society of America.

Yeo, G., & Gallagher-Thompson, D. (Eds.). (1996). *Ethnicity and the dementias*. Bristol, PA: Taylor & Francis.

Yeo, G., Gallagher-Thompson, D., & Lieberman, M. (1996). Variations in dementia characteristics by ethnic category. In G. Yeo & D. Gallagher-Thompson (Eds.), *Ethnicity and the dementias* (pp. 21–30). Bristol, PA: Taylor & Francis.

Ying, Y. W., & Hu, L. T. (1994). Public outpatient mental health services: Use and outcome among Asian Americans. *American Journal of Orthopsychiatry, 64*, 448–455.

Young, B.B.C. (1980). The Hawaiians. In J. F. McDermott, W. S. Tseng, & T. W. Maretzki (Eds.), *People and cultures of Hawaii: A psychocultural profile* (pp. 5–24). Honolulu: University Press of Hawaii.

Young, J. J., & Gu, N. (1995). *Demographic and socio-economic characteristics of elderly Asian and Pacific Island Americans*. Seattle, WA: National Asian Pacific Center on Aging.

Yu, E.S.H., & Liu, W. T. (1992). U.S. national health data on Asian Americans and Pacific Islanders: A research agenda for the 1990s. *American Journal of Public Health, 82*, 1645–1652.

This chapter was originally published in the November 1998 issue of *Health & Social Work*, Vol. 23, Number 4, pp. 262–274.

# 12

## The Effect of
## Functional Disability
## on Service Utilization

### Implications for Long-Term Care

LEE R. SLIVINSKE,
V. L. FITCH and
N. W. WINGERSON

The number of elderly people aged 65 and over is growing, as is their demand for services (Brody, 2004; Hobbs & Damon, 1997; Chappell & Knysacz, 1996; Dwyer, Barton & Vogel; Kolanty, & Bohnfield, 1997; Manton, Corder, & Stallard, 1997; Wiener & Illston, 1994). As a result, reliable and valid criteria are required for determining their need for services (Kempen & Summerfeir, 1996; Spector & Kemper, 1994; Williams et al., 1991). This criteria has become an important concern regarding managed care initiatives at federal, state, and local governments and private insurance companies attempt to establish disability tests to determine eligibility for entry into portions of the long-term services network for elderly people (Cowand & Vogel; Duncan, & Grauo, 1995; Hudson, 1996; Kane, Saslow, & Brundage, 1991; Rischovsky & Newman, 1990; Robert & Norgard, 1996; Spector, 1991; Stone & Murtaugh, 1990).

Numerous amendments to Medicare, Medicaid, Title XX of the Social Security Act, and Title III of the Older Americans Act regarding eligibility requirements have been proposed during the past decade (Binstock, 1994; Shearer, 1989; Spector,

# 12

# The Effect of Functional Disability on Service Utilization

Implications for Long-Term Care

LEE R. SLIVINSKE,
V. L. FITCH, and
N. W. WINGERSON

The number of elderly people age 65 and over is growing and so is their demand for services (Brody, Litvin, Hoffman, & Kleban, 1995; Cornman & Kingson, 1996; Emlet & Hall, 1991; Lianov, Kohatsu, & Bohnstedt, 1991; Manton, Corder, & Stallard, 1993; Wiener & Illston, 1994). As a result, reliable and valid criteria are required for determining the actual need for services (Kempen & Suurmeijer, 1990; Spector & Kemper, 1994; Williams et al., 1991). This criteria has become an important concern regarding managed care initiatives as federal, state, and local governments and private insurance companies attempt to establish disability tests to determine eligibility for entry into portions of the long-term services network for elderly people (Coward, Vogel, Duncan, & Uttavo, 1995; Hudson, 1996; Kane, Saslow, & Brundage, 1991; Reschovsky & Newman, 1990; Robert & Norgard, 1996; Spector, 1991; Stone & Murtaugh, 1990).

Numerous amendments to Medicare, Medicaid, Title XX of the Social Security Act, and Title III of the Older Americans Act regarding eligibility requirements have been proposed during the past decade (Binstock, 1994; Shearer, 1989; Spector,

1991). States also are enacting legislation to screen nursing home applicants and limit other benefits to those considered to have the greatest need (Inverson, 1986; Justice, 1988; Spector, 1991). In addition, private insurers also are offering a variety of policies to cover long-term, in-home, and other care (Capitman & Sciegaj, 1995; Health Insurance Association of America, 1989; Stone & Murtaugh, 1990; Temkin-Greener & Meiners, 1995).

The eligibility criteria selected will have a tremendous effect on the service delivery system and the care provided for elderly people. These criteria will influence which elderly people are entitled to have access to the system, the composition and amount of services provided, and the allocation of resources to cover the cost of service provision (Capitman & Sciegaj, 1995; Kempen & Suurmeijer, 1990; Spector, 1991).

In the past and often today, the eligibility criteria proposed have been indicators of independent functioning. Typically, these eligibility criteria included measures of activities of daily living (ADLs) and instrumental activities of daily living (IADLs) (Spector, 1991; Spector & Kemper, 1994; Stone & Murtaugh, 1990). ADLs generally are the ability to eat, dress, walk, toilet, and bathe, activities considered necessary for a person to care for himself or herself directly or independently. IADLs, which include the ability to shop, prepare meals, do housework, take medication, and the like, often are used to assess the ability of elderly people to remain self-reliant and to successfully negotiate their environment (Kempen & Suurmeijer, 1990). A disability in one or more of those areas has been the criterion proposed to determine eligibility for a variety of services and programs (Stone & Murtaugh, 1990).

More recent studies and reports have recognized the importance of examining the ef-

fect of cognitive impairment and disruptive behaviors on eligibility for long-term care and other services (Bass, Looman, & Ehrlich, 1992; Kane et al., 1991; Leutz, Abrahams, & Capitman, 1993; Pruchno et al., 1995; Spirrison & Pierce, 1993; U.S. Bipartisan Commission on Comprehensive Health Care, 1990). Those examining such effects note that individuals who suffer from dementias, neurological syndromes, or cognitive deficits have a need for care and services that is just as great and important as the need of those experiencing ADL–IADL problems (Bass & Noelker, 1987; Spector, 1991). Similarly, elderly people who steal compulsively, wander, throw temper tantrums, or engage in other disruptive behaviors also may require assistance and supervision (Brill, Drimmer, Morgan, & Gordon, 1995; Kane et al., 1991; Spector, 1991). Thus, eligibility criteria theoretically should include an assessment of cognitive and behavioral impairments, particularly if constant supervision is indicated, as well as ADL–IADL measures of functional disability (Kane et al., 1991; U.S. Bipartisan Commission on Comprehensive Health Care, 1990). The debate continues, but whatever eligibility process is used, it must be simple to administer, easy to understand, and reliable and valid (Leutz et al., 1993; Rabiner, Mutran, & Stearns, 1995).

This study examined the efficacy of using ADL–IADL dependencies and cognitive and behavioral impairments as eligibility criteria for entry into portions of the service network of elderly people. Specifically, four different approaches in determining eligibility were examined. These included measuring individual ADL–IADL limitations, counting the number of ADL–IADL disabilities, using Likert-type ADL–IADL scales, and using a comprehensive eligibility model.

The research design used three comparison groups of service recipients. Included were people receiving long-term care in nursing homes, people receiving assistance at home, and people participating in other community-based services such as those provided by multipurpose centers and meal sites. Fredman, Droge, and Rabin (1992) considered the inclusion of comparison groups to be essential in determining actual disability and service utilization patterns. These comparison groups also permitted the gathering of baseline data useful for an examination of the disabilities possessed by current system users. This study provides data that may permit a future comparison of disabilities possessed by current and future elderly consumers if universal preadmission screening were used.

## Method

### Sample

We selected a purposive sample of facilities that represented three general types of long-term care—institutional, in-home/home health, and community based. Three nursing homes, two in-home/home health agencies, two multipurpose centers, and a regional meal site were used in this study. All elderly individuals receiving services from those facilities during the course of this study were asked to be participants. Of these 1,439 consumers, 547 people (38 percent) agreed to participate. No pattern for reason for refusal to participate was noted in any of the settings. Participants' average age was 74.02 years (SD = 7.13), and average formal education was 10.5 years (SD = 1.84). Nearly four-fifths (77.5 percent) were female; 94.0 percent were white (Table 12-1). Approximately 64 percent of the sample had annual incomes below $9,999, 31.3 percent had incomes between $10,000 and $19,999, and 4.4 percent had incomes greater than $20,000. Regard-

TABLE 12-1. Demographic Characteristics of Respondents (N = 547)

| Variable | % |
|---|---|
| Gender | |
| Female | 77.5 |
| Male | 22.5 |
| Annual income ($) | |
| 0–4,999 | 21.2 |
| 5,000–9,999 | 43.0 |
| 10,000–14,999 | 22.0 |
| 15,000–19,999 | 9.3 |
| 20,000 and over | 4.4 |
| Employment status | |
| Retired | 94.5 |
| Full-time, part-time | 4.5 |
| Seeking employment | 1.0 |
| Race | |
| White | 94.0 |
| African American | 6.0 |
| Marital status | |
| Single | 7.3 |
| Married | 30.5 |
| Separated | .4 |
| Divorced | 4.2 |
| Widowed | 57.6 |
| Service type | |
| Nursing home | 30.7 |
| In-home/home health care | 35.1 |
| Community services only | 34.2 |

ing employment, 94.5 percent were retired, 4.5 percent were working part- or full-time, and 1.0 percent were actively seeking employment. About 58 percent were widowed, 30.5 percent were married, and 11.9 percent were separated, divorced, or single. In addition, 30.7 percent resided in nursing homes, 35.1 percent received in-home/home health care, and 34.2 percent used community-based services (Table 12-1).

### Measurement

Three sets of measures were used in this study. The first two were subjective and evaluative measures of ADL–IADL, physical health, social resources, morale, religiosity, economic resources, overall level of functioning, personal control, memory deficits, and behavioral problems. Subjective measures consisted of the elderly person's self-assessment of his or her state or condition in each of the above mentioned areas, and evaluative measures consisted of the judgments of professional staff in these same areas.

Six Likert-type scales were used to measure physical health (12 items), social resources (13 items), morale (20 items), religiosity (11 items), economic resources (10 items), and ADL–IADL (13 items). The alpha reliability coefficients of the scales ranged from .80 to .94. All scales, including ADL–IADL measures, were taken from the Wellness Index, which measured overall level of functioning. The Wellness Index had a theta reliability coefficient of .77. Prior examination of the Wellness Index and scales revealed both the index and the scales to have acceptable reliability as well as validity. For a complete discussion of the procedures used to establish their reliability and validity, see Slivinske, Fitch, and Morawski (1996).

The reliability of the ADL and IADL items on the ADL–IADL scale also were assessed separately for the purposes of this study. ADL items consisted of difficulties in eating, dressing, bathing, walking, toileting, and getting in and out of bed without assistance. Cronbach's alpha for this portion of the scale was .94. The alpha reliability coefficient for the IADL items, which included problems with shopping, meal preparation, housework, taking medications, money management, and transportation, was .86. The items in both scales were modeled after those routinely used in various disability measures. Five ADLs and cognitive and behavioral measures were recommended for use by the U.S. Bipartisan Commission on Comprehensive Health Care (1990), and Kempen and Suurmeijer (1990) suggested 18 separate ADL–IADL categories. Multidimensional subscales are being identified and examined within ADL–IADL scales (Fitzgerald, Smith, Martin, Freedman, & Wolinsky, 1993). At this time there appears to be no consensus about which specific measures should be used.

Personal control was measured using the 35-item Perceived Control Scale (PCS). The PCS was developed by Ireys (1979) to measure individuals' perceived capacity to bring about change in their immediate environment. The reliability and validity of the scale were assessed on a sample of 59 adults in varying situations and at varying times. Split-half reliability coefficients, ranging from .75 to .86, were obtained, in addition to test–retest reliability coefficients, which ranged from .72 to .89. Concurrent validity of the scale was examined by comparing PCS scores to those obtained on the Nowicki-Duke Locus of Control Scale for adults (Nowicki & Duke, 1974). It was found to be acceptable ($r = -.41$, $p < .05$, $n = 59$). A thorough discussion of the procedures used may be found in Ireys (1979).

We measured self-assessment of level of functioning with a five-point Likert-type item with categories ranging from 5 = excellent to 1 = very poor. Self-assessment of memory and behavioral problems was measured with dichotomous "yes/no" responses. Similarly, professional staff evaluated participants' level of functioning, physical health, social resources, morale, religiosity, economic resources, and ADLs and IADLs, using five-point Likert-type items. Regarding memory and behavior problems, staff responded to items that had dichotomous categories identical to those described above. The third set of variables consisted of the demographic characteristics used in this study. Two additional measures, occupational status and medical insurance, also were obtained.

## Results

Several study variables, including gender, marital status, occupational status, and race

**TABLE 12-2. Original Means and Standard Deviations of All Study Variables (N = 547)**

| Variable | M | SD |
|---|---|---|
| Self-assessment | | |
| ADL–IADL | 49.01 | 9.52 |
| Physical health | 43.00 | 7.52 |
| Social resources | 51.42 | 6.00 |
| Morale | 72.95 | 8.22 |
| Religiosity | 42.91 | 6.84 |
| Economic resources | 33.87 | 7.44 |
| Level of functioning | 3.66 | 0.80 |
| Personal control | 113.87 | 11.51 |
| Memory deficits | .12 | 0.33 |
| Behavioral problems | .05 | 0.22 |
| Evaluative assessment | | |
| ADL–IADL | 3.87 | 0.93 |
| Physical health | 3.54 | 0.85 |
| Social resources | 3.94 | 0.75 |
| Morale | 3.91 | 0.81 |
| Religiosity | 3.92 | 0.71 |
| Economic resources | 3.58 | 0.71 |
| Level of functioning | 3.71 | 0.81 |
| Personal control | 3.95 | 0.89 |
| Memory deficits | .13 | 0.04 |
| Behavioral problems | .06 | 0.25 |
| Age | 74.02 | 7.13 |
| Gender[a] | .22 | 0.04 |
| Marital status[a] | .31 | 0.05 |
| Occupational status[a] | .29 | 0.05 |
| Race[a] | .06 | 0.24 |
| Income | 2.33 | 0.88 |
| Educational level | 10.50 | 1.84 |
| Medical insurance | 1.82 | 0.91 |

a. Coded as 0 and 1 and treated as interval level.

were represented as indicator or dummy variables coded as 0 or 1 to permit their inclusion in the analyses that follow (see Table 12-2). In subsequent univariate and multivariate procedures, highly interrelated (.68 and higher) and nonnormally distributed variables were excluded from certain analyses. These variables included self-assessed memory and behavioral problems, evaluative level of functioning, personal control, behavioral problems, and race.

As would be expected, the percentage of respondents experiencing difficulties increases in each category of ADL–IADLs, as well as the subjective and evaluative components of cognitive and behavioral problems, as service type progresses from community services only to in-home/home health to nursing-home care (Table 12-3). Walking without assistance was the ADL problem experienced by the largest percentage of people across all service categories (18.8 percent, 9.5 percent, and 2.9 percent, respectively), and needing help with housework was the greatest IADL concern (25.6 percent, 24.7 percent, and 9.3 percent). Regarding cognitive and behavioral problems, 11.2 percent and 5.7 percent, respectively, of those in nursing homes were evaluated as having deficits, whereas 9.0 percent and 4.4 percent in this setting perceived themselves as having problems in these areas. The percentages in the remaining service categories (in-home/home health and community-based services) also were much smaller (2.7 percent and 0 percent), as predicted.

The first method of eligibility determination was examined using chi-square analyses. These revealed that all ADL–IADL disability measures, as well as perceived and evaluated cognitive problem variables, were significantly associated with service type ($p < .001$). Cramer's Vs ranged from .25 to .59, and the amount of variation explained ranged from 6 percent to 35 percent.

These analyses revealed that needing assistance shopping (IADL) explained the greatest amount of variation (35 percent), and needing help bathing (ADL) and walking (ADL) tied for the second largest amount (21 percent). The variable that explained the least amount of variation (6 percent) was needing assistance eating (ADL).

Similarly, mean levels of ADLs, IADLs, ADL–IADLs combined, and cognitive and behavioral problems (self-assessed and evaluated) were calculated for each service type. All mean levels of disabilities increased across

**TABLE 12-3. Percentage of Functional Disabilities and Cognitive and Behavioral Difficulties, by Service Type (N = 547)**

| Variable | Nursing Home (n = 168) | In-Home/ Home Health Care (n = 192) | Community Services Only (n = 187) | Cramer's V |
|---|---|---|---|---|
| ADLs | | | | |
| Eating | 5.9 | 3.7 | 0.2 | .25* |
| Dressing | 10.8 | 3.3 | 0.2 | .41* |
| Grooming | 8.2 | 3.1 | 0.4 | .33* |
| Walking | 18.8 | 9.5 | 2.9 | .46* |
| Bed | 13.0 | 5.7 | 0.0 | .44* |
| Bathing | 14.3 | 4.9 | 0.7 | .46* |
| Toileting | 11.5 | 4.8 | 1.1 | .37* |
| IADLs | | | | |
| Shopping | 25.4 | 21.4 | 4.0 | .59* |
| Meals | 22.9 | 16.5 | 3.1 | .54* |
| Housework | 25.6 | 24.7 | 9.3 | .45* |
| Medications | 18.1 | 10.8 | 1.5 | .48* |
| Money management | 13.7 | 10.6 | 2.0 | .36* |
| Transportation | 22.5 | 13.7 | 3.1 | .53* |
| Cognitive problems | | | | |
| Self-assessed | 9.0 | 2.7 | .4 | .36 |
| Evaluated | 11.2 | 1.6 | .2 | .47 |
| Behavioral problems | | | | |
| Self-assessed | 4.4 | .5 | 0.0 | — |
| Evaluated | 5.7 | .4 | .2 | — |

*$p < .001$

the service categories, as expected (Table 12-4). Overall, those in nursing homes had the most problems, those receiving in-home/home health services had fewer problems, while those receiving community-based services had the least. The apparent tie of mean levels of evaluated behavioral problems between community services only and in-home/home health care is an artifact of the rounding procedures used. The raw data were in the intended direction.

Participants in nursing homes averaged approximately three ADL problems and four IADL problems; mean levels of perceived and evaluated behavioral and cognitive problems ranged from .36 to .14. Those receiving in-home/home health care on average experienced one ADL problem and three IADL difficulties and had negligible

cognitive and behavioral difficulties. And those in the community centers averaged less than one combined ADL–IADL difficulty, with virtually no behavioral or cognitive difficulties (Table 12-4).

We used one-way analysis of variance analyses to assess the second method of eligibility determination. They revealed that there were significant associations between the average number of functional disabilities (ADLs, IADLs, ADL–IADLs combined, and evaluated cognitive problems) and service type ($p < .001$). Eta$^2$ was calculated for these items. Of all these measures, IADL difficulties explained the greatest amount of variation (50 percent) with service type. ADLs–IADLs combined explained the next largest amount of variation (44 percent), ADLs somewhat less variation (26 percent),

**TABLE 12-4. Overall Mean Levels of Functional Disabilities and Cognitive and Behavioral Difficulties, by Service Type (N = 547)**

| | No. of ADLs | No. of IADLs | No. of ADLs–IADLs | ADLs Likert Format | IADLs Likert Format | ADLs–IADLs Likert Format | Cognitive Problems | | Behavioral Problems | |
| | | | | | | | Self-Assessed | Evaluated | Self-Assessed | Evaluated |
|---|---|---|---|---|---|---|---|---|---|---|
| Nursing home[a] | 2.68* | 4.17* | 6.86* | 23.95* | 17.21* | 41.17* | .29 | .36* | .14 | .18 |
| In-home/home health[a] | .99* | 2.78* | 3.78* | 27.86* | 20.34* | 48.20* | .08 | .05* | .02 | .01 |
| Community services only[a] | .16* | .67* | .83* | 31.25* | 25.64* | 56.89* | .01 | .01* | .00 | .01 |
| Eta | .51 | .71 | .67 | .57 | .70 | .67 | — | .47 | — | — |

Note: — = not applicable.
a. Post hoc comparisons = $p < .05$.
*$p < .001$.

with evaluated cognitive problems the least (22 percent). Differences between all service type groupings in each category also were significant ($p < .05$).

When the Likert-type scales for ADLs, IADLs, and ADL–IADLs combined were analyzed, all results were virtually identical. Therefore, the ordering of the amount of variation explained for these measures remained the same. These measures represented the third type of eligibility determination.

A multiple group, step-wise discriminant function analysis was used to examine the fourth method of eligibility determination, which simultaneously included all major study variables (see Table 12-5). Two significant functions emerged ($p < .001$), which respectively explained 53 percent, and an additional 23 percent, of the variation with service type. The standardized discriminant function coefficients were rotated to aid in the interpretation of the two functions. Progressing from community-based services only through in-home/home health care to institutionalization, the profile described by the first function was as follows: Participants in nursing homes, as expected, reported more ADL–IADL problems than those receiving in-home/home health care, who experienced more difficulties than those consuming community-based services only. Following the same pattern, those in institutions tended to be widowed and to have fewer evaluated economic resources and less income, lower levels of evaluated and self-assessed social resources, lower assessments of overall functioning, and greater evaluative religiosity. Similarly, the second function showed that those in institutions were evaluated as having greater levels of ADL–IADL difficulty compared with people receiving in-home/home health care. Likewise, the latter group manifested greater levels of ADL–IADL difficulty compared with those participating in community-based services. People receiving in-home/home health care also were assessed by professional staff as having more memory problems, poorer physical health, and problems with morale than those in community-based services. Their educational levels were lower, they were least likely to have medical insurance, and they tended to be female. The participants themselves also rated their physical health and morale as lower. Overall, both functions combined explained 76 percent of the variation and correctly classified 73 percent of the cases by service type.

**TABLE 12-5. Rotated Standardized Discriminant Function Coefficients for Study Variables in Predicting Service Type ($N = 547$)**

| Function 1 Variable | Coefficient | Function 2 Variable | Coefficient |
|---|---|---|---|
| ADLs–IADLs (P) | .89 | ADLs–IADLs (E) | .63 |
| Marital status | .50 | Memory (E) | −.62 |
| Economic resources (E) | .30 | Physical health (E) | .43 |
| Social resources (E) | .25 | Educational level | −.26 |
| Level of functioning (P) | .22 | Morale (E) | .24 |
| Income | .19 | Physical health (P) | .19 |
| Social resources (P) | .16 | Gender | .18 |
| Religiosity | −.13 | Insurance | .17 |
| | | Morale (P) | .13 |
| $\chi^2(1, 34) = 549.75, p < .011, r = .73$ | | $\chi^2(1, 16) = 141.31, p < .001, r = .48$ | |
| Classification accuracy | 72.58% | | |

*Note: P = self-assessed or perceived, E = evaluated.*

## Discussion

This study compared different methods of assessing disabilities across three service types. Analyses revealed that each method had utility in distinguishing those receiving community-based, in-home/home health, and nursing home care. In univariate analyses every ADL–IADL limitation was capable of discriminating between participants in each level of long-term care. Nursing home residents were more impaired than in-home/home health care recipients, who in turn had more difficulties than community-based services consumers. This finding is consistent with that of Fredman, Droge, and Rabin (1992) and provides support for using ADL and IADL criteria in determining eligibility for long-term care. Bathing, walking, transferring, dressing, toileting, grooming, and eating were all independently associated with service type, as were shopping, preparing meals, transportation, taking medication, housework, and money management. Therefore, any ADL or IADL limitation or combination shown in the analyses could be used to screen recipients for these long-term care services.

When the method used was that of counting the number of specific ADL and IADL difficulties, similar results were obtained. In other words, participants in nursing homes had higher mean levels of ADL, IADL, and ADL–IADL combined limitations compared with those receiving in-home/home health care. Likewise, participants in in-home/home health care had greater mean levels of problems than those in community-based care. This finding provides support for those who suggest models that use counting the number of a variety of ADL, IADL, or ADL–IADL problems (Kane et al., 1991; Spector, 1991; Stone & Murtaugh, 1990).

Eligibility models using Likert-type ADL, IADL, and ADL–IADL combined scales also

were able to differentiate among people in each level of care. Here, as in the other models discussed, the mean disability levels across each group were significantly different and in the intended direction. The data provide support for those who suggest that Likert-type ADL, IADL, or ADL–IADL measures should be used (Katz, Ford, Jackson, & Jaffe, 1963; Kempen & Suurmeijer, 1990; Lawton & Brody, 1969; Williams et al., 1991).

Support also was found for the proposition that cognitive and behavioral problems must be included in eligibility criteria for long-term care (Alzheimer's Association, 1990; Kane et al., 1991; Leutz et al., 1993; Spirrison & Pierce, 1993; U.S. Bipartisan Commission on Comprehensive Health Care, 1990). In each service category the number of self-assessed and evaluative memory and behavioral problems increased as expected. Univariate analyses revealed significant differences among the service groupings for self-assessed and evaluative cognitive difficulties. There were not enough cases in each category to test the relationship for any behavioral problem variables.

Finally, when the comprehensive model of eligibility determination was examined, eight variables loaded significantly on the first function explaining the relationship to service type. Those variables included self-assessed ADLs–IADLs, level of functioning and social resources, evaluated economic resources, social resources, and religiosity as well as marital status and income level. Nine variables loaded significantly on the second function: evaluated ADLs–IADLs, memory, physical health and morale, perceived physical health and morale, educational level, gender, and insurance. This approach, which used a variety of multiple indicators, including demographic characteristics, was somewhat similar to the approaches used by Duffy and MacDonald (1990); Greene and Ondrich

(1990); Jette, Branch, Sleeper, Feldman, and Sullivan (1992); and Robert and Norgard (1996). This approach shows that many additional factors, such as marital status, economic and social resources, educational level, gender, insurance, and morale, are related to long-term care service types as well. The variables most strongly associated with service type, however, in each function, respectively, were perceived ADLs–IADLs and evaluated ADLs–IADLs. A combined ADL–IADL measure was used as the individual measures were too highly intercorrelated.

The major limitation of this study concerns the representativeness of this sample of elderly adults. Data were gathered for only 38 percent of all eligible to participate. Thus, although these findings were considered to represent the patterns of disability for participants receiving services from the facilities who agreed to participate, they may not generalize to other service recipients of those facilities or of other agencies. The disability measures themselves are another major concern in this study. As mentioned in the instrumentation section, there appears to be no consensus about which specific measures should be used. Although this study used seven ADL and six IADL measures, as well as measures for cognitive and behavioral disabilities, data were not gathered about using the telephone (IADL) or being able to do one's own laundry (IADL).

## Policy and Practice Recommendations

This study on functional disability as it relates to long-term care provides information that is useful to researchers, policymakers, and practitioners. It provides data about the level of disabilities among people currently in three levels of the long-term care continuum. Practitioners and researchers may compare disability levels in their populations

of interest to those in this study. In addition, should universal screening be used, these data would provide useful baseline information.

The focus on these four methods of determining eligibility for different levels of long-term care adds detail to the literature about eligibility measures and permits cross comparison of the methods' effectiveness as eligibility determinants. Although all methods could successfully differentiate consumers in each level of care, the comprehensive one advocated here was most successful overall. Although more costly initially, over time cost effectiveness might be achieved by knowledgeable planning. For example, a more precise placement strategy would be possible if an eligibility determination method were used that correctly classifies 73 percent of the cases by service type. Furthermore, a more objective and standardized method of eligibility determination would ensure greater equity of access. In an era of managed care and scarce resources, the most accurate and comprehensive system of eligibility determination should be used. The type of information derived therefrom is not meant to replace the judgments of trained clinicians but to enhance the precision of the eligibility determination process.

At first it may appear that the most prudent path would be to focus only on counting or otherwise measuring ADL–IADL limitations and identifying a cut-off score for eligibility. Realistically speaking, specific eligible elderly people could have many ADL–IADL limitations but have a number of informal service providers who currently meet their needs. So, although eligible to receive all services, in actuality they do not need them. On the other hand, elderly people with fewer ADL–IADL limitations who are not eligible to get access to the system may lack the social or other resources to meet their needs and will needlessly suffer the consequences. In times of limited resources, policymakers need to be particularly aware that programs and services for elderly people must be not only fiscally sound but also practical and target those in need.

Some proposals before Congress suggest that only basic ADLs and measures of cognitive and behavioral disabilities are sufficient to provide the best method to determine eligibility. This study and others show that there are eligibility screening procedures that explain more variation and appear to be more accurate classifiers than simple ADL–IADL or cognitive and behavioral disability measures. The comprehensive eligibility determination model advocated here appears to have great potential in this regard. It is possible to make comparisons, within one's own agency, budget, and philosophy, of the various methods suggested or actually being used. The approach that examines all important facets of an elderly person's functional limitations and resources will be more cost-efficient and effective in the long term.

Clearly defined criteria for level of care assignments can lead to effective, appropriate care to meet client needs. The results of this study indicate that social work practitioners can confidently use the four methods examined to assess an elderly client's long-term needs. Examination of the type or number of ADL–IADL limitations and use of Likert-type scales have utility. Social work assessment through use of the comprehensive eligibility model allows for contextual factors to be taken into account for the most accurate assessment of services indicated. Because both perceived and evaluated ADLs–IADLs can be used as eligibility criteria, the social work practitioner may engage the elderly client and his or her family actively in the assessment process. This, itself, is a potentially empowering experience. Similarly, assessment of contextual factors—marital, social, physical, spiritual, economic, educational, cognitive, and gender-related—allows a valuable level of client and family engagement in the assessment process. The practitioner can better intervene toward optimal client services utilization when there is accurate assessment with engaged participants.

The comprehensive model will help practitioners recognize and better understand the presenting pattern of disabilities that elderly people experience. Elderly people need to avoid premature dependence, to capitalize on their own strengths, and to prepare for their futures. These objectives (Walker, 1996) can be met with the assistance of practitioners thoroughly informed about their clients' functional limitations and resources. Practitioner care and social advocacy can be enhanced through data concerning elder care needs (Carlton-LaNey, 1997). A comprehensive method of eligibility determination for long-term care can provide rich data about elder disabilities and resources useful in service planning and program development. Continued research needs to be conducted to determine the best method of eligibility determination if a universal screening device is implemented nationwide.

## Conclusion

A number of general conclusions can be drawn from this study. First, each of the models does have utility and can be used for determining eligibility for long-term care. Examination of the amounts of variation explained reveals that the best single indicator was shopping (IADL). The next best indicator was evaluated memory (cognitive problems), with walking and bathing (ADLs) tied for third. The individual IADLs, as a group, explain the most variation, with cognitive problems and ADLs explaining less.

When we used additive indices, which either count the number of limitations in each category or use Likert-type scaling, the results are virtually identical. As a group, each ADL, IADL, and ADL–IADL combined measure, which counts the number of disabilities, explains more variation than any individual measure, with the exception of shopping (IADL), meals (IADL), and transportation (IADL). When Likert scaling was used, more variation was explained with only one exception: shopping (IADL). The results were identical when examining only the scales themselves. Numerical and Likert IADL indices explained the most variation; numerical and Likert ADL–IADLs combined, the next, with ADLs, both numerical and Likert, third.

Finally, the most variation was explained (76 percent) when all study variables were included. The comprehensive eligibility model includes measures of perceived ADL–IADLs, level of functioning, social resources, physical health and morale, evaluated economic resources, social resources, religiosity, ADL–IADLs, memory, physical health and morale, as well as marital status, income, educational level, gender, and insurance.

🌿🌿🌿

## References

Alzheimer's Association. (1990). *Annual public policy forum: Background on public policy issues—Eligibility for long-term care key issues.* Washington, DC: Author.

Bass, D. M., Looman, W. J., & Ehrlich, P. (1992). Predicting the volume of health and social services: Integrating cognitive impairment into the modified Andersen framework. *Gerontologist, 32,* 33–43.

Bass, D. M., & Noelker, L. S. (1987). The influence of family caregivers on elder's use of in-home services. *Journal of Health and Social Behavior, 28,* 184–196.

Binstock, R. H. (1994). Changing criteria in old-age programs. *Gerontologist, 34,* 726–730.

Brill, P. A., Drimmer, A. M., Morgan, L. A., & Gordon, N. F. (1995). The feasibility of conducting strength and flexibility programs for elderly nursing home residents with dementia. *Gerontologist, 35,* 263–266.

Brody, E. M., Litvin, S. J., Hoffman, C., & Kleban, M. H. (1995). Mental status of caregiving daughters and co-residence with dependent parents. *Gerontologist, 35,* 75–85.

Capitman, J., & Sciegaj, M. (1995). A contextual approach for understanding individual autonomy in managed community long-term care. *Gerontologist, 35,* 533–540.

Carlton-LaNey, I. (1997). Social workers as advocates for elders. In M. Reisch & E. Gambill (Eds.), *Social work in the 21st century* (pp. 285–296). Thousand Oaks, CA: Pine Forge.

Cornman, J. M., & Kingson, E. R. (1996). Trends, issues perspectives, and values for the aging of the baby boom cohorts. *Gerontologist, 36,* 33–35.

Coward, R. T., Vogel, W. B., Duncan, R. P., & Uttavo, R. (1995). Should intrastate funding formulae for the Older Americans Act include a rural factor? *Gerontologist, 35,* 24–34.

Duffy, M. E., & MacDonald, E. (1990). Determinants of functional health of older persons. *Gerontologist, 30,* 503–509.

Emlet, C. A., & Hall, A. M. (1991). Integrating the community into geriatric case management: Public health interventions. *Gerontologist, 31,* 556–560.

Fitzgerald, J. F., Smith, D. M., Martin, D. K., Freedman, J. A., & Wolinsky, F. D. (1993). Replication of the multidimensionality of activities of daily living. *Journal of Gerontology: Social Sciences, 48,* S28–S31.

Fredman, L., Droge, J. A., & Rabin, D. L. (1992). Functional limitations among home health care users in the National Health Interview Survey Supplement on Aging. *Gerontologist, 32*, 641–646.

Greene, V. L., & Ondrich, J. I. (1990). Risk factors for nursing home admissions and exits: A discrete-time hazard function approach. *Journal of Gerontology: Social Sciences, 45*, S250–S258.

Health Insurance Association of America. (1989). *Long-term care: An emerging employee concern.* Washington, DC: Author.

Hudson, R. B. (1996). The changing face of aging politics. *Gerontologist, 36*, 33–35.

Inverson, L. H. (1986). *A description and analysis of state preadmission screening programs.* Excelsior, MN: Interstudy Center for Aging and Long-Term Care.

Ireys, H. T. (1979). *Components of situationally specific perceived personal control.* Unpublished doctoral dissertation, Case Western Reserve University, Cleveland.

Jette, A. M., Branch, L. G., Sleeper, L. A., Feldman, H., & Sullivan, L. M. (1992). High-risk profiles for nursing home administration. *Gerontologist, 32*, 634–640.

Justice, D. (1988). *State long-term care reform: Development of community care systems in six states.* Washington, DC: National Governors Association, Center for Policy Research.

Kane, R. L., Saslow, M. G., & Brundage, J. (1991). Using ADLs to establish eligibility for long-term care among the cognitively impaired. *Gerontologist, 31*, 60–66.

Katz, S., Ford, A. B., Jackson, B. A., & Jaffe, M. W. (1963). Studies of illness in the aged. The Index of ADL: A standardized measure of biological and social function. *JAMA, 185*, 914–919.

Kempen, G.I.J.M., & Suurmeijer, T.P.B.M. (1990). The development of a hierarchical polychotomous ADL–IADL scale for noninstitutionalized elders. *Gerontologist, 30*, 497–502.

Lawton, M. P., & Brody, E. M. (1969). Assessment of older people: Self-maintaining and instrumental activities of daily living. *Gerontologist, 9*, 179–188.

Leutz, W., Abrahams, R., & Capitman, J. (1993). The administration of eligibility for community long-term care. *Gerontologist, 33*, 92–104.

Lianov, L., Kohatsu, N., & Bohnstedt, M. (1991). Referral outcomes from a community-based preventive health care program for elderly people. *Gerontologist, 31*, 543–547.

Manton, K. G., Corder, L., & Stallard, E. (1993). Changes in the use of personal assistance and special equipment from 1982 to 1989: Results from the 1982 and 1989 NLTCS. *Gerontologist, 33*, 168–176.

Nowicki, S., & Duke, M. (1974). A locus of control scale for non-college as well as college adults. *Journal of Personality Assessment, 38*, 136–137.

Pruchno, R. A., Smyer, M. A., Rose, M. S., Hartman-Stein, P. E., & Henderson-Laribee, D. L. (1995). Competence of long-term care residents to participate in decisions about their medical care: A brief, objective assessment. *Gerontologist, 35*, 622–629.

Rabiner, D. J., Mutran, E., & Stearns, S. C. (1995). The effect of channeling on home care utilization and satisfaction with care. *Gerontologist, 35*, 186–195.

Reschovsky, J. D., & Newman, S. J. (1990). Adaptations for independent living by older frail households. *Gerontologist, 30*, 543–552.

Robert, S., & Norgard, T. (1996). Long-term care policy based on ADL eligibility criteria: Impact on community dwelling elders not meeting the criteria. *Journal of Gerontological Social Work, 25*(3/4), 71–91.

Shearer, G. (1989). *Long-term care: Analysis of public policy options.* Washington, DC: Brookings Institution.

Slivinske, L. R., Fitch, V. L., & Morawski, D. P. (1996). The Wellness Index: Developing an instrument to assess elders' well-being. *Journal of Gerontological Social Work, 25*(3/4), 185–204.

Spector, W. D. (1991). Cognitive impairment and disruptive behaviors among community based elderly persons: Implications for targeting long-term care. *Gerontologist, 31*, 51–60.

Spector, W. D., & Kemper, P. (1994). Disability and cognitive impairment criteria: Targeting those who need the most home care. *Gerontologist, 34*, 640–651.

Spirrison, C. L., & Pierce, P. S. (1992). Psychometric characteristics of the Adult Functional Adaptive Behavior Scale (AFABS). *Gerontologist, 32*, 234–239.

Stone, R. J., & Murtaugh, C. M. (1990). The elderly population with chronic functional disability: Implications for home care eligibility. *Gerontologist, 30*, 491–496.

Temkin-Greener, H., & Meiners, M. R. (1995). Transitions in long-term care. *Gerontologist, 35*, 196–206.

U.S. Bipartisan Commission on Comprehensive Health Care, The Pepper Commission. (1990). *A call for action: Final report.* Washington, DC: U.S. Government Printing Office.

Walker, R. J. (1996). Caregiver stress, long-term care, and future social work practice. In P. R. Raffoul & C. A. McNeece (Eds.), *Future issues for social work practice* (pp. 125–138). Needham Heights, MA: Allyn & Bacon.

Wiener, J. M., & Illston, L. H. (1994). Health care reform in the 1990s: Where does long-term care fit in? *Gerontologist, 34*, 402–408.

Williams, J. H., Drinka, T.J.K., Greenberg, J. R., Farrell-Holtan, J., Euhardy, R., & Scharm, M. (1991). Development and testing of the Assessment of Living Skills and Resources (ALSAR) in elderly community dwelling veterans. *Gerontologist, 31*, 84–91.

This chapter was originally published in the August issue of *Health & Social Work*, Vol. 23, Number 3, pp. 175–185.

# 13

# Standardized Screening of Elderly Patients' Needs for Social Work Assessment in Primary Care

## Use of the SF-36

BARBARA BERKMAN,
SUSAN CHAUNCEY HORKY, WILLIAM HOLMES,
ANN DANIELS, EVELYN BONANDER,
SUZANNE SAMPSON, and MARK ROBINSON

Growth of outpatient primary health care services has expanded significantly since the early 1980s because of increasing numbers of elderly patients presenting with multiple chronic health problems, advanced technology enabling the substitution of outpatient for inpatient procedures, reimbursement incentives, and consumer demand (American Hospital Association, 1990–91). Concomitantly there has been an increase in the average annual number of outpatient physician visits per elderly person. The average person age 65 or older, in good or excellent health, visits his or her physician an average of four times per year, but if the individual is in fair or poor health, his or her visits increase to 9.4 times annually. The average annual visits increase by one-third with the population ages 85 years and older (Schick & Schick, 1994). Current trends project a rise in outpatient visits of 106 percent by 2000 (American Hospital Association, 1990–91).

Fewer hospitalizations, as well as decreased lengths of stay in the hospital, have resulted in increased frailty in elderly patients seen in primary care settings (Berkman et al., 1996). Chronic illnesses and their consequences, as well as a variety of psychological ailments (that is, emotional disorders and stress), appear as the major personal and social health problems encountered by health care professionals in working with the elderly people in primary care (Berkman et al., 1996). Chronically ill or disabled elderly people need extensive environmental support services and continuing care planning if they are to remain in the community. However, elderly people in need of such community services often have been overlooked by their physicians, whose traditional diagnostic focus on physiological issues is too restrictive to enable assessment of the overall health concerns of their patients (Azzarto, 1993; Badger et al., 1994; Sloane, 1991). Physicians' difficulties in diagnosing psychosocial problems are compounded by the fact that they reportedly spend less average time per visit with their older patients, leaving little time to accurately diagnose the complicated needs of the elderly patients. Lack of time also limits a doctor's ability to consult with an elderly patient's family, let alone make referrals and coordinate community service needs (Clarke, Neuwirth, & Bernstein, 1986; Gropper, 1988). Unfortunately, extending the initial visit time is not possible for many physicians because of the growing limitations on reimbursement and the mandate to see more patients (Badger et al., 1994; Schauffler & Rodriguez, 1993; Sloane, 1991).

When psychosocial needs go unmet through misdiagnosis, lack of detection, lack of treatment and follow-up, elderly patients are at risk of further health problems that can lead to physical deterioration, reduced independence, and eventually to the need for more intensive and expensive services (Shearer, Simmons, White, & Berkman, 1995). Inadequate assessment also can lead to inappropriate long-term care and unnecessary institutional placements. Medical management of the frail elderly patient requires a comprehensive approach that includes careful assessment of complex medical problems and functional capabilities, social supports, and emotional well-being.

Social work screening and assessment of psychosocial and environmental needs of patients in primary care provide valuable patient information in busy physician practices, where doctors do not have time to interpret both the physical and psychological meaning of each somatic complaint (Azzarto, 1993; Berkman et al., 1996). However, the process of screening is often lengthy and labor intensive, thus expensive—involving activities such as conducting interviews, reviewing records, and making direct observations. Attention must now be given to the use of standardized screening tools that will offer an accurate and efficient early prediction of whether a patient needs a social work assessment because of psychosocial health care risks (Azzarto, 1993; Berkman et al., 1996; Clarke et al., 1986; Shearer et al., 1995; Zedlewski, Barnes, Burt, McBride, & Meyer, 1989). In addition to the importance of standardized measures for reliable identification of psychosocial problems, use of these tools could provide standardized documentation across patient groups (Van Hook, Berkman, & Dunkle, 1996).

Many in the health professions (Ware & Sherbourne, 1992) are proposing the use of standardized conceptual definitions and measurements in which the focus is on health-related components of quality of life that are important to patients, such as, Did the treatment improve mobility, return the patient to work, improve his or her mental state? The value of health-related quality-of-life (HRQL) standardized measures for social work is that they expand health care screening and assessment beyond the physiological to the use of multistage diagnostic screening using multidimensional factors (Berkman & Maramaldi, in press). There is growing recognition of the need to go beyond traditional physiological variables to include the other psychosocial components of HRQL that, of course, are of importance to social work practice.

Bringing this perspective to social work requires explicit selection and measurement of those dimensions of HRQL most relevant to the goals of social work interventions. In addition, standardization is essential if social workers are to have reliability and validity in screening and is prerequisite for valid detection of clinically important differences among patients. However, social workers in health care settings have had little experience in using standardized questionnaires. Thus, it is important to study the usefulness, as well as the limitations, of standardized measures as a means to screen for psychosocial needs. Social work practitioners can then make an informed decision on whether to adopt this model of screening.

## The Question for Study

The traditional relationship between social work services and primary care physicians' practices in the outpatient clinics at Massachusetts General Hospital (MGH) is a referral-based system in which the physician or nurse refers the elderly person and his or her family to the Social Service Department when problems in the home situation are recognized, usually at point of breakdown. This system, prevalent in most outpatient clinics, limits the number of patients identified. On the average fewer than 10 percent of patients are referred, and referrals that are made are episodic and crisis oriented. This crisis orientation limits the social work time available

for helping the patient and family, restricting the options available to meet patient needs. This practice can result in a dissatisfied consumer, misuse of physician time, inefficient use of physician expertise, and significant amounts of rework by social workers. Early identification by social workers of patients in need of community and hospital nonmedical services is necessary to improve delivery of services to patients and families. Meeting patients' psychosocial needs is necessary for enhancement of their quality of life.

This study examines the viability of using a new model for screening primary care elderly patients with psychosocial needs, the use of a standardized health-related quality-of-life (HRQL) questionnaire (SF-36) to predict need for social work assessment. This standardized HRQL questionnaire allows the patient to self-assess his or her social, environmental, emotional, and functional needs (Ware & Sherbourne, 1992). The study addresses whether the SF-36 can be used as a screen for patients in need of social work assessment independent of traditional social work–specific screening questions. (In other words, is it possible to eliminate social work–specific questions because one or more of the scales on the SF-36 tap the same problem area?) In addition, we explored the question of how a social worker would use the standardized HRQL questionnaire in screening for patients in need of services: Which SF-36 scale scores were significantly related to the social worker's judgment of who needed an assessment?

## Method

Physicians from the 10 MGH Primary Care Practice Groups were asked by the Social Service Department for permission to give their elderly patients a self-administered questionnaire to assess functional and psychosocial needs. Two primary care practice groups agreed to participate, representing 16 physicians. Two convenience methods were used to select the study's sample. In the first approach, during the first three months of study, the clinics' office staff were requested to hand out the questionnaires to all patients 65 years and older while they waited for their medical appointments. Each questionnaire had a cover letter from their physician explaining the project and requesting participation. Although 950 patients ages 65 and older were scheduled for appointments during this time period, there was no way to ascertain the actual number of questionnaires distributed. Only 200 questionnaires were returned. This limitation in the dissemination plan led to the decision that 300 additional questionnaires would be mailed to patients before their scheduled appointments. Questionnaires were mailed based on a computer-generated list of all patients, 65 years of age or older, who were scheduled for appointments at the two participating practice groups during the second three months of the study. Three hundred randomly selected patients were mailed questionnaires. These questionnaires were accompanied by a physician cover letter requesting participation, with a postage-paid response envelope.

The study's final sample size of 313 patients was a combined total of the 200 respondents who completed questionnaires in the doctors' waiting rooms and the 113 who returned questionnaires from the mailing. There was no way to determine the rate of completed questionnaires in the office sample because there were no hard data on the number of questionnaires actually distributed in the offices. However, both groups were based on a population of patients for a three-month period, and the mailed-questionnaire group was a random sample. There was a 38 percent rate of return from the mailing. The questionnaire included the 36 questions comprising the eight SF-36 scales and 21 social work–specific questions traditionally used in screening.

## SF-36

The SF-36 is a health-related quality-of-life questionnaire constructed to survey health status (Ware & Sherbourne, 1992). This survey instrument is based on an increasing consensus in health care that values the "centrality" of the patient's point of view in monitoring medical care outcomes (Ware, Snow, Kosinski, & Gandek, 1993). It measures how a patient functions in the context of his or her life and how a health problem may be affecting the patient's ability to perform a job or a task or how she or he relates to family and friends. There are 36 questions, which when grouped comprise eight scales: limitations in physical activities due to health problems, limitations in social activities because of physical/emotional problems, limitations in usual role activities due to physical health problems, bodily pain, general mental health (that is, psychological distress and well-being), limitations in usual role activities due to emotional problems, vitality (that is, energy and fatigue), and general health perceptions.

The measure is constructed for self-administration by people 14 and older or may be administered by a trained interviewer in person or by telephone. The questionnaire can be filled out in 10 to 15 minutes. For each scale, responses to questions are summed and scores are converted to a scale of one to 100 with the higher scores indicating the best functioning level or overall well-being. The SF-36 is a standardized measurement that has been found reliable in measuring various health factors. A study found coefficients for the multi-item health scale to range from 0.81

to 0.88, thereby supporting the reliability of this scale (Stewart, Hays, & Ware, 1988). The researchers further studied reliability with two subsamples, those with less than a high school education and those over 75 years of age. Results showed similar findings for all groups with ranges from 0.76 to 0.89 for both subgroups, thus lending weight to the sensitivity and reliability of this measure. Factor analysis has supported the construct validity of the SF-36 scales (Ware et al., 1993). Previous empirical studies also have shown that the SF-36 effectively measures factors related to physical and mental health. Clinical tests of validity also were performed based on criteria used to form mutually exclusive patient groups. The fact that the instrument is standardized, is brief, can be self-administered, and is easy to score all contribute to its usefulness to social workers as a clinical measurement of effect of illness on health-related quality of life (Van Hook et al., 1996).

### Social Work–Specific Questions

The 21 social work screening questions, which were used in addition to the SF-36 questions, were specific problems that social workers traditionally use in screening patients for psychosocial need. Supported by a John A. Hartford grant at Huntington Memorial Hospital in Pasadena, California, the questions were developed by interdisciplinary focus groups so that they specifically related to issues of concern to social workers in screening and assessing elderly patients in primary care (Berkman et al., 1996). The 21 social work–specific questions focused on two broad categories: (1) functional status (physical, social, and mental health), and (2) socioeconomic and environmental factors (see Table 13-1). The focus group members believed the social work–specific questions had face and content validity (Berkman et al.,

**TABLE 13-1. Social Work–Specific Screening Factors**

Difficulties in

  a.  doing the laundry
  b.  doing light housework
  c.  following any dietary restrictions
  d.  getting about in your home
  e.  getting to appointments
  f.  going shopping
  g.  managing money/paying bills
  h.  preparing food
  i.  taking medications
  j.  using the telephone

Difficulties with

  a.  alcohol/drug abuse
  b.  appetite
  c.  concentration
  d.  dizziness
  e.  falling
  f.  hearing
  g.  memory
  h.  sex
  i.  sleeping
  j.  urinary incontinence
  k.  vision

1996). Construct validity is supported by the fact that significant correlations were found between patients' answers to questions and theoretically expected directions of responses (Berkman et al., 1996). Although no formal tests of reliability were conducted, the preciseness of the social work–specific questions tends to support the assumption of reliability. Before they were used in this study, a focus group of social workers at MGH reviewed the 21 social work–specific questions, previously used in California, and agreed they served as an excellent screen of psychosocial needs in primary care. Thus, patient questionnaires included the SF-36 questions and the 21 social work–specific psychosocial questions, so that we could assess whether the eight standardized SF-36 scales could serve as an independent screen of some or all of the psychosocial needs.

## Social Worker's Use of SF-36 Scales in Screening

To explore the question of which SF-36 scale scores were significantly related to the social worker's judgment of who needed an assessment, the following procedure was used. After the questionnaires were returned, the SF-36 questions were separated from the social work–specific questions. The social worker assigned to the primary care unit determined which elderly patients needed an assessment on the basis of her screening of the patients' answers to the SF-36 questions. Although the social worker reviewed the patients' responses, she did not know the actual SF-36 scale scores, because those scores were calculated later during computer analyses. Her judgment was conceptual, based on her professional view of the patients' responses to the questions.

### Analysis

The primary goal of analysis was to determine whether the SF-36 scales could be used independently (without social work–specific questions) as a screen of psychosocial needs. It was important to determine whether patients' self-reported problems on social work–specific questions were correlated with poorer HRQL scores as measured by the SF-36 scales. A social work–specific question was only considered for exclusion from future screening if patients reporting problems on that specific question had significantly lower mean scores (than patients not reporting the problem) on five or more of the eight SF-36 scales and if those patients reporting the specific problem made up a significantly larger proportion of those who scored under 50 (than those patients not reporting the problem) on the same SF-36 scales. When both criteria were met, consideration was given to

the assumption that the SF-36 could serve as an independent screen for the social work–specific psychosocial question and that the specific question could be excluded from future screening tools.

How the social worker would use the SF-36 scales to screen for psychosocial need of assessment was a secondary focus for analyses. The question addressed was, Which of the eight SF-36 scales were most related to the social worker's decision that an assessment was needed? $t$ test was used to compare differences on SF-36 scale scores between those patients who were identified as needing assessment and those who were not. The relative risk ratio was computed for each SF-36 scale. In addition to the low scores on scales that always seem to generate an intervention, the other scales with the largest relative risks were identified.

## Findings

The data in this study indicate that nine of the 21 social work–specific problems were significantly related to poorer HRQL scores as measured by the SF-36. The following social work–specific psychosocial problems were significantly correlated ($p \leq .001$) with poorer HRQL scores on a minimum of five SF-36 scales: appetite, falling, food preparation, getting about the home, doing housework, doing laundry, shopping, taking medications, and getting to appointments. These nine problems met both criteria for possible exclusion from future screening. The SF-36 does not adequately tap other specific physical and mental difficulties that might indicate the need for a social work assessment. The problems reported in sleeping, memory, compliance with dietary restrictions, concentration, alcohol or drug abuse, hearing, sex, dizziness, managing money, vision, urinary incontinence, and use of telephone were not significantly correlated with SF-36 scale scores.

## Relationship of Social Work Screening Decisions and SF-36 Scale Scores

Thirty-six percent of the patients were identified by the social worker as needing further assessment. Although the social worker did not know what the patients' scores on the SF-36 scales were at the time of her screening review, there was a significant relationship between mean scores on each of the eight SF-36 scale and screening statuses. Patients screened as needing an assessment by the social worker had significantly lower mean scores ($p \leq .0001$) than those not determined to need as assessment (Table 13-2).

## Relative Risk Ratios

The relative risk ratios related to screening decisions for each SF-36 scale were calculated, and the scores with the highest relative risks were physical functioning, bodily pain, vitality, mental health, social functioning, and general health. Patients whose scores

were less than 50 on the SF-36 scales of physical functioning, bodily pain, and mental health were always screened as needing an assessment by the social worker. Those patients who scored less than 50 in vitality had a 132 times greater chance of being screened as needing an assessment. Those patients who scored less than 50 on social functioning and on general health were 35 and 39 times, respectively, more likely to be screened as needing an assessment. Two SF-36 scales, role physical and role emotional, had relative risk ratios of less than 15 (Table 13-3).

## Implications of Findings

Findings have shown that the SF-36 clearly captures some important psychosocial risk factors in elderly patients, such as problems with instrumental activities of daily living (IADLs), which social workers traditionally screen to determine need for assessment. Thus, it is suggested that specific social work questions in these functional areas could be eliminated from a future screening tool, facilitating the goal of keeping the questionnaire brief and user-friendly as well as standardized for IADL needs.

Methodological issues related to the validity of the remaining 12 social work–specific questions, reflecting other physical and men-

**TABLE 13-2. Significant Differences in Mean SF-36 Scores for Patients Screened as Needing an Assessment and Those Not Needing an Assessment by the Social Worker**

| SF-36 Scale | Needs Assessment (M) | Does Not Need Assessment (M) |
| --- | --- | --- |
| Physical functioning | 49.48 | 84.39 |
| Role physical | 38.96 | 81.31 |
| Role emotional | 54.50 | 89.37 |
| Bodily pain | 54.46 | 81.56 |
| Vitality | 46.10 | 72.55 |
| Mental health | 65.74 | 82.83 |
| Social function | 63.66 | 93.62 |
| General health | 52.50 | 76.77 |

*Note:* All mean differences were significant at a minimum of $p \leq .0001$

**TABLE 13-3. SF-36 Scales, Significantly Related to Need for Assessment, with Largest Relative Risk Ratios**

| Significant Scales | Relative Risk Ratio |
| --- | --- |
| SF-36 Physical functioning < 50 | * |
| SF-36 Bodily pain < 50 | * |
| SF-36 Mental health < 50 | * |
| SF-36 Vitality < 50 | 132 |
| SF-36 Social functioning < 50 | 35 |
| SF-36 General health < 50 | 39 |

*Note:* * = Relative risk ratio was not computed, because all patients scoring below 50 were assessed.

tal functioning areas, may explain why these factors did not correlate with the SF-36 scales. For example, questions regarding problems with dizziness, sleep, hearing, drug and alcohol abuse, and sex required simply a yes or no response. (Yes, meaning difficulties exist in this area; or no, there are no difficulties in this area.) This type of simple categorical question leaves little room for variance. It requires that the respondent state that a problem exists or does not exist. Thus, it may not allow for specificity of the true picture of the subject's sense of difficulty. A physical and mental functioning question that asks "Do you have problems with your memory?" or "Do you have problems with sex?" would clearly be harder for the elderly person to answer unequivocally, compared with a specific IADL question that would ask "Do you have difficulty doing laundry or light housework?" Thus, these questions may have lost the specificity necessary to show any significant differences in the extent of the problem, thus limiting the chance for correlation with the SF-36 scores.

Concomitantly, many of these mental and physical functioning difficulties could be considered sensitive topics that an elderly person might not be so willing to admit exists. For example, difficulties with memory and concentration have stereotypically been associated with senility, and drug and alcohol abuse and difficulties with sex are topics that the elderly person might not be comfortable in addressing. Asking about these questions in a more sensitive standardized fashion may elicit more valid discriminating responses. In the future study of the use of the SF-36, it will be important to refine the remaining 12 social work–specific questions. In addition, other focused standardized measures that address psychosocial issues should be tested, such as the Prime MD (Spitzer et al., 1994), to see if they address the additional areas of need not identified through the SF-36.

One limitation of this exploratory study was the use of a sample that was self-selected on many levels. The sample consisted of elderly individuals who were scheduled for appointments with primary care physicians. Generalizability was limited to the two group practices that agreed to participate. In the first part of the study the secretaries were inconsistent in handing out the questionnaires, distributing them to patients on the basis of their own idiosyncratic judgment of who might need or not need services, rather than to all patients 65 and older. In addition, the mailed questionnaires were limited to those respondents who agreed to answer and return them, even though the mailed survey was based on a random sample.

There may also be limitations in how the questionnaire was used. The respondents who received mailed questionnaires may not have completed the questionnaire independently, having had a family member, caretaker, or friend help fill it out. The individual elderly participant may not have filled out the form honestly because he or she did not want to be labeled as sick, needy, or unable to live independently. Some of the elderly people may not have been able to fill out the SF-36 because of their limited educational level, cognitive impairment, or lack of English-speaking ability. Because of the makeup of this study population, many people of color and low-income people were excluded. The SF-36 used in this study was directed toward white, Anglo-Saxon patients. At the time of the study, culturally sensitive study forms in other languages were not available. These versions have now been developed for Hispanic populations and should be tested in a future study.

The exploration of how the social worker would use the SF-36 questions proved interesting, although only qualified interpretations should be made because of the limitations in method. It is not surprising that there was a significant increase in patients identified as needing an assessment under the new model of screening, because under the traditional referral system so few patients reach social work services. In addition, the fact that the social worker's decision making was closely related to six of the SF-36 scales is not surprising, because the questions making up each of these scales are very similar to the psychosocial questions that social workers address in screening. A limitation was that there was funding for only one social worker to screen whether an assessment was needed. This social worker brought to the study her own personal workstyle, ethics, and skills. As a highly trained professional, 15 years post-master's degree, who had worked with primary care patients for five years, she made every effort to give consistent unbiased decisions, based on her review of the patients' responses to the questionnaires.

It is not unusual for there to be only one social worker covering a large number of primary care practices. However, usually the coverage is based on a limited referral system in which the doctors, nurses, patients, or family members request social work services for situations that have reached a crisis in psychosocial need. The model of coverage in this project differed in that the project social worker reviewed the patients' answers to the SF-36 questions and, independent of referral, made a screening decision as to whether assessment was warranted. It is clear that this social worker was able to use the SF-36 as a screen and that certain scales were reflective of the way she made screening judgment.

Further study is needed to demonstrate the validity of the SF-36 as a standardized screen for identifying patients in need of social work services. Such a study should have multiple social workers using the SF-36 in screening and would need to address the predictive validity of its use through follow-up on whether an assessment then indicated the need for social work intervention.

## Conclusion

Chronic illness, its functional consequences, and a number of psychological problems appear to be the major personal and social health care problems that patients bring into the primary care setting. A missed or misdiagnosed problem or psychosocial risk factor is costly to both the patient and the health care system. Presently, many patients relying on their primary physicians for psychosocial supports are not getting their needs met. Social workers using reliable and valid standardized screening mechanisms to identify patients in need of psychosocial assessment can offer timely appropriate services to meet the identified psychosocial needs, saving the patient and doctor time and money and lowering the patient's health care claim costs (Azzarto, 1993; Clarke et al., 1986; Gropper, 1988; Loomis, 1988). Greater attention must be given to the testing and use of standardized screening tools in social work that use predictive factors that can result in assessment of patients at risk for psychosocial needs.

The SF-36 is one such standardized approach that will help social work identify patients with significant IADL problems resulting in poorer HRQL. Social work needs to continue to develop and adopt standardized approaches to screening. Screening in primary care settings using a standardized health-related quality-of-life questionnaire should result in improved relationships with patients by providing earlier intervention, enabling efficient linkages with needed services, and saving time for the doctor, office staff, and the patient through quick access to assistance.

🌾 🌾 🌾

## References

American Hospital Association. (1990–91). *Hospital statistics.* Chicago: Author.

Azzarto, J. (1993). The socioemotional needs of elderly family practice patients: Can social workers help? *Health & Social Work, 18,* 40–48.

Badger, L. W., DeGruy, F. V., Hartman, J., Plant, M. A., Leeper, J., Anderson, R., Ficken, R., Gaskins, S., Maxwell, A., Rand, E., & Tietze, P. (1994). Patient presentation, interview content, and the detection of depression by primary care physicians. *Psychosomatic Medicine, 56*(2), 128–135.

Berkman, B., & Maramaldi, P. (in press). Use of standardized measures in agency-based research and practice. *Social Work in Health Care 22*(3).

Berkman, B., Shearer, S., Simmons, J., White, M., Robinson, M., Sampson, S., Holmes, W., Allison, D., & Thomson, J. (1996). Ambulatory elderly patients of primary care physicians: Functional, psychosocial and environmental predictors of need for social work care management. *Social Work in Health Care, 22*(3), 1–20.

Clarke, S. S., Neuwirth, L., & Bernstein, R. H. (1986). An expanded social work role in a university hospital-based group practice: Service provider, physician educator, and organizational consultant. *Social Work in Health Care, 11*(4), 1–16.

Gropper, M. (1988). A study of the preferences of family practitioners and other primary care physicians in treating patients' psychosocial problems. *Social Work in Health Care, 13*(2), 75–91.

Loomis, J. F. (1988). Case management in health care. *Health & Social Work, 13,* 219–225.

Schauffler, H. H., & Rodriguez, T. (1993). Managed care for preventative services: A review of policy options. *Medical Care Review, 50*(2), 153–197.

Schick, F., & Schick, R. (1994). *Statistical handbook on aging Americans.* Phoenix: Oryx Press.

Shearer, S., Simmons, J. W., White, M., & Berkman, B. (1995). Physician partnership project: Social work case managers in primary care. *Continuum, 15*(4), 1–5.

Sloane, P. (1991). Changes in ambulatory care with patient age: Is geriatric care qualitatively different? *Family Medicine, 23*(1), 40–43.

Spitzer, R., Williams, J., Kroenke, K., Linzer, M., deGruy, F., III, Hahn, S., Brody, D., & Johnson, J. (1994). Utility of a new procedure for diagnosing mental disorders in primary care: The PRIME-MD 1000 study. *JAMA, 272,* 1749–1756.

Stewart, A. L., Hays, R., & Ware, J. (1988). Communication: The MOS short-form general health survey—Reliability and validity in a patient population. *Medical Care, 26,* 724–735.

Van Hook, M. P., Berkman, B., & Dunkle, R. (1996). Assessment tools for general health care settings: PRIME-MD, OARS, and SF-36. *Health & Social Work, 21,* 230–234.

Ware, J. E., & Sherbourne, C. D. (1992). The MOS 36-item short form health survey (SF-36): Conceptual framework and item selection, Part I. *Medical Care, 30,* 473–481.

Ware, J. E., Snow, K. K., Kosinski, M., & Gandek, B. (1993). *SF36 health survey manual and interpretation guide.* Boston: New England Medical Center, Health Institute.

Zedlewski, S. R., Barnes, R. O., Burt, M. K., McBride, T. D., & Meyer, J. (1989). *The needs of the elderly in the 21st century.* Washington, DC: Urban Institute.

This chapter was originally published in the February 1999 issue of *Health & Social Work,* Vol. 24, Number 1, pp. 9–16.

# 14

## Preparation for Oncology Settings

### What Hospice Social Workers Say They Need

PAMELA J. KOVACS and
LAURA R. BRONSTEIN

An estimated 1.2 million Americans will be diagnosed with cancer in 2000 (American Cancer Society, 2000). Such a diagnosis will irrevocably change their lives. Health care social workers will work with many of these patients, their families, and their friends as they face these changes. In hospitals, oncology clinics, nursing homes, hospices, and homes, social workers will help patients adjust to an initial diagnosis and an uncertain prognosis and future, cope with the physical and emotional components of treatment, try to trust and enjoy life after remission, or live with the dying process that half of those diagnosed with cancer must face.

Hospice social workers, in particular, spend a greater percentage of their time with terminal cancer patients than do social workers in many other settings, becoming involved when a person has been given six months or less to live and is no longer pursuing aggressive, curative treatment (Beresford, 1993). Instead, palliative care, focusing on pain management and symptom control and the psychosocial and spiritual needs of the patient and family, becomes the treatment of choice. According to the National Hospice Organization (NHO), approximately 2,700 hospices in the United States and Puerto Rico served 390,000 patients in 1995,

78 percent of whom had a cancer diagnosis. In fact, of the people dying from cancer in the United States, about one of every three receives hospice care (NHO, 1997).

Medicare hospice regulations mandate that hospice services be provided by an interdisciplinary team composed of at least the core members, which include a doctor of medicine or osteopathy, a registered nurse, a social worker, and a pastoral or other counselor (Martinez, 1996). Johanson and Johanson (1996) summarized the general qualifications for a hospice social worker as follows: (1) BSW from an accredited school of social work; (2) MSW or MS/MA in marriage and family counseling (recommendations of NHO); (3) minimum of one to three years' supervised experience in health care; (4) ability to work with and contribute to an interdisciplinary team; (5) understanding and compassion toward patients and families; and (6) knowledge of community resources available to patients and their families. They noted that qualifications may vary depending on licensure and certification requirements specific to a given state.

Because social workers are core interdisciplinary team members, it is important to know how well prepared they are for hospice positions. In this article we report the results of a study conducted with hospice social workers to explore the influence of social work education, training, and personal and professional experience on their work, as well as their needs for continuing education.

## Background

For decades medical social workers and social work educators have discussed how best to prepare, supervise, and continue educating social workers for health care settings (Berkman & Carlton, 1985; Caroff &

Mailick, 1985; Dickinson, Sumner, & Frederick, 1992; Falck, 1978; Rehr & Caroff, 1986; Rossen, 1987). In reviewing this literature several themes emerged: (1) the importance of collaboration (Abramson & Mizrahi, 1996; Carroll, 1980; Netting & Williams, 1997) and the role of social workers on interdisciplinary teams (Cowles & Lefcowitz, 1992); (2) the need for specialized knowledge about medical terminology (Miller & Dane, 1990; Weiner, 1990), death and dying (Dane & Miller, 1990; Zelinsky & Thorson, 1983), and other health–related issues; and (3) the value of generalist social work training (Alperin, 1985).

With regard to collaboration, although the literature on interdisciplinary practice showed that social workers collaborate with a wide range of professionals, it is those in health and school settings with whom social workers have been collaborating the longest and those in health and mental health settings with whom collaboration has taken on increasing importance (Abramson & Rosenthal, 1995). Interested in how schools of social work prepared students for the role of collaborator, Kane (1990) surveyed programs in 1974 and learned that "the majority attempted to introduce this content through the practicum and the overall curriculum" (p. 799). More recent studies addressed the nature of these collaborative efforts between physicians and social workers (Abramson & Mizrahi, 1996; Netting & Williams, 1997).

Generalist versus specialist training for social workers in health settings is an ongoing discussion in the literature (Alperin, 1985; Bailis, 1985; Berkman, 1985; Caroff & Mailick, 1985; Dinerman, Schlesinger, & Wood, 1980; Lane, 1982). As early as 1975 the Council on Social Work Education recommended strengthened curricula for social work in the health field and linkages with medical centers and other schools for health professionals (Caroff & Mailick, 1985). This recommendation was balanced by the council's commitment to generalist training for all social work students.

To better understand the needs of social work students completing field placements in oncology settings, Sormanti (1994) conducted focus groups of oncology social workers serving as field instructors. Among other themes, she identified gaps in the curricula of schools of social work that negatively affected the total learning experience of students in oncology and other medical settings. More specifically, the consensus was that schools of social work were "responsible for initiating and perpetuating an extremely limited definition of clinical work that does not adequately recognize the connection between physical and mental health" (Sormanti, p. 80).

## The Study

With these themes in mind, we solicited hospice social workers' opinions to better understand what effect their formal education, informal on-the-job training, and other professional and personal experiences had in preparing them for work with oncology patients. We used a combination of closed- and open-ended questions to broaden our understanding.

### Method

In September 1995 we administered a survey to hospice and hospital social workers at the State of Florida Oncology Social Workers Annual Conference, designed to ascertain their views of their training for oncology social work. Thirty responses served as a pilot test for a larger national study, the results of which are reported here. Feedback from the pilot study helped refine the instrument that was mailed by NHO with its quarterly mailing to its social work membership known as the Social Work Section Group, of which one of the authors is a member. The survey was one page in length, with instructions on the reverse side. A brief description of the study encouraging social workers' participation was also included in the accompanying NHO newsletter. We received surveys from 108 social workers of the 366 to whom it was sent, resulting in a 30 percent response rate.

### Data Analysis

Closed-ended questions were analyzed using descriptive statistics. Qualitative responses were analyzed through the use of grounded theory techniques as developed by Glaser and Strauss (1967). Responses to the open-ended survey data were coded and categorized. Constant ongoing and concurrent analysis occurred until identified patterns and themes emerged. Saturation of the data led to the following themes: the perceived value of generalist and specialist training; the value of cross-disciplinary training and skills in collaboration; and the importance of other-than-professional training, including personal experiences.

### Limitations

Although benefiting from the endorsement and minimal cost of including our questionnaire in the NHO mailing, this inclusion limited the length of our survey. The questionnaire may have been an incentive to busy social workers who might be more inclined to participate in a brief, less time-consuming study, but the fact that it was not its own separate mailing and had no follow-up reminder may have contributed to the relatively low response rate.

Social workers are core members of all hospice interdisciplinary teams as determined by Medicare regulations (Johanson & Johanson, 1996). At the time of the study, there were more than 2,700 hospices in the United States (NHO, 1997) involving many more social workers than those who choose to join the Council of Hospice Professionals through NHO. Those who responded may be representative of members, but we have no way of knowing if they are representative of the greater number of hospice social workers who are not members, thereby restricting the generalizability of the findings reported here. Because inclusion of our survey with this NHO mailing was dependent on limiting it to one page and in light of the known homogeneity of the hospice social work population (predominantly white, female, and between the ages of 25 and 45), we omitted questions on basic demographic data. Respondents were asked to identify the number of years they had spent practicing in various health-related settings, but the categories were not discrete enough to provide a total number of years of social work experience.

## Results

### Demographic Characteristics of Respondents

Respondents represented all geographic regions in the United States with the fewest (5 percent, $n = 5$) from the northwest and the most (21 percent, $n = 23$) from the central states. Respondents were asked to respond "yes" or "no" to whether they had a BSW or an MSW degree. Of the 108 respondents, 88 percent ($n = 95$) reported having MSW degrees, 34 percent ($n = 37$) reported having BSW degrees, 22 percent ($n = 24$) reported having both BSW and MSW degrees, and 11 percent ($n = 12$) reported having only a BSW degree.

Interested in learning more about who supervises hospice social workers, we asked respondents, "Have you supervised social workers or students in an oncology setting?" and if so to indicate the number of years. A little over half (52 percent, $n = 56$) had experience as supervisors in an oncology setting, and thus their responses may reflect the perspective of having been both a student as well as a supervisor of students. For those with supervisory experience, the mean number of years supervising was 3.79 ($SD = 3.19$), with a range of 1 to 20 years.

### Generalist versus Specialist Training

The responses to a number of questions spoke to the benefit of a combined generalist and specialist training for oncology social work in a hospice setting. In the pilot study, respondents were asked an open-ended question about which courses in their formal social work training were most helpful. The choices given in this study included the four core courses: (1) practice, (2) human behavior, (3) policy, and (4) research, and the four electives most frequently listed by respondents in the pilot study. When asked which social work courses were the most helpful in preparing them for their hospice work, respondents reported practice (required generalist or core course work) to be most helpful, followed by electives (medical social work, family treatment, and crisis intervention). Another required course, human behavior, followed the electives in usefulness in preparation. Required courses in research and policy received the lowest rankings in terms of their helpfulness in preparation for the oncology setting (Table 14-1).

Social workers were also asked to identify previous experiences (professional or personal) that had been helpful in preparing them for oncology social work. Respondents most often mentioned the illness of a

**TABLE 14-1. Social Work Courses Ranked in Order of Helpfulness in Oncology Social Work**

| Course | M |
| --- | --- |
| Methods of direct practice | 2.21 |
| Medical social work | 2.35 |
| Family treatment | 2.69 |
| Crisis intervention | 2.90 |
| Human behavior | 3.05 |
| Group work | 3.36 |
| Research | 4.00 |
| Policy | 4.23 |

*Note:* Respondents were asked to rank these courses from 1 to 5 (1 = most helpful to 5 = least helpful) "in order of their helpfulness in your work in oncology."

family member or a friend (31 percent, $n = 34$). The second most frequently mentioned experience was social work in other medical settings (10 percent, $n = 11$), followed by professional medical training (9 percent, $n = 10$) and social work in other (nonmedical) settings in which they worked with individuals and families (7 percent, $n = 8$). More specifically, one respondent cited "inpatient psychiatric hospital, street work with gangs, drug abuse, and violent families" as helpful experience in preparing to work with oncology patients. Responses to this question echoed responses to the question about social work courses, in which respondents again valued both generalist (professional social work practice in nonmedical settings) and specialist training (professional practice in medical settings and other professional medical training).

Yet despite the value of both generalist and specialist training, it was the more specialized training that social workers indicated was inadequate. In response to the open-ended question asking which body of knowledge was lacking in their education, the largest group of social workers (22 percent, $n = 24$) identified death, dying, and bereavement, and the second largest group (12 percent, $n = 13$) indicated knowledge about interventions specifically relevant to their patients. Twenty-

five percent ($n = 3$) of those with only a BSW ($n = 12$) responded to this question with content typically emphasized in the "concentration year" of an MSW program, including two who mentioned one-to-one clinical work with clients. This response makes sense given that BSW programs do not cover specialized content as the concentration year of MSW programs do.

### *The Value of Cross-Disciplinary Training and Preparation for Collaboration*

Respondents were asked to identify what they considered to be vital on-the-job training (as distinct from classroom education) for beginning oncology social workers. Most necessary according to respondents was knowledge about the medical setting, including medications, charts, and medical terminology (19 percent, $n = 20$), again validating the importance of specialized knowledge. Second, training related to working in a host setting, such as collaborating with physicians and nurses and understanding teamwork dynamics, was considered vital on-the-job training (15 percent, $n = 16$). More specifically, respondents wrote, "Understanding the medical hierarchy," "Time to shadow people of different disciplines," and "Working with the doctors—hearing how they explain to and proceed with the patients—that's where many issues stem from."

Related to respondents' identified need for training on interdisciplinary collaboration was the finding that 9 percent (the third largest category of responses to this question) noted the value of an additional degree in the medical field (that is, medical technology, nursing, and the like) when asked what previous training had been useful in preparing them for oncology social work. Responses included "Before receiving my social work degree, I was an RN—this is the experience that has helped me in my hospice role," and

"My master's in rehab counseling was the most useful preparation for work in oncology." Because these comments came in response to an open-ended question about previous helpful experiences, the importance of this as the third largest category of responses was impressive.

### Relevance of Other-Than-Professional Training

Hospice social workers responding to this survey placed an extremely high value (noted by a 32 percent, $n = 34$ response to an open-ended question) on the role of family members' and friends' illness in preparing them for oncology social work. This was especially noted by those with only a BSW ($n = 12$) in which 54 percent ($n = 7$) responded to the open-ended question about previous relevant experiences by citing a personal experience with death or illness. Many mentioned the death or illness of people close to them, including parents and children. Many also noted the positive role hospice played in their lives and the desire to "give back" and help others. In addition, 14 percent ($n = 15$) responded to this same question by highlighting the importance of what they learned from patients. These data point to the need to help social workers integrate their personal experiences with loss in their professional work.

## Implications

This survey revealed three major findings with implications for future practice, education, and research. Although the advantages of combined generalist–specialist training and the importance of interdisciplinary collaboration have been pointed out in earlier literature, the following findings from this study have been less well documented: medical social workers' comfort with their generalist training and desire for more specialist training, skills in working with teams viewed as something learned on the job as opposed to in the classroom, and the perceived importance of personal life experience in this work.

### Implications for Practice

Hospice social workers in our sample emphasized the need for increased knowledge about the medical aspect of their work, including the medical process, terminology, paperwork, and so forth. This need points to a role for supervisors in developing orientations that introduce workers to this information (Abramson, 1993). In addition, respondents noted the importance of the interdisciplinary team and being able to function as an effective team player. This issue could be addressed using a thoughtful orientation, the ongoing pairing of professionals from different disciplines who can learn from each other over time, and social work leadership in facilitating the work of interdisciplinary teams.

The last finding, the importance of personal experiences, argues for the need to pay closer attention to thoughtful integration of the personal and professional experiences in practice. Although this is a spoken value in social work, supervisors and workers vary in their abilities and willingness to integrate these two "worlds," leaving open the possibility that personal experiences will influence practice, but in a reactive manner as opposed to in a thoughtful, proactive way that is most helpful to clients. In the interest of staff development and morale and indirectly enhanced patient care, agency directors and supervisors are encouraged to provide opportunities for all team members to discuss difficult cases, address problems among staff members, and process the overlap of personal and professional issues.

## Implications for Education

The findings point to implications for classroom, field, on-the-job, and continuing education. That respondents considered their required research and policy courses to be least helpful in their preparation, although not unusual for practitioners, is of concern. To be in compliance with the social work code of ethics and to practice sound, empirically based social work, clinicians need skills and knowledge to conduct research as well as to interpret and influence policy. The literature reflects important efforts to help social work students integrate policy and practice (Hart, 1989; Humphreys et al., 1993; Meenaghan & Gruber, 1986; Wyers, 1991) and research and practice (Blythe & Briar, 1985; Olsen, 1990; Reinherz, Regan, & Anastas, 1983). The results of this survey, however, serve as a reminder of this ongoing challenge.

Also of importance is the finding that the most frequently noted gap in the respondents' academic preparation was content on loss and grief. Because social workers deal with people of all ages experiencing loss, change, and grief secondary to divorce, illness and death, natural disasters, foster care and adoption, immigration, and numerous other life events, we recommend integrating this content related to coping with loss and change in a variety of courses. Too often this content is covered only in human behavior classes when discussing late adulthood, rather than being related to life events across the lifespan in practice as well as in human behavior classes.

Further implications for social work education argue for more in-depth opportunities for specialized knowledge in the classroom, whether by integrating this into concentration-year core courses or by increasing the availability of electives. In particular, on the basis of the findings of this study, schools are encouraged to offer content on social work in health care settings, family intervention, and crisis intervention. In addition, findings suggested providing proactive training for interdisciplinary collaboration, supporting Reese and Sontag's (1997) recommendation that interdisciplinary collaboration in health care settings be taught in schools of social work. Schools also should focus on structuring interdisciplinary classroom experiences and expanding opportunities for joint degree programs in which teamwork is taught and modeled. These suggestions also can be extended into the field where social work field instructors in hospices (and other health care settings) consciously teach required specialized knowledge. Spitzer and Nash (1996) summarized the history of this dialogue on how best to prepare social workers for health care settings and presented recommendations for enhancing such integration of field and classroom experiences. They, as well as Christ (1996), addressed the need for collaboration between schools and agencies, especially in light of the need for cost containment in education and in health care environments.

A number of model programs have been implemented around the country, geared to actualize related goals through continuing education that integrates on-the-job training. The Columbia University School of Social Work developed a model for interdisciplinary geriatric health care but found that rather than incorporating it into the MSW program, it was best taught as "a continuing education, post-graduate experience" (Solomon & Mellor, 1992, p. 175). A similar program in gerontological social work is affiliated with the Social Work Department at Beth Israel Hospital in Boston (Eckert, Hubner, Kapust, & Mayer, 1996). Another example, also in the area of gerontology, is the postgraduate interdisciplinary training model conducted by the Hunter/Mount Sinai Geriatric Education

Center. Here, an interdisciplinary faculty helps social workers and members of nine other health care disciplines acquire an interdisciplinary knowledge and skill base for work in geriatric settings. Based on the belief that there is not time or space in the MSW curriculum for this training, the training occurs as part of a free 50-hour continuing education program. A critical part of this training is educating participants on how to bring the knowledge they acquire back to their own agencies and to serve as educators of interdisciplinary gerontology (Solomon & Mellor, 1992).

In addition to the examples of continuing education programs in health care, the Network in Aging of Western New York was conceived in 1980 "as an umbrella organization to provide a cooperative framework for educational institutions, elderly consumers, students, and service providers engaged in the provision of health and social service support to elderly people in Western New York" (Karuza, Calkins, Duffey, & Feather, 1988, p.148). In addition, national, state, and local chapters of NASW, organizations of health care social workers, societies for social work administrators in health care, associations of oncology social workers, and the NHO are just some of the organizations that address the continuing education of health care social workers. Through these organizations practitioners and social work educators could enhance the practice of oncology social work and provide these professionals with "what they say they need" as well as help ensure that social work education remains in touch with the needs of practitioners.

### Implications for Research

Future studies should explore in more detail the content that was helpful in social workers' professional training, eliciting from them the course in which this content was covered.

Field placements should be inquired about in greater depth to better understand the effect of these experiences in career choices and opportunities as well as to prepare students for this work. The educational needs of social workers who assist with end-of-life issues in any setting should be surveyed. Additional research should pursue the continuing education opportunities that hospice social workers feel they need to further enhance their work. The numerous organizations representing health care social workers mentioned earlier should be involved in future research as participants and recipients of findings. Schools of social work should collaborate with organizations representing practitioners to conduct research that enhances practice. These organizations, in turn, can continue to ensure that academic research is relevant and reaches practitioners.

### Conclusion

Social workers as members of interdisciplinary hospice teams have the privilege and the challenge of addressing psychosocial needs of terminally ill cancer patients and their families and friends. Results from a national survey of hospice social workers support the combined generalist–specialist approach in preparing them for their work and indicate a need for increased attention to interdisciplinary collaboration. An interesting finding that stands out argues for an ongoing focus on integrating personal experience with the social workers' professional practice. In addition to graduates' academic and field preparation, findings suggest that continuing education of hospice and other health care social workers dealing with people living with and dying from cancer is important for continuing growth and success in this work.

## References

Abramson, J. S. (1993). Orienting social work employees in interdisciplinary settings: Shaping professional and organizational perspectives. *Social Work, 38,* 152–157.

Abramson, J. S., & Mizrahi, T. (1996). When social workers and physicians collaborate: Positive and negative interdisciplinary experiences. *Social Work, 41,* 270–281.

Abramson, J. S., & Rosenthal, B. B. (1995). Interdisciplinary and interorganizational collaboration. In R. L. Edwards (Ed.-in-Chief), *Encyclopedia of social work* (19th ed., Vol. 2, pp. 1479–1489). Washington, DC: NASW Press.

Alperin, D. (1985). Hospice social work: Support for generalist training. *Social Work in Health Care, 10*(3), 119–122.

American Cancer Society (2000). Statistics. [Online]. Available: www.cancer.org/statistics/index.html.

Bailis, S. (1985). What social work students need to know to begin practice in health care. In B. Berkman & T. O. Carlton (Eds.), *The development of health social work curricula: Patterns and process in three programs of social work education* (pp. 61–68). Boston: MGH Institute of Health Professions.

Beresford, L. (1993). *The hospice handbook.* Boston: Little, Brown.

Berkman, B. (1985). Basic competencies and knowledge base needs for social work practice in health care. In B. Berkman & T. O. Carlton (Eds.), *The development of health social work curricula: Patterns and process in three programs of social work education* (pp. 22–33). Boston: MGH Institute of Health Professions.

Berkman, B., & Carlton, T. O. (1985). *The development of health social work curricula: Patterns and process in three programs of social work education.* Boston: MGH Institute of Health Professions.

Blythe, B. J., & Briar, S. (1985). Developing empirically based models of practice. *Social Work, 30,* 483–488.

Caroff, P., & Mailick, M. D. (1985). Health concentrations in schools of social work: The state of the art. *Health & Social Work, 10,* 5–14.

Carroll, M. (1980). Collaboration with social work clients: A review of the literature. *Child Welfare, 59,* 407–417.

Christ, G. H. (1996). School and agency collaboration in a cost conscious health care environment. *Social Work in Health Care, 24*(1/2), 53–72.

Cowles, L. A., & Lefcowitz, M. J. (1992). Interdisciplinary expectations of the medical social worker in the hospital setting. *Health & Social Work, 17,* 57–65.

Dane, B. O., & Miller, S. O. (1990). AIDS and dying: The teaching challenge. *Journal of Teaching in Social Work, 4*(1), 85–100.

Dickinson, G. E., Sumner, E. D., & Frederick, L. M. (1992). Death education in selected health professions. *Death Studies, 16,* 281–289.

Dinerman, M., Schlesinger, E. G., & Wood, K. M. (1980). Social work roles in health care: An educational framework. *Health & Social Work, 5*(4), 13–20.

Eckert, J. W., Hubner, M. K., Kapust, L. R., & Mayer, J. B. (1996). A post-master's program in gerontological social work: Fulfilling a practice need in health care. *Social Work in Health Care, 24*(1/2), 137–152.

Falck, H. S. (1978). Social work in health settings. *Social Work in Health Care, 3*(4), 395–403.

Glaser, B., & Strauss, A. (1967). *The discovery of grounded theory.* Chicago: Aldine.

Hart, A. F. (1989). Teaching policy to the clinical master's student: A historical approach. *Journal of Teaching in Social Work, 3*(2), 35–45.

Humphreys, N., Lake, S., Demont, P., Hollidge, C., Mangiardi, P., Nol, J., Rudd, J., Stalker, C., & Twomey, J. (1993). Integrating policy and practice: The contribution of clinical social work. *Smith College Studies in Social Work, 63,* 177–185.

Johanson, G. A., & Johanson, I. V. (1996). The core team. In D. C. Sheehan & W. B. Forman (Eds.), *Hospice and palliative care: Concepts and practice* (pp. 31–40). Sudbury, MA: Jones & Bartlett.

Kane, R. A. (1990). Interprofessional education and social work: A survey. In K. W. Davidson & S. C. Clarke (Eds.), *Social work in health care: A handbook for practice* (pp. 799–810). Binghamton, NY: Haworth Press.

Karuza, J., Calkins, E., Duffey, J., & Feather, J. (1988). Networking in aging: A challenge, model, and evaluation. *Gerontologist, 28,* 147–155.

Lane, H. J. (1982). Toward the preparation of social work specialists in health care. *Health & Social Work, 7,* 230–234.

Martinez, J. M. (1996). The interdisciplinary team. In D. C. Sheehan & W. B. Forman (Eds.), *Hospice and palliative care: Concepts and practice* (pp. 21–30). Sudbury, MA: Jones & Bartlett.

Meenaghan, T., & Gruber, M. (1986). Social policy and clinical social work education: Clinicians as social policy practitioners. *Journal of Social Work Education, 22,* 38–45.

Miller, S. O., & Dane, B. O. (1990). AIDS and social work: Curricula development in an epidemic. *Journal of Social Work Education, 26,* 177–186.

National Hospice Organization. (1997). *Hospice fact sheet.* Alexandria, VA: Author.

Netting, F. E., & Williams, F. G. (1997). Case manager–physician collaboration: Implications for professional identity, roles, and relationships. *Health & Social Work, 21,* 216–224.

Olsen, L. (1990). Integrating a practice orientation into the research curriculum: The effect of knowledge and attitudes. *Journal of Social Work Education, 26,* 155–161.

Reese, D. J., & Sontag, M. (1997, March). *Preparing students to articulate the social work role on the interdisciplinary team.* Paper presented at Council on Social Work Education Annual Program Meeting, Chicago, IL.

Rehr, H., & Caroff, P. (1986). *A new model in academic-practice partnership: Multi-instructor and institutional collaboration in social work.* Lexington, MA: Ginn Press.

Reinherz, H., Regan, J. M., & Anastas, J. W. (1983). A research curriculum for future clinicians: A multimodel strategy. *Journal of Social Work Education, 19,* 35–41.

Rossen, S. (1987). Hospital social work. In A. Minahan (Ed.-in-Chief), *Encyclopedia of social work* (18th ed., Vol. 1, pp. 816–821). Silver Spring, MD: National Association of Social Workers.

Solomon, R., & Mellor, M. J. (1992). Interdisciplinary geriatric education: The new kid on the block. *Journal of Gerontological Social Work, 18*(3/4), 175–186.

Sormanti, M. (1994). Fieldwork instruction in oncology social work: Supervisory issues. *Journal of Psychosocial Oncology, 12*(3), 73–87.

Spitzer, W. J., & Nash, K. B. (1996). Educational preparation in contemporary health care social work practice. *Social Work in Health Care, 24*(1/2), 9–34.

Weiner, A. (1990). Incorporating AIDS content across the BSW curriculum. *Journal of Social Work Education, 26,* 162–176.

Wyers, N. L. (1991). Policy-practice in social work: Models and issues. *Journal of Social Work Education, 27,* 241–250.

Zelinsky, L. F., & Thorson, J. A. (1983). Educational approaches to preparing social work students for practice related to death and dying. *Death Education, 6,* 313–322.

This chapter was originally published in the February 1999 issue of *Health & Social Work,* Vol. 24, Number 1, pp. 57–64.

# 15

# The Effectiveness of
# Social Work with Older
# People and Their Families

## A Meta-analysis of Conference Presentations

AMANDA M. GRENIER
and KEVIN M. GOREY

A recent meta-analysis of 88 published studies evaluating social work interventions found them to be effective (Gorey, 1996). This research concluded that nearly eight of every 10 clients (78 percent) who engaged social work services did better than the typical nonparticipating client. This index of social work's average interventive effect size was estimated to be significant in both a statistical and practical clinical or policy sense. Moreover, Gorey's meta-analysis of the extant social work research literature of the 1990s essentially replicated the overall findings of similar reviews from the 1970s and 1980s (Reid & Hanrahan, 1982; Rubin, 1985; Thomlison, 1984; Videka-Sherman, 1988).

The consistent inference has been that social work services are helpful (that is, that they significantly ameliorate, alleviate, or solve the client- and worker-identified problem) to the vast majority of people who use them. There is a plausible alternative explanation for the touted effectiveness of social work, though, and that is that because the meta-inferences of Gorey and others were primarily based on the summarization of published research, it may be that their overall positive findings are solely explainable by the tendency for peer-reviewed journals to print "significant" or nonnull findings. This potential "file drawer problem" (Rosenthal, 1979), or publication bias, has not yet been adequately accounted for in reviews of the research on the effectiveness of social work practice. The present meta-analysis of conceptually similar, although unpublished, social work research findings will do so. Also, by focusing on gerontological practice, it will integratively review a field of social work that has not previously been so summarized.

We are aware of only one study on the potential potency of publication bias among the social work research literature (de Smidt & Gorey, 1997). In fact, de Smidt and Gorey's meta-analysis of unpublished graduate student research (dissertations and theses) suggested that publication bias could probably be rejected as a salient alternative explanation for social work's observed effectiveness. However, although direct evidence is not available on this score, one may conjecture that some (and perhaps many) of the student authors who formed their "unpublished" sampling frame, particularly those hoping to become academics, may already have been experiencing "publish or perish" pressure. If so, there may be a greater tendency among them to report "significant" results that may be more "publishable" later, during their early academic careers, in peer-reviewed journals. The meta-analysis reported in this article sought to empirically clarify this question by systematically replicating a recent review of published research on the effectiveness of social work (Gorey, 1996) and a similar review of dissertations and theses (de Smidt & Gorey, 1997) using another source of unpublished research, conference presentations.

## Method

Recent (1990 to 1996) conference presentations from the annual scientific meetings of

the Gerontological Society of America (GSA) that reported empirical findings on the effectiveness of gerontological social work (work with older people and their families) were this review's sampling frame. This largest of the field's annual professional conferences accepted manuscript abstracts at a rate of 88 percent in 1996; none were disqualified simply on the basis of nonsignificant findings, and acceptance rates for the years 1990 to 1995 were reported to be similar to the 1996 rate (personal communication with S. E. Gordon, GSA Director of Conferences, July 22, 1996). Forty-two conference presentations were selected from Volumes 30 (1990) to 36 (1996) of *The Gerontologist* (see Sample Presentations list following the References). The sample of studies for meta-analysis comprises the abstracts of these presentations. This meta-analysis exactly replicated Gorey's (1996) previous analysis based on published research in its use of the subject key word search scheme and the calculation of a scale-free effect size metric, the $r$ index (interpretable as Pearson's $r$), for each study as well as its summarization across the 42 studies (Cooper, 1989; Light & Pillemer, 1984). Abstracts affiliated with schools of social work or social welfare that met these criteria were included, as well as other multidisciplinary ones in which social workers were involved in theory development or service delivery.

## Results

### Sample Description

The 42 conference presentations typically (86 percent) had samples of fewer than 200 client participants (median = 89; combined intervention and comparison groups ranged widely from one to 14,000). All except one Canadian study were carried out in the United States. They also all, except one single-system design, used group research designs to evaluate direct, face-to-face interventions with individuals (34 percent), small groups (49 percent), or families (17 percent). Study designs included pre- (one group prepost, 42 percent), quasi- (comparison group, 34 percent), and true experiments (randomized control group, 24 percent).

These unpublished studies were similar to their published counterparts (Gorey, 1996) in all of these descriptive characteristics except one. The studies reported at the annual GSA meetings were less likely than their published counterparts to have evaluated organizational or community practice (where the units of analyses were larger than individuals—for example, programs or communities; none versus 27 percent, respectively) [$\chi^2(1, N = 130) = 14.16, p < .01$]. This variable was not, however, found to be associated with intervention effect size among the previously reviewed published studies, so by definition (for a third variable to confound a bivariate relationship it must minimally be associated with both of them) it cannot confound this study's unpublished–published effect size comparison.

### Effectiveness of Gerontological Social Work Interventions

In combining the results of the 42 conference presentations, our review essentially replicated the general effectiveness of social work interventions found by the previous review of published social work research; we found a mean $r$ index of .240 (95 percent confidence interval [CI] of .163, .317) (Table 15-1). Conversion to Cohen's (1988) $U_3$—a statistic that compares all of an intervention group's outcome measure scores with a comparison group median score—allows for the inference that about two-thirds (69 percent) of the older clients or their caregiving family members who participated in an intervention did better than the average client in a comparison group.

**TABLE 15-1. The Effectiveness of Social Work Interventions with Older People and Their Families: Conference Presentations Compared with Published Research**

| Effect Size Statistic | Conference Presentations[a] | Published | |
|---|---|---|---|
| | | All | Gerontological[b] |
| Studies (n) | 42 | 88 | 20 |
| Minimum r | .000 | −.380 | .020 |
| Maximum r | .997 | .962 | .941 |
| Mean r | .240 | .356 | .345 |
| SD | .253 | .261 | .239 |
| r (95 percent CI) | .163, .317 | .302, .411 | .240, .450 |
| Cohen's $U_3$ | 68.9% | 77.7% | 76.9% |

*Note:* CI = confidence interval. Conference presentations versus all published studies [$t(128) = 2.42, p < .05$] or versus published gerontological studies [$t(60) = 1.59, p < .10$], both one-tailed.

a. Sample included studies of social work with older people themselves (25 studies, 60 percent), with caregivers (13 studies, 31 percent), and simultaneously with both (four studies, 9 percent). The majority of the therapeutic interventions with elders and supportive ones with caregivers were based on generalist, systemic, or task-centered frameworks (57 percent); the remainder were cognitive or behavioral theory based. Specific interventive methods ranged widely from less formal individual life review or supportive group work to more structured methods such as cognitive–behavioral group work or task-centered case management. Effect size was not found to differ significantly by these client or treatment factors.

b. Adapted from Gorey (1996).

Not surprisingly, this review of conference presentations produced a somewhat smaller (10 percent attenuation) average effect size (69 percent) than the one based on all of the published studies (78 percent) or the specifically gerontological ones (77 percent). However, although the overall unpublished–published between-group comparison was statistically significant ($p < .05$), the meta-analytic comparison of unpublished and published research on the effectiveness of gerontological social work only approached significance ($p < .10$). Both similarly infer gerontological social work's interventive effectiveness (70 percent to 75 percent positive change associated with the intervention); both had $p$s of less than .05 (combined probability; 95 percent CIs did not include the null). Publication bias does not seem to saliently confound the generally positive inferences of social work effectiveness that have arisen from the profession's peer-reviewed publications.

## Discussion

Recently available unpublished research on social work intervention (1990 to 1996) provides the basis for generally inferring its effectiveness. On the basis of 42 studies presented at the GSA's annual scientific meetings, 69 percent of older clients or their caregivers participating in an intervention do better than the average client in a comparison group. Moreover, this overall finding closely replicates that of a recent meta-analysis of the published research on the effectiveness of social work (Gorey, 1996), as well as another based on unpublished dissertations and theses (de Smidt & Gorey, 1997).

In a sense, the present article is an extension of these previous ones. Taken together, they demonstrate in a quite unequivocal fashion that publication bias does not potently confound the generally positive inferences about social work's effectiveness that have been reported in peer-reviewed publications. Social workers can be confident in the validity of the notion that their services, and in this instance gerontological social work services, are practically helpful to seven to eight of every 10 clients who use them. This consistent conclusion is not explainable merely by the tendency of social work journals to report positive findings.

Taken together, this series of meta-analyses, which summarize the findings of more than 150 studies on the effectiveness of social work interventions in the 1990s, converge on the strong inference that such work is helpful for most clients who engage in it. But what of those for whom social work services are ineffective, an estimated two of every 10 social work clients? Answers to questions about their specific needs and the provision of effective services to them ought to be the mission of the next generation of social work research (de Smidt & Gorey, 1997). Social workers need to extend the population and contextual validity of their professional knowledge base. Having favorably answered the question of social work's overall effectiveness, we must now learn how the effects of specific interventions are moderated by specific client, worker, intervention, and other situational characteristics.

It should be noted that even though studies presented at a conference are clearly categorically definable as unpublished at the time of their presentation, they may subsequently be published in the profession's journals or elsewhere. To the extent to which this review's sample of presentations has thus penetrated the professional literature, its hypothesized independent variable (unpublished versus published) will misclassify studies. Such misclassification bias does not potently confound this review's central finding for the following reasons. First, at the time of this writing, computer searches of *Social Work Abstracts, Psychological Abstracts, Sociological Abstracts, Nursing Abstracts,* and *Index Medicus* revealed that although eight (19 percent) of the conference presentations were subsequently published (Feather, 1993; Fishback & Lovett, 1992; Gottesman, Peskin, Kennedy, & Mossey, 1991; Hebert, Leclerc, Bravo, Girouard, & Lefrancois, 1994; Kemp, Corgiat, & Gill, 1992; Rodman, Gantz, Schneider, & Gallagher-Thompson, 1991; Smith, Tobin, & Toseland, 1992; Toseland, Labrecque, Goebel, & Whitney, 1992), support for the criterion validity of this review's unpublished–published operational definition remained [$r = .86$, converted from $\chi^2(1, N = 130) = 96.29$, $p < .01$ (34 of 42 unpublished versus none of 88, Gorey, 1996; $(r = \chi^2/n)^{1/2}$, Cooper, 1989)]. Second, exclusion of these eight subsequently published presentations did not result in substantively different meta-analytic inferences. Finally, neither did exclusion of the 15 conference presentations from 1995 or 1996 (those most likely to presently be in review or in press). So we are confident that this review validly sampled unpublished social work research.

## References

Cohen, J. (1988). *Statistical power analysis for the behavioral sciences* (2nd ed.). Hillsdale, NJ: Lawrence Erlbaum.

Cooper, H. M. (1989). *Integrating research: A guide for literature reviews* (2nd ed.). Newbury Park, CA: Sage Publications.

de Smidt, G. A., & Gorey, K. M. (1997). Unpublished social work research: Systematic replication of a recent meta-analysis of published intervention efficacy research. *Social Work Research, 21,* 58–62.

Feather, J. (1993). Factors in perceived hospital discharge planning effectiveness. *Social Work in Health Care, 19*(1), 1–14.

Fishback, J. B., & Lovett, S. B. (1992). Treatment of chronic major depression and assessment across treatment and follow-up in an elderly female. *Clinical Gerontologist, 12,* 31–40.

Gorey, K. M. (1996). Social work intervention effectiveness research: Comparison of the findings from internal versus external evaluations. *Social Work Research, 20,* 119–128.

Gottesman, L. E., Peskin, E., Kennedy, K., & Mossey, J. (1991). Implications of a mental health intervention for elderly mentally ill residents of residential care facilities. *International Journal of Aging and Human Development, 32,* 229–245.

Hebert, R., Leclerc, G., Bravo, G., Girouard, D., & Lefrancois, R. (1994). Efficacy of a support group program for caregivers of demented patients in the community: A randomized controlled trial. *Archives of Gerontology and Geriatrics, 18,* 1–14.

Kemp, B. J., Corgiat, M., & Gill, C. (1992). Effects of brief cognitive–behavioral group psychotherapy for older persons with and without disabling illness. *Behavior, Health, and Aging, 2,* 21–28.

Light, R. J., & Pillemer, D. B. (1984). *Summing up: The science of reviewing research.* Cambridge, MA: Harvard University Press.

Reid, W. J., & Hanrahan, P. (1982). Recent evaluations of social work: Grounds for optimism. *Social Work, 27,* 328–340.

Rodman, J. L., Gantz, F. E., Schneider, J., & Gallagher-Thompson, D. (1991). Short-term treatment of endogenous depression using cognitive–behavioral therapy and pharmacotherapy. *Clinical Gerontologist, 10,* 81–84.

Rosenthal, R. (1979). The "file drawer problem" and tolerance for null results. *Psychological Bulletin, 86,* 638–641.

Rubin, A. (1985). Practice effectiveness: More grounds for optimism. *Social Work, 30,* 469–476.

Smith, M. F., Tobin, S. S., & Toseland, R. W. (1992). Therapeutic processes in professional and peer counseling of family caregivers of frail elderly people. *Social Work, 37,* 345–351.

Thomlison, R. J. (1984). Something works: Evidence from practice effectiveness studies. *Social Work, 29,* 51–57.

Toseland, R. W., Labrecque, M. S., Goebel, S. T., & Whitney, M. H. (1992). An evaluation of a group program for spouses of frail elderly veterans. *Gerontologist, 32,* 382–390.

Videka-Sherman, L. (1988). Meta-analysis of research on social work practice in mental health. *Social Work, 33,* 325–338.

## Sample Presentations

*All abstracts of papers presented at the annual scientific meetings of the Gerontological Society of America are published in* The Gerontologist.

Abraham, I. L. (1991). Effects of a cognitive group intervention on cognition, depression, hopelessness and life satisfaction in nursing home residents [Abstract]. *Gerontologist, 31,* 153

Ambinder, A., Mittelman, M., Mackell, J., Shulman, E., Steinberg, G., & Ferris, S. (1990). Relationship between coping strategies and depression in aged caregivers [Abstract]. *Gerontologist, 30,* 369A.

Beckette, C. D., Haug, M. R., Musil, C. M., Morris, D. L., & Clapp, M. K. (1995). The effects of social support on anxiety in elderly African-Americans and whites with a chronic illness [Abstract]. *Gerontologist, 35,* 152.

Caserta, M., Lund, D., Miller, J., & Feinaeur, L. (1990). The effectiveness of a family counselling program for older adults and their children living in intergenerational households [Abstract]. *Gerontologist, 30,* 203A.

Elliot, L. B., Eggert, G. M., Wamsley, B., & Teri, L. (1994). Reducing stress and burden for caregivers of Alzheimer's patients using a behaviour management intervention [Abstract]. *Gerontologist, 34,* 49.

Factor, A., & Richter, P. (1991). Evaluating the effectiveness of in-home mental health services to the resistant elderly [Abstract]. *Gerontologist, 31,* 366.

Feather, J. (1991). Determinants of perceived hospital discharge planning effectiveness [Abstract]. *Gerontologist, 31,* 346.

Fishback, J. B., & Lovett, S. B. (1991). Treatment of chronic major depression, and assessment over treatment and follow-up, in an elderly female [Abstract]. *Gerontologist, 31,* 64.

Fitzpatrick, T. R. (1992). Stress and well-being among the frail elderly: The effect of social

and recreational services [Abstract]. *Gerontologist, 32,* 55.

Gallagher-Thompson, D., Coon, D., & Thompson, L. W. (1996). Anger expression by type of treatment interaction predicts treatment outcome in family caregivers [Abstract]. *Gerontologist, 36,* 218.

Gottesman, L., Peskin, E., Kennedy, K., & Mossey, J. (1990). Implications of a mental health intervention for elderly mentally ill residents of RCFs [Abstract]. *Gerontologist, 30,* 148A.

Greene, R., Ferrano, E., & Zarit, S. H. (1995). Caregiver satisfaction with adult day care services for relatives with dementia [Abstract]. *Gerontologist, 35,* 156.

Gunther, J. S., Taylor, M., Calkins, E., & Karuza, J. (1996). Outcomes of dynamics system exercise class for older adults with arthritis [Abstract]. *Gerontologist, 36,* 331.

Haight, B. K., & Michel, Y. (1996). Examining the effects of the life review in nursing home residents over time [Abstract]. *Gerontologist, 36,* 37.

Hebert, R., Bravo, G., Leclerc, G., Girouard, D., & Lefrancois, R. (1992). Efficacy of a support group program for caregivers of demented patients: An experimental study [Abstract]. *Gerontologist, 32,* 267.

Ho, P. S., Stegall, M. B. H., & Wan, T. T. H. (1993). Effects of use of case-managed formal in-home services on the quality of life of the community-based frail elderly [Abstract]. *Gerontologist, 33,* 299–300.

Holdren, M. E., & Karuza, J. (1996). Therapy effectiveness and patient satisfaction for older adults served by private practice network [Abstract]. *Gerontologist, 36,* 143.

Kaus, C. R., & Mandel, R. G. (1994). Effects of focused reminiscence on cognition, affect, and social orientation in dementia residents [Abstract]. *Gerontologist, 34,* 141.

Kemp, B. (1990). Brief group cognitive/behavioral therapy for depressed older persons with and without chronic illness [Abstract]. *Gerontologist, 30,* 97A.

Kimboko, P. J. (1990). Impact of empowerment interventions on well-being of hard-to-serve elderly [Abstract]. *Gerontologist, 30,* 172A.

Laliberte, L., & Mor, V. (1993). Impact of preventive services on health and health practices among the elderly [Abstract]. *Gerontologist, 33,* 128.

Leach-McMahon, A. (1990). Effects of intervention strategies for adult children caring for elderly parents [Abstract]. *Gerontologist, 30,* 15A.

Lombardo, N. E., Berrol, C., Katz, S., & Ooi, W. L. (1996). Improving mood in frail elders in adult day care and nursing homes through dance/movement therapy [Abstract]. *Gerontologist, 36,* 40.

Miller, M., Nelson, P., Bullick, P., Sonnier, M., Olson, D., Lynch, J., & Willenbring, M. (1992). An outpatient clinic approach in case management of the medically ill elderly alcoholic [Abstract]. *Gerontologist, 32,* 256.

Morrow-Howell, N., Judy, L., & Becker, S. (1996). Evaluation of an intervention for elders at risk of suicide [Abstract]. *Gerontologist, 36,* 354.

Naleppa, M. J., & Reid, W. J. (1996). Task-centered case management: Field testing an intervention [Abstract]. *Gerontologist, 36,* 124–125.

Neuschatz, S., Shaban, K., Gaines, C., & Lewis, C. (1996). Interdisciplinary case management: Its effectiveness and efficiency [Abstract]. *Gerontologist, 36,* 120.

Rodman, J. (1991). Short-term treatment of a complicated bereavement using a combination of cognitive–behavioral psychotherapy and pharmacotherapy [Abstract]. *Gerontologist, 31,* 95.

Rodman, J., Gantz, F., & Schneider, J. (1990). Short-term treatment of endogenous depression using a combination of cognitive behavioral therapy for depressed older persons with

and without chronic illness [Abstract]. *Gerontologist, 30,* 97A.

Rubenstein, L. Z., Wieland, S. A., & Sui, A. L. (1990). Effectiveness of geriatric assessment programs: Meta-analysis of controlled trials [Abstract]. *Gerontologist, 30,* 181–182A.

Schieberl, J. E. (1995). Support group participation and subjective well-being among caregivers of stroke patients [Abstract]. *Gerontologist, 35,* 151–152.

Smith, G. C., Toseland, R. W., & Tobin, S. (1990). A three month follow-up of peer and professional counseling for family caregivers [Abstract]. *Gerontologist, 30,* 368–369A.

Smith, J., Shua-Haim, J. R., Shua-Haim, V., & Gross, J. S. (1996). The impact of social worker evaluation on length of stay (LOS) in hospitalized elderly: A prospective study [Abstract]. *Gerontologist, 36,* 119.

Spier, B. E., & McGrew, J. (1996). Evaluation of the PACE exercise program to improve quality of life of arthritis patients [Abstract]. *Gerontologist, 36,* 107.

Steffen, A., Futterman, A., & Gallagher-Thompson, D. (1991). Comparative outcomes of two interventions for caregivers with major depressive disorder [Abstract]. *Gerontologist, 31,* 369.

Toseland, R., Engelhardt, J., Jue, D., & Dwyer, P. (1993). Effectiveness of managed care for elderly outpatients [Abstract]. *Gerontologist, 33,* 299.

Toseland, R., Engelhardt, J., & O'Donnell J. (1994). Effectiveness and efficiency of GEM care for frail elderly outpatients [Abstract]. *Gerontologist, 34,* 177–178.

Toseland, R., Labrecque, M., & Goebel, S. (1990). The effectiveness and efficiency of a caregiver support program [Abstract]. *Gerontologist, 30,* 369A.

Westfried, E. (1995). Group psychotherapy and young older adults: A case study with implications for future cohort groups of older adult women [Abstract]. *Gerontologist, 35,* 113.

Woods, P., Francis, J., McIntyre, K., Ashley, J., Ooi, W., Volicer, L., & Camberg, L. (1996). Family-centered intervention to increase engagement among Alzheimer's patients [Abstract]. *Gerontologist, 36,*144.

Wroblewski, H. A. (1990). Healthy lifestyle change attempts of older adults through a holistic approach [Abstract]. *Gerontologist, 30,* 140A.

Yamada, H. (1992). The effect of emotional social support on the well-being of caregivers [Abstract]. *Gerontologist, 32,* 267.

This chapter was originally published in the March 1998 issue of *Social Work Research*, Vol. 22, Number 1, pp. 60–64.

# 16

# Creating Cost-Efficient Initiatives in Social Work Practice in the Cardiac Program of an Acute Care Hospital

CATHERINE KOHM,
DIANE NEIL-POLLINGER,
and FATIMA SHERIFF

The dramatic changes in federal–provincial funding for health care outlined in the 1989 federal budget have had a profound effect on hospitals in Ontario province (Gilchrist, 1997). By November 1995 it was clear that hospital funding would decrease by 1.3 billion Canadian dollars over three years. This 18 percent reduction was staged in 5 percent, 6 percent, and 7 percent increments over the period 1995 to 1998 (Ministry of Health, Ontario, 1996). Combined with other environmental pressures and advancements in medical–surgical practices, this reduction in funding initiated a surge of restructuring, re-engineering, and reshaping of initiatives in health care organizations.

Many measures were implemented to cope with these fiscal pressures, ranging from layoffs, bed closures, decreased length of stays, increased ambulatory programs to multiskilling. And yet, along with these changes, continuous quality improvement remained a pivotal concern for staff and management (Jirsch, 1993).

As the Cardiac Program at Toronto General Hospital (TGH), part of the University Health Network (UHN) went through a re-engineering process, the Department of Social Work concur-rently attempted to look for efficiencies. This article describes the three-fold results within the cardiovascular surgical division: (1) the creation of a one-page application form to streamline the cardiac rehabilitation application process, (2) the assignment of a specific role for the resource specialist of the Department of Social Work in assisting with applications for rehabilitation, and (3) the development and distribution of an information package on cardiac rehabilitation to patients and families. These three initiatives resulted in benefits for patients and families, for the social workers, and for the program.

## The Cardiovascular Surgical Service at TGH, UHN

The Cardiac Program of TGH is a quaternary care program in clinical service, research, and teaching. Its cardiovascular surgical (CVS) division serves a multi-ethnic patient population from the Greater Toronto Area and surrounding communities. CVS also accepts out-of-province and out-of-country referrals.

Currently, 28 intensive care beds and 55 ward beds accommodate cardiac surgical patients in a newly renovated area within the hospital. The number of cardiac surgeries performed during the past several years has increased steadily. In the fiscal year 1996–97, there were 2,342 cardiac surgeries completed; in 1997–98, this number grew to 2,502 surgeries. In 1998–99, the forecast was 2,726 surgeries.

Two full-time, master's level–trained social workers are assigned by the Department of Social Work to the cardiac program. The CVS division accounts for approximately two-thirds of their workload. Cardiovascular surgical patients requiring social work services are referred by staff to the social workers. Social work services include

- psychosocial assessments
- supportive, adjustment, and crisis counseling regarding hospitalization, and coping with heart disease
- assistance with planning for continuing care
- provision of information about and linkage with community resources
- patient–family education
- consultation to the treatment team.

In addition to clinical work, teaching and research account for approximately 20 percent of social work practice.

For cardiac patients who have little social support, planning for continuing care may include an application to one of the local rehabilitation hospitals that provide a cardiac rehabilitation program. Facilitating both applications and transfers to these rehabilitation hospitals has been a significant and necessary part of the social work role within the CVS division.

## The Resource Specialist

The Discharge Office, located in the Department of Social Work, created the position of resource specialist to allow social work staff to spend more time with patients and families. The office has one full-time resource specialist whose focus is resource finding and follow-up of patients waiting for alternate levels of care. The resource specialist

1. creates, monitors, and communicates information from "the resource bank" of community resources to facilitate timely discharge and appropriate posthospital care

2. reviews, monitors, and follows up with alternate level of care applications and accepts bed calls from receiving facilities

3. provides direct assistance to patients and families locating resources and supports as requested by social workers.

The resource specialist has an undergraduate degree, plus a social service diploma from a community college. Additional skills include communication, time management, and client advocacy. These distinct qualifications ensure that there is a clear role distinction between the social workers, educated at the master's level, and the resource specialist.

The advantages of this system include

• an increase in the amount of clinical time available to social workers for work with patients and families
• a tracking system for information on applications to Alternate Level of Care (ALC), including discharge data, e.g., length of hospital stay
• improved linkages to the community
• an extensive data base of resources for all staff.

## Initiative 1:
## One-Page Application Form

The cardiac program performed 2,502 surgeries in fiscal year 1997–98. Of these 2,502 patients approximately 12 percent, or 300 patients, required a period of postoperative rehabilitation at one of two local rehabilitation centers. Each of these centers has a program of education, exercise, and monitoring that is designed to help the patient and family adjust to the recent surgery and achieve a level of activity that allows the patient to return home safely.

The process of admission to these facilities traditionally has required a four-page application form to be completed by the physician, nurse, and social worker, in consultation with the patient. With the permission of the patient, the application form is then faxed to both facilities by a discharge secretary. The rehabilitation facility contacts the discharge office when a bed becomes available, and the patient is transferred on the preappointed day.

The review of this process identified the application form as cumbersome and repetitive. Many patients requiring rehabilitation have a diagnosis of arterial coronary bypass (ACB) or valve surgery, are elderly, and have inadequate or unavailable social support. Initially in postoperative recovery, they typically require assistance with their activities of daily living, assistance or supervision with ambulation, and psychoeducation regarding recovery. These patients commonly follow predictable stages of progression in their recovery. Accordingly, staff found themselves rewriting the same information describing the patient's medical and functional levels and outlining identified needs on the application for cardiac rehabilitation.

In 1995, in collaboration with one of the rehabilitation facilities, the Department of Social Work arranged meetings of health care teams from both settings to exchange information and develop a better understanding of the goals of acute care and post-acute care for surgical cardiac patients. The results of these meetings included an application form that was reduced from four pages to one page for ACB and valve surgery patients and an education package for patients shared between the two facilities. By 1996 collaboration with the second rehabilitation facility resulted in the immediate acceptance of the shortened application form. Our acute care hospital guaranteed to take patients back who were not able to cope with the rehabilitation program or who became acutely ill and required readmission.

The shortened application form has increased efficiencies and allowed the social workers to spend more time with patients and less time doing repetitive paper work. Time-saving gains were recognized also by nurses and physicians. The benefits to the cardiovascular surgical division and the hospital were two-fold: (1) maintenance of quality of service delivery and (2) cost reduction. It is estimated that the shortened application form has resulted in an annual cost savings of $9,900 through reduction in professional and support staff time and printing costs.

The ongoing collaborative efforts of the cardiac program social workers, the Department of Social Work, and the rehabilitation hospitals ensured that quality of service delivery was maintained through streamlining the rehabilitation application process.

## Initiative 2:
## Use of the Resource Specialist

Further efficiencies were realized when, in August 1998, the resource specialist took on the task of completing the one-page cardiac rehabilitation application. The cardiac social worker now triages all requests for social work postcardiac surgery and refers those who do not have complex issues to the resource specialist. The resource specialist then meets with the patient and

- assesses the patient's suitability for the rehabilitation program
- explains the program
- ensures that the information pamphlet is given to the patient
- completes the one-page application form
- documents the intervention on the patient's medical chart.

From the Rehabilitation Center's perspective, ACB and valve surgery patients are identified easily because of the one-page form. Patients who are more complex in their rehabilitation needs still have a four-page application completed on their behalf by the cardiac social worker to communicate all the necessary information.

In summary, the introduction of the resource specialist created a staffing skill mix appropriate to the tasks involved in planning a continuum of care for patients and families.

## Initiative 3:
## Information Pamphlet

In June 1997, with the streamlined rehabilitation application process in place, cardiac social workers and management focused on examining further opportunities for efficiencies. Patient orientation to cardiac rehabilitation was targeted for review, given the high number of patients requiring application to rehabilitation hospitals after their surgery.

Social work practice at that time involved an individual interview with each patient and family about the cardiac rehabilitation programs. This orientation usually took place on the first or second day following surgery to facilitate timely submission of the application and reduce waiting time for admission.

The central activity in the orientation interview was information provision; the information provided was essentially the same for the majority of patients. The repetitive nature of this orientation allowed us to consider the provision of this information in the form of an information package on cardiac rehabilitation for patients and families.

We reviewed the literature on adult education and reminded ourselves that adults learn best if they feel there is a need to learn and if there are opportunities for them to be participants (Gessner, 1989). We recognized that patients' abilities to learn vary from one recovery phase to another and differ among individuals (Allan, 1998). With input from our nursing colleagues, we decided on an information pamphlet combined with a shortened interview with the social worker to deal with patients' concerns and comments.

**TABLE 16-1. Results of Patient Questionnaire (*N* = 22)**

| Variable | No. of "Yes" Replies | % of Total |
|---|---|---|
| People who found the information helpful | 19 | 86 |
| People who had other questions/concerns apart from the written information | 5 | 23 |
| People who preferred to read the information rather than see a video | 18 | 82 |
| People who had comments | 5 | 23 |

The pamphlet was both practical and cost-efficient. The patient could read the pamphlet at his or her leisure, could share the pamphlet with his or her family so that all were informed, and could keep it for review at any time. The interview, scheduled at the time that the application form was signed by the patient, provided the opportunity for the patient to participate directly, ask questions, identify concerns, and receive responses. It also allowed the social worker to adjust the intervention to the varying stages of a patient's ability to learn.

For patients whose primary language is other than English, often there is a family member who can speak English and provide translation. A logical next step is to translate the pamphlet into other languages.

The information package, accompanied by a questionnaire on its usefulness was pilot tested over four months beginning at the end of August 1998. Of the patients that were handed the package and questionnaire, 77 percent actually read the material. The results (Table 16-1) indicated that the majority of patients and their families who had read the information found the information helpful in understanding the steps and issues involved, had no other questions or concerns about the information, and preferred to read the information rather than see a video. We concluded that the combined information package and shortened interview format met our goal of streamlining the process of providing information to patients and families

about cardiac rehabilitation without compromising the quality of care.

Throughout the pilot, social workers monitored their time spent with patients in the shortened interviews. The results of this tracking identified that approximately five to 12 minutes of social work time per patient is saved by using the combined pamphlet and shortened interview. Over the four months, this amounted to a saving of from eight to 19.2 hours.

## Summary and Conclusion

All three cost-saving initiatives—the creation of a one-page application form to streamline the rehabilitation application process, the use of the resource specialist to assist with applications, and the development of an information package on cardiac rehabilitation—reflect a process whereby a creative idea, generating planning, activities, and follow-up, resulted in a measurable effective change in practice. This process truly translated strategy into action (Kaplan, 1996) and is vital to the current rethinking in health care of how best to do our work (Coan, 1994). Because of this process, social workers in the cardiovascular surgical division of the cardiac program are better equipped to respond to the psychosocial needs of a growing cardiac population in a fiscally restrained environment.

🌿 🌿 🌿

## References

Allan, R. (1998). *Heart failure workbook*. Unpublished manuscript, York University, Nursing Science Practicum, Toronto.

Coan, T. (1994). Reengineering the organization: An approach for discontinuous change. *Quality Management in Health Care, 2*(3), 15–26.

Gessner, B. A. (1989). Adult education: The cornerstone of patient teaching. *Nursing Clinics of North America, 24,* 589–595.

Gilchrist, J. G. (1997, Spring). How did we get from "then" to "now"? *OASW Newsmagazine,* pp. 2, 4.

Jirsch, D. (1993, Winter). Patient-focused care: The systemic implications of change. *Healthcare Management Forum, 6*(4), 27–32.

Kaplan, R. S. (1996). *The balanced scorecard: Translating strategy into action.* Boston: Harvard Business School Press.

Ministry of Health, Ontario. (1996, February 23). *Backgrounder.* Toronto, Ontario: Author.

This chapter was originally published in the May 2000 issue of *Health & Social Work*, Vol. 25, Number 2, pp. 149–152.

# 17

# Short-Term Persistent Depression Following Hip Fracture

## A Risk Factor and Target to Increase Resilience in Elderly People

SHERYL ITKIN ZIMMERMAN,
H. DAVID SMITH, ANN GRUBER-BALDINI,
KATHLEEN M. FOX, J. RICHARD HEBEL,
JOHN KENZORA, GERALD FELSENTHAL,
and JAY MAGAZINER

Maximizing recovery following hip fracture presents an important clinical challenge. In 1990, 1.66 million hip fractures occurred worldwide; by 2050 an estimated 6.26 million people will suffer a fracture each year (Cooper, Campion, & Melton, 1992). Approximately 300,000 hip fractures occur annually in the United States (U.S. Congress, Office of Technology Assessment, 1994). Depending on the domain under study and the method of measurement, an estimated 25 percent to 75 percent of people ambulating before their fracture cannot walk without assistance or achieve their previous level of independent living within the year following fracture (Zimmerman, Fox, & Magaziner, 1995). Also, depression is especially prevalent in this population, with between one-third and one-half of patients exhibiting substantial depressive symptomatology during hospitalization. Of concern is that depression is a well-known risk factor associated with failure to return to prefracture levels in walking and other activities (Billig, Ahmed, & Kenmore, 1988; Cobey, et al., 1976;

Magaziner, Simonsick, Kashner, Hebel, & Kenzora, 1990; Mossey, Knott, & Craik, 1990; Mutran, Reitzes, Mossey, & Fernandez, 1995; Roberto, 1992).

Because many people experience reactive depression following illness or trauma, it is important to understand the role of chronicity in predicting health outcomes. One study of hip fracture recovery found that depressive symptoms that were persistently elevated through one year postfracture were related to poor physical functioning outcomes and that people with symptoms that resolved by six months postfracture fared no worse than those displaying no depressive symptoms (Mossey et al., 1990). This finding, that persistently depressed people are at risk of poor outcomes, is intriguing. Perhaps the individuals who are not depressed or those whose depression resolves constitute a resilient cohort.

## Resilience: Depression and Recovery Following Hip Fracture

Recovery following hip fracture presents an opportunity for tertiary prevention to lessen disability subsequent to fracture. Risk factors that increase the probability of poor recovery after hip fracture are multiple; besides depression, they include age; male gender; concomitant disease; delirium; dementia; having sustained a major fall; poor postfracture balance, gait, and mobility; poor social support before and after fracture; longer hospital stay; and rehospitalization after discharge (Beals, 1972; Fox et al., 1998; Gill, Robison, & Tinetti, 1997; Magaziner, Simonsick, Kashner, Hebel, & Kenzora, 1989; Magaziner et al., 1990). Risk factors for depression in elderly people also are multiple and include age, female gen-

der, unmarried or widowed marital status, less than a high school education, economic hardship, concomitant disease, cognitive impairment, functional disability, poor social support, history of psychiatric illness, retirement, few interests, negative attitude toward aging, loneliness, poor self-esteem, low personal control, stressful life events, and low life satisfaction (Burke, Burke, Regier, & Rae, 1990; Callahan & Wolinsky, 1995; "Diagnosis and treatment of depression in late life: NIH consensus development panel on depression in late life," 1992; Foster, 1997; Mirowsky & Ross, 1992; Parmelee, Katz, & Lawton, 1992; Weissman, Bland, & Canino, 1996). For hip fracture and depression, markedly fewer factors have been demonstrated to be protective; social support and self-efficacy are notable exceptions (Dean, Kolodny, & Wood, 1990; Krause, Liang, & Yatomi, 1989; Magaziner et al., 1990). To the extent that common risk and protective factors can be identified for these conditions, people who are at highest risk of poor recovery might be identified (Table 17-1). The effects of age and gender differ for depression and fracture, but people with concomitant disease, cognitive impairment, functional disability, and poor social support may be especially likely to exhibit poor adaptation and poor outcomes— thereby constituting a cohort especially at risk. Being able to identify such people would facilitate the development and targeting of effective intervention programs to maximize recovery. Therefore, the aims of the current investigation were to identify the relationship between depression following hip fracture and functional recovery at one year and to investigate which characteristics discriminate people who are at greatest risk of poor outcomes, based on affective status.

**TABLE 17-1. Common Risk and Protective Factors for Depression in Elderly People and Recovery Following Hip Fracture**

|  | *Depression* | *Hip Fracture* |
|---|---|---|
| Risk Factors | Age (younger) | Age (older) |
|  | Gender (female) | Gender (male) |
|  | Concomitant disease | Concomitant disease |
|  | Cognitive impairment | Cognitive impairment |
|  | Functional disability | Postfracture balance, gait, mobility |
|  | Social support (deficient) | Social support (deficient) |
| Protective Factors | Social support (high) | Social support (high) |

## Methods

### Study Population

As part of a study of hip fracture recovery in community dwellers ages 65 and older admitted to eight Baltimore area hospitals (1990 to 1991), 682 people were enrolled, 308 for whom depression assessments during hospitalization and at two months postfracture were conducted; of these, 12-month outcome data were available for 272 people (88 percent).

### Data Collection

Participants were interviewed during their hospitalization for hip fracture and at their residence at two and 12 months postfracture. Information about prefracture status was obtained while the participants were hospitalized. Depressive symptomatology was assessed by participant self-report at hospitalization and two months postfracture. For some other data, proxies provided prefracture or 12-month recovery information in physical activities of daily living (PADLs), instrumental activities of daily living (IADLs), or social functioning if participants were unable to be interviewed; most missing data related to social functioning prefracture ($N = 8$) and at 12 months postfracture ($N = 22$). Subject-proxy response comparability for

physical and instrumental activities of daily living and social activity scales for hip fracture patients is very high, with intraclass correlation values of .60 to .85 (Magaziner, Simonsick, Kashner, & Hebel, 1988; Magaziner, Zimmerman, Gruber-Baldini, Hebel, & Fox, 1997).

### Measures

*Depression.* The Center for Epidemiologic Studies Depression Scale (CES-D) (Radloff, 1977), a 20-item measure of depressive symptomatology used widely in studies of elderly people, was administered to participants during hospitalization and at two months postfracture. This scale has high internal consistency, good test–retest reliability, high concurrent validity when assessed against clinical and self-report criteria, and evidence of construct validity. It includes symptoms on which a diagnosis of clinical depression is based, but which also may accompany other diagnoses. The items comprise four factors (depressive affect, somatic activity, positive affect, and an interpersonal factor) and are answered on a four-point scale ranging from 0 = rarely to 3 = most or all the time. Scores range from 0 to 60, with higher scores indicating more symptoms. Scores of 16 or more have a higher probability of clinical depression.

*Physical Function.* Information about PADLs was obtained with a modified version of the Functional Status Index (Jette, 1980), to which was added lower extremity activities of relevance to hip fracture recovery. Information referred to assistance used in the past week to perform 15 activities (that is, walk one block, walk across a room, climb five steps, get into a car, get in and out of bed, rise from a chair, put on a shirt, button a shirt, put on pants, put on socks and shoes, get in and out of a bath or shower, wash self, get on and off the toilet, feed self, groom self).

*Instrumental Function.* IADLs were assessed with a modified version of the Older Americans Resources and Services Instrument (Fillenbaum, 1988), which asked participants how they performed seven activities, rather than asking them to rate their ability to perform them (that is, travel, shop, use the telephone, prepare meals, do housecleaning, handle money, take medicine). Questions referred to whether the individual was independent in each activity during the preceding two-week period.

*Social Function.* Items related to social functioning incorporated 12 functions of a passive or active nature and solitary or social nature (that is, watch television, read, go to religious services, attend meetings, participate in sports, go to movies, go to museums, work at a hobby, play cards, go on pleasure drives, go to a family member or friend's home for a meal, do volunteer work) (House, Robbins, & Metzner, 1982). Questions referred to the number of these 12 activities in which participants engaged over the preceding two weeks.

*Other Measures.* Other measures included the Mini-Mental State Examination (MMSE) (Folstein, Folstein, & McHugh, 1975), a measure of cognitive impairment administered during hospitalization, in which scores range from 0 to 30, with 0 to 16 indicating

impaired cognition, 17 to 23 indicating moderately impaired cognition, and 24 and higher indicating intact cognitive function. Also, the burden of comorbid disease was determined by chart abstract of the presence of 13 preexisting major conditions from which a weighted index was derived, representing a modified version of the Charlson Index (Charlson, Pompei, Ales, & MacKenzie, 1987); the resulting comorbidity score ranged from 0 to 9, with higher scores indicating more illness. In addition, data were collected on age, gender, race, education, and marital status.

### Data Analysis

CES-D scores, measured in hospital and at two months postfracture, were used to create four groups on the basis of persistence of depressive symptoms. The standard cutpoint of 16 was used to discriminate people with high versus low depressive symptoms; participants whose CES-D scores were 15 or lower on both occasions were categorized as not depressed, and participants whose scores were 16 or higher at both times were considered persistently depressed. Resolved depression and incident depression groups included those whose scores changed across the cutpoint between hospitalization and two-month follow-up.

Functional outcomes referred to physical, instrumental, and social functioning at one year postfracture. PADLs and IADLs were assessed in reference to whether the individual could perform the task independently; activities were coded to represent dichotomous categories with 0 representing independent functioning and 1 indicating dependence. The ability to perform individual tasks as well as a summary score for both PADLs and IADLs was examined. Social functioning referred to the number of social activities in which the participant took part; these data also were analyzed in reference to individual items and a total summary score. When a summary score was created, the total was derived by adding the number of activities for which the individual required assistance (PADLs and IADLs) and the number of 12 activities in which the individual participated (social function). If more than 25 percent of the items were missing, the score was not computed; if fewer than 25 percent of the items were missing, the denominator was adjusted and a proportioned score was derived. When predicting outcomes, only individuals who performed the activity prefracture were included in the analyses. Summary scores were not computed for participants who were dependent in all PADLs or IADLs prefracture or who did not participate in any social activities, because recovery (that is, improvement to a prior, improved state of function) was not likely for these individuals.

To evaluate the relationship between persisting depression and functional outcomes at 12 months, the summary score and individual items were examined. Multiple linear regression was used for the summary score, controlling for age, gender, race, education, marital status, comorbidities, cognitive status, and prefracture PADLs, IADLs and social functioning. For individual items, in which the outcome was categorical, logistic regression models were used, controlling for prefracture function on the individual item. Additional covariates could not be included because of power constraints and difficulties having the models converge; however, these covariates typically exert their influence on prefracture function, which was controlled. For these models, persistence groupings were entered using a dummy coding system with the not-depressed group serving as the reference category. To examine predictors of de-

pression, analysis of variance was used to determine prefracture differences between the four persistence of depression groups, and Students' *t* tests were used to examine potential differences between depression groupings in reference to mean functional summary scores.

## Results

### *Participants*

Participants were 80 percent female, 95 percent white, and between ages 65 and 96 (mean age = 79.3 years, $SD$ = 7.1) (Table 17-2). Fifty-eight percent were widowed, and they had an average education of 11.6 years ($SD$ = 3.7). During hospitalization, the majority (73 percent) demonstrated good cognitive function.

**TABLE 17-2. Characteristics of the Sample (*N* = 272)**

| Characteristic | N | % | M | SD |
|---|---|---|---|---|
| Female | 217 | 80 | | |
| White | 259 | 95 | | |
| Marital status | | | | |
|   Married | 87 | 32 | | |
|   Widowed | 159 | 58 | | |
|   Other | 26 | 10 | | |
| Cognitive status[a] | | | | |
|   Impaired | 8 | 3 | | |
|   Moderately impaired | 63 | 23 | | |
|   Intact | 198 | 73 | | |
| Age | | | 79.3 | 7.1 |
| Education | | | 11.6 | 3.7 |
| Comorbidity[b] | | | 1.4 | 1.4 |
| Physical functioning[c] | | | 2.9 | 3.4 |
| Instrumental functioning[d] | | | 2.1 | 2.0 |
| Social functioning[e] | | | 4.5 | 1.9 |

    a. Hospital status, based on Mini-Mental State Examination; data are missing for three participants.
    b. Modified Charlson Index score; number represents a weighted score of 13 conditions.
    c. Reported prefracture functioning; number of 15 activities for which participant is dependent.
    d. Reported prefracture functioning; number of seven activities for which participant is dependent.
    e. Reported prefracture functioning; number of 12 activities in which participant participated.

Mean prefracture dependency scores were 2.9 of 15 PADLs ($SD$ = 3.4) and 2.1 of 7 IADLs ($SD$ = 2.0); participants engaged in 4.5 of 12 social activities ($SD$ = 1.9). Participants for whom complete data were available differed from others ($p < .01$) in that they were younger (mean age 79.3 versus 82.1), had more education (11.6 years versus 10.4 years) and less comorbid burden (Charlson score 1.4 versus 1.8), and were less cognitively impaired (mean MMSE score 25 versus 24), functionally impaired (mean PADL score 2.9 versus 4.6; mean IADL score 2.1 versus 3.7), and socially impaired (mean number of activities 4.5 versus 3.7) at baseline.

### Persistence of Depression

Almost half (48 percent) of the participants were depressed during hospitalization; by two months, half of these cases resolved. The largest subgroup was composed of the people who were not depressed at either hospitalization or two-months postfracture (43 percent); the smallest group was composed of the 9 percent who became depressed at two months (Table 17-3).

**TABLE 17-3. Percentage of Participants Reporting Depression and Persistence of Depression through Two Months Postfracture ($N$ = 272)**

|  | N | (%) |
|---|---|---|
| Depressed postfracture (hospital)[a] | 131 | 48 |
|   Depressed at two months | 66 |  |
|   Not depressed at two months | 65 |  |
| Not depressed postfracture (hospital) | 141 | 52 |
|   Depressed at two months | 23 |  |
|   Not depressed at two months | 118 |  |
| Persistence of depression[b] |  |  |
|   Persistent depression | 66 | 24 |
|   Resolved depression | 65 | 24 |
| No depression | 118 | 43 |
| Incident depression | 23 | 9 |

a. CES-D scores of 16 or greater indicate depression.
b. Persistence is determined as per in-hospital and two-months postfracture assessment.

*Functional Status at 12 Months: Summary Indices.* Depression at two months was significantly related to poorer physical functioning (PADLs) at 12 months; the adjusted mean score for the number of activities for which participants required assistance was 7.4 (incident depression) and 6.6 (persistent depression), compared with 5.4 (no depression) and 5.7 (resolved depression) for those who were not depressed at two months (Table 17-4). For IADLs, pairwise post hoc $t$ tests revealed that those who were persistently depressed had significantly poorer functioning at 12 months than the not-depressed group and those whose depression resolved ($M$ = 3.4 compared with 2.7 and 2.5). Depression that resolved was not a significant predictor for either PADL or IADL function at one year. No significant differences were found for social functioning, although those who became depressed at two months displayed a trend toward participating in fewer social activities ($M$ = 4.1) than all others.

*Functional Status at 12 Months: Individual Items.* All PADL, IADL, and social function items that made up summary scores were analyzed individually to examine whether particular types of activities were affected. Adjusted odds ratios at level $p < .05$ are reported in Table 17-5. The persistently depressed group recovered more poorly than the not-depressed group in the majority of PADLs, including both upper- and lower-extremity functions. Also, compared with the not-depressed group, participants whose depression resolved were at increased risk in one activity, and those with incident depression were at increased risk in four activities. One of seven IADLs demonstrated greater risk for those who were persistently depressed (that is, meal preparation) compared with those who were not depressed. Participants who became depressed at two months had a higher risk of not participat-

**TABLE 17-4. Multiple Regression of Depression Category on PADL, IADL and Social Functioning Summary Scores: Adjusted Mean Scores at 12 Months Postfracture[a]**

| | PADLs (N = 206) | IADLs (N = 160) | Social (N = 209) |
|---|---|---|---|
| No depression | 5.4 | 2.7 | 4.5 |
| Incident depression | 7.4[c, d] | 3.1 | 4.1 |
| Resolved depression | 5.7 | 2.5 | 4.5 |
| Persistent depression | 6.6[b] | 3.4[b, e] | 4.6 |

*Note:* PADL = physical activities of daily living; IADL = instrumental activities of daily living.

a. Adjusted for age, gender, race, education, marital status, comorbidities, Mini-Mental State Examination score, and prefracture PADLs, IADLs, and social functioning.

b. $p < .05$ for comparison with no depression group.

c. $p < .01$ for comparison with no depression group.

d. $p < .05$ for comparison with resolved depression group.

e. $p < .01$ for comparison with resolved depression group.

ing in one activity (that is, attending religious services) compared with people who were not persistently depressed.

*Prediction of Persistent Depression: Baseline Scores.* There was no statistically significant relationship between age, gender, race, marital status, education, or prefracture comorbid or IADL status and persistence of depression.

Participants who were persistently depressed had lower cognitive and prefracture PADL and social function than those who were not depressed (Table 17-6). The persistently depressed group was more cognitively impaired than those with incident depression. Participants whose depression resolved also were significantly more impaired in PADLs than

**TABLE 17-5. Bivariate Logistic Regressions of Depression Category on Dependence in Individual PADLs and IADLs and Participation in Individual Social Function Activities at 12 Months Postfracture**

| Activity | N | Incident Depression AOR | 95% CI | Resolved Depression AOR | 95% CI | Persistent Depression AOR | 95% CI |
|---|---|---|---|---|---|---|---|
| PADLs (of 15 activities)[a] | | | | | | | |
| Get into car | 226 | | | | | 2.09* | (1.01, 4.33) |
| Get in and out of bed | 257 | 3.74* | (1.33, 10.53) | | | 4.33*** | (2.07, 9.07) |
| Rise from a chair | 225 | 4.25* | (1,40, 12.92) | | | 2.24* | (1.09, 4.62) |
| Put on a shirt | 262 | | | | | 6.70*** | (2.33, 19.20) |
| Button a shirt | 256 | | | | | 4.21* | (1.28, 13.84) |
| Put on pants | 259 | | | | | 3.12** | (1.40, 6.96) |
| Take shower (wash) | 260 | 3.12* | (1.12, 8.73) | | | 1.96* | (1.01, 3.78) |
| Get on and off toilet | 258 | 4.88* | (1.34, 17.86) | 2.18* | (1.08, 4.40) | 2.22* | (1.10, 4.47) |
| Groom self (brush) | 260 | | | | | 5.17** | (1.81, 14.73) |
| IADLs (of 7 activities)[a] | | | | | | | |
| Prepare meals | 197 | | | | | 3.57** | (1.49, 8.56) |
| Social function (of 12 activities)[a] | | | | | | | |
| Religious services | 114 | .11** | (0.02, 0.57) | | | | |

*Note:* PADL = physical activities of daily living; IADL = instrumental activities of daily living; AOR = adjusted odds ratio; CI = confidence interval.

a. Adjusted for prefracture function on that item (independent or with assistance; participate or not participate). Reference category is no depression. Seven models failed to reach convergence (walk one block, climb five stairs, feed self, go to museums, participate in sports, do volunteer work, watch television). The only activities reported are those for which $p < .05$.

*$p < .05$. **$p < .01$. ***$p < .001$.

**TABLE 17-6. Analysis of Variance Comparing Baseline Depression Categories by Demographic Variables and Mean Baseline Function (N = 272)**

| | Cognitive Status (MMSE) | Prefracture PADLs | Prefracture Social |
|---|---|---|---|
| No depression | 25.8 | 2.1 | 4.8 |
| Incident depression | 26.4 | 3.0 | 4.4 |
| Resolved depression | 25.3 | 3.3[a] | 4.5 |
| Persistent depression | 24.2[b, d] | 3.9[c] | 3.9[b] |

Note: MMSE = Mini-Mental State Examination; PADL = physical activities of daily living. There were no significant relationships between depression categories and age, gender, race, marital status, education or prefracture comorbid or IADL status.

a. $p < .05$ for comparison with no depression group.
b. $p < .01$ for comparison with no depression group.
c. $p < .001$ for comparison with no depression group.
d. $p < .05$ for comparison with incident depression group.

the not-depressed group. Pairwise post hoc $t$ tests revealed no significant differences between participants whose depression resolved and those who remained persistently depressed.

## Discussion

Participants who were persistently depressed through two months following hip fracture exhibited poorer recovery than those whose depression resolved and those who were not initially depressed. Participants with incident depression at two months also exhibited poor recovery, but analyses could not examine whether incident depression predated poor functioning or was a concomitant of it. Information about persistence over a short period (that is, two months) is useful to target early assessment and treatment to an especially high-risk group. Although earlier research demonstrated a similar risk, it assessed depression through six or 12 months postfracture; this classification does not lend itself to early intervention, and it confounds the temporal nature of the relationship because both persistence and functioning were assessed simultaneously. The similarity of that study to the present one is noteworthy, however. In the current study, 24 percent of

all hip-fracture patients remained persistently depressed through two months postfracture; this figure is comparable to the 22 percent who remained depressed through 12 months in the prior work (Mossey et al., 1990). What matters is not whether depression increases or decreases between assessments, whether its normal course is to oscillate, whether it is reactive or chronic, or whether ensuing events between those times influenced its pattern, but that the persistence of this depression constitutes a risk factor for poor outcomes following hip fracture. Depression during hospitalization, by itself, is not predictive of later functional status: This group displayed increased risk in only one PADL and in no summary indices.

People who are persistently depressed are notably nonresilient and least able to ward off the negative consequences of a hip fracture. In this study, the available prefracture and baseline variables (age, gender, race, marital status, education, and cognitive and prefracture comorbid, PADL, IADL, and social function) did not differentiate individuals who were persistently depressed from those whose depression resolved by two months postfracture. These variables represent the common risk and protective factors for depression and recovery following hip fracture as listed on Table 17-1, yet they did not enable prediction of the most at-risk individuals. Hankin and Locke (1982), Hornstra and Klassen (1977), and Callahan, Hui, Nienaber, Musick, and Tierney (1994) had similar difficulty identifying characteristics that place individuals at risk of persistent depression. In the present study, methodological and analytical considerations explain, in part, why persistently depressed individuals could not be distinguished on the basis of risk and protective factors. Most notably, social support was indicated by marital status and social interaction. These indicators do not reflect degree of contact with the social network or size of the social network, both of which are predictive for recovery following hip fracture (Magaziner et al., 1990). Also, multiple risk factors for recovery were not controlled, including severity of fracture, amount of time between fracture and fixation, type of surgical repair, nutritional status, and surgical and postoperative complications. An additional limitation of the study, namely, that data could not be obtained for the most impaired patients, is likely to have confounded the findings; participants scored significantly lower on all listed risk factors, except male gender.

## Implications for Social Work Research and Practice

It is intriguing that this study found that the effects of persistent depression were pervasive across 10 PADLs and IADLs and were not specific to lower extremity functions expected to be most affected by the fracture. For example, being persistently depressed was associated with an increased risk of dependence in dressing, grooming, and meal preparation. The effect of persistent depression across these less fracture-specific domains suggests these findings might extend beyond an elderly hip-fracture population and may relate to the demands imposed on a frail elderly population by a sudden change in health status. Indeed, depression coexists with many other health states, and it exerts a similar effect across conditions (Dunham & Sager, 1994). In this view, the fracture, or other condition, constitutes the critical life event for which persistent depression is a risk factor for poor outcomes. Whether persistence, risk factors, and protective factors are similar across health states, and whether their influence is direct, indirect, additive, or interactive awaits investigation. Certainly, when an elderly person suffers a traumatic illness or experience, practitioners should assess depression and the risk factors for depression and recovery. To the extent that treatment resources may be limited, services might be targeted to the people who are persistently depressed through two months. Ongoing assessment of these individuals can elucidate the course and effects of depression that persist beyond two months. Also warranting further investigation is that social functioning was not impaired in a manner similar to PADLs and IADLs; it is curious that this at-risk population demonstrated resilience in their maintenance of social activities.

Knowing that support reduces depression (Dean et al., 1990), that decreases in support lead to increases in depression (Lin & Ensel, 1984), and that satisfaction with social support reduces depression (Krause et al., 1989) offers areas for social work intervention. Mobilizing social support will lessen its risk potential and heighten its protective effect for both depression and recovery. Social work group treatment has been effective for posttrauma recovery, but it is difficult for impaired hip-fracture patients to leave their homes early in the recovery process; in this regard, technology-based group treatment conducted by telephone conference call is a promising avenue to benefit elderly people recovering from hip fracture. It has become commonplace for multiple people to call into a single telephone line, and doing so overcomes barriers to face-to-face contact presented by physical limitations and difficulties with transportation (Schopler, Abell, & Galinsky, 1998). Advances in technology, such as hands-free use and augmented volume, make this modality especially applicable to older, frail populations. Social support could be facilitated by other means as well. For patients who are not as housebound, more active social engagement could be encouraged. Many elderly individuals find emotional support working in hospital gift shops or similar settings, a role that can increase feelings of self-efficacy and self-worth. It is worth considering programs to lessen isolation preceding fracture, such as through community efforts to promote volunteerism. Finally, social support to hip-fracture patients can be facilitated by support provided to their caregivers and other family members. These individuals can be encouraged and enabled to obtain respite and to learn to recognize their own internal cues as to when it is necessary. Family members also can learn to identify the limits of their caretaking role and thereby limit the patient's dependence, which could otherwise initiate a course of learned helplessness (Beaver & Miller, 1985).

Additional applications of social work treatment are multiple and include psychotherapy, the provision of concrete services, and environmental modification. Maximizing feelings of control, autonomy, and independent functioning is a promising avenue to lessen depression and facilitate recovery; concrete services and environmental modification are especially beneficial to facilitate independent function. Impaired mobility postfracture makes it difficult to travel and shop; arranging for transportation and other supportive services, including assistive de-

vices, is empowering. Modification of the home environment is less often considered as a social work intervention postfracture, but it does further recovery. Often, furniture can be rearranged in a room, and items in cupboards, to allow independent function and lessen difficult tasks such as reaching and bending. Ability to rise from a chair and toilet can be dramatically improved by provision of hard chairs with arms and elevated toilet seats. Finally, psychiatric and medical consultation for medication use or alternative therapies may be considered.

Depression is a common problem in elderly people (Koenig & Blazer, 1992), and one-half of all hip-fracture patients report depressive symptomatology immediately postfracture. More is known about risk than protective factors related to depression in elderly people and recovery following hip fracture. Further search for factors underlying resilience is likely to be especially fruitful if it examines known and presumed protective factors, including social support and disposition, such as self-efficacy (Garmezy, 1985). The search for dispositional factors might begin with the known relationship between motivation and expectations and functional recovery (Borkan & Quirk, 1992; Furstenberg, 1986; Resnick, Zimmerman, Magaziner, & Adelman, 1998). If the factors that affect resilience can be identified, intervention can be targeted in one of two ways: on common risk factors for depression in elderly people to lower the risk of persistent depression (Roberts, Kaplan, Shema, & Strawbridge, 1997) or on focused efforts to improve functional ability in persistently depressed people (Callahan et al., 1994). It is important to remember that there is nothing inherent in the aging process itself that impairs resilience (Foster, 1997).

# References

Beals, R. K. (1972). Survival following hip fracture: Longitudinal follow-up of 607 patients. *Journal of Chronic Disease, 25*, 235–244.

Beaver, M. L, & Miller, D. (1985). *Clinical social work with the elderly: Primary, secondary and tertiary intervention.* Homewood, IL: Dorsey Press.

Billig, N., Ahmed, S. W., & Kenmore, P. I. (1988). Hip fracture, depression, and cognitive impairment: A follow-up study. *Orthopaedic Review, 17*, 315–320.

Borkan, J. M., & Quirk, M. (1992). Expectations and outcomes after hip fracture among the elderly. *International Journal of Aging and Human Development, 34*, 339–350.

Burke, K. C., Burke, J. D., Regier, D. A., & Rae, D. S. (1990). Age at onset of selected mental disorders in five community populations. *Archives of General Psychiatry, 47*, 511–518.

Callahan, C. M., Hui, S. L., Nienaber, N. A., Musick, B. S., & Tierney, W. M. (1994). Longitudinal study of depression and health services use among elderly primary care patients. *Journal of the American Geriatrics Society, 42*, 833–838.

Callahan, C. M., & Wolinsky, F. D. (1995). Hospitalization for major depression among older Americans. *Journal of Gerontology: Medical Sciences, 50A*, M196–M202.

Charlson, M. E., Pompei, P., Ales, K. L., & MacKenzie, C. R. (1987). A new method of classifying prognostic comorbidity in longitudinal studies: Prognostic development and validation. *Journal of Chronic Disease, 40*, 373–383.

Cobey, J. C., Cobey, J., Conant, L., Ulrich, W., Greenwald, W., & Southwick, W. (1976). Indicators of recovery from fractures of the hip. *Clinical Orthopaedics and Related Research, 117*, 258–262.

Cooper, C., Campion, G., & Melton, L. J. (1992). Hip fractures in the elderly: A worldwide projection. *Osteoporosis International, 2*, 285–289.

Dean, A., Kolodny, B., & Wood, P. (1990). Effects of social support from various sources on depression in elderly persons. *Journal of Health and Social Behavior, 31*, 148–161.

Dunham, N. C., & Sager, M. A. (1994). Functional status, symptoms of depression, and the outcomes of hospitalization in community-dwelling elderly patients. *Archives of Family Medicine, 3*, 676–681.

Fillenbaum, G. G. (1988). *Multidimensional functional assessment of older adults: The Duke Older Americans Resources and Services Procedures.* Hillside, NJ: Lawrence Erlbaum.

Folstein, M. F., Folstein, S. E., & McHugh, P. R. (1975). "Mini-mental state:" A practical method for grading the cognitive state of patients for the clinician. *Journal of Psychiatric Research, 12*, 189–198.

Foster, J. R. (1997). Successful coping, adaptation and resilience in the elderly: An interpretation of epidemiologic data. *Psychiatric Quarterly, 68*, 189–219.

Fox, K. M., Hawkes, W. G., Hebel, J. R., Felsenthal, G., Clark, M., Zimmerman, S. I., Kenzora, J. E., & Magaziner, J. (1998). Mobility after hip fracture predicts health outcomes. *Journal of the American Geriatrics Society, 46*, 169–173.

Furstenberg, A-L. (1986). Expectations about outcome following hip fracture among older people. *Social Work in Health Care, 11*, 33–47.

Garmezy, N. (1985). Stress-resistant children: The search for protective factors. In J. E. Stevenson (Ed.), *Recent research in developmental psychopathology* (pp. 213–233). Tarrytown, NY: Pergamon Press.

Gill, T. M., Robison, J. T., & Tinetti, M. E. (1997). Predictors of recovery in activities of daily living among disabled older persons living in the community. *Journal of General Internal Medicine, 12*, 757–762.

Hankin, J. R., & Locke, B. Z. (1982). The persistence of depressive symptomatology among prepaid group practice enrollees: An exploratory study. *American Journal of Public Health*, 72, 1000–1007.

Hornstra, R. K., & Klassen, D. (1977). The course of depression. *Comprehensive Psychiatry*, 18, 119–125.

House, J. M., Robbins, C., & Metzner, H. L. (1982). The association of social relationships and activities with mortality: Prospective evidence from the Tecumseh Community Health Study. *American Journal of Epidemiology*, 116, 123–140.

Jette, A. M. (1980). Functional Status Index: Reliability of a chronic disease evaluation instrument. *Archives of Physical and Medical Rehabilitation*, 61, 395–401.

Koenig, H. G., & Blazer, D. G. (1992). Epidemiology of geriatric affective disorders. *Clinical Geriatric Medicine*, 8, 235–251.

Krause, N., Liang, J., & Yatomi, N. (1989). Satisfaction with social support and depressive symptoms: A panel analysis. *Psychology and Aging*, 4, 88–97.

Lin, N., & Ensel, W. M. (1984). Depression-mobility and its social etiology: The role of life events and social support. *Journal of Health and Social Behavior*, 25, 176–188.

Magaziner, J., Simonsick, E., Kashner, T. M., & Hebel, J. R. (1988). Patient-proxy response comparability on measures of patient health and functional status. *Journal of Clinical Epidemiology*, 41, 1065–1074.

Magaziner, J., Simonsick, E. M., Kashner, T. M., Hebel, J. R., & Kenzora, J. E. (1989). Survival experience of aged hip fracture patients. *American Journal of Public Health*, 79, 274–278.

Magaziner, J., Simonsick, E. M., Kashner, T. M., Hebel, J. R., & Kenzora, J. E. (1990). Predictors of functional recovery one year following hospital discharge for hip fracture in the aged: A prospective study. *Journal of Gerontology: Medical Sciences*, 45, M101–M107.

Magaziner, J., Zimmerman, S. I., Gruber-Baldini, A. L., Hebel, J. R., & Fox, K. M. (1997). Proxy reporting in five areas of functional status. *American Journal of Epidemiology*, 146, 418–428.

Mirowsky, J., & Ross, C. E. (1992). Age and depression. *Journal of Health and Social Behavior*, 33, 187–205.

Mossey, J. M., Knott, K., & Craik, R. (1990). The effects of persistent depressive symptoms on hip fracture recovery. *Journal of Gerontology: Medical Sciences*, 45, M163–M168.

Mutran, E. J., Reitzes, D. C., Mossey, J., & Fernandez, M. E. (1995). Social support, depression, and recovery of walking ability following hip fracture surgery. *Journal of Gerontology: Social Sciences*, 50B, S354–S361.

NIH Consensus Development Panel on Depression in Late Life. (1992). Diagnosis and treatment of depression in late life. *JAMA*, 268, 1018–1024.

Parmelee, P. A., Katz, I. R., & Lawton, M. P. (1992). Incidence of depression in long-term care settings. *Journal of Gerontology: Medical Sciences*, 47, M189–M194.

Radloff, L. S. (1977). The CES-D Scale: A self-report depression scale for research in the general population. *Applied Psychological Measurement*, 1, 385–401.

Resnick, B., Zimmerman, S. I., Magaziner, J., & Adelman, A. (1998). Utilization of the apathy evaluation scale as a measure of motivation in the elderly. *Rehabilitation Nursing*, 23, 141–147.

Roberto, K. A. (1992). Elderly women with hip fractures: Functional and psychosocial correlates of recovery. *Journal of Women and Aging*, 4, 3–21.

Roberts, R. E., Kaplan, G. A., Shema, S. J., & Strawbridge, W. J. (1997). Prevalence and correlates of depression in an aging cohort: The Alameda County study. *Journal of Gerontology: Social Sciences*, 52B, S252–S258.

Schopler, J. H., Abell, M. D., & Galinsky, M. J. (1998). Technology-based groups: A review and conceptual framework for practice. *Social Work*, *43*, 254–267.

U.S. Congress, Office of Technology Assessment. (1994). *Hip fracture outcomes in people age 50 and over* (Background paper. OTA-BP-H-120). Washington, DC: U.S. Government Printing Office.

Weissman, M. M., Bland, R. C., & Canino, C. J. (1996). Cross-national epidemiology of major depression and bipolar disorder. *JAMA*, *276*, 293–299.

Zimmerman, S. I., Fox, K. M., & Magaziner, J. (1995). Psychosocial aspects of osteoporosis. *Physical Medicine and Rehabilitation Clinics of North America*, *6*, 441–453.

This chapter was originally published in the September 1999 issue of *Social Work Research*, Vol. 23, Number 3, pp. 187–196.

# 18

## Adequacy of Discharge Plans and Rehospitalization among Hospitalized Dementia Patients

### SHERRY M. CUMMINGS

During the past two decades regulatory and marketplace forces have combined to exert increasing pressure on hospitals to curtail expenditures and conserve health care resources. To remain financially viable, hospitals are undergoing major structural reorganizations and are continuing efforts to shift their focus from acute inpatient care to more cost-effective outpatient services. The trend toward decreased length of stay (LOS) that began with the introduction of diagnosis related groups (DRGs) in 1983 has been strengthened by the financial pressure exerted on hospitals by the managed care health system (Robinson, 1996). In this environment discharge planning has become an increasingly critical activity. The challenge of developing a comprehensive plan of care to meet patients' post-discharge needs is heightened not only by the decreased amount of time available in which to plan but also by the increasingly complex set of problems brought to the inpatient setting by an expanding elderly patient population.

In addition to acute illnesses that result in hospitalization, elderly people experience a high prevalence of chronic illness and functional disabilities that complicate the recovery process. The growth in the number of elderly people has been accompanied by an increase in the number of people with Alzheimer's disease and other related dementias. Such people require comprehensive aftercare to address not only medical and functional needs but also cognitive and social deficits. This combination of medical illnesses and incapacities experienced by cognitively impaired elderly people often creates a complex constellation of post-discharge needs (Cox & Verdieck, 1994) because of patients' varying levels of cognitive impairment, the need to involve family members in aftercare planning, and the need to secure services designed to address the special requirements of cognitively impaired people. Not surprisingly, dementia patients have an extended LOS. Whereas the duration for the average hospital stay for patients is 3.8 days, patients with a dementia typically stay 9.4 days (Health Care Information Analysts, Inc., 1998).

Adequate discharge planning for dementia patients is critical if hospitals are to meet the challenge of remaining financially viable while serving the needs of a rapidly growing older population. Inadequate discharge plans may result in insufficient post-discharge care and, therefore, readmission to the hospital. Researchers have found that cognitive impairment and a decline in cognitive functioning are associated with greater aftercare needs (Travis, Moore, & McAuley, 1991) and early readmissions (Severson et al., 1994; Weiler, Luben, & Chi, 1991). Readmission of elderly people can have serious consequences. Studies indicate that older people who must be readmitted are more severely ill and more functionally dependent than they were during their first admission (Berkman, Walker, Bonander, & Holmes, 1992). In light of this fact, it is not surprising that rehospitalizations drive up health care expenditures. The cost of a readmission ranges from 24 percent to 55 percent higher than the cost of the original inpatient stay (Berkman & Abrams, 1986).

Given the heavy and increasing emphasis on continued patient care and recuperation in the post-discharge environment, information about the adequacy of discharge plans to meet patients' post-hospitalization needs is crucial. Earlier follow-up studies on adequacy of discharge plans focused either on patients admitted to medical units (Proctor & Morrow-Howell, 1990; Proctor, Morrow-Howell, Albaz, & Weir, 1992; Simon, Showers, Blumenfield, Holden, & Wu, 1995; Steun & Monk, 1990) or on general patients admitted throughout a hospital system (Morrow-Howell, Proctor, & Berg-Weger, 1993; Wolock, Schlesinger, Dinerman, & Seaton, 1987). Although cognitive impairment has been linked with complications in the discharge planning process and less-than-adequate discharge plans, no studies have examined the adequacy of plans developed specifically for cognitively impaired patients.

The purpose of this study was to measure the adequacy of discharge plans developed for elderly dementia patients and to expand the understanding of factors related to the adequacy of these plans. Adequate continuity of care should maximize independent patient functioning (Muenchow & Carlton, 1985) and the patient's potential for wellness (Buckwalter, 1985). It is important to note that an adequate plan must address the medical and the psychosocial needs of post-discharge patients (Morrow-Howell, Proctor, & Mui,1991). Roberts (1975) incorporated these concepts and stated that effective aftercare compensates for the disabling effects of any current state of illness or disability. These effects may be physical, medical, emotional, or social. Colerick and George (1986) added another dimension, which is especially important when dealing with dementia patients. They argued that an adequate aftercare plan not only maximizes patient functioning and wellness but does so "without jeopardizing quality of life for the caregiver" (p. 493). Drawing on these concepts, the definition of discharge plan adequacy used for this study was "the ability of the plan to counteract the disabling effects, whether medical, functional, or emotional, of an illness or disability without jeopardizing caregiver well-being."

## Discharge Planning Adequacy

Studies that have examined the effect of aftercare plans on discharged patients point to sizeable percentages of patients (ranging from 25 percent to 35 percent) for whom adequate discharge plans were not developed, as judged by the patients, families, and discharge planners (Morrow-Howell et al., 1993; Proctor et al., 1992; Soskolne & Auslander, 1993). Given the complexity of elderly patients' medical conditions and the difficulty inherent in establishing effective aftercare plans for such patients, it is not surprising that elderly patients have a high rate of readmission. Rates of readmission for elderly patients reported in the literature range from 8 percent to 37 percent depending on the primary diagnosis of the patient and on the time period analyzed (Berkman & Abrams, 1986; Evans & Hendricks, 1993; Thomas & Holloway, 1991).

Some researchers have examined the association between patient characteristics and discharge plan outcomes. Study results indicate that cognitive impairment is associated with less than adequate discharge plans (Morrow-Howell et al., 1993), increased risk of institutionalization (Cox, 1996b), and early readmissions (Severson et al., 1994). Problematic behaviors often associated with dementia, such as agitation, wandering, aggressiveness, and sleep or wake cycle disturbances, are linked not only with hospitalization but also with the institutionalization of dementia patients (Cox & Verdieck, 1994; Haley, Brown, & Levine, 1987). In addition, being male (Fethke, Smith, & Johnson, 1986), being widowed (Fethke et al., 1986; Morrow-Howell et al., 1991), having longer hospital stays (Berkman & Abrams, 1986), and exhibiting an increased number of patient diagnoses (Fethke et al., 1986; Proctor & Morrow-Howell, 1990) all have been related to increased risk of poor post-discharge outcomes.

Family members are critical to the discharge planning for dementia patients, because many patients are unable to comprehend their illness and are unable to adequately understand the consequences of various discharge plan options. Thus, family members are looked on as necessary partners in the planning process and as invaluable resources to discharged dementia patients. To develop effective and timely discharge plans, families must be able to quickly absorb new information and decide on a course of action. This ability can be compromised, however, if caregivers have not fully acknowledged the nature and consequences of the disease. Teusink and Mahler (1984) noted that caregiver denial of an Alzheimer's disease diagnosis and the related prognosis can make "realistic assessment, decision-making and treatment planning impossible" (p. 153). To realistically plan for patients' future needs, family members also must be able to accurately gauge their own ability to care for the patient after discharge. At times, families deny their need for assistance in caring for the patient and then become overinvolved in an effort to compensate for patient deficiencies (Lindoerfer, 1991). One study of discharge planning outcomes reported social workers' concerns that patient care was too demanding for caregivers or soon would overwhelm the caregivers as a reason for lower ratings of plan adequacy (Morrow-Howell et al., 1993).

According to recent studies, lack of affordable and available resources decreases discharge plan adequacy (Morrow-Howell et al., 1993) and increases the risk of rehospitalization (Morrow-Howell et al., 1991; Simon et al., 1995) and institutionalization (Collins, King, & Kokinakis, 1994). These findings may be particularly relevant to dementia patients. Medicare provides funding for home health services for patients with acute care needs. The primary services needed by dementia patients, however, are for chronic rather then acute needs. Therefore, these patients often must rely on private resources or do without. Patients requiring nursing home (NH) placement also confront difficulties. Because of the high cost of NHs, many elderly people must rely on Medicaid to cover the costs of NH care. It is often very difficult, however, to find a Medicaid bed for a hospitalized dementia patient, especially a patient with agitated behaviors. For this reason dementia patients, at times, are admitted to NHs that are less than optimal or geographically distant from their home, community, and family. Whether the dementia patient is returning home or being admitted to an NH, issues of resource affordability and availability are critical.

In summary, the dementia patient's very limited ability to participate in planning and the need to fully involve family members often complicates the discharge planning process. In addition, the difficulty of developing an adequate plan is often compounded by the high level of care needed to maintain elderly people with dementia after discharge and by the lack of resources available to support these patients and their caregivers. The goals of the present research study were to measure the adequacy of the overall discharge plans developed for elderly patients with de-

mentia; to examine the relationship between discharge planners' ratings of adequacy and the readmission status of dementia patients; and to expand the understanding of patient, family, and resource factors related to the adequacy of discharge plans for dementia patients.

## Method

This study used a prospective research design. Data regarding the discharge plans of patients hospitalized on the neuropsychiatry unit of a geriatric hospital affiliated with a major university were collected. All patients from the neuropsychiatry unit who were discharged during the period of August 1996 through February 1997 with a diagnosis of dementia ($n = 167$) were considered for inclusion in this study. Patients who were transferred to another unit or to another hospital were excluded, as were patients whose primary caregiver was a paid professional. Given these criteria the initial participant pool consisted of 154 patients. Twelve caregivers refused to provide needed information, and 11 patients died before the completion of the study. Therefore, the final participant pool consisted of 131 patients.

Four social workers who developed the discharge plans for unit patients captured patient demographics; recorded discharge plan characteristics; evaluated patient-, family-, and resource-related factors; and rated the adequacy of the discharge plan at the time of discharge. The social workers involved were trained in the use of the discharge planning survey and participated in a pilot study using a draft survey instrument. The reliability of the social workers' assessments was further enhanced by the social work department's practice protocol and by the study protocol. The social workers interviewed all patients and their family members within 48 hours of their admission to the unit and completed a psychosocial assessment. The reason for admission and the patient's current living environment, formal and informal supports, and family history were reviewed. This assessment became a part of the patient's medical record. The social workers kept in close contact with family members to discuss and develop the discharge plan and to provide individual and family counseling, as needed. In addition, the social workers participated in family conferences along with the physician and other relevant staff to discuss test and treatment results, patient prognosis, and discharge plan recommendations. Through all these measures the social workers developed an understanding of the patient's aftercare needs and the family's emotional readiness and practical abilities to carry out the discharge plan. In addition, the study protocol directed the social workers to complete their portion of the discharge planning survey at the time of the patient's discharge. The promptness of the social workers' completion of the survey and the availability of the medical chart, which remained on the unit throughout the day of discharge, helped enhance the accuracy of their responses.

The social workers also identified the patient's primary caregiver, that is, the family member or friend who worked with the social worker and the hospital team to develop the discharge plan and who assumed principal responsibility for the execution of the discharge plan. The study author contacted the primary caregivers one month after patient discharge by telephone and asked them to complete questionnaires that included questions about the patient's readmission status and changes in the patient's cognitive, functional, emotional, and behavioral levels, and about the caregivers' experience of burden. The discharge planning survey instrument and questionnaire were developed through the participation of

knowledgeable social workers and a thorough review of relevant literature. The execution of a pilot study provided additional feedback from the discharge planners and primary caregivers.

## Measures

### Independent Variables

At the time of discharge the social worker responsible for the development of the patient's discharge documented patient demographics and assessed patient-, family-, and resource-related variables hypothesized to be associated with plan adequacy. Social workers indicated the presence of these variables by placing a check mark next to the factors that were present. They also rated the degree of complication presented by each factor checked using a five-point Likert scale ranging from 1 = minor complication to 5 = extreme complication. Patient-related factors included patient's gender, age and marital status, LOS, admitting diagnoses, number of diagnoses, problematic patient behaviors, and heavy care (Table 18-1). Race was not included because of the relatively small number of people of color admitted to the study hospital. Family-related factors included relationship of caregiver to patient, family conflict, caregiver's denial of diagnosis, prognosis and functional impairment status, insufficient caregiver support system, and caregiver unrealistic about own ability to provide care. Resource-related factors included discharge to a nondementia-specific NH or personal care home (PCH), needed resources unavailable, and needed resources unaffordable (Table 18-1).

### Dependent Variables

Adequacy of the discharge plan was conceptualized as the ability of the discharge plan

**TABLE 18-1. Operational Definitions of Independent Variables**

**Patient-related factors**

*Marital status*—married, single, widowed, or divorced

*LOS*—number of days from admission to discharge

*Admitting diagnosis*—diagnosis listed in medical chart as reason for patient's admission

*Number of diagnoses*—number of diagnoses listed in the patient's history and physical completed at admission

*Problematic behaviors*—agitation, wandering, verbal or physical aggressiveness, or sleep–wake cycle disturbance

*Heavy care*—need for extensive hands on assistance or the requirement for consistent nursing attention

**Family-related factors**

*Relationship of caregiver*—spouse, daughter, son, other family member, friend

*Family conflict*—disagreement or arguments among or between family members involved in a patient's care

*Denial of diagnosis*—lack of intellectual or emotional acceptance of the given diagnosis of dementia or Alzheimer's disease

*Denial of prognosis*—lack of intellectual or emotional acceptance of the degenerative nature of the dementia and of the effect that the illness will have on the patient's cognitive and functional abilities

*Denial of functional impairment status*—lack of intellectual or emotional acceptance of the extent of the patient's current cognitive and functional disabilities

*Insufficient support system*—caregiver's lack of necessary emotional or practical assistance to carry out his or her caregiving responsibilities

*Unrealistic about ability to provide care*—caregiver's overestimation of his or her own ability to provide the structure, supervision, and assistance required by the patient to maintain the patient's physical and emotional health without jeopardizing his or her own

**Resource-related factors**

*Nondementia NH–PCH*—the NH or PCH to which the patient is discharged does not contain a specialized unit or program for dementia residents

*Resources unaffordable*—patient does not have the necessary private funds and does not qualify for available government funds to secure services and resources to meet his or her needs

*Resources unavailable*—services and resources required by the patient do not exist in the geographic area to which the patient has access, or if they do exist a waiting list prevents their use by the patient.

*Note:* NH = nursing home; PCH = personal care home.

to counteract the disabling effects, whether medical, cognitive, functional, or emotional, of the patient's illness or disability as rated by the social worker (discharge planner) at the time of discharge. Adequacy was measured using a five-point Likert scale, with 1 = very inadequate, 2 = less than adequate, 3 = adequate, 4 = more than adequate, and 5 = extremely adequate. One month after discharge telephone follow-up was conducted with the primary caregivers who were asked

to assess the adequacy of the discharge plan using the same five-point Likert rating. The Likert scale being used for this study is based on those developed by Proctor and colleagues (1990, 1992, 1995). Readmission to a hospital was defined as the patient's readmission to any hospital after discharge from the study hospital. Readmission was measured by asking caregivers whether patients had been admitted to any hospital since their discharge from the study hospital.

## Results

Descriptive statistics were used to summarize patient demographics, discharge plan characteristics, and adequacy scores. Bivariate statistics were used to test the significance of relationships among patient-, family-, and resource-related factors and social work adequacy ratings and between these variables and patient readmission status. Last, multiple regression techniques were performed to develop beginning models explaining the combinations of variables that influence social workers' perceptions of plan adequacy and rates of readmission.

### Demographics

Study patients were primarily widowed white females. The vast majority of patients were admitted with a primary diagnosis of dementia with agitation and were covered by Medicare. The relationship of the primary caregiver to the patient was that of an adult child in more than half of the cases. The mean LOS in the hospital for the patients included in this study was 15.5 days ($SD$ = 9.6, range = 3–70 days). (See Table 18-2 for patient demographics.) Patient and caregiver demographics and social worker adequacy ratings were compared for patients who were excluded because the caregivers refused to participate or could not be reached. The only significant differences found were in caregiver gender and the relationship of the caregiver to the patient. A greater number of excluded patients had male caregivers who were adult sons.

### Discharge Plan Characteristics

The majority of the patients (61.1 percent) were discharged to the same setting in which they were living before their admission. Pa-

**TABLE 18-2. Patient Demographics**

| Characteristic | % |
|---|---|
| Gender | |
| Male | 38.9 |
| Female | 61.1 |
| Race | |
| White | 84.7 |
| African American | 14.5 |
| Hispanic | 1.0 |
| Marital status | |
| Married | 36.6 |
| Widowed | 52.7 |
| Single | 6.1 |
| Divorced | 4.6 |
| Insurance | |
| Medicare | 98.5 |
| Medicaid | 33.1 |
| Private | 54.6 |
| Caregiver | |
| Child | 52.7 |
| Spouse | 14.5 |
| Other family member | 24.4 |
| Friend | 3.1 |
| Diagnoses | |
| Dementia and agitation | 73.3 |
| Dementia | 22.1 |
| Depression | 10.7 |

tients' particular discharge destinations included NHs (68.7 percent), own homes or that of a relative (22.1 percent), and PCHs (9.2 percent). Of the patients going to NHs, 58 percent were admitted to nondementia-specific or general units. Method of NH payment included Medicaid (52.2 percent), private funds (32.2 percent), and Medicare (15.6 percent). All of the patients who entered PCHs did so as private pay residents. The majority of patients returning home received assistance from a home health care agency (82.8 percent). These patients received the services of RNs (92.0 percent), nursing assistants (44.0 percent), paid companions (36.0 percent), occupational therapists (32.0 percent), and physical therapists (28.0 percent).

## Adequacy Ratings

Social workers rated 35.1 percent of the discharge plans as less than adequate or very inadequate. Forty-eight percent of the plans were judged as being adequate while 16.8 percent were seen as more than adequate or extremely adequate. Pearson's correlations coefficients were computed to determine which of the independent variables were significantly related to social worker adequacy ratings. Significant patient factors included LOS ($r = .213, p < .05$), heavy care ($r = -.275, p < .01$), and problematic behaviors ($r = -.188, p < .05$). Significant family factors included unrealistic beliefs about ability to provide care ($r = -.363, p < .0001$), denial of functional impairment status ($r = -.345, p < .0001$), denial of prognosis ($r = -.295, p < .001$), denial of diagnosis ($r = -.278, p < .001$), and insufficient caregiver support ($r = -.241, p < .01$). Last, significant resource factors included nondementia NH–PCH ($r = .595, p < .0001$), resources unaffordable ($r = -.318, p < .0001$), and resources unavailable ($r = -.262, p < .01$).

## Rates of Readmission

In this study 24 of the patients (18.3 percent) were readmitted to a hospital one month after their discharge from the study hospital. To determine which of the independent variables were significantly related to patient readmission chi-square analyses were computed for categorical-level variables and $t$ tests for ratio-level variables. Adequacy rating was treated as an independent variable in this analysis for the purpose of assessing social workers' abilities to discriminate between successful and unsuccessful discharge plans (Table 18-3).

## Multivariate Analysis

Stepwise multiple regression analysis was computed to determine the degree to which social workers' perceptions of specific patient, family, and resource risk factors influenced their ratings of plan adequacy. Logistic regression techniques were used to measure the degree to which specific patient-, family-, and resource-related factors and social workers adequacy ratings predict readmission. Prior to entering variables into the model, all independent variables were examined for multicollinearity. Variance inflation factors and tolerance levels indicated no multicollinearity problems.

*Factors Predicting Adequacy Ratings.* Stepwise multiple regression techniques were used to determine the factors that influenced social workers' ratings of plan adequacy. Only those independent variables that had a significant bivariate relationship with the dependent variable were included in the regression analysis. As a result, 10 variables—(1) heavy care, (2) LOS, (3) denial of diagnosis, (4) denial of prognosis, (5) insufficient support system, (6) unrealistic attitudes about ability to provide care, (7) denial of functional impairment status, (8) resources unaffordable, (9) resources unavailable, and (10) nondementia NH–PCH—predicting social worker adequacy ratings were entered into the regression model for social worker adequacy ratings. The final model included nondementia NH–PCH, denial of diagnosis, denial of functional impairment status, LOS, and resources unavailable ($R^2 = .496, p < .0001$). Therefore, patients who were admitted to a nondementia-specific NH or PCH, had a longer LOS, were not able to obtain needed resources, and whose caregiver had difficulty accepting the patient's diagnosis and level

**TABLE 18-3. Factors Impacting Patient Readmission Status**

| Categorical-Level Factors | % of Total | % Readmitted (n = 24) | % Not Readmitted (n = 107) | $\chi^2$ |
|---|---|---|---|---|
| Patient's gender (n = 131) | | | | |
| Male (n = 51) | 38.9 | 62.5 | 33.6 | 6.86** |
| Heavy care (n = 21) | 16.0 | 33.3 | 12.1 | 6.53** |
| Deny functional impairment (n = 34) | 26.0 | 45.8 | 21.5 | 6.04* |
| Deny prognosis (n = 19) | 14.5 | 29.2 | 11.2 | 5.09* |
| Insufficient support (n = 22) | 16.8 | 37.5 | 12.1 | 9.01** |
| Caregiver unrealistic (n = 29) | 22.1 | 41.7 | 17.8 | 6.50** |

| Ratio-Level Factors | Readmitted | | Not Readmitted | | t value |
|---|---|---|---|---|---|
| | M | SD | M | SD | |
| Social worker adequacy rating | 2.3 | .61 | 2.9 | .84 | 3.80*** |

*$p < .05$. **$p < .01$. ***$p < .001$.

of functional impairment received lower social worker adequacy ratings. These variables explain 50 percent of the variance in social workers' adequacy ratings. The variable contributing the largest increment to $R^2$ was discharge to a nondementia-specific NH unit or PCH (Table 18-4).

*Factors Predicting Readmission.* Logistic regression analysis was computed to determine factors predictive of readmission (Table 18-5). Logistic regression was used because of the dichotomous nature of the dependent variable. Seven variables had a significant and sufficiently strong bivariate relationship to be entered into the model for predicting

patient readmission. These variables included patient requiring heavy care, problematic patient behaviors, insufficient caregiver support system, unrealistic about own ability to provide care, denial of the patient's level of functional impairment, patient gender, and social worker adequacy ratings. Social worker adequacy ratings ($p < .01$), patient gender ($p < .01$), and caregiver support ($p < .05$) were all significant and included in the final model ($R^2 = .18$). Patients who received lower social worker adequacy ratings were men; these men, whose caregiver lacked social support, had higher rates of readmission.

**TABLE 18-4. Summary of Stepwise Regression Analysis for Variables Predicting Social Worker Adequacy Ratings (N = 131)**

| Variable | B | SE B | β | Increment to $R^2$ |
|---|---|---|---|---|
| Discharge to a nondementia-specific NH unit or PCH | .822 | .122 | .463 | .36 |
| Denial of patient's functional impairment | −.440 | .138 | −.228 | .07 |
| Needed resources not available | −.497 | .144 | −.231 | .03 |
| Length of stay | .016 | .006 | .174 | .02 |
| Denial of diagnosis | −.484 | .229 | −.152 | .02 |

Note: NH = nursing home; PCH = personal care home.
$R^2 = .50$, $p < .0001$.

**TABLE 18-5. Summary of Logistic Regression Analysis for Variables Predicting Readmission ($N = 131$)**

| Variable | B | SE B | p |
|---|---|---|---|
| Social worker rating | −1.04 | .36 | .01 |
| Patient gender | 1.43 | .53 | .01 |
| Insufficient support | −1.24 | .61 | .05 |

## Discussion

Although this study addresses a gap in discharge planning research by focusing on the outcome of aftercare plans for elderly dementia patients, it has some limitations. The limitations include the survey instrument used, the scope of the independent variables, and the homogeneity of the sample. Reliance on individuals' (social workers') perceptions of discharge plan adequacy is another limitation of this study. Perception of plan adequacy is a subjective measure that may be influenced by individuals' roles, understandings of the situation, and desires for the patient. No established measures were available to measure the study variables, however. For this reason, the assessments of the social workers who were the staff people most familiar with the discharge plan characteristics and the patient and caregiver discharge needs were used. In addition, an objective measure, rate of readmission, was included.

The patient, family, and resource factors used in this study do not represent all possible factors that may affect the development of an adequate discharge plan. Because of the sample size, only a limited number of variables could be examined. The factors used were selected because of their relevance, as demonstrated in the literature and by knowledgeable social workers' experience, to discharge planning with cognitively impaired patients. Adequacy is a complex and multidimensional construct, however. Other types of factors could have been used. In particular, variables that have been linked to discharge planning adequacy for nondemented elderly patients should be explored to examine their effect on those with dementia. Such variables include physical disabilities (Morrow-Howell et al., 1993), insufficient communication between patient and staff (Bull, 1994), insurance guidelines (Proctor & Morrow-Howell, 1990), patients' emotional health (Showers, Simon, Blumenfield, & Holden, 1995), and severity or complexity of illness ratings (Thomas & Holloway, 1991).

Limitations also exist because of the homogeneity of the sample. The majority of patients admitted to the study hospital were white and had midlevel incomes. It must be recognized that dementia patients and caregivers from various racial and socioeconomic backgrounds may have different strengths and needs; and therefore, alternate factors may be involved in the development of adequate discharge plans for these patients. The majority of study participants also had moderate to severe dementia. Therefore, the results of this study should not be generalized to patients with mild dementia.

The results of this study indicate that social workers are able to effectively predict which discharge plans will be successful and which will not. At a time when continued vigorous efforts are being made to reduce acute health care costs, the ability to predict discharge plan failure and patient rehospitalization is a critical skill. Social workers can contribute a valuable service by carefully evaluating the adequacy of discharge plans and then by clearly communicating the results of their assessment to the health care team. Interdisciplinary teams that have a member who is able to effectively distinguish between adequate and inadequate plans will be better positioned to work with patients and families on aftercare issues. At a time when the field of medical social work is under increasing attack, it is critical that hospital social workers recognize the unique skills they possess, that they clearly communicate the results of their judgments to health care teams, and that they actively participate in the development of programs that target and assist patients at risk of discharge plan failure. In particular, the development and evaluation of follow-up programs that target identified "at-risk" patients are greatly needed.

Results from this study indicate that the adequacy of discharge plans for dementia patients is negatively affected by a dearth of available and affordable resources and by complications experienced by familial caregivers. Medicare and Medicaid focus on provision of services to those with acute care demands and do not reimburse for services to assist those with chronic care needs. Affordable home care, adult day care, assisted-living facilities and dementia-specific nursing home units are needed to adequately meet the needs of people with dementia. Findings from this study suggest that admission to a nondementia-specific nursing home unit decreases discharge plan adequacy. Results from studies comparing the efficacy of Alzheimer's special care units and traditional care units have found that patients admitted to special care units create fewer behavioral disturbances (Bellelli et al., 1998), exhibit better social functioning (Swanson, Maas, & Buckwalter, 1994), experience less discomfort, and are transferred less frequently to acute medical settings (Volicer et al., 1994). Unfortunately, many dementia-specific units are private pay and, therefore, not available to a large percentage of dementia patients. Options for providing needed long-term health care, such as the creation of a public–private long-term care insurance program (Torres-Gil, 1998), require serious and prompt attention. Many states also are cur-

rently engaged in heated debates concerning the nature and extent of long-term care provision. Until policymakers squarely confront long-term health care issues, the needs of dementia patients and their caregivers will not be addressed in a sufficient and consistent manner. Social workers must join with those in other professions and with aging-related organizations to form coalitions that advocate on behalf of dementia patients and their families at both the national and state levels.

Family members' abilities to participate with hospital staff in the development of effective aftercare plans are hampered not only by the lack of available resources for dementia patients but also by the condensed period of time available to absorb new information and make critical decisions. When dementia patients are not able to engage actively in the development and execution of discharge plans, hospital personnel rely on family members to execute this crucial function. However, family members are not always prepared to fill such a role. With the increasing reduction in LOS, the amount of time that social workers have to help family members work through their feelings related to the illness and its prognosis is limited. As patients' LOS continues to decline, serious attention must be paid to the unintended consequences that this shortened time has for family members, and, thus, for patients' continuity of care after discharge. Medical personnel often assess patients with a dementia multiple times during the course of their illness. It is rare, however, that an evaluation is conducted of the family's ability to understand and deal with the patient's diagnosis or his or her deteriorating functional and cognitive abilities. Unfortunately, neglect of such critical issues may pave the way for future problems in patient care. To prevent the development of crises in patient care related to family factors, the concept of dementia assessment should be expanded to include thorough family evaluations throughout the duration of patient care.

Additional research is needed to increase understanding of factors related to discharge plan failure for hospitalized dementia patients. The current study identified factors related to social workers' ratings of discharge plan adequacy and to rates of readmission for dementia patients. The proportion of variance in adequacy ratings and readmission rates explained by these factors is modest, although significant given available knowledge in this area. Continued exploration of these and other factors is needed to identify dementia patients who may be at greatest risk of poor post-discharge outcomes.

Future studies should also include a greater representation of people of color. Differences have been found between white and African American caregivers' initial plans about discharge for their relatives with dementia and among the factors that influence the caregivers' final decisions (Cox, 1996a). People from diverse cultural and socioeconomic backgrounds may possess unique needs and strengths that affect their response to similar situations differently. Elderly people and caregivers of color, for example, often have fewer economic resources than do white people. This reality may affect their access to needed services negatively and, therefore, the adequacy of their aftercare plans. On the other hand, people of color come from cultures that also have pronounced areas of strength. African Americans and Hispanics, for example, place a high value on relationships in the extended family. Such informal supports may bolster elderly people's and caregivers' ability to respond to illness and also may provide services necessary to support elderly people and caregiver well-being (Wood & Parham, 1990). Gain-

ing a clearer understanding of the factors that contribute to discharge plan success or failure for patients from various cultures would enable discharge planners to construct aftercare plans for diverse groups of patients more effectively and more appropriately evaluate the efficacy of these plans.

## References

Bellelli, G., Frisono, G. B., Bianchetti, A., Boffelli, S., Guerrini, G. B., & Scotuzzi, A. (1998). Special care units for demented patients: A multicenter study. *Gerontologist, 38*, 456–462.

Berkman, B., & Abrams, R. D. (1986). Factors related to hospital readmission of elderly cardiac patients. *Social Work, 31*, 99–103.

Berkman, B., Walker, S., Bonander, E., & Holmes, W. (1992). Early unplanned readmissions to social work of elderly patients: Factors predicting who needs follow-up services. *Social Work in Health Care, 17*, 103–119.

Buckwalter, K. C. (1985). Exploring the process of discharge planning: Application to the construct of health. In E. McClelland, K. Kelly, & K. C. Buckwalter (Eds.), *Continuity of care: Advancing the concept of discharge planning* (pp. 5–10). Orlando, FL: Grune & Stratton.

Bull, M. J. (1994). Patients' and professionals' perception of quality of discharge planning. *Journal of Nursing Care Quality, 8*, 47–61.

Colerick, E. J., & George, L. K. (1986). Predictors of institutionalization among caregivers of patients with Alzheimer's disease. *Journal of the American Geriatrics Society, 34*, 493–498.

Collins, C., King, S., & Kokinakis, C. (1994). Community service issues before nursing home placement of persons with dementia. *Western Journal of Nursing Research, 16*, 40–56.

Cox, C. (1996a). Outcomes of hospitalization: Factors influencing the discharges of African

American and white dementia patients. *Social Work in Health Care, 23*, 23–38.

Cox, C. B. (1996b). Discharge planning for dementia patients: Factors influencing caregiver decisions and satisfaction. *Health & Social Work, 21*, 97–104.

Cox, C., & Verdieck, M. J. (1994). Factors affecting the outcomes of hospitalized dementia patients: From home to hospital to discharge. *Gerontologist, 34*, 497–504.

Evans, R. L., & Hendricks, R. D. (1993). Evaluating hospital discharge planning: A randomized clinical trial. *Medical Care, 31*, 358–370.

Fethke, C. C., Smith, I. M., & Johnson, N. (1986). Risk factors affecting readmission of the elderly into the health care system. *Medical Care, 24*, 429–437.

Haley, W. E., Brown, S. L., & Levine, E. G. (1987). Family caregiver appraisals of patient behavioral disturbance in senile dementia. *Clinical Gerontologist, 6*, 25–34.

Health Care Information Analysts, Inc. (1998). *Length of stay by diagnosis: United States, 1998.* Baltimore: Author.

Lindoerfer, S. J. (1991). Treatment of families of the neurologically impaired aged. In R. L. Dippel & J. T. Hutton (Eds.), *Caring for the Alzheimer's patient* (pp. 119–128). Virginia Beach, VA: Golden Age Books.

Morrow-Howell, N., Proctor, E. K., & Berg-Weger, M. (1993). Adequacy of informal care for elderly patients going home from the hospital: Discharge planner perspectives. *Journal of Applied Gerontology, 12*, 188–205.

Morrow-Howell, N., Proctor, E. K., & Mui, A. C. (1991). Adequacy of discharge plans for elderly patients. *Social Work Research & Abstracts, 27*(1), 6–13.

Muenchow, J. D., & Carlton, B. B. (1985). Evaluating programs of discharge planning. In E. McClelland, K. Kelly, & K. C. Buckwalter (Eds.), *Continuity of care: Advancing the concept of discharge planning* (pp. 149–159). Orlando, FL: Grune & Stratton.

Proctor, E. K., & Morrow-Howell, N. (1990). Complications in discharge planning with Medicare patients. *Health & Social Work, 15*, 45–54.

Proctor, E. K., Morrow-Howell, N., Albaz, R., & Weir, C. (1992). Patient and family satisfaction with discharge plans. *Medical Care, 30*, 262–275.

Proctor, E. K., Morrow-Howell, N., Kitchen, A., & Wang, Y.-T. (1995). Pediatric discharge planning: Complications, efficiency, and adequacy. *Social Work in Health Care, 22*(1), 1–18.

Roberts, I. (1975). *Discharged from hospital.* London: Royal College of Nursing.

Robinson, J. C. (1996). Decline in hospital utilization and cost inflation under managed care in California. *JAMA, 276*, 1060–1064.

Severson, M. A., Smith, G. E., Tangalos, E. G., Peterson, R. C., Kokmen, E., Ivnik, R. J., Atkinson, E. J., & Kurland, L. T. (1994). Patterns and predictors of institutionalization in community-based dementia patients. *Journal of the American Geriatrics Society, 42*, 181–185.

Showers, N., Simon, E. P., Blumenfield, S., & Holden, G. (1995). Predictors of patient and proxy satisfaction with discharge plans. *Social Work in Health Care, 22*, 19–35.

Simon, E. P., Showers, N., Blumenfield, S., Holden, G., & Wu, X. (1995). Delivery of home care services after discharge: What really happens. *Health & Social Work, 20*, 5–14.

Soskolne, V., & Auslander, G. K. (1993). Follow-up evaluation of discharge planning by social workers in an acute-care medical center in Israel. *Social Work in Health Care, 18*, 23–49.

Steun, C., & Monk, A. (1990). Discharge planning: The impact of Medicare's prospective payment on elderly patients. *Journal of Gerontological Social Work, 15*, 149–165.

Swanson, E. A., Maas, M. L., & Buckwalter, K. C. (1994). Alzheimer's residents' cognitive and functional measures: Special and traditional care comparisons. *Clinical Nursing Research, 3*, 27–41.

Teusink, J. P., & Mahler, S. (1984). Helping families cope with Alzheimer's disease. *Hospital and Community Psychiatry, 35*, 152–156.

Thomas, J. W., & Holloway, J. J. (1991). Investigating early readmission as an indicator for quality care studies. *Medical Care, 29*, 377–394.

Torres-Gil, F. (1998, February 15). Today's Medicaid program won't survive grayer America. *Atlanta Journal-Constitution*, p. F4.

Travis, S. S., Moore, S. R., & McAuley, W. J. (1991). A comparison of hospitalization experiences for demented and nondemented elders: Findings of a retrospective chart review. *Journal of Gerontological Social Work, 17*, 35–46.

Volicer, L., Collard, A., Hurley, A., Bishop, C., Kern, D., & Karon, S. (1994). Impact of special care units for patients with advanced Alzheimer's disease on patients' discomfort and costs. *Journal of the American Geriatrics Society, 42*, 597–603.

Weiler, P., Luben, J., & Chi, I. (1991). Cognitive impairment and hospital use. *American Journal of Public Health, 81*, 1153–1157.

Wolock, I., Schlesinger, E., Dinerman, M., & Seaton, R. (1987). The posthospital needs and care of patients: Implications for discharge planning. *Social Work in Health Care, 12*, 61–76.

Wood, J. B., & Parham, I. A. (1990). Coping with perceived burden: Ethnic and cultural issues in Alzheimer's caregiving. *Journal of Applied Gerontology, 9*, 325–339.

This chapter was originally published in the November 1999 issue of *Health & Social Work*, Vol. 24, Number 4, pp. 249–259.

# 19

# Adequacy of Home Care and Hospital Readmission for Elderly Congestive Heart Failure Patients

ENOLA K. PROCTOR,
NANCY MORROW-HOWELL,
HONG LI, and PETER DORE

The development of discharge plans for post-acute care is a central activity for acute care social workers. A substantial literature reflects assumptions that the product of discharge planning should be care arrangements that meet patients' needs and prevent early readmission to acute care facilities (Morrow-Howell, Proctor, & Mui, 1991). From the perspectives of cost and quality of care, early readmission to acute care is viewed widely as one of the most serious problems in health services and one that discharge planning can help prevent. The repeated hospitalization of chronically ill individuals is a significant contributor to the high costs of care; such costs make up a major proportion of Medicare expenditures (Anderson & Steinberg, 1984). Furthermore, readmission is viewed as an indicator of poor outcomes of home care (Leibson, Naessens, Campion, Krishan, & Ballard, 1991; Mason, Bedwell, Vander Zwagg, & Runyan, 1980; Robinson & Barbaccia, 1982). Home care after discharge is burdensome for families and the health care system (Naylor et al., 1994), especially because patients are discharged earlier and sicker

(Rogers et al., 1990). Appropriate post-hospital care is viewed as important to pre-venting readmission (Naylor et al., 1994), lessening family burden, and contributing to patient recovery (Anderson, Hanson, & DeVilder, 1996).

Although earlier studies highlighted the problem of readmission and pointed to pa-tients at high risk of early readmission, most have ignored social and environmental fac-tors (Lockery, Dunkle, Kart, & Coulton, 1994) and have failed to elucidate the spe-cific problems with posthospital care that prevent maintenance in community care (Anderson et al., 1996). Thus, studies that address the adequacy of home care in rela-tion to hospital readmission are needed (Legge & Reilly, 1980; Robinson & Barbaccia, 1982). Such studies have the po-tential to reveal the contribution of care ar-rangements, which social workers help develop, to one of the most costly and wide-spread problems in health care.

## Readmission Rates and Associated Factors

Readmission among elderly people with chronic degenerative illness is, to some de-gree, inevitable—even with careful discharge planning and follow-up (Andrews, 1986). Although risk of readmission is heightened for previously admitted patients (Anderson et al., 1990) and for elderly people (Ander-son & Steinberg, 1984; Fethke, Smith, & Johnson, 1986; Gooding & Jette, 1985), pa-tients with congestive heart failure (CHF) have among the highest readmission rates (Kane, 1994). Reported readmission rates for elderly CHF patients varied from 29 percent in three months (Rich & Freedland, 1988) to 42 percent in four months (Berkman, Dumas, Gastfriend, Poplawski, & South-worthe, 1987) to 44 percent in six months

(Krumholz et al., 1997). The readmission rate was 47 percent in three months for patients ages 70 or older (Vinson, Rich, Sperry, Shah, & McNamara, 1990). The risk of readmis-sion for older CHF patients appeared to be greatest shortly after discharge (Rich & Freedland, 1988). Since 1983 and the incep-tion of the Prospective Payment System, the highest increases in readmission rates were observed during the first seven days after dis-charge. Epstein, Bogen, Dreyer, and Thorpe (1991) found that readmission increased by 13 percent at seven days, 8 percent at 14 days, and 5 percent at 30 days.

Earlier studies identified a variety of fac-tors associated with readmission, including hospital factors (Anderson & Steinberg, 1985) and patient demographic factors such as gender (Anderson et al., 1996; Anderson & Steinberg, 1985; Fethke et al., 1986; Krumholz et al., 1997; Leibson et al., 1991; Zook, Savickis, & Moore, 1980), age (Ander-son & Steinberg, 1984, 1985; Leibson et al., 1991), marital status (Fethke et al., 1986), race (Anderson & Steinberg, 1985), and socioeco-nomic status (Anderson & Steinberg, 1984, 1985). Other studies pointed to clinical fac-tors, such as recurrent or chronic disease (Ashton et al., 1987; Holloway, Thomas, & Shapiro, 1988; Smith, Norton, & McDonald, 1985, Victor & Vetter, 1985; Vinson et al., 1990), cognitive impairment (Hulka, Kupper, Cassel, & Efird, 1975), readiness for initial discharge (Ashton et al., 1987; Victor & Vetter, 1988), and functional ability (Berkman et al., 1987; Holloway et al., 1988), especially ability to ambulate (Schwartzberg, 1982). Finally, social–psychological factors such as stress (Berkman & Abrams, 1986), life satis-faction (Fethke et al., 1986), and compliance with therapy (Graham & Livesley, 1983) were related to readmission, as was discharge to home rather than to institutional settings (Lockery et al., 1994).

The literature contains frequent references to the role of posthospital care in preventing readmission. This focus is consistent with shortened hospital stays and with readmission risk shortly after discharge. Studies show that 40 percent to 50 percent of readmissions are linked to social problems and lack of community services (Andrews, 1986; Gooding & Jette, 1985; Graham & Livesley, 1983; Mason et al., 1980; Robinson, 1983). Rich and Freedland (1988), who speculated that increased use of home care services might contribute to lower readmission rates, cited the importance of directly testing the relationship between posthospital care and readmission (Kane, 1994; Martens & Mellor, 1997).

Discharge to home, rather than to institutional settings—which presumably provide higher levels of care and closer medical monitoring—has been associated with higher readmissions (Fethke et al., 1986; Gooding & Jette, 1985; Kane, 1994; Leibson et al., 1991). These findings have been interpreted as possibly signaling problems with the adequacy of home care. Some studies have addressed the relationship between caregiving factors and readmission. Schwartzberg (1982) found that older adults who lived alone were more likely to be hospitalized sooner than those who lived with elderly or younger family members. Yet Narain et al. (1988) found that elderly patients with no caregiver—probably the most functional—had the lowest readmission rates. This finding signals the importance of controlling for health status in studies of readmission.

Other investigators have attempted to assess directly the effect of adequacy of posthospital care on readmission. One approach has been to assess the extent to which posthospital care meets patient needs. Ashton et al. (1987) tried to determine the extent to which patient needs for treatment,

assistance, and observation could be met in the posthospital environment. However, they grossly assessed need–environment match, noting that direct assessment would have required data from patient and caregiver interviews, which they lacked. They found no significant relationship between need–environment match and readmission. Mamon et al. (1992) reported that patients with unmet needs after discharge were more likely to be rehospitalized within three months after discharge.

Other studies have examined services received in posthospital care. Berkman and Abrams (1986) found less readmission among older cardiac patients who received formal care postdischarge. Although Victor and Vetter (1985) found that those with higher use of home help were more likely to be readmitted than those with lower levels of service, the difference in service use might be, in fact, a function of disability. Neither of these studies controlled for sickness or impairment. And Graham and Livesley (1983) found that failure to conduct a functional assessment before discharge and inadequate rehabilitation services were associated with some "preventable" cases of readmission. They concluded that "inadequate medical management and social problems precipitated early readmission more often than unavoidable clinical deterioration did" (Graham & Livesley, 1983, p. 405). Williams and Fitton (1988) found that, in addition to relapse of original condition and development of new medical problems, problems encountered by caregivers and problems with posthospital services contributed to readmission. Finally, focusing on follow-up medical care, Ashton et al. (1987) found that arrangement of appropriately timed follow-up medical care was related to readmission.

The importance of postdischarge care in preventing readmission among elderly people is reflected also in the studies of experimental treatments aimed at reducing readmission. Recent evidence shows that interventions aimed at increasing telephone contact with medical providers and increasing patient knowledge about CHF, nutrition, and medications reduced readmissions (Rich et al., 1995; West et al., 1997). However, because the interventions were packages or programs, the studies have not yet determined the relative importance of various components of the experimental interventions (Rich et al., 1993). Evidence that many chronically ill elderly people require intensive follow-up after discharge leads some investigators to conclude that greater attention needs to be directed to home care (Naylor et al., 1994).

Few studies have addressed specifically the role of home care in preventing readmission among elderly people with CHF (Kornowski et al., 1995). This study addresses that issue by assessing patient-perceived adequacy of formal and informal assistance in meeting needs related to skilled-nursing tasks and functional activities of living.

## Method

The study used a prospective design to track Medicare patients with heart disease after their discharge from a large midwestern urban hospital through 14 weeks of post-acute home care. The analyses were constructed to test literature-driven hypotheses about the relationship between home care adequacy and readmission.

### Sample

All Medicare patients meeting the following criteria were approached for consent during their hospital stay: diagnosed with CHF, served by a hospital social worker, and discharged home between July 1990 and October 1991. During the 16 months of data collection, social workers forwarded the names of 362 patients who met the criteria to research staff; 298 patients (82 percent) consented. Fifteen percent of the consenting patients died before discharge or were discharged to a nursing home. Thus, 253 patients were available for the study at the time of discharge.

One diagnosis was chosen for study, consistent with the recommendation that studies of care needs, service use, and outcomes be conducted within disease categories to increase the accuracy of findings (Benjamin, 1992; Kane, Kane, Illston, & Eustis, 1994). CHF was chosen because it is a leading chronic disease among elderly people, is associated with limitations in activities and physical dependency (Brody, Brock, & Williams, 1987; May, Kelly, Mendlein, & Garbe, 1991; U.S. Department of Health and Human Services, 1987), contributes to more readmissions among Medicare recipients than any other diagnosis (Krumholz et al., 1997), and is the most common diagnosis for patients served by home health agencies (Williams, Mackay, & Torner, 1991).

The second criterion, served by a social worker, was used to enhance the likelihood that participants would have formal and informal services in place postdischarge. This criterion was appropriate because of the study's focus on the adequacy of posthospital care relative to readmission. As with other studies of discharge planning and post-acute care conducted in teaching hospitals, it is patients with higher needs and more complicated arrangements for formal services who receive discharge planning from social workers, whereas uncomplicated discharges involving only formal care usually are handled by physicians (Naylor et al., 1994). A more inclusive approach, such as studying all elderly people with CHF, would have been less efficient in that it would have yielded high numbers of participants who left the hospital with no formal services required and such low levels of need that variability in adequacy of care would be constrained. Hospital records were used to estimate that about 30 percent of patients over age 65 with CHF were referred to social workers during the study.

Because of the study's focus on home care, the third criterion ensured inclusion of only elderly people who were discharged back to the community rather than to nursing homes. To enhance generalizability, individuals who were cognitively impaired or too ill to participate in the interview were retained in the sample; family collaterals, identified by the social worker as the people most familiar with the patient, were interviewed in such cases, which made up about 35 percent of cases.

### Procedures

Data were collected through three protocols. First, hospital-based research assistants (RA) gathered demographic and insurance data from hospital records. Second, geriatric nurse practitioners gathered data on medication compliance in an in-home interview two weeks postdischarge. Third, trained interviewers conducted structured telephone interviews with participants (or family collaterals, in the case of participants with cognitive impairment) at two weeks postdischarge, to collect data on receipt of formal and informal home care, socioeconomic status, and health functioning. Information about hospital readmission was collected during subsequent telephone calls at six, 10, and 14 weeks after discharge. Readmission also was monitored through routine checks of hospital records. If the check revealed that a participant was readmitted before the scheduled two-week observation period, an interview was conducted immediately to assess health status and service arrangements that were in place before the readmission. The telephone interview for postdischarge data collection was pretested; test–retest reliability was determined, through a Kappa statistic, to be at least .80 for all variables (Proctor, Morrow-Howell, & Chadiha, 1993). The nurse in-home interview schedule was pretested and continually monitored for interrater reliability through a Kappa statistic; reliability was at least .80 on all variables.

### Measurement of Variables

For purposes of sample description, demographic variables (age, gender, race, and marital status) were measured from hospital records. Medicaid, Medicare, and private insurance status were gathered from social work records. The Hollingshead Index of Social Class (Hollingshead, 1957) was used to measure socioeconomic status; this measure uses education and occupation to rate participants' socioeconomic status, with scores ranging from 11 to 77; higher scores indicate lower socioeconomic status.

*Dependent Variable: Readmission.* Readmission was monitored for participants in the sample in two ways. First, an RA monitored hospital records daily to identify study participants who were readmitted. In such cases the RA visited the patient's room to administer a readmission questionnaire. Second, to provide for situations in which the patient was readmitted to other than the study hospital or was readmitted to the study hospital but was missed by the RA, participants were asked in each telephone interview (two, six, 10, and 14 weeks), "Have you been home continuously since we last talked?" If not, questions were asked to determine readmission status. Thus, a strength of tracking patients through telephone interviews was the ability to assess readmission to other hospitals; most earlier studies have documented readmission only to the same institution, thereby risking severe underestimation of the number of readmissions (Krumholz et al., 1997). Each patient received a dichotomous disposition score of "readmitted" or "continued community stay." Patients were coded "readmitted" if they reported or were found to have experienced a hospital readmission at any of the two, six, 10, or 14 week observations. These analyses address first readmissions only.

*Independent Variable: Adequacy of Care.* A ratio measure of adequacy of care served as the major independent variable of interest (see Morrow-Howell, Proctor, & Doré, 1998, for measurement details). The definition of home care in this study includes both informal and formal health and social services provided in the home (Kavesh, 1986). Through a structured assessment at two weeks postdischarge, the respondent provided information on the type and amount of formal and informal services received in each of 14 activity areas (bathing, toileting, grooming, walking, transferring, dressing, eating, taking medication, preparing meals, shopping, getting around, housekeeping, managing money, and administering medical treatment), in which he or she needed assistance (areas where he or she was not independent). For the quantity score in each area, respondents were asked, "How often are you without help for (for example, bathing) when you need it?" Responses were rated on a scale of one to four, with one = "without help at most times" and four = "always enough help." For the quality score, respondents were asked, "How good is the help you receive with (for example, bathing)?" Responses were rated on a scale of one to four, from poor to excellent. Test–retest reliability on this self-reported information was established, with weighted

Kappas over .80 (Morrow-Howell et al., 1998). From this information, a ratio measure was derived across all need areas, reflecting for a given respondent how well needs were met in terms of quantity and quality of assistance vis-à-vis a "desired" level. The sum of the actual quantity and quality ratings serves as the numerator, with the denominator composed of the services received, weighted with the highest quality and quantity ratings. That is, the denominator is the product of the number of need areas and eight, the maximum scores possible for quantity (four = always enough help) plus the maximum score possible for quality (four = excellent quality). The score ranges from zero to one, with higher values reflecting more adequate care. The obtained scores ranged from .46 to 1.00 ($M$ = .88, $SD$ = .11). Although family collaterals provided information for the adequacy measure in 35 percent of cases, adequacy scores did not vary by respondent [$F(1, 251)$ = 1.32, $p$ = .27].

*Control Variables.* Patient health status and medication compliance were used as control variables. Two measures of health status were bed days and self-rated health, each assessed in the two-week telephone interview. Bed days were measured through participant response to the question, "How many days in the past two weeks have you stayed in bed because of your health?" This measure is consistent with that of Stewart, Ware, Brook, and Davies-Avery (1978), who cited its advantage of precision in information from respondents. Self-rated health was measured by respondent's answer to the question, "How would you rate your health today? Poor, fair, good, or excellent?" This single-item measure has been used to measure perceived health since the late 1950s, and evidences reliability, reproducibility, and stability (Ware, Davies-Avery, & Donald, 1978). Medication compliance was assessed by participant response to two questions administered during an in-home interview by a geriatric nurse two weeks postdischarge. The nurse asked, "Sometimes people have trouble remembering to take all their medications. During the past week, have you missed any of your tablets?" and, "Do you take your medicine at the same time every day?" Responses were coded and summed, so that higher scores reflected greater compliance.

### Calculation of Readmission Rates

Readmission rates were calculated for each observational period as well as for the 14-week postdischarge period overall. Final disposition was calculated, to reflect whether over the course of the 14 weeks of observation the patient was ever readmitted.

### Analysis

The effect of care adequacy was tested through logistic regression, with readmission as a dichotomous (yes–no) dependent variable, reflecting whether the participant was ever readmitted during the 14 weeks of observation. For the dependent variable "ever readmitted," independent variables were care adequacy, medication compliance, bed days, and self-rated health, as measured at two weeks postdischarge. This is consistent with the study's focus on care received in the immediate post-acute care period.

### Results

A description of the study participants is presented in Table 19-1. The sample disproportionately included African American elderly people because African American elderly people are more likely to have heart disease from hypertension and because of the location of the study hospital. The hospital was a large, urban hospital, serving an inner-city population that was disproportionately African American. Also, at similar levels of dependency, African Americans are more likely than their white counterparts to be discharged to their homes rather than a nursing home (Morrow-Howell & Proctor, 1994). Because the hospital is located near low-income communities, the percentage of participants without Medi-gap insurance or with both Medicare and Medicaid was higher than that in the national population of elderly people. In a 1987 nationally representative sample of elderly people, 8.5 percent had Medicaid, and 12.9 percent had no supplemental insurance (Short, 1990).

TABLE 19-1. Sample Description (N = 253)

| Characteristic | % |
|---|---|
| Sex | |
|   Male | 41.4 |
|   Female | 58.6 |
| Race | |
|   White | 51.5 |
|   Not white | 48.5 |
| Marital Status | |
|   Married | 36.4 |
|   Not married | 63.6 |
| Medicaid | |
|   Yes | 18.5 |
|   No | 81.5 |
| Medicare | |
|   Yes | 98.7 |
|   No | 1.3 |
| Private insurance | |
|   Yes | 56.3 |
|   No | 43.7 |

| Variable | M | SD | Range |
|---|---|---|---|
| Age (years) | 77.4 | 7.2 | 65–98 |
| Medication compliance | 1.5 | .75 | 0–2 |
| SES (Hollingshead Index) | 56.7 | 5.4 | 11–77 |
| Days spent in bed | 3.6 | 5.4 | 0–16 |
| Self-rated health | 2.1 | .82 | 1–4 |
| Adequacy of care | .88 | .11 | .46–1.0 |

Note: SES = socioeconomic status.

## Readmission Rates

By 14 weeks postdischarge, 42 percent of patients discharged home were readmitted. Wave-specific readmission rates were 12.9 percent at two weeks, 17.4 percent at six weeks, 14.6 percent at 10 weeks, and 11.3 percent at 14 weeks. It should be noted that these latter rates are based on an increasingly small sample—those who had remained in community care until the observation period and did not die.

## Test of Hypothesis

The results of the logistic regression model support the study hypothesis (Table 19-2). Adequacy of care was significantly related to readmission ($p = .04$). Controlling for health and compliance, patients with more adequate care experienced significantly lower rates of readmission. The odds ratio of .05 indicates that a person with an adequacy measure of zero is 20 times more likely (in terms of odds) to be readmitted than is a person with an adequacy measure of one. With more realistic values, as the adequacy score drops from the mean .88 to .78 (a 10 percent change, approximately the standard deviation), the odds of readmission are 25 percent greater.

Self-rated health and medication compliance also significantly affected readmission. Every one-unit increase in compliance with the medication regimen reduces the odds of readmission by nearly half (.47), and a one-unit increase in self-rated health reduces the odds of being readmitted by one-third (.35).

## Discussion

The measurement of adequacy of home care used in this study is based on patient self-report, not on professional evaluation or objective assessment of predefined criteria. Although these different measurement approaches may yield different assessments of adequacy, patient perceptions of the quality of care remain important and are believed to constitute a significant influence on health care outcomes (Ware, 1992).

These findings raise implications for research, policy, and practice. Our study adds to the growing body of literature highlighting the vulnerability to poor outcomes

**TABLE 19-2. Summary of the Logistic Analysis Results**

| Factor Estimate and Probability | Ever Readmitted Readmitted (n = 90) Not Readmitted (n = 128) | | |
|---|---|---|---|
| | Parameter Estimate | p | Odds Ratio (95% CI) |
| Intercept | 4.1400 | .0024 | 62.8 (4.4–902.9) |
| Days in bed | –.0154 | .5915 | .99 (.93–1.0) |
| Self-rated health | –.4290 | .0274 | .65 (.44–.95) |
| Medication compliance | –.6268 | .0021 | .53 (.36–.80) |
| Adequacy of care | –2.9812 | .0394 | .05 (.003–.85) |

*Notes:* Any discrepancies in sample size from Table 1 are due to missing data on independent variables. CI = confidence interval.

among elderly patients in the immediate postdischarge period (Naylor et al., 1994). The elderly CHF patients had high rates of readmission to acute care. These readmission rates are consistent with some earlier reports (Anderson et al., 1990; Fethke et al., 1986) but are considerably higher than those reported for CHF patients just a few years ago. Rich and Freedland (1988), who also studied older CHF patients in St. Louis, found that within three months 21.7 percent had experienced one readmission; in our sample, nearly twice as many were readmitted within three months. The sampling approach targeting those referred for social work discharge planning is likely to have produced a more dependent and perhaps sicker sample than elderly CHF patients whose discharge to their homes did not require professional discharge planning. Unfortunately, the hospital record did not include variables assessed through our study; therefore, we could not compare the study sample to those not served by social workers with respect to postdischarge functioning, health status, or readmission. Yet if this sample was more impaired, adequate home care may be of greater importance. The findings are more reflective of dependent elderly patients typically served by hospital social workers. Social workers employed in hospitals may need to demonstrate the vulnerability of their clients, who often make up the most needy subset of a particular diagnostic or demographic group, for high-risk and high-cost outcomes such as readmission.

The findings indicate that the elderly people with CHF most likely to be readmitted are those who, during the first two weeks after discharge, were sicker, were less compliant with prescribed medication regimens, and received less-than-adequate home care. These findings are consistent with evidence that systematic discharge planning for home care may

begin to affect readmission among medically ill elderly people as early as two weeks following hospital discharge (Naylor et al., 1994).

Although confidence in these findings will be strengthened by their replication in future studies, they point to some important implications for hospital social workers. The findings suggest that a key social work activity—the careful assessment of day-to-day needs postdischarge and arrangements to meet those needs—may help prevent hospital readmission. Although considerable research has addressed demographic and clinical factors associated with readmission, this may be the first study to demonstrate a relationship between the adequacy of home care in the immediate posthospital period and readmission. Social workers bear primary responsibility for developing plans for posthospital care. Yet few studies have attempted to demonstrate the contribution of social work activities and products to more distal outcomes that have significance in terms of the cost and effectiveness of the larger system of health care. This study is an example of the type of research with potential to demonstrate the contribution of social work to national and organizational priorities in health service, such as optimizing quality, enhancing patient outcomes, and reducing unnecessary health expenditures.

The findings also suggest some implications for the individual practitioner. Our assessment of adequacy of care was very detailed with respect to domain of need and to issues of quality and quantity of care. In the same vein, it may be important for social workers to take a detailed approach to assessment and planning for post-acute care. For example, rather than simply ask, "Who will help take care of you?" the assessment and planning should focus on specific activities of daily living, such as taking medications, preparing meals, assisting with functions of toileting, transfer, and walking. For each activity, the social worker may need to assess how often potential caregivers can provide assistance and how well they can perform specific caregiving tasks. Akin to our assessment of adequacy, discharge planners need to assess the quantity and quality of assistance in specific domains and develop plans to meet day-to-day needs through formal in-home services and through the care of family and friends.

Because we measured compliance with medication regimens only at two weeks postdischarge, our data did not permit exploration of the relationships among compliance, health status, and adequacy of care. In future studies that measure each of these constructs repeatedly over time, it may be possible to examine how adequacy of care may affect compliance as an intermediate outcome that in turn affects health status and readmission. That is, it will be important for future studies to examine how adequacy of care affects health status and readmission, perhaps through ensuring that medications are taken according to the prescribed regimens, that meals are prepared consistent with dietary guidelines, and that a minimum activity level is maintained through periodic transfer and moving about.

Findings suggest the importance of implementing practice and policy guidelines aimed at enhancing the adequacy of home care. Home care in the period immediately after discharge needs to be recognized as an important "transitional" component in the continuum of care. Practices and policies directed toward preventing readmission are likely to have significant economic benefit for hospitals and insurers (Anderson & Steinberg, 1985; Naylor et al., 1994), especially for groups with predictable, high-cost readmission, such as the older CHF patients in this study.

## References

Anderson, G., Steinberg, E. P., Whittle, J., Powe, N. R., Antebi, S., & Herbert, R. (1990). Development of clinical and economic prognoses from Medicare claims data. *JAMA, 263,* 967–972.

Anderson, G. F., & Steinberg, E. P. (1984). Hospital readmissions in the Medicare population. *New England Journal of Medicine, 311,* 1349–1353.

Anderson, G. F., & Steinberg, E. P. (1985). Predicting hospital readmissions in the Medicare population. *Inquiry, 22,* 251–258.

Anderson, M. A., Hanson, K. S., & DeVilder, N. W. (1996). Hospital readmissions during home care: A pilot study. *Journal of Community Health Nursing, 13*(1), 1–12.

Andrews, K. (1986). Relevance of readmission of elderly patients discharged from a geriatric unit. *Journal of the American Geriatrics Society, 34*(l), 5–11.

Ashton, C. M., Wray, N. P., Dunn, J. K., Scheurich, J. W., DeBehnke, R. D., & Friedland, J. A. (1987). Predicting readmission in veterans with chronic disease: Development and validation of discharge criteria. *Medical Care, 25,* 1184–1189.

Benjamin, A. (1992). An overview of in-home health and supportive services for older persons [References]. In M. G. Ory & A. P. Dunckler (Eds.), *In-home care for older people: Health & supportive services* (pp. 9–52). Newbury Park, CA: Sage Publications.

Berkman, B., & Abrams, R. D. (1986). Factors related to hospital readmission of elderly cardiac patients. *Social Work, 31,* 99–103.

Berkman, B., Dumas, S., Gastfriend, J., Poplawski, J., & Southworthe, M. (1987). Predicting hospital readmission of elderly cardiac patients. *Health & Social Work, 12,* 221–228.

Brody, J. A., Brock, D. B., & Williams, T. F. (1987). Trends in the health of the elderly population [Review]. *Annual Review of Public Health, 8,* 211–234.

Epstein, A. M., Bogen, J., Dreyer, P., & Thorpe, K. E. (1991). Trends in length of stay and rates of readmission in Massachusetts: Implications for monitoring quality of care. *Inquiry, 28,* 19–28.

Fethke, C. C., Smith, I. M., & Johnson, N. (1986). "Risk" factors affecting readmission of the elderly into the health care system. *Medical Care, 24,* 429–437.

Gooding, J., & Jette, A. M. (1985). Hospital readmissions among the elderly. *Journal of the American Geriatrics Society, 33,* 595–601.

Graham, H., & Livesley, B. (1983). Can readmissions to a geriatric medical unit be prevented? *Lancet, 1,* 404–406.

Hollingshead, A. (1957). *Four factor index of social status.* Unpublished manuscript.

Holloway, J. J., Thomas, J. W., & Shapiro, L. (1988). Clinical and sociodemographic risk factors for readmission of Medicare beneficiaries. *Health Care Financing Review, 10*(l), 27–36.

Hulka, B. S., Kupper, L. L., Cassel, J. C., & Efird, R. L. (1975). Medication use and misuse: Physician–patient discrepancies. *Journal of Chronic Diseases, 28*(l), 7–21.

Kane, R. A., Kane, R. L., Illston, L. H., & Eustis, N. N. (1994). Perspectives on home care quality. *Health Care Financing Review, 16*(l), 69–89.

Kane, R. L. (1994). *A study of post-acute care: Final report May 1994.* Minneapolis: Institute for Health Services Research.

Kavesh, W. N. (1986). Home care: Process, outcome, cost. *Annual Review of Gerontology & Geriatrics, 6,* 135–195.

Kornowski, R., Zeefi, D., Averbuch, M., Finkelstein, A., Schwartz, D., Moshkovitz, M., Weinreb, B., Hershkovitz, R., Eyal, D., Miller, M., Levo, Y., & Pines, A. (1995). Intensive home-care surveillance prevents hospitalization and improves morbidity rates among elderly patients with severe congestive heart failure. *American Heart Journal, 129,* 762–766.

Krumholz, H. M., Parent, E. M., Tu, N., Vaccarino, V., Wang, Y., Radford, M. J., & Hennen, J. (1997). Readmission after hospitalization for congestive heart failure among Medicare beneficiaries. *Archives of Internal Medicine, 157,* 99–104.

Legge, J. S., & Reilly, B. J. (1980). Home health services for previously hospitalized and non-hospitalized patients with circulation ailments: A research note. *Home Health Care Services Quarterly, 1*(3), 85–91.

Leibson, C. L., Naessens, J. M., Campion, M. E., Krishan, I., & Ballard, D. J. (1991). Trends in elderly hospitalization and readmission rates for a geographically defined population: Pre- and post-prospective payment. *Journal of the American Geriatrics Society, 39,* 895–904.

Lockery, S. A., Dunkle, R. E., Kart, C. S., & Coulton, C. J. (1994). Factors contributing to the early rehospitalization of elderly people. *Health & Social Work, 19,* 182–191.

Mamon, J., Steinwachs, D. M., Fahey, M., Bone, L. R., Oktay, J., & Klein, L. (1992). Impact of hospital discharge planning on meeting patient needs after returning home. *Health Services Research, 27*(2), 155–175.

Martens, K., & Mellor, S. (1997). A study of the relationship between home care services and hospital readmission of patients with congestive heart failure. *Home Healthcare Nurse, 15*(2), 123–129.

Mason, W. B., Bedwell, C. L., Vander Zwagg, R., & Runyan, J. W. (1980). Why people are hospitalized: A description of preventable factors leading to admission for medical illness. *Medical Care, 18,* 147–163.

May, D. S., Kelly, J. J., Mendlein, J. M., & Garbe, P. L. (1991). Surveillance of major causes of hospitalization among the elderly, 1988. *MMWR CDC Surveillance Summaries, 40*(l), 7–21.

Morrow-Howell, N., & Proctor, E. (1994). Discharge destinations of Medicare patients receiving discharge planning: Who goes where? *Medical Care, 32,* 486–497.

Morrow-Howell, N., Proctor, E., & Doré, P. (1998). Adequacy of care: The concept and its measurement. *Research on Social Work Practice, 8,* 86–102.

Morrow-Howell, N., Proctor, E. K., & Mui, A. (1991). Adequacy of discharge plans for elderly patients. *Social Work Research & Abstracts*, 27(1), 6–13.

Narain, P., Rubenstein, L. Z., Wieland, G., Rosbrook, B., Strome, L., Pietruszka, F., & Morley, J. (1988). Predictors of immediate and 6-month outcomes in hospitalized elderly patients: The importance of functional status. *Journal of the American Geriatrics Society, 36*, 775–783.

Naylor, M., Brooten, D., Jones, R., Lavizzo-Mourey, R., Mezey, M., & Pauly, M. (1994). Comprehensive discharge planning for the hospitalized elderly. *Annals of Internal Medicine, 1200*, 999–1006.

Proctor, E. K., Morrow-Howell, N., & Chadiha, L. *Adequacy of home care for chronically ill elderly.* R01-HS-06406-01. In Final Report to the Agency for Health Care Policy & Research. Rockville, MD: U.S. Department of Health & Human Services, Public Health Services, Agency for Health Care Policy & Research, 1993.

Rich, M., Beckham, V., Wittnerg, G., Leven, C., Freedland, K., & Carney, R. (1995). A multidisciplinary intervention to prevent the readmission of elderly patients with congestive heart failure. *New England Journal of Medicine, 333*, 1190–1195.

Rich, M. W., & Freedland, K. E. (1988). Effect of DRGs on three-month readmission rate of geriatric patients with congestive heart failure. *American Journal of Public Health, 78*, 680–682.

Rich, M. W., Vinson, J. M., Sperry, J. C., Shah, A. S., Spinner, L. R., Chung, M. K., & Davila-Roman, V. (1993). Prevention of readmission in elderly patients with congestive heart failure: Results of a prospective, randomized pilot study. *Journal of General Internal Medicine, 8*, 585–590.

Robinson, B. C. (1983). Validation of a Caregiver Strain Index. *Journal of Gerontology, 38*, 344–348.

Robinson, B. C., & Barbaccia, J. C. (1982). Acute hospital discharge of older patients and external control. *Home Health Care Services Quarterly, 3*(1), 39–57.

Rogers, W. H., Draper, D., Kahn, K. L., Keeler, E. B., Rubenstein, L. V., Kosecoff, J., & Brook, R. H. (1990). Quality of care before and after implementation of the DRG-based prospective payment system: A summary of effects. *JAMA, 264*, 1989–1994.

Schwartzberg, J. G. (1982). Home health care and rapid rehospitalization. *Home Health Care Services Quarterly, 3*(1), 25–37.

Short, P. (1990). *Estimates of the uninsured population, calendar year 1987.* Rockville, MD: U.S. Public Health Service.

Smith, D. M., Norton, J. A., & McDonald, C. J. (1985). Nonelective readmissions of medical patients. *Journal of Chronic Diseases, 38*(3), 213–224.

Stewart, A., Ware, J., Brook, R., & Davies-Avery, A. (1978). *Conceptualization and measurement of health of adults in the Health Insurance Study: Vol. II. Physical health in terms of functioning.* Santa Monica, CA: Rand.

U.S. Department of Health and Human Services. (1987). Long-term care for the functionally dependent elderly (Vital and Health Statistics, Series 13, No. 104). Hyattsville, MD: Author.

Victor, C. R., & Vetter, N. J. (1985). The early readmission of the elderly to hospital. *Age & Aging, 14*, 37–42.

Victor, C. R., & Vetter, N. J. (1988). Preparing the elderly for discharge from hospital: A neglected aspect of patient care? *Age & Aging, 17*, 155–163.

Vinson, J. M., Rich, M. W., Sperry, J. C., Shah, A. S., & McNamara, T. (1990). Early readmission of elderly patients with congestive heart failure [see comments]. *Journal of the American Geriatrics Society, 38*, 1290–1295.

Ware, J. (1992). *Measures for a new era of health assessment: Measuring functioning and well-being.* Durham, NC: Duke University Press.

Ware, J. E., Davies-Avery, A., & Donald, C. A. (1978). *Conceptualization and measurement of health for adults in the Health Insurance Study: Vol. V. General health perception.* Santa Monica, CA: Rand.

West, J. A., Miller, N. H., Parker, K. M., Senneca, D., Ghandour, G., Clark, M., Greenwald, G., Heller, R., Fowler, M., & DeBusk, R. (1997). A comprehensive management system for heart failure improves clinical outcomes and reduces medical resource utilization. *American Journal of Cardiology, 79*(1), 58–63.

Williams, B. C., Mackay, S. A., & Torner, J. C. (1991). Home health care: Comparison of patients and services among three types of agencies. *Medical Care, 29,* 583–587.

Williams, E. I., & Fitton, F. (1988). Factors affecting early unplanned readmission of elderly patients to hospital. *British Medical Journal, 297,* 784–787.

Zook, C. J., Savickis, S. F., & Moore, F. D. (1980). Repeated hospitalization for the same disease: A multiplier of national health costs. *Health & Society, 58,* 454–471.

This chapter was originally published in the May 2000 issue of *Health & Social Work*, Vol. 25, Number 2, pp. 87–96.

# IV
# Self-Fulfillment

People of all ages need to continually experience challenges and stimulation and to pursue opportunities for full development of their potential. These experiences and activities require access to the educational, cultural, spiritual, and recreational resources of society. To this end, it is especially noteworthy that some subgroups of older people are effectively denied other opportunities because their daily lives revolve so heavily around meeting the needs for care of others. Familial obligations to care are very unevenly distributed by gender, race, and socioeconomic factors. Although caring for others can be highly fulfilling, it can be burdensome as well.

This section emphasizes the frequently overlooked extent to which the "unpaid caregiving work of older persons," while usually highly valued within families, is both unacknowledged and undervalued by the larger society. While elders themselves typically give caregiving roles powerful meaning and derive vital sustenance from them in their daily lives, the extent to which other elders do not share such compelling obligations seems also remarkable. Certain groups today—especially grandmothers in African American and Latino families–are highly likely to be "drafted" into caring for grandchildren and other ill and often marginalized family members who have literally no one else to rely upon.

Two ground-breaking articles in this section highlight the health costs for such elders. This first is landmark research on African American family care by Esme Fuller-Thomson and Meredith Minkler, examining the health needs of African American grandparents raising grandchildren. Using a randomized sample drawn from the 1987–88 and 1992–94 waves of the National Survey of Families and Households, they compare non-caregiving African American grandparents with African American grandparents who provided care for six months or more. While the health profile of African American elders is troubling, they find the health of African American grandparent caregivers especially troubling.

Most of the caregiving grandparents have physical limits in walking, lifting, and climbing stairs that would make it difficult to fulfill normal parenting duties, such as lifting and bathing children, taking them on outings, and participating in other normal activities. The authors identify an urgent need for local Afrocentric health promotion and social services, and make very specific recommendations for practitioners and researchers. These are especially relevant to advocates working to redress the Temporary Assistance to Needy Families (TANF) restrictions on grandparents who are now often inappropriately mandated to accept employment.

In the second article, Denise Burnette examines the unmet needs and service use among a purposive sample of 74 Latino custodial grandparent caregivers in New York City. Study participants tended to be unmarried, middle-aged and older women who were monolingual Spanish-speaking and had very low levels of educational attainment and income. Nearly all were connected to the formal service system yet still had many unmet needs. Lack of knowledge was a major barrier to service use, but other factors predicting unmet needs included low education, poor health, high levels of life stress, and lack of reliable help with child rearing. Given the multiple population identities subsumed under the category Hispanic, this article highlights the great need for more research in different cities and in rural areas on the needs

of caregiving elders and programs to assist them in these important tasks.

Along this same vein, Cynthia Cannon Poindexter and Nathan Linsk examine the experiences of older women of color caring for children and adults with HIV infection. Exploring in-depth interviews with 19 caregivers, they identify the hardships these caregivers encounter in having to manage both the stigma of this disease and their own resultant isolation. This group of hidden caregivers receives little supplemental support from family, friends, pastors, or social services. Contrary to the researchers' expectations, few of these caregivers had experienced overt discrimination simply because they had carefully avoided disclosing the diagnoses except to a few highly trustworthy people. In poignant detail these women describe the heartbreak of hiding the diagnosis, avoiding even the name of the illness, to protect their loved ones and themselves from the thoughtless paranoia of others. Unable usually even to share with their religious congregations, and embarrassed at the biases they had harbored previously themselves, most found participation in research an important way of reducing their own isolation. In "the current political climate regarding public assistance, and the subsequent burden on informal support providers, social workers need more information about how to support the older caregivers who are providing so much." These authors identify urgent needs for social workers to reach out, assess the needs of such caregivers, and offer services and support groups that are accessible and relevant. We must devise environments that are safe enough for older people to disclose the presence of HIV in the home and family and assure that such caretakers get appropriate support.

Caregiving's burden is sometimes recognized more in the "unusual" caregiver than in normative caregiving, the bulk of which is provided by middle-aged women. Betty Kramer's longitudinal study followed husbands caring for wives with Alzheimer's disease for a one-year period. Focusing on family care and addressing male spouses, Dr. Kramer highlights issues too often overlooked in regard to female caregivers. The husbands sort into two outcome groups, those whose wives moved to a nursing home and those whose wives continued to live at home, with the research examining the comparative changes in stressors, resources, and psychological well-being of husbands in the two groups. Dr. Kramer identifies unique conflicts for the male spouse caregivers that resulted in depression within both groups, with the continuing care group adapting somewhat better over time to their wives' memory and behavior problems. Kramer also identifies the importance of worry about finances, especially among those who had institutionalized their wives and were incurring nursing home expenses.

Kramer advises social workers to share new knowledge of the experience of caregiving with male caregivers just beginning to face this situation and with those considering placement of their wives. Such men also need more intensive supports and interventions than they get and help to discover alternatives to nursing home placement that can also lower physical strain. Linking those considering placement with those who have already done so would also be helpful.

And so the challenges faced by husbands of women with dementia highlight the long-term difficulties faced also by women caring for husbands, parents, and other relatives, and compounded in the lives of women of color. These elders are "the hidden army," as Poindexter and Linsk point out, of older people providing personal care and emotional support to children, youths, adults and other elders. Yet, care work is also fulfilling work, as distinctly highlighted in the work of Rhoades and MacFarlane (1999) on older persons who have chosen to provide foster care to adults with mental illness. None of it should ever be taken for granted.

## References

Rhoades & MacFarlane (1999, November). Caregiver Meaning: A study of caregivers of the mentally ill, *Health & Social Work, 24* (4), 291–298.

# 20

# African American Grandparents Raising Grandchildren

## ESME FULLER-THOMSON
## and MEREDITH MINKLER

Social workers, health care providers, and mental health care providers working in large inner-city clinics in the late 1980s reported a marked increase in the number of missed appointments, stress-related conditions, and exacerbation of previously controlled hypertension and diabetes among their middle-age and older female patients (Davis, 1993; Miller, 1991; Minkler & Roe, 1993). On further investigation it became apparent that many of these patients had recently assumed custody of grandchildren or great-grandchildren. The 1990 census revealed that what social workers and services providers were finding mirrored a much larger national trend. The 1980s indeed saw a 44 percent increase in the number of children living with grandparents or other relatives. In a third of these homes, neither parent was present (Saluter, 1992), typically making the grandparent the sole or primary caregiver.

Although grandparent caregiving includes all racial and ethnic minority groups, it is particularly prevalent in African American families. By the mid-1990s, 13.5 percent of African American children were living with grandparents or other relatives (Lugaila, 1998), compared with 6.5 percent of Hispanic children and 4.1

percent of white children. Almost 30 percent of African American grandmothers and about 14 percent of African American grandfathers reported having had primary responsibility for raising a grandchild for at least six months at some point in their lives (Szinovacz, 1998), compared with 10.9 percent of all grandparents (Fuller-Thomson, Minkler, & Driver, 1997).

This article examines differences in physical and mental health status between African American grandparents raising grandchildren and those who are not involved in this caregiving role. This discussion builds on our earlier study of grandparent caregivers, using a national data set, but it is unique in that it explores the physical and mental health of the growing subpopulation of African American grandparents who are raising grandchildren.

## Review of the Literature

### Increase in Grandparent-Headed Households

The rapid growth in the number of children formally placed with relatives can be traced in part to federal and state laws and policies, beginning in 1979, which had the effect of encouraging or requiring that a preference be given to next-of-kin in the placement of foster children. In many of the most populated parts of the United States, fully one-half of the children in out-of-home placements are in "kinship care" or formal placements with relatives (Brooks, Webster, Berrick, & Barth, 1998). But policies promoting kinship care do not explain the concomitant increase social workers also have seen in the number of children who have been informally "going to live with grandma"—a trend that has continued into the late 1990s (Harden, Clark, & Maguire, 1997; Minkler,

1999). A variety of social factors have contributed to the increase. Prominent among these are drug abuse (particularly the epidemic of cocaine use in the 1980s), the rise in households headed by single parents, teenage pregnancy and youth unemployment (Burnette, 1997; Harden et al., 1997), HIV/AIDS (Joslin & Harrison, 1998), and a sixfold increase in the rate of female incarceration from 1980 to 1995 (U.S. Department of Justice, 1997).

### Grandparent Caregiving among African Americans

Several factors help explain the disproportionate number of African American children living in the care of grandparents. Historically, the extended family was the primary West African family structure at the time of slavery (Scannapieco & Jackson, 1996). The immediate needs of children who were separated from their parents during slavery promoted continued reliance on extended family caregiving (Sudarkasa, 1981; Wilson, 1989). In the United States, during the first half of the 20th century, poverty, oppression, racism, and the consequent lack of opportunity in the South led to great migration of African Americans to the North in pursuit of employment. It was commonplace for grandparents to remain in the South to care for children while the middle generation established themselves in Northern cities (Sudarkasa, 1981; Wilson, 1989). Subsequently and continuing through the 1960s, urban parents often would send their children in summer to grandparents and other extended family in the South. These visits allowed the new generation to remain closely connected with their grandparents and other relatives in the South and to be exposed to cultural traditions.

In contrast, as Burton and Dilworth-Anderson (1991) have noted, contemporary grandparent caregiving often occurs in response to crises such as incarceration of children's mothers, HIV/AIDS, and substance abuse. These reasons for caregiving frequently carry with them a stigma for the whole family, including grandparent caregivers. Extended families, churches, and other supports that historically have helped African Americans cope with racism and other adversities (Gibbs, 1991) are in place for many grandparent caregivers and will be discussed later; however, the stigma attached to AIDS and drug abuse also has led to social isolation from peers and not infrequently from churches in the African American community (Generations United, 1998; Poe, 1992).

### Health Problems Associated with Grandparent Caregiving

Although caring for one's grandchildren brings many rewards, including "keeping the family together" (Burton, 1992; Jendrek, 1994; Minkler & Roe, 1993; Poe, 1992), it also has been associated with potentially serious physical and mental health problems. Key among these is depression, which, as Walker and Pomeroy (1996) noted, is one of "the more enduring effects of caregiving" (p. 247). Recent analysis of the National Survey of Families and Households (NSFH) multicultural sample found that 25 percent of all grandparent caregivers had clinically relevant levels of depression (Minkler, Fuller-Thomson, Miller, & Driver, 1997). Depression may develop because of difficulties in balancing multiple work, family, and social responsibilities at a time when many grandparents had hoped to have more time to themselves. The increased demands on caregivers' time and finances may be particularly disheartening when contrasted with noncaregiving grandparents' increasing freedom and leisure time.

Earlier qualitative studies among African American grandparents raising grandchildren (Burton, 1992; Minkler & Roe, 1993; Poe, 1992) have suggested that such depression also may be triggered by sorrow that results from distressing circumstances surrounding the onset of care (such as the substance abuse, incarceration, or death of the adult child). Walker and Pomeroy (1996) suggested that symptoms of depression, in fact, may reflect the caregivers' "normal distress" and grief (p. 248). Whether depression or grief, however, the elevated rates of psychological distress reported among African American grandparent caregivers are noteworthy.

Adverse physical health outcomes and functional health limitations also have been associated with primary caregiving for a grandchild, including exacerbation of pre-existing chronic conditions, comorbidity, declines in self-assessed health, and limitations in one or more activities of daily living (Burnette, 1999b; Miller, 1991; Minkler & Fuller-Thomson, 1999a; Minkler & Roe, 1993; Strawbridge, Wallhagen, Shema, & Kaplan, 1997). To untangle the unique effects of caregiving on health, it is essential to take into account the fact that older African Americans have, on average, more physical health problems because of, in part, racism, oppression, and poverty. In fact, African American women experience greater morbidity and mortality than all other groups of women (Gaston, Barrett, Johnson, & Epstein, 1998). Consequently, African American caregivers must be compared with noncaregiving African Americans, rather than with the general population of noncaregivers.

The great majority of studies on grandparent caregivers to date have used small nonrepresentative samples, and hence their results cannot be generalized (for example, Burnette, 1999b; Burton, 1992; Minkler &

Roe, 1993; Shore & Hayslip, 1994). Studies that have used representative data sets (for example, Chalfie, 1994; Fuller-Thomson et al., 1997; Minkler & Fuller-Thomson, 1999a, 1999b; Minkler et al., 1997; Szinovacz, 1998) have not focused their research on African American grandparent caregivers. With the use of a nationally representative subsample of African Americans, we sought to address this gap and answer the question, "How do African American caregiving grandparents differ with respect to demographic and physical and mental health characteristics from African American grandparents who are not raising a grandchild?"

## Methods

Two cycles of the NSFH were conducted, the first from 1987 through 1988 and the second from 1992 through 1994. In the first cycle 13,008 people were interviewed, 2,390 of whom were African American. African Americans and other ethnic minority groups were oversampled in the NSFH to allow subanalysis by race. To adjust for this over-sampling, as well as oversampling related to nontraditional families and recently married people and to deal with the problem of non-response, a weighting variable was constructed by the NSFH. This weighting represents a sample that is demographically representative of the continental United States. (For a more in-depth discussion of the NSFH, see Sweet, Bumpass, & Call, 1988.) In the second cycle 10,008 people were reinterviewed, including 1,723 or 72 percent of the original African American respondents. The analyses reported here are based on the second cycle of data collection.

The original multiracial NSFH sample had 3,477 grandparents in the second cycle of data collection, 173 of whom were caregivers. (For detailed discussions of custodial caregiving in the general population, see Fuller-Thomson et al., 1997; Minkler & Fuller-Thomson, 1999a; Minkler et al., 1997). The subsample here is restricted to African American grandparents who were raising a grandchild during the 1990s ($n$ = 78) and a comparison sample of African American grandparents who had never been primary caregivers for a grandchild ($n$ = 485). Custodial grandparents were defined as those who replied in the affirmative to the question "For various reasons, grandparents sometimes take on the primary responsibility for raising a grandchild. Have you ever had the primary responsibility for any of your grandchildren for six months or more?" Grandparents who reported that they had begun or ended caregiving during the 1990s were the subgroup of primary interest in this investigation. To avoid confounding the analysis, grandparents who previously had provided care but who were no longer doing so during the 1990s were excluded.

Because we restricted the analyses to the African American subsample of the original survey, the weighting variable required modification. To allow for appropriately weighted comparisons in the African American sub-sample, we divided the weighting variable by the mean value of that variable for this group (Statistics Canada, 1996). This technique allows the overall sample size of African Americans to remain constant, but it "takes into account the unequal probabilities of selection" (p. 28). Caregivers and noncaregivers were then compared and contrasted on demographic and physical health and mental health characteristics. Chi-square tests were used for nominal and ordinal variables, and independent $t$ tests were used for interval- and ratio-level variables.

Depression was measured using a modified 12-item version of the Center for Epidemiological Studies Depression Scale (CES-D) (Radloff, 1977). The full CES-D is a self-report measure of current symptoms of depression, developed for use in large-scale community-based studies. The CES-D scale has excellent concurrent validity, good internal consistency, and acceptable test–retest reliability (Devins & Orme, 1985; Radloff, 1977). The correlation between the full CES-D and the 12-item CES-D is 0.88 (Fuller-Thomson, 1995). The traditional cut-point that suggests clinically relevant levels of depressive symptoms in the full CES-D is a score of 16 or higher. Although the 12-item CES-D used in this study has a much smaller range (0–36) than the full 20-item CES-D (0–60), we conservatively chose to retain the full CES-D cut-point of 16. Because we retained this cut-point, the possibility of identifying respondents as depressed when they would not be so identified on the full CES-D was minimized (false positives), but the true level of depression may have been underestimated (false negatives).

## Results

African American custodial grandparents of the 1990s tended to begin caregiving when the grandchildren were very young. More than half (53.6 percent) began when the grandchildren were younger than one year old, and an additional 20.5 percent undertook care when the grandchildren were between the ages of one and five; 17.5 percent began caregiving when the child was between five and 10 years old, and the remaining 8.4 percent undertook care when the child was 11 years old or older.

The findings of this study indicate that there are marked differences between caregiving grandparents and noncaregiving grandparents in the African American community (Table 20-1). Three-fourths of caregiving grandparents were widowed, divorced, separated, or never married, compared with

**TABLE 20-1. Comparative Demographic Profile of African American Custodial Grandparents versus African American Noncustodial Grandparents of the 1990s**

| Variable | % Noncaregiving Grandparents (n = 495) | % Caregiving Grandparents (n = 78) |
|---|---|---|
| Marital status in 1993 | | |
| Widowed, divorced, separated, or never married | 51.7 | 76.9*** |
| Married | 48.3 | 23.1 |
| Mean age in 1993 | 55.6 | 58.3† |
| Gender | | |
| Male | 45.1 | 23.1*** |
| Female | 54.9 | 76.9 |
| Education level in 1993 | | |
| Grade 11 or less | 45.6 | 50 |
| Grade 12 or higher | 54.4 | 50 |
| Geographic region in 1988 | | |
| South | 56.6 | 50.0 |
| Elsewhere | 43.4 | 50.0 |
| Urban or rural status in 1988 | | |
| Nonstandard metropolitan area (rural) | 19 | 20.5 |
| Standard metropolitan area (urban) | 81.0 | 79.5 |
| Income in 1988 | | |
| Median income | $27,889 | $21,163* |
| Families below poverty line | 25.4 | 47.1*** |
| Families above poverty line | 74.6 | 52.9 |
| Mean number of grandchildren | 5.3 | 8.2** |

*Note:* Chi-square tests were used for nominal variables, and independent *t* tests were used for ratio-level variables.
† *p* < .10. *\*p* < .05. *\*\*p* < .01. *\*\*\*p* < .001.

one-half of noncaregivers. Caregivers were also more likely to be female (77 percent compared with 55 percent), to have more grandchildren (on average, 8.2 grandchildren compared with 5.3 grandchildren), and to be poorer. Almost half lived below the poverty line, compared with one-quarter of noncaregiving grandparents.

African American caregivers were significantly more likely than their noncaregiving peers to have limitations in four of the five activities of daily living (ADL) investigated (Table 20-2). Caregivers had more problems moving around inside the house and doing day-to-day tasks. The levels of limitation were quite substantial, with 29 percent of

**TABLE 20-2. Comparative Profile of Health-Related Variables for African American Custodial Grandparents Compared with African American Noncustodial Grandparents in the 1990s**

| Variable | % Noncaregiving Grandparents (n = 495) | % Caregiving Grandparents (n = 78) |
|---|---|---|
| Physical or mental conditions limit respondent's ability to care for personal needs such as bathing, dressing, eating, or going to the bathroom? | | |
| Does not limit at all | 84.4 | 78.7 |
| Limits a little | 9.6 | 10.7 |
| Limits a lot | 6 | 10.6 |
| Move about inside the house? | | |
| Does not limit at all | 81.1 | 65.8* |
| Limits a little | 12.2 | 20.5 |
| Limits a lot | 6.7 | 13.7 |
| Do day-to-day tasks? | | |
| Does not limit at all | 75.1 | 54.8** |
| Limits a little | 15.6 | 27.4 |
| Limits a lot | 9.4 | 17.8 |
| Climb a flight of stairs? | | |
| Does not limit at all | 68.4 | 47.2*** |
| Limits a little | 19.6 | 23.6 |
| Limits a lot | 12.0 | 29.2 |
| Walk six blocks? | | |
| Does not limit at all | 66.8 | 44.6*** |
| Limits a little | 16.8 | 16.2 |
| Limits a lot | 16.4 | 39.2 |
| Limitation of at least one ADL | | |
| No limitations | 57.3 | 36.5*** |
| Some limitation of at least one ADL | 42.7 | 63.5 |
| Mean number of ADL limitations (n = 525) | 1.2 | 2.1*** |
| Health status | | |
| Very poor or poor | 9.2 | 8.1† |
| Fair | 25.1 | 36.5 |
| Good or excellent | 65.7 | 55.4 |
| Depression | | |
| Categorized as depressed using modified CES-D | 20.8 | 36.8 |
| Not depressed | 79.2 | 63.2** |
| Mean score on CES-D | 9.0 | 11.5* |

*Notes:* ADL = activities of daily living. CES-D = Center for Epidemiological Studies Depression Scale (Radloff, 1977). Chi-square tests were used for nominal and ordinal-level variables. Independent $t$ tests were used for interval and ratio-level variables.

† $p < .10$. * $p < .05$. ** $p < .01$. *** $p < .001$.

caregivers reporting "a lot of limitation" climbing a flight of stairs and two of five caregivers indicating that they had a lot of limitation walking six blocks. Approximately two-thirds of caregivers had at least one limitation, and the mean number of limitations was two. No significant differences were found between African American caregivers and noncaregivers with respect to self-reported health status or with their reported ability to bathe, dress, and provide other personal care.

African American caregivers also had more symptoms of depression compared with their noncaregiving peers, with more than one-third of caregivers reporting clinically relevant levels of depression, compared with one-fifth of noncaregivers.

## Discussion

There are several limitations to this study. First, the relatively small sample size of African American grandparent caregivers in the NSFH prohibited us from taking advantage of the longitudinal character of the data to explore causation. As a result, we were able to report only on associations and had no information on whether these factors were causally related to grandparent caregiving status and, if so, in which direction the relationship flowed. Second, the NSFH did not allow us to distinguish between caregivers raising one grandchild and those raising two or more grandchildren. Smaller, nonrandom studies in New York (Joslin & Brouard, 1995); Oakland, California (Minkler & Roe, 1993); and elsewhere have suggested that many African American grandparents may be raising more than one grandchild, particularly in inner-city neighborhoods. Because the financial, emotional, and physical consequences of raising several children may be even more substantial than those associated with raising one, further study in this area is war-

ranted. Third, the NSFH did not provide information on whether grandparents had legal custody of the grandchildren. This information is critical because grandparents raising grandchildren in the formal foster care system are eligible for significantly greater benefits than those without the "kinship care" designation. Furthermore, some grandparents without legal custody may avoid obtaining any government assistance because they fear that the child will be taken into nonfamilial foster care.

Finally, the NSFH data set did not enable an examination of why individuals become grandparent caregivers, and it did not allow us to understand the reason for the elevated risk for depression and ill health among African American grandparents compared with their noncaregiving peers.

## Implications for Social Work Research and Practice

Despite these limitations our study was able to outline a health profile of African American grandparents raising grandchildren, and that profile was troubling. Caregivers had, on average, two limitations of their ADL, twice as many as were experienced by noncaregiving grandparents. More than 50 percent had trouble climbing stairs or walking six blocks. Because 75 percent of the grandparents undertook custodial care when the child was younger than five years old, when the physical aspects of child-rearing typically are most strenuous, the consequences of these limitations may be particularly problematic.

The extent of physical limitations among African American caregiving grandparents has a number of implications for social work practice and research. Social workers who have caregiving grandparents as clients need to be attentive particularly to current health problems and the possibility that the extensive demands of caregiving may exacerbate these conditions. Devices for assistance, home modifications, and in-home support services should be made easily accessible to grandparent caregivers in need. Similarly, respite services should be made far more available to grandparents, and their child care component should include relief from some of the more physically demanding tasks of caregiving, such as bathing young children and taking them on outings.

Grandparents who are in the poorest health and those raising children they perceive as having physical or behavioral problems may be among the least likely to seek and receive counseling and other help for themselves (Burnette, 1999a; Shore & Hayslip, 1994). More targeted outreach to such grandparents and the creation of "one-stop shopping" centers, where grandparents can receive mental and physical health care and services for their grandchildren and themselves, may be critical for effective service delivery (Generations United, 1998; Minkler, 1999). An Afrocentric neighborhood-based health promotion center (Elliott Brown, Jemmott, Mitchell, & Walton, 1998) holds considerable promise for this population of older African Americans. These holistic services agencies could offer direct services, information, and referral for mental and physical health needs of caregiving grandparents, support groups, exercise and wellness workshops; coordinate babysitting exchanges; and provide legal advice on custody and access issues. African American grandparents' willingness to use social services and health centers and the cultural appropriateness of services they receive are enhanced by hiring staff who live in the community (Harvey & Rauch, 1997).

The high levels of depressive symptoms for African American grandparent caregivers in this study (37 percent) underscores the need for high-quality and culturally sensitive psychotherapeutic interventions, including support groups designed to reinforce and build on the strengths of African American grandparents and to address their unmet needs. Detroit's Project GUIDE ("Assisting Intergenerational Families," 1993), a comprehensive program of services, support, and cultural enrichment for African American grandparents and the grandchildren in their care, which grew out of the drug epidemic, provides an excellent example of an intervention that meets many of these criteria.

Social workers assisting grandparent-headed households also should stay abreast of pre-existing resources such as the grandparent information center (GIC) of the American Association of Retired Persons (AARP). The GIC, for example, maintains a database of approximately 500 grandparent caregiver support groups in all 50 states (personal communication with M. Hollidge, director, AARP GIC, June 4, 1999) and can put social work professionals and grandparents themselves in touch with programs and services in their geographic areas. If further research indicates that the grandparents' depression is primarily a grief reaction from loss associated with caregiving, the focus of social work interventions should be on coping with grief rather than managing long-term depression (Walker & Pomeroy, 1996). More effective involvement of African American churches in the provision of support and assistance to grandparents raising grandchildren also is needed. As several observers have noted, the shame often associated with two major causes of the increase in grandparent caregiving—substance abuse and HIV/AIDS—has resulted in the tendency for many African American churches to shy away from greater involvement in this area (Generations United, 1998). Social workers can play an important role in bringing visibility to the work of churches that have helped address the needs of grandparent caregivers in these situations and in helping to find culturally appropriate and comfortable ways for other churches to follow their example.

The fact that fully half of the grandparent caregivers in this study were living below the poverty line underscores the importance of studying and responding to grandparent caregiving within a broad sociostructural framework. Indeed, many of the causes of the increase in grandparent caregiving nationally (for example, incarceration of one or both parents, the rise in single parent-headed households, and the epidemics of substance abuse and AIDS) are tied in fundamental ways to the continued and often interconnected problems of poverty and racism in our society (Gibbs, 1991). The rapid increase in incarceration rates of women, for example, has affected disproportionately low-income African American women and their families (Dressel & Barnhill, 1994). Similarly, the disproportionate rates of single parent-headed households among African Americans reflect, in part, the continued loss of men's relative economic advantage as breadwinners—a loss that has been far more pronounced in the African American community as a result of institutionalized racism and oppression (Ozawa, 1994). Serious efforts to address the factors contributing to the rise in intergenerational households headed by grandparents cannot be made without a concomitant commitment to confronting these underlying problems.

Of immediate salience in this regard are the potential effects of the 1996 welfare reform legislation on low-income grandparents raising grandchildren. As Mullen (1997) has pointed out, the legislative changes incorporated in the Personal Responsibility and Work Opportunity Reconciliation Act of 1996 (P.L. 104-193) (which removed the entitlement status of Aid to Families with Dependent Children and replaced the latter with the Temporary Assistance to Needy Families [TANF] program), "were never designed with grandparent-headed households in mind." Despite this oversight, a growing proportion of TANF recipients are grandparents and other relatives, particularly in the inner city. TANF regulations that establish five-year lifetime benefit limits, impose a work requirement after two years, and require teenage mothers to live at home as a condition of receiving aid may have the effect of increasing the number of grandparents who become primary caregivers to their grandchildren (Minkler, Berrick, & Needell, 1999; Mullen, 1997). As frontline workers, social workers are among the first professionals to become aware of the ramifications of TANF for their clients. Policymakers need to be apprised of these ramifications, with suggestions on how to improve the policies so they take less of a toll on our nation's grandparents. Social workers also are well situated to alert researchers of the need for further investigation into and data collection on neglected caregiving issues (Gaston et al., 1998). Both qualitative and quantitative longitudinal studies on the effect of TANF on African American grandparents are critical as we attempt to assess the consequences of welfare reform for the growing number of intergenerational households headed by grandparents.

As suggested earlier, further social work research should attempt to examine also the legal custody status of the children being provided care by African American grandparents and its effect (mediated through differential access to resources and so forth) on grandparents' health and well-being. Finally, studies are needed to determine the extent to which the elevated depression rates found in grandparent caregivers may in fact be a function of grief as has been found with other forms of caregiving (Walker & Pomeroy, 1996). Taking a cue from Walker and Pomeroy's study of the experience of caregivers of people with dementia, instruments (for example, The Grief Experience Inventory [Sanders, Mauger, & Strong, 1985] and the Beck Depression Inventory [Beck, Steer, & Garbin, 1988]) that enable the delineation of the role of grief in influencing depression scores should be used.

## Conclusion

In focusing on grandparents as surrogate parents to their grandchildren, this study inadvertently may have reinforced the common misconception that grandparent caregiving is "a black issue" and that this role is in fact common in the African American community. As Hunter and Taylor (1998) pointed out, "research on black grandparents has historically been couched within the public discourse on black families and social policy" (p. 70). In contrast to the majority of research on white grandparents, studies of black grandparenthood tend to stress the roles of grandparents within a context of family crisis. Much further research is needed on the 71 percent of African American grandmothers and 86 percent of grandfathers (Szinovacz, 1998) who never serve as surrogate parents to their grandchildren. The results should be publicized widely to help counter these misconceptions. At the same time, however, the needs of those African American grandparents raising grandchildren are deserving of continued attention from researchers and increased attention from policymakers and social work practitioners. As Gibbs (1991) explained, issues such as grandparent caregiving in African American communities "can be better understood if they are conceptualized as an interaction between historical patterns of adaptation, current social policies, environmental stress, and coping strategies utilized by black family members" (p. 328). Davis, Aguilar, and Jackson (1998) suggested that social workers can play a key role in "raising substantive questions about social justice" (p. 83) and in advocating for change in policies that may adversely affect women who make low wages and their families. As the findings of this study make clear, such advocacy should include work with and on behalf of the growing number of grandparents, many of them African American, who are raising their grandchildren.

## References

Assisting intergenerational families in drug crisis: Detroit's Project GUIDE. (1993). *Brookdale Grandparent Caregiver Information Project Newsletter, 2*(1), 1–2.

Beck, A. T., Steer, R. A., & Garbin, M. G. (1988). Psychometric properties of the Beck Depression Inventory: Twenty-five years of evaluation. *Clinical Psychology Review, 8*, 77–100.

Brooks, D., Webster, D., Berrick, J. D., & Barth, R. (1998). *An overview of the child welfare system in California: Today's challenges and tomorrow's interventions.* Berkeley: University of California, Center for Social Services Research.

Burnette, D. (1997). Grandparents raising grandchildren in the inner city. *Families in Society, 78*, 489–499.

Burnette, D. (1999a). Custodial grandparents in Latino families: Patterns of service use and predictors of unmet needs. *Social Work, 44*, 22–34.

Burnette, D. (1999b). Physical and emotional well-being of custodial grandparents in Caribbean Latino families. *American Journal of Orthopsychiatry, 69*, 305–318.

Burton, L. (1992). Black grandmothers rearing children of drug-addicted parents: Stressors, outcomes and social service needs. *Gerontologist, 32,* 744–751.

Burton, L. M., & Dilworth-Anderson, P. (1991). The intergenerational roles of aged black Americans. *Marriage and Family Review, 16*(3/4), 311–330.

Chalfie, D. (1994). *Going it alone: A closer look at grandparents parenting grandchildren.* Washington, DC: American Association of Retired Persons.

Davis, E. (1993, March 20). Keynote address. Presented at the Annual Meeting of Generations United, Washington, DC.

Davis, K. E., Aguilar, M. A., & Jackson, V. (1998). Save low-income women and their children first. *Health & Social Work, 23,* 83–86.

Devins, G. M., & Orme, C. M. (1985). Center for Epidemiological Studies Depression Scale. In Daniel J. Keyser and Richard C. Sweetland (General Editors) *Test Critiques* (Vol. 2, pp. 144–160). Kansas City, MO: Westport.

Dressel, P., & Barnhill, S. (1994). Reframing gerontological thought and practice: The case of grandmothers with daughters in prison. *Gerontologist, 34,* 685–690.

Elliott Brown, K. A., Jemmott, F. E., Mitchell, H. J., & Walton, M. L. (1998). The Well: A neighborhood-based health promotion model for black women [Practice Forum]. *Health & Social Work, 23,* 146–153.

Fuller-Thomson, E. (1995). *Poignant loss or painless transition?: The effect of parental death upon adult children.* Unpublished doctoral dissertation, University of California, Berkeley.

Fuller-Thomson, E., Minkler, M., & Driver, D. (1997). A profile of grandparents raising grandchildren in the United States. *Gerontologist, 37,* 406–411.

Gaston, M. H., Barrett, S. E., Johnson, T. L., & Epstein, L. G. (1998). Health care needs of medically underserved women of color: The role of the Bureau of Primary Health Care. *Health & Social Work, 23,* 86–96.

Generations United. (1998). *Grandparents and other relatives raising children: An intergenerational action agenda.* Washington, DC: Author.

Gibbs, J. (1991). Developing intervention models for black families: Linking theory and research. In H. E. Cheatham & J. B. Stewart (Eds.), *Black families: Interdisciplinary perspectives* (pp. 325–351). New Brunswick, NJ: Transaction Books.

Harden, A. W., Clark, R. L., & Maguire, K. (1997). *Informal and formal kinship care.* Washington, DC: U.S. Department of Health and Human Services.

Harvey, A. R., & Rauch, J. B. (1997). A comprehensive Afrocentric rites of passage program for black male adolescents. *Health & Social Work, 22,* 30–38.

Hunter, A., & Taylor, R. J. (1998). Grandparenthood in African American families. In M. Szinovacz (Ed.), *Handbook on grandparenthood* (pp. 70–86). Westport, CT: Greenwood Press.

Jendrek, M. P. (1994). Grandparents who parent their grandchildren: Circumstances and decisions. *Gerontologist, 34,* 206–216.

Joslin, D., & Brouard, A. (1995). The prevalence of grandmothers as primary caregivers in a poor pediatric population. *Journal of Community Health, 20,* 383–401.

Joslin, D., & Harrison, R. (1998). The "hidden patient": Older relatives raising children orphaned by AIDS. *Journal of the American Women's Medical Association, 53,* 65–76.

Lugaila, T. (1998). *Marital status and living arrangements, March 1997* (Current population reports, Series P20, No. 506). Washington, DC: U.S. Government Printing Office.

Miller, D. (1991, November). *The "Grandparents Who Care" support project of San Francisco.* Paper presented at the Annual Meeting of the Gerontological Society of America, San Francisco.

Minkler, M. (1999). Intergenerational households headed by grandparents: Contexts, realities, and implications for policy. *Journal of Aging Studies, 13*(2), 199–218.

Minkler, M., Berrick, J. D., & Needell, B. (1999). The impacts of welfare reform on California grandparents raising grandchildren: Reflections from the field. *Journal of Aging and Social Policy, 10*(3), 45–63.

Minkler, M., & Fuller-Thomson, E. (1999a). The health of grandparents raising grandchildren: Results of a national study. *American Journal of Public Health, 89*, 1384–1389.

Minkler, M., & Fuller-Thomson, E. (1999b). Second time around parenting: Factors predictive of grandparents becoming caregivers for their grandchildren. *International Journal of Aging and Human Development, 50*, 185–198.

Minkler, M., Fuller-Thomson, E., Miller, D., & Driver, D. (1997). Depression in grandparents raising grandchildren. *Archives of Family Medicine, 6*, 445–452.

Minkler, M., & Roe, K. M. (1993). *Grandmothers as caregivers: Raising children of the crack cocaine epidemic*. Newbury Park, CA: Sage Publications.

Mullen, F. (1997, October). *Grandparents raising grandchildren: Public benefits and programs*. Paper presented at the Generations United, AARP symposium on grandparents and other relatives raising children, Washington, DC.

Ozawa, M. N. (1994). Women, children and welfare reform. *Affilia, 9*, 338–359.

Personal Responsibility and Work Opportunity Reconciliation Act, 1996, P.L. 104-193, 110 Stat. 2105.

Poe, L. M. (1992). *Black grandparents as parents*. Berkeley, CA: Author.

Radloff, L. S. (1977). The CES-D Scale: A self-report depression scale for research in the general population. *Applied Psychological Measurement, 1*, 385–401.

Saluter, A. F. (1992). Marital status and living arrangements: March 1991. *Current population reports* (Series P-20, No. 461). Washington, DC: U.S. Government Printing Office.

Sanders, C., Mauger, P., & Strong, P. (1985). *A manual for the Grief Experience Inventory*. Palo Alto, CA: Consulting Psychologists Press.

Scannapieco, M., & Jackson, S. (1996). Kinship care: The African American response to family preservation. *Social Work, 41*, 190–196.

Shore, R. J., & Hayslip, B. (1994). Custodial grandparenting: Implications for children's development. In A. E. Gottfried & A. W. Gottfried (Eds.). *Redefining families: Implications for children's development* (pp. 171–218). New York: Plenum Press.

Statistics Canada. (1996). N.P.H.S. public use microdata documentation. Ottawa, Canada: Author.

Strawbridge, W. J., Wallhagen, M. I., Shema, S. J., & Kaplan, G. A. (1997). New burdens or more of the same? Comparing grandparent, spouse and adult child caregivers. *Gerontologist, 37*, 505–510.

Sudarkasa, N. (1981). Interpreting the African heritage in Afro-American family organization. In H. P. McAdoo (Ed.), *Black families* (pp. 37–53). Beverly Hills, CA: Sage Publications.

Sweet, J., Bumpass, L., & Call, V. (1988). *The design and content of the National Survey of Families and Households* (NSFH Working Paper No. 1). University of Wisconsin—Madison, Center for Demography and Ecology.

Szinovacz, M. E. (1998). Grandparents today: A demographic profile. *Gerontologist, 38*, 37–52.

U.S. Department of Justice. (1997). *Prisoners in 1996* (Report No. NCJ164619). Washington, DC: Bureau of Justice Statistics.

Walker, R. J., & Pomeroy, E. C. (1996). Depression or grief: The experience of caregivers of people with dementia. *Health & Social Work, 21*, 247–254.

Wilson, M. N. (1989). Child development in the context of the black extended family. *American Psychologist, 44*, 380–385.

This chapter was originally published in the May 2000 issue of *Health & Social Work*, Vol. 25, Number 2, pp. 109–118.

# 21

# Custodial Grandparents in Latino Families

## Patterns of Service Use and Predictors of Unmet Needs

### DENISE BURNETTE

During the past quarter century, the number of children ages 18 and under who live in households headed by grandparents has increased by more than 50 percent, from 2.2 million in 1970 to 3.9 million in 1997 (Lugaila, 1998). Moreover, whereas the number of children living with grandparents with neither parent present increased by only 6 percent during this period, it nearly tripled from a half million in 1990 to 1.5 million in 1997 (Lugaila, 1998). A combination of social and health problems—for example, joblessness, child abuse and neglect, teenage pregnancy, HIV/AIDS, and particularly substance abuse—has contributed to this rapid growth of skipped-generation families.

At present, just over one in 10 grandparents in the United States assumes parental responsibility for a grandchild for at least a six-month period at some point in his, or more likely her, life (Fuller-Thomson, Minkler, & Driver, 1997). Custodial grandparents are from all racial and ethnic groups, socioeconomic levels, and geographic regions. Nationally, 68 percent are white, 29 percent are African American, 10 percent are Hispanic (of any race), 2 percent are Asian/Pacific Islander, and 1 percent are American Indian (Chalfie, 1994). However, African Americans were nearly twice as likely in 1991 to be grandparent caregivers as their white counterparts (9 percent compared with 5 percent), and more than 12 percent of African American children lived with grandparents, compared with 5.8 percent of Hispanic and 3.6 percent of white children (U.S. Bureau of the Census, 1991).

Previous studies of custodial grandparents either have focused on African Americans (Burton, 1992; Dressel & Barnhill, 1994; Minkler & Roe, 1993) or whites (Jendrek, 1994) or compared the two groups (Solomon & Marx, 1995). Studies by Joslin and Brouard (1995), Shore and Hayslip (1994), and Fuller-Thomson et al. (1997) included small numbers of Latinos but did not examine this group in analyses. However, Latino national origin groups are heavily concentrated in large cities (Chapa & Valencia, 1993), where the social and economic contexts of family life may result in more similar rates between Latino and African American households of skipped-generation families.

A recent study by the New York City Center for Policy on Aging reported comparable proportions of African American (6 percent) and Latino (4.4 percent) elderly people living in grandparent–grandchild-only households, compared with only 0.8 percent of same-aged whites (Cantor & Brennan, 1993). And Joslin and Brouard (1995) found similar rates of grandparent caregiving in predominantly African American Central Harlem (9.7 percent) and primarily Hispanic East Harlem (7.3 percent) in a random sample drawn from low-income pediatric clinics in New York City.

This article examines the self-identified needs, patterns of service use, and predictors of unmet needs among a sample of Latino grandparent caregivers in New York City. Referring to a long-standing debate in ger-

ontology about the relative importance of age versus need in policy formulation and service delivery for older adults (Neugarten, 1982), Dressel and Barnhill (1994) argued that the role-related needs of custodial grandparents often supersede age-related needs. Research on foster parents, especially kinship foster parents, provides helpful insights on these role-related needs. However, about two-thirds of relative-caregivers are grandparents, who tend to be older than either parents or foster parents (Chalfie, 1994; Harden, Clark, & Maguire, 1997), and a disproportionate number are poor women of color (Berrick, Barth, & Needell, 1994; Chalfie, 1994; LeProhn, 1994). Some needs and service use patterns thus are expected to be linked to chronological age and developmental life stage and to the effects of current and cumulative economic disadvantage.

## Literature Review

A full discussion of foster and kinship care is beyond the scope of this article; refer to Harden et al. (1997) and the entire volume of *Families in Society* ("Foster and Kinship Care," 1997) for recent reviews. Of relevance here is the level of support needed to fulfill the caregiver role. Two closely related events led to the designation and phenomenal growth of a kinship foster-parent status, with benefits on par with nonkin foster parents, in the child welfare system. The Supreme Court decision in *Miller v. Youakim* (1979) determined that relatives caring for Aid to Families with Dependent Children (AFDC) eligible children and whose homes met other state regulations were eligible for federal foster care benefits, and the Adoption Assistance and Child Welfare Act of 1980 (P.L. 96-272), passed the next year, called for placing children in the most "family-like setting" possible. The American Public Welfare Association estimated that 483,000 children were in substitute care at the end of 1995—a 75 percent increase since the end of 1985 (Tatara, 1995). About one-third of these children were wards of the state living in formal kinship foster care homes (Harden et al., 1997).

Research confirms that the needs and welfare of children in kinship foster care are indeed similar to those in foster care (Berrick et al., 1994; Dubowitz, Feigelman, & Zuravin, 1993). Moreover, a study at a private agency in Philadelphia found that needs of kinship families who remained outside the child welfare system were "strikingly similar" to the needs of those who moved into formal foster care (McLean & Thomas, 1996). Despite their similar needs, however, families with informal arrangements, who greatly outnumber those in formal care, function outside the purview of government policy and regulations with much lower levels of support. As a result, this group is expected to have a high level of unmet service needs. Only 6 percent of Latino grandparents in the present study were in the formal kinship foster care system.

What are the service needs across these different caregiver statuses? Studies of grandparent caregivers identified a range of needs (American Association of Retired Persons, 1995; Burnette, 1997; Burton, 1992; Minkler & Roe, 1993; Takas, 1993), many of which overlapped those of foster care providers (Administration on Children, Youth, and Families, 1989): financial support; parent skills training; preventive and restorative health and mental health services for children; training for care of children with special needs; knowledge of laws and regulations that govern placement; child care and respite for caregivers who work; skills to manage new family roles and relationships; support in individual and family crises; issues of visitation,

reunification, and permanency planning; and help coordinating services across multiple delivery systems. In addition, services to grandparent caregivers should be geared to the dynamics of kin placement and to salient life experiences, including age, life stage, and race and ethnicity. Latino grandparents share many of the life circumstances and needs of other custodial grandparents of color, including reasons for child rearing, stage of individual and family development, norms of intergenerational shared child rearing, late life physical and emotional problems, family conflict, and low financial resources, as well as potential health and psychological benefits of child rearing (Burton, 1992; Minkler & Roe, 1993). On the other hand, language, ethnic values and identity, and immigrant and acculturation status, although they confer special strengths in many arenas, create unique needs and barriers to access and use of health and social services for Latino grandparents (Zambrana, 1995).

For example, nonwhite elderly people from ethnic minority groups tend persistently to underuse formal services for which they are eligible to meet health and social services needs (Angel & Angel, 1992; Krause & Goldenhar, 1992). This pattern appears to result from a combination of personal, social, cultural, structural, and environmental factors. Multivariate models examining predictors of and barriers to service use among older adults report that need for services explains most of the variance in use and that enabling factors such as education, income, and social supports may facilitate use (Coulton & Frost, 1982; Nelson, 1993; Wallace, Campbell, & Lew-Ting, 1994). Another strong predictor of use is knowledge of services (Starrett, Bresler, Decker, Walters, & Rogers, 1990), which tends to be greater in high-density ethnic areas (Holmes,

Holmes, Steinbach, Hausner, & Rocheleau, 1979). And although acculturation may not play a key role in these locales, low English proficiency tends to impede knowledge and access (Krause & Goldenhar, 1992). Finally, the relative effect of specific predictors on service use by older Latinos also varies by national origin group (Burnette & Mui, 1995; Starrett, Wright, Mindel, & Tran, 1989).

## Method

### Sample

Data for this study are from a purposive sample of 74 middle-aged and older Latinos in New York City who were primary caregivers of their grandchildren or great-grandchildren. The inclusion criteria were self-identification as member of a Latino ethnic group, age 50 or older, and an extended family member with major or sole responsibility for at least one related minor child (one godchild was also named). Other people could live in the household, but the respondent had to identify him- or herself as the primary caregiver. Recruitment was targeted in geographic areas and health and social services agencies with high proportions of Latino residents and clients. Posters were widely distributed to child welfare, aging, and family services agencies; schools; churches; pediatric and geriatric clinics; housing projects; and senior and community centers. Several key leaders in the Latino community publicly endorsed the study, encouraging recruitment and participation. Finally, booths in neighborhood street fairs were used, along with agency open houses and public service announcements and interviews on Spanish language radio programs to advertise the study.

### Data Collection and Instruments

*Interviewers.* Six bilingual, bicultural interviewers were trained in the purpose and pro-

cedures of the study (Tom-Orme, 1991). Five were social workers, and the other was a sociology graduate student. Four were Puerto Rican, one Colombian, and one Costa Rican. Four were women. All interviewers had experience working with older Latinos, and when possible, they were matched to respondents on the basis of language (Cardenas & Arce, 1982), gender (Markides, Liang, & Jackson, 1990), and national origin. Face-to-face interviews lasted one to two hours, and most (88 percent) were conducted in Spanish in the grandparents' homes. Grandparents received $20 for participation, which clearly served as an incentive, and an opportunity to get information on resources and services. The commitment and skill of the interviewers in obtaining and completing interviews and ensuring high-quality data were essential, particularly given the sensitive nature of many of the questions.

*Translation.* Noting that direct translations of measures may not be culturally or linguistically appropriate for low-income, ethnic-minority populations, Zambrana (1991) recommended that bilingual people of the same ethnic origin as the study population who are experienced in the community translate and review the instrument to ensure correct colloquial words, symbolic meaning, and word structure. This method offers a viable alternative to direct back translation, which, according to Zambrana, makes unwarranted assumptions that threaten the validity of data.

Thus, the data collection instrument was first translated by an experienced Latina translator. An interviewer who had also worked as a translator and had extensive social work experience with low-income Latinos then scrutinized each question closely. Several items were revised as a result, and further adjustments were made on the basis of three pretest interviews. Finally, each completed interview schedule was evaluated for possible problems in interpretation or understanding.

*Measures.* Data were collected on socio-demographic characteristics, household income, acculturation, health and mental health status, life stressors, household composition, informal social supports, knowledge, need for and use of formal services, current circumstances and contact with grandchildren's parents, and personal concerns for oneself and family. Several items were drawn from studies of African American grandparent caregivers by Burton (1992) and Minkler and Roe (1993). Variables used in the present analysis were operationalized as discussed in the following paragraphs.

### Dependent Variable

A list of 16 health and social services spanning income maintenance, child welfare, aging, and family services systems was compiled. Following the protocol of the *1988 Survey of Hispanic Elderly People*, respondents were asked whether they had used each service during the preceding year and whether they presently needed the service. A measure of "unmet needs" was then calculated for each service (have not used service but need it = 1) and these values were summed to create a composite measure of unmet needs. Because of skewness, the variable was dichotomized (at least one unmet need = 1) in the multivariate model. A measure of unmet needs was used rather than "use versus nonuse," because all but one grandparent had used at least one service. This is not surprising given the extent of their needs and the breadth of services examined. "Number of services used" also was deemed an unsuitable outcome, because providers and insurance policies exercise increasing control over services, and it was unclear how well this measure captures the adequacy of services for meeting needs (Wallace et al., 1994).

### Independent Variables

*Economic Status.* Poverty status was used rather than annual household income, because income is an eligibility criterion for some services (Wallace et al., 1994), and this measure was also skewed. Poverty status (poverty, near poverty at or below 125 percent of poverty, and extreme poverty at or below 75 percent of poverty) was determined by adjusting income for household size using estimates of national poverty thresholds for February 1996 (U.S. Bureau of the Census, 1995).

*Health Status.* Self-rated health status was assessed on a Likert-type scale as excellent = 1, good = 2, fair = 3, and poor = 4. It was then recoded to excellent or good = 1 and fair or poor = 0, because 70 percent of respondents rated their health as either fair or poor.

*Life Stressors.* Eleven stressful life events were scored dichotomously (experienced during past year = 1), then summed: death of spouse, close family member, or close friend; change in marital, health, or financial status; change in where you live or household composition; illness of household member; self or spouse retired; and family discord (range = 0 to 8, $M = 2.36$, $SD = 1.70$).

*Informal Supports.* A full household enumeration was obtained by asking how many of the following currently lived with respondent: spouse, parents (in-law), daughters (in-law), sons (in-law), sisters (in-law), brothers (in-law), other relatives, friends, and unrelated adults. Sixty-eight percent of households were two-generational, consisting of grandchildren plus grandparents, and nearly half (46 percent) of these households included only one grandparent.

Methodological literature on social support underscores the need to establish dimensions of this structurally complex and functionally specific construct in different populations and contexts. A principal components analysis with varimax rotation was used to explore the factor structure of seven informal support measures. The analysis yielded a three-factor solution (eigenvalues > 1.0) accounting for 66.5 percent of the variance: (1) size of family network (number of children and grandchildren in New York City area and number of people in household), (2) availability and reliability of help with child care (current help with child rearing available and will be available indefinitely), and (3) socialization (has a confidante and visits with family and friends four or more times per week, in person or by telephone).

*Language Acculturation.* Language acculturation was assessed with a 12-item scale from the San Luis Valley Hispanic Health and Aging Study (Baxter, Hoag, & Hamman, 1994). Items included self-assessed ability to speak, read, write, and understand English and Spanish (well = 1, fair = 2, poorly/not at all = 3) and language spoken in four social contexts (family, friends, neighbors, work) (mostly/only English = 1, Spanish and English equally = 2, mostly/only Spanish = 3) ($\alpha$ = .87; $M$ = 17.9, $SD$ = 5.5). Control variables were age (60+ = 1, because 60 determines eligibility for most services authorized by the Older Americans Act of 1965 [P.L. 89-73]), educational attainment, and number of services used. As expected, educational attainment and acculturation were highly correlated ($r$ = .43, $p$ < .001), and only educational level was retained in the model (Krause & Goldenhar, 1992). Finally, although Puerto Ricans had lived in the United States longer than Dominicans and had higher levels of education [$t(63)$ = 2.18, $p$ <.05] and language acculturation [$t(60)$ = 6.39, $p$ < .001], these two main groups did not differ otherwise, and national origin was not included in the model.

### Logistic Regression Analysis

Logistic regression was used because the dependent variable was dichotomous and had a skewed distribution. At least 10 cases were needed per independent variable in the logistic model (Concato, Feinstein, & Holford, 1993), and statistical power was adequate (Borenstein & Cohen, 1988). With seven variables in the regression model, a medium effect size of .15 to be detected, and a .10 probability level (because of a relatively small sample and the exploratory nature of the study), a sample size of 72 yielded statistical tests with a power level of .80. Two cases were dropped because of missing data. A correlation matrix of independent variables showed values ranging from .01 to .30 with most less than .15, suggesting that multicollinearity was not a problem (Berry & Feldman, 1990).

The logistic coefficients indicate the direction and magnitude of an independent variable's association with an outcome measure. They are interpreted as in ordinary least-squares regression, with parameter estimates indicating the change in log odds of being in a category with a unit change in the independent variable, while controlling for the effects of other variables in the model. The probability of having an unmet need was estimated by calculating the odds ratio through the antilogs of the parameter estimate of each independent variable, giving a further interpretation of relative effect. Thus, an odds ratio of 1.58 means that a respondent was 58 percent more likely to have an unmet need than not, whereas an odds ratio of .30 would indicate a 70 percent less likelihood.

### Results

#### Respondent Characteristics

Ages ranged from 50 to 78, with a mean of 63—22 percent of grandparents were age 70 or older. Nearly all were women, and most were from Puerto Rico or the Dominican Republic. The balance were from Cuba, Ec-

**TABLE 21-1. Sociodemographic Characteristics (*N* = 74)**

|  | n | % | M | SD |
|---|---|---|---|---|
| Age |  |  | 63.1 | 7.0 |
| Years in United States |  |  | 35.1 | 13.6 |
| Gender |  |  |  |  |
| Female | 69 | 93.2 |  |  |
| Male | 5 | 6.8 |  |  |
| National origin |  |  |  |  |
| Puerto Rican | 44 | 59.5 |  |  |
| Dominican | 21 | 28.4 |  |  |
| Other Latin American | 9 | 12.2 |  |  |
| Marital status |  |  |  |  |
| Never married | 5 | 6.8 |  |  |
| Married | 16 | 21.6 |  |  |
| Widowed | 18 | 24.3 |  |  |
| Divorced/separated | 35 | 47.3 |  |  |
| Education |  |  |  |  |
| No formal education | 5 | 6.8 |  |  |
| 1st–4th grade | 14 | 18.9 |  |  |
| 5th–7th grade | 16 | 21.6 |  |  |
| 8th grade/some high school | 19 | 25.7 |  |  |
| High school graduate | 10 | 13.5 |  |  |
| Some college/graduate | 10 | 13.5 |  |  |
| Annual household income ($) |  |  |  |  |
| Under 7,500 | 40 | 54.1 |  |  |
| 7,500–10,499 | 11 | 14.9 |  |  |
| 10,500–13,499 | 11 | 14.9 |  |  |
| 13,500–16,499 | 2 | 2.7 |  |  |
| 16,500–19,499 | 5 | 6.8 |  |  |
| 19,500 and over | 5 | 6.8 |  |  |
| Adjusted poverty level |  |  |  |  |
| Below 75% poverty threshold | 54 | 73.0 |  |  |
| Below 100% poverty threshold | 60 | 81.1 |  |  |
| Below 125% poverty threshold | 69 | 93.2 |  |  |

uador, Guatemala, Honduras, Nicaragua, or Panama. Respondents had been in the United States on average 35 years (*SD* = 13.6) (Table 21-1), yet fewer than one in five reported speaking English well (not shown in table).

Study participants had very low levels of formal education and household income. Fewer than one in three had graduated high school, and 93 percent were poor or near poor by federal poverty standards. Indeed, using adjusted household income, 81 percent lived in households with incomes below the poverty line, and almost three-quarters lived in extreme poverty (Table 21-1).

Grandparents were rearing on average two children (ranging from 1 to 5) whose ages ranged from 4 months to 18 years (*M* = 9.8, *SD* = 4.4) (not shown in table). Half the 150 children in the 74 families came into grandparent care at or within one year of birth. About one-third of care arrangements were informal, 56 percent involved legal guardianship or legal custody, and 6 percent were enrolled in the kinship foster care program.

## Patterns of Service Use

Financial support for basic needs, including Aid to Families with Dependent Children

(AFDC) and child nutrition programs, were the most widely used services for children. More than half the grandparents had obtained counseling for a grandchild, one-third had used health services for a grandchild's special (nonroutine) health needs, and 27 percent had used special education. Fifteen percent of grandparents in the study had participated in parent education, and one in four had received education about substance abuse or HIV/AIDS. Forty-one percent had sought legal assistance with issues such as custody and visitation (Table 21-2).

The most frequently used aging service was health care, which often serves as an entry point into the services delivery system— 85 percent of grandparents reported help with a physical ailment. Nearly half had participated in individual counseling, 42 percent had attended a grandparent support group, and 10 percent had used marital or family counseling. The relatively high use of support groups no doubt reflects the fact that 27 grandparents were recruited from these groups, although 15 of these recruits were identified for the study and for a new support group simultaneously.

Grandparents had used an average of six services each, yet 80 percent still reported at least one unmet need ($M = 3.0$, $SD = 2.6$). Most unmet needs were for information and support services, including toll-free hot lines, support groups, respite child care, parent education, and legal help. When queried about unmet needs not listed, grandparents named decent, affordable housing most often, followed by cash and in-kind financial assistance (especially food stamps and Medicaid), child care, neighborhood safety, camps and enrichment programs for children and youths, rehabilitation for adult children, and translation services. Several identified pressing needs for items such as food, clothing, infant formula, and diapers. The most frequently named barrier to service use was lack

of knowledge about available services. Other major obstacles were ineligibility, unaffordability, and language and cultural barriers.

The multivariate model of predictors of unmet need are presented [model $\chi^2(7, N = 72) = 19.4$, $p < .01$]. Seven independent variables, selected from the literature review and bivariate analyses, were entered into the model (Hosmer & Lemeshow, 1989). Educational attainment, self-rated health status, life stressors, and reliable support with child rearing were significant predictors of unmet need. Grandparents who reported greater life stress during the preceding year were 77 percent more likely and those in excellent or good health were 77 percent less likely to identify unmet needs. Similarly, grandparents who had more education and those with child-related supports were 74 percent and 72 percent less likely, respectively, to have unmet needs (Table 21-3).

## Discussion

As the number of grandparent-maintained families increases, social workers in aging, child welfare, and family services, as well as those working in a wide range of substantive areas, are likely to encounter grandparent caregivers and their families. Empirical data on the needs of these families, many of whom experience myriad long-term problems that often predate the onset of caregiving (Fuller-Thomson et al., 1997; Strawbridge, Wallhagen, Shema, & Kaplan, 1997) are limited. So, too, is knowledge about the availability, physical and cultural accessibility, and adequacy of available services to meet these needs. This article has examined formal services use and predictors of unmet services needs in a nonprobability sample of 74 Latino grandparent caregivers in New York City. Findings suggest several important points for assessment and intervention with these caregivers, and to the extent that their role-

**TABLE 21-2. Patterns and Barriers to Service Use**

| | Used Services | | Unmet Need for Service | | Reasons for Unmet Need (listed in tied/descending order of frequency) |
|---|---|---|---|---|---|
| | n | % | n | % | |
| Child special health need | 24 | 32.4 | 3 | 4.1 | Did not know of service<br>Could not afford service<br>Not eligible for service |
| Special education/tutoring | 20 | 27.0 | 9 | 12.2 | No openings—wait listed<br>Grandchild resistant<br>Could not afford service |
| Counseling for grandchild | 39 | 52.7 | 6 | 8.1 | Did not know of service<br>Grandchild resistant<br>No openings—wait listed<br>Language/culture barrier<br>Child too young |
| Legal assistance | 30 | 40.5 | 19 | 25.7 | Did not know of service<br>Not to traumatize family<br>Could not afford service |
| Health service for grandparent | 63 | 85.1 | — | — | Did not know of service<br>Could not afford service<br>Language/culture barrier |
| Counseling for grandparent | 34 | 45.9 | 9 | 12.2 | Did not know of service<br>Language/culture barrier<br>No child care |
| Marital/family counseling | 7 | 9.5 | 10 | 13.5 | Language/culture barrier<br>Did not know of service<br>Could not afford service<br>No child care<br>Family resistant |
| Grandparent support group | 31 | 41.9 | 29 | 39.2 | Did not know of service<br>No transportation<br>Language/culture barrier<br>Not enough time |
| Respite child care services | 4 | 5.4 | 24 | 32.4 | Did not know of service<br>Could not afford service<br>Not eligible for service<br>Not trust strangers |
| Parent education/parent skills training | 11 | 14.9 | 24 | 32.4 | Did not know of service<br>Language/culture barrier<br>No transportation<br>Not enough time |
| AFDC | 53 | 71.6 | 8 | 10.8 | Did not know of service<br>Not eligible for service |
| Foster care services | 5 | 6.8 | 4 | 5.4 | Did not know of service<br>Language/culture barrier |
| Nutrition (school lunch, WIC, food stamps) | 61 | 82.4 | 10 | 13.5 | Did not know of service<br>Not eligible for service<br>Culture (food preference)<br>Not applied but intend to |
| Homemaker services | 11 | 14.9 | 18 | 24.3 | Did not know of service<br>Not eligible for service<br>Trouble scheduling |
| Toll-free hot line | 3 | 4.1 | 35 | 47.3 | Did not know of service<br>Ashamed/embarrassed |
| Drug/AIDS education | 20 | 27.0 | 15 | 20.3 | Did not know of service<br>Ashamed/embarrassed<br>Not interested/afraid<br>Not enough time |

*Note:* — = not available.
Number of services used: $M = 5.6$, $SD = 2.3$.
Number of grandparents with one or more unmet needs: $n = 59$ (79.7 percent).
Number of unmet needs: $M = 3.0$, $SD = 2.6$.

TABLE 21-3. Logistic Regression of Unmet Service Need

| Variable | $\beta$ | SE | Odds Ratio | 90% CI |
|---|---|---|---|---|
| Age (60+ = 1) | .24 | .80 | 1.27 | −1.07, 1.56 |
| Education | −.32 | .19 | .26* | −.63, .01 |
| Poverty (yes = 1) | −.49 | .96 | .61 | −2.07, 1.1 |
| Health (excellent/good = 1) | −1.46 | .81 | .23* | −2.78, −.12 |
| Life stressors | .57 | .30 | 1.77** | .10, 1.06 |
| Child-related support | −1.26 | .71 | .28* | −2.44, −.09 |
| Number of services used | .03 | .18 | 1.03 | −.27, .33 |

Intercept = 4.24 ($SE$ = 2.5); Model $\chi^2$(7, $N$ = 72) = 19.4, $p$ = .006.
*$p$ < .10. **$p$ < .05.

based needs overlap with those of similarly situated grandparents in other racial or ethnic groups, findings may also be more generally relevant.

The exploratory nature of the study, which is a first investigation of this population, and the lack of a viable sampling frame for random selection dictated the choice of a purposive sample. Research scholars of ethnic aging have discussed methodological problems inherent in sampling rare populations like ethnic minority groups and elderly people, where sampling errors result from both nonrandom strategies and insufficient sample sizes (Jackson, 1989; Kalton & Anderson, 1989). A further problem with this study population is that grandparent caregiver status must be inferred, usually from living arrangements in public data sources such as the *Current Population Survey*. Although these sources are suitable for secondary analysis, they often lack the variables of interest to a researcher.

Studies of small or geographically isolated groups require special sampling designs (La Veist, 1995). Markides et al. (1990) suggested several alternative strategies—for example, random sampling from households in high-density ethnic group locales, which ensures the inclusion of group members that represent significant sources of variation, for example, social class, national origin, and time in the United States. As Chapa and Valencia (1993) pointed out, the geographic scope and focus of research on Latinos may be appropriately limited to states, cities, or other locales with high concentrations of Latinos or specific national origin groups. Use of sampling strategies such as these would yield more representative samples in future studies.

The selection strategy used in the present study probably resulted in a sample of grandparents who are relatively "better off" than those not connected with the formal service system. Most participants were unmarried Puerto Rican and Dominican women in their early 60s with very low levels of educational attainment and household income. They appeared to fare worse than their counterparts in studies of custodial grandparents in other racial or ethnic groups on these factors. The 27 percent high school completion rate in this study compares with 57 percent in a national sample (Fuller-Thomson et al., 1997) and 40 percent and 47 percent in purposive samples of African American grandparents in studies by Minkler and Roe (1993) and Burton (1992), respectively. Even more troubling is the 81 percent poverty rate, which compares to national estimates of 20 percent (Fuller-Thomson et al., 1997), 27 percent (Chalfie, 1994), and 30 percent (Solomon & Marx, 1995).

The only significant sociodemographic predictor of unmet need was level of education. Previous studies of older Latinos indicated that education may operate through illiteracy and low English proficiency (Krause & Goldenhar, 1992; Wallace et al., 1994). Greater attention to adult literacy programs, English language classes, and bilingual workers could help diminish unmet needs that stem from this barrier. Family income and poverty status also usually are associated with service use by older Latinos. Neither influenced the likelihood of unmet needs in this study, probably because income levels were so uniformly low. The extreme level of poverty among these families has profound implications for the well-being of each generation in the family and raises timely policy issues.

Analyzing the likely impact of welfare reform on New York City's elderly people, Busch (1997) predicted three groups will be most adversely affected by the Personal Responsibility and Work Opportunity Reconciliation Act of 1996 (P.L. 104-193)—elderly immigrants, grandparents raising grandchildren, and older adults who contribute to and depend on pooled resources in multigenerational households. Latino grandparent caregivers are especially vulnerable to the dictates of this legislation, and aggressive monitoring and advocacy for this population are needed as these policies are implemented and evaluated.

Closer inspection of services used and reasons for nonuse also provide information for targeted planning, programming, and policy. Study participants appeared to have greater access to and fewer unmet needs for child-related services such as health, education, and counseling, presumably because information on these services was more readily available through familiar community institutions such as schools and clinics. In keeping with

Dressel and Barnhill's (1994) argument that custodial grandparents' needs may be more role than age related, most unmet needs in this study were for information and support services related to child rearing, for example, support groups, respite child care, and parent education. Interestingly, the need for a Spanish-speaking toll-free hot line was named most often. Mutual aid and support groups for grandparent caregivers have proliferated nationwide (AARP, 1994), and telephone groups or "buddies" may be another venue to meet the information and socialization needs of grandparents who cannot attend groups.

Other significant variables in the multivariate model also provide directions for practice. Stressful life events had the strongest effect on unmet needs. Most events that study participants reported were related to loss, and strategies for assessment and intervention with grandparent caregivers should consider the high likelihood of multiple, serious losses. Another important type of life stress not explored in this or other studies of custodial grandparenting to date, but deserving of increased attention, is the daily hassles associated with child care, especially under strained conditions (Kanner, Coyne, Schaefer, & Lazarus, 1981).

Consistent with previous studies of Latino elders, poor health was another significant predictor of unmet needs. Although most grandparents had used health services, they had multiple chronic conditions that seemed to require ongoing medical attention. Social workers can improve access to health services by decreasing barriers such as inadequate income and insurance; promoting individual and programmatic sensitivity to cultural norms, customs, and beliefs (De La Rosa, 1989); and maximizing the influence of lay referral structures to promote the use of professional services by elderly people of color

(Birkle & Reppucci, 1983). Another crucial aspect of health status that studies of grandparent caregivers have not yet addressed, but that has major implications for current and ongoing caregiving capacity, is functional status.

Of the three informal support factors identified in these data, only availability of reliable help with child rearing activities, a type of role-specific, instrumental support, was associated with lower levels of unmet need. As noted earlier, social support is a multidimensional concept that is most appropriately assessed in the context of need (Lubben & Gironda, 1996). Thus, the specificity of this finding is not surprising and suggests that practitioners' efforts to bolster support networks might well be targeted to services in this area.

Finally, the main obstacle to service use was lack of knowledge about available services. Knowledge is the single most mutable factor for increasing service use; improving general knowledge about services while targeting outreach to people with the greatest needs also can compensate for some of the structural barriers to use. Services for skipped-generation families are spread over a vast, uncoordinated system of aging, child welfare, family, health care, and income maintenance services, with different eligibility criteria and variable entry points. Targeting and coordinating efforts in local communities could help reduce obstacles such as lack of child care, transportation, and language differences and better enable Latino grandparents engaged in the challenging long-term care of their grandchildren to participate in and use their own natural support systems (Delgado & Humm-Delgado, 1982).

## References

Administration on Children, Youth, and Families. (1989). *The national survey of current and former foster parents* (DHHS 105-89-1602). Washington, DC: Author.

Adoption Assistance and Child Welfare Act of 1980, P.L. 96-272, 94 Stat. 500.

American Association of Retired Persons. (1994, Winter). *The AARP Grandparent Information Center Newsletter, 1*(1). Washington, DC: Author.

American Association of Retired Persons. (1995). *Grandparents as caregivers: Options for improving access to federal public benefit programs*. Washington, DC: Author.

Angel, J., & Angel, R. J. (1992). Age at immigration, social connections, and well-being among elderly Hispanics. *Journal of Aging and Health, 4*, 480–499.

Baxter, J., Hoag, S., & Hamman, R. F. (1994, November 19). *Social networks of rural, elderly Hispanic and non-Hispanic white persons. The San Luis Valley Hispanic Health and Aging Study*. Paper presented at the 47th Annual Scientific Meeting of the Gerontological Society of America, Atlanta.

Berrick, J. D., Barth, R. P., & Needell, B. (1994). A comparison of kinship foster homes and family foster homes: Implications for kinship foster care as family preservation. *Children and Youth Services Review, 16* (1/2), 35–63.

Berry, W., & Feldman, S. (1990). *Multiple regression in practice*. Newbury Park, CA: Sage Publications.

Birkle, R. C., & Reppucci, N. D. (1983). Social networks, information-seeking, and the utilization of services. *American Journal of Community Psychology, 11*(2), 185–205.

Borenstein, M., & Cohen, J. (1988). *Statistical power analysis: A computer program*. Hillsdale, NJ: Lawrence Erlbaum.

Burnette, D. (1997). Grandparents raising grandchildren in the inner city. *Families in Society, 78*, 489–499.

Burnette, D., & Mui, A. C. (1995). In-home and community-based service use by three groups of elderly Hispanics: A national perspective. *Social Work Research, 19,* 197–206.

Burton, L. M. (1992). Black grandparents rearing grandchildren of drug-addicted parents: Stressors, outcomes and social service needs. *Gerontologist, 32,* 744–751.

Busch, A. (1997). *The impact of welfare reform on the elderly of New York City.* New York: Council of Senior Centers and Services of New York City, Inc.

Cantor, M., & Brennan, M. (1993). *Growing older in New York City in the 1990s* (Vol. 2). New York: New York City Center for Policy on Aging of the New York Community Trust.

Cardenas, G., & Arce, C. (1982). The National Chicano Survey: Recruiting bilingual interviewers. In W. T. Liu (Ed.), *Methodological problems in minority research* (pp. 41–59). Chicago: Pacific/Asian American Mental Health Research Center.

Chalfie, D. (1994). *Going it alone: A closer look at grandparents parenting grandchildren.* Washington, DC: American Association of Retired Persons.

Chapa, J., & Valencia, R. R. (1993). Latino population growth, demographic characteristics, and educational stagnation: An examination of recent trends. *Hispanic Journal of Behavioral Sciences, 15,* 165–187.

Concato, J., Feinstein, A. R., & Holford, T. R. (1993). The risk of determining risk with multivariate models. *Annals of Internal Medicine, 118,* 201–210.

Coulton, C., & Frost, A. K. (1982). Use of social and health services by the elderly. *Journal of Health and Social Behavior, 23,* 330–339.

De La Rosa, M. (1989). Health care needs of Hispanic Americans and the responsiveness of the health care system. *Health & Social Work, 14,* 104–113.

Delgado, M., & Humm-Delgado, D. (1982). Natural support systems: Source of strength in Hispanic communities. *Social Work, 27,* 83–89.

Dressel, P. L., & Barnhill, S. K. (1994). Reframing gerontological thought and practice: The case of grandmothers with daughters in prison. *Gerontologist, 34,* 685–691.

Dubowitz, H., Feigelman, S., & Zuravin, S. (1993). A profile of kinship care. *Child Welfare, 72,* 153–169.

Foster and kinship care: A special focus. (1997). *Families in Society* (Special issue), *78*(5).

Fuller-Thomson, E., Minkler, M., & Driver, D. (1997). A profile of grandparents raising grandchildren in the United States. *Gerontologist, 37,* 406–411.

Harden, A. W., Clark, R., & Maguire, K. (1997). *Informal and formal kinship care* (Report for the Office of the Assistant Secretary for Planning and Evaluation, Task Order HHS-100-95-0021). Washington, DC: U.S. Department of Health and Human Services.

Holmes, D., Holmes, M., Steinbach, L., Hausner, T., & Rocheleau, B. (1979). Use of community-based services in long-term care of older minority persons. *Gerontologist, 19,* 389–397.

Hosmer, D., & Lemeshow, S. (1989). *Applied logistic regression.* New York: John Wiley & Sons.

Jackson, J. S. (1989). Methodological issues in survey research on older minority adults. In M. P. Lawton & A. R. Herzog (Eds.), *Special research methods for gerontology* (pp. 137–161). Amityville, NY: Baywood.

Jendrek, M. P. (1994). Grandparents who parent their grandchildren: Circumstances and decisions. *Gerontologist, 34,* 206–216.

Joslin, D., & Brouard, A. (1995). The prevalence of grandmothers as primary caregivers in a poor pediatric population. *Journal of Community Health, 20,* 383–401.

Kalton, G., & Anderson, D. (1989). Sampling rare populations. In M. P. Lawton & A. R. Herzog (Eds.), *Special research methods for gerontology* (pp. 7–30). Amityville, NY: Baywood.

Kanner, A. D., Coyne, J. C., Schaefer, C., & Lazarus, R. (1981). Comparison of two modes of stress assessment: Daily hassles and uplifts versus major life events. *Journal of Behavioral Medicine, 4*, 1–39.

Krause, N., & Goldenhar, L. M. (1992). Acculturation and psychological distress in three groups of elderly Hispanics. *Journal of Gerontology, 47*, S279–S288.

LaVeist, T. A. (1995). Data sources for aging research on racial and ethnic groups. *Gerontologist, 35*, 328–339.

LeProhn, N. S. (1994). The role of kinship foster parent: A comparison of relative and non-relative foster parents. *Children and Youth Services Review, 16*(1/2), 65–84.

Lubben, J., & Gironda, M. (1996). Assessing social support networks among older people in the United States. In H. Litwin (Ed.), *The social networks of older people: A cross-national analysis* (pp. 143–161). Westport, CT: Praeger.

Lugaila, T. (1998). *Marital status and living arrangements: March 1997* (Current Population Report Series, P20-506). Suitland, MD: U.S. Bureau of the Census.

Markides, K. S., Liang, J., & Jackson, J. S. (1990). Race, ethnicity, and aging: Conceptual and methodological issues. In R. Binstock & L. George (Eds.), *Handbook on aging and the social sciences* (3rd ed., pp. 112–129). San Diego: Academic Press.

McLean, B., & Thomas, R. (1996). Informal and formal kinship care populations: A study in contrasts. *Child Welfare* (Special issue), 75, 489–505.

*Miller v. Youakim*, 440 U.S. 125 (1979).

Minkler, M., & Roe, K. M. (1993). *Forgotten caregivers: Grandmothers raising children of the crack cocaine epidemic.* Newbury Park, CA: Sage Publications.

Nelson, M. (1993). Race, gender, and the effect of social supports on the use of health services by elderly individuals. *International Journal of Aging and Human Development, 37*, 227–246.

Neugarten, B. (Ed.). (1982). *Age or need? Public policies for older people.* Beverly Hills, CA: Sage Publications.

Older Americans Act of 1965, P.L. 89-73, 79 Stat. 218, 42 USC §§ 3001 et seq.

Personal Responsibility and Work Opportunity Reconciliation Act of 1996, P.L. 104-193, 110 Stat. 2105.

Shore, R. J., & Hayslip, B., Jr. (1994). Custodial grandparenting: Implications for children's development. In A. E. Gottfried & A. W. Gottfried (Eds.), *Redefining families: Implications for children's development* (pp. 171–218). New York: Plenum Press.

Solomon, J. C., & Marx, J. (1995). To grandmother's house we go: Health and school adjustments of children raised solely by grandparents. *Gerontologist, 35*, 386–394.

Starrett, R. A., Bresler, C., Decker, J. T., Walters, G. T., & Rogers, D. (1990). The role of environmental awareness and support networks in Hispanic elderly persons' use of formal social services. *Journal of Community Psychology, 18*, 218–227.

Starrett, R. A., Wright, R., Mindel, C. H., & Tran, T. V. (1989). The use of social services by Hispanic elderly: A comparison of Mexican American, Puerto Rican, and Cuban elderly. *Journal of Social Service Research, 13*(1), 1–25.

Strawbridge, W. J., Wallhagen, M. I., Shema, S. J., & Kaplan, G. A. (1997). New burdens or more of the same? Comparing grandparent, spouse, and adult child caregivers. *Gerontologist, 37*, 505–510.

Takas, M. (1993). *Kinship care and family preservation: A guide for states in legal and policy development.* Washington, DC: American Bar Association, Center on Children and the Law.

Tatara, T. (1995, March). U.S. child substitute care flow data and the race/ethnicity of children in care for FY 1993, along with recent trends in the U.S. child substitute care populations. In *VCIS Research Notes, 113.* Washington, DC: American Public Welfare Association.

Tom-Orme, L. (1991). The search for insider–outsider partnerships in research. In M. L. Grady (Ed.), *Primary care research: Theory and methods* (DHHS, AHCPR Pub. No. 91-0011, pp. 229–233). Rockville, MD: U.S. Department of Health and Human Services.

U.S. Bureau of the Census. (1991). *Current population reports: Marital status and living arrangements: March 1990* (Series P-20, No. 450). Washington, DC: U.S. Government Printing Office.

U.S. Bureau of the Census. (1995). *Money income and poverty status of families and persons in the United States.* Washington, DC: U.S. Department of Commerce.

Wallace, S. P., Campbell, K., & Lew-Ting, C. Y. (1994). Structural barriers to the use of formal in-home services by elderly Latinos. *Journal of Gerontology, 49,* S253–S263.

Zambrana, R. E. (1991). Cross-cultural methodological strategies in the study of low-income racial ethnic populations. In M. L. Grady (Ed.), *Primary care research: Theory and methods* (DHHS, Public Health Service, AHCPR Pub. No. 91-0011, pp. 221–227). Rockville, MD: U.S. Department of Health and Human Services.

Zambrana, R. (Ed.). (1995). *Understanding Latino families.* Thousand Oaks, CA: Sage Publications.

This chapter was originally published in the January 1999 issue of *Social Work*, Vol. 44, Number 1, pp. 22–34.

# 22

# HIV-Related Stigma in a Sample of HIV-Affected Older Female African American Caregivers

CYNTHIA CANNON POINDEXTER
and NATHAN L. LINSK

People who have HIV disease (refers to the trajectory of the illness that is caused by the retrovirus, whether symptomatic or asymptomatic; symptomatic, or end-stage HIV disease, often is referred to as AIDS) tend to experience a series of unpredictable medical, emotional, and social crises (Poindexter, 1997a); therefore, the trajectory of HIV-affected caregiving also is uncertain and often anxiety provoking (Brown & Powell-Cope, 1991, 1993; Cates, Graham, Boeglin, & Tielker, 1990; Jankowski, Videka-Sherman, & Laquidara-Dickinson, 1996; Land, 1996; Lego, 1994; Lesar, Gerber, & Semmel, 1995). HIV caregiving is an especially salient issue for communities of color, women, and older people for the following reasons. HIV disease has affected children, youths, and adults in racial and ethnic minority groups disproportionately (Anderson, 1990; Brown, Mitchell, & Williams, 1992; Duh, 1991; Jenkins, 1992; Magana & Magana, 1992; Michaels & Levine, 1992, 1993; Thomas & Quinn, 1994). Therefore, when HIV-infected family members return home in the final stages of the disease, or when children who are orphaned by HIV disease need parenting, the older people who become caregivers are likely to be members of an ethnic minority group (Joslin, 1995; Lloyd, 1989). Second, as is the case with informal caregiving in general, caregivers for individuals with HIV are predominately women (Ogu & Wolfe, 1994). Third, many family caregivers to children, youths, and adults with HIV disease are older people, who may be especially unprepared for the burdens of providing care within the context of a highly stigmatized illness (Allers, 1990; Levine, 1993; Linsk, 1994; Muschkin & Ellis, 1993; Ory & Zablotsky, 1993). Older women of color as informal caregivers also face the multiple jeopardies of race or ethnicity, poverty, socioeconomic status, age, and gender (Minkler & Stone, 1985; Okazawa-Rey, 1994), in addition to the difficulties of HIV-related care.

Because HIV-affected older caregivers are understood insufficiently by researchers (Brabant, 1994) and by service providers and advocates in the fields of aging and HIV (Linsk, 1994; Lloyd, 1989), research and service programs are needed to understand and address their needs better (Gutheil & Chichin, 1991; McKinlay, Skinner, Riley, & Zablotsky, 1993; Mellins & Ehrhardt, 1994). The project discussed in this article explored the perceptions and experiences of 19 older female HIV-affected caregivers of color regarding a cluster of relevant variables concerning HIV-related stigma. The purpose of the research was to understand better the effect of anticipated, perceived, and actual discrimination on HIV caregiving.

## Background on Stigma

*Stigma*, defined as "undesired differentness" or "spoiled identity," describes a negative, moral, or judgmental definition of a person or social situation, often connected to discrediting, disgrace, blame, and ascription of responsibility for the condition (Goffman, 1959, 1963). Stigma is part of a cultural system of shared meanings, typologies, or schemas that allow people to interpret the world, control behavior, respond to differences, explain danger or inferiority, or express disapproval (Coleman, 1986; Goffman, 1963; Jones et al., 1984; Page, 1984).

A wide variety of situations, diseases, and social issues include stigma as a concern. Examples of topics seen as stigmatized social problems include criminal behavior (DeVinney & Thomas, 1980), poverty (Alex, 1995), illiteracy (Beder, 1991), receiving public aid (Mills, 1996; Moffitt, 1983; Ranney & Kushman, 1987), suicide (Solomon, 1982), and using alcohol (Rather, 1991) or crack cocaine (Fullilove, Lown, & Fullilove, 1992). A variety of physical or medical states also can be stigmatized, such as involuntary childlessness or infertility (Miall, 1989, 1994; Whiteford & Gonzalez, 1995), epilepsy (Chaplin, Floyd, & Lasso, 1993; Iphofen, 1990; Jacoby, 1994; Schneider, 1988), deafness (Flexer & Wood, 1984), obesity (Robinson & Bacon, 1996), and other physical impairments (Cahill & Eggleston, 1995; Fine & Asch, 1988; Frank, 1988; Hahn, 1988; Royse & Edwards, 1989; Susman, 1994). Individuals also can be stigmatized for having mental retardation (Angrosino, 1992; Birenbaum, 1992; Szivos & Griffiths, 1990), being diagnosed with a mental illness (Lefley, 1989; Mechanic, McAlpine, & Rosenfield, 1994), growing old (Luken, 1987), or having a terminal illness (Epley & McCaghy, 1978). Finally, stigmas may be attached to being adopted (March, 1996), being raped (Weidner & Griffitt, 1983), being victimized by child sexual abuse (Coffey, Leitenberg, & Henning, 1996; Feiring, Taska, & Lewis, 1996; Tomlin, 1992), or having a same-gender sexual orientation (Coleman & Remafedi, 1989; Herek & Capitanio, 1996).

There are three related concepts, which comprise a set of issues to be considered in any stigmatized situation: associative stigma, internalized stigma, and stigma management. *Associative stigma*, which Goffman (1963) called "courtesy stigma," is ascribed to people who are voluntarily attached as caregivers or acquaintances to people who are stigmatized. Examples of issues that produce stigma by association include homosexuality (Neuberg, Smith, & Hoffman, 1994; Sigelman, Howell, Cornell, Cutright, & Dewey, 1991), dying (Posner, 1976), mental illness (Greenberg, Greenberg, McKee, Brown, & Griffin-Francell, 1993), mental retardation (Birenbaum, 1992), and dementia (Blum, 1991). *Internalized stigma*, or accepting the discrediting of one's worth conveyed by society, can occur without the experience of overt mistreatment and can lower a person's sense of self-esteem and prestige, because he or she is aware of the threat of censure and rejection (Jones et al., 1984). *Stigma management* is central to coping with carrying a stigma; that is, being aware of the real or potential negative reactions of others and attempting to minimize their effects (Jones et al., 1984; Page, 1984). The stigmatized person who strives to manage the stigma must consider the problems of concealment, disclosure, "passing" as normal, secrecy, information management, and social visibility (Goffman, 1963; Page, 1984).

## HIV-Related Stigma

HIV-infected people and their caregivers experience a particular type of stigma, which Herek and Glunt (1988) labeled "AIDS-related stigma" to designate a level of discrimination and prejudice that is deeper than that experienced by individuals with other types of illnesses or social problems. HIV is perceived as a demeaning disease of marginalized groups (Baker, 1992; Cadwell, 1994; Laryea & Gien, 1993; Novick, 1997) and thus adds to the existing stigma of being marginalized. Marginalization and HIV-related stigma together contribute to difficulty in adjustment and obtaining support (Herek & Glunt, 1988). As Land (1996) explained, one reason for the stress of HIV caregiving stems from the psychosocial context of victim blaming, ascribed low societal status, and defining HIV-affected populations as likely to experience multiple problems.

HIV-related stigma has been well documented since Herek and Glunt coined the phrase nearly a decade ago. There is ample evidence of negative or punitive attitudes among the public (Borcher & Rickabaugh, 1995; Herek & Capitanio, 1992, 1993; Lang, 1991; O'Hare, Williams, & Ezoviski, 1996; St. Lawrence, Husfeldt, Kelly, Hood, & Smith, 1990) and among helping professionals such as physicians, nurses, and social workers (Denker, 1990; Eliason, 1993; Faugier & Wright, 1990; Hall, 1992; Longo, Sposs, & Locke, 1990; "Many Found Daunted by Clients with HIV," 1995; Marshall & O'Keefe, 1995; Peate, 1995; Sherer & Goldberg, 1994; Siminoff, Erlen, & Lidz, 1991; Wiener & Siegel, 1990). HIV-infected people have reported suffering the negative psychological and social effects of societal stigma (Crandall & Coleman, 1992; Lang, 1991; Laryea & Gien, 1993; Longo, Sposs, & Locke, 1990). In addition, there is evidence that children in HIV-affected families suffer from associative HIV-related stigma (Cameron, 1994; Fair, Spencer, & Wiener, 1995), as do caregiving parents of HIV-infected adults (McGinn, 1996). A recent study found through a meta-analysis of 21 studies that HIV-related stigma exceeds stigma caused by other illnesses (Crawford,

1996). In addition, as potent and real as HIV-related stigma is, there is also evidence of internalized stigma among people with HIV and their caregivers, causing them to anticipate and expect discrimination and ostracism if they disclose the presence of HIV (Crandall, 1991; Green, 1995).

HIV disclosure can result in loss of social support (Hoffman, 1996; Kadushin, 1996; Lang, 1991; Lesar, Gerber, & Semmel, 1995). The social isolation stemming from HIV-related stigma may be exacerbated for women (Semple et al., 1993; Stuntzner-Gibson, 1991), for elderly people (Solomon, 1996), and for people of color (Boyd-Franklin, Aleman, Jean-Gilles, & Lewis, 1995). Because the stigmatization of adults and children with HIV infection often extends to their caregivers, families can become isolated and find it difficult to seek or locate support (Gutheil & Chichin, 1991; Jankowski et al., 1996; Kreibick, 1995; Lesar, Gerber, & Semmel, 1995; Lippmann, James, & Frierson, 1993; Mellins & Ehrhardt, 1994; Melvin & Sherr, 1993; Ogu & Wolfe, 1994; Powell-Cope & Brown, 1992). Caregivers may respond to the HIV-related stigma and hostility of their network and society by withdrawing, ignoring their own social needs, and becoming further isolated (Perreault, Reidy, Taggart, Richard, & Savard, 1992). The lack of HIV disclosure can increase stress (McDonell, Abell, & Miller, 1991) and complicate grieving (Brown & Powell-Cope, 1993; Dane, 1991; Walker, Pomeroy, McNeil, & Franklin, 1996).

Because HIV caregivers are likely to experience direct, perceived, and associative stigma, questions regarding HIV-related discrimination and stigma were included in a larger exploratory study of the experiences of HIV-affected older caregivers of color. This article addresses three research questions: (1) What is the evidence of HIV-related stigma in this population of HIV-affected caregivers? (2) How did the experience of HIV-related stigma affect these caregivers? and (3) What are the connections between HIV-related disclosure, HIV-related support, and HIV-related stigma?

## Method

Nineteen older female African American HIV-affected caregivers in the Chicago area participated from January to August 1996 in one-time semistructured qualitative interviews regarding their perceptions of and experiences with HIV-related stigma (during the interviews, the researchers referred to the respondents by their last names and titles [for example, Mrs. Johnson]; respondents were assigned first names [pseudonyms] in the transcripts and tables for the purpose of making them more real to the researchers and readers). These caregivers were recruited primarily through fliers distributed in HIV-related social and health agencies. Most often, a family member with HIV or a case manager would inform the caregiver of the study. Initial inclusion criteria were over age 50, self-defined as being not white, and currently caring for adult children who were infected with HIV or minor children who were infected with HIV or affected by the HIV status of their family members. Because participant recruitment proved to be very difficult, the initial guidelines were eased as the study progressed. The age criterion was expanded, because we received calls from four women in their middle to late forties who self-identified as older and qualified in other ways. Researchers also decided to broaden the definition of care recipient after receiving calls from three eager respondents who were caring for individuals who were not their children or grandchildren. Most of the caregivers were providing care at the time; however, five had cared for a person with HIV who had died within the previous year, and one had cared for someone who had died two years before.

Interviews were open ended and used a checklist as a guide to ensure content comparability. Examples of checklist questions related to stigma are: "What concerns have you had about HIV?" "What concerns have others had about HIV?" "How has HIV affected your family?" "Whom have you told about your loved ones' HIV status? Why or why not?" and "Tell me a story about how you or your family members have had negative responses or have experienced discrimination about AIDS."

All interviews were audiotaped with the written consent of the respondents and transcribed verbatim (in transcribing the interviews and in reproducing the remarks of the respondents, the researchers tried to be true to the words, phrases, styles, and pronunciations of the interviewees to represent them accurately, to convey the tone and affect of their statements, and to preserve the elegance of their expression). Field notes, observations, researcher comments, methodological difficulties and successes, and a summary of the respondent's story were all added to the document containing the transcription of the tape (as per Lofland & Lofland, 1995). This entire interview record was included in the coding and data analysis. *Coding* refers to the researchers' inserting labels, which would later be used for computer word searches and sorts, into the interview document. Words and phrases that served as summaries of meaning were placed in brackets at the beginning of the phrase, sentence, or paragraph that made up the unit of analysis. The first stage codes were simply descriptive (for example, "family rejected them after disclosure"); the second stage codes were categorical (for example, "disclosure—family"); and the third stage drew conclusions about the respondents' experiences as a whole (for example, "disclosure with stigma"). Additional details concerning recruitment, content of interviews, sampling method, and sample delineation appear elsewhere (Linsk & Poindexter, 2000; Poindexter, 1997b).

## Respondents

The researchers were funded to locate and study older caregivers of color who were providing care for family members infected with HIV. We sought respondents who were beginning to confront their own aging process and therefore aimed for people over 50. As previously discussed, the convenience sampling method and the difficulty in recruitment led to a sample with some heterogeneity; however, all met basic study criteria.

Seventeen of the women were African American, one was Mexican, and one was Filipino. Ages ranged from 44 to 80, with a mean age of 61. Length of time in HIV caregiving ranged from three months to 11 years. Thirteen respondents were caring for or had been caring for their HIV-infected adult children, six of whom had died. Four interviewees were taking care of an HIV-infected minor grandchild; in each of these cases, the mother of the minor was HIV infected as well or had died from AIDS. The remaining two interviewees were caring for other adults: one for a male lover and another for her sister (for further information about the context of and reasons for their caregiving, see Linsk & Poindexter, 2000; Poindexter, 1997b; Poindexter, Linsk, & Warner, 1999).

## Findings on HIV-Related Stigma and Disclosure

Whether the respondents had stories to tell concerning HIV-related discrimination depended on whether they had disclosed the presence of HIV in the family. There was a continuum ranging from no HIV disclosure to full HIV disclosure. Within this disclosure continuum there were varying experiences with HIV-related stigma, ranging from no awareness of discrimination to the experience of ostracism. We noticed four categories of disclosure and stigma: (1) disclosure of HIV with the experience of HIV-related stigma, (2) no HIV disclosure and thus no HIV-related stigma, (3) selective and controlled HIV disclosure because of internalized stigma and concern about associative stigma, and (4) full disclosure of HIV with no HIV-related stigma. The last three categories have been grouped as "no overt HIV-related stigma reported." This array shows where these 19 respondents were placed in this disclosure and stigma interaction (Table 22-1).

### *Disclosure with Stigma*

Five caregivers said that they had experienced rejection and censure from most of their family and friends after the HIV disclosure. They explained that their families abandoned them and the individuals with HIV they cared for

when the diagnosis was revealed. For example, Florence commented on her family's disappearance when her daughter was very ill from AIDS complications.

> My whole family got afraid. . . . They wouldn't even go see her. She begged them, please, "Momma, tell them." Celeste said of her family: "They stopped coming over since they found out Tonya had it [HIV]."

One grandmother had been rejected completely by her own family because of the HIV diagnoses of her daughter, brother, and granddaughter:

> My daughter, my only surviving daughter told me she was sick and tired of me. . . . It's annoying how I had to remove a lot of things, like family pictures. I had to take all that stuff down. . . . There's too much pain. Too much pain, you know (Daisy).

Alma told of a confrontation with a family member:

> I had some words with my brother. Because he went to see him in the hospital. And he came back and told me that he told Michael he shouldn't be kissing people. . . . I told him, I said, "Well, if you 'fraid a him, don't go 'round him. Don't go out there telling him not to touch," I said. "Don't go 'round him."

TABLE 22-1. HIV Disclosure and Stigma Interaction (N = 19)

| Reported Stigma | Experience with HIV Disclosure and HIV-Related Stigma | No. of Caregivers |
|---|---|---|
| Overt HIV-related stigma reported | Experienced stigma with disclosure to family or friends | 5 |
| No overt HIV-related stigma reported | No disclosure and no stigma; fear of stigma | 2 |
| | Selective disclosure with little or no stigma; fear of stigma | 11 |
| | Person with HIV went public; caregiver experienced no stigma | 1 |

Jen was disgusted with how some members of her family treated the person with HIV. She attributed their behavior to irrational fear of HIV transmission:

> You know, like my niece with that jar shit. He got to drink out a jar when he come there. Or they don't want to hug him, like it can rub off. Or they don't want to go in the bathroom after he been in. . . .That's silliness. You know?

Three of the respondents who lost family contact and support said that they also lost friends because of HIV disclosure. For example, Daisy said, "I don't have friends, family. None of them want to have anything to do with us. . . . Because of her illness." Jen, caring for her lover, was angry that her female friends had been especially harsh when she told them of his diagnosis and wondered why she was staying with him:

> If you're my friend, if I like it, you supposed to love it. If you're really my friend. . . . You know, so I don't listen to what people say anymore.

Celeste explained that she did not have anything in common with her former friends:

> I don't feel the same. Because I know that they'll be going on with their lives, and none of my friends' children have HIV. And they sit around talking about people with AIDS.

### Little or No Disclosure, No Stigma

Because of the well-documented existence of HIV-related stigma and its adverse effect on HIV caregivers, researchers anticipated that these respondents would have incidents of HIV-related discrimination to discuss. It was surprising that this was seldom the case: 14

reported that they had not directly experienced the effects of HIV-related stigma. One of them, to be discussed in more detail, was caring for someone who had gone public about her HIV status. The other 13 gave the following reasons for their lack of direct experience with HIV-related discrimination: They had told no one about HIV being in the family, had been selective and careful about whom they did tell, or had not been forthcoming about the HIV diagnosis. This is indicative of stigma management—they had not given anyone the chance to mistreat them because of HIV. This is demonstrated by the following interchange:

> *Interviewer*: So, you haven't had, you haven't felt a lot of negativity from other people.

> *Nell*: Uh-huh. Because they don't know. They just think she got rheumatory arthritis.

Two respondents had disclosed the HIV diagnosis to no one at all and thus had no stigma to report. Eleven of the respondents had disclosed the HIV diagnosis, but had made careful decisions about whom to tell and had experienced little or no discrimination as a result. Many of these caregiving women were aware of and afraid of the possible effects of stigma and explained their reluctance to disclose as an unwillingness to face censure or moral judgment. The following comments illustrate this:

> 'Cause, see, they don't understand. . . . You know, they think, because she in my home, that I might have AIDS (Nell).

> · · ·

> 'Cause I, you know, I didn't want them to tell me, oh, these peoples will come out and tell you, no, God didn't mean for you to be like that, God don't like that, and all that. And I don't want to hear that. I don't want

to hear that. . . . 'Cause people feel so differently when it comes to things like that, you know. They don't want a see it my way, you know. And I just kept it to myself (Faye).

The one instance in this sample of going public is worthy of notice, because it is an exception in a mostly closeted sample. Carol cared for her 44-year-old grandniece Nora. Carol reported that Nora approached her with a desire to help other women through public disclosure about her HIV status. Although Carol did not herself make a decision to go public, she understood, admired, and supported the desire of her care recipient to do so. Carol reported the following about Nora's decision:

> It was surprising to her to see so many black women were still, they weren't coming out [about having HIV]. So, somebody asked her to appear on TV. And she called me. She says, "How would it feel if I go public?" I said, "Public, how?" She said, "Momma, there's so many women out there, especially black women, that are not aware of what's out there for them, and they're hiding it. . . . If I can go on TV and let them know I've lived with this a couple years, that'll help a lot of them. . . . Do you have a problem with this?" I said, "No." . . . And I was never more proud of her at that moment. . . . And that started it. But I think she's done a tremendous job.

This caregiver could not describe any ramifications that resulted from stigma. She stated that, although acquaintances commented on Nora's media appearances, they never spoke about the reason for these television interviews: "People call me to say 'Nora's on TV!', but they never say she has HIV. They never say that." Going public can

mitigate the effects of stigma (Jones et al., 1984), and perhaps a person does not notice or care about public opinion as much when a secret is not being protected. It is also possible that the members of Carol's social network did not feel that they had permission to say "HIV" to Carol until she broached the subject herself.

### Respondents' Awareness of HIV-Related Stigma

Whether they had themselves experienced the effects of HIV stigma, most interviewees were cognizant of its existence and did not approve of how people with HIV are sometimes regarded or treated. Thirteen of the women commented on HIV-related stigma in some way, noticing how neighbors, friends, families, churches, schools, society, and service systems chastise or shun people with HIV and their family members. When discussing the negative attitudes and actions that people with HIV often encounter, several respondents spoke with empathy for HIV-infected individuals and had a view that AIDS was no different from other diseases or a sense that people with HIV were often treated unjustly. Examples follow for each of these aspects:

The comments of caregivers who showed empathy and awareness of rejection follow.

> 'Cause there's no situation in the world like this. 'Cause when you turn your back on somebody for havin' it, and you're supposed to love 'em, that destroys people (Jen).

. . .

> There are so many hundreds and thousands of peoples that don't even want their children around, even if their children die, they won't even come to the funeral. . . . They

won't do nothin' for them. 'Cause he had a friend, and his friend said, the boy's mother . . . wouldn't even come to visit him. . . . And when I see people that have AIDS, you know . . . it's just something that's kinda hurtin', you know. To see that they runnin' around out there by theyself and they got nobody. Relatives or nobody want to be with 'em (Faye).

. . .

Some people have AIDS don't have anybody to love them. . . . And then she had a friend that has AIDS . . . that he said his daughter and them, they don't come and see him, because they found out he got AIDS (Sheryl).

. . .

There are so many cases of how parents treat their children. I had a young lady. . . [tell me] how her mother wouldn't even let her children go near. . . . She told this outta her own mouth, with tears running down her cheeks. How they treated her (Florence).

. . .

I went through this with my cousin. Some of his friends, you know . . . they were mean. And he was so sad. . . . And so, after that, he changed his phone number. His pastor came to see him, but his friends stopped. So, I just knew (Belle).

Caregivers whose sentiments were that AIDS is no different from other diseases said the following:

I just look at it like another sickness. Another illness. Just like cancer, leukemia, whatever. That's the way I look at it. Because it's just another illness. Something you can't help. Something you didn't ask

to have. But it's there. That's the way I look on it (Lacy).

. . .

It hurts me so bad. I've met people whose families won't accept them. . . . If you're sick, you're sick (Carol).

Caregivers who responded with a sense of justice explained:

I don't see nothin' to be ashamed of. And to be against somebody. . . . I can't see nobody mistreatin' somebody, whether you got AIDS or whether you haven't. I just don't see it. We don't know what we're gonna leave here with (Faye).

. . .

I don't shy nobody. You never know what you're gonna have. It's best to always treat people right (Lacy).

Two respondents were vocal early in their interviews about their confidentiality and disclosure concerns. In one instance, before the interviewer could present the consent form, the respondent asked if the conversation would remain confidential. When Belle was told about the consent and confidentiality procedures, she responded that you can never be too careful where HIV was concerned and said, "I don't know, that's just me, I didn't want it exposed, you know." As the researcher was introducing the study to Anna by explaining that the purpose of the interview was to gather information from older people who were caring for family members with AIDS, Anna quickly motioned for silence and whispered, "We don't use that word." After the interviewer verified that it was the word "AIDS" that was objectionable, Anna explained that there was a family member downstairs and that no one in the family knew what her ill son's diagnosis was. Later in the interview she said about the stigma of the word "AIDS": "It's a terrible word to hear, as you know."

## Other Indicators of HIV Disclosure–Stigma Interaction

Several other observations generated by this research are indicative of the influence of HIV-related stigma in the lives of the caregivers: hiding the nature of the illness, reports of HIV-infected adult care recipients attempting to avoid or postpone disclosure, not telling anyone in church, their own past prejudice against individuals with HIV and their families, and intense desire to participate in the study as a way to lessen their isolation.

### *Hiding the Diagnosis*

The literature on stigma management refers to attempts to "pass" as normal. For HIV-affected families passing entails ascribing the family member's illness to some other cause. Six of the respondents handled the wish to avoid stigma and censure by hiding the diagnosis from neighbors and friends and, in one case, from family. Three of them said it was cancer. Other "diagnoses" given were tuberculosis and pneumonia, rheumatoid arthritis, and leukemia. Two of them expressed some regret or defensiveness at having hidden the nature of the disease.

None of the four caregivers for HIV-infected minor children had disclosed the child's status to other children in the school or neighborhood, although the teacher and principal had been told. Similarly, none of the four grandparent caregivers told the HIV-infected child of the diagnosis, in an effort to protect the children from feeling stigmatized.

### *Reluctance of Person with HIV to Disclose*

Twelve of the caregivers shared stories about how adult HIV-infected family members were afraid to disclose to them and to others. The reasons for this hesitancy, as perceived by the caregivers, fell into two broad categories: (1) fear of rejection, ridicule, or bad treatment (six individuals) and (2) desire on the part of the care recipient to protect the family or caregiver (two people). Four of these respondents were not specific about the motivations of the person with HIV; they simply knew that disclosure of diagnosis was unwanted. Three of the caregivers spoke about their decisions to disclose to close friends or family members even though they were asked by the HIV-positive adult not to share the diagnosis with anyone; the reason for the disclosure was to garner emotional support. As Dorothy explained, "I couldn't carry it by myself. It was too deadly. . . . I told them. I need to share, too, you know."

### *Lack of Disclosure in Churches*

Although most stated clearly how important church participation and spirituality was for them (Poindexter, 1997b; Poindexter, Linsk, & Warner, 1999), respondents varied in their disclosure patterns to churches. Eleven of those who attended church had disclosed to no one in their churches, including the pastor. Two had told only the pastor, and two had told the pastor and a few church members. Two had gone public in their churches, but with differing responses—one noticed no ramifications, and one was disappointed that none of the church members visited her daughter when she was in the hospital and nursing home. These findings coincide with the conclusions of Boyd-Franklin et al. (1995)

regarding African Americans finding strength in their church involvement but not sharing the HIV diagnosis. The stated reasons for not disclosing to churches were because the presence of HIV was considered by the caregiver or care recipient to be a private matter, the caregiver did not feel the need for the congregation's support, or because the respondent feared the ramifications of disclosure.

### Respondents' Own Previous Prejudice

Other evidence for the presence of HIV-related stigma came from three respondents who spoke introspectively and honestly about their own biases in the past against people with HIV. They spoke of how having it in their families had changed their perspectives completely. Many spoke of their regret at their initial intolerance and judgmental attitudes; one respondent felt that God was punishing her for her old attitudes by giving her two family members with HIV.

### Research Participation as a Means to Lessen Isolation

The research experience itself illuminated the dynamic of HIV-related stigma in the lives of caregivers in two ways: participants did not come forward readily, but when they did they were extremely anxious to share their stories. The isolation of these caregivers and limited opportunities for emotional and social support were evident in the way that several of the respondents seemed to feel compelled to connect with the research project and tell their stories. For example, although confidentiality was of concern to most of them, the majority of them were so eager to be heard that they started talking in depth before hearing about the details of the project or reviewing or signing the consent for participation and taping. Interviewers frequently had to interrupt the narrative flow to insist on getting a signature on the consent form. The four respondents in their forties either exaggerated their ages upward or declined to tell us their ages over the telephone; they all had the fliers that announced the eligibility as age 50 or over. There seemed to be a strong desire to be heard, possibly out of a need to pass on the care recipients' legacy and to bear witness to the unique struggles and special relationships. As Florence said, "I want the world to know about it. Can you, would you see to that?"

### Summary

Most individuals in this sample did not experience HIV-related stigma, a result that was counter to what the researchers expected to find. Only five reported ostracism from family; three of those felt that they also lost contact with friends because of the disclosure of HIV. Although most respondents did not report the experience of overt HIV-related stigma, its influence was felt. Thirteen of 19 individuals carefully chose whether to disclose and whom they would tell about the presence of HIV; this was done primarily because they were afraid of the ramifications of the telling. They either told no one or told only a few trusted people. Clearly, the prospect of HIV-related stigma, stemming from either moral judgment or fear of transmission, was significant for these caregivers, and they managed disclosure accordingly. These caregivers were attuned acutely to HIV-related stigma and experienced some isolation or rejection because of this phenomenon.

## Discussion

Data from this study support the existence of AIDS-related stigma as a deeper level of perceived, anticipated, and experienced discrimination. For example, given the choice of acknowledging their family members' illness as "AIDS" or another stigmatized condition like "cancer," several of these caregivers chose the label that they determined to be the lesser of two evils. Although the researchers were surprised at the lack of overt discrimination experienced by these HIV-affected caregivers, this finding is explained by the fact that most of the participants had not disclosed the diagnosis. The dynamic interaction of fear of stigma and reticence to disclose form a self-limited cycle: Disclosure of HIV must precede being the target of overt HIV-related stigma, yet it is often the fear of stigma that precludes disclosure. Because of the anticipation of HIV-related stigma, most respondents did not widely disclose the HIV diagnosis, if at all. Consequently, they could neither experience overt HIV-related discrimination nor receive support that acknowledged their struggles as HIV-affected caregivers. Therefore, because of lack of HIV disclosure as a result of fear of HIV-related stigma, not only was overt discrimination regarding HIV avoided, but their social and emotional support for their HIV caregiving also was reduced. They were protected from stigma, but at the cost of being further isolated.

The findings of this study are related to associative stigma, internalized stigma, and stigma management. The caregivers had taken on associative HIV stigma and were highly aware of its possible ramifications, even though they themselves were not HIV infected. The respondents had internalized the presence of HIV-related stigma in society to the extent that they governed their own disclosure decisions based on their anticipation of discrimination. They managed the stigma by managing HIV disclosure, supporting Powell-Cope and Brown's (1992) findings in an earlier qualitative study of HIV-affected caregivers.

Because of unexpected difficulties with sample development, the researchers concluded that potential participants were not readily open to talking to strangers and that agency personnel who serve HIV-infected people were possibly protective of the caregivers. If there had not been stringent guarantees of confidentiality, it is likely that the recruitment process would have been longer and more arduous. Difficulty with recruitment of participants has implications for further research efforts and is another indicator of HIV-related stigma. Older HIV-affected caregivers of color in metropolitan areas evidently are not rare—they are hidden.

Future research must further contrast the experience of having HIV or being associated with someone who has HIV with the experience of other conditions. In addition, because HIV-related stigma was first labeled in 1988, explorations of how HIV-related stigma has or has not changed over the past decade are necessary. It is also vital to begin to examine the impact of multiple stigmas on the population of caregivers who may be struggling simultaneously with classism, sexism, ageism, racism, homophobia, and HIV-related stigma. It was evident in this sample that some of the individuals with HIV had asked their caregivers not to disclose their HIV diagnosis; therefore, research is needed on how much of the lack of caregiver disclosure about HIV is the result of the fear of HIV-related stigma on the part of the HIV-infected person.

Other issues for future projects include how HIV-affected caregivers weigh and evaluate HIV disclosure decisions, why some caregivers fear HIV disclosure, and how they internalize HIV-related stigma. In addition, given earlier indications that HIV disclosure may be more problematic for elderly people than for younger groups (Solomon, 1996) and more difficult for families of color than for white families (Baker, 1992; Boyd-Franklin et al., 1995; Brown et al., 1992; Gant & Ostrow, 1995; Icard, Schilling, El-Bassel, & Young, 1992), these assertions need to be tested by comparing the stigma management strategies of older caregivers of color with those of younger caregivers and white caregivers. This study did not compare the sample of older female African American caregivers of people with HIV with any other group (for example, younger, male, or white caregivers). Future projects should include other groups for comparisons.

This research also raised questions regarding what may allow an individual or family to go public. There is little insight about this in the literature—only one article on AIDS caregivers going public was found (Powell-Cope & Brown, 1992). Future studies should explore how people with HIV and their caregivers are affected when energy is no longer spent on maintaining secrecy and managing stigma.

We agree with Levy (1993) that for clients who are stigmatized for any reason, assistance with stigma management can be offered as part of social work services. This is particularly vital for social workers who serve people with HIV and their associates. Practitioners can help their HIV-affected clients control information disclosure, make decisions about whom to tell, positively adjust or reframe their views of their medical and social status, develop communication skills to attempt to enhance the empathy of others, and appropriately confront those who persecute them (Levy, 1993).

In addition, social workers in health care and social services settings should be more cognizant of the hidden army of older women who are providing personal care and emotional support to children, youths, and adults with HIV. The caregivers in this sample were reluctant to come forward but were eager to share their stories and ask for assistance when they were given a chance to talk. But practitioners in HIV service organizations are far more likely to meet individuals with HIV infection than to meet their caregivers. Therefore, social workers in the HIV field should ask HIV-infected clients about who is caring for them, assess the service needs of the informal caregivers, offer aggressive outreach to the caregivers, tailor support groups and other programs to caregivers, and make support more accessible and relevant. Social workers who serve elderly people should strive to provide an environment that is safe enough for older people to disclose the presence of HIV in the home or family and should be prepared to provide services or refer them to appropriate support.

## Conclusion

Facing this growing pandemic, the current political climate regarding public assistance, and the subsequent burden on informal support providers, social workers need more information about how to support the older caregivers who are providing so much of the personal care for people with HIV. Because the literature has paid limited attention to the emerging topic of the older caregivers of family members with HIV, most of the program planning for them is being guided by practice wisdom and anecdotal evidence. Although these sources are useful, a broader perspective drawn from systematic analyses of caregivers' opinions is needed.

The stigmatized status that has been ascribed to people with HIV in our society over the past 15 years has serious implications, such as discrimination, difficulty in obtaining care, and lack of social support. The most important implication of this study of HIV-related stigma, therefore, is that major societal and structural shifts are required so that HIV can be brought "out of the closet." There is an interaction between sexism, ageism, racism, classism, homophobia, and HIV stigma that produces a potent form of oppression and that heightens the fear, uncertainty, grieving, and confusion of older caregivers of color. It is a tragedy that these caregivers and their HIV-positive loved ones often live in terror of disclosure and, thus, do not gain access to informal and formal support because of this fear.

A social work response will continue to be needed urgently. HIV disease, sadly, will be a concern for many decades. The profession must assist society in changing its treatment of and attitudes toward people with HIV and their caregivers. As Gilmore and Somerville (1994) suggested, our society must overcome the "us versus them" orientation and the metaphors of scapegoating that characterize HIV-related stigma, fear, and discrimination. And society must realize that we are all HIV-affected and are all essentially living with AIDS. Social workers must continue to be on the forefront of education of individuals, systems, and the public to eliminate pervasive HIV stigma.

## References

Alex, A. Y. (1995). Myths about race and the underclass: Concentrated poverty and "underclass" behaviors. *Urban Affairs Review*, *31*, 3–19.

Allers, C. T. (1990). AIDS and the older adult. *Gerontologist*, *30*, 405–407.

Anderson, G. R. (Ed.). (1990). *Courage to care: Responding to the crisis of children with AIDS*. Washington, DC: Child Welfare League of America.

Angrosino, M. V. (1992). Metaphors of stigma: How deinstitutionalized mentally retarded adults see themselves. *Journal of Contemporary Ethnography*, *21*, 171–199.

Baker, L. S. (1992). The perspective of families. In M. L. Stuber (Ed.), *Children with AIDS* (pp. 147–161). Washington, DC: American Psychiatric Press.

Beder, H. (1991). The stigma of illiteracy. *Adult Basic Education*, *1*(2), 67–78.

Birenbaum, A. (1992). Courtesy stigma revisited. *Mental Retardation*, *30*, 265–268.

Blum, N. S. (1991). The management of stigma by Alzheimer family caregivers. *Journal of Contemporary Ethnography*, *20*, 263–284.

Borcher, J., & Rickabaugh, C. A. (1995). When illness is perceived as controllable: The effects of gender and mode of transmission on AIDS-related stigma. *Sex Roles*, *33*, 657–668.

Boyd-Franklin, N., Aleman, J., Jean-Gilles, M. M., & Lewis, S. Y. (1995). Cultural sensitivity and competence. In N. Boyd-Franklin, G. L. Steiner, & M. G. Boland (Eds.), *Children, families, and HIV/AIDS: Psychosocial and therapeutic issues* (pp. 53–59). New York: Guilford Press.

Brabant, S. (1994). An overlooked AIDS affected population: The elderly parent as caregiver. *Journal of Gerontological Social Work*, *22*(1/2), 131–145.

Brown, G., Mitchell, J., & Williams, S. B. (1992). The African American community. In M. L. Stuber (Ed.), *Children with AIDS* (pp. 21–32). Washington, DC: American Psychiatric Press.

Brown, M. A., & Powell-Cope, G. M. (1991). AIDS family caregiving: Transitions through uncertainty. *Nursing Residency*, *40*, 338–345.

Brown, M. A., & Powell-Cope, G. M. (1993). Themes of loss and dying in caring for a family member with AIDS. *Residential Nursing Health*, *16*, 179–191.

Cadwell, S. (1994). Twice removed: The stigma suffered by gay men with AIDS. In S. A. Cadwell, R. Burnham, & M. Forstein (Eds.), *Therapists on the front line: Psychotherapy with gay men in the age of AIDS* (pp. 3–24). Washington, DC: American Psychiatric Press.

Cahill, S. E., & Eggleston, R. (1995). Reconsidering the stigma of physical disability: Wheelchair use and public kindness. *Sociological Quarterly*, *36*, 681–698.

Cameron, T. (1994). Children orphaned by AIDS: Providing homes for a most vulnerable population. *AIDS and Public Policy Journal*, *9*, 29–35.

Cates, J. A., Graham, L. L., Boeglin, D., & Tielker, S. (1990, April). The effect of AIDS on the family system. *Families in Society*, pp. 195–201.

Chaplin, J. E., Floyd, M., & Lasso, R. Y. (1993). Early psychosocial adjustment and the experience of epilepsy: Findings from a general practice survey. *International Journal of Rehabilitation Research*, *16*, 316–318.

Coffey, P., Leitenberg, H., & Henning, K. (1996). Mediators of the long-term impact of child sexual abuse: Perceived stigma, betrayal, powerlessness, and self-blame. *Child Abuse & Neglect*, *20*, 447–455.

Coleman, E., & Remafedi, G. (1989). Gay, lesbian, and bisexual adolescents: A critical challenge to counselors. *Journal of Counseling and Development*, *68*(1), 36–40.

Coleman, L. M. (1986). Stigma: An enigma demystified. In S. C. Ainlay, G. Becker, & L. M. Coleman (Eds.), *The dilemma of difference: A multidisciplinary view of stigma* (pp. 211–232). New York: Plenum Press.

Crandall, C. S. (1991). AIDS-related stigma and the lay sense of justice. *Contemporary Social Psychology*, *15*(2), 66–67.

Crandall, C. S., & Coleman, R. (1992). AIDS-related stigmatization and the disruption of

social relationships. *Journal of Social and Personal Relationships*, *9*, 163–177.

Crawford, A. M. (1996). Stigma associated with AIDS: A meta-analysis. *Journal of Applied Social Psychology*, *26*, 398–416.

Dane, B. O. (1991, February). Anticipatory mourning of middle-aged parents of adult children with AIDS. *Families in Society*, pp. 108–115.

Denker, A. L. (1990). Stigma and the nursing care of children with AIDS (Abstract no. S.D.877). *International Conference on AIDS*, *6*, 309.

DeVinney, D. J., & Thomas, K. B. (1980). The stigma associated with various criminal offenses in hiring decisions. *Journal of Employment Counseling*, *17*, 301–305.

Duh, S. V. (1991). *Blacks and AIDS: Causes and origins*. Newbury Park, CA: Sage Publications.

Eliason, M. J. (1993). AIDS-related stigma and homophobia: Implications for nursing education. *Nurse Educator*, *18*(6), 27–30.

Epley, R. J., & McCaghy, C. H. (1978). The stigma of dying: Attitudes toward the terminally ill. *Omega*, *8*, 379–392.

Fair, C. D., Spencer, E. D., & Wiener, L. (1995). Healthy children in families affected by AIDS: Epidemiological and psychosocial considerations. *Child and Adolescent Social Work Journal*, *12*, 165–181.

Faugier, J., & Wright, S. (1990). Homophobia, stigma and AIDS—An issue for all health care workers. *Nurse Practitioner*, *3*(2), 27–28.

Feiring, C., Taska, L. S., & Lewis, M. (1996). A process model for understanding adaptation to sexual abuse: The role of shame in defining stigmatization. *Child Abuse & Neglect*, *20*, 767–782.

Fine, M., & Asch, A. (1988). Disability beyond stigma: Social interaction, discrimination, and activism. *Journal of Social Issues*, *44*(1), 3–21.

Flexer, C., & Wood, L. A. (1984). The hearing aid: Facilitator or inhibitor of auditory interaction. *Volta Review*, *86*, 354–361.

Frank, G. (1988). Beyond stigma: Visibility and self-empowerment of persons with congenital limb deficiencies. *Journal of Social Issues*, *44*, 95–115.

Fullilove, M. T., Lown, E. A., & Fullilove, R. E. (1992). Crack 'hos and skeezers: Traumatic experiences of women crack users. *Journal of Sex Research, 29*, 275–287.

Gant, L. M., & Ostrow, D. G. (1995). Perceptions of social support and psychological adaptation to sexually acquired HIV among white and African American men. *Social Work, 40*, 215–224.

Gilmore, N., & Somerville, M. A. (1994). Stigmatization, scapegoating, and discrimination in sexually transmitted disease: Overcoming "them" and "us." *Social Science and Medicine, 39*, 1339–1358.

Goffman, E. (1959). *The presentation of self in everyday life*. Englewood Cliffs, NJ: Prentice Hall.

Goffman, E. (1963). *Stigma: Notes on the management of spoiled identity*. Englewood Cliffs, NJ: Prentice Hall.

Green, G. (1995). Attitudes towards people with HIV: Are they as stigmatizing as people with HIV perceive them to be? *Social Science and Medicine, 41*, 557–568.

Greenberg, J. S., Greenberg, J. R., McKee, D., Brown, R., & Griffin-Francell, C. (1993). Mothers caring for an adult child with schizophrenia: The effects of subjective burden on maternal health. *Family Relations, 42*, 205–211.

Gutheil, I. A., & Chichin, E. R. (1991). AIDS, older people, and social work. *Social Work, 16*, 237–244.

Hahn, H. (1988). The politics of physical differences: Disability and discrimination. *Journal of Social Issues, 44*(1), 39–47.

Hall, B. A. (1992). Overcoming stigmatization: Social and personal implications of the human immunodeficiency virus diagnosis. *Archives of Psychiatric Nursing, 6*, 189–194.

Herek, G. M., & Capitanio, J. P. (1992). AIDS-related stigma persists in the United States (Abstract no. PoD 5811). *International Conference on AIDS, 8*(2), D524.

Herek, G. M., & Capitanio, J. P. (1993). Public reactions to AIDS in the United States: A second decade of stigma. *American Journal of Public Health, 83*, 574–577.

Herek, G. M., & Capitanio, J. P. (1996). "Some of my best friends": Intergroup contact, concealable stigma, and heterosexuals' attitudes towards gay men and lesbians. *Personality and Social Psychology Bulletin, 22*, 412–424.

Herek, G. M., & Glunt, E. K. (1988). An epidemic of stigma: Public reactions to AIDS. *American Psychologist, 43*, 886–891.

Hoffman, M. A. (1996). *Counseling clients with HIV disease*. New York: Guilford Press.

Icard, L., Schilling, R. F., El-Bassel, M., & Young, D. (1992). Preventing AIDS among black gay men and black gay and heterosexual intravenous drug users. *Social Work, 37*, 440–445.

Iphofen, R. (1990). Coping with a "perforated life": A case study in managing the stigma of petit mal epilepsy. *Sociology, 24*, 447–463.

Jacoby, A. (1994). Felt versus enacted stigma: A concept revisited: Evidence from a study of people with epilepsy in remission. *Social Science and Medicine, 38*, 269–274.

Jankowski, S., Videka-Sherman, L., & Laquidara-Dickinson, K. (1996). Social support networks of confidants of people with AIDS. *Social Work, 41*, 206–312.

Jenkins, B. (1992). AIDS/HIV epidemics in the black community. In R. L. Braithwaite & S. E. Taylor (Eds.), *Health issues in the black community* (pp. 55–63). San Francisco: Jossey-Bass.

Jones, E. E., Farina, A., Hastarf, H. H., Markus, H., Miller, D. T., & Scott, R. A. (1984). *Social stigma: The psychology of marked relationships*. New York: W. H. Freeman.

Joslin, D. (1995, Winter). Older adults as caregivers in the HIV/AIDS epidemic. *Coalition on AIDS in Passaic County Newsletter*. (Available from Coalition on AIDS in Passaic County [CAPCO], CAPCO Resource Center, 100 Hamilton Place, Room 707, Paterson, NJ 07505).

Kadushin, G. (1996). Gay men with AIDS and their families of origin: An analysis of social support. *Health & Social Work, 21*, 141–149.

Kreibick, T. (1995). Caretakers' support group. In N. Boyd-Franklin, G. L. Steiner, & M. G. Boland (Eds.), *Children, families, and HIV/AIDS: Psychosocial and therapeutic issues* (pp. 167–178). New York: Guilford Press.

Land, H. (1996). The social and psychological contexts of HIV/AIDS caregiving. In V. J. Lynch & P. A. Wilson (Eds.), *Caring for the HIV/AIDS caregiver* (pp. 1–16). Westport, CT: Auburn House.

Lang, N. (1991). Stigma, self-esteem, and depression: Psychosocial responses to risk of AIDS. *Human Organization, 50*(1), 66–72.

Laryea, M., & Gien, L. (1993). The impact of HIV-positive diagnosis on the individual: Part 1. Stigma, rejection, and loneliness. *Clinical Nursing Residency, 2,* 245–266.

Lefley, H. P. (1989). Family burden and family stigma in major mental illness. *American Psychologist, 44,* 556–560.

Lego, S. (1994). AIDS-related anxiety and coping methods in a support group for caregivers. *Archives of Psychiatric Nursing, 8,* 200–207.

Lesar, S., Gerber, M. M., & Semmel, M. I. (1995). HIV infection in children: Family stress, social support, and adaptation. *Exceptional Children, 62,* 224–236.

Levine, C. (Ed.). (1993). *Orphans of the HIV epidemic.* New York: United Hospital Fund.

Levy, A. J. (1993). Stigma management: A new clinical service. *Families in Society, 74,* 226–231.

Linsk, N. L. (1994). HIV and the elderly. *Families in Society, 75,* 362–372.

Linsk, N., & Poindexter, C. (2000). Older caregivers for family members with HIV/AIDS: Reasons for caring. *Journal of Applied Gerontology, 19*(2), 181–202.

Lippmann, S. B., James, W. A., & Frierson, R. L. (1993). AIDS and the family: Implications for counseling. *AIDS Care, 5,* 71–78.

Lloyd, G. A. (1989, Fall). AIDS and elders: Advocacy, activism, & coalitions. *Generations,* pp. 32–35.

Lofland, J., & Lofland, L. H. (1995). *Analyzing social settings* (3rd ed.). Belmont, CA: Wadsworth.

Longo, M. B., Sposs, J. A., & Locke, A. M. (1990). Identifying major concerns of persons with acquired immunodeficiency syndrome: A replication. *Clinical Nurse Specialist, 4*(1), 21–26.

Luken, P. C. (1987). Social identity in later life: A situational approach to understanding old age stigma. *International Journal of Aging and Human Development, 25,* 177–193.

Magana, J. R., & Magana, H. A. (1992). Mexican-Latino children. In M. L. Stuber (Ed.), *Children with AIDS* (pp. 33–43). Washington, DC: American Psychiatric Press.

Many found daunted by clients with HIV. (1995, September). *NASW News,* p. 15.

March, K. (1996). Perception of adoption as social stigma: Motivation for search and reunion. *Journal of Marriage and the Family, 57,* 653–660.

Marshall, P. A., & O'Keefe, J. P. (1995). Medical students' first-person narratives of a patient's story of AIDS. *Social Science and Medicine, 40,* 67–76.

McDonell, J. R., Abell, N., & Miller, J. (1991). Family members' willingness to care for people with AIDS: A psychosocial assessment model. *Social Work, 36,* 43–53.

McGinn, F. (1996). The plight of rural parents caring for adult children with HIV. *Families in Society, 77,* 269–278.

McKinlay, J. B., Skinner, K., Riley, J. W., & Zablotsky, D. (1993). On the relevance of social science concepts and perspectives. In M. W. Riley, M. G. Ory, & D. Zablotsky (Eds.), *AIDS in an aging society* (pp. 127–146). New York: Springer.

Mechanic, D., McAlpine, D., & Rosenfield, S. (1994). Effects of illness attribution and depression on the quality of life among persons with serious mental illness. *Social Science and Medicine, 39,* 155–164.

Mellins, C. A., & Ehrhardt, A. A. (1994). Families affected by pediatric acquired immunodeficiency syndrome: Sources of stress and coping. *Journal of Developmental and Behavioral Pediatrics, 15*(3), S54–S60.

Melvin, D., & Sherr, L. (1993). The child in the family: Responding to AIDS and HIV. *AIDS Care, 5*, 35–42.

Miall, C. E. (1989). Reproductive technology versus the stigma of involuntary childlessness. *Social Casework, 70*, 43–50.

Miall, C. E. (1994). Community constructs of involuntary childlessness: Sympathy, stigma, and social support. *Canadian Review of Sociology and Anthropology, 31*, 392–421.

Michaels, D., & Levine, C. (1992). Estimates of the number of motherless youth orphaned by AIDS in the United States. *JAMA, 268*, 3456–3461.

Michaels, D., & Levine, C. (1993). The youngest survivors: Estimates of the number of motherless youth orphaned by AIDS in New York City. In C. Levine (Ed.), *Orphans of the HIV epidemic* (pp. 3–12). New York: United Hospital Fund.

Mills, F. B. (1996). The ideology of welfare reform: Deconstructing stigma. *Social Work, 41*, 391–395.

Minkler, M., & Stone, R. (1985). The feminization of poverty and older women. *Gerontologist, 25*, 351–357.

Moffitt, R. (1983). An economic model of welfare stigma. *American Economic Review, 73*, 1023–1035.

Muschkin, C. G., & Ellis, M. (1993). Migration in search of family support: Elderly parents as caregivers for persons with AIDS. *Program abstracts*. New Orleans: Gerontological Society of America.

Neuberg, S. L., Smith, D. M., & Hoffman, J. C. (1994). When we observe stigmatized and "normal" individuals interacting: Stigma by association. *Personality and Social Psychology Bulletin, 20*, 96–109.

Novick, A. (1997). Stigma and AIDS: Three layers of damage. *Journal of the Gay and Lesbian Medical Association, 1*(1), 53–60.

Ogu, C., & Wolfe, L. R. (1994). *Midlife and older women and HIV/AIDS*. Washington, DC: American Association of Retired Persons.

O'Hare, T., Williams, C. L., & Ezoviski, A. (1996). Fear of AIDS and homophobia: Implications for direct practice and advocacy. *Social Work, 41*, 51–58.

Okazawa-Rey, M. (1994). Grandparents who care: An empowerment model of health care. In A. Dula & S. Goering (Eds.), *"It just ain't fair": The ethics of health care for African Americans"* (pp. 221–233). New York: Praeger.

Ory, M. G., & Zablotsky, D. (1993). Notes for the future: Research, prevention, care, public policy. In M. W. Riley, M. G. Ory, & D. Zablotsky (Eds.), *AIDS in an aging society* (pp. 202–216). New York: Springer.

Page, R. (1984). *Stigma*. London: Routledge & Kegan Paul.

Peate, I. (1995). A question of prejudice: Stigma, homosexuality and HIV/AIDS. *Professional Nursing, 10*, 380–383.

Perreault, M., Reidy, M., Taggart, M. E., Richard, L., & Savard, N. (1992, July). Needs assessment of natural caregivers of people with HIV or AIDS (Abstract no. PoB 3436). *International Conference on AIDS, 8*(2), B159.

Poindexter, C. C. (1997a). In the aftermath: Serial crisis intervention with persons with HIV. *Health & Social Work, 22*, 125–132.

Poindexter, C. (1997b). *Stigma and support as experienced by HIV-affected older minority caregivers*. Unpublished doctoral dissertation, University of Illinois at Chicago.

Poindexter, C., Linsk, N., & Warner, S. (1999). "He listens . . . and never gossips": Spiritual coping without church support among older, predominately African American caregivers of persons with HIV. *Review of Religious Research*.

Posner, J. (1976). Death as a courtesy stigma. *Essence, 1*(1), 39–48.

Powell-Cope, G. M., & Brown, M. A. (1992). Going public as an AIDS family caregiver. *Social Science and Medicine, 34*, 571–580.

Ranney, C. K., & Kushman, J. F. (1987). Cash equivalence, welfare stigma, and food stamps. *Southern Economic Journal, 53*, 1011–1027.

Rather, B. C. (1991). Disease versus social-learning models of alcoholism in the prediction of alcohol problem recognition, help seeking, and stigma. *Journal of Drug Education, 21,* 119–132.

Robinson, B. E., & Bacon, J. G. (1996). The "if only I were thin" treatment program: Decreasing the stigmatizing effects of fatness. *Professional Psychology, Research and Practice, 27,* 175–183.

Royse, D., & Edwards, T. (1989). Communicating about disability: Attitudes and preferences of persons with physical handicaps. *Rehabilitation Counseling Bulletin, 32,* 203–209.

Schneider, J. W. (1988). Disability as moral experience: Epilepsy and self in routine relationships. *Journal of Social Issues, 44*(1), 63–78.

Semple, S. J., Patterson, T. L., Temoshok, L. R., McCutchan, J. A., Straits-Troster, K. A., Chandler, J. L., & Grant, I. (1993). Identification of psychobiological stressors among HIV-positive women. *Women and Health, 20,* 15–36.

Sherer, R., & Goldberg, D. (1994). HIV disease and access to care: A crisis within a crisis. In A. Dula & S. Goering (Eds.), *"It just ain't fair": The ethics of health care for African Americans* (pp. 149–164). New York: Praeger.

Sigelman, C. K., Howell, J. L., Cornell, D. P., Cutright, J. D., & Dewey, J. C. (1991). Courtesy stigma: The social implications of associating with a gay person. *Journal of Social Psychology, 131,* 45–56.

Siminoff, L. A., Erlen, J. A., & Lidz, C. W. (1991). Stigma, AIDS and quality of nursing care: State of the science. *Journal of Advanced Nursing, 16,* 262–269.

Solomon, K. (1996). Psychosocial issues. In K. M. Nokes (Ed.), *HIV/AIDS and the older adult* (pp. 33–46). Washington, DC: Taylor & Francis.

Solomon, M. (1982). The bereaved and the stigma of suicide. *Omega, 13,* 377–387.

St. Lawrence, J. S., Husfeldt, B. A., Kelly, J. A., Hood, H. V., & Smith, S. (1990). The stigma of AIDS: Fear of disease and prejudice toward gay men. *Journal of Homosexuality, 19*(3), 85–101.

Stuntzner-Gibson, D. (1991). Women and HIV disease: An emerging social crisis. *Social Work, 36,* 22–28.

Susman, J. (1994). Disability, stigma, and deviance. *Social Science and Medicine, 38,* 15–22.

Szivos, S. E., & Griffiths, E. (1990). Group processes involved in coming to terms with a mentally retarded identity. *Mental Retardation, 28,* 333–341.

Thomas, S. B., & Quinn, S. C. (1994). The AIDS epidemic and the African-American community: Toward an ethical framework for service delivery. In A. Dula & S. Goering (Eds.), *"It just ain't fair": The ethics of health care for African Americans* (pp. 75–89). New York: Praeger.

Tomlin, S. S. (1992). Stigma and incest survivors. *Child Abuse & Neglect, 15,* 557–566.

Walker, R. J., Pomeroy, E. C., McNeil, J. S., & Franklin, C. (1996). Anticipatory grief and AIDS: Strategies for intervening with caregivers. *Health & Social Work, 21,* 49–57.

Weidner, G., & Griffitt, W. (1983). Rape: A sexual stigma? *Journal of Personality, 51,* 152–166.

Whiteford, L. M., & Gonzalez, L. (1995). Stigma: The hidden burden of infertility. *Social Science and Medicine, 40,* 27–36.

Wiener, L. S., & Siegel, K. (1990). Social workers' comfort in providing services to AIDS patients. *Social Work, 35,* 18–25.

This chapter was originally published in the January 1999 issue of *Social Work*, Vol. 44, Number 1, pp. 46–61.

# 23

## Husbands Caring for Wives with Dementia

### A Longitudinal Study of Continuity and Change

## BETTY J. KRAMER

The older adult population is expected to more than double between now and 2040, tripling the number of people age 85 years and older (Stone, 1999). This trend, combined with the social and health care needs that accompany advanced age, poses present and imminent challenges to the social work profession. Of particular concern is the growing magnitude of diseases that cause dementia and affect more than 7 million people age 65 years and older in the United States (U.S. House Select Committee on Aging, 1987) and the social and health care implications of these diseases. Health care social workers in community and institutional settings serve in the role of strengthening and supporting family members caring for people with dementia. Therefore, it is essential that practitioners understand the effects and the dynamic and changing nature of caregiving so that interventions may be tailored appropriately to meet the needs of those at various junctures in the caregiving experience. For example, competent nursing home social workers must be knowledgeable about the psychosocial effects of placement on caregivers so they can develop appropriate and supportive services for family members. Family caregiving research has made much progress in identifying the effects of caregiving; however, this body of knowledge has been constrained in two important ways. First, the predominant focus of earlier research has been on women, but several trends are likely to put increasing demands on caregiving men (Kaye & Applegate, 1990b). Second, the few studies that have focused on the male caregiver have been cross-sectional (for example, Chang & White-Means, 1991; Harris, 1995; Kramer, 1997a), seriously limiting the conclusions that can be drawn regarding the changing nature of the male caregiving experience.

## Transition to Nursing Home Care

Increasingly, researchers and health care practitioners have become aware of the strains associated with the transition to nursing home care and the central role played by family members in institutional settings (King, Collins, Given, & Vredevoogd, 1991; Zarit & Whitlatch, 1992). Placing a family member in a nursing home is one of the most difficult and challenging decisions facing family caregivers (King et al., 1991). Numerous studies document that this is a particularly arduous event for spouses who are less likely than adult children to institutionalize the care receiver (Colerick & George, 1986; Montgomery & Kosloski, 1994) and who experience poorer well-being than adult children both before and after admission (King et al., 1991). Although several cross-sectional studies have compared caregivers in the community with caregivers who have relatives in nursing homes (see Novak & Guest, 1992; Pratt, Schmall, Wright, & Hare, 1987; Stephens, Kinney, & Ogrocki, 1991), little empirical attention has been given to the transition from family care to institutional care. In response to these and the previously discussed limitations, the study discussed in this article used the conceptual model described below to examine the experiences of

husbands caring for wives with dementia. More specifically, the purpose of the study was to examine and contrast changes or stability in husbands who continued to provide care in the community with those who placed their spouses in nursing homes during a one-year period.

## Conceptual Model

Because this study examines changes over time for both husbands who placed their spouses in nursing homes and husbands who continued to provide care for their spouses in the community, the conceptual framework used to guide this study synthesizes the empirical findings from comparative studies of these samples with theoretical considerations and empirical findings regarding caregiver stress and adaptation. It is modified from the frameworks used in two earlier studies on institutionalization (Montgomery & Kosloski, 1994; Pruchno, Michaels, & Potashnik, 1990) and from a conceptual model of caregiver adaptation that draws on multiple relevant theoretical perspectives (Kramer, 1997b). According to this model, primary stressors, resources, appraisals of role strain, and psychological well-being undergo specified directional changes over time, according to whether a transition (that is, placing a spouse in a nursing home) has occurred.

*Stressors.* In the context of caregiving, stressors are conceptualized as the care receiver's impairments and illness symptoms that typically include functional, behavioral, and cognitive indicators. One might assume that such indicators are no longer stressors for those who place a family member in a nursing home because they no longer assume primary care responsibilities. However, Pearlin, Mullan, Semple, and Skaff (1990) proposed that these functional impairments and memory and behavioral problems are stressors not only because the caregiver may be providing necessary assistance relative to the impairments, but also because they influence the potential for communicating and relating to the care receiver and serve as painful reminders of the "changed persona of the patient" (p. 587). Indeed, Stephens et al. (1991) reported that a majority of caregivers with family members in nursing homes reported that cognitive limitations continued to cause strain. The wear-and-tear hypothesis proffers that caregivers experience a gradual increase in stressors over time (Townsend, Noelker, Deimling, & Bass, 1989). Two published studies reported that objective stressors in the form of functional status (that is, activities of daily living) increased over time for both continuous caregivers and caregivers who placed a family member in a nursing home (Schulz & Williamson, 1991; Zarit, Todd, & Zarit, 1986). Findings relative to stressors involving memory and behavior problems were not as complementary. For example, Schulz and Williamson (1991) reported that memory and behavior problems were more pronounced over time for male caregivers in the continuing care group and for the nursing home group. Alternatively Zarit et al. (1986) found that these stressors remained stable among the continuing care group but declined slightly among husbands who had placed their spouses in nursing homes.

Another stressor of relevance to nursing home placement concerns financial strains. The high cost of institutionalization is of great concern to most families. Today's cohort of older men typically has taken responsibility for managing family finances and has expressed concerns about the financial strain of institutional care (Kaye & Applegate, 1990a).

*Resources.* It is widely acknowledged that physical and social resources play a central role in understanding caregiver outcomes,

and these are important considerations in social work assessments. Studies that have drawn comparisons between community and nursing home caregivers reported that caregivers who had placed relatives in nursing homes had more health problems and perceived greater negative effects on their health than those providing care in the community (Deimling & Poulshock, 1985; Pratt et al., 1987). Because these samples did not differentiate between spousal and nonspousal caregivers or control for age and gender, it is possible that these findings reflect potential differences between older (that is, spouses) and younger (that is, adult child) caregivers. As a result, it is unclear how physical resources change for husband caregivers over time and how health is influenced by the transition to institutional care. We do know that many husbands have health problems that limit their caregiving abilities (Kaye & Applegate, 1990b) and that husbands who continue to provide care over time are physically at risk in a number of ways. Structural factors in the caregiving situation, such as lack of time to sleep and physically draining caregiving tasks (for example, lifting and bathing), may contribute to the poorer health found among older caregivers (Gallant & Connell, 1998). Such constraints are likely to diminish among older caregivers who place their spouses in nursing homes.

To date, few published studies have examined changes in social resources of husband caregivers, although there is evidence that social support declines over time for community-dwelling male caregivers (for example, see Schulz, Williamson, Morycz, & Biegel, 1991). Research concerning the role of social resources as they relate to nursing home versus community care, using heterogeneous samples, has revealed contradictory evidence. For example, two studies reported enhanced social resources among nursing home caregivers in terms of fewer restrictions in social activities (Stephens et al., 1991) and greater satisfaction with social and leisure activities (Colerick & George, 1986), whereas another study reported more restrictions in social activities after placement (Deimling & Poulshock, 1985). It is plausible that nursing home placement alleviates time constraints placed on caregivers and allows husbands more time to invest in social relationships.

*Appraisal of Role Strain. Appraisal* may be defined as "an evaluative process that determines why and to what extent a particular transaction or series of transactions between the person and the environment is stressful" (Lazarus & Folkman, 1984, p. 19). One approach to evaluating the appraisal of role strain that seems particularly relevant to older men who have not been socialized to adopt the caregiving role is the extent to which functional status limitations and memory and behavior problems are viewed as stressful. Given the progressive nature of dementia, the wear-and-tear hypothesis suggests that husbands who continue in the caregiving role appraise functional impairments and memory and behavior problems as more stressful over time. However, one published study that examined changes in appraisals reported that memory and behavior problems were perceived as less stressful over time for husbands who had placed a spouse in a nursing home and husbands who continued to provide care in the community (Zarit et al., 1986). For the nursing home caregivers, this finding is not surprising given that institutionalization may provide some relief from the strains that precipitated placement. For the community caregivers, Zarit et al. reasoned that over time and through experience the husbands learned how to manage and tolerate better the stressors that confronted them.

*Depression.* One prevailing hypothesis about the effects of nursing home placement on the spousal caregiver predicts that insti-

tutionalization itself is a traumatic event that engenders emotional distress (King et al., 1991). This hypothesis was supported by Zarit and Whitlatch (1993), who reported that one-half of the nursing home caregivers surveyed had high levels of mental health symptoms after placement, although mean levels of symptoms did not vary between nursing home and community caregivers. The few longitudinal studies that have examined changes in depression over time and after placement have revealed inconsistent findings. Some have reported stability in depression scores (King et al., 1991), whereas others have reported slight decreases after placement (Wright, 1994). Rosenthal and Dawson (1991) found that within the first month after admission, nearly 50 percent of spouses met the criteria for depression. Zarit and Whitlatch (1992) differentiated among husbands, wives, and adult children and reported that both husbands and wives tended to remain stable or increase in levels of depressive symptoms regardless of placement status. Similarly, Schulz and Williamson (1991) reported that men providing care in the community became significantly more depressed over time.

## Research Question and Hypotheses

The research question addressed in this study is: How do the patterns change over time for husbands who maintain their caregiving role in the community compare with those of husbands who place their spouses in nursing homes in terms of caregiving stressors, resources, appraisals, and psychological well-being? I hypothesized that

• stressors relative to the spouse's functional status and memory and behavior problems (MBP) increase over time for both groups of husbands.

• financial worry remains stable among the continuing care group but is greater and increases over time for the nursing home group.

• health and satisfaction with social activities declines among the continuing care group but improves for the nursing home group.

• functional impairments and MBP are appraised as less stressful over time for both groups of husbands.

• depression remains stable or increases among the continuing care group and increases among the placement group.

## Method

### Sample

The original study sample was made up of 74 husbands who were primary caregivers currently residing at home with their wives diagnosed with dementia. A multimethod approach to participant recruitment that included community agencies, geriatric evaluation services, notices in the public media, and word of mouth was used. The mean age of 72 among husbands was similar to that found in a national study of family caregivers (Stone, Cafferata, & Sangl, 1987). Although there was considerable variation with respect to education, more than half (54 percent) had some post–high school training. The majority (78 percent) were retired, and the largest percentage of caregivers reported annual household incomes of $10,000 to $19,000 (33 percent), with the median ranging from $20,000 to $29,000. The sample represented an exclusively white population. The mean duration of spousal illness was 78 months.

### Procedures

Caregivers were contacted approximately one year after the initial interview and were asked about the condition and current status of their spouses. Except in cases where the wife was deceased, the caregiver was asked if he was willing to be interviewed again. As with the initial interview, face-to-face interviews were conducted with eligible husbands at the time and site of their convenience. The interviews lasted approximately 60 minutes.

Those who participated in the follow-up interview included 60 percent of the original sample ($n$ = 43), who continued to provide care to their spouses in the community and 10 percent ($n$ = 14) of the original sample, who had institutionalized their spouses. The remaining husbands who were not involved in the follow-up study included those who were deceased ($n$ = 2), those who were too ill ($n$ = 2), those whose spouse was deceased ($n$ = 7), those who had moved ($n$ = 2), and those who did not wish to participate ($n$ = 4). Analyses comparing caregivers included in the follow-up study with those not included indicated that the respondents were better educated ($t$ = –2.18, $p$ < .01), had not been married as long ($t$ = 2.52, $p$ < .05), and had higher incomes ($t$ = –2.54, $p$ < .05) than those not included in follow-up. Among time 2 (T2) respondents, there were no differences at time 1 (T1) between those who continued to provide care in the home and those who had institutionalized their spouses in terms of age, education, income, duration of spouse's illness, duration of caregiving, and duration of marriage.

### Measures

*Stressors.* The Katz Index of Activities of Daily Living (ADL) (Katz, Ford, Moskowitz, Jackson, & Jaffee, 1963) measure calls for a dichotomous rating of six ADL functions (that is, bathing, dressing, toileting, transferring, remaining continent, and feeding) in terms of whether the individual performs the activity without assistance. The scale was scored for the number of ADL limitations, which could range from zero to six. Instrumental activities of daily living (IADL)—that is, higher level self-care tasks (Lawton & Brody, 1969)—were assessed by asking caregivers to indicate whether their spouses were independent in using the telephone, going shopping, preparing meals, taking medicine, handling money, doing laundry, and driving. The scale was scored for the number of limitations, which could range from zero to eight. A 17-item version of the Memory and Behavior Problems Checklist (MBPC) (Zarit & Zarit, 1987) was used as a measure of stressors or degree of level of impairment and disruptive behaviors, and it could range from zero to 68. To assess financial strain, husbands were asked the following question: Do the financial expenses involved in caring for your wife worry you a great deal, somewhat, or not at all? Responses ranged from 1 = not at all to 3 = a great deal.

*Resources.* Health was measured using a three-point self-rated measure in which husbands were asked whether their physical health was now better, about the same, or worse than it had been in the preceding year, with higher scores indicating worse health. Satisfaction with social participation was assessed using measures developed by George and Gwyther (1986). Caregivers rated their satisfaction with the frequency and quality of their social–recreational participation (that is, phone contacts and visits with family and friends, church and club attendance, time spent in personal hobbies, and relaxing). The subjective assessments were summed to form a scale measuring satisfaction with social participation. Many of the scale items correlated with the amount of tangible social support and assistance that caregivers received (Clipp & George, 1990), and significant correlations with the adequacy of social support available to caregivers supported the construct validity of this scale (Clipp & George, 1990).

*Caregiver Appraisal.* With the use of the approach by Haley, Levine, Brown, and Bartolucci (1987), for each item on the ADL, IADL, and MBPC for which caregivers reported a disability, husbands were asked to rate their personal appraisal of the stressfulness of that problem. Each reaction rating was made on a scale ranging from not at all stressful = 0 to extremely stressful = 3. For each of these three scales, the average stressfulness rating was computed.

*Psychological Well-Being.* Caregiver depression was measured using the Center for Epidemiologic Studies–Depression Scale (CES–D), which was designed to identify individuals at risk of depression (Radloff, 1977). Respondents were asked how often during the past week they had experienced each of 20 symptoms, with responses given on a four-point scale ranging from 0 = less than one day to 3 = five to seven days. The CES–D yields scores ranging from 0 to 60, with a cutoff of 16 found to be the most valid indicator of depression.

These measures have been used commonly in caregiver research and were chosen for their adequate psychometric properties. Cronbach's coefficient alphas for the study scales, which measure the internal consistency of the measures (DeVellis, 1991), all ranged from .74 to .89 for T1 and T2.

### Plan of Analysis

The primary research question addressed in this study is concerned with the patterns of change from T1 to T2 in stressors, resources, appraisals, and psychological well-being for husbands providing continuing care in the community compared with husbands who have placed their spouses in nursing homes. A series of 2 × 2 repeated analysis of variance (ANOVA) measures (time × placement status) were performed for each stressor, resource, appraisal, and psychological well-being indicator. To ensure that the significant interactions were interpreted correctly, means were graphed and inspected, and univariate tests were used to further evaluate the effects. The standard alpha level of .05 defined the statistical significance. Given the small sample size, trend level effects also were noted, but should be interpreted cautiously.

## Findings

### Comparison of In-Home and Nursing Home Groups at T1

Before I examine changes over time, it is useful to compare the two groups at the point at which they initially entered the study. Husbands who had placed their wives in nursing homes were caring for wives with greater impairments in IADL and MBP, were more worried about financial expenses, and appraised ADL and MBP as more stressful at T1 than husbands who continued to provide care in the home (Table 23-1). There were no differences at T1 among those who con-

tinued to provide care in the home and those who had institutionalized their spouses in terms of one stressor indicator (that is, ADL), both resource variables (that is, health and satisfaction with social activities), appraisal of IADL, and caregiver depression.

### Patterns of Change for In-Home and Nursing Home Groups

The first two hypotheses examined changes in stressors, and the results from the ANOVAs are reported in Table 23-2. In support of the first hypothesis, there was a trend level effect for the time × placement status interaction concerning stressors relative to ADL functioning. Paired $t$ tests revealed significant increases in ADL spousal dependency between T1 and T2 for both the continuing care group ($t = -.07, p < .01$) and the nursing home group ($t = -3.39, p < .01$); however, graphing of the mean scores indicated that the amount of increase in the ADL stressor was greater for the nursing home group than for the continuing care group.

**TABLE 23-1. Mean Group Comparisons for Time 1 Stressor, Resource, Appraisal, and Well-Being Indicators**

| Variable | Continuously at Home (n = 43) | Moved to Nursing Home (n = 14) | Statistic |
|---|---|---|---|
| Stressors | | | |
| ADL | 2.97 | 3.43 | $t = -.85$ |
| IADL | 6.88 | 7.79 | $t = -2.70^{**}$ |
| MBP | 18.98 | 25.00 | $t = -2.23^{*}$ |
| Financial worry | 1.86 | 2.36 | $t = -2.38^{*}$ |
| Resources | | | |
| Health | 2.16 | 2.21 | $t = -.25$ |
| Social activity satisfaction | 17.04 | 15.57 | $t = .75$ |
| Appraisals | | | |
| ADL appraised as stressful | .76 | 1.47 | $t = -2.85^{**}$ |
| IADL appraised as stressful | .54 | .83 | $t = -1.53$ |
| MBP appraised as stressful | .98 | 1.28 | $t = -1.87†$ |
| Well-being (depression) | 13.65 | 15.86 | $t = .66$ |

Notes: ADL = activities of daily living; IADL = instrumental ADL; MBP = memory and behavior problems.
† $p < .10$. *$p < .05$. **$p < .01$.

**TABLE 23-2. Repeated ANOVA Measures of Changes in Stressors, Resources, Appraisals, and Psychological Well-Being of Caregivers**

| | At Home (n = 43) | Nursing Home (n = 14) | Time F | Place F | Time x Place F |
|---|---|---|---|---|---|
| | | | | Significance | |
| Variable | | | | | |
| **Stressors** | | | | | |
| Activities of daily living T1 | 2.97 | 3.43 | 24.78*** | NS | 4.68† |
| Activities of daily living T2 | 3.51 | 4.79 | | | |
| Instrumental ADL T1 | 6.88 | 7.79 | 6.10* | 2.92† | NS |
| Instrumental ADL T2 | 7.18 | 8.00 | | | |
| Memory & behavioral problems T1 | 18.98 | 25.00 | 4.45* | NS | 7.27 ** |
| Memory & behavioral problems T2 | 19.60 | 19.86 | | | |
| Financial worry T1 | 1.86 | 2.36 | NS | 3.54† | NS |
| Financial worry T2 | 1.79 | 2.07 | | | |
| **Resources** | | | | | |
| Health T1 | 2.16 | 2.21 | 5.07* | 2.82† | 5.07* |
| Health T2 | 2.16 | 1.64 | | | |
| Social activity satisfaction T1 | 17.04 | 15.57 | 3.57† | NS | 4.52* |
| Social activity satisfaction T2 | 16.88 | 18.36 | | | |
| **Appraisals** | | | | | |
| ADL appraised as stressful T1 | .76 | 1.47 | 31.49*** | NS | 14.46*** |
| ADL appraised as stressful T2 | .55 | .40 | | | |
| IADL appraised as stressful T1 | .54 | .83 | 16.00*** | NS | 7.74** |
| IADL appraised as stressful T2 | .44 | .26 | | | |
| MBP appraised as stressful T1 | .98 | 1.28 | 30.23*** | NS | 12.27** |
| MBP appraised as stressful T2 | .83 | .60 | | | |
| **Well-being** | | | | | |
| Depression T1 | 13.65 | 15.86 | NS | NS | 3.53† |
| Depression T2 | 12.40 | 17.36 | | | |

*Notes:* Place = placement status; NS = not significant; ADL = activities of daily living; IADL= instrumental activities of daily living; MBP = memory and behavior problems.

† $p < .10$. *$p < .05$. **$p < .01$. ***$p < .001$.

Mean scores for IADL indicated continued impairment over time for both groups; however, the time × placement interaction failed to reach significant levels, which may have been due to a ceiling effect because the IADL scores of the nursing home group were all at maximum levels at T2. Although there was a significant interaction for MBP, the paired $t$ test for the continuing care group was not significant, suggesting that MBP did not change dramatically during the one-year period. Contrary to the expectation, there was a significant decline in MBP in the nursing home group ($t = 2.59, p < .05$). A regression to the mean as a result of the higher scores of the nursing home group on MBP at T1 may have contributed to the decline.

The second hypothesis predicted that financial worry would remain stable for the continuing care group but would be greater and will increase for the nursing home group. There was a trend level effect for placement status, indicating that the nursing home group was more concerned about financial worries (Table 23-2). Contrary to the expectation, there was no time × placement interaction for financial worry. The nursing home group was more worried about finances than the continuing care group, but there was no change over time noted.

The third hypothesis predicted that health and satisfaction with social activities would decline among the continuing care group but would improve over time for the nursing home group. Both of these caregiver resources had significant time × placement status interactions (Table 23-2). Univariate tests revealed that health and social activity satisfaction remained stable for the continuing care group. In partial support of this hypothesis, univariate tests revealed that both resource variables improved for the placement group. The reduced health score indicates that health was perceived as improved ($t = 2.51, p < .05$), and the increased social activity score indicates that husbands reported more satisfaction with their social and recreational activities after placement ($t = -2.43, p < .05$).

The fourth hypothesis specified that functional impairments and MBP would be appraised as less stressful over time for both groups. Significant two-way interactions for time × placement status were found for each of the appraisal items. In support of the fourth hypothesis, paired $t$ tests revealed that husbands in the community appraised ADL ($t = 1.99, p < .05$) and MBP ($t = 2.30, p < .05$) as less stressful over time. Not surprisingly, husbands who placed their wives in a nursing home appraised ADL ($t = 4.39, p < .001$), IADL ($t = 2.63, p < .05$), and MBP ($t = 3.91, p < .01$) as significantly less stressful after placement. Indeed, graphing of means suggested that the decline in appraised stress was greater for the nursing home group than for the continuing care group.

The final hypothesis predicted that depression would remain stable or increase among the continuing care group and will increase among the placement group. The repeated ANOVA measures for caregiver depression-by-placement status revealed a trend level effect for the two-way interaction for time × placement status ($F = 3.53, p < .10$). Contrary to the expectation, there was a trend level effect for decreased depression among the continuing care group ($t = 1.84, p < .10$). The mean-level depression score for the nursing home group increased from 15.86 to 17.36 (Table 23-2), which is above the cutoff for depression, but this increase was nonsignificant. It should be noted that a very large difference would have had to occur to have the power to detect a small effect given the few placement cases.

## Discussion

This study sought to understand the comparative changes in stressors, resources, appraisals, and psychological well-being between husbands who continue to provide care for their wives with dementia and husbands who place their wives with dementia in nursing homes after one year. Perhaps the most intriguing findings pertain to the differential patterns that emerged for the two groups of husbands investigated in this study. For husbands who continued to provide care for their wives in their homes, there appeared to be a pattern of adaptation. Theories of adaptation propose that all beings have an innate drive to maintain a state of equilibrium (Selye, 1974). Systems theory refers to this process as "homeostasis," whereby systems function to self-regulate and restore balance when under stress (Anderson & Carter, 1990). Thus, the adaptation hypothesis proposes that caregivers adapt to the strains of caregiving and either maintain or improve in well-being over time (Lawton, 1996; Schulz et al., 1991). In the current study, although stressors actually increased and resources remained stable, husbands in the continuing care group appraised functional limitations of their spouses as less stressful and reported lower levels of depression over time. This pattern of adaptation is consistent with earlier research reporting that husbands tolerated stressors better over time (Zarit et al., 1986) and maintained stable depression levels over a two-year period (Zarit & Whitlatch, 1992).

In contrast to this pattern of stable resources and improved psychological well-being, a very different pattern emerged for husbands who placed their spouses in a facility. As hypothesized, the husbands' physical and social resources actually improved after placement. It was apparent through several comments made by the husbands that after placement they experienced less physical strain of providing care and had more time to enjoy social and recreational activities. For example, some men commented on the lightened physical load as illustrated in these comments: "I feel physically better now." "The stress is less physical. Now I have a smile on my face when I see her. Last year all she saw was a grouch." "I feel so relieved that she's getting the care that she needs. There are things about this situation that aren't so pleasant but what else can you do? I have more energy now."

Interestingly, although resources were improved and appraisals of stressors were lessened, husbands who placed their spouses in a nursing home reported no change in their psychological well-being. Indeed the average depression score for 50 percent of these husbands at T2 was at or above the cutoff score that is indicative of risk of clinical depression. Theories of adaptation and stress and coping have emphasized the essential role of resources and appraisals for mediating the effect of stressful life events on psychological well-being (Kramer & Vitaliano, 1994). It seems counterintuitive that improvements in these two domains could occur without effecting positive changes in psychological well-being. One possible explanation is that

this finding simply reflects a bereavement process that began in anticipation of and that follows the transition to nursing home placement. Rosenthal and Dawson (1991) observed high levels of depression and grief responses among wives who had recently institutionalized their spouses and likened the transition to the bereavement experience. Zarit and Whitlatch (1993) found that spouses who had placed their husband or wife reported fewer constraints on their time but had higher levels of depression than community-dwelling spouses.

According to crisis theory, when caregiving challenges escalate and no longer respond to the customary repertoire of coping responses available to the husband caregiver, he is likely to enter an active crisis state, marked by disorganization and disequilibrium. The outcome of a crisis is likely to be either a return to the previous, precrisis situation or a persisting disruption, referred to as a "transition state" (Weiss, 1976). Transitions (that is, institutionalization), which follow periods of crisis, represent permanent changes in the individual's life organization and identity, which often result in a sense of loss, depression, and mourning (Golan, 1986). Transitions are more likely to be defined as loss when they are perceived to affect the person's life space (that is, personal relationships, home environment) (Golan, 1986). Several husbands commented on the effect on their life space through the loneliness they felt without their wives.

It is noteworthy that 32 percent of the husbands who continued to provide care and 50 percent of the husbands who had placed their spouses in a nursing home were at or above the cutoff indicative of risk of clinical depression. These rates are two to four times as high as the rates (14 percent to 16 percent) found among representative middle and older adult populations (Eaton & Kessler,

1981; Frerichs, Aneshensel, & Clark, 1981). Husbands in this study voiced two major risk factors for depression (that is, social isolation and financial concerns) (Friedman & Sjogren, 1981). Given that married women are known to be at greater risk of depressive symptoms of sadness than married men (Newmann & Watson, 1992), the high rate of depressive symptoms among husbands in this study is striking. These high depression levels may reflect the detrimental effects of losing one's partner to a dementia, an effect that is most challenging to older husbands who typically rely on their wives for intimate emotional and social support. Alternatively, another plausible explanation for the high depression levels is that these husbands were just as depressed before taking on the caregiving role. Data are not available concerning depression levels prior to caregiving, and so caution must be used in interpreting these findings.

One variable that has not been included in many earlier caregiving studies, which may be particularly salient to the husband caregiver, is financial concern. Schulz and Williamson (1991) found that concern about financial resources appeared to be an important predictor of depression among male caregivers. Financial concern was greatest among those facing the placement decision and did not appear to change over time. When asked to share recommendations they would make to policymakers, nearly 60 percent of the 14 men who placed their wives in nursing homes expressed concerns about the high cost of care and issues relevant to finances. One man stated, "In most cases I think the money problems are the greatest concern to people. I've worked hard to make my money and I wish there was some way I could keep it." Another shared his belief, "The average husband would appreciate special funding. It's frightening to think total life

savings would be wiped out." Others voiced similar concerns and suggested that caregivers should have financial protection, that expenses should be tax deductible, that spousal impoverishment laws should be improved, and that nursing homes should be more "affordable."

## Limitations

Although this exploratory study takes an important first step in understanding possible patterns of change over time experienced by husbands caring for wives with dementia, it is necessary to acknowledge that several limitations restrict conclusions that may be drawn. The most notable limitation includes the nonrepresentative and small nature of the sample. Although there was greater variation in the original sample, those who dropped out were less educated and had lower incomes than those who participated in the follow-up. This sample consisted of white men who had at least some high school education and incomes above the poverty line. A major disadvantage of small samples is their likely failure to detect meaningful differences. Yet even in this very small sample, several significant findings were noted. As is characteristic of most earlier caregiver research, the lack of precaregiving data, the limited number of data points, and the limited time encompassed by this study restrict the inferences that can be drawn regarding patterns of change and their meaning. In addition, it cannot be concluded with any degree of certainty that the differential changes of the groups across time were functions of the difference between the groups, or whether the two groups were simply different to begin with. Another limitation of this study is its reliance on self-report data, particularly for the stressor variables, which may have been influenced by the husbands' emotional states. To obtain a more definitive understanding of the patterns of change among husband caregivers, conducting prospective, multiwave longitudinal research; using probability data; and relying on self-report and more objective measures are recommended. I hope these findings will stimulate replication studies and additional investigation of the older male caregiver, who has been largely neglected in the literature and who may possess distinct needs and experiences. Qualitative investigations should be conducted to further enhance understanding of how the transition to nursing home placement influences the male caregiver experience.

## Implications for Practice

As discussed, the exploratory nature of this study suggests that further work be done to replicate these findings. Replication of the findings may have several important implications for practice. First, social workers who work with caregivers in the community may use this information to inform husbands about the changes they might anticipate after placement. For example, one task of the gerontological social worker is to help husbands struggling with the placement decision to problem solve and to evaluate the pros and cons of this alternative (Cole, Griffin, & Ruiz, 1986). Some of the potential benefits for the caregiver might be more time for social and recreational activities and less physical strain. Such changes might allow a husband to have more energy and be more present with his spouse once the demands for care have been lessened through placement. Second, more intensive supports and interventions might be needed to help the husband cope with the transition of placing his spouse in a facility. Skills for assessing and treating depressive symptoms and finding ways to help husbands cope with their grief and potential loneliness

would be essential in this effort. Social workers might be advised to consider linking a husband who has placed his spouse in a nursing home and has adjusted to that transition with a husband who is in the process of doing so. Third, and most important, the implications suggest that social workers need to evaluate further and assist husbands in uncovering alternatives to nursing home placement. The resources that were available to these husbands in terms of potential alternatives to placement are unknown. But optimally, social workers should focus on the needs and desires of the individual client and help the client explore creative solutions to challenging problems. If researchers uncover through further investigation that nursing home placement is indeed associated with elevated depressive symptoms of the older husband, there may be a need to develop more appealing and acceptable alternatives. Current social policies provide few financially feasible options to institutional care for people with dementia, which appears to weigh heavily on husbands' minds. We know that although families show great preference for home care, "Medicaid continues to show a strong institutional bias, with more than 80% of the $50 billion spent on long-term care in 1995 going to nursing homes and institutions of people with cognitive disabilities" (Stone, 1999, p. 3). With the rapidly approaching demographic explosion of older people who are primary consumers of long-term care services, it is essential that social workers take a more active role first in helping understand the long-term care values and preferences of older husbands, and second in helping to inform the policies and to shape the optimal services that will be congruent with these values and preferences. Ideally, the available options and supports will enhance well-being, rather than detract from it.

# References

Anderson, R. E., & Carter, I. (1990). *Human behavior in the social environment: A social systems approach*. New York: Aldine de Gruyter.

Chang, C. F., & White-Means, S. I. (1991). The men who care: An analysis of male primary caregivers who care for frail elderly at home. *Journal of Applied Gerontology, 10*, 343–358.

Clipp, E. C., & George, L. K. (1990). Caregiver needs and patterns of social support. *Journal of Gerontology, 45*, S102–S111.

Cole, L., Griffin, K., & Ruiz, B. (1986). A comprehensive approach to working with families of Alzheimer's patients. In R. Dobrof (Ed.), *Social work and Alzheimer's disease* (pp. 27–39). New York: Haworth Press.

Colerick, E. J., & George, L. K. (1986). Predictors of institutionalization among caregivers of patients with Alzheimer's disease. *Journal of the American Geriatrics Society, 34*, 493–498.

Deimling, G. T., & Poulshock, S. W. (1985). The transition from family in-home care to institutional care: Focus on health and attitudinal issues as predisposing factors. *Research on Aging, 7*, 563–576.

DeVellis, R. F. (1991). *Scale development: Theory and applications*. Newbury Park, CA: Sage Publications.

Eaton, W. W., & Kessler, L. G. (1981). Rates of symptoms of depression in a national sample. *American Journal of Epidemiology, 114*, 528–538.

Frerichs, R. R., Aneshensel, C. S., & Clark, V. A. (1981). Prevalence of depression in Los Angeles County. *American Journal of Epidemiology, 113*, 691–699.

Friedman, J., & Sjogren, T. (1981). Assets of the elderly as they retire. *Social Security Bulletin, 44*(1), 16–31.

Gallant, M. P., & Connell, C. M. (1998). The stress process among dementia spouse caregivers: Are caregivers at risk for negative health behavior change? *Research on Aging, 20*, 267–297.

George, L. K., & Gwyther, L. P. (1986). Caregiver well-being: A multidimensional examination of family caregivers of demented adults. *Gerontologist, 26*, 253–259.

Golan, N. (1986). Crisis theory. In F. J. Turner (Ed.), *Social work treatment: Interlocking theoretical approaches* (3rd ed., pp. 296–340). New York: Free Press.

Haley, W., Levine, E., Brown, S., & Bartolucci, A. (1987). Stress, appraisal, coping and social support as predictors of adaptational outcome among dementia caregivers. *Psychology and Aging, 2*, 323–330.

Harris, P. B. (1995). Differences among husbands caring for their wives with Alzheimer's disease: Qualitative findings and counseling implications. *Journal of Clinical Geropsychology, 1*, 97–106.

Katz, S., Ford, A., Moskowitz, R., Jackson, B., & Jaffee, M. (1963). Studies of illness in the aged. The index of ADL, a standardized measure of biological and psychosocial functioning. *JAMA, 185*, 914–919.

Kaye, L. W., & Applegate, J. S. (1990a). *Men as caregivers to the elderly: Understanding and aiding unrecognized family support*. Lexington, MA: Lexington Books.

Kaye, L. W., & Applegate, J. S. (1990b). Men as elder caregivers: Building a research agenda for the 1990s. *Journal of Aging Studies, 4*, 289–298.

King, S., Collins, C., Given, B., & Vredevoogd, J. (1991). Institutionalization of an elderly family member: Reactions of spouse and nonspouse caregivers. *Archives of Psychiatric Nursing, 5*, 323–330.

Kramer, B. J. (1997a). Differential predictors of strain and gain among husbands caring for wives with dementia. *Gerontologist, 37*, 239–249.

Kramer, B. J. (1997b). Gain in the caregiving experience: Where are we? What next? *Gerontologist, 37*, 218–232.

Kramer, B. J., & Vitaliano, P. P. (1994). Coping: A review of the theoretical frameworks and the measures used among caregivers of individuals with dementia. *Journal of Gerontological Social Work, 23*(1/2), 151–174.

Lawton, M. P. (1996). The aging family in a multigenerational perspective. In G.H.S. Singer, L. E. Powers, & A. L. Olson (Eds.), *Family, community, and disability: Redefining family support, innovations in public-private partnerships* (pp. 135–149). Baltimore: Paul H. Brookes.

Lawton, M. P., & Brody, E. (1969). Assessment of older people: Self-maintenance instrumental activities of daily living. *Gerontologist, 9,* 179–186.

Lazarus, R., & Folkman, S. (1984). *Stress, appraisal, and coping.* New York: Springer.

Montgomery, R. J., & Kosloski, K. (1994). A longitudinal analysis of nursing home placement for dependent elders cared for by spouses vs adult children. *Journal of Gerontology: Social Sciences, 49,* S62–S74.

Newmann, J. P., & Watson, D. (1992). Gender, marital status, and depression. *Research in Community and Mental Health, 7,* 125–152.

Novak, M., & Guest, C. (1992). A comparison of the impact of institutionalization on spouse and nonspouse caregivers. *Journal of Applied Gerontology, 11,* 379–394.

Pearlin, L. I., Mullan, J. T., Semple, S. J., & Skaff, M. M. (1990). Caregiving and the stress process: An overview of concepts and their measures. *Gerontologist, 30,* 583–591.

Pratt, C., Schmall, V., Wright, S., & Hare, J. (1987). The forgotten client: Family caregivers to institutionalized dementia patients. In T. H. Brubaker (Ed.), *Aging, health, and family: Long-term care* (pp. 197–213). Newbury Park, CA: Sage Publications.

Pruchno, R. A., Michaels, E., & Potashnik, S. L. (1990). Predictors of institutionalization among Alzheimer disease victims with caregiving spouses. *Journal of Gerontology: Social Sciences, 45,* S259–266.

Radloff, L. (1977). The CES—D scale: A self-report depression scale for research in the general population. *Applied Psychological Measurement, 1,* 385–401.

Rosenthal, C. J., & Dawson, P. (1991). Wives of institutionalized elderly men: The first stage of the transition to quasi-widowhood. *Journal of Aging and Health, 3,* 315–334.

Schulz, R., & Williamson, G. M. (1991). A 2-year longitudinal study of depression among Alzheimer's caregivers. *Psychology and Aging, 6,* 569–578.

Schulz, R., Williamson, G. M., Morycz, R. K., & Biegel, D. E. (1991). Costs and benefits of providing care to Alzheimer's patients. In S. Spacapan & S. Oskamp (Eds.), *Helping and being helped: Naturalistic studies* (pp. 153–181). Newbury Park, CA: Sage Publications.

Selye, H. (1974). *Stress without distress.* Philadelphia: Lippincott.

Stephens, M. A. P., Kinney, J. M., & Ogrocki, P. K. (1991). Stressors and well-being among caregivers to older adults with dementia: The in-home versus nursing home experience. *Gerontologist, 31,* 217–223.

Stone, R. (1999). Long-term care: Coming of age in the 21st century. In J. Olson & K. Bogenschneider (Eds.), *Wisconsin family impact seminars briefing report: Long-term care—State policy perspectives* (pp. 3–11). Madison: University of Wisconsin—Madison, School of Human Ecology.

Stone, R., Cafferata, G., & Sangl, J. (1987). Caregivers of the frail elderly: A national profile. *Gerontologist, 27,* 616–626.

Townsend, A., Noelker, L., Deimling, G., & Bass, D. (1989). Longitudinal impact of interhousehold caregiving on adult children's mental health. *Psychology and Aging, 4,* 393–401.

U.S. House Select Committee on Aging. (1987, January). *Exploring the myths: Caregiving in America.* Washington, DC: U.S. Government Printing Office.

Weiss, R. S. (1976). Transition states and other stressful situations: Their nature and programs for their management. In G. Caplan & M. Killilea (Eds.), *Support systems and mutual help: A multidisciplinary exploring* (pp. 213–232). New York: Grune & Stratton.

Wright, L. K. (1994). AD spousal caregivers: Longitudinal changes in health, depression and coping. *Journal of Gerontological Nursing, 20*(10), 33–45, 48.

Zarit, S. H., Todd, P. A., & Zarit, J. M. (1986). Subjective burden of husbands and wives as caregivers: A longitudinal study. *Gerontologist, 26,* 260–266.

Zarit, S. H., & Whitlatch, C. J. (1992). Institutional placement: Phases of the transition. *Gerontologist, 32,* 665–672.

Zarit, S. H., & Whitlatch, C. J. (1993). The effects of placement in nursing homes on family caregivers: Short and long term consequences. *Irish Journal of Psychology, 14,* 25–37.

Zarit, S. H., & Zarit, J. (1987). *The Memory and Behavior Problems Checklist-1987R and the Burden Interview* (Technical Report). University Park: Pennsylvania State University.

This chapter was originally published in the May 2000 issue of *Health & Social Work*, Vol. 25, Number 2, pp. 97–107.

# V
# Dignity

❧ ❧ ❧

Elders have the right to live in dignity, with security and freedom from exploitation and physical and mental abuse. They should be treated fairly regardless of their age, gender, racial or ethnic background, disability, or functional or mental impairments, and they should be valued independently of their economic contributions. These values highlight the importance to older people of the right to maintain their own home life and to make their own choices in maintaining the construction of their daily lives—whether living in one's own private space or in congregate care or even in a medical care facility.

The articles in this section emphasize the fundamental decisions older people make about where and how to live and the attenuated rights that other family members have to influence those decisions. These articles draw attention to the importance of maintaining control in one's home on a daily basis, even when the home is owned by others, and when older persons rely upon relatives and home care professionals to carry on with normal activities and participate in pleasurable events.

In this vein, James Reinardy and Rosalie Kane report on a representative sample of 439 cognitively intact older Oregonians who have experienced the new choices in late life offered to them by that state's initiation in the 1980s of an extensive range of foster care alternatives. Comparing retrospectively the decisions of elders who chose nursing homes and those who chose foster care, they explore the alternatives that were considered, the circumstances leading to the move, and the residents' perceptions

351

of the decision-making process and who influenced it. Significant differences were found in the characteristics of settings that each group deemed important, the circumstances surrounding the need to relocate, the nature of the search process, the people influencing it, and the perceived control over the decision. This article highlights many important aspects of social work practice in the high proportion of nursing home residents who got there following an acute care hospitalization, a situation in which pressure and urgency reduces the patient's sense of control or subsequent satisfaction. Many who felt the decision had been made by others showed no sign of having protested it. The authors emphasize the importance of making decisions directly with older clients, working hard to communicate with them, and not undercutting their dignity by relying overly on family to make decisions. Decisions about where to live are too important to be left to hospital discharge planners; they should be a flexible and continuous function of planning, not a hasty but irrevocable choice.

Marcia Egan and Goldie Kadushin are interested in similar issues of client self-determination in their exploratory study of the professional functions and ethical concerns raised by 118 social workers in home care agencies in Wisconsin and Tennessee. They note that social workers in home health care perform a wider array of professional functions with a more diverse population of patients than previously documented. Workers most often experienced ethical concerns related to self-determination, barriers to access to services, implementation of advance directives, and assessment of mental competence. Ethical concerns were raised by the influence of reimbursement incentives; practices having mainly elderly clients; and caseloads of clients with complex problems. Comparing

the experiences of social workers in proprietary and nonprofit agencies, workers in proprietary agencies rated barriers to access as their most important ethical concern; such ratings occurred significantly more frequently than did similar ratings by workers in nonprofit agencies. Like Reinardy and Kane, Egan and Kadushin mention the need to develop more formalized mechanisms to ensure full attention and continuity of care for patients transitioning from hospitalization to home care.

Perhaps the most important decisions that the older person should be able to make with autonomy and a sense of control are those concerning death. As noted by Egan and Kadushin, concerns about older patients' mental competence run high among practitioners in home care. The next article provides a very helpful framework for both assessment and intervention with terminally ill people who may experience depression or express a desire to die. Ruth Anne Van Loon notes that terminally ill patients who make "desire to die" statements may be expressing depression, suicidal intent, or coping. It is incumbent on social workers to evaluate such meanings by assessing patients for both depression and suicide risk, in order to distinguish those using such statements to cope or to indicate a rational choice for suicide. Only through accurate differentiation among meanings can the clinician design appropriate interventions. Through excellent development of schematics, criteria, and risk factors, Van Loon provides useful clinical guidance for differential assessment of these key issues. Her assessment of the usefulness of "desire-to-die" talk is especially compelling in light of societal obligation to listen to and engage with dying persons so that they will have a good death.

Finally, in the last article, Colleen Galambos explores the many complicated decisions raised by medical technology around options for patient treatment and for death itself. Galambos describes two legislative efforts aimed at preserving end-of-life autonomy: the Patient Self-Determination Act adopted by Congress in 1991 and the Uniform Health Care Decisions Act, a model state code recommended for enactment by all the states. Both provisions provide a more comprehensive approach to planning advance directives. The first requires that health care facilities furnish written information on treatment options, and right-to-die and advance directives to all adult patients upon admission. It assumes that such information will prompt discussion between patients, their families, and their physicians. The latter, when adopted by all the states, would result in more consistency across states. Galambos describes the many aspects of this proposed legislation, defining advance directives, surrogate, guardian, and other terms, and clarifying the difficulties with consistently getting such information into patient records and getting medical practitioners to honor patient wishes. The article urges social workers to advocate for passage of the Uniform Health Care Decisions Act in all 50 states.

An overriding theme in these articles is the innate right of adults to make their own decisions. Related to this is the importance of maintaining a sense of personal control. Even when older adults prefer to designate decisions to a trusted relative or friend, they should be able to exercise their own preferences in that designation.

# 24

# Choosing an Adult Foster Home or a Nursing Home

## Residents' Perceptions about Decision Making and Control

JAMES REINARDY and
ROSALIE A. KANE

Given the current emphasis on cost containment, quality of life, and alternatives to nursing homes for older people with long-term care needs, family-like settings (often called adult foster care programs) are an appealing policy option for cost and quality considerations. Yet compared with their knowledge about nursing homes, policymakers' and practitioners' knowledge about adult foster care programs, their clientele, and, in particular, the decision to enter such a residential setting is scant. This article explores the circumstances of the decision to move to a foster home rather than a nursing home through the retrospective perceptions of cognitively intact residents who had moved to each setting.

We take as a given that the decisions to move to any residential long-term care setting are complex and multiply determined and made in a social context where family members and others have potential to influence those decisions. This article also examines what residents consider important in seeking a care setting, aspects of the decision-making process, and the residents' sense of control over that decision. Of particular interest is how the decision-making process might influence resident satisfaction and social participation in either care site.

Social workers are involved as advisors to older people and their families as they make life transitions—and particularly to those making such transitions from hospital settings. Any systematic information about care decisions for options less known than the nursing home should help refine social work practice.

## Nursing Homes

Nursing homes are well known to health and social services professionals as the long-term care service for elderly people that accounts for the vast majority of public funding. A *nursing home* is defined, somewhat circularly, as a residential health care facility that meets the federal requirements for certification for payment under Medicare and Medicaid and any additional state licensure requirements. These standards have evolved since their initial enactment in 1965, particularly since the implementation of the Nursing Home Reform Act of 1987 (P.L. 100-203), which grew out of the Institute of Medicine (1986) report on the quality of nursing homes. Nursing home standards are organized in categories such as administrative practices, environmental concerns, quality of care, quality of life, residents' rights, and infection control. Federal regulations that articulate some minimum nursing standards and staffing standards for training of nursing assistants also have been enacted. Within these requirements, nursing homes vary in size and other attributes. For the most part, however, they are modeled on hospitals, with the preponderance of accommodations being shared and a predominance of nursing routines (Gamroth, Semradek, & Tornquist, 1995; Kane & Caplan, 1990).

## Adult Foster Care

Although adult foster care in the United States has been traced back to colonial times, when boarding homes provided meals and laundry, foster care specifically for older adults with disabilities is a fairly recent development (Sherman & Newman, 1979). The confusing variation of names—for example, family care homes, residential care, "homes plus," supportive care, board and care—and regulatory definitions associated with this type of arrangement complicate investigation of adult foster care. The most recent national study of adult foster care (Folkemer, Jensen, Lipson, Stauffer, & Fox-Grage, 1996) standardized a definition to include targeting adults unable to live independently because of physical or mental impairments or disabilities and who need supervision or personal care; offering 24-hour supervision, protection, and personal care besides room and board; serving a designated small group (ordinarily from one to six); and providing a homelike, family-like environment with a caregiver often residing in the home.

Mehrotra and Kosloski (1991) identified four common assumptions underlying foster care placement: (1) Nursing homes have detrimental psychological and social effects; (2) a family setting is inherently superior to an institutionalized setting; (3) adult foster care homes represent a "least restrictive care environment"; and (4) foster care is a desirable part of a continuum of long-term care. They also noted unresolved issues, such as the need for appropriate targeting and program goal setting. In a survey to which 42 states and the District of Columbia responded, Folkemer et al. (1996) found that 26 states had definitions of foster care that met their more stringent definitions of giving personal care. Of these, most state foster home programs served fewer than 1,000 residents, all but seven served mostly publicly subsidized clientele, and only five states served a majority of private-pay residents. Twenty states supplemented the Supplemental Security Income benefit standard to support adult foster care, and eight used Medicaid waivers to support direct care in adult foster homes. As Hudson, Dennis, Nutter, Gallaway, and Richardson (1994) pointed out, few states collect data on the health and functioning of adult foster care residents.

## Setting for the Study

Oregon is ideal for the present study of location decisions for two reasons: (1) Adult foster care is well established as a middle-class as well as a low-income alternative form of long-term care (Kane, Kane, Illston, & Nyman, 1991), and (2) adults with substantial disability levels receive foster care in Oregon foster homes. Indeed, Folkemer et al. (1996) found that Oregon was one of only five states with a preponderance of private-pay residents in adult foster care and was the only state with a program of substantial size in comparison to its nursing home population. Thus, we knew there would be some overlap in characteristics of residents in foster homes and nursing homes in terms of functional and care needs.

Regulations define an Oregon adult foster home as a family-style home in a residentially zoned area that provides care to a maximum of five elderly or disabled people. Foster home caregivers are required to attend 18 hours of preservice training, supplemented by 10 hours of yearly training (Ladd & Hannum, 1992). Since 1982 care for the service component of adult foster homes (as opposed to room and board) in Oregon could be reimbursed under the Medicaid waiver for eligible residents. Indeed, the state stimulated the development of adult foster care as part of its effort to divert people from nursing homes. Initially the state imposed few regulations. But by the 1990s the homes were classified into three levels (depending on the training and background of the provider) that differ according to maximum impairment limitations of the adults they can serve. Staff members in adult foster homes provide personal assistance and supervision and, under Oregon's Nurse Delegation Act (Oregon Board of Nursing, 1993), may perform nursing tasks if a nurse trains them and certifies their competence (Kane, O'Connor, & Olsen Baker, 1995). Thus, most adult foster care programs administer medications to the residents and provide routine nursing services.

Public officials at state and local levels in Oregon view adult foster care as an alternative service that consumers can choose rather than a niche on the continuum for those not yet "needing" nursing homes. Funding imperatives, therefore, drive placement decisions less in Oregon than in other states, because multiple options are available under Medicaid for people with comparable disabilities. Information constraints for both consumers and their advocates and advisors, of course, may limit the extent to which less familiar alternatives are genuine options.

Although adult foster care in Oregon is a real alternative to nursing homes, it by no means replaces them. The populations in the two settings overlap, but a 1991 study (Kane et al., 1991) showed that the foster care population was less impaired on average. However, all foster care residents reimbursed by Medicaid must be eligible for nursing homes based on their functioning, and Kane and colleagues found that the privately paying foster care residents had more disabilities than the Medicaid clientele (Kane et al., 1991; Stark, Kane, Kane, & Finch, 1995).

The widespread acceptance of adult foster care homes in Oregon is underscored because more private-pay residents use them than Medicaid-supported clients do. In 1995 about two-thirds of Oregon's approximately 10,000 adult foster care residents were paying privately, a proportion that has characterized the program from the beginning, although the absolute numbers of foster care have grown steadily.

Because adult foster care in Oregon is a large, mature program serving people with a wide range of incomes and disability levels, it provides an opportunity to investigate issues surrounding the decision to enter a foster home compared to a nursing home.

In Oregon almost all nursing home beds are licensed as intermediate care facilities (ICFs). The distinction between ICFs and skilled nursing facilities (SNFs) disappeared for quality purposes with the regulatory changes of 1987, which eliminated any difference in standards for the two settings, although Medicare will cover only those deemed to need SNF care in facilities certified for skilled nursing care. However, the ratio between ICFs and SNFs and the reimbursement accorded to each has always been a matter of state policy. Well before we began our study, Oregon had developed two classifications for ICFs based on acuity and had almost eliminated the SNF designation, which was reserved for a handful of residents in extremely grave medical circumstances. Therefore, in drawing our sample, we used ICF residents only to achieve more direct comparability with foster care residents.

## Relocation and Decision Making

Relocation studies typically are divided into studies about relocation within the community, from the community to institutions, and between institutions (Schulz & Brenner, 1977). The distinctions blur, however, as new options are added to the housing–care continuum, such as community care, retirement communities, and various types of support- ive settings (Armer, 1993; Netting & Wilson, 1991). Most early studies investigated relocation per se, focusing on adverse outcomes, especially mortality and morbidity (see, for example, Aldrich & Mendkoff, 1963; Lawton & Yaffe, 1970; Pablo, 1977). More recent approaches study the predictors of adjustment and positive and negative outcomes (Armer, 1993; Coulton et al., 1988; Lieberman & Tobin, 1983; Mirotznik & Ruskin, 1985; Pohl & Fuller, 1980; Reinardy, 1992, 1995). There is no existing literature on why people choose one form of long-term care over another, including the relationship of social work practitioners to that decision.

On the other hand, decision making and control over the decision to move have received recent attention in the long-term care literature, particularly in studies of relocation to nursing homes. Associations have been found between control or perceived choice and such postadmission outcomes as adaptation and adjustment, satisfaction with posthospital care, psychological distress, satisfaction with nursing home services, participation in activities, higher physical functioning, decreased pain, reduced use of medications, life satisfaction, depression, and health status (Armer, 1993; Gallagher & Walker, 1990; Harel & Noelker, 1982; Lieberman & Tobin, 1983; Pohl & Fuller, 1980; Reinardy, 1992, 1995; Rodin, 1986a, 1986b). The theoretical frameworks used to explain the relationship between control and postadmission well-being differ. It is important for practitioners, however, to realize that control may stem from a perceived sense of "mastery" over the task—seeing oneself at the center of the decision—as well as from the use of coping and management skills such as working through the steps of the decision process and absorbing adequate information about the new environment and alternatives (Lieberman & Tobin, 1983; Schulz & Brenner, 1977). Taken together, the evidence suggests that social workers should support both approaches in helping their elderly clients maintain a sense of control over the residential moves that they make for health purposes.

In the present study, using an existing data set, we were able to obtain some direct perceptions of cognitively intact elderly respondents about the preferences and circumstances surrounding their move and the factors influencing the move. In addition, the data shed light on the themes found in the literature about how decision and control affect residents' well-being. The study, therefore, affords an opportunity to learn more about the lived experiences of the clientele whom social workers serve at times of great personal crisis and disruption.

## Method

### *Respondents and Data Collection*

We collected the data as part of a study to develop and evaluate the effects of Oregon's foster care program compared to its nursing home program on functional abilities to perform activities of daily living (ADLs) (Kane et al., 1991). We sampled 405 foster care and 402 ICF residents from four geographic areas, chosen to represent urban and rural populations (including the Portland area) and to reflect state characteristics such as bed-to-population ratios and both public and private-pay residents. We selected foster homes from the four geographic areas, and all of the residents in each sampled foster home were interviewed. We sampled ICFs proportionally to the ICF supply in each of the four geographic areas and interviewed 10 residents from each ICF sampled.

We conducted in-person interviews at the foster homes and the nursing homes. Because we were interested in the experiences as perceived by the older people themselves, this article considers only those sufficiently

cognitively intact to be interviewed without proxy informants. The resulting sample for analysis consisted of 439 respondents, 260 adult foster care residents (or 64 percent of the original sample) and 179 nursing home residents (or 45 percent of the original sample), a difference that reflects the much higher levels of cognitive impairment measured among the nursing home residents. To make the determination of cognitive incapacity, the interviewers visited all the sampled residents in person and administered the Short Portable Mental Status Questionnaire (Pfeiffer, 1975); if this 10-point scale had more than four errors, family members and facility staff were interviewed as proxies for specific questions.

### *Measures*

*Variables Regarding Relocation.* The analysis presented here relies particularly on questions about the resident's decision to move to the setting. These include the health, social, and economic circumstances surrounding the move (presented as lists of items to which residents agreed or disagreed about the presence of each); the characteristics of the setting that residents perceived as important in the decision to move to the particular setting (also presented as a list, including items such as location, activity programs, rehabilitation programs, price, and homelike setting); consideration of one or more other residential alternatives before moving; key actors, both professional and informal, influencing the move; residents' perceptions of their own control over the decision to move; and the residents' satisfaction with the relocation decision.

We measured degree of control by an ordinal question: "All in all, how much did you control the decision to move to this foster (nursing) home? Would you say, 'I had almost complete control over the decision,' 'I had some control over the decision,' or 'I had little or no control over the decision.'" To clarify further the closed-ended variable on control, we asked respondents an open-ended question: "Please tell me a bit about how it happened that you moved from _____ to NAME OF PLACE."

*Dependent Variables.* Resident satisfaction and social participation were dependent variables for analyses of the effect of perceived control over the location decision. We measured satisfaction with services on an eight-item scale ($\alpha$ = .84) with four-point Likert ratings for each item. Respondents were asked how satisfied they were in the following areas: food, room, daily care, daily activities, amount of time to see family and friends, medical care, physical safety, and the safety of personal possessions. Activities within the residence were measured on an eight-item scale ($\alpha$ = .71) with three-point ratings of 1 = never, 2 = sometimes, or 3 = often for each item. The activities included were watching television, talking to other residents, reading books or newspapers, doing hobbies, chatting with staff, playing cards or other games, participating in activities organized by the foster care or nursing home, and helping with cooking or other housekeeping.

*Covariates.* The interview protocol largely used fixed-choice questions and for some variables used established scales to collect data on functional abilities, mood and outlook, cognitive status, and use of health services. We captured physical functioning in an ADL score derived from a six-item scale ($\alpha$ = .88) that mirrored the assessment that Oregon uses in its statewide Medicaid waiver program: The items were ability to move around both in and out of doors, to transfer to bed and chair, to bathe, to dress oneself, to use the toilet alone, and to feed oneself. All were measured on a three-point range,

from "without help," through "need some help," to "depend completely or almost completely" on help.

We measured cognitive status by the Short Portable Mental Status Questionnaire (MSQ) (Pfeiffer, 1975). Mood and outlook were measured by a battery of questions adapted from a scale that has been developed by Ware and used in a large study of outcomes of nursing home residents (Kane, Bell, Riegler, Wilson, & Kane, 1983).

## Analysis

We used frequencies and percentages to describe demographic characteristics of both adult foster care and nursing home respondents and to summarize findings related to influences and circumstances surrounding the decision to move. The chi-square test and, where appropriate, chi-square–based measures of association were used to compare sample characteristics and findings between the two types of residents. Bivariate comparisons were made within each of the samples to determine whether residents' characteristics and the circumstances surrounding the move were associated with the degree of self-perceived control over the decision to move.

Control over the decision was the independent variable in regression models testing whether control over the move at admission was associated with satisfaction with services and degree of activity in the residence. Scores from the satisfaction scale and the activities scale were used as the dependent variables. We entered several other variables into the model to control for differences in social, physical, and mental status that might affect satisfaction or activity. These were gender, source of payment (public or private pay), marital status (married or not married), age, place admitted from (hospital, home, facility similar to current residence, or other), physical health status, functional status, cognitive status, and psychological mood. For physical health, variables indicated diagnoses in certain disease groups: cardiovascular diseases, musculoskeletal diseases, and diseases of the nervous system. Scores from the MSQ controlled for cognitive functioning, because some residents who were able to be interviewed were nonetheless somewhat cognitively impaired. We constructed two dichotomous variables from two ordinal questions in the mood and outlook battery. They indicate whether respondents answered that they "always or almost always" were depressed or that they "never or almost never" felt that there were things to look forward to.

Finally we performed content analysis of the respondents' verbatim comments on how they came to move to the care setting to gain a richer understanding of the residents' experience. We examined the content categories in relation to the degree of control that the respondents indicated in the categorical question.

### Limitations

Like many relocation studies, this study is based on a cross-sectional, retrospective view of the relocation experience, whereas postadmission experiences may influence the residents' perceptions of the preadmission process. Also, we have no baseline data to control for health and cognitive status at the time of the move. However, we did look for patterns that might suggest reconstructed perceptions of the move. Length of stay was entered into the equations to detect any association between time of residence and the effect of control on the dependent variables, and no such interactions were found. The results are generalizable only to the residents

sufficiently cognitively intact to participate in or recall the relocation process.

### Findings

#### Characteristics of Respondents

Respondents in nursing homes and adult foster care were similar in demographic characteristics: Most were female, currently not married, ages 75 to 84, and overwhelmingly white (97 percent, not in table). Most had lived at their current residence for under two years (Table 24-1).

Three major areas in which the foster care residents and nursing home residents differed were place admitted from, physical health, and ADLs. The foster home residents were much less likely to have been admitted from hospitals (11 percent compared with 38 percent). On the other hand, 24 percent of foster home residents had been admitted from other foster homes, whereas only 6 percent of nursing home residents had moved there from other nursing homes. Also, more of the foster care residents came from other types of settings—mainly residential care—or residential care facilities (that is, board and care home with limited personal care services). It is striking, however, that many of the foster home residents had experienced nursing homes and nursing home residents had experienced foster homes immediately before their move to their present location. Had we inquired about all previous locations, we expect that even a higher proportion of respondents would have experienced both settings.

Although the foster care group included some people with serious disabilities, on average it had significantly less disability than the nursing home group. Across all ADLs, nursing home residents had more need for help, both "some help" ($p < .001$) and "complete help" ($p < .001$). They also were more

**TABLE 24-1. Respondent Characteristics**

| Characteristic | In Foster Care Homes (N = 260) | | In Nursing Homes (N = 179) | |
|---|---|---|---|---|
| | n | % | n | % |
| Age (years) | | | | |
| Less than 75 | 64 | 25 | 37 | 22 |
| 75–84 | 137 | 54 | 92 | 54 |
| 85 or older | 54 | 21 | 41 | 24 |
| Marital status | | | | |
| Married | 27 | 10 | 33 | 18 |
| Not married currently | 233 | 90 | 146 | 82 |
| Gender | | | | |
| Male | 58 | 23 | 51 | 29 |
| Female | 199 | 77 | 127 | 71 |
| Education | | | | |
| 8 years or less | 119 | 47 | 85 | 48 |
| 9–12 years | 80 | 31 | 43 | 24 |
| More than 12 years | 56 | 22 | 48 | 27 |
| Relocated from** | | | | |
| Own home | 53 | 20 | 49 | 27 |
| Hospital | 30 | 11 | 69 | 38 |
| Similar type of setting[a] | 63 | 24 | 11 | 6 |
| Different type of relocation setting[b] | 114 | 44 | 50 | 28 |
| Primary payment source | | | | |
| Private pay | 140 | 56 | 80 | 49 |
| Medicaid | 114 | 44 | 50 | 28 |
| Number of ADLs requiring some help | | | | |
| 0–1 | 221 | 85 | 96 | 54 |
| 2–3 | 22 | 9 | 26 | 14 |
| 4 or more | 16 | 6 | 57 | 32 |
| Length of stay (months) | | | | |
| 6 or fewer | 71 | 31 | 46 | 28 |
| 7–20 months | 79 | 34 | 45 | 27 |
| More than 20 | 83 | 35 | 76 | 45 |
| Diagnosis | | | | |
| Heart condition* | 54 | 21 | 53 | 30 |
| Stroke | 50 | 19 | 34 | 19 |
| Skeletal–muscular* | 41 | 16 | 45 | 25 |
| Dementia | 39 | 15 | 37 | 20 |

Note: Numbers may not add to totals in some cases because of missing values.

a. The foster home residents coming from other foster homes and the nursing home residents coming from other nursing homes are counted in this category.

b. The nursing home residents coming from foster care and the foster care residents coming from nursing homes are counted in this category, and a few residents coming from institutions such as state mental hospitals.

*$p \leq .05$. **$p \leq .01$.

likely to have been diagnosed with prevalent health problems such as heart disease or fractured hip. Fifteen percent of respondents in foster homes and 20 percent of respondents in nursing homes had a dementia diagnosis (even after removing the proxy interviews required for 35 percent of the foster care residents and 55 percent of the nursing home residents).

### Relocation Decision

Forty-three percent of the foster care residents saw themselves as having had complete or almost complete control over the decision to move; 30 percent indicated some control; and 27 percent said that they had little or no control, a significant difference from the nursing home residents ($p < .001$) (Table 24-2). With these residents the pattern reversed itself: The largest category was made up of those who claimed they had little or no control.

Thirty-six percent of foster care residents had considered one or more other foster homes before choosing the current one, not significantly different from the portion of nursing home residents who had considered other nursing homes. Foster care and nursing home residents differed on whether they

considered the decision to move to have been a good one. Although a high percentage of both groups agreed that the decision had been good, more foster care residents answered affirmatively than did nursing home residents ($p \leq .01$).

For foster care residents, the two major groups influencing the decision to move were family members and physicians (Table 24-2). For nursing home residents, family members also were most likely to influence the move, but influence from physicians was more likely ($p \leq .001$) and from case managers less likely ($p \leq .01$) than was the case for the foster care residents. The difference

**TABLE 24-2. Respondents' Relocation Decision Variables**

| Variable | In Foster Care Homes (N = 260) | | In Nursing Homes (N = 179) | |
|---|---|---|---|---|
| | n | % | n | % |
| Control over decision to move*** | | | | |
| Almost complete | 109 | 43 | 45 | 26 |
| Some | 78 | 30 | 45 | 26 |
| Little or none | 69 | 27 | 84 | 48 |
| More than one home considered | 85 | 36 | 71 | 44 |
| Decision to move a good one** | 242 | 94 | 144 | 85 |
| People influencing decision | | | | |
| Family member | 157 | 62 | 116 | 66 |
| Physician*** | 72 | 29 | 77 | 47 |
| Home health nurse | 18 | 7 | 18 | 11 |
| Hospital discharge planner | 22 | 9 | 24 | 15 |
| Social worker | 44 | 18 | 27 | 16 |
| Case manager* | 17 | 7 | 17 | 10 |
| Circumstances before move | | | | |
| Overnight hospital stay*** | 115 | 46 | 112 | 64 |
| Sickness requiring extensive care | 55 | 22 | 49 | 28 |
| Accident/injury | 78 | 31 | 57 | 33 |
| Falls** | 69 | 27 | 66 | 38 |
| Memory loss | 63 | 25 | 37 | 21 |
| Serious new illness | 53 | 21 | 37 | 21 |
| Life changes before move | | | | |
| Death of spouse | 29 | 12 | 19 | 11 |
| Death of caregiver | 23 | 9 | 10 | 6 |
| Caregiver moved away | 28 | 11 | 11 | 6 |
| Loss of income/financial difficulties | 35 | 14 | 18 | 16 |

*Note:* Percentages may be slightly off because of missing values.
*$p \leq .05$. **$p \leq .01$. ***$p \leq .001$.

highlights the alternative admission routes taken by the two groups; nursing home residents more frequently entered through the acute care system. Both foster care and nursing home respondents reported social workers, discharge planners, and home health–public health nurses as being far less likely to influence the decision.

For foster care residents, the most frequent change in health circumstances was an overnight stay in a hospital (46 percent), followed by the occurrence of an injury or accident (31 percent), frequent falls (27 percent), worries about memory loss (25 percent), sickness requiring extensive care at home (22 percent), and a serious new illness (21 percent). These percentages were similar to those of the nursing home group, although foster care residents were less likely to have experienced a hospital stay ($p \leq .001$) or frequent falls ($p \leq .01$).

There were no significant differences between foster care and nursing home residents regarding changes in life circumstances. For both groups, death of a spouse and financial difficulty were most frequently mentioned; 48 percent of foster care residents and 41

percent of nursing home residents had experienced none of the suggested events, including an unspecified "other" category. The primary issue is the comparability between those ending up in the two settings in terms of key factors that often precipitate a long-term care move. Although the numbers experiencing any event are relatively small, the key issue is the comparability.

Residents were presented with a list of 10 specific attributes and were asked if each was important in deciding to move to "this" home (Table 24-3). Supervision and safety (92 percent), home-like atmosphere (91 percent), privacy (82 percent), and flexible routine (76 percent) were most often mentioned by the foster care residents. Supervision and safety also had the highest rating by the nursing home group (86 percent), but this was followed by personal assistance care (81 percent), medical care (78 percent), and cost of care (69 percent). Home-like atmosphere ($p \leq .001$), privacy ($p \leq .001$), and flexible routine ($p \leq .001$) were more important to the foster care residents; medical care ($p \leq .05$) and physical rehabilitation ($p \leq .01$), to the nursing home residents.

TABLE 24-3. Factors Respondents Considered Important in Relocation Setting

| Factor Viewed As Important | In Foster Care Homes (N = 260) | | In Nursing Homes (N = 179) | |
|---|---|---|---|---|
| | n | % | n | % |
| Home-like atmosphere*** | 223 | 91 | 96 | 53 |
| Location/neighborhood | 158 | 64 | 101 | 62 |
| Personal assistance | 191 | 76 | 132 | 81 |
| Medical care* | 169 | 68 | 127 | 78 |
| Supervision and safety | 227 | 92 | 140 | 86 |
| Privacy*** | 204 | 82 | 92 | 58 |
| Flexible routine*** | 181 | 76 | 68 | 46 |
| Cost of care | 177 | 74 | 108 | 69 |
| Organized activities* | 80 | 33 | 70 | 44 |
| Physical rehabilitation** | 67 | 28 | 64 | 41 |

Note: Numbers may not add to totals because of missing data.
*$p \leq .05$. **$p \leq .01$. ***$p \leq .001$.

### Perceived Control over the Decision

The only demographic variable associated with perceived control was education. A low, positive association ($p < .05$; $\delta = .17$) was found between years of education and degree of control for the foster care residents. For the nursing home residents, those admitted from acute care hospitals were more likely to indicate low control over the decision than those with other sources of admission ($p < .005$; Cramer's V = .24), whereas those admitted from their own homes were more likely to indicate high control ($p < .02$; Cramer's V = .20).

When control was cross-tabulated with the types of people perceived as influencing the decision, perceived control was related to family influence for both foster home and nursing home residents. Residents who were influenced by family members were less likely to indicate that they were in control of the decision (foster care: $p < .02$; Cramer's V =.18; nursing home: $p < .004$; Cramer's V = .25). For example, of foster care residents who indicated little or no control, 67 percent were influenced by family, and 33 percent were not. No associations were found between control and changes in life circumstances, but we found three associations for changes in health conditions prior to the move. Foster care residents who were aware of experiencing memory loss prior to the move were less likely to perceive themselves as having been in control ($p < .01$; Cramer's V = .20). And nursing home residents who had an overnight hospital stay or who had experienced a serious new illness also perceived less control ($p < .02$; Cramer's V = .21 and $p < .01$; Cramer's V = .22, respectively).

Surprisingly, no association was found between perceived control and consideration of more than one alternative home in making their decision. There was an association, however, between thinking that the decision to move was a good one and control. For both foster care and nursing home residents, those who said that the move was good were more likely to perceive themselves in control of the decision ($p < .01$; Cramer's V =.18 and $p < .001$; Cramer's V = .33, respectively).

### Relationship of Control to Satisfaction and Activity

The regression model was initially run on all respondents ($N = 439$), but interaction was found between control over the decision and type of residence (foster care as opposed to nursing home). Subsequent runs for satisfaction as the dependent variable (Table 24-4) and for activities in the new setting as the dependent variable (Table 24-5), were therefore done separately for the foster care and nursing home residents. All four of the regression equations were significant ($p < .01$ to $p = .000$) with a moderate amount of variance explained ($R^2$s from .16 to .27). Control over the decision was significant, however, only for the foster care residents. In the nursing home group, grade school education (a dummy variable representing the questionnaire's categories of "completed grade school" and "did not complete grade school") was associated with higher satisfaction ($p < .01$), as was higher ADL functioning ($p < .005$). For the nursing home activity equation, those with greater disabilities, less education, and little to look forward to participated less in activities.

For foster care residents, "almost complete" control predicted greater satisfaction with services ($p < .005$), as well as more activity in the home ($p < .005$), and "some" control predicted satisfaction with services ($p < .05$). Lower educational attainment also predicted greater satisfaction ($p < .01$), and residents admitted from their own home or

TABLE 24-4. Regressions for Scores in Satisfaction for Residents of Foster Care Homes and Nursing Homes ($N$ = 439)

| Independent Variable | Foster Care Homes $\beta$ | Nursing Homes $\beta$ |
|---|---|---|
| Age | −0.0119 | −0.0051 |
| Nervous system diagnosis | −0.0078 | −0.3371 |
| Cardiovascular/musculoskeletal diagnosis | −0.0325 | −0.6085 |
| Complete control | −1.9570****[a] | −1.3628 |
| Some control | −1.1361*[a] | 0.2581 |
| ADL score | 0.0942 | 0.2233*** |
| Mental status score | −0.0248 | −1.0241 |
| From same type facility | −1.0983 | 0.2184 |
| From hospital | −1.9539* | 0.2311 |
| From own home | −1.6488** | 0.2167 |
| Male | −0.6440 | 1.0751 |
| Married | −0.4421 | 0.6336 |
| Medicaid payment status | 0.5748 | −0.6726 |
| Less than grade school education | −1.0269 | −1.4364** |
| Depressed mood | 1.0965 | 0.1714 |
| Little hope | 0.3435 | 1.0917 |
| | $R^2$ = 0.16 | $R^2$ = 0.24 |
| | $F$ = 2.218*** | $F$ = 1.989* |

Note: ADL = activity of daily living.
a. The beta is negative because low numbers represent higher satisfaction on the scale.
*$p \leq .05$. **$p \leq .01$. ***$p \leq .001$. ****$p \leq .0001$.

the hospital were found to be more satisfied than those with other sources of admission ($p < .01$ and $p < .05$, respectively). For the activity equation, older age ($p < .05$), functional disability, ($p < .001$), and cognitive impairment ($p < .05$) predicted less activity, whereas those who had been admitted from similar homes tended to participate more in activities ($p < .05$).

Because the relationship between perceived control and the dependent variables was significant for the adult foster care residents, we ran an interactive model to test the hypothesis that control might have a greater effect on those who considered more than one home as an alternative. Considering more than one home had no effect on either satisfaction or activity. We also ran models to test whether place admitted from might interact with perceived control. One source of admission was found significant: the model

testing interaction between control and admission from their own homes. Control was associated with higher satisfaction for residents who entered adult foster care from their own homes ($R^2$ = .18; $F$ = 2.89; significance of home × high control = .05)

## Qualitative Findings

Content analysis of the open-ended question on "how it happened that you moved here" helped to shed light on what the respondents meant by control.

### Foster Care Residents

For foster care residents who claimed that they had almost complete control over the decision to move, a strong majority of answers, about 85 percent, fell within the major approaches to control described in our

**TABLE 24-5. Regressions for Scores in Activity for Residents of Foster Care Homes and Nursing Homes (N = 439)**

| Independent Variable | Foster Care Homes $\beta$ | Nursing Homes $\beta$ |
|---|---|---|
| Age | −0.0346 | −0.0162 |
| Nervous system diagnosis | −0.5023 | 0.1018 |
| Cardiovascular/musculoskeletal diagnosis | −0.0958 | 0.8947 |
| Complete control | 1.2630*** | 0.1742 |
| Some control | 0.2095 | 0.1062 |
| ADL score | −0.3375**** | −0.1383* |
| Mental status score | −0.1470* | 0.0191 |
| From same type of facility | 1.1888 | −0.3185 |
| From hospital | 0.7973 | −0.3446 |
| From own home | 0.8904 | −0.0150 |
| Male | −0.2923 | −0.3463 |
| Married | −0.6154 | 0.4047 |
| Medicaid payment status | 0.3528 | 1.6800* |
| Less than grade school education | 0.1105 | 1.1088* |
| Depressed mood | −1.3424 | −2.5946 |
| Little hope | −0.5719 | −1.4599* |
| | $R^2 = 0.27$ | $R^2 = 0.19$ |
| | $F = 4.938$*** | $F = 2.04$** |

*Note:* ADL = activity of daily living.
*$p < .05.$ **$p < .01.$ ***$p < .001.$ ****$p < .0001.$

literature review: a sense of mastery or coping strategies. Some respondents emphasized mastery over the decision and let it go at that: "My family never tells me what to do," "I decided myself," "I wanted this home despite my daughter's suggestion to live in another home." In the majority of responses, however, residents did not speak directly to making the decision, but focused on the home as a better alternative or on the desirability of moving to this particular home (coping strategies): "Couldn't stand it at the nursing home," "Daughter helped me pick this one close to her home," "My wife was here," "Had met the owner and loved her."

The comments of foster care residents who claimed to have little or no control contrasted sharply with those of the first group. About 80 percent of the responses related to the notion of mastery, almost all suggesting that someone other than themselves was in control of the decisions: "My daughter made

me get out," "My son just picked me up and brought me here," "I got kicked out of the other foster home." Although a few of the comments, fewer than 10 percent, suggested some coping strategies ("My wife is here."), most described a decision that they did not work through: "My daughter made all the arrangements," There was "no room at my granddaughter's so she arranged for me to come here."

The comments of foster residents who indicated "some control" over the move appeared to fall between the extremes described above. Most spoke about influence or help from family or others: "My oldest daughter did most of it," "My daughter said she knew of a nice home and we'll go out and see the place." About 20 percent dwelt on the reasons for the move without mentioning anyone's influence; about the same percentage spoke as if the arrangements had been made for them. If anything, this group appeared closer to those who claimed "no control" than those who indicated it was their own decision.

### Nursing Home Residents

In comparison to the foster care group, there were no sharp contrasts across the three categories of nursing home residents: those with complete, some, or little control over the decision. And in general the notions of mastery and coping strategies were not illustrated as forcefully in their comments. For example, none of the remarks of the nursing home residents who fell in the high control category suggested a strong sense of mastery, as was the case for the foster care residents. In fact their answers appeared closer to those of foster care respondents who mentioned some control. There was control but it was qualified; many dwelled on help received from others in making the decision or on why the move was necessary. Again, in contrast to foster care residents, those who claimed little or no control on the fixed-item question did not focus on notions of being forced to move or being tricked into the decision. Rather their comments tended toward a simple acknowledgment that someone else, usually a family member, had made the decision: "My family put me here and said I'd like it," "My brother made most of the decisions while I was in the hospital."

## Discussion

The study shows substantial differences between interviewable residents in adult foster care and interviewable residents in nursing homes in the circumstances precipitating the move, the nature of the search, in perceived control, and in the attributes of the setting deemed important. The qualitative analysis shows dramatically that high proportions of residents in both settings perceived that they

had been manipulated into the move or that the move had been inevitable with little opportunity for choice. Nursing home residents were flatter in the way they described this than were foster care residents.

Moving to a long-term care residence is an important life transition. The findings of this study suggest that in Oregon moving to an adult foster care home—at least in contrast to moving to a nursing home—can be an experience that allows many elderly people to see themselves in control and that such perceived control is associated with higher satisfaction and activity following the transition. The findings also suggest that, in making their decision, most older adults see foster care as a distinct alternative to nursing care, appealing to their needs for a home-like atmosphere, privacy, and flexible routines.

Why the finding that nursing home residents were less likely than foster care residents to perceive themselves in control of the move? The nursing home residents tended to relocate to long-term residence from the acute care sector, and admission from acute care was also associated with less control over the decision to move. Perhaps the acute care sector had its own momentum, channeling patients into nursing home care without the time or conditions that are necessary to encourage the older person to feel in control over the decision.

The study found an association between control and measures of satisfaction and activity for the foster care residents only, not the nursing home residents. Again, perhaps the large percentage of admissions from acute care hospitals in the nursing home group compared with the proportion of foster care residents making the decision at home accounted for this differential effect of control on the dependent variables. An additional explanation may be found in the nature of control and its association with adverse effects. Perhaps people hand over control to trusted others without negative impact, when they feel circumstances to be beyond their competence or control (Thompson, 1981). The comments of the nursing home residents, unlike the comments of the foster care residents, did not reflect the extremes of mastery over the move or being forced to move. Many mentioned that the decision was made by others, but without their protest. Patients in acute care settings, given the pressing conditions of health and circumstance, might have been more willing to delegate decision making to those whom they know and trust.

Social workers and nurses who work as hospital discharge planners and as community-based case managers need to be more sensitive to the importance of facilitating the older person's sense of control over the move. This need is underscored by our finding that both foster care and nursing home residents view family members as providing a major influence on the move—but one that appears to dampen rather than support a sense of control. Reliance on family members to make decisions may have negative effects on elderly people's later perceived well-being.

From a practice perspective, practitioners may need to give more thought to placing more emphasis on working directly with the older person rather than concentrating principally on family members, who are often more accessible. Notions that the "family is the client" may be counter-productive. Although the implications of family systems theory are particularly salient when working with older adults, it is also most important to work with them as clients in their own right. Certainly it is necessary to deal directly with the feelings of helplessness that placement often engenders. It is also important to systematically encourage clients to consider the attributes of care settings that are impor-

tant to *them*. Using lists such as those used in this retrospective study may be helpful to anchor such discussion.

It also seems that practice patterns have not yet caught up with the range of options available to seniors in a state like Oregon, or the dynamic value of their choices. Note that more than a few foster care residents had been in nursing homes and vice versa and that most of these foster care residents had moved from a different foster home. (One imagines that some of these moves reflect the resident's choice, taking advantage of the flexibility of the program to move to a preferred setting, whereas others might reflect rejection by the setting.)

Hospital discharge planning, as historically and currently too often practiced, seems much too limited a concept to reach and serve best the seniors who could benefit from help with relocation decisions. Our findings seem to call for a more flexible and continuous function of planning as opposed to a one-time and hasty discharge plan made from the hospital. Hospitalizations are short, post-acute and subacute care occur in a variety of step-down locations, and posthospital location decisions need not be painted as irrevocable choices. Some assistance with reviewing and making new long-term care decisions may be needed for people in a wide range of long-term care locations. Perhaps this continuity can be found in case managers in public or private programs. Another potential is that personnel, including social workers, in managed care organizations can assist older people with the dynamic process of decision making related to their care regardless of their current physical location. At the very least, if nursing homes are used deliberately in lieu of hospitalizations or as sites for short-term rehabilitation, clients and family members must be made aware that nursing homes are not perceived as a final destination.

## Conclusion

Practitioners have long had an uneasy feeling that the haste and sense of crisis associated with hospital discharge creates a poor circumstance for life decision making. Similarly, decision advisors will need to exert care that the current emphasis on clinical pathways and computerized decision trees for identifying the best placement for patients in managed care systems not omit the person from a highly personal decision. This study suggests that even in a state that has, through public policy, expanded the range of possible decisions for those who must relocate for long-term care, the way the older person participates in the decision can influence the postdecision outcomes.

In this cross-sectional study, we have incomplete data on the history of relocations for the respondents. Our data cannot tell us where in the sequence of decision making clients are more likely to see the decision as out of their control. Nor can the data tell us, once clients have lost control over the relocation process, whether they can regain that sense of control in subsequent moves. The current context of care seems to offer a wider range for residential decisions and more opportunities to make sequential decisions. Further clinical and health services research could help illuminate those patterns.

❦ ❦ ❦

## References

Aldrich, C. K., & Mendkoff, E. (1963). Relocation of the aged and disabled: A mortality study. *Journal of the American Geriatric Society, 11*, 185–194.

Armer, J. (1993). Elderly relocation to a congregate setting: Factors influencing adjustment. *Issues in Mental Health Nursing, 14*, 157–172.

Coulton, J. C., Dunkle, R. E., Chow, J., Haug, M., & Vielhaber, D. P. (1988). Dimensions of post-hospital care decision-making: A factor analytic study. *Gerontologist, 28*, 218–223.

Folkemer, D., Jensen, A., Lipson, L., Stauffer, M., & Fox-Grage, W. (1996). *Adult foster care for the elderly: A review of state regulatory and funding strategies: Volume 1* (No. 9604A). Washington, DC: American Association of Retired Persons, Public Policy Institute.

Gallagher, E., & Walker, G. (1990). Vulnerability of nursing home residents during relocations and renovations. *Journal of Aging Studies, 4*(1), 31–46.

Gamroth, L. M., Semradek, J., & Tornquist, E. M. (Eds.). (1995). *Enhancing autonomy in long-term care: Concepts and strategies.* New York: Springer.

Harel, Z., & Noelker, L. (1982). Social integration, health, and choice. *Research on Aging, 4*, 97–111.

Hudson, J., Dennis, D., Nutter, R., Gallaway, B., & Richardson, G. (1994). Foster family care for elders. *Adult Residential Care Journal, 8*(2), 65–76.

Institute of Medicine. (1986). *Improving the quality of care in nursing homes.* Washington, DC: National Academy Press.

Kane, R. A., & Caplan, A. L. (1990). *Everyday ethics: Resolving dilemmas in nursing home life.* New York: Springer.

Kane, R. A., Kane, R. L., Illston, L., & Nyman, J. (1991). Adult foster care for the elderly in Oregon: A mainstream alternative to nursing homes? *American Journal of Public Health, 81*, 1113–1120.

Kane, R. A., O'Connor, C., & Olsen Baker, M. (1995). *Delegation of nursing activities: Implications for patterns of long-term care.* (Report prepared for American Association of Retired Persons). Minneapolis: University of Minnesota.

Kane, R. L., Bell, R., Riegler, S., Wilson, A., & Kane, R. A. (1983). Assessing the outcomes of nursing-home patients. *Journal of Gerontology, 38*, 385–393.

Ladd, R., & Hannum, C. (1992). Oregon's adult foster care program—A model for community-based long-term care for elderly and disabled. *Community Alternatives, 4,* 171–184.

Lawton, M. P., & Yaffe, S. (1970). Mortality, morbidity, and voluntary changes in residence on the well-being of older people. *Journal of the American Geriatric Society, 18,* 823–831.

Lieberman, M. A., & Tobin, S. S. (1983). *The experience of old age: Stress, coping, and survival.* New York: Basic Books.

Mehrotra, C., & Kosloski, K. (1991). Foster care for older adults: Issues and evaluations. *Home Health Care Quarterly, 12,* 115–136.

Mirotznik, J., & Ruskin, A. P. (1985). Interinstitutional relocation and its effect on psychosocial status. *Gerontologist, 25,* 265–270.

Netting, F., & Wilson, C. (1991). Accommodation and relocation decision making in continuing care retirement communities. *Health & Social Work, 16,* 266–273.

Nursing Home Reform Act of 1987, P.L. 100-203, *U.S. Statutes at Large, 101,* 1330.

Oregon Board of Nursing. (1993). *Oregon administrative regulations 851-47-010(23).* Portland: Author.

Pablo, R. Y. (1977). Intra-institutional relocation: Its impact on long-term care patients. *Gerontologist, 17,* 426–435.

Pfeiffer, E. (1975). A short portable mental status questionnaire for the assessment of organic brain deficit in elderly patients. *Journal of the American Geriatric Society, 23,* 433–441.

Pohl, J. M., & Fuller, S. S. (1980). Perceived choice, social interaction, and dimensions of morale of residents in a home for the aged. *Research in Nursing and Health, 3,* 147–157.

Reinardy, J. (1992). Decisional control in moving to a nursing home: Post-admission adjustment and well-being. *Gerontologist, 32,* 96–103.

Reinardy, J. (1995). Relocation to a new environment: Decisional control and the move to a nursing home. *Health & Social Work, 20,* 31–38.

Rodin, J. (1986a). Aging and health: Effects of the sense of control. *Science, 233,* 1271–1276.

Rodin, J. (1986b). Health, control, and aging. In M. M. Baltes & P. B. Baltes (Eds.), *The psychology of control and aging* (pp. 139–165). Hillsdale, NJ: Lawrence Erlbaum.

Schulz, R., & Brenner, G. (1977). Relocation of the aged: A review and theoretical analysis. *Journal of Gerontology, 32,* 323–333.

Sherman, S. R., & Newman, E. S. (1979). Foster family care for the elderly: Surrogate family or mini institution? *International Journal on Aging and Human Development, 10,* 165–176.

Stark, A., Kane, R. L., Kane, R. A., & Finch, M. (1995). Effect on physical functioning of care in adult foster homes and nursing homes. *Gerontologist, 35,* 648–655.

Thompson, S. C. (1981). Will it hurt less if I can control it? A complex answer to a simple question. *Psychological Bulletin, 90,* 89–101.

This chapter was originally published in the November 1999 issue of *Social Work,* Vol. 44, Number 6, pp. 571–585.

# 25

# The Social Worker in the Emerging Field of Home Care

## Professional Activities and Ethical Concerns

MARCIA EGAN and
GOLDIE KADUSHIN

Social workers face challenges in defining their professional function as the locus of health care delivery shifts from a hospital-based, inpatient focus to an outpatient, community-based model (Berger et al., 1996; Berkman, 1996; Dhooper, 1997; Keigher, 1997; Netting & Williams, 1996; Rosenberg, 1994; Simmons, 1994). Consistent with this emphasis on community-based care, one of the fastest growing segments of the health care delivery system is home health (Balinsky, 1994; Benjamin, 1993). Medicare spending for home health services increased 31 percent a year to $16.7 billion in 1996 from $3.3 billion in 1990 (Pear, 1997). This growth in home health services is a response to cost containment pressures on hospitals to discharge patients more quickly; liberalized regulations governing reimbursement and licensing of home care agencies; increasing numbers of elderly people; a growing population of children with chronic illnesses living into young adulthood; the AIDS epidemic; a shift in the dominant diseases from acute to chronic disorders; limited access to nursing home beds; and the development of sophisticated medical technology that can be used outside of the hospital setting (Balinsky, 1994; Benjamin, 1993; Bishop & Skwara, 1993; Davitt & Kaye, 1996; Haddad, 1992; Malone-Rising, 1994; Schmid & Hasenfeld, 1993).

Home care has many advantages; it provides an alternative to institutionalization and enhances autonomy by allowing people to receive care in their own homes. On the other hand, the provision of home care is stressful because of conflicts between caregivers and patients, limited community resources, restrictions on the type and amount of care funded, and the challenges to personal autonomy that arise as a result of the effects of chronic and acute illnesses. These tensions in home health care produce ethical dilemmas for patients, families, and professionals (Callopy, 1990).

However, in spite of the expansion of home health services, the ethical dilemmas associated with the delivery of home care, and the need to clearly define the social work function in community-based settings, the only empirically based articles on the subject of social workers in home care, with one exception (Kerson & Michelsen, 1995), were published in the 1980s (Fessler & Adams, 1985; Levande, Bowden, & Mollema, 1987; Vincent & Davis, 1987). Empirically based research on social work practice in home health agencies is essential to help the profession explain its function to other disciplines, to educate practitioners and students for community-based practice, and to serve as the basis for the development and measurement of outcomes for social work practice in home health. This article presents the results of a survey of social workers employed in proprietary and nonprofit home health agencies in Tennessee and Wisconsin regarding their practice activities and ethical concerns.

## The Context of Social Work in Home Care

Policies that determine reimbursement in home health agencies for social work services are likely to influence the activities and ethical issues experienced by social workers. For example, Binney, Estes, and Ingman (1990) documented the influence of the medical model on the formulation of Medicare policy related to home care. Consistent with this emphasis on the medical model, social work services are not reimbursed under Medicare unless they are prescribed by a physician, the patient is receiving some type of skilled (nursing, speech, occupational, or physical therapy) service, the patient is homebound, and services are necessary to resolve a medical problem (Health Care Financing Administration, 1992). Only direct patient contact, not indirect services such as care planning or care coordination, are reimbursable social work activities under Medicare (personal communication, Medicare provider representative, June 18, 1997). The recently enacted Balanced Budget Act of 1997 (P.L. 105-33), which requires beneficiaries to copay for home health services, is likely to create even more problems in gaining access to home health care, particularly for low-income elderly and disabled people.

Another source of public funding for home health care for very poor elderly people, children, and patients with HIV/AIDS is Medicaid. However, under Medicaid, social work services in home health are reimbursable only if there is a federal waiver program in place (Balinsky, 1994). In Wisconsin and Tennessee, the two states surveyed in this study, there were no such waivers (Tennessee Rules and Regulations, Chapter 1200-13-12-04; Wisconsin Administrative Code, HFS 107.11). Patients with HIV are also eligible for home health care coverage, including social services, through the Ryan White Comprehensive AIDS Resources Emergency Act of 1990 (P.L. 101-381), if these funds are granted to the states and they are available to the home health care agency.

The final source of coverage for home care is private insurance. Although the home care features of private long-term care insurance vary depending on the payer, most policies closely approximate Medicare's home health provisions, and coverage of nonmedical supportive services of any duration remains the exception rather than the rule (Benjamin, 1993). Only 4 percent to 5 percent of elderly people and even fewer young or middle-aged adults have long-term care insurance (Balinsky, 1994).

Whether a home health agency is a proprietary or a nonprofit organization may affect the extent to which reimbursement influences the practice patterns of social workers (Ellenbecker, 1995; Shuster & Cloonan, 1991; Williams, 1994; Williams, Mackay, & Torner, 1991). As a result of the passage of the Omnibus Budget Reconciliation Act of 1981 (P.L. 97-35), allowing Medicare and Medicaid reimbursement to proprietary agencies, the number of these agencies grew rapidly and now constitute 43 percent of certified Medicare agencies (Benjamin, 1993; National Association for Home Care, 1997). Nonprofit agencies may receive funds from philanthropy or tax revenues; proprietary agencies depend entirely on reimbursement from private insurance, Medicare, and Medicaid or privately paying clients. The mission of the nonprofit agency is altruistically oriented toward meeting the needs of the community and the client, whereas proprietary agencies have been viewed as motivated by self-interest and profit making (Williams, 1994). Thus, it

might be anticipated that reimbursement issues would more strongly influence the practice of the social worker in the proprietary rather than the nonprofit agency.

A final variable influencing the functions of social workers in home care is the changing population of clients receiving home care services. Although the elderly population continues to be the largest consumer of home care, there has been an increase in the population of users under age 65. The 1993 National Home and Hospice Care Survey found that 25 percent of patients receiving home care services were under age 65 (Strahan, 1994). The increase in survival rates of chronically ill children and adults and advances in high-technology home care contribute to an increasing number of children and adults under age 65 receiving care in their own homes (Balinsky, 1994; Haddad, 1992; Kaye & Davitt, 1995). In addition, home care has become a critical component in the care of AIDS patients, most of whom are young or middle-aged adults (Balinsky, 1994).

## The Functions of Social Workers in Home Care

Empirically based information on the functions performed by social workers in home care is scarce. Two case studies that examined social work activities in a single agency found that social workers are clinical case managers, linking patients and families to formal and informal sources of support and providing emotional support to help them resolve feelings related to loss, the burden of caregiving, and the need to readjust relationships in the face of illness and disability (Kerson & Michelsen, 1995; Levande et al., 1987).

A separate group of articles discussed social work practice in home health care from a conceptual perspective. Simmons (1994) identified care coordination, health education, counseling, assessment, and skill in facilitating decision making related to ethical issues as the core activities of social workers in a community-based setting. Dhooper (1997) focused on care coordination as the primary practice activity of social workers in home health.

## Ethical Dilemmas in Home Care

Several ethical issues have been identified as distinctive to the provision of home care. The most frequently discussed ethical problem in home care is the issue of patient autonomy or self-determination (Arras & Dubler, 1994; Callopy, 1988; Callopy, Dubler, & Zuckerman, 1990; Dubler, 1990; Kane & Caplan, 1993; Robbins, 1996; Zuckerman, Dubler, & Callopy, 1990). When clients tolerate a high level of risk to remain at home, client autonomy may conflict with the professional obligation to protect clients from harm or beneficence (Hofland, 1993). Patient autonomy may also be eroded as patients experience increasing frailty and depend on others for assistance with the basic activities of life. In this situation, caregivers may confuse physical limitations in implementing choices with the cognitive ability to make choices (Callopy, 1988; Callopy et al., 1990). Finally, because the majority of home care is provided by family members (Kane & Reinardy, 1990), balancing the patients' and families' rights to self-determination is often an ethical issue (Arras & Dubler, 1994; Callopy et al., 1990; Dubler, 1990; Haddad, 1992).

The right to exercise self-determination is based on the ethical requirement that the client has the decisional capability to make the choice in question. Kane and Caplan (1993) found that issues related to the assessment of decisional capacity created the strongest moral dilemmas for case managers providing home care. Decisional capacity fluctuates and also is decision specific: A person may not be able to balance a checkbook but may be capable of caring for herself at home (Wolf, 1993). Questions of decisional capacity also are more likely to be raised when clients choose a plan different from what family or professionals consider to be in the patient's best interest (Ryden, 1993). The assessment of decisional capacity may be particularly difficult to make in the home where "clients are seen only intermittently, in surroundings bolstered by family and familiar routines" (Callopy et al., 1990, p. 8). Problems in assessing decisional capacity may also create ethical dilemmas in implementing advance directives, because advance directives do not become operational until a patient is assessed as incapacitated or unable to make and communicate decisions (Davitt & Kaye, 1996).

The conflict between restricted resources and client need (Haddad, 1992) is another ethical concern in home care. Although all types of home care services are inadequately funded, the dominance of medical services as the funding priority in home care means that there may be particular barriers to the provision of nonmedical supportive services when clients have social needs but no simultaneous or related need of skilled medical care (Binney et al., 1990; Callopy et al., 1990; Macklin & Callahan, 1990).

Several ethical concerns have been mentioned less frequently in the literature. Kane (1993) discussed ethical issues related to confidentiality and the circumstances under which providers and family members should receive information about a competent client without the client's consent. It is argued that such disclosures are ethical only when they are necessary to prevent serious harm to clients, family members, or professional caregivers. Ethical issues related to abuse and neglect arise when professionals impose their own values on clients who appear exploited or neglected rather than helping clients make informed choices for themselves (Asch, 1993; Dresser, 1993).

The literature on the tasks performed by social workers in home care is based largely on examinations of social workers in single agencies or on conceptual articles. Furthermore, although the literature documents a large number of potential ethical conflicts in home care, only one of the studies reviewed (Davitt & Kaye, 1996) is based on a social work sample. Finally, in spite of the increase in the number of proprietary agencies, none of the literature reviewed examined how practice patterns or ethical concerns are influenced by the variable of auspice.

## Study Design and Sampling Procedures

A 38-item survey questionnaire was developed from a review of the literature (Browne, Smith, Ewalt, & Walker, 1996; Davitt & Kaye, 1996; Fessler & Adams, 1985; Proctor, Morrow-Howell, & Kaplan, 1996; Simon, Showers, Blumenfield, Holden, & Wu, 1995; Vincent & Davis, 1987) and in consultation with social workers employed in home health agencies. Social workers were asked to indicate whether they engaged in 13 direct and indirect practice activities, how often these activities typically occurred (daily, twice a week, once a week, monthly), and how many hours in a typical week these activities required. Respondents also were asked to rate how often they experienced 11 ethical concerns on a scale ranging from 0 = never to 4 = very often. A separate closed-ended question asked workers to indicate whether they met regularly with hospital dis-

charge planners regarding referrals. The question was included because research suggests that discharge plans made in the hospital are frequently not implemented in the community, and there is a consequent need to facilitate better continuity of care by improving communication between hospital discharge planners and home health care professionals (Proctor et al., 1996; Simon et al., 1995). The survey also asked for demographic information about the respondents, their caseloads, and agencies.

The questionnaire was sent to social workers in all home health agencies listed as providing social work services ($N = 232$) (McBrayer, Slade, & Heller-Bramblett, 1996) in Wisconsin and Tennessee. This listing identifies types of services provided and agency auspice (proprietary, nonprofit, or government). Nonrespondents were contacted three weeks after the initial mailing to increase the response rate and collect information about address changes, agency closures, and duplication in the listing. Nine percent of the nonrespondents in proprietary agencies and 4 percent in nonprofit and government agencies were found to have been absorbed by other home health organizations, duplicated on the list, or to have worked for facilities that had closed. Thus, only 216 of the original sample of agencies were found to be potentially eligible for the study.

Questionnaires were received from 118 social workers, resulting in an overall response rate of 55 percent, which is considered sufficient for analysis and reporting (Rubin & Babbie, 1996). Comparison of the auspice of the social workers' agencies in the adjusted sampling of agencies with the sample obtained revealed that the sample obtained was representative and thus could be considered unbiased (Rubin & Babbie, 1996) (Table 25-1).

**TABLE 25-1. Analysis of Eligible Sample and Obtained Sample**

| Auspice | Original No. Questionnaires Sent | No. of Respondents Eligible | % | No. Responses Received | % |
|---|---|---|---|---|---|
| Proprietary | 121 | 110 | 50.9 | 54 | 46.6 |
| Nonprofit | 91 | 87 | 40.3 | 53 | 45.7 |
| Government | 20 | 19 | 8.8 | 9 | 7.8 |
| Total | 232 | 216 | 100.0 | 116 | 100.0 |

Note: Percentages may not add to 100 due to rounding. Two surveys did not identify auspice.

## Findings

### Characteristics of Social Workers, Caseloads, and Agencies

The 213 social workers ranged in age from 23 to 63 years, averaging 37.2 years ($SD$ = 8.9). Most of the social workers in these agencies were employees (81 percent) rather than contracted workers (19 percent). The majority also were female (93 percent). The social workers averaged 7.4 years of practice ($SD$ = 6.2, range = less than one year to 29 years) prior to work in home health, and 4.2 years ($SD$ = 3.5, range = less than one year to 20 years) of practice in home health. The majority (77 percent, $n$ = 90) of social workers had at least one social work degree. One-fifth (20.8 percent) had a bachelor's degree and two-fifths (41.6 percent) had a master's degree in social work. Far less frequent were practitioners with both social work degrees (14.6 percent). Nearly 18 percent had a bachelor's degree in a field other than social work, 3 percent of respondents had a master's degree in another field, and 3 percent had undergraduate degrees in nursing.

Over one-third (35.0 percent) of the social workers provided services exclusively to elderly populations (Table 25-2). The remaining practitioners had caseloads of clients from diverse population groups in addition to elderly patients (Table 25-2). A typical caseload size was 30 patients per month ($SD$ = 22.5).

Although the range of caseload size was wide (1 to 120), few of the workers ($n$ = 7) had caseloads over 60 patients per month.

Agencies were evenly divided between proprietary (46.6 percent, $n$ = 54) and nonprofit (45.7 percent, $n$ = 53) auspices. Over half of the social workers were from proprietary (22.4 percent, $n$ = 26) or nonprofit (31.9 percent, $n$ = 37) free-standing private agencies (Table 25-3). Being a contracted worker rather than an employee was significantly associated ($p$ = .03) with employment in a proprietary agency [$\chi^2(1)$ = 4.7]. No significant differences or associations between social workers in proprietary and nonprofit auspices were found on education, years of experience prior to or in home health, or caseload size. However, caseload composition varied somewhat by agency auspice. For instance, more social workers in nonprofit settings saw nonelderly adults, HIV patients, and children than those in proprietary settings. Conversely, more social workers in proprietary agencies had exclusively elderly caseloads (Table 25-2).

### Data Analysis

Data on the 13 practice activities were analyzed to determine which were identified as a component of practice, how frequently they occurred, and how much time they required. Those respondents who practiced fewer than two days per week or were administrators

**TABLE 25-2. Distribution of Patient Population Served and Social Workers' Agency Auspice**

| Auspice | Only Elderly Clients (%) | Distribution within Diverse Caseload (%) | | | | |
|---|---|---|---|---|---|---|
| | | Adults | People with HIV | Children | Organ Recipients | All Groups (%) |
| Total (n = 117)[a] | 35.0 | 88.0 | 28.9 | 19.7 | 7.9 | 13.2 |
| Proprietary (n = 54) | 38.9 | 78.9 | 27.2 | 18.2 | 12.1 | 15.2 |
| Nonprofit (includes government agencies) (n = 61)[b] | 32.8 | 95.0 | 29.0 | 21.9 | 2.4 | 12.2 |

a. Missing value = 1.
b. Missing value = 2.

without direct practice responsibility (n = 8) were eliminated from the latter two analyses and all further analyses. Data from workers in government agencies were included in the nonprofit auspice group. The association of activities and auspice and caseload composition (solely elderly and diverse) were analyzed by chi-square computations. Workers' hours invested in practice activities in proprietary and nonprofit agencies were compared by t test analysis, as were comparisons of ratings of ethical concerns.

### Practice Activities of Practitioners in Home Health

There was a high degree of consensus (over 90 percent) that respondents performed functions such as coordination of services, assessment, counseling, interagency collaboration, and home visits. Over three-fifths or more of the respondents performed these activities twice a week or more often (Table 25-4). Other items had less consensus, but 89 percent advocated for services for patients, 86 percent participated in care planning, 86 percent educated coworkers about social work, and 74 percent provided health education. Two of these tasks, health education and advocating for services, were performed by approximately two-thirds of the respondents twice a week or more often. The remaining tasks were performed less frequently (Table 25-4). Respondents indicated a strong concern with ethical issues: 85 percent of social workers discussed ethical dilemmas with coworkers and approximately 40 percent had these discussions at least weekly (that is, 20 percent, twice a week to daily, and 19 percent, once a week).

There was unanimous agreement among social workers in proprietary agencies that assessment, home visits, and interagency collaboration were components of practice

**TABLE 25-3. Distribution of Auspice and Agency Type (N = 116)**

| Auspice | % of Total Sample | Distribution of Agency Type | |
|---|---|---|---|
| | | Free-Standing/ Private | Division of Larger Organization |
| Proprietary (n = 54) | 46.6 | 22.4 | 24.1 |
| Nonprofit (n = 53) | 45.7 | 31.9 | 13.8 |
| Government (n = 9) | 7.8 | NA | 7.8 |
| Total | 100.0 | 54.3 | 45.7 |

Note: Percentages may not add to 100 due to rounding. NA = not applicable.

(Table 25-4). In addition, more social workers in proprietary agencies than in nonprofit settings identified assessment, home visits, providing health education, collaboration, coordination of services, advocating for patients, and care planning as components of their practice (Table 25-4). However, only more frequently providing health education and advocating for patients were significantly ($p = .05$ and $p = .02$) associated with employment in a proprietary agency (Table 25-4). In addition, social workers in proprietary agencies invested significantly more time providing health education [$t(39) = 2.417, p = .02$] (Table 25-4). Having a diverse caseload was significantly associated with more frequent assessments ($p = .01$) and discussions of ethical dilemmas with coworkers ($p = .05$) (Table 25-4).

Only one of five respondents met with hospital discharge planners about referrals of patients into home health care. Significantly more social workers in nonprofit settings ($p = .02$) met with discharge planners than those in proprietary settings [$\chi^2(1) = 5.6, p = .02$].

Social workers also rated how often they experienced 11 ethical concerns on a continuum from 0 = never to 4 = very often) (Table 25-5). Concerns about self-determination were, on average, rated as occurring most often ($M = 2.78$). Advance directives ($M = 2.71$), assessment of mental competence ($M = 2.69$), and barriers to access of services ($M = 2.68$) were rated as occurring nearly as often (Table 25-5). Barriers to access of services was a consistent concern in that all respondents indicated that this issue occurred.

On average, social workers in proprietary agencies rated ethical concerns as occurring more often than those in nonprofit settings (Table 25-5). In particular, those in proprietary agencies rated concerns about barriers to access of services as occurring significantly ($p = .005$) more often [$t(105) = 2.84, p = .005$]

(Table 25-5). Statistically significant differences were found between workers with diverse as opposed to elderly caseloads regarding their experience of ethical concerns related to self-determination [$t(104) = 2.13, p = .04$] and to advance directives [$t(106) = 2.43, p = .02$]. In each instance, those with diverse caseloads reported these concerns more often (Table 25-5).

## Discussion

The research found a high degree of consensus among respondents regarding practice activities such as coordination of services, assessment, counseling, interagency collaboration, and home visits. These tasks have been previously identified in the literature as components of the social work function in home care (Kerson & Michelsen, 1995; Levande et al., 1987). However, the study also identified additional components of social work practice in home care that have not been previously documented. For instance, a majority of the social workers indicated that they frequently advocated for patients and provided health education. Over 80 percent of workers also engaged in care planning and educating coworkers about social work, although these tasks occurred less frequently. These additional tasks suggest that social work practice in home care involves a wider range of activities and, by implication, knowledge and skills than previously discussed in the literature.

An interesting finding is that a majority of the respondents discussed ethical dilemmas with coworkers and that approximately two-fifths had such conversations at least weekly. That social workers experience a pervasive concern with ethical issues is not surprising given the large number of potential ethical dilemmas that can arise in home care. This finding also raises concerns about the

**TABLE 25-4. Practice Activity Components and Frequency of Activity Occurrence**

| Practice Activities | % of Workers Identifying Practice Activity | | | Distribution of Occurrence of Activities (n = 104) | | | |
|---|---|---|---|---|---|---|---|
| | % Total Sample (n = 114) | % Proprietary Agencies (n = 48) | % Nonprofit (n = 56) | % Twice/week to daily | % Once/week | % Monthly | Hours (M) |
| Direct patient activities | | | | | | | |
| Direct assessment | 95 | 100 | 89 | 80[a] | 3 | 16 | 6.7 |
| Home visits after assessment | 94 | 100 | 91 | 69 | 10 | 20 | 9.6 |
| Counseling patients and families | 95 | 90 | 98 | 79 | 9 | 13 | 5.4 |
| Providing health education to patient families | 74 | 78 | 70 | 62[b] | 13 | 26 | 4.1[c] |
| Indirect patient activities | | | | | | | |
| Collaboration among agencies | 95 | 100 | 86 | 77 | 11 | 11 | 4.9 |
| Coordination of services | 94 | 92 | 88 | 93 | 0 | 4 | 5.6 |
| Advocating for services for patients | 89 | 86 | 90 | 67[d] | 12 | 21 | 3.7 |
| Care planning | 86 | 96 | 81 | 19 | 39 | 42 | 2.1 |
| Discussing ethical dilemmas with coworkers | 85 | 90 | 84 | 20[e] | 19 | 60 | 1.5 |
| Contacting managed care organizations | 51 | 40 | 58 | 26 | 14 | 61 | 1.0 |
| Contacting reimbursement organizations | 24 | 18 | 32 | 33 | 18 | 50 | 1.0 |
| Organizational/professional activities | | | | | | | |
| Educating coworkers about social work | 86 | 98 | 79 | 39 | 14 | 46 | 2.0 |
| Participating in policy/procedure and planning | 40 | 47 | 36 | 13 | 23 | 65 | 1.2 |

a. Association by population; $\chi^2(3) = 11.23$, $p = .01$.
b. Association by auspice; $\chi^2(3) = 7.72$, $p = .05$.
c. Difference by auspice; $t(39) = 2.417$, $p = .02$ (proprietary $M = 5.7$, nonprofit $M = 3.1$).
d. Association by auspice; $\chi^2(3) = 10.06$, $p = .02$.
e. Association by population; $\chi^2(3) = 7.66$, $p = .05$.

TABLE 25-5. Social Workers' Ethical Concerns in Total Sample and by Auspice and Population

| Ethical Concern | M (n = 107) | SD | Range | By Auspice | | | | | By Population | | | | |
|---|---|---|---|---|---|---|---|---|---|---|---|---|---|
| | | | | Proprietary (M) | Non-profit (M) | t | df | p | Diverse Caseload (M) | Only Elderly (M) | t | df | p |
| Self-determination | 2.78 | 1.04 | 0–4 | 2.86 | 2.78 | .75 | 103 | .463 | 2.94 | 2.54 | 2.13 | 104 | .035 |
| Barriers to access to services | 2.68 | .83 | 1–4 | 2.90 | 2.46 | 2.84 | 105 | .005 | 2.69 | 2.71 | -.128 | 106 | .898 |
| Advance directives | 2.71 | 1.02 | 0–4 | 2.73 | 2.75 | -.147 | 106 | .881 | 2.90 | 2.42 | 2.43 | 106 | .016 |
| Assessment of mental competence | 2.69 | .91 | 0–4 | 2.73 | 2.53 | 1.13 | 106 | .260 | 2.63 | 2.59 | 2.59 | 107 | .795 |
| Unmet needs | 2.52 | .90 | 0–4 | 2.65 | 2.47 | 1.01 | 106 | .310 | 2.54 | 2.56 | -.095 | 106 | .928 |
| Truth telling | 2.13 | 1.01 | 0–4 | 2.39 | 1.96 | 2.08 | 105 | .131 | 2.20 | 2.02 | .875 | 107 | .383 |
| Confidentiality | 2.02 | 1.05 | 0–4 | 2.10 | 1.97 | .65 | 106 | .515 | 2.18 | 1.76 | 2.05 | 106 | .143 |
| Rationing of services | 1.98 | .99 | 0–4 | 2.10 | 1.91 | .977 | 104 | .331 | 1.94 | 2.08 | -.677 | 106 | .499 |
| Elder abuse | 1.76 | .75 | 0–4 | 1.84 | 1.66 | 1.27 | 103 | .206 | 1.73 | 1.78 | -.313 | 104 | .754 |
| Terminating services due to limits of reimbursement | 1.54 | 1.10 | 0–4 | 1.67 | 1.46 | .969 | 103 | .335 | 1.65 | 1.39 | 1.16 | 107 | .247 |
| Right to die | 1.62 | .97 | 0–4 | 1.64 | 1.61 | .175 | 106 | .861 | 1.64 | 1.46 | 1.17 | 104 | .248 |

extent and adequacy of administrative and supervisory support to help social workers resolve these issues. Did social workers turn to coworkers because supervisors were not available to discuss these issues or because supervisors did not have the ability to resolve these issues competently?

The auspice of the social workers' agencies was slightly associated with practice activities. Social workers in proprietary agencies provided health education and advocated for services for clients significantly more frequently than social workers in nonprofit settings. The greater frequency of advocacy activities among social workers in proprietary than in nonprofit agencies may be attributable to the fact that proprietary agencies may be more likely than nonprofit agencies to refuse to provide social work services when those services are not reimbursed. Social workers may thus be advocating for clients more frequently in proprietary agencies because clients are denied access to services more frequently in these settings.

The finding that social workers in proprietary settings provided health education more frequently and invested more time in this activity than social workers in nonprofit settings can also be attributed to reimbursement criteria. Social work services are not reimbursed under Medicare unless they are necessary to resolve a medical problem. Medicare may be more willing to reimburse for a service such as health education, which has an obvious medical focus, than for other social work services less directly related to the patient's medical condition such as counseling.

Although practice activities were also generally similar among practitioners with only elderly clients as opposed to diverse populations in their caseloads, social workers with diverse caseload populations performed assessment tasks significantly more frequently than workers with only elderly clients. The assessment of elderly Medicare clients may be standardized to a greater extent than the assessment of younger clients with more complex medical and psychosocial needs, such as HIV patients, organ recipients, or patients receiving high-technology care, whose medical conditions and crises may require more hospitalizations and, thus, more frequent assessments as they return to home care. Social workers with diverse caseloads also discussed ethical dilemmas significantly more often with coworkers than those with only elderly patients, reflecting the greater variety of ethical issues that may arise with a diverse caseload, as well as the emergence of new ethical dilemmas given the use of sophisticated medical technology among younger patients.

Finally, the fact that few respondents met with discharge planners suggests that social workers in home care do not generally consider this task a component of their job. The finding that more social workers in nonprofit agencies did so may reflect the more altruistic commitment of nonprofit agencies to client well-being or the greater reluctance of proprietary agencies to engage in nonreimbursable activities (Williams, 1994).

The most frequent ethical concerns that workers confronted in their practice were related to self-determination, barriers to access to services, implementation of advance directives, and the assessment of mental competence. The frequency of concerns about self-determination is not surprising given the emphasis of the biopsychosocial model on client empowerment and the challenges faced by home-bound, chronically ill clients in an environment of restricted resources (Brown & Furstenberg, 1992; Callopy et al., 1990; Netting & Williams, 1996). Social worker concerns about barriers to access of services can be understood in the context of the "medicalization" of home care and the fact that access to social services is contingent on the receipt of skilled medical care (Binney et al., 1990; Callopy et al., 1990; Zuckerman et al., 1990). In a situation where patients do not have a skilled medical need but require social work services, the agency may have to choose to provide social work services without reimbursement or discontinue services.

The frequency of ethical concerns related to advance directives and the assessment of mental competence is consistent with the findings of a recent study that only 67 percent of home care agencies reported having policies on the implementation of advance directives and only 42 percent had policies on how to handle clients with questionable decision-making capacity (Davitt & Kaye, 1996). In the absence of clearly articulated policies, it may be difficult for social workers to make decisions about implementing advance directives or to know when to activate an advance directive.

The higher frequency of concerns over barriers to access to services in proprietary agencies may relate to the fact that nonprofit agencies are more willing than proprietary agencies to provide nonreimbursable services. However, it may also be true that because social workers in proprietary settings advocated for services for clients more frequently, they had more opportunities than nonprofit social workers to experience denials of requests for services and so experienced barriers to service as an ethical issue more often.

Social workers with diverse as opposed to only elderly clients in their caseloads rated ethical concerns related to self-determination and advance directives as significantly more frequent. One possible explanation of these findings may relate to ethical issues raised by the use of complex technology in home care. Compared with patients who are receiving routine home care, high-technology patients are likely to be younger and living with a sup-

port person who can supervise the regimen of care (Kaye & Davitt, 1995). Because complex medical technology places an enormous burden on caregivers—disrupting lives, careers, and emotional balance—it may create a severe conflict between the self-determination of the caregiver and the patient (Arras & Dubler, 1994). High-technology patients also are more likely than other patients to experience serious and urgent complications in the home. Davitt and Kaye's (1996) finding that home health agencies lack policies regarding the implementation of advance directives may create ethical dilemmas for providers if a patient experiences an acute episode and no advance directive has been executed or the advance directive is not available.

In summary, the findings of this study indicate that social work practice in home care is complicated, involving a wide range of activities. Ethical concerns related to self-determination, barriers to access to service, implementation of advance directives, and the assessment of mental competence were rated as occurring most often. Practice activities and the occurrence of ethical issues were influenced by reimbursement mechanisms as well as by caseload population.

## Implications for Social Work Practice

This is the first published survey to examine the activities and ethical concerns of social workers in home health care. Caution should be exercised in generalizing the findings of this study to the population of social workers in home health agencies because the findings are not based on a random sample of the population. Nevertheless, the findings suggest several implications for social work practitioners, educators, and administrators.

With regard to practice, the findings indicate that social work practice in home care is more complex and multifaceted than documented in earlier research. The practice approach evident in this study appears to be a variation of, rather than a "pure" approach to, generalist practice. The "pure" generalist engages systems on a problem-by-problem basis (Parsons, Hernandez, & Jorgensen, 1988; Tolson, Reid, & Garvin, 1994). The type of generalist practice documented in this study is patient centered, with the social worker simultaneously engaging multiple systems (that is, patient, family, community, and organization) to resolve the patient's difficulty. This work requires a sophisticated practitioner with the skills to engage and integrate practice at several system levels.

A second implication of the study for practice is the need for social work practitioners in home and acute care settings to develop more formalized mechanisms to ensure continuity of care for patients making the transition from the hospital to the community. Participation of home care social workers at patient care rounds in hospitals that refer a high volume of patients to the home care agency may be one mechanism for facilitating necessary continuity of care.

With regard to education, the study suggests that social work preparation for practice in home care will require an understanding of issues that influence health care practice at individual, family, community, and organizational levels. The finding that the majority of practitioners had diverse caseloads suggests that practice courses should emphasize the effect of chronic illness on individuals and families across the life cycle. To prepare social workers for the tasks of health education, counseling, and assessment and to work with patients receiving high-technology home care, it will also be important for practice courses to emphasize an understanding of, and an ability to integrate, physiological data. Because practice

activities and ethical concerns were associated with reimbursement mechanisms, workers will need to understand issues related to reimbursement and how to negotiate with reimbursement systems. Finally, courses to prepare students for multisystemic case management should be developed because coordination of services and interagency collaboration were frequent social work activities.

Content related to ethics and the resolution of ethical dilemmas should be a strong component of health care practice courses. However, a recent survey of the syllabi used to teach health care practice courses in graduate schools accredited by the Council on Social Work Education found that only 62 percent of courses included a unit on ethics. Among those courses that did include such a unit, required readings related to advance directives were included in 42 percent, and readings related to self-determination were included in 19 percent of the syllabi. The survey found no required readings related to barriers to access to services or the assessment of mental competence (Kadushin & Egan, 1997). The development of ethical content related to the concerns identified as occurring frequently in this study should be a priority for social work educators preparing students for practice.

The findings with regard to ethical concerns also suggest that home care social workers require administrative and supervisory support in resolving such issues. Supervisors of social workers in home care agencies need to be aware of ethical issues as an area to target in supervisory sessions. It may also be necessary for administrators to provide workers with access to continuing education opportunities through conferences and in-service training.

The level of concern about ethical issues documented in this survey suggests that future research should examine levels of job satisfaction among social workers in home care. In light of Siefert, Jayaratne, and Chess's (1991) finding of a relationship between conflict with professional values and levels of job satisfaction among health care workers and the findings of this study that workers in proprietary agencies may be more vulnerable to such conflicts than those in nonprofit settings, future research should also compare the job satisfaction of social workers in proprietary and nonprofit home health agencies.

ᴑ  ᴑ  ᴑ

## References

Arras, J., & Dubler, N. (1994). Bringing the hospital home: Ethical and social implications of high-tech home care. *Hastings Center Report, 24* (Special suppl.), S19–S28.

Asch, A. (1993). Abused or neglected clients—Or abusive or neglectful service systems? In R. Kane & A. Caplan (Eds.), *Ethical conflicts in the management of home care* (pp. 113–121). New York: Springer.

Balanced Budget Act of 1997, P.L. 105-33, 111 Stat. 251.

Balinsky, W. (1994). *Home care: Current problems and future solutions.* San Francisco: Jossey-Bass.

Benjamin, A. E. (1993). A historical perspective on home care policy. *Milbank Quarterly, 71,* 129–166.

Berger, C. S., Cayner, J., Jensen, G., Mizrahi, T., Scesny, A., & Trachtenberg, J. (1996). The changing scene of social work in hospitals: A report of a national study by the Society for Social Work Administrators in Health Care and NASW. *Health & Social Work, 21,* 167–177.

Berkman, B. (1996). The emerging health care world: Implications for social work practice and education. *Social Work, 41,* 541–551.

Binney, E., Estes, C., & Ingman, S. (1990). Medicalization, public policy and the elderly: Social services in jeopardy? *Social Science and Medicine, 30,* 761–771.

Bishop, C., & Skwara, K. C. (1993). Recent growth of Medicare home health. *Health Affairs, 12,* 95–110.

Brown, J. T., & Furstenberg, A. L. (1992). Restoring control: Empowering older patients and their families during health care crisis. *Social Work in Health Care, 17,* 81–101.

Browne, C., Smith, M., Ewalt, P., & Walker, D. (1996). Advancing social work practice in health settings: A collaborative partnership for continuing education. *Health & Social Work, 21,* 267–276.

Callopy, B. (1988). Autonomy in long term care: Some crucial distinctions. *Gerontologist, 28* (Special suppl.), 10–17.

Callopy, B. (1990). An introduction to home care: What are the issues? In C. Zuckerman, N. Dubler, & B. Callopy (Eds.), *Home health care options* (pp. 3–23). New York: Plenum.

Callopy, B., Dubler, N., & Zuckerman, C. (1990). The ethics of home care: Autonomy and accommodation. *Hastings Center Report, 20* (Special suppl.), 1–16.

Davitt, J., & Kaye, L. (1996). Supporting patient autonomy: Decision making in home health care. *Social Work, 41,* 41–50.

Dhooper, S. (1997). *Social work in health care in the 21st century.* Thousand Oaks, CA: Sage Publications.

Dresser, R. (1993). Values and perspectives on abuse: Unspoken influences on ethical reasoning. In R. Kane & A. Caplan (Eds.), *Ethical conflicts in the management of home care* (pp. 121–127). New York: Springer.

Dubler, N. (1990). Accommodating the home care client: A look at rights and interest. In C. Zuckerman, N. Dubler, & B. Callopy (Eds.), *Home health care options* (pp. 141–165). New York: Plenum.

Ellenbecker, C. (1995). Profit and non-profit home health care agency outcomes: A study of one state's experience. *Home Health Care Services Quarterly, 15*, 47–60.

Fessler, S. R., & Adams, C. G. (1985). Nurse–social worker role conflict in home health care. *Journal of Gerontological Social Work, 9*(1), 113–121.

Haddad, A. M. (1992). Ethical problems in home healthcare. *Journal of Nursing Administration, 22*, 46–51.

Health Care Financing Administration. (1992). *Medicare home health agency manual*. Washington, DC: U.S. Government Printing Office.

Hofland, B. (1993). Use of facts to resolve conflicts between beneficence and autonomy. In R. Kane & A. Caplan (Eds.), *Ethical conflicts in the management of home care* (pp. 36–45). New York: Springer.

Kadushin, G., & Egan, M. (1997). Educating students for a changing health care environment: An examination of health care practice course content. *Health & Social Work, 22*, 211–222.

Kane, R. (1993). Uses and abuses of confidentiality. In R. Kane & A. Caplan (Eds.), *Ethical conflicts in the management of home care* (pp. 147–158). New York: Springer.

Kane, R., & Caplan, A. (Eds.). (1993). *Ethical conflicts in the management of home care*. New York: Springer.

Kane, R., & Reinardy, J. (1990). Family caregiving in home care. In C. Zuckerman, N. Dubler, & B. Callopy (Eds.), *Home health care options* (pp. 89–113). New York: Plenum.

Kaye, L., & Davitt, J. K. (1995). Provider and consumer profiles of traditional and high-tech home health care: The issue of differential access. *Health & Social Work, 20*, 262–271.

Keigher, S. (1997). What role for social work in the new health care practice paradigm? [National Health Line]. *Health & Social Work, 22*, 149–156.

Kerson, T., & Michelsen, R. (1995). Counseling homebound clients and their families. In L. Kaye (Ed.), *New developments in home care services for the elderly: Innovations in policy, program*

*and practice* (pp. 159–190). New York: Haworth Press.

Levande, D. I., Bowden, S. W., & Mollema, J. (1987). Home health services for dependent elders: The social work dimension. *Journal of Gerontological Social Work, 11*, 5–17.

Macklin, R., & Callahan, D. (1990). Some examples to consider. In C. Zuckerman, N. Dubler, & B. Callopy (Eds.), *Home health care options* (pp. 217–252). New York: Plenum.

Malone-Rising, D. (1994). The changing face of long-term care. *Community Health Nursing and Home Health Nursing, 29*, 417–429.

McBrayer, S., Slade, V., & Heller-Bramblett, P. (1996). *The national health care blue book*. Atlanta: Billian.

National Association for Home Care. (1997). *Basic statistics about home care 1996* (Online), http://www.nah.org/Consumer/hcstats.html.

Netting, F. E., & Williams, F. G. (1996). Case manager–physician collaboration: Implications for professional identity, roles, and relationships. *Health & Social Work, 21*, 216–224.

Omnibus Budget Reconciliation Act of 1981, P.L. 97-35.

Parsons, R., Hernandez, S., & Jorgensen, J. (1988). Integrated practice: A framework for problem solving. *Social Work, 33*, 417–421.

Pear, R. (1997, June 25). Senate backs rise in Medicare costs for wealthy aged. *The New York Times*, pp. A1, A14.

Proctor, E., Morrow-Howell, N., & Kaplan, S. (1996). Implementation of discharge plans for chronically ill elders discharged home. *Health & Social Work, 21*, 30–40.

Robbins, D. (1996). *Ethical and legal issues in home health and long-term care*. Gaithersburg, MD: Aspen.

Rosenberg, G. (1994). Social work, the family and the community. *Social Work in Health Care, 20*, 7–20.

Rubin, A., & Babbie, E. (1996). *Research methodologies for social work*. Monterey, CA: Brooks/Cole.

Ryan White Comprehensive AIDS Resources Emergency (CARE) Act of 1990, P.L. 101-381, 42 U.S.C.A. §§ 300ff–111. (West, 1991, & Supp. 1997).

Ryden, M. (1993). Clinical determination of competency and existential advocacy. In R. Kane & A. Caplan (Eds.), *Ethical conflicts in the management of home care* (pp. 68–75). New York: Springer.

Schmid, H., & Hasenfeld, Y. (1993). Organizational dilemmas in the provision of home-care services. *Social Service Review, 67,* 40–54.

Shuster, G., & Cloonan, P. (1991). Home health nursing care: A comparison of not-for-profit and for-profit agencies. *Home Health Care Services Quarterly, 12,* 23–36.

Siefert, K., Jayaratne, S., & Chess, W. (1991). Job satisfaction, burnout, and turnover in health care social workers. *Health & Social Work, 16,* 193–202.

Simmons, J. (1994). Community based care: The new health social work paradigm. *Social Work in Health Care, 20,* 35–46.

Simon, E. P., Showers, N., Blumenfield, S., Holden, G., & Wu, X. (1995). Delivery of home care services after discharge: What really happens. *Health & Social Work, 20,* 5–14.

Strahan, G. W. (1994). An overview of home health and hospice care patients: Preliminary data from the 1993 National Home and Hospice Care Survey. *Advance Data, 256,* 2–11.

Tennessee Rules and Regulations, Chapter 1200-13-12-04 (1994, 1995, and 1996, revised).

Tolson, E., Reid, W., & Garvin, C. (1994). *Generalist practice: A task-centered approach.* New York: Columbia University Press.

Vincent, P., & Davis, J. (1987). Functions of social workers in a home health agency. *Health & Social Work, 12,* 213–219.

Williams, B. (1994). Comparison of services among different types of home health agencies. *Medical Care, 32,* 1134–1152.

Williams, B., Mackay, S., & Torner, J. (1991). Home health care: Comparison of patients and services among three types of agencies. *Medical Care, 29,* 583–587.

Wisconsin Administrative Code (HFS 107.11, 1997).

Wolf, S. (1993). Beyond the double agent: Toward a systemic ethics of case management. In R. Kane & A. Caplan (Eds.), *Ethical conflicts in the management of home care* (pp. 59–68). New York: Springer.

Zuckerman, C., Dubler, N., & Callopy, B. (Eds.). (1990). *Home health care options.* New York: Plenum.

This chapter was originally published in the February 1999 issue of *Health & Social Work,* Vol. 24, Number 1, pp. 43–55.

# 26

## Desire to Die in Terminally Ill People

### A Framework for Assessment and Intervention

RUTH ANNE VAN LOON

*"I wish I could die. I'm no good to anyone like this. . . . don't get any better. What's the point of this? I just wish I could die."*

Statements like these are familiar to social workers and others who care for people with terminal illness. Termed "desire for death," "desire to die," or "suicide talk," they are expressions of the wish for death. Although prevailing practice encourages the person with terminal illness to acknowledge the inevitability of death and to discuss related feelings, indications that a person *wants* to die can produce confusion and fear in professionals and family members alike. Is the patient depressed? Is he or she planning to end his or her life? Is he or she asking for help in doing that? Or is this "just talk"? And, anyway, is it not normal to feel this way under these circumstances? These questions produce heightened emotion when considered in the context of current public debates about the right to die and assisted suicide.

Desire-to-die statements may serve a number of functions for people with terminal illness. They may be expressions of depression or suicidal ideation, they may be a way of coping, they may express a spiritually based acceptance of death, or they may be an indication of a rational choice for suicide. *Depression* is used in this instance to indicate a severe and persistent disorder that impairs social functioning rather than a mood characterized by sadness and discouragement (American Psychiatric Association, 1994). *Suicidal ideation* includes thoughts and statements about intentionally ending one's life (Ivanoff, 1991). *Coping* means the strategies, including verbalizations, that people use to alleviate stress. To intervene appropriately, social workers need to understand the meaning behind a particular patient's desire-to-die statement. This article presents a framework for making these evaluations through assessment for depression and suicide intent in people with terminal illness and outlines appropriate interventions.

Two assumptions underlie this framework. (1) Expressing a desire for death is assumed to be common and therefore a "normal" response to, and way of coping with, terminal illness. Many people who come into contact with terminally ill patients, including professionals, however, find these statements disconcerting and react by changing the subject, contradicting the patient, or offering unrealistic reassurance. This can make patients less inclined to express feelings and can limit opportunities to discuss upsetting emotions and allay fears. (2) A desire for death is commonly thought to be the result of depression, and many people, including patients and professionals, consider depression a normal and expected response to terminal illness (Brody, 1997; Brugha, 1993; Valente, Saunders, & Cohen, 1994). The empirical evidence suggests that it is not, but the assumption of normality means that depression is often neglected and untreated in the terminally ill (Billings & Block, 1995) and that opportunities to improve the quality of life for this population are missed.

## Desire to Die, Depression, and Suicide in Terminally Ill Individuals

Anecdotal reports suggest that expressions of a desire to die are common among ter-

minally ill individuals, but recent research presents a more complex picture. Brown et al. (1986) found that 23 percent of palliative care patients had desire for death or expressed suicidal ideation, and Owen et al. (1992) found that one-third of cancer patients had considered suicide. More than 44 percent of patients admitted to a palliative care unit expressed at least an occasional wish to die, but at follow-up two weeks later, only 8.5 percent continued to express this wish (Chochinov et al., 1995).

Desire to die has been linked with depression in some studies. All patients expressing desire for death in Brown et al.'s (1986) study were depressed, and a majority of those with a consistent wish to die were depressed in Chochinov et al.'s (1995) study. Owen et al. (1994) found that depression was correlated with desire for death, but not with contemplation of suicide. Furthermore, although pain and lack of family support could exacerbate depression (Chochinov et al., 1995), these factors were not linked directly to the desire to die (Breitbart, Rosenfeld, & Passik, 1996; Chochinov et al., 1995).

Estimating the extent of depression among terminally ill people is important because of the role depression plays in producing desire for death. Depression rates reported in the literature range from 5 or 6 percent to 40 percent (Chochinov, Wilson, Enns, & Lander, 1994). These rates depend in part on the criteria used in diagnosing depression, as well as the point in the illness when the assessment is made. For example, 77 percent of patients severely disabled by cancer were depressed, compared with 23 percent whose physical functioning was better (Bukberg, Penman, & Holland, 1984). Two sets of criteria, the Research Diagnostic Criteria and Endicott's symptom-substitution criteria, produced quite different rates of depression among palliative care patients, 13 percent and 26 percent (Chochinov et al., 1994). Despite conflicting data, most commentators maintain that a rate of depression of 10 percent to 25 percent can be expected (Billings & Block, 1995; Brugha, 1993; Valente et al., 1994).

Desire-to-die statements sometimes reflect suicidal ideation, and terminally ill people are at greater risk of suicide. The suicide rate for men with AIDS is 7.4 times that of demographically similar men without AIDS (Marzuk, 1994). Men with cancer have an increased risk of suicide vis à vis the general population, 2.9 compared to 1.3; the risk for women with cancer is 1.9 compared to 0.9 for the general population. Those with head and neck, lung, breast, urogenital, and gastrointestinal cancers are at greatest risk (Marzuk, 1994).

These studies suggest that the desire to die may be a transient phenomenon for most terminally ill patients, but that for a small but significant group the wish for death is stable, with depression as an associated factor. Al-though the risk of depression among patients with terminal illness may be less than commonly thought, both depression and the possibility of suicide are significant sources of stress for these patients, their family members, and caregivers.

## Framework for Assessment and Intervention

Depression and suicide intent should be considered for all patients. This process differentiates depressed patients who are suicidal from those who are not. (Figure 26-1 depicts the process of assessment and intervention with patients expressing a desire for death.) Also, patients who are not depressed and express a desire to die as a way of coping or as an expression of their acceptance of death can be distinguished from those who may have made a rational choice to end their lives.

**FIGURE 26-1. Framework for Assessment and Intervention in "Desire-to-Die" Talk**

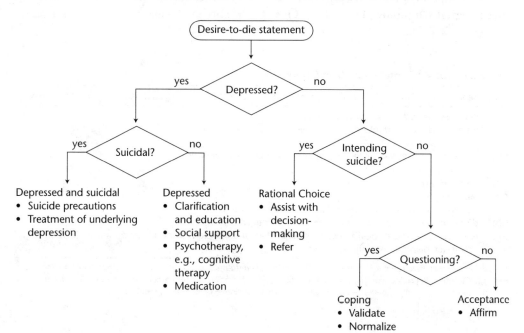

### Assessment of Depression in Terminally Ill People

Assessing depression in the terminally ill is complicated. DSM-IV criteria for major depression are inadequate for this group, because diagnosis depends on somatic symptoms that are difficult to distinguish from symptoms caused by terminal illness (Billings & Block, 1995; Melvin, Ozbek, & Eberle, 1995; Valente et al., 1994). These symptoms include changes in weight or appetite, sleep disturbance, changes in psychomotor functioning, fatigue, and cognitive disturbances. Thinking about death is another symptom common to people with terminal illness as well (Table 26-1)

To correct this problem, several authors have proposed alternatives to the DSM criteria for depression for use with people with serious medical conditions (Cavanaugh, Clark, & Gibbons, 1983; Endicott, 1984; Valente et al., 1994), including those with terminal illness (Billings & Block, 1995; Chochinov et al., 1995). In general, the alternate criteria eliminate or minimize the somatic symptoms and emphasize a range of psychological symptoms (Table 26-2). One problem with these criteria is that the assessor must determine whether certain psychological responses are more intense or persistent than might be expected for seriously ill people or for the particular person being assessed. This implies that there is a normative response to terminal illness, which has not been established, and requires knowledge of the person's pre-illness functioning, which may not be available.

Chochinov (cited in Brody, 1997) suggested that directly asking patients about depression can produce accurate information. Patients can be asked simply whether their reactions to the illness and situation are reasonable or too much (Brugha, 1993) and about their mood. If a patient reports depressed feelings or unreasonable reactions to the illness, follow-up questions can ascertain the persistence of a depressed mood.

### Assessment of Suicide Risk in Depressed Patients

Suicide assessment starts with confronting suicidal thoughts and statements directly. Patients may make frank statements about

---

**TABLE 26-1. DSM-IV Criteria for Major Depression**

*The presence of five or more of the following symptoms for at least two weeks; either (1) or (2) must be present:*

| | |
|---|---|
| (1) | depressed mood, most of the day, nearly every day. |
| (2) | markedly diminished interest or pleasure in all or almost all activities most of the day, nearly every day. |
| (3[†]) | significant weight loss or gain or decrease or increase in appetite. |
| (4[†]) | insomnia or hypersomnia. |
| (5[†]) | psychomotor agitation or retardation. |
| (6[†]) | fatigue or loss of energy. |
| (7) | feelings of worthlessness or excessive or inappropriate guilt. |
| (8[†]) | diminished ability to think or concentrate, or indecisiveness. |
| (9[†]) | recurrent thoughts of death, recurrent suicidal ideation without a specific plan, or suicide attempt or specific plan for committing suicide. |

*Source:* American Psychiatric Association. (1994). *Diagnostic and statistical manual of mental disorders—Fourth Edition.* Washington, DC: Author. Reprinted with permission from DSM-IV, Fourth Edition. © 1994 American Psychiatric Association.

† Symptoms commonly experienced by patients with terminal illness regardless of psychiatric status.

**TABLE 26-2. Criteria for Depression in People with Serious Medical Illness**

- Somatization, unexpected poor functioning, or poor pain and symptom control.[a]
- Symptoms such as dysphoria; feelings of helplessness, hopelessness, or worthlessness; guilt; loss of self-esteem; or wish to die are severe, persistent, out of character, pervasive, and excessive.[a]
- Fearfulness or depressed appearance in face or body posture.[b]
- Social withdrawal or decreased talkativeness.[b]
- Brooding, self-pity, pessimism.[b]
- Lack of reactivity of mood in situations that would normally be pleasurable; cannot be cheered up, doesn't smile, no response to good news or funny situations.[b]
- Feels like a failure.[c]
- Loss of interest in people.[c]
- Feels punished.[c]
- Has suicidal ideas.[c]
- Persistent negativism; no "connection" with caregivers.[a]

a. *Source:* Billings, J. A., & Block, S. (1995). Depression. *Journal of Palliative Care, 11,* 48–54.
b. *Source:* Endicott, J. (1984). Measurement of depression in patients with cancer. *Cancer, 53,* 2243–2248.
c. *Source:* Cavanaugh, S., Clark, D. C., & Gibbons, R. D. (1983). Diagnosing depression in the hospitalized medically ill. *Psychosomatics, 24,* 809–815.

killing themselves, but more often they express suicidal thoughts and feelings in vague, veiled, or even nonverbal ways, such as keeping the book *The Final Exit* (Humphry, 1991) on the coffee table or a gun by the bedside. Social workers should respond empathically, but directly with statements such as "You sound pretty hopeless. Have you been considering suicide?" Although clinicians and others sometimes fear that this may introduce the idea of suicide as an option, direct inquiry is recommended (Ivanoff, 1991). Patients who are not considering suicide often are surprised, even offended, by this question and are emphatic in their denials. Others for whom suicide is a concern receive permission to have a discussion they may be unable to initiate.

Suicide assessment continues with understanding a patient's intent and determining whether a plan has been made. Patients' motivation for considering suicide vary. Some patients are looking for help, reassurance, or the opportunity to talk about what they are experiencing and are unable to express these requests directly. Other patients are seeking deliverance from pain, other symptoms, or what they consider an intolerable situation. Still others are hoping to relieve overburdened caregivers. Motivation and goals can be discovered by asking patients questions such as "How would things be different if you committed suicide?"

Finding out whether a patient has a definite suicide plan can be accomplished by asking questions such as "Have you thought about or decided how you would commit suicide?" If the patient has, the specifics of the plan should be determined, including the method and means, time and place, and others who may know or be involved. The availability of the means, such as a gun or pills, and the patient's physical ability to carry out the plan also should be assessed. Suicide plans that are specific, use methods that have higher degrees of lethality such as shooting, and have poor probability of postattempt discovery or reversibility carry the greatest risk of imminent danger.

Risk factors for suicide also should be evaluated (Table 26-3), including general risk factors and those unique to terminal illness, such as changes in medical or psychosocial status and dealing with chronicity.

**TABLE 26-3. Risk Factors for Suicide in Terminally Ill People**

History/Pre-Existing Factors
- previous suicide attempt[a]
- history of psychiatric illness, especially depression and psychosis[a]
- family history of suicide[a]
- parallel circumstances in family members or close friends
- substance abuse[a]
- personality traits such as aggressiveness, impulsivity, rigidity
- borderline personality disorder, antisocial personality disorder[a]
- male, especially over age 65[b]
- white[a]
- HIV/AIDS[c]

Change in Medical Status
- altered mental state, particularly depression, anxiety, psychosis, and delirium[c]
- change in physical condition or functioning, especially when this results in dependency[c]
- discontinuation of treatment due to ineffectiveness

Change in Psychosocial Status
- change in family/caregiver support or situation[c]
- self-imposed isolation[c]
- "giving away" possessions
- feelings of humiliation or loss[c]
- financial insolvency[c]
- relocation[c]

Dealing with Chronicity
- recognition that symptoms are intractable[c]
- decline in quality of life

a. *Source:* Fremouw, W. J., de Perczel, M., & Ellis, T. E. (1990). *Suicide risk: Assessment and response guidelines.* New York: Pergamon Press.
b. *Source:* Clark, D. C., & Fawcett, J. (1992). Review of empirical risk factors for evaluation of the suicidal patient. In B. Bongar (Ed.), *Suicide: Guidelines for assessment, management, and treatment* (pp. 16–48). New York: Oxford University Press.
c. *Source:* Marzuk, P. M. (1994). Suicide and terminal illness. *Death Studies, 18,* 497–512.

## Interventions with Patients Who Are Depressed

Terminally ill patients who are depressed can benefit from a number of interventions, both pharmacological and psychosocial. The first steps in alleviating depression are to address pain and other symptoms and to clarify the patient's understanding of his condition and prognosis, as symptomatic relief and accurate understanding may ease a patient's fears and promote feelings of control. Patients, however, may have difficulty communicating concerns in these areas to the health care team. Social workers can teach patients how to ask questions of doctors and other professionals and can act as advocates in conveying patients' concerns. Social support also may relieve depression. Social workers can interpret a patient's needs for support to family members and others in his social network and help them determine ways to enhance support. Additional support may be found through referrals to other agencies.

Although a number of psychotherapeutic modalities are effective in the treatment of depression (Turnbull, 1991), cognitive therapy may be of particular value to terminally ill patients with depression (Billings &

Block, 1995; Valente et al., 1994) because of its time-limited nature and focused approach to achieving well-defined goals. Cognitive therapy offers ways to identify and correct specific faulty beliefs and perceptions that contribute to depression. For example, the social worker might challenge a patient's belief that she is useless and a burden to others by helping her identify ways she is important to her family. Similarly, a patient might be offered a definition of hope as maintaining a good quality of life rather than being cured. In using these techniques, however, the social worker must guard against appearing unrealistically optimistic.

Medications for treating depressed patients with limited life expectancies are available, and some patients may benefit from these. Antidepressants and the faster-acting psychostimulants have been shown to be effective (see Billings & Block, 1995, for a review). Social workers can be instrumental in referring patients for medication evaluations. They also may need to counsel patients on the benefits of a trial of medication, as terminally ill patients are sometimes reluctant to take additional medication.

### Interventions with Patients Who Are Depressed and Suicidal

Depressed patients who are suicidal require immediate attention. If a patient is in imminent danger of harming herself, hospitalization should be considered. However, admitting a terminally ill patient to a psychiatric facility often is not possible. A patient might be admitted to a medical floor under a suicide observation protocol, but mental health services in these facilities may be limited.

When a patient remains at home, a number of precautions should be taken. Some authorities (Ivanoff, 1991) recommend the use of a no-suicide contract, which involves eliciting an agreement from the patient that she will make no attempt to take her life within a limited time frame (generally until the next contact with the social worker) and that she will call for help when feeling overwhelmed. The efficacy of these contracts has not been established, and some critics suggest that their primary effect is to relieve worker anxiety, not change patient behavior (Fremouw, de Perczel, & Ellis, 1990; Goldblatt, 1994). However, they may serve as the means for initiating problem solving and devising safety plans (Fremouw et al., 1990; Goldblatt, 1994). As the social worker and patient discuss what the patient will do when feeling suicidal, the social worker should state explicitly that he or she must inform the health care team and family members and other caregivers about the situation. As most health care agencies serving this population have an on-call system that rotates among a number of staff members, managing these contracts is complicated. All staff need to be informed of the contract and trained to respond. However, a no-suicide contract should not be seen as a guarantee of safety, and other measures must be taken.

Safe proofing the home is a primary goal. Social workers need to educate family members and caregivers and enlist their cooperation in removing the means of suicide from the home and supervising medications that may be used in a suicide attempt. They also should be counseled to increase their support to the patient. A family's need for support also will likely increase during this time, and social workers need to be prepared for this demand on their time and skills.

### Interventions with Patients Who Are Not Depressed

Although some patients who express a desire for death are depressed, more are not

(Chochinov et al., 1995). Three patterns can be seen among these patients: (1) those who make desire-to-die statements as a way of coping; (2) those who are expressing an acceptance of death based on religious, spiritual, or philosophical beliefs; and (3) those who are considering or have made a choice to end their lives. As with depressed patients, careful assessment is the first step in determining a patient's intention.

### Desire-to-Die Talk as Coping

Some patients make statements about desiring death as a way of coping with their circumstances. These statements may be used to promote feelings of control, invite a discussion of existential concerns, or elicit help.

Feelings of personal control are jeopardized by terminal illness. Patients often feel loss of control as the disease progresses, symptoms change or worsen, and options narrow. Patients may suggest that suicide is a choice they are considering. These statements are often future-oriented, such as "when things get too bad, I'll just end it," indicating that they have some kind of marker in mind about when they would take action.

Other statements suggest that patients wish to discuss existential concerns, such as the meaning or quality of life, which are difficult to raise directly. They may ask "Haven't I suffered enough?" as a way of thinking about "What is the meaning of my suffering?" or "What's the point of life like this?" as a way of saying "I find the quality of my life unacceptable." Patients also may express these feelings in a more positive manner, saying "I've lived a good life. I'm ready to go," as a way of inviting reflection on the meaning of life.

Still other statements may reflect patients' requests for help, particularly with symptoms that seem unbearable or with feelings that

threaten to overwhelm them. These requests can be direct: "Can't you give me something to end it now?" or indirect: "I'm going to end it all before I become too disabled."

Determining whether a patient is using desire-to-die talk as a way of coping becomes clearer if depression has been ruled out and if these expressions are transient. These statements also seem to be characterized by a questioning or struggling quality. The social worker can be more confident of coping as a source of these statements through an exploration of their meaning with the patient.

The goal for intervention with these patients is normalization, which involves attending to and validating these expressions and the feelings behind them. By actively offering patients opportunities to discuss prognosis, dying, and existential concerns, social workers can demonstrate their comfort with these issues and provide relief to patients. Attempts also can be made to promote control over their circumstances and reframe the meaning of independence. Patients who are debilitated and physically dependent may still be able to be involved in decision making about schedules and other aspects of daily life.

### Desire-to-Die Talk as Acceptance

Some patients' desire-for-death statements indicate acceptance of death. A statement such as "I'm ready for God to take me home" reflects an assurance based in religious faith. Similarly, others may express a readiness for death that is rooted in a spiritual or philosophical stance; "death is just another part of life" may be such an expression. Affirmation of these beliefs is the social worker's task with these patients. If a patient desires, the social worker also can involve clergy or a faith community to provide pastoral counseling or religious rites.

### *Desire-to-Die Talk and Rational Choice*

Occasionally, social workers encounter patients who make desire-to-die statements and who are neither depressed nor using their statements as a way of coping. These patients express a well-thought-out and persistent belief that suicide is their best option, a phenomenon termed "rational choice."

Several authors (Forstein, 1994; Siegel, 1986; Werth, 1995) have outlined the components of a rational choice for suicide that can be used in assessment (Table 26-4). An important element is ruling out depression, other psychological disturbances, and substance abuse, all of which may impair thinking and judgment. Examining the patient's process and time frame for decision making, by asking how long he has felt that way and what factors have gone into making the choice, can assist in differentiating between impulsive and deliberate actions.

Social workers face ethical issues when working with patients who have made a rational choice for suicide. Discussions about terminally ill patients ending their lives often revolve around the issue of assisted suicide, although patients in this position may develop plans for suicide without assistance from others. Social workers have expressed arguments both for and against the legality

of assisted suicide (Boyle, 1997; Callahan, 1994, 1997; Canady, 1997; Smokowski & Wodarski, 1996). NASW has taken the position that the value of client self-determination is pre-eminent in these cases and "affirms the right of the individual to determine the level of his or her care" at the end of life, including suicide (NASW, 1997, p. 60). "Social workers should be free to participate or not" in these end-of-life discussions "depending on their own beliefs, attitudes, and value systems" (NASW, 1997, p. 61), but should refer patients and families elsewhere if they choose not to participate. The possibility of criminal charges prohibits social workers from actually participating in an assisted suicide, but they may be present if the client requests this and if "legally permissible" (NASW, 1997, p. 61). Miller et al. (1998) offered a model for assessing requests for assistance with suicide which considers concerns about diagnosis, treatment, symptoms, and needs for care, as well as the individual and family's cultural context and psychosocial functioning.

Agencies serving terminally ill people need to discuss the issues of rational choice and assisted suicide and develop protocols for responding to patients who have considered these options. Social workers need to make sure that patients clearly understand what

**TABLE 26-4. Components of a Rational Choice for Suicide**

- The person has a realistic assessment of the situation.[a]
- The person's mental processes are unimpaired by psychological illness or severe emotional distress.[a]
- The person has a motivation that would be understandable to a majority of uninvolved community members.[a]
- The decision is deliberated and reiterated over a period of time.[b]
- Whenever possible, the decision should involve the person's significant others.[b]
- A substance abuse disorder or acute intoxication precludes rationality as described above.[c]

a. *Source:* Siegel, K. (1986). Psychosocial aspects of rational suicide. *American Journal of Psychotherapy, 40,* 405–418.
b. *Source:* Werth, J. L. (1995). Rational suicide reconsidered: AIDS as an impetus for change. *Death Studies, 19,* 65–81.
c. *Source:* Forstein, M. (1994). Suicidality and gay men. In S. A. Caldwell, R. A. Burnham, & M. Forstein (Eds.), *Therapists on the front line: Psychotherapy with gay men in the Age of AIDS* (pp. 111–145). Washington, DC: American Psychiatric Press.

they and other agency staff will and will not do, particularly about maintaining or breaking confidentiality and the extent of participation in supporting or helping someone end his or her life.

## Implications for Social Work Practice

Desire-to-die statements have many meanings for people who are terminally ill. Careful assessment can differentiate among those meanings and help social workers intervene appropriately. Screening of all patients who express a desire to die for depression can lead to beneficial interventions for those who are depressed as well as for those who are not. Depression is not inevitable for terminally ill patients, and they can benefit from a variety of psychosocial and pharmacological interventions, making their accurate identification imperative. On the other hand, patients who are not depressed can benefit from having their feelings validated and normalized, particularly in light of a general reluctance to respond to these sorts of difficult statements.

❧ ❧ ❧

## References

American Psychiatric Association. (1994). *Diagnostic and statistical manual of mental disorders* (4th ed.). Washington, DC: Author.

Billings, J. A., & Block, S. (1995). Depression. *Journal of Palliative Care, 11,* 48–54.

Boyle, D. P. (1997). Should social workers participate in assisted suicide? Yes. In B. A. Thyer (Ed.), *Controversial issues in social work practice* (pp. 179–184). Boston: Allyn & Bacon.

Breitbart, W., Rosenfeld, B. D., & Passick, S. D. (1996). Interest in physician-assisted suicide among ambulatory HIV-infected patients. *American Journal of Psychiatry, 153,* 238–242.

Brody, J. E. (1997, June 18) Personal health. *New York Times,* p. B11.

Brown, J. H., Henteleff, P., Barakat, S., & Rowe, C. J. (1986). Is it normal for terminally ill patients to desire death? *American Journal of Psychiatry, 143,* 208–211.

Brugha, T. A. (1993). Depression in the terminally ill. *British Journal of Hospital Medicine, 50,* 175, 177–181.

Bukberg, J., Penman, D., & Holland, J. C. (1984). Depression in hospitalized cancer patients. *Psychosomatic Medicine, 46,* 199–212.

Callahan, J. (1994). The ethics of assisted suicide. *Health & Social Work, 19,* 237–244.

Callahan, J. (1997). Assisted suicide, community, and the common good. *Health & Social Work, 22,* 243–245.

Canady, K. (1997). Should social workers participate in assisted suicide? No. In B. A. Thyer (Ed.), *Controversial issues in social work practice* (pp. 185–190). Boston: Allyn & Bacon.

Cavanaugh, S., Clark, D. C., & Gibbons, R. D. (1983). Diagnosing depression in the hospitalized medically ill. *Psychosomatics, 24,* 809–815.

Chochinov, H. M., Wilson, K. G., Enns, M., & Lander, S. (1994). Prevalence of depression in the terminally ill: Effects of diagnostic criteria and symptom threshold judgments. *American Journal of Psychiatry, 151,* 537–540.

Chochinov, H. M., Wilson, K. G., Enns, M., Mowchun, N., Lander, S., Levitt, M., & Clinch, J. J. (1995). Desire for death in the terminally ill. *American Journal of Psychiatry, 152,* 1185–1191.

Clark, D. C., & Fawcett, J. (1992). Review of empirical risk factors for evaluation of the suicidal patient. In B. Bongar (Ed.), *Suicide: Guidelines for assessment, management, and treatment* (pp. 16–48). New York: Oxford University Press.

Endicott, J. (1984). Measurement of depression in patients with cancer. *Cancer, 53,* 2243–2248.

Forstein, M. (1994). Suicidality and gay men. In S. A. Cadwell, R. A. Burnham, & M. Forstein (Eds.), *Therapists on the front line: Psychotherapy with gay men in the Age of AIDS* (pp. 111–145). Washington, DC: American Psychiatric Press.

Fremouw, W. J., de Perczel, M., & Ellis, T. E. (1990). *Suicide risk: Assessment and response guidelines*. New York: Pergamon Press.

Goldblatt, M. J. (1994). Hospitalization of the suicidal patient. In A. A. Leenaars, J. T. Maltsberger, & R. A. Neimeyer (Eds.), *Treatment of suicidal people* (pp. 153–165). Washington, DC: Taylor & Francis.

Humphry, D. (1991). *The final exit*. Eugene, OR: Hemlock Society.

Ivanoff, A. (1991). Suicide and suicidal behavior. In A. Gitterman (Ed.), *Handbook of social work practice with vulnerable populations* (pp. 677–709). New York: Columbia University Press.

Marzuk, P. M. (1994). Suicide and terminal illness. *Death Studies, 18*, 497–512.

Melvin, T. A., Ozbek, I. N., & Eberle, D. E. (1995). Recognition of depression. *Hospice Journal, 10*, 39–46.

Miller, P. J., Hedlund, S. C., & Murphy, K. A. (1998). Social work assessment at end of life: Practice guidelines for suicide and the terminally ill. *Social Work in Health Care, 26*, 23–36.

National Association of Social Workers. (1997). *Social work speaks* (4th ed.). Washington, DC: NASW Press.

Owen, C., Tennant, C., Levi, J., & Jones, M. (1992). Suicide and euthanasia: Patient attitudes in the context of cancer. *Psycho-oncology, 1*, 79–88.

Owen, C., Tennant, C., Levi, J., & Jones, M. (1994). Cancer patients' attitudes to final events in life: Wish for death, attitudes to cessation of treatment, suicide and euthanasia. *Psycho-oncology, 3*, 1–9.

Siegel, K. (1986). Psychosocial aspects of rational suicide. *American Journal of Psychotherapy, 40*, 405–418.

Smokowski, P. R., & Wodarski, J. S. (1996). Euthanasia and physician assisted suicide: A social work update. *Social Work in Health Care, 23*, 53–65.

Turnbull, J. E. (1991). Depression. In A. Gitterman (Ed.), *Handbook of social work practice with vulnerable populations* (pp. 165–204). New York: Columbia University Press.

Valente, S. M., Saunders, J. M., & Cohen, M. Z. (1994). Evaluating depression among patients with cancer. *Cancer Practice, 2*, 65–71.

Werth, J. L. (1995). Rational suicide reconsidered: AIDS as an impetus for change. *Death Studies, 19*, 65–81.

This chapter was originally published in the November 1999 issue of *Health & Social Work*, Vol. 24, Number 4, pp. 260–268.

# 27
# Preserving End-of-Life Autonomy

## The Patient Self-Determination Act and the Uniform Health Care Decisions Act

### COLLEEN M. GALAMBOS

Advances in medical treatment have increased the ability to sustain life artificially. These advances complicate health care decision making for patients, family members, concerned people, and health care providers. Treatment options and end-of-life decisions are replete with ethical conflicts and dilemmas for all involved individuals. Now, more than ever, sound practice and policy that protects end-of-life autonomy for clients are needed to guide and direct practitioners, clients, family members, and other interested individuals.

This article describes and discusses the Patient Self-Determination Act (PSDA) and the Uniform Health Care Decisions Act (UHCDA), two legislative efforts that focus on the preservation of end-of-life autonomy. Available empirical evidence is used to analyze the PSDA critically, and the PSDA is compared to the UHCDA. The implications of each act are discussed, and suggestions for research, policy, and practice are provided for the social work practitioner.

## Patient Self-Determination Act

In an effort to preserve end-of-life autonomy and reduce the costs of unwanted medical treatment, the PSDA was enacted as part of the deficit reduction effort of the Omnibus Budget Reconciliation Act of 1990 (P.L. 101-508). Effective December 1, 1991, the PSDA requires that health care facilities receiving Medicare and Medicaid funding provide written information on treatment options, right-to-die information, and advance directives to adult patients on admission or enrollment to a health care facility (Madson, 1993; Wolf, 1991). This information must specifically address the patient's legal rights concerning medical care, including the right to refuse treatment, advance directive options, and any relevant written policies of the institution (Madson, 1993; Wolf, 1991).

According to the PSDA, the health care provider has the additional responsibility to document the existence of advance directives in the patient's medical record, ensure compliance with state laws, maintain organizational policies and procedures, and provide community and staff education on advance directives. The regulations also stipulate that health care provided to a patient cannot be conditional on the existence of advance directives (Madson, 1993; Wolf, 1991). The PSDA applies to a variety of health care delivery systems, including hospitals, skilled nursing facilities, hospices, home health care agencies, and health maintenance organizations. The underlying assumption of the PSDA is that increased awareness and information on advance directives will generate discussion between people and their health care providers and result in an increase in completed advance directives (Silverman, Tuma, Schaeffer, & Singh, 1995).

The term *advance directive* is defined as a "written instruction, such as a living will or durable power of attorney for health care,

recognized under State law and relating to the provision of such care when the individual is incapacitated" (Osman & Perlin, 1994, p. 246). Generally, there are two types of advance directives: (1) instruction directives that provide self-initiated written instructions on life-sustaining treatments that the person desires under certain types of clinical situations and (2) proxy directives that appoint an individual to make health care decisions for the person in the event of incapacitation.

## Identified Problems and Impact of the Patient Self-Determination Act

### Few People Enact Advance Directives

Since the enactment of the PSDA, research conducted on advance directives indicates that few people issue advance directives and that those who do tend to come from a white, female, middle-to-upper socioeconomic background (U.S. General Accounting Office [GAO], 1995). It has been reported that only 9 percent of patients under age 30 have an advance directive, compared with 35 percent of patients over age 75 (U.S. GAO, 1995). Two studies report less participation and increased discomfort among the African American population related to both completion of these documents and acceptance of the concept of advance directives (Caralis, Davis, Wright, & Marcial, 1993; Silverman et al., 1995). These factors were attributed to skepticism about the intent of an advance directive (Caralis et al., 1993; Silverman et al., 1995).

One intention of the PSDA is to increase the number of completed advance directives through educational programs. Although education may be a major component of the act, several research studies refute the benefits of education and indicate that increased education does not expand the number of people completing advance directives (High, 1993; Silverman et al., 1995; Weinberg & Brod, 1995). Completion rates for advance directives remain at the rate of 4 percent to 15 percent despite the PSDA's emphasis on education (Weinberg & Brod, 1995). It is important to note here that, although the PSDA legislated community education, no funds were appropriated to assist in the implementation of these programs. This lack of funds may have affected the quality of educational efforts negatively.

### Advance Directive Education Targets ElderlyPeople

An inherent problem in the implementation of the PSDA is that the emphasis on dissemination of information and completion of advance directives has concentrated on the elderly population (U.S. GAO, 1995). There is an assumption that elderly people are more likely to desire advance directives. However, several research studies point out that elderly people prefer informal discussions with family members to the completion of a formalized advance directive process (Cohen-Mansfield et al., 1991; Fairman, 1992; High, 1988, 1993; Madson, 1993; Roe, Goldstein, Massey, & Pascoe, 1992). Several studies discussed the tendency for older adults to delay the completion of advance directives to a future time and to defer to others to make health care decisions in times of need (Cohen-Mansfield et al., 1991; High, 1993; Roe et al., 1992). These findings highlight the importance of family involvement in health care and end-of-life decision making.

A documented benefit of the PSDA is that the provision of education on advance directives stimulates discussion among family members and health care providers about end-of-life decisions. Bailly and DePoy (1995) reported that discussions about end-of-life decisions with family members increased in frequency and intensity after attendance at educational programs on advance directives. Information and educational programs about the importance of advance directives may be more effective if targeted to younger, healthier people. At least one study that compared attitudes on advance directives between adults and physicians indicated that patients believed discussions about advance directives should occur at younger ages, when individuals are still healthy (Johnston, Pfeifer, & McNutt, 1995).

### Variation in the Implementation of Advance Directives

Research and experience have indicated that there is a wide variation in the extent to which advance directives are implemented by health care professionals and organizations. For instance, most health care agencies are in compliance with the development and distribution of information on advance directives (U.S. GAO, 1995). One study indicated that most facilities that were part of the research sample complied with the administrative requirements of the PSDA, including the development of written policies and procedures on advance directives, the development of written materials on advance directives and the distribution of this information to patients on admission to the facility, and the provision of staff training on advance directives (U.S. GAO, 1995).

However, data also indicate that health care agencies were less compliant in the area of documenting advance directives in the patient's medical record. In addition, only two-thirds of the facilities that participated in the study planned or were planning community education events on advance directives (U.S. GAO, 1995).

Another identified concern associated with advance directives is that they are not always followed. Although health care facilities are mandated by the PSDA to implement a patient's advance directive, there is documented noncompliance with this requirement (U.S. GAO, 1995). GAO identified several reasons for this problem. One is that the advance directive may not be followed because health care providers are unaware of its existence. Broadwell, Boisaubin, and Dunn's (1993) research pointed out that a number of patients kept the only copy of their advance directive in a safe deposit box. In addition, in a 1992 survey of health care facilities, only 60 percent of patients with advance directives had the actual copy in their medical record (U.S. Department of Health and Human Services, 1993). Advance directives are not always transferred with the patient from one health care provider system to another. A study of one nursing home facility indicated that advance directives were transferred to the hospital in only one-third of the cases of individuals who had enacted them (U.S. GAO, 1995).

Despite the existence of an advance directive, physicians may not always honor the directive. Ely, Peters, and Zweig's (1992) research suggested that when the directive conflicted with family opinion, the majority of physicians surveyed indicated that they would comply with the family's preference rather than the written directive. Other research suggests that when physician values conflicted with a patient's directive, the physician's opinion prevailed. Data from a recent study showed that 39 percent of doctors surveyed had ended life-sustaining treatment without the consent of the patient or family, 3 percent indicated making the decision over the objection of a patient's family, and 34 percent declined to withdraw life support despite a family's wishes (Asch, Hansen-Flaschen, & Lanken, 1995).

Another problem identified with the implementation of advance directives is that sometimes individuals designate a health care agent as a surrogate decision maker and fail to make health care preferences known to this

agent (Weinberg & Brod, 1995). This study also indicated that only a small percentage of study participants had given a copy of their advance directive to their surrogate decision maker.

## The Uniform Health Care Decisions Act

In an attempt to resolve some of the inherent problems of the PSDA, in 1993 the National Conference of Commissioners on Uniform State Laws drafted the Uniform Health Care Decisions Act. The act was approved by the American Bar Association and recommended for enactment in all states in 1994.

The UHCDA is a comprehensive advance care document designed to provide uniformity and a minimum level of standards in statutes across state lines. Presently, each state operates under a different advance directive regulation, which often results in conflicts between statutes in different states (Uniform Law Commissioners, 1994). Conflicts often arise when an advance care directive enacted according to one state statute is implemented under another state law. These situations occur as a result of relocation or when an individual may live in one state but receive health care in a different state. Conflicts and confusion also may occur when family members or others designated as proxies or surrogate decision makers live in another state and are more familiar with the statute in the state in which they reside. If enacted in all 50 states, the UHCDA would provide consistency across state lines. This consistency would help reduce conflicts and confusion surrounding the advance directive process within different geographic areas.

The UHCDA promotes autonomous decision making in that it acknowledges the right of individuals to make health care decisions in all circumstances. Included in the decision making is the right to decline health care and to direct that health care be discontinued. This right extends to any and all health care decisions that might arise. When an individual chooses a surrogate or agent to act in his or her behalf, the surrogate is extended the authority to make all health care decisions for the individual (Uniform Law Commissioners, 1994). These provisions support client self-determination and address many of the implementation problems that have been identified with attempts to enact advance directives in health care facilities.

The act authorizes health care decisions to be made by an agent designated by the individual when the individual cannot or chooses not to make his or her own decisions. This agent may be a designated surrogate, family member, or close friend when the individual has no appointed guardian. According to this act, a court may be granted agent status as the decision maker of last resort (Uniform Law Commissioners, 1994). This provision supports and acknowledges elderly people who prefer to defer decision making to another. In an attempt to simplify the advance directives process, the UHCDA allows for the enactment of an advance directive to be either written or oral. The one exception is that a power of attorney for health care must be written but no longer needs to be witnessed (Uniform Law Commissioners, 1994).

Compliance by health care providers and institutions is addressed in the UHCDA. Providers are mandated to comply with an advance directive (Uniform Law Commissioners, 1994). In addition, the UHCDA is structured such that decisions about an individual's health are based on an individual's own wishes and values. An agent or surrogate who makes health care decisions must make them according to written instructions and other wishes of the individual to the extent that they are known. In guardianship

cases, a guardian must comply with an individual's instructions. A guardian cannot revoke an individual's directive without court approval. When the intentions of the individual are unknown, decisions must be made "in accordance with the best interest of the individual, but in light of the individual's personal values known to the agent or surrogate" (Uniform Law Commissioners, 1994, p. 6). These provisions safeguard end-of-life autonomy for the patient.

Finally, the UHCDA further advances self-determination through the inclusion of a procedure for the resolution of disputes. When irreconcilable conflicts exist, the act permits a court to hear and render a decision on the matter and specifies who may bring a petition to the court (Uniform Law Commissioners, 1994). This provision provides a resource for individuals when patients or family members have disagreements with health care providers over honoring enacted advance directives.

## The Uniform Health Care Decisions Act and the Patient Self-Determination Act: A Comparison

A comparison of the UHCDA and the PSDA reveals both similarities and differences and also reveals that the two acts complement each other. If used simultaneously, both legislative initiatives would greatly enhance end-of-life decision making. The UHCDA has a more comprehensive approach to the issue of advance directives than the PSDA. Whereas the specific focus of the PSDA is to provide information about advance directives, the UHCDA attempts to address specific problems in the implementation of advance directives.

The basic premise of both the PSDA and the UHCDA is to preserve end-of-life autonomy. However, the UHCDA advances autonomous decision making through its specific attempts to preserve an individual's known values, desires, and directives within both the surrogate decision-making process and in its attempts to ensure institutional and provider compliance.

The UHCDA also expands the concept of autonomy from the individual only to include family and surrogates in the decision-making process. Although decisions are based on individual preferences, family members and surrogates play a prominent role in this process. This approach addresses the fact that some individuals, particularly elderly people, prefer family members and close friends to make decisions for them.

A documented concern about advance directives is that people prefer more informal means to express wishes. The UHCDA attempts to provide more informality to the process by allowing oral directives to be honored. This provision may enhance individual participation in the enactment of advance directives.

As mentioned previously, despite the increased educational and discussion efforts prompted by the PSDA and despite the existence of advance directives, physicians often do not follow enacted directives. The UHCDA contains two mechanisms that serve to increase compliance with an individual's wishes and reduce incidents when decisions are made contrary to the advance directive. There are provisions within the UHCDA that direct facilities to comply with patient instructions, and there is a mechanism whereby disputes can be addressed within a court process.

It should be noted here that even with these additional safeguards, compliance is not guaranteed. A health care provider has the right to decline to honor an advance directive in two situations: (1) for reasons of conscience, if the directive conflicts with institution policy or values, and (2) if the in-

struction is contrary to accepted health care standards. However, individuals must be informed of these conflicts, and reasonable efforts must be made to transfer the individual to a facility that can honor the directive. Even with these provisions, it may not always be possible to transfer an individual to another facility. In addition, reasonable effort implies that some type of judgment must occur to determine reasonableness. It is in these types of situations that the court mechanism for dispute resolution is helpful in protecting individual autonomy.

Similar to the PSDA, the UHCDA attempts to promote constancy throughout the country and across state lines. The major difference is that the PSDA is federally legislated, whereas the UHCDA is a model state statute. Each state may choose whether to replace its own advance directive mandates with the UHCDA. Currently, only five states have enacted modified versions of the UHCDA. Clearly, the UHCDA would have a stronger, more consistent effect if it too were federally mandated.

Unlike the PSDA, the UHCDA does not address the educational promotion of advance directives. However, both acts working simultaneously will provide more opportunity for autonomy in end-of-life decisions. Each legislative initiative focuses on different but necessary steps in the process of end-of-life decision making. The PSDA provides an educational focus and the UHCDA concentrates on implementation concerns. Together, the acts serve as mechanisms that support the rights of an individual to be informed and to enact an advance directive.

## Implications for Social Workers

The social work profession has a long-established history of work with families. This expertise places social workers in the unique position of having the knowledge, skill, and opportunity to generate discussions on advance directives with both individuals and families. It has been suggested that social workers are often the preferred staff member to discuss advance directives with patients (Osman & Perlin, 1994; Sachs, 1994). Social workers are taking lead roles in the implementation of educational programs and providing counseling on advance directives in nursing homes, life care communities, and hospitals. Social workers also can take a lead role in practice settings where clients are generally well and healthy.

Increased educational opportunities and discussions on advance directives are needed for younger individuals and individuals who are still healthy. It is interesting to note that the two most controversial court cases dealing with end-of-life decisions, those of Karen Ann Quinlan and Nancy Cruzan, involved two women under age 30 who unexpectedly became seriously ill and unresponsive.

Providing information earlier in a client's life allows people the opportunity to discuss advance directives with family members and significant others and to engage in measured deliberations about their own wishes for end-of-life decisions. This approach assists in the development of an emotional readiness for the death and dying process. It encourages thinking and discussion about end-of-life decisions at a time when thought processes are clearer, individuals are not in crisis, and time is more abundant. Providing information about advance directives to people who are healthy removes a level of anxiety that is produced when discussions occur on admission to health care facilities at a time when individuals are coping with both an illness and the emotions related to it. Educational programs could be organized and implemented in churches, synagogues, or other religious institutions, physician's offices or health care clinics, community centers, or educational settings.

Because autonomy and self-determination are acknowledged professional values, advocating for individual rights and respecting diversity of interests, lifestyles, and cultures as they relate to advance directives is common ground for social work practice. Social workers are in a position to play a key role in ensuring that individual concerns and differences are addressed in advance care planning. Advocacy includes protecting the right of individuals who choose not to enact an advance directive as well as helping individuals develop directives that are unique to their situations.

To advance autonomy in end-of-life decisions, social workers need to advocate for the passage of the UHCDA in each of the 50 states. Both state and national campaign endeavors are necessary to advance this cause. Also, advocacy efforts are needed to procure additional funding for community educational programs associated with the PSDA. There is a particular need for community education for younger, healthy individuals and for workshops that focus on how to communicate with significant others and health care professionals about advance directives.

The legislative development of the UHCDA to a national act is needed to ensure consistency in statutes and approaches across the 50 states. The development of the UHCDA into a national statute will ensure its adoption in all 50 states. A multidisciplinary and citizen effort is needed to be successful in this area. Social workers can assist by providing their expertise to the process and in organizing citizen involvement and lobbying efforts toward this cause.

### Further Research Needed

Because both the PSDA and the UHCDA are relatively recent legislative initiatives, additional research is needed to learn more about the effect of end-of-life autonomy on organizations, programs, and the individual.

Studies that focus on end-of-life autonomy and its relationship to psychosociocultural issues, implementation issues, and the effect of educational programs on beliefs, attitudes, and behavior toward end-of-life decision making would enhance our understanding of how to assist clients, family members, other concerned individuals, and health care professionals to exercise self-determination.

In the realm of psychosociocultural issues, additional research that examines the meaning socially diverse groups attach to the enactment of advance directives is needed. Data that are more sensitive to cultural diversity and contain provisions for honoring diversity could be used to develop future legislation on end-of-life decision making. Because older adults tend to defer end-of-life decision making to family members, the profession could benefit from more knowledge about the roles and dynamics associated with family involvement in this process, including identification of factors associated with a surrogate decision maker's being informed of end-of-life decisions, how health care professionals respond to surrogate decision makers, and the psychosocial dynamics related to making decisions for another. Because preliminary research showed that people believed that discussions about advance directives should occur at earlier ages, more information that examines age factors and end-of-life decision making is needed. Information on the relationship between completing an advance directive and attitudes about death also is needed.

Related to implementation factors and the enactment of end-of-life decision making, research that examines the availability of the advanced directive to health personnel, the failure of physicians to carry out patients' wishes, the dynamics associated with communicating information about advance directives, and the preference of some patients for informal instructions should continue. More studies in these areas will increase understanding of how organizations, programs, and health care personnel can be more responsive to end-of-life decision making.

Previous research has both refuted and supported the benefits of education on end-of-life decision making. Therefore, additional research that examines the effect of counseling and educational programs on beliefs, attitudes, and behaviors related to this process would provide social workers with more insight into the types of programs and approaches that have been effective in assisting clients with these issues.

## Conclusion

The PSDA and the UHCDA are important recent legislative efforts aimed at promoting autonomy in end-of-life decisions. Although each act has its limitations, the two together offer a comprehensive approach to advance care planning. Opportunities exist for social workers to implement and provide educational and counseling programs related to the PSDA, UHCDA, and advance care planning. Social workers also can advocate for individual rights in the advance directive process on micro, mezzo, and macro levels. Additional lobbying efforts are needed to enact the UHCDA and to ensure appropriation of funds for community education. Finally, further research is needed to enhance understanding of the dynamics associated with end-of-life decision making. The technologically changing health care industry provides the impetus for social workers to increase their involvement in the protection of end-of-life-autonomy for all clients.

# References

Asch, D. A., Hansen-Flaschen, J., & Lanken, P. N. (1995). Decisions to limit or continue life sustaining treatment by critical care physicians in the United States: Conflicts between physician's practices and patient's wishes. *American Journal of Respiratory and Critical Care Medicine, 151,* 288–292.

Bailly, D. J., & DePoy, E. (1995). Older people's responses to education about advance directives. *Health & Social Work, 20,* 223–228.

Broadwell, A. W., Boisaubin, E. V., & Dunn, J. K. (1993). Advance directives on hospital admission: A survey of patient attitudes. *Southern Medical Journal, 86*(2), 165–168.

Caralis, P. V., Davis, B., Wright, K., & Marcial, E. (1993). The influence of ethnicity and race on attitudes toward advance directives, life-prolonging treatments, and euthanasia. *Journal of Clinical Ethics, 4,* 155–165.

Cohen-Mansfield, J., Rabinovich, B. A., Lipson, S., Gerber, B., Fein, A., & Weisman, S. (1991). The decision to execute a durable power of attorney for health-care and preferences regarding the utilization of life-sustaining treatments in nursing home residents. *Archives of Internal Medicine, 151,* 289–294.

Ely, J. W., Peters, P. G., & Zweig, S. (1992). The physician's decision to use tube feedings: The role of the family, the living will, and the Cruzan decision. *Journal of the American Geriatric Society, 40,* 471–475.

Fairman, P. R. (1992). Withdrawing life sustaining treatment. *Archives of Internal Medicine, 152,* 25–27.

High, D. M. (1988). All in the family: Extended autonomy and expectations in surrogate health-care decision-making. *Gerontologist, 28* (Suppl.), 46–51.

High, D. M. (1993). Why are elderly people not using advance directives? *Journal of Aging and Health, 5,* 497–515.

Johnston, S. C., Pfeifer, M. P., & McNutt, R. (1995). The discussion about advance directives: Patient and physician opinions regarding when and how it should be conducted. *Archives of Internal Medicine, 155,* 1025–1030.

Madson, S. K. (1993). Patient Self-Determination Act: Implications for long-term care. *Journal of Gerontological Nursing, 19*(21), 15–18.

Omnibus Budget Reconciliation Act of 1990, P.L. 101-508, § 4206, 4751, 104 Stat. 1388, 1388-115, 1388-204.

Osman, H., & Perlin, T. M. (1994). Patient self-determination and the artificial prolongation of life. *Health & Social Work, 19,* 245–252.

Roe, J. M., Goldstein, M. K., Massey, K., & Pascoe, D. (1992). Durable power of attorney for health-care: A survey of senior center participants. *Archives of Internal Medicine, 152,* 292–296.

Sachs, G. (1994, November/December). Increasing the prevalence of advance care planning. *Hastings Center Report* (Special Suppl.), S13–S16.

Silverman, H. J., Tuma, P., Schaeffer, M. H., & Singh, B. (1995). Implementation of the Patient Self-Determination Act in a hospital setting. *Archives of Internal Medicine, 155,* 502–510.

Uniform Law Commissioners. (1994). *Uniform Health-Care Decisions Act.* Chicago: National Conference of Commissioners on Uniform State Laws.

U.S. Department of Health and Human Services. (1993). *Patient advance directives, early implementation experience.* (OEI 06-9101130). Washington, DC: Author.

U.S. General Accounting Office. (1995). *Patient Self-Determination Act providers offer information on advance directives but effectiveness uncertain,* (GAO/HEHS-95-135). Washington, DC: U.S. Government Printing Office.

Weinberg, J. K., & Brod, M. (1995). Advance medical directives: Policy perspectives and practical experiences. *Journal of Ethics, Law, and Aging, 1*(1), 15–35.

Wolf, S. M. (1991). Sources of concern about the Patient Self-Determination Act. *New England Journal of Medicine, 325,* 1666–1672.

This chapter was originally published in the November 1998 issue of *Health & Social Work,* Vol. 23, Number 4, pp. 275–281.

# Afterword

The organization of this text, as with the International Year of Older Persons itself, highlights the challenges facing the helping professions in reaching elders and their families, not in the name of charity, but through balanced, normative, and reciprocal relationships across generations, communities, and social institutions. These articles underscore some ugly inequities in certain life chances that persist into old age for certain people disadvantaged in American society. Inequities deriving from race, gender, socioeconomic status, and early life opportunities have certainly restricted the independence and self-fulfillment open to adults now living in late life.

Participation in the mainstream of life will be of less concern to the recently retired white-collar worker than to the 92-year-old woman isolated by sensory impairments in a third floor walkup apartment, but participation with and connection to others is vitally important to both of their life chances. Self-fulfillment, or even enjoying a whole television program, may be a luxury to a 70-year-old woman whose grandchildren have just moved permanently into her home. But the inequitable distribution of caregiving responsibilities and burdens is starkly apparent against the other inequities that glare at us when seen against the backdrop of extreme age. National policies could redress some of such inequities by extending Medicare coverage to include prescription drugs for all older persons and skilled nursing care and therapies to all homebound patients. Medicaid could mandate the coverage of personal care for all persons with disabilities. The federal government could fund the creation of new culturally appropriate resource centers for multigenerational families and for family caregivers needing relief and support.

The vast socioeconomic differences within the elderly population, like the intergenerational differences inherent in the 40-year age span they encompass, and the related morbidity and mortality differentials all captured in the term elderly are profound. As the entire society ages, becoming more sensitized to our generational differences, so we hope will we recognize our common human needs. All of us as humans share these needs to become and remain independent, to participate with and be valued by others, to care and be cared for, to see our dreams fulfilled, and to enjoy the dignity and respect that come from a life lived well.

# Index

Note: Numbers in italics indicate tables and figures.

# About the Editors

**Sharon M. Keigher, PhD, ACSW,** is professor, School of Social Welfare, University of Wisconsin–Milwaukee. She has an AM and PhD from the University of Chicago School of Social Service Administration. She is the current editor-in-chief of *Health & Social Work* and the past chair of the Social Research, Policy, and Practice section of the Gerontological Society of America.

**Anne E. Fortune, PhD,** is professor, School of Social Welfare, University at Albany, State University of New York. She has an AM and PhD from the University of Chicago School of Social Service Administration. She is the current editor-in-chief of *Social Work Research*.

**Stanley L Witkin, PhD,** is professor, Department of Social Work, University of Vermont. He has an MSW and PhD from the University of Wisconsin–Madison. He is the current editor-in-chief of *Social Work*.

# About the Contributors

**Robin E. Ahern, MSW, LSW,** is a PhD student, School of Social Work, University of Illinois, Urbana-Champaign, Champaign, IL.

**Barbara Berkman, DSW, LICSW,** is Helen Rehr/Ruth Fizdale Professor, School of Social Work, Columbia University, New York, NY.

**Mercedes Bern-Klug, MSW, MA,** is senior research associate and doctoral student, University of Kansas Medical Center/Center on Aging, Kansas City, KS.

**Evelyn Bonander, MSW, ACSW,** is executive director of social services, Massachusetts General Hospital, Boston, MA.

**Kathryn L. Braun, DrPH,** is associate professor of public health and director, Center on Aging, John A. Burns School of Medicine, University of Hawaii at Manoa, Honolulu, HI.

**Laura R. Bronstein, PhD, ACSW,** is assistant professor, School of Education and Human Development, Binghamton University, Binghamton, NY.

**Colette V. Browne, DrPH,** is associate professor, School of Social Work, University of Hawaii at Manoa, Honolulu, HI.

**Denise Burnette, PhD,** is associate professor, School of Social Work, Columbia University, New York, NY.

**Hong-jer Chang, PhD,** is assistant professor, Fu-Jen Catholic University, Hsia Chuang City, Taipei, Taiwan.

**Sherry M. Cummings, PhD, LCSW,** is assistant professor, College of Social Work, University of Tennessee, Nashville, TN.

**Ann Daniels, PhD, LICSW, ACSW, BCD,** is clinical director of social services, Massachusetts General Hospital, Boston, MA.

**Caroline Dawson, BSN, MSN, MPA,** is a doctoral student, School of Social Welfare, University at Albany, State University of New York, Albany, NY.

**Peter Doré, MA,** is a database administrator, Center for Mental Health Services Research, George Warren Brown School of Social Work, Washington University, St. Louis, MO.

**Marcia Egan, PhD, MSW,** is associate professor, College of Social Work, University of Tennessee, Memphis, TN.

**David J. Ekerdt, PhD,** is professor of sociology, University of Kansas, Lawrence, KS.

**Gerald Felsenthal, MD,** is chief, Department of Rehabilitation Medicine, Sinai Hospital, Baltimore, MD.

**V. L. Fitch, PhD, LISW,** is director, School of Social Work, University of Akron, OH.

**Kathleen M. Fox, PhD,** is executive vice president, Managed Edge, New York, NY.

**Esme Fuller-Thomson, PhD,** is I. Anson Assistant Professor, Faculty of Social Work, University of Toronto, Toronto, Ontario, Canada.

**Colleen M. Galambos, DSW, ACSW, LCSW-C,** is associate professor, University of Tennessee College of Social Work, Knoxville, TN.

**Todd Gerber, MS,** is research scientist, New York State Department of Health, Albany, NY.

**Susan Gieryic, MSW,** is research specialist, New York State AIDS Institute, Menands, NY.

**Kevin M. Gorey, PhD, CSW,** is associate professor, School of Social Work, University of Windsor, Windsor, Ontario, Canada.

**Stephen Gorin, PhD,** is professor, Social Work Program, Plymouth State College, Plymouth, NH, and part-time executive director, New Hampshire Chapter, National Association of Social Workers, Concord, NH.

**Amanda M. Grenier, MSW,** is a doctoral candidate, School of Social Work, McGill University, Montreal, Quebec, Canada.

**Ann Gruber-Baldini, PhD,** assistant professor, Department of Epidemiology and Preventive Medicine, University of Maryland School of Medicine, Baltimore, MD.

**Vincent Guilamo-Ramos, MSW, ACSW,** is a doctoral candidate, School of Social Welfare, State University of New York at Albany, Albany, NY.

**J. Richard Hebel, PhD,** is professor, University of Maryland School of Medicine, Baltimore, MD.

**M.C. "Terry" Hokenstad, PhD,** is the Ralph S. and Dorothy P. Schmitt Professor and professor of international health, Mandel School of Applied Social Sciences, Case Western Reserve University, Cleveland, OH.

**William Holmes, PhD,** is visiting associate professor, Department of Sociology, University of Massachusetts, Boston, MA.

**Susan Chauncey Horky, MSW, LCSW, LICSW,** is faculty social worker, University of Florida Pediatric Pulmonary Center, Gainesville, FL.

**Robert B. Hudson, PhD,** is professor and chair, Department of Social Welfare Policy, School of Social Work, Boston University, Boston, MA.

**Goldie Kadushin, PhD, ACSW,** is associate professor, School of Social Welfare, University of Wisconsin–Milwaukee, Milwaukee, WI.

**Rosalie A. Kane, PhD, ACSW,** is professor and director, Division of Health Services Research & Policy, School of Public Health, University of Minnesota, Minneapolis, MN.

**John Kenzora, MD,** is professor, orthopaedic surgery, University of Maryland School of Medicine, Baltimore, MD.

**Catherine Kohm, MEd, RN, BA,** is clinical utilization manager, The University Health Network, Toronto Western Hospital, Toronto, Ontario, Canada.

**Pamela J. Kovacs, PhD,** is assistant professor, School of Social Work, Virginia Commonwealth University, Richmond, VA.

**Betty J. Kramer, PhD,** is associate professor, School of Social Work, University of Wisconsin–Madison, Madison, WI.

**Hong Li, PhD,** is assistant professor, University of Illinois at Urbana-Champaign, Champaign, IL.

**Nathan L. Linsk, PhD, ACSW,** is professor and principal investigator of the Midwest AIDS Training and Education Center, Jane Addams College of Social Work, University of Illinois at Chicago, Chicago, IL.

**Yat-Sang Lum PhD,** is assistant professor, School of Social Work, University of Minnesota, St. Paul, MN.

**Jay Magaziner, PhD,** is professor and director, Division of Gerontology, University of Maryland School of Medicine, Baltimore, MD.

**Philip McCallion, PhD, ACSW,** is director, Center for Research on Aging, School of Social Welfare, University at Albany, State University of New York, Albany, NY.

**Meredith Minkler, DrPH,** is professor of health and social behavior, School of Public Health, University of California, Berkeley, CA.

**Nancy Morrow-Howell, PhD,** is associate professor, George Warren Brown School of Social Work, Washington University, St. Louis, MO.

**Elizabeth J. Mutran, PhD,** is professor, School of Public Health, University of North Carolina at Chapel Hill, Chapel Hill, NC.

**Shankar Nair, MBA,** is a PhD student, School of Business, University of Illinois, Urbana-Champaign, Champaign, IL.

**Diane Neil-Pollinger, MSW, CSW,** is professional practice leader and social worker for the cardiac program, University Health Network, Toronto General Hospital, Toronto, Ontario, Canada.

**Martha N. Ozawa, PhD,** is Bettie Bofinger Professor of Social Policy, George Warren Brown School of Social Work, Washington University, St. Louis, MO.

**Cynthia Cannon Poindexter, PhD,** is assistant professor, School of Social Work, Boston University, Boston, MA.

**Enola K. Proctor, PhD, LCSW,** is Frank J. Bruno Professor of Social Work, George Warren Brown School of Social Work, Washington University, St. Louis, MO.

**Dona J. Reese, PhD, LCSW,** is assistant professor, Department of Social Work, University of North Dakota, Grand Forks, ND.

**James Reinardy, PhD, MSW,** is associate professor, School of Social Work, University of Minnesota, Minneapolis, MN.

**Donald C. Reitzes, PhD,** is professor and chair, Department of Sociology, Georgia State University, Atlanta, GA.

**Mark Robinson, CNE,** is systems administrator, Massachusetts General Hospital, Boston, MA.

**Anita Rosen, PhD,** is project coordinator-SAGE-SW, Council on Social Work Education, Alexandria, VA.

**Suzanne Sampson, BS, RN,** is administrator, Alzheimer's Research Lab, Massachusetts General Hospital/Harvard Medical School, Charlestown, MA.

**Joleen D. O'Faire Schrock, MSW,** is clinical coordinator, Elon Homes for Children at Kennedy Campus, Charlotte, NC.

**Fatima Sheriff, BSC (hon.), SSW,** is clinical utilization coordinator, The University Health Network, Toronto Western Hospital, Toronto, Ontario, Canada.

**Darcy Clay Siebert, MSW, LCSW, CEAP,** is a doctoral candidate, School of Social Work, University of North Carolina at Chapel Hill, Chapel Hill, NC.

**Lee R. Slivinske, PhD,** is professor, Department of Social Work, Youngstown State University, Youngstown, OH.

**H. David Smith, PhD,** is assistant professor of psychology, Department of Psychology, Middlebury College, Middlebury, VT.

**Jeanette C. Takamura,** is assistant secretary for aging at the U.S. Department of Health and Human Services, Washington, DC, and former deputy director of health and director of the executive office on aging, State of Hawaii.

**Ronald W. Toseland, PhD,** is director and professor, Ringel Institute of Gerontology, School of Social Welfare, University at Albany, State University of New York, Albany, NY.

**Huan-yui Tseng, PhD,** is assistant professor, Department of Social Work, Shih-Chien University, Taipei, Taiwan.

**Ruth Anne Van Loon, PhD, ACSW, LISW,** is assistant professor, School of Social Work, University of Cincinnati, Cincinnati, OH.

**Claudia Warren-Wheat, MSW, LCSW,** is intake coordinator, Peachtree Hospice, Atlanta, GA.

**Deborah Schild Wilkinson, PhD,** is assistant professor, School of Social Work, University of Michigan, Ann Arbor, MI.

**N.W. Wingerson, PhD, LISW,** is assistant professor, School of Social Work, University of Akron, OH.

**Sheryl Itkin Zimmerman, PhD,** is associate professor, School of Social Work, University of North Carolina at Chapel Hill, Chapel Hill, NC.

# ORDER THESE INNOVATIVE RESOURCES ON AGING FROM NASW PRESS

**Aging and Social Work:** *The Changing Landscapes,* Sharon M. Keigher, Anne E. Fortune, and Stanley L Witkin, Editors.

*Aging and Social Work* gathers a wide-reaching collection of 31 articles about aging into one unique resource. It offers theory, research and case studies about the needs, issues, and challenges faced by the senior population. This vibrant collection signals the start of a new discussion about seniors and the role of social work in meeting their diverse needs.

*ISBN: 0-87101-326-6. Item #3266. $39.99.*

**Gerontology for Health Professionals:** *A Practice Guide, 2nd Edition,* Florence Safford and George I. Krell, Editors.

Here is the new edition of the best-selling guide for working with elderly people—filled with expert guidance and proven interventions. You'll learn to better assess physical, mental, psychological, and social function . . . and to plan interventions for common problems caused by dementia, grief and loss, and more. New to the second edition are three chapters that address the increasing challenges of elder abuse, AIDS and elderly people, and advance directives.

*ISBN: 0-87101-283-9. Item #2839. $24.95.*

**The Field of Adult Services:** *Social Work Practice and Administration,* Gary M. Nelson, Ann C. Eller, Dennis W. Streets, and Margaret L. Morse, Editors.

*The Field of Adult Services* helps define the complex world of adult services delivery by examining the specialized body of values, knowledge, and skills that constitute the field. Includes numerous tables, charts, and case examples to illustrate complex information so that it is easily grasped.

*ISBN: 0-87101-250-2. Item #2502. $34.95.*

**Social Work Speaks, 5th Edition,** *NASW Policy Statements, 2000-2003.*

The latest unabridged collection of policy statements adopted by the Delegate Assembly, NASW's key policy-making body, in August 1999. New policy statements include Correctional Social Work, Environmental Policy, Technology and Social Work, Transgender and Gender Identity Issues, and more.

*ISBN: 0-87101-318-5. Item #3185. $39.99.*

**Humane Managed Care?** *Anita Lightburn and Gerald Schamess, Editors.*

*Humane Managed Care?* takes the lead in the national debate on health care in the United States. As no other book on health care issues today, this volume has fostered dialogue among human services professionals and consumers.

*ISBN: 0-87101-294-4. Item #2944. $29.95.*

**Health & Social Work.**

*Health & Social Work* journal delivers current information through articles grouped by special themes such as aging, managed care, substance abuse, and diversity. Journal articles also cover research, policy, specialized services, in-service training, and other topics that affect the delivery of health care services.

*ISSN: 0360-7283. Published quarterly in February, May, August, and November. NASW Member (#4001) $45.00; NASW Student Member (#4101) $30.00; Individual Nonmember (#4201) $79.95; Library/Institution (#4301) $99.95.*

***(Order form and information on reverse side)***

# ORDER FORM

| Qty. | Title | Item # | Price | Total |
|---|---|---|---|---|
| ___ | Aging and Social Work | 3266 | $39.99 | _____ |
| ___ | Gerontology for Health Professionals | 2839 | $24.95 | _____ |
| ___ | The Field of Adult Services | 2502 | $34.95 | _____ |
| ___ | Social Work Speaks, 5th Edition | 3185 | $39.99 | _____ |
| ___ | Humane Managed Care? | 2944 | $29.95 | _____ |
| ___ | Health & Social Work | | | |
| ___ | NASW Member | 4001 | $45.00 | _____ |
| ___ | NASW Student Member | 4101 | $30.00 | _____ |
| ___ | Individual Nonmember | 4201 | $79.95 | _____ |
| ___ | Library/Institution | 4301 | $99.95 | _____ |

**POSTAGE AND HANDLING**
Minimum postage and handling fee is $4.95.
Orders that do not include appropriate postage
and handling will be returned.

**DOMESTIC:** Please add 12% to orders under $100
for postage and handling. For orders over $100
add 7% of order.

**CANADA:** Please add 17% postage and handling.

**OTHER INTERNATIONAL:** Please add 22% postage and
handling.

| | Total |
|---|---|
| Subtotal | _____ |
| Postage and Handling | _____ |
| DC residents add 6% sales tax | _____ |
| MD residents add 5% sales tax | _____ |
| Total | _____ |

❏ **Check** or **money order** (payable to NASW Press) for $ _____.

❏ **Credit card**
    ❏ NASW Visa* | ❏ Visa | ❏ NASW MasterCard* | ❏ MasterCard | ❏ Amex

_____    _____
Credit Card Number      Expiration Date

Signature _____
            *Use of these cards generates funds in support of the social work profession.*

Name _____

Address _____

City _____ State/Province _____

Country _____ Zip _____

Phone _____ E-mail _____

NASW Member # (if applicable) _____

*(Please make checks payable to NASW Press. Prices are subject to change.)*

NASW PRESS
**P. O. Box 431**
**Annapolis JCT, MD 20701**
**USA**

**Credit card orders call**
**1-800-227-3590**
(In the Metro Wash., DC, area, call 301-317-8688)
**Or fax your order to 301-206-7989**
**Or order online at http://www.naswpress.org**

*Visit our Web site at http://www.naswpress.org.*      ASW1000